# Pedophilia

Jay R. Feierman
Editor

# Pedophilia
## Biosocial Dimensions

With 70 Illustrations

041₀₀₃

Springer-Verlag
New York Berlin Heidelberg London
Paris Tokyo Hong Kong Barcelona

Jay R. Feierman
Department of Psychiatry
University of New Mexico
   and
Department of Behavioral Medicine
Presbyterian Healthcare Services
Albuquerque, New Mexico 87112, USA

Library of Congress Cataloging-in-Publication Data
Pedophilia : biosocial dimensions / Jay R. Feierman, editor.
     p.     cm.
   Includes bibliographical references.
   ISBN 0-387-97243-9 (alk. paper)
   1. Pedophilia.   2. Child molesting.   3. Sociobiology.
I. Feierman, Jay R.
HQ71.P38     1990
306.77 – dc20                                              90-9458

Printed on acid-free paper

Camera-ready copy provided by the editor and prepared by The Type Tailor/CanyonLand
Graphics, Grand Junction, Colorado.
Printed and bound by Edwards Brothers, Ann Arbor, Michigan.
Printed in the United States of America.

9   8   7   6   5   4   3   2

ISBN 0-387-97243-9 Springer-Verlag New York Berlin Heidelberg
ISBN 3-540-97243-9 Springer-Verlag Berlin Heidelberg New York

# Contents

## Background

## Evolution

## Cause

## Function

## Development

## Conclusion

# Contributors

*Connie M. Anderson,* Department of Anthropology, Hartwick College, Oneonta, New York 13820, USA

*Craig Bielert,* Department of Psychology, SUNY College, Oneonta, New York 13820, USA

*Vern L. Bullough,* Office of the Dean, Faculty of Natural and Social Sciences, SUNY College, Buffalo, New York 14222, USA

*Bruno D'Udine,* Museo di Storia Naturale e Laboratorio, Università di Parma, I-43100 Parma, Italy

*Milton Diamond,* Department of Anatomy and Reproductive Biology, John A. Burns School of Medicine, University of Hawai'i, Honolulu, Hawai'i 96822, USA

*Herman Dienske,* TNO Primate Center, 2280 HV Rijswijk, The Netherlands

*Michael Domjan,* Department of Psychology and Institute for Neurological Sciences, University of Texas at Austin, Austin, Texas 78712, USA

*Michael J. Dougher,* Department of Psychology, University of New Mexico, Albuquerque, New Mexico 87131, USA

*Irenäus Eibl-Eibesfeldt,* Forschungsstelle für Humanethologie in der Max-Planck-Gesellschaft, D-8138 Andechs, Federal Republic of Germany

*Jay R. Feierman,* Department of Psychiatry, University of New Mexico and Department of Behavioral Medicine, Presbyterian Healthcare Services, Albuquerque, New Mexico 87112, USA

*Randall J. Garland,* Department of Psychology, University of New Mexico, Albuquerque, New Mexico 87131, USA

*Brian A. Gladue,* Department of Psychology, North Dakota State University, Fargo, North Dakota 58103, USA

*Sigrid Hopf,* Max-Planck-Institut für Psychiatrie, D-8000 München 40, Federal Republic of Germany

*John B. Hutchison,* MRC Neuroendocrine Development and Behaviour Group, Institute of Animal Physiology, BABRAHAM, Cambridge CB2 4AT, United Kingdom

*Rosemary E. Hutchison,* MRC Neuroendocrine Development and Behaviour Group, Institute of Animal Physiology, BABRAHAM, Cambridge CB2 4AT, United Kingdom

*Wade C. Mackey,* Division of Humanities, El Paso Community College, El Paso, Texas 79998, USA

*Gerhard Medicus,* Forschungsstelle für Humanethologie in der Max-Planck-Gesellschaft, D-8138 Andechs, Federal Republic of Germany and Landes-Nervenkrankenhaus Hall in Tirol, A-6060 Hall in Tirol, Austria

*John Money,* Johns Hopkins University and Hospital, Baltimore, Maryland 21205, USA

*Paul Okami,* Independent Researcher, New York, New York 10024, USA

*Anne Pusey,* Department of Ecology and Behavioral Biology, University of Minnesota, Minneapolis, Minnesota 55455, USA

*Wulf Schiefenhövel,* Forschungsstelle für Humanethologie in der Max-Planck-Gesellschaft, D-8138 Andechs and Wissenschaftskolleg zu Berlin, D-1000 Berlin 33, Federal Republic of Germany

*Donald C. Silva,* Institutional Affiliation Withheld at the Request of the Author

*David M. Taub,* Department of Psychiatry and Behavioral Sciences, Medical University of South Carolina, Charleston, South Carolina 29425 and Laboratory Animal Breeders & Services (LABS), Yemassee, South Carolina 29945, USA

*Frans B. M. de Waal,* Wisconsin Regional Primate Research Center, University of Wisconsin, Madison, Wisconsin 53715-1299, USA

*Gail Zivin,* Department of Psychiatry and Human Behavior, Jefferson Medical College, Philadelphia, Pennsylvania 19107, USA

# Introduction

## The Reason for this Volume

If we were to judge the seriousness of a psychosocial problem by the attention that the popular media give to it, we would have to conclude that the modern world is in the midst of an epidemic of pedophilic child sexual abuse. One can scarcely go more than a few weeks in any large metropolitan area without reading about one of the community's upstanding citizens discovered to have been sexually involved with children or adolescents.

The attention that the popular media give this topic is paralleled by the attention that it receives in the social sciences, where literally dozens of books and more than a thousand articles have been published on it in the past few years. In fact, "child sexual abuse," along with "co-dependency" and "dysfunctional family," have become the avant-garde psychological cliches of the decade. However, most of the lay and professional literature, although voluminous, reflect a narrow anthropo-, ethno-, and chronocentrism that precludes any real understanding of the topic with anything more than the preconceptions of our times.

The writing is anthropocentric because the topic often is discussed as though humans were the only species in which sexual behavior between adults and nonadults is found. The writing is ethnocentric because the behavior is discussed as though it were, somehow, peculiar to Western industrialized societies. The writing is chronocentric because the behavior is discussed as though it were a recent development in the history of the human species. All of these "-centrisms" obscure the fact that the behavior is seen in other species, societies, and times and has to be understood within these broader contexts.

The behavioral-science disciplines that have contributed the most significantly to our current understanding of this topic have been sociology and social psychology (e.g., David Finkelhor's *Child Sexual Abuse* and Mark Cook's *Adult Sexual Interest in Children*). Numerous practitioners have based clinical interventions on the data base and knowledge generated by these disciplines. This volume adds to this data base by including new, biosocial contributions from the perspectives of history, political science, sexology, biology, primatology, anthropology, experimental and developmental psychology, and psychiatry. What results is a transspecies, transcultural, and transhistorical perspective that gives new biosocial insights into the roots of pedophilia as the phenomenon is found in contemporary industrialized societies.

## Biosocial Perspective

Human behavior, like human anatomy, has evolved. The major mechanisms that account for this evolutionary process are natural, sexual, and kin selection, all of which are explained later in this volume. Selected behavior that leads to an increased chance for the individual to survive and reproduce is called "adaptive behavior," or simply, "an adaptation." As a result, almost all humans who are alive today are individuals who exhibit a repertoire of adaptive behaviors. Because of our current understanding of the evolutionary process, the biosocial perspective systematically asks the question, **Is** or **was** a particular behavior adaptive? It is legitimate to ask the question regarding **any** human behavior, including some aspects of adult human sexual behavior with children and adolescents.

Many social scientists would argue that the determinants of adult human sexual behavior with children and adolescents simply are culturally transmitted across generations by social learning. This view has been the predominant perspective in the sociological and social-psychological literature on the subject to date. This volume will expand upon this view by developing the thesis that aspects of the behavior result from an interaction of genetic and nongenetic determinants and that in many instances, there is strong support that some of the genetic determinants were subjected to positive selective pressures or were the by-products of selective pressures in our evolutionary past. This realization is perhaps the single most important contribution of this volume and is of more than academic interest, inasmuch as it not only suggests why there is a proclivity towards the behavior in some individuals but it also suggests a rational strategy by which heuristic questions and future hypotheses can be formulated.

The biosocial perspective augments the previously published literature on pedophilia, much of which is published under the category "Child Sexual Abuse" in the lay and professional literature. The perspective of most of the child sexual abuse literature is that of cultural transmission through social learning, a perspective that is strongly influenced by the emerging but still nascent discipline of victimology. One of the central theoretical tenets of victimology is the perpetuation of the behavior, perpetuation that occurs, it is said, because the primary determinant of one's being a child sexual abuser as an adult is that one was sexually abused as a child.

This volume critically examines the biases under which the data that form the basis of this fundamental tenet of victimology are collected, as well as critically examining the actual data, and comes to the conclusion that, contrary to the popular belief that is based on victimology theory, being sexually involved with an adult as a child is neither a necessary nor a sufficient cause of the engaging in sexual behavior with a child as an adult. Clearly, alternative perspectives are in order.

## Terminology

The title of this volume, "Pedophilia," is the word that the popular media give to any kind of sexual behavior between an adult and a legally underage person. However, the more scientific definition of the term "pedophilia" is "sexual attraction to prepubertal children." The term for actual sexual behavior between an adult and a prepubertal child is "pedosexual behavior." Sexual attraction to adolescents is called "ephebophilia" (the synonym is "hebephilia"), and actual sexual behavior between an adult and an adolescent is called "ephebosexual behavior." All of these specific attractions and behaviors are discussed separately in this volume under the rubric "Pedophilia."

Because of the biosocial perspective of this volume, a vocabulary was chosen that allows numerous species, including humans, to be described with the same terms. For example, the term "male" is used in place of "man" or "boy." The term "female" is used in place of "woman" or "girl." Likewise, the term "individual" is used in place of "person." Although these terms may appear to be somewhat awkward at times, the overall effect of having a common terminology with which to describe the behavior of humans as well as nonhumans outweighs the disadvantages.

Incest is defined in this volume as sexual behavior between any two individuals who are first-degree relatives and, therefore, are related to each other by 0.5. This category includes relationships between parents and offspring and between brothers and sisters. Incestuous behavior does not imply that one of the individuals is a child or an adolescent, because much incestuous behavior takes place between first-degree relatives both of whom are adults. When incestuous behavior involves a child or an adolescent, the adult is engaging in pedo- or ephebosexual behavior. Such an adult may or may not be a pedo- or an ephebophile.

The tendency in the clinical literature has been to not consider most adults who engage in sexual behavior with children and adolescents as being pedo- or ephebophiles, inasmuch as pedo- and ephebophilia previously have been assumed to be the result of either previous childhood victimization or mental derangement. This volume will question both of these assumption, inasmuch as the major "roots" of pedo- and ephebophilia are found neither in the previous childhood exposure to sexual behavior with an adult nor in the minds of the seriously mentally ill. Rather, the bulk of the determinants of pedo- and ephebophilia are embedded in the phylogenetic, i.e., the evolutionary, past of all humans.

In addition to the very sensitive issue of incest, there is also a very sensitive and somewhat strained relationship between adult homosexual males and adult, androphilic pedo- and ephebosexual males. An awareness of the nature of this relationship has resulted in the use of the terms "androphilic" and "gynephilic" in this volume rather than "homosexual" and "heterosexual" to describe the sex of the individuals to whom pedo- and ephebosexual males are sexually attracted.

## Contents and Organization of this Book

The volume is organized in six parts, the middle four of which represent ethologist Niko Tinbergen's suggestions regarding the areas of inquiry that one has to address if one is going to understand a particular behavior.

### Background

In **Chapter 1**, "A Biosocial Overview . . . ," Feierman develops a biosocial basis by which selected aspects of human sexual attraction and behavior in general can be understood and then puts pedo- and ephebosexual behavior within this context. In **Chapter 2**, "History . . . ," Bullough places adult human sexual behavior with children and adolescents into the historical context of Western civilization and concludes that such behavior, in contrast to popular belief, is at an all-time low level of occurrence. In **Chapter 3**, "Sociopolitical Biases in the Contemporary Scientific Literature . . . ," Okami shows how the use of the nascent discipline of victimology, as a basis with which to understand all adult human sexual behavior with children and adolescents, serves more as a sociopolitical vehicle for the values of some of its users than as a scientific model with which to understand the phenomenon.

### Evolution

In **Chapter 4**, "The Phylogeny of Male/Female Differences . . . ," Medicus and Hopf show how an understanding of the evolutionary history of male/female differences can help in explaining why pedo- and ephebophilia are largely adult male phenomena. In **Chapter 5**, "Dominance, Submission, and Love: . . . ," Eibl-Eibesfeldt explains how the origins of pedo- and ephebophilia can be found in the dominant/submissive sexuality of our reptilian ancestors as well as in parental love. In **Chapter 6**, "Adolescent/Adult Copulatory Behavior in Nonhuman Primates," Anderson and Bielert document that a low frequency of copulatory sexual behavior between adults and nonadults is widespread among our primate ancestors and that the patterns of who copulates with whom can be predicted to some degree with a knowledge of the species as well as of the socioecology of the particular social group. In **Chapter 7**, "Mechanisms of Inbreeding Avoidance . . . ," Pusey describes the two main biosocial mechanisms of inbreeding avoidance in nonhuman primates: separation of close relatives (by death or dispersal) and suspension of mating (by prolonged familiarity) between close kin living in the same social group. These biosocial mechanisms predate the emergence of humans and, therefore, of age-of-consent laws and incest taboos.

## Cause

In **Chapter 8**, "The Modification of Sexual Behavior Through Imprinting: . . . ," D'Udine describes how adult sexual preferences in rodents can be predictably and permanently altered through experimental manipulation of their early environment by cross-fostering among different species. In **Chapter 9**, "The Modification of Sexual Behavior Through Conditioning: . . . ," Domjan demonstrates experimentally in the Japanese quail that even in adulthood, sexual behavior can be modified in some degree through conditioning to inanimate objects. In **Chapter 10**, "Hormones and Neuroendocrine Factors . . . ," Gladue reviews the literature on neuroendocrine correlates of sexual orientation in humans and suggests how these same techniques can be used to study the neuroendocrine correlates of age orientation. In **Chapter 11**, "Adult-Male/Juvenile Association . . . ," Mackey, using a comparative field approach among many societies, argues that the consistency and predictability of certain nonsexual temporal associations of adult males with children and adolescents across diverse societies suggests that such behavior is a species-characteristic trait of humans.

## Function

In **Chapter 12**, "The Concept of Function . . . ," Dienske discusses the possible answers and their biophilosophical implications that result from asking the ethologically justified question, Is there a function of adult human sexual behavior with children and adolescents? In **Chapter 13**, "The Functions of Primate Paternalism: . . . ," Taub reviews the various functions of adult-male/nonadult associations in nonhuman primates. In **Chapter 14**, "Sociosexual Behavior . . . Among Bonobos," de Waal shows how sexual behavior functions in regulating interindividual tension among all age and sex combinations in bonobos (pygmy chimpanzees), a species of living primates that is one of the genetically closest to humans. In **Chapter 15**, "Ritualized Adult-Male/Adolescent-Male Sexual Behavior in Melanesia,"

Schiefenhövel discusses the functions of a behavior that is considered criminal in Western industrialized societies but is both normative and obligatory in some Melanesian societies. In **Chapter 16**, "Selected Cross-Generational Sexual Behavior in Traditional Hawai'i: . . . ," Diamond presents a sexual ethnography, with emphasis on adult/nonadult sexual behavior, of a non-Western society known even to most nonanthropologists.

## Development

In **Chapter 17**, "Pedophilia: . . . New Phylism Theory as Applied to Paraphilic Lovemaps," Money shows how pedophilia (and ephebophilia) can be understood in terms of a transposition of the parenting and mating "phylisms." In **Chapter 18**, Silva—the pseudonym for an incarcerated, androphilic pedo- and ephebosexual physician with specialty training in both pediatrics and child psychiatry—describes his own sexual development and adult behavior, giving a unique, personal insight into the development of pedo- and ephebophilia. This chapter should be particularly helpful to individuals reading this volume who have little previous knowledge of the topic. In **Chapter 19**, "The Abused/Abuser Hypothesis . . . ," Garland and Dougher critically review the literature concerning what now must be considered the most widespread misconception about child sexual abuse: that being sexually involved with an adult as a child or an adolescent will cause one to be sexually attracted to children and adolescents in adulthood. In **Chapter 20**, "Sexual Development at the Neurohormonal Level: . . . ," Hutchison and Hutchison critically review sexual brain differentiation and sexual development in terms of the role of androgens, the male sex hormones. In **Chapter 21**, "The Complexity of the Concept of Behavioral Development: A Summary," Zivin reviews and synthesizes the latest concepts concerning behavioral development in general and applies them to our current, rather simplistic views on how pedo- or ephebosexual behavior develops.

## Conclusion

In **Chapter 22**, "Human Erotic Age Orientation: A Conclusion," Feierman develops a biosocial understanding of why "pedophilia" and "ephebophilia" are perceived, categorized, and labeled. The processes of the "neotenization" of nubile females and "nubility perpetuation" of any-age, reproductively competent females are examined in their relationship to pedo- and ephebophilia. It is argued that to date, although aspects of pedo- and ephebophilia appear to be phylogenetically adaptive, the entire behavioral repertoire—in the context in which it is seen in modern industrialized societies—is best conceptualized as a by-product of selection. The chapter concludes with the optimistic hope that through acceptance, compassion, and understanding, pedo- and ephebophiles will be provided the help they need in order to conform their behavior to the expectations of the societies in which they live.

## Acknowledgments

The impetus to produce this volume came from the International Society for Human Ethology, some of whose members suggested that human ethology, the biology of human behavior, had to demonstrate its usefulness in a clinically relevant area. The editor of this volume, who at the time was the Membership Chair of the Society and had worked clinically for more than 10 years as a psychiatrist with adults who had been sexually involved with children and adolescents, suggested that the subject matter that now composes this volume was worthy of consideration.

In the summer of 1987, The Servants of the Paraclete, a Catholic religious order, generously supported the convening of the Society in the order's secluded retreat facilities in Jemez Springs, New Mexico, where this very sensitive topic was addressed. Approximately 50 behavioral scientists from seven countries met for a week in Jemez Springs to try to further the understanding of the phenomenon. The respective final versions of many of the chapters in this volume reflect the thinking of numerous individuals in attendance at the Symposium. For their contributions, specific appreciation is expressed to Mark Cook, Kathryn J. Dolan, David Finkelhor, Suzanne G. Frayser, Robert W. Goy, J. Stephen Heisel, Jane B. Lancaster, Joan A. Nelson, Hilda and Seymour Parker, Donald Pfaff, Susan Phipps-Yonas, Theo G.M. Sandfort, Albert Yonas, and others. Approximately half of the individuals who presented papers at that meeting were invited to submit revised manuscripts, and in addition, a number of individuals not in attendance at Jemez Springs also were invited to submit manuscripts. From these submitted manuscripts, this volume was developed. Without the support of the International Society for Human Ethology and The Servants of the Paraclete, the volume never would have come to fruition.

The Vista Hill Foundation, San Diego, California, generously provided financial and secretarial support for the editor during 1983-1987, which made it possible for the Jemez Springs Symposium to be organized and to take place. Presbyterian Healthcare Services in Albuquerque, New Mexico, has supported the editing of the volume with secretarial staff and office space for the editor in 1988 and 1989.

Susan Weiss has overseen the entire project during a three-year period. Her organizational, editing, and writing skills are reflected in almost every aspect of the volume.

Finally, this work is dedicated to all of the adults, adolescents, and children whose lives have been affected, in one way or another, by the topic that is addressed in this volume.

Jay R. Feierman, M.D.
Corrales, New Mexico

October 31, 1989

# 1
# A Biosocial Overview of Adult Human Sexual Behavior with Children and Adolescents

Jay R. Feierman
*Department of Psychiatry*
*University of New Mexico*
 *and*
*Department of Behavioral Medicine*
*Presbyterian Healthcare Services*
*Albuquerque, New Mexico 87112*

## Introduction

### Sex, Culture, and the Biosocial Perspective

The word "sex" usually captures people's attention when it occurs in book titles, magazine articles, and newspaper headlines, especially when the word is referring to sexual behavior that falls outside a socially acceptable boundary. Interestingly, such boundaries appear to be somewhat arbitrary, inasmuch as a given society can ignore or rigidly enforce the transgressions of its members over very short periods of historical time (see Bullough, this volume). In addition, neighboring societies can and often do have very different boundaries that pertain to the "with whom" and "what context" aspects of sexual behavior.

Until now, science has had less an understanding of the biosocial factors that determine and regulate adult human sexual behavior with children and adolescents than it has had an understanding of the culturally transmitted boundary markers, such as age-of-consent laws and incest taboos. This volume is more concerned with sexual **behavior** per se and its biosocial determination and regulation than with the culturally transmitted, humans-created, age-of-consent laws and incest taboos. There already is a large body of literature on the age-of-consent laws as well as on the cultural variations and correlations of the incest taboos.

Sexual reproduction between a parent and that individual's adolescent or adult offspring is extremely rare in any species under **natural** conditions, and nonhuman species do not have culturally transmitted age-of-consent laws or incest taboos, which commonly are believed to prevent such behavior in humans (see Pusey, this volume). Yet, to some degree, the very same "wild" animals under certain conditions of **captivity**—as well as domesticated animals in barnyards, backyards, and pastures—often will mate with their own adolescent or adult offspring. Sexual behavior, as this example shows, therefore, is context dependent. This context dependency also may have relevance in the understanding of adult human sexual behavior with children and adolescents, whether the child or adolescent is related to the adult who is involved in the behavior or not, inasmuch as many humans do not live under socioecological conditions that even resemble natural conditions, i.e., the context in which their genotypes evolved.

In the nonhuman primates that have been and are being adequately studied under natural and seminatural conditions, even though parent/offspring mating is observed infrequently at any age of the offspring, other copulatory, as well as noncopulatory, forms of sexual behavior between related and nonrelated adults and juveniles are common and predictable and appear to have adaptive functions, depending on the particular species (see Anderson and Bielert, this volume; de Waal, this volume; Pusey, this volume). That this behavior is predictable, functional, and seemingly adaptive in some nonhuman primates suggests that there are biosocial factors that predate human culture (i.e., age-of-consent laws and incest taboos), factors that both determine and regulate species-typical, adult/juvenile sexual behavior. This volume seeks to elucidate these same types of biosocial determining and regulating factors in the human species.

The biosocial perspective around which this volume is organized has provided useful insights into other socially unacceptable behavior, such as infanticide, homicide, child abuse, rape, incest, and adultery. The biosocial perspective asks several questions: Is or was a given behavior or category of behavior maladaptive or adaptive? If it is or was adaptive, how is this determined, and how did it evolve? What factors influence its regulation and dysregulation? "Adaptive," as it is used in the biological sense, simply means "the facilitating of getting one's genes into the next generation." Adaptive behavior can be legal or illegal, moral or immoral, socially acceptable or socially unacceptable.

## Sexual Behavior

This volume is mainly about sexual **behavior**.[1] "Sexual behavior" can be defined in several ways, such as (a) "any behavior performed during measurable or observable sexual arousal," (b) "any behavior that uses copulatory motor patterns," (c) "any behavior that involves touching (one's own or others') genitals," and (d) "any behavior that signals, by species-specific movements, an internal readiness, or mood, to mate." There is a contrasting point of view that espouses that all humans are sexual beings and, therefore, that **all** behavior that an individual engages in is sexual. This definition of "sexual behavior" is so broad that it loses all usefulness.

Most reported adult human sexual behavior with children and adolescents concerns sexual behavior involving adult males rather than adult females, by a ratio of approximately 10:1 (Abel et al., 1987; Gebhard et al., 1965; Linder and Seliger, 1947). This volume does not address the involvement of adult females because too little information currently is known and has been written about the topic.

Although differences in the processes through which males and females are socialized have been proposed as explanations of this behavioral sex difference (Finkelhor, 1984; Maccoby and Jacklin, 1974), there are also many complementary biosocial explanations (see Eibl-Eibesfeldt, this volume; Gladue, this volume; Hutchison and Hutchison, this volume; Mackey, this volume; Medicus and Hopf, this volume; Taub, this volume). Since behavioral sex differences are seen in both social and nonsocial nonhuman primates (Mitchell, 1979) as well as in almost all other well-studied nonprimate species (Wickler, 1973), the explanatory adequacy of "differential socialization" alone, devoid of biology, is questionable.

In order to understand adult human sexual behavior with children and adolescents, this author finds it useful to divide sexual behavior into the three traditional phases, **proceptive, receptive,** and **conceptive,** but to define these phases in terms of their functions (i.e., their effects) in a biosocial-communications context rather than in terms of their structure, which is more traditional:

1.  **Proceptive behavior** functions in eliciting sexual behavior by an uncommitted individual.

2.  **Receptive behavior** functions in the mutual acknowledgement of ongoing or impending sexual behavior.

3.  **Conceptive behavior** is the performing of species-typical, sexual, behavioral motor patterns that are used in consummating an adult-male/adult-female sexual relationship.

Many human societies have names as well as ritualized rights of passage for the formal transition through the three phases—e.g., maidenhood, engagement, and marriage—with ornamental acknowledgement of each phase in the form of hair style, clothing, and jewelry. However, in contrast to the months to years that elapse as one moves through the phases in the context of formal engagement and marriage, the transition from the proceptive to the conceptive phase can take minutes to hours when the relative permanency of a relationship or the creation of heirs are not issues.

## Sexual Motivation and Mood

"Motivation" means "the total of all factors, both internal and external to the individual, that increase the probability of a particular behavior's occurring." "Mood" is a subset of motivation; it encompasses some of the internal factors only and is synonymous with the ethological concept "a specific, internal readiness to act" (see Eibl-Eibesfeldt, 1975). In this volume, in which new empirical data are introduced and old empirical data are reviewed, the material that is presented is organized around a biosocial, theoretical framework that will help interested persons better understand not only the behavior involved but also, at least to some modest degree, motivational factors and moods. Readers of this volume with legal interests may want to understand both internal and external "motives." Clinicians may want to know more about internal moods, which are self-perceived as "feelings," and external "risk factors." These areas, which often overlap, are addressed in this volume, at least to the extent that they relate to or are predictive of behavior.

## Sexual Interactants

To understand adult human sexual behavior with children and adolescents, one must address sexual awareness, attention, arousal, and behavior in the **interactants**. The term "interactants" may disturb some readers, inasmuch as there has been a trend in the clinical literature on child sexual abuse to conceptualize adult/child and adult/adolescent sexual behavior within a victimological paradigm (see Okami, this volume). In that paradigm, the child or adolescent is seen as the passive "victim" of the "perpetrator's" "sexual aggression" (e.g., Burgess et al., 1978; Finkelhor, 1984). This terminology is not used in this volume. Rather, purely descriptive terms are used.

The most obvious difference between the victimological and the biosocial paradigms is the role of the child or adolescent. The biosocial paradigm sees the child or adolescent as an active interactant. This interactant role is **not** equivalent to saying that a child or an adolescent is making a free-will choice or is morally responsible for engaging in sexual behavior with an adult. It is a value judgement of the author of this chapter/editor of this volume that in any relationship in which there is a large dominance or power differential between the interactants, clearly, the more dominant and more powerful individual must accept full moral and legal responsibility.

## Sexual Attraction

One cannot even begin to understand sexual behavior in any species, but especially in the human species, without including the term "sexual attraction." The term is broader in meaning than "**mate choice**" (Bateson, 1983), "**sexual preference**" (Bell et al., 1981), and "**sexual choice**" (Remoff, 1984). Sexual attraction, too, is context dependent in the human species, in that attributes considered desirable in a sexual partner are not necessarily the same as attributes considered desirable in a marital partner. However, in either context, individuals usually are sexually attracted to other individuals who are neither too similar to nor too dissimilar from themselves.

**Sexual attraction** can be operationally defined as the
1. **awareness of** or
2. **attention given to** or
3. behavioral **association with** or
4. **courtship** behavior **displayed towards** another specific individual or class of individuals (in person, representation, or fantasy)
5. **that is associated with** either observable or measurable physiological **sexual arousal** in the body of the perceiving individual.

Although there are modal, societal standards of sexual attractiveness for categories of individuals—e.g., sexually attractive adult male, sexually attractive adult female—individuals who represent the best examples of these standards cannot elicit sexual attraction in every adult of the opposite sex who is aware of and pays attention to them. John Money developed the concept "**lovemap**" to accommodate this idiosyncracy of individual sexual attraction. A lovemap is defined as follows: ". . . **a developmental representation or template in the mind and in the brain depicting the idealized lover and the idealized program of sexuoerotic activity projected in imagery or actually engaged in with that lover**" (Money, 1986, p. 290). The lovemap is discussed in more detail in the next section of this chapter, titled "The Lovemap," and in Money (this volume). In ethological conceptualization, the lovemap would be represented in the brain by the **stimulus filter**[2] (Lorenz, 1981).

The first four components of sexual attraction will be discussed separately in the remainder of this subsection, and the fifth component, sexual arousal, will be discussed separately in the subsection "Sexual Arousal," which concludes this section.

### Awareness

The awareness of an individual or of a class of individuals must start with one's noticing the presence of that individual or class of individuals. Certain stimuli enter or remain in one's awareness more than do other stimuli, based upon the stimulus filters of innate releasing mechanisms, previous experience, the context, and the mood (Lorenz, 1981). It is reasonable to assume that there would be awareness of the presence of an individual or of a class of individuals towards whom there is sexual attraction, especially if a sexual context and mood were present. Sexual awareness usually is not noticeable or measurable by an outside observer.

## Attention

Attention means "the sensory monitoring of the behavior of an individual or of a class of individuals either continuously or intermittently." An individual does not have to be aware that he or she is being monitored. When individuals behave in such a way as to cause others (not sexually committed to them) to pay attention to them and when the basis of the attention is sexual attraction, such attention-eliciting behavior satisfies the functional definition of proceptive behavior (Moore, 1985). The acknowledgement by one individual that someone is paying attention to him or her is the beginning of communication (Smith, 1977). Communication becomes courtship when the attention between two individuals becomes both alternating and escalating and is accompanied by certain species-specific, mood-specific, stereotyped, proceptive expressive behaviors, as well as by mixed or alternating approach-and-avoidance eye-contact behaviors, which are the preadapted, adult/adult version of the culturally universal childhood-expressed game "peek-a-boo."

## Behavioral Association

Behavioral association, the next indicator of sexual attraction, can take two forms: increased time or decreased space between two individuals. In both time and space, the association often starts under contexts and pretexts that do not reveal that, at least for one of the interactants, the underlying motivation is sexual attraction. One individual often increases behavioral association with another individual before any real communication or relationship has begun. Behavioral association is not a communicative interaction unless both individuals have acknowledged (vocally or nonvocally) that they are paying attention to each other. When it is communication, behavioral association is often used as proceptive behavior by both males and females.

In the special case of adult human sexual behavior with children and adolescents, social institutions that are founded on adult/child and adult/adolescent association, such as youth groups, are a proceptive means through which the **pedophile** (an adult who is sexually attracted primarily to prepubertal children) and the **ephebophile** (an adult who is sexually attracted primarily to adolescents[3]) can associate in a socially acceptable context with children and adolescents who are not related to the adult.

## Courtship Behaviors

Courtship behaviors are a sequential, alternating and escalating series of species-specific, mood-specific, ritualized behaviors that signal mutual sexual receptivity (i.e., they are receptive-phase behavior) between two individuals (Morris, 1970; Tinbergen, 1960). Courtship is **escalating** intimacy over time where, in order for courtship to continue, the behavior of one interactant has to be responded to by the other interactant with escalation, rather than with de-escalation or with no response. Escalation signals the other interactant's opportunity to escalate in return. De-escalation signals termination. No response and mixed messages (e.g., "Your words say 'no' but your eyes say 'yes.'") are ambiguous signals that test the intensity of the other interactant's motivation.

Perper (1985), in a nonsystematic but nevertheless insightful way, describes four behaviors that compose the escalating temporal sequence of human receptive-phase courtship: (1) **talk** to each other, (2) **turn** in space, (3) **touch** each other, and (4) **synchronize** movements. Performed alone or without the specific sequence of 1,2,3,4, without alternation, and without escalation, these behaviors are not courtship and, therefore, are not predictive of ensuing human, interindividual, conceptive-phase sexual behavior.

## Sexual Arousal

At a purely physiological level, within the context of the Masters-and-Johnson-defined **sexual response cycle**, sexual arousal shows a definite cross-cultural commonality among all adults. There are some differences both within and between the two sexes, however (Masters and Johnson, 1966). (See Figure 1.1a and 1.1b.)

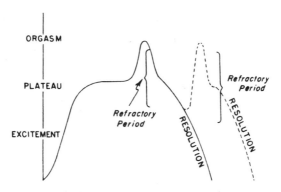

Figure 1.1a.    Stages of the human male sexual response cycle. (Source: W.H. Masters and V.E. Johnson, *Human sexual response* [Boston: Little, Brown and Company, 1966], p. 5.) (Reprinted with the permission of the Masters & Johnson Institute.)

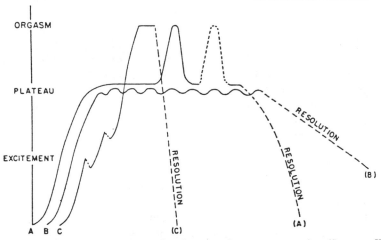

Figure 1.1b. Stages of the human female sexual response cycle. (Source: W.H. Masters and V.E. Johnson, *Human sexual response* [Boston: Little, Brown and Company, 1966], p. 5.) (Reprinted with the permission of the Masters & Johnson Institute.)

For example, the human female has the potential for multiple orgasms within a sexual response cycle and a greater variance in that cycle compared to the male. These differences are not of much significance in the understanding of the adult male sex bias in adult human sexual behavior with children and adolescents, however, because orgasm, which differentiates the male and female sexual response cycles, occurs during the conceptive phase of interindividual sexual behavior. The adult male sex bias in adult human sexual behavior with children and adolescents is more a reflection of the proceptive-phase differences between males and females.

Sexual arousal can be defined and measured by several different means, one of which is verbal self-report. Verbal self-report of sexual arousal may be accurate when one is sexually attracted to socially appropriate-age persons of the opposite sex. In all other cases, verbal self-report is highly suspect at best, inasmuch as it is very easy for the person making the self-report not only to deceive the person listening to the report but also to deceive him- or herself as well. In the case of adult human sexual behavior with children and adolescents, the inherent lack of certainty is especially true and is the reason for the use of penile plethysmography to measure and define sexual arousal (see Freund et al., 1989).

## The Lovemap

One's own idiosyncratic lovemap (already defined in the previous section in the subsection "Sexual Attraction") is made up of the animate, inanimate, and contextual attributes, associated with other individuals, to which one is sexually attracted. Since lovemaps vary greatly among individuals, classifying some of the factors believed to contribute to lovemap variability may give insight into the yet to be fully understood determinants of adult human sexual attraction to children and adolescents.

Three sets of factors contribute to some of the lovemap variability:

1. Two sources of stimulus familiarity—**phylogeny**[4] and **ontogeny**,[5]
2. One property of the stimulus—the **capacity to evoke initial-stimulus appetence**[6] **in the perceiver**, and
3. One property of the nervous system—**stimulus discriminative ability**[7]

(The two properties will be discussed subsequently.)

The qualifying term "initial" is used before "stimulus appetence" because, after the perceiving individual's initial encounter with a phylogenetically familiar or unfamiliar sexual-arousal-associated-with stimulus,[8] previously unfamiliar and neutral, animate, inanimate, or contextual stimuli can be conditioned into ontogenetically familiar, sexually evocative status through pairing with the initial sexual arousal. The age at which one encounters conditioned sexual stimuli determines whether or not such stimuli will become part of the lovemap (see D'Udine, this volume, for early-age and Domjan, this volume, for late-age experimental animal models). This sexual-conditioning effect will be discussed in this chapter in regard to adult heterosexual males.

For reasons that will be explained later in the chapter, the human male lovemap is largely coded and stored in a visual format. The analysis of visual stimulus patterns and their sexual relevance is processed in neural tissue whose response to both familiar and novel stimuli will vary among individuals, based on genetic differences in the reactivity of the tissue itself

|  | INITIAL-STIMULUS APPETENCE | STIMULUS DISCRIMIN-ABILITY |
|---|---|---|
| **PHYLOGENETIC FAMILIARITY** | high | low |
| **ONTOGENETIC FAMILIARITY** | low | potentially high |

Figure 1.2. Relationship of phylogenetic and ontogenetic familiarity to initial-stimulus appetence and stimulus discriminability.

as well as on previous exposure of the tissue to stimuli with varying degrees of phylogenetic or ontogenetic familiarity to the perceiving individual.

Whether or not the familiarity is on the basis of phylogeny (known by the species, historically) or ontogeny (known by the individual, developmentally) has an effect on the capacity of a stimulus to evoke **initial**-stimulus appetence. Phylogenetically familiar stimuli, such as the shape of a nubile[9] female, evoke a higher degree of **initial**-stimulus appetence but have a lower degree of stimulus discriminability; in contrast, ontogenetically made-familiar sexual stimuli, such as a particular pattern of lace, evoke a lower degree of **initial**-stimulus appetence but have a higher degree of stimulus discriminability (see Figure 1.2). Ontogenetically made-familiar stimuli, such as lace, which evoke low initial-stimulus appetence, can be incorporated into an individual's lovemap, however, as will be discussed in relation to "secondary-stimulus appetence."

## Capacity of a Stimulus To Evoke Initial-Stimulus Appetence

The stimuli that have a capacity to evoke a high degree of initial-stimulus appetence in a perceiver are not arbitrary. Rather, they derive from those attributes whose variations, over eons of evolutionary time (i.e., through phylogeny), have been associated with variance in fitness and about which the species already is familiar. Initial stimuli that have affected fitness positively over eons of evolutionary time usually evoke a high degree of initial-stimulus appetence.

There appear to be two major attributes some of the variations of which evoke initial-stimulus appetence: biological age and sex (usually perceived as gender attributes). That is, the two most fitness-relevant attributes in a potential sexual partner are the age of the individual and the sex of the individual. Evolution should have shaped human populations so that the "average adult male" has an initial-stimulus appetence for the attributes found in nubile females. Surely, the average adult male's genetic material has encountered this combination of attributes before, and adult males who attended to these attributes perceptually left more offspring than did adult males who ignored them.

## Stimulus Discriminative Ability

Initial-stimulus appetence evolved so that individuals would be attracted to those attributes whose variations positively affected fitness in those individuals' evolutionary past. However, stimuli usually are complex, and to attend to those features of stimuli that are associated with optimal fitness requires that the degree of stimulus discriminative ability be optimized.

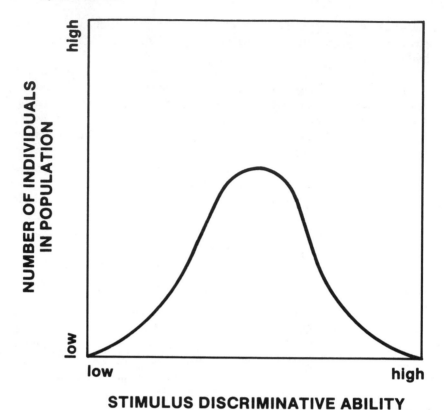

Figure 1.3. Distribution of the trait "discriminative ability" in a hypothetical population.

Stimulus discriminative ability, in this context, is a measure of the degree to which the numerous animate, inanimate, and contextual attributes of, or that are associated with, another individual can be matched to the numerous attributes in the prototype in one's lovemap, with the assumption that the closer the match, the more the erotosexual attraction. Stimulus discriminative ability is primarily a measure of the ability of the perceiving individual's nervous system to discriminate—it is not a property of, but may be limited by the discriminability of, the stimulus. Since in humans the lovemap is constructed in early childhood and does not become activated in the service of fertile mating until several years later, it is unlikely that any new individual ever could completely resemble the lovemap in all animate, inanimate, and contextual attributes.

If stimulus discriminative ability as a perceptual/physiological trait is distributed normally in the population (as a first-order approximation), there will be some individuals whose stimulus discriminative ability will be lower than optimum (left half of curve in Figure 1.3) and other individuals whose stimulus discriminative ability will be higher than optimum (right half of curve in Figure 1.3), so that the "average male" (center of curve in Figure 1.3) will have the optimum degree of stimulus discriminative ability.[10]

Individuals with higher than optimum stimulus discriminative ability can attend to minor details in the attributes of and associated with other individuals when appetitively searching for individuals who fit their lovemap. These individuals often have a sexual attraction to very specific, ontogenetically made-familiar, conditioned sexual stimuli, inasmuch as phylogeny can code only generalities in the innate stimulus filters of the recipient. In ontogeny, the degree to which a conditioned sexual stimulus can be discriminated (i.e., made to match the lovemap) is limited only by the discriminative ability of the perceiver and the discriminability of that which is being perceived.

A **secondary-stimulus appetence** can develop for a sexually conditioned, early in development encountered, ontogenetically made-familiar animate, inanimate, or contextual attribute in the lovemap, such as lace or black leather, whose potency can be as strong as or stronger than the initial phylogenetically familiar stimulus.[11] An early in development encountered, ontogenetically made-familiar, highly potent secondary stimulus, such as an inanimate attribute, that evokes a strong secondary-stimulus appetence is called a paraphilic[12] "fetish."

The development of strong secondary-stimulus appetences can occur because, once the phylogenetically familiar stimulus has been optimized for fitness, stimulus potency increases with stimulus discrimination, as will be shown subsequently. Some paraphiles can appetitively discriminate sexual stimuli to such a degree, i.e., search for and find the stimuli that very closely resemble the attributes in their lovemaps, that the stimuli have extraordinary, addiction-like, idiosyncratic sexual potency. Sexual-stimulus discrimination is the mechanism by which **type paraphilias** develop, and the propensity to develop them is correlated functionally with sexual stimulus discriminative ability and, mechanistically, with the degree to which the brain is defeminized in utero, as will be developed later in this chapter in the section titled "Adult/Child and Adult/Adolescent Sexual Behavior Versus Sexual Abuse."

Some pedo- and ephebophiles, who are sexually attracted to the highly discriminable, visual animate attributes of very particular stages of development of hairless or of budding secondary sexual characteristics, respectively, are thus attracted to children and adolescents on the basis of a type paraphilia.

Individuals who are endowed with lower than optimum stimulus discriminative ability (see left half of curve in Figure 1.3) attend only to major generalities in the phylogenetically familiar attributes of other individuals when appetitively searching for individuals who fit their lovemap. These appetitively searching individuals have an attraction only to phylogenetically familiar stimuli, inasmuch as ontogenetically made-familiar, conditioned stimuli cannot become potent enough in themselves to elicit

Figure 1.4. Oystercatcher reacting to giant egg (supranormal stimulus) in preference to normal egg (foreground) and herring gull's egg (left). (From N. Tinbergen, *The study of instinct,* Oxford University Press, 1951, p. 45. Reprinted with the permission of the publisher.)

sexual arousal because these individuals' low discriminative ability does not allow them to move to the right half of the curve in Figure 1.3. These individuals can increase the potency of sexual stimuli only through searching for supranormal stimuli.

## Supranormal Stimuli

In addition to increasing as a result of increased stimulus discrimination, stimulus potency also increases when attributes become **"supranormal stimuli"** (Tinbergen, 1951), where the stimuli are phylogenetically familiar but are supranormally exaggerated in size (i.e., extra large or extra small) and are therefore more potent. (See Figure 1.4.) Attraction to supranormal stimuli is the mechanism by which **size paraphilias** develop. For reasons that will be mechanistically developed later in the chapter, individuals whose brains are highly masculinized are sexually attracted to the submissive aspects of "smallness," whereas individuals whose brains are highly unmasculinized are sexually attracted to the dominant aspects of "largeness." Some pedophiles, who are sexually attracted to the smallness of the whole child or to the child's primary or secondary sexual characteristics, fall into the category of size paraphiliacs.

## Degree of Stimulus Discrimination,
## Stimulus Fitness, and Stimulus Potency

There is a relationship between the three variables—degree of stimulus discrimination, stimulus fitness, and stimulus potency—that is shown in Figure 1.5. Although it may be limited by the discriminability of the stimulus, the degree of stimulus discrimination is reflective of one's innate stimulus discriminative ability and is the independent variable. Based on the degree of stimulus discrimination, an individual would obtain varying degrees of stimulus fitness and stimulus potency, which are considered to be the dependent variables.

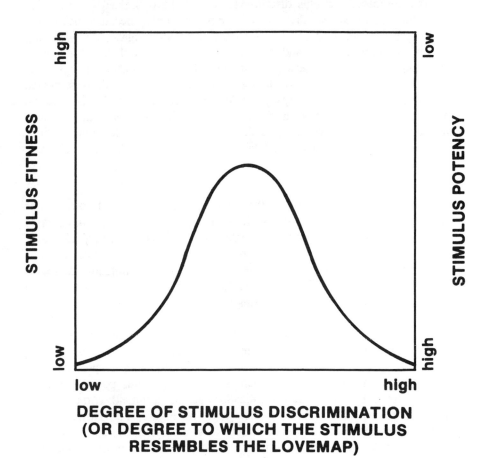

Figure 1.5. Relationship of stimulus fitness and stimulus potency to the degree of stimulus discrimination in the perceiving individual.

## Stimulus Fitness

Stimulus fitness is the effect on overall, lifetime fitness of one's being sexually attracted to naturally found stimuli using a given level of stimulus discrimination. The most general attributes that the average heterosexual male would attend to in locating a fertile individual—female sex and reproductive age—would require a very low level of stimulus discrimination. Female sex and nubile age would require a higher level, followed by female sex, nubile age, and good health; then female sex, nubile age, good health, and high status; then female sex, nubile age, good health, high status, and good education; and so on. Because of the potential for an almost never-ending range in the degree of stimulus discrimination (i.e., the degree to which the stimuli match the prototype in the lovemap), there obviously is an optimum degree of stimulus discrimination that optimizes fitness in the perceiving individual.

The degree of stimulus discrimination must be optimized in order that fitness be optimized **in the average human male,** because being too indiscriminate could lead to sexual attraction to individuals who were not even of the opposite sex and fertile. Being too discriminate, conversely, could lead to the male's turning down potential opportunistic matings. It is assumed that the reproductive strategy that evolved and optimized human male fitness protects and helps provision the offspring of the best fertile female who chooses him as a mate (see Remoff, 1984) and, at the same time, allows the male to not turn down uncommitted mating opportunities with other willing fertile females (Daly and Wilson, 1983; Symons, 1979).

## Stimulus Potency

Stimulus potency reflects the amount of stimulus necessary for achieving a standard response, such as a certain degree of measurable sexual arousal. Stimulus potency is analogous to the pharmacological use of the term "potency," as in "drug potency." The relationship among stimulus potency, stimulus fitness, and degree of stimulus discrimination is shown graphically in Figure 1.5. Note that as the degree of stimulus discrimination increases (i.e., the stimulus increasingly resembles the lovemap), stimulus potency initially decreases and then increases, because the basis of discrimination switches from phylogenetic to ontogenetic familiarity at the top of the bell-shaped curve in Figure 1.5. For example, a particular nubile female will deviate from the ideal nubile female phylogenetic prototype the more in detail she is perceived, which is why her stimulus potency actually decreases from the perceptual idealization in the left-hand corner to the perceptual reality at the top of the curve in Figure 1.5. However, the potential resemblance of a particular female to idiosyncratic, ontogenetically made-familiar, conditioned stimuli or attributes in the lovemap means that stimulus potency can potentially increase as stimulus discrimination increases on the right-hand side of Figure 1.5. This situation would occur when both the particular female and the prototype female in the lovemap have idiosyncratic animate or inanimate attributes or contexts in common. The more the resemblance, the higher the degree of stimulus discrimination and the higher the potency.

Natural selection has maximized stimulus fitness when stimulus potency (of a particular stimulus/attribute) is minimized with the result that attraction to appropriate (multi-stimulus/-attribute) **individuals** rather than to isolated stimuli or attributes of individuals is insured.

As is shown in Figure 1.6, there is a positive correlation between the number of near[13] optimally-discriminated-for-fitness stimuli or attributes and the total stimulus potency or overall desirability of an **individual**. A perceived individual in whom many stimuli or attributes were near optimally-discriminated-for-fitness could have a higher total stimulus potency or overall desirability value to a perceiving individual than another individual in whom only one stimulus or attribute was nearly maximally discriminated. The ability to maximize stimulus potency by minimizing or maximizing stimulus discrimination (i.e., the two tails of the curve in Figure 1.5) is the mechanism by which males, more so than females, can dissociate sexual eroticism (potency is maximized) from erotic affectual bonding (fitness is potentially maximized). Males accomplish this by perceptually focusing on one highly discriminated animate, inanimate, or contextual stimulus (attribute) that closely resembles their lovemap. In contrast, the steep rise in the slope of the curve in Figure 1.6, once a critical number of near optimally-discriminated-for-fitness stimuli have been accrued, reflects the potentially fitness maximizing process of forming an erotic affiliative bond with an individual (i.e., "falling in love") rather than merely being sexually attracted to an individual's attributes.

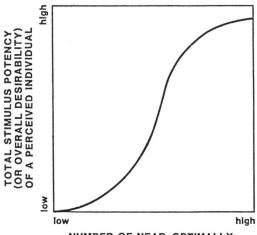

Figure 1.6. Relationship of total stimulus potency (or overall desirability) of a perceived individual to the number of near optimally-discriminated-for-fitness stimuli by a perceiving individual.

## Relationship to Love

Someone's idiosyncratic lovemap is that individual's ideal representation of another individual with whom the first should fall in love. This concept is true even if, through variable hormonal or life experience, the latter individual is not of the complementary sex or is not fertile.[14] Whereas one can perform sexual behavior with a wide variety of individuals, one can fall in love only with an individual whose attributes closely resemble the attributes in one's lovemap. For some adult males, the age of individuals in their lovemap, for reasons that will be partially explained in this volume, is the age of children (pedophilia) and adolescents (ephebophilia).

The erotic love of children and adolescents by an adult has three characteristics that differentiate it from the usual type of adult/adult love:

1. The love between the adult and the child or adolescent is not necessarily of the same kind to both of them.
2. There is a very limited time during which the love can remain erotic for the adult.
3. The child or adolescent can be an extremely potent sexual stimulus for the adult.

# Adult/Child and Adult/Adolescent Sexual Behavior within the Context of Reproductive Behavior

## Reproductive Behavior

Philosophers, biologists, and theologians of all persuasions have struggled with the question, What is the purpose of life? If one looks for the common element in all of their writings, one would find the conclusion that the purpose of life is to propagate life. The process by which life propagates life is called "reproductive behavior," and because the process expands on the purpose, that process is important to **all** individuals in a society, including pedophiles, ephebophiles, and even chaste celibates.

Reproductive behavior is not simply sexual behavior that is open to the possibility of or results in pregnancy! **Reproductive behavior** can be defined as "any behavior that promotes one's genetic propagation." Sexual behavior (e.g., copulating) accomplishes only a small part of reproductive behavior. Humans, in contrast to many simpler forms of life, are required to carry a pregnancy to term, to give birth to a live infant, and to provide a large amount of biparental care in order that an offspring be raised optimally to an age at which that offspring can genetically propagate.

## Nonsexual Reproductive Behavior

One of the most important contributions from the field of sociobiology—which is the synthesis of ethology, population genetics, and behavioral ecology—has been the concepts **"inclusive fitness"**[15] (Hamilton, 1964) and **"kin selection"**[16] (Smith, 1964). These concepts are especially important in the understanding of the nonsexual reproductive behavior of individuals who sexually reproduce themselves at a less-than-average rate. However, one should not assume that pedophiles and ephebophiles or individuals who engage in pedo- or ephebosexual behavior fall into this category, since the relevant data for making such a determination have not been collected.

## Inclusive Fitness and Kin Selection

The concepts "inclusive fitness" and "kin selection" developed when biologists tried to understand the "purpose of life" of sterile castes of insects. Another, slightly different way of asking the same question would be, why would individuals in a sterile-insect caste work to care for a brood that was not their own? The answer came through the realization that reproductive behavior is getting one's genes into the next generation, irrespective of whose genitals make the transfer. For example, if as a result of meiosis, there are 50% of an adult's genes in every one of his or her own offspring, then there are 25% of an adult's genes in every one of his or her nephews and nieces. Helping a relative's offspring is almost as beneficial in relation to evolution as is helping one's own offspring, whether the relative is a bee or a human.

Since pedo- and ephebophilia (and pedo- and ephebosexual behavior) sometimes involve sociosexual behavior between relatives, it is a testable hypothesis that such behavior evolved through mechanisms of kin selection by raising the inclusive fitness of one or both of the interactants (see Anderson and Bielert, this volume; Taub, this volume; de Waal, this volume). Kin selection may be a mechanism by which pedo- and ephebophilia evolved, because adult human males evolved in the presence of related children and adolescents. In the hunter-gatherer bands in which humans evolved, under conditions in which nubile females changed bands, an adult male would be related to the majority of children and adolescents encountered in his natal band. Kin selection also could have been involved under the alternative condition in which reproductive-age males changed bands, because a nonprocreative "alternative strategy" for some (pedo- and ephebophile) males would be to stay in their natal band and assist their sister's offspring, to whom they also are genetically related.[17] (See Pusey, this volume.) Thus, pedo- and ephebophilia could have evolved by mechanisms associated with kin selection but, in larger modern societies, now involve relationships between adult males and children and adolescents to whom the males are not genetically related.

Of course, alternative hypotheses are that pedo- and ephebosexual behavior are the results of nonselected random mutation or genetic drift or are simply a by-product of selection for some other trait, such as heterosexuality. These hypotheses will be developed in the subsection "Pedo- and Ephebophilia," which is found later in this chapter. (See Gould and Lewontin, 1979.)

Finally, pedo- and ephebosexual behavior may be psychopathological, maladaptive responses to mental derangement or social dysregulation and may actually lower the fitness of both of the interactants. In the absence of conclusive data allowing the refutation of any of these hypotheses, it is reasonable to at least discuss and eventually test them all. Random change and the by-product hypothesis are difficult to test and refute. There are not enough demographic data to test the genetic drift hypothesis, but it is a reasonable hypothesis, inasmuch as parental investment and care are not distributed equally among geographically diverse societies.

The "adaptationist" (also known as "selectionist") hypothesis will be discussed in this section; the by-product hypothesis will be discussed in the subsection "Pedo- and Ephebophilia," referred to previously on this page; and the pathology hypothesis will be discussed in the subsection "Harm," which is found in the section "Adult/Child and Adult/Adolescent Sexual Behavior Versus Sexual Abuse."

Inclusive fitness and kin selection are related to reproductive behavior, which, from a biosocial perspective, can be divided into (a) mating effort, (b) parturition, and (c) parental investment (see Betzig et al., 1988). Whereas it is difficult to conceptualize adult human sexual behavior with children and adolescents as having much to do with parturition, aspects of both mating effort and parental investment appear to be involved and will be discussed subsequently, following a brief discussion of some of the functions of nonprocreative sexual behavior.

## Nonprocreative Sexual Behavior

Sexual behavior that is nonprocreative is "possible" only if one does not assume that all sexual behavior is "practice" and that such practice eventually facilitates heterosexual, procreative intercourse, i.e., mating. Nonprocreative sexual behavior among humans appears to have two major adaptive functions: affiliation and drive reduction. Affiliation also is called "attachment" (Bowlby, 1969) and "bonding." See Eibl-Eibesfeldt (this volume) for a discussion of affiliation, attachment, bonding, and love. There also are minor, culturally transmitted, society-specific functions, such as occur in Polynesia (Diamond, this volume) and in Melanesia (Schiefenhövel, this volume). Among pygmy chimpanzees (bonobos), it is fairly clear that another function of sexual behavior is interindividual tension regulation (de Waal, this volume).

### Affiliation

The affiliative function of nonprocreative sexual behavior in humans is proposed because most human sexual behavior between two opposite-sex, fertile individuals is not open to procreation. As a result of concealed ovulation and continuous sexual receptivity, the human female affords the human male the time and opportunity to form an affiliative bond with her. A bonded male is more likely to help protect and provision young offspring than is a nonbonded male.

Because of the context in which interindividual sexual behavior evolved, one outcome of a protracted sexual relationship between almost any two individuals (of any sex or age) is a certain degree of affiliation. If affiliation is considered as being a primary drive, separate from sex and hunger (Bowlby, 1969), then for some adults, one potential functional outcome of sexual behavior with children and adolescents is affiliation with them (see Dienske, this volume).

### Drive Reduction

Humans are a very sexual primate, with a sex drive that often surpasses their copulatory opportunities. This condition creates another function of orgasmic human sexual behavior: the reduction of the sexual drive while one is engaged in behavior that is not even open to procreation.

Nonprocreative sexual behavior includes most noncontracepted and all contracepted heterosexual intercourse, some types of self- as well as mutual masturbation, fondling, and homosexual, heterosexual, and pedo- and ephebosexual behavior.

## Adult/Child and Adult/Adolescent Sexual Behavior as Mating Effort

Because males and females have such different reproductive strategies, the question, Can aspects of adult/child and adult/adolescent sexual behavior be, or be derived from, mating effort? will be considered, first in adult males and then separately in male and in female children and adolescents. Because of the ages and the relationships of the interactants who are addressed in this volume, mating effort and parental investment, two components of reproductive behavior, are not as easily separable as they would be with other interactants.

### Adult Males

Sexual behavior between an adult male and a male or a female child or adolescent could be actual mating effort for the adult male if (a) an adult male impregnates an adolescent female or (b) an adult male uses pedophilic and ephebophilic affiliative behaviors to demonstrate high, nonovertly sexual, paternal-investment-like qualities to the child's or adolescent's mother and, thereby, gains sexual access to her as a form of sexual selection on her part. This male strategy has been suggested for some species of baboons as well as for humans.

It is also possible that, in regard to the adult, adult/child and adult/adolescent sexual behavior **derives** from mating effort. The "object" of one's sexual desires may be under the control of open genetic programs[18] that specify relative age and relative gender of individuals towards whom one is attracted but that are under (natural) selection pressures to allow individual life experience to influence the specifics of mate selection (see D'Udine, this volume).

### Male Children and Adolescents

There certainly was a time in the history of Western civilization when adult male tutors and their young male students learned more than the new Pythagorean theorem together (see Bullough, this volume). In ancient Greece, adult male tutors experientially taught their pubescent male students about genital sexual behavior, and parents sought out the best teacher they could for their sons. Even today, there is some evidence that male-adult/male-child and male-adult/male-adolescent sexual behavior may be more prevalent but less reported than similar behavior with female children and adolescents (Abel et al., 1987). Such sexual behavior could be considered mating-effort practice for the younger interactant, but there is no published evidence that such practice is needed or increases later fitness.

### Female Children and Adolescents

To an adolescent female, the same "practice" that may make an adolescent male "perfect" can easily make her pregnant. However, in terms of mating effort, adolescent pregnancy (but not necessarily single, nonkin-assisted parenthood) may be an adaptive reproductive strategy for some socioeconomically disadvantaged females in socially stratified, industrialized societies, given their limited reproductive options (Draper and Harpending, 1982; Harpending et al., 1987; Lancaster and Hamburg, 1986; Lancaster et al., 1987). In many pregnancies among socioeconomically disadvantaged adolescents, the fathers contribute little if anything to the provisioning of the offspring. As a result, to these female adolescents the important male attributes would be the ones that could be transmitted genetically. Male age would not be a factor except that older males would have had more of a chance to demonstrate their genetic worth than would younger males.

If the sexual behavior is both procreative and incestuous[19] (sexual behavior between two first-degree relatives, who are related to each other by 1/2), the detrimental effects of inbreeding are of almost as much biological significance to the adult male as they are to the potentially fertile, adolescent female, since the reproductive success of both of them is dependent upon the fitness of the same progeny. As a result, there are biological mechanisms that prevent natural fathers and their daughters from being sexually attracted to each other at any age (see Parker and Parker, 1986; Shepher, 1983; Wolf and Huang, 1980; Pusey, this volume).[20]

It is a testable hypothesis that in incestuous as well as in nonincestuous, but nevertheless related individuals (e.g., uncles, grandfathers, cousins), nonprocreative (i.e., noncoital) sexual behavior between an adult male and a related female child or adolescent could increase the inclusive fitness of both the adult male and the female child or adolescent, by hastening the female child's or adolescent's onset of actual reproduction. Weakly in support of this hypothesis is the finding that socioeconomically disadvantaged females, who make up the bulk of females having teenage pregnancies, are **reported** in numerous studies to be involved sexually during their childhood and adolescence with both related and nonrelated adult males more than are nonsocioeconomically disadvantaged females (e.g., Finkelhor, 1984). The sampling biases of socioeconomic class as well as numerous intervening variables make this correlation open to numerous interpretations, however.

If an offspring were produced by an adult male and an adolescent female who were related to each other by 1/4-1/8, the inclusive fitness of both of them would be maximized. This outcome predicts a high degree of sexual attraction and behavior between adult males and nubile females who are distant relatives.

It has been proposed that there is a critical period in the psychosexual development of adolescent females during which time the female, through an open genetic program, learns by imitation of her mother the most adaptive reproductive strategy to pursue (Draper and Harpending, 1982). If this notion is true, then it requires that the adolescent female have a more than passive role in determining her own reproductive destiny.

## Adult/Child and Adult/Adolescent Sexual Behavior as Parental Investment

Trivers (1972) defines parental investment as "**any investment by the parent in an individual offspring that increases the offspring's chance of surviving (and hence reproductive success) at the cost of the parent's ability to invest in other offspring.**"

In some well-studied species of nonhuman primates, there is evidence that adult/juvenile **sexual** behavior may be a type of parental investment (Anderson and Bielert, this volume; Hopf, 1979). It is a fact that, among humans, some adults sexually interact with children and adolescents, including children and adolescents who are relatives. This subsection is simply exploring parental investment as a "biological motive" for this behavior.

There are two basic questions:

1. Can any aspect of adult human sexual behavior with children and adolescents **be** parental investment today? and
2. Do aspects of adult human sexual behavior with children and adolescents derive from behavior that **was** parental investment in humans' evolutionary past?

Currently, data are not available to answer these two questions definitively. Nevertheless, some of the components of parental investment, collectively called "nurturing behavior," are seen in both pedo- and ephebophilia and can be considered and discussed as (1) comforting and contact, (2) feeding, (3) grooming, (4) protecting, and (5) teaching, in the effort being made to answer these questions.

### Comforting and Contact Behavior

Comforting and contact behavior to conspecifics (members of the same species) appears to be a basic characteristic of adult humans, with adult females comforting and contacting infants more than adult males do. Males, however, also contribute to comforting and contact of children and adolescents.

Comforting is a type of bodily contact that involves caressing and rocking or patting movements, often with the body of the comforter and of the individual being comforted moving or swaying in unison, which is the phylogenetically preadapted origin of the synchrony, or matching phase, of adult/adult courtship. Fondling, which is one of the most frequent pedophilic behaviors, uses the same motor patterns as comforting behavior—i.e., caressing and so forth—but is associated with sexual arousal, at least on the part of the fondler. Young children (ages 3-6) actively seek, more than give, comforting behavior. Children that comfort tend to be female rather than male, and they tend to be over 6 years of age.

Among many nonhuman primates (e.g., rhesus and pigtail macaques), the ability to parent successfully in adulthood is contingent upon parent- (or parent-surrogate-) contact behavior during childhood. In the squirrel monkey (*Saimiri*), captivity-raised individuals of both sexes in mixed-sex peer groups were not even able to conceive unless they had been allowed, when they were juveniles, to have **sexual** contact with opposite-sex adults (Hopf, 1979, personal communication). It is reasonable to expect, therefore, that human infants and children should be selected (by natural selection) to first **elicit** and then actively **seek** comforting behaviors from adults. These outcomes, indeed, are what are found.

Regarding the adult male who is sexually aroused by comforting types of behavior with a child or an adolescent (i.e., fondling), if Trivers's definition of parental investment is used, such behavior can be considered to be actual parental investment on the part of the adult male only if (a) the child or adolescent is a biological relative **and** (b) the sexual behavior improves the future reproductive success of the child or adolescent **and** (c) the investment (in time and energy) by the adult male is taking away a resource from a sibling or another close relative. That these criteria will be met is possible in some female children and adolescents who are pursuing an early-mating-effort type of reproductive strategy. (However, it is improbable that these criteria will be met—as has been discussed in this section in the subsection "Female Children and Adolescents," which is found in the greater subsection "Adult/Child and Adult/Adolescent Sexual Behavior as Mating Effort.")

## Feeding

Since it is quite natural for adults to provision and feed children and adolescents and since such adult/child and adult/adolescent feeding behavior is the preadapted, phylogenetic origin of part of adult/adult courtship ritual, it is easy to see how the feeding and provisioning of children and adolescents could predispose some adult males to sexual behavior. Feeding and mating have functional proximity[21] in the hierarchy of behavioral organization. In true pedophiles and ephebophiles, feeding often plays a major role in the proceptive and receptive phases of their courtship behavior. The public image of the "child molester" who with candy lures children who are strangers to him from playgrounds into sexual activity is legend, but this image describes the behavior of a pedosexual psychopath more than the behavior of a true pedophile.

## Grooming

Grooming behavior, in the context of parental care, consists of the bodily care behaviors that an adult does for a child, such as cleaning after elimination, bodily washing, and skin, hair, and nail care. In nonhuman primates, both kin and nonkin social bonds are formed and reinforced by grooming, and there is a very predictable species-specific pattern of who grooms whom.

Adult humans groom each other's hair and massage each other for a variety of reasons including relaxation, social intimacy, affiliation, and sexual gratification. One effect or potentially adaptive function of grooming, for whatever stated motive, is that it puts two individuals (the groomer and the groomed) into intimate physical contact with each other, contact that is similar to the physical proximity of parent and child or of two adult individuals engaged in the intimate, physical contact stage of courtship.

## Protecting

Young of all species, whether prey or predator, are not able to care for themselves to the same degree that adults of the same species are. Therefore, in all species in which there is parental care, the mother protects the young. In fact, in multimale species[22] of primates, such as humans, all adult males of the social group, at least to some degree, protect all of the young. This behavior is especially well developed in some of the higher primates (see Mackey, this volume; Taub, this volume).

The same motor patterns in the same context are used by adult human males to protect both adult females and their young offspring. These aggressive motor patterns must lie in relative "functional proximity" to sexual motor patterns to the degree that they are both associated with adult females. As a result, protecting children and adolescents may facilitate a sexual mood in some males who have the other preconditions for pedo- or ephebophilia. As a corollary, being in a sexual mood may, in some males, facilitate feelings of wanting to protect younger or weaker members of the social group.

## Teaching

The higher an organism is on the phylogenetic scale, the greater the role is of individual as well as social or observational learning. In associational learning, which usually occurs in the lone individual (and by means of which the individual is "self-taught"), previously neutral stimuli can become associated with reward or reinforcement and acquire the capacity to elicit responses. Observational learning, which is present in some birds and all primates and is the major mechanism of cultural transmission, also is a means of "self-teaching" in that there need not be any intent to teach by anyone, even though social association is required. In humans, the concept "teach" implies a deliberate modification of another individual's behavior. To some degree, all human parents teach their children.

In simple societies, most of what a child has to learn to become an adult can be taught by its parents. However, in more complex societies with a specialized division of labor, children and adolescents are taught by professional teachers who have parent-like relationships with their students. The professional teacher/parent surrogate, therefore, has an intimate relationship with a child or an adolescent to a degree that used to be reserved for a biological parent.

Adults can teach and give children and adolescents skills and resources for upward social mobility as well as teaching them pedagogical facts. In a sample of male androphilic (andro = male sex; philia = love of) pedo- and ephebophiles involved in ongoing sexual relationships with 11- to 16-year-old males, the pedo- and ephebophiles came from significantly higher socioeducational levels than did the young males' fathers or stepfathers (Sandfort, 1981). In numerous industrialized Western metropolises, there is a documented tradition of wealthy male patrons "subsidizing" lower socioeconomic status pubescent males in return for sexual favors. The sexual component of the more traditional teacher/student relationships of ancient Greece is legend to the extent that pedo- and ephebophilia often are called "Greek love."

Because the previously discussed inbreeding-avoidance mechanisms, which protect children and parents from becoming sexually attracted to each other, would not operate with teachers and their students, all such mentoring types of relationships are at risk of becoming sexual.

## Comparison of Pedophiles and Ephebophiles to Individuals with Other Age and Sexual Orientations Throughout the Life Span

### Coding and Storing of the Lovemap

Some attributes that compose the human lovemap are amenable to being coded and stored in the brain on the basis of their structure: shape, texture, color, movement, and odor. It will be shown that although males primarily code and store the attributes that compose their lovemap on the basis of structure, there are other attributes composing the lovemap in males that are coded and stored in a nonstructural way that first requires processing at a higher level of neural integration.

The female lovemap is not primarily coded and stored on the basis of structure; rather, attributes are coded and stored in such a way as to first require processing at higher levels of neural integration.

How the attributes of the lovemap are coded and stored in neural tissue, i.e, whether they are coded and stored on the basis of structure or processed at a higher level of neural integration first, has a profound effect on the capacity of the attributes of the lovemap to act as sexually provocative stimuli to which other, previously neutral stimuli can be conditioned to sexually evocative status. Attributes that can be stored as part of the male lovemap on the basis of their structure can act as conditioning agents (i.e., unconditioned stimuli) much more so than can attributes whose coding and storage first require processing at higher levels of neural integration. Because their lovemap comprises structurally coded and stored attributes, it is males more than females in whom resides the capacity for the conditioning of an array of previously neutral, animate, inanimate, and contextual, structurally codable and storable stimuli to sexually evocative status.[23]

Each new structurally codable and storable stimulus in the array that is conditioned to sexually evocative status will be slightly less potent and, therefore, have slightly less capacity to similarly condition other, previously neutral stimuli. A hierarchy of sexually evocative, animate, inanimate, and contextual stimuli is created, with each stimulus that is closer to the actual lovemap having more sexually evocative potency. This hierarchy-building process is one of the neuroethological mechanisms by which an appetitive behavior (searching for a female mate) eventually leads to a consummatory behavior (mating) in a heterosexual human male. This process also is one of the neuroethological mechanisms that underlie male, more so than female, proneness to paraphilias.

According to the theory of the lovemap (Money, 1986), the initial stimuli that make up the human male lovemap are acquired in early childhood, well before puberty. As part of the acquisition process, certain aspects of the lovemap, such as the relative age and gender of individuals towards whom one is sexually attracted, are partly innate; other aspects of the lovemap itself, such as idiosyncratic, specific preferences, are almost entirely dependent on individual life experiences. Obviously, life experiences vary from male to male. Similarly, there is every reason to believe that, as a result of genetic variability and of intrauterine hormonal variability, the innate elements of the lovemap, too, are different in different males.

As was noted previously, the lovemap comprises attributes that are coded and stored in two ways: (1) on the basis of the attributes' perceived structure and (2) on the basis of nonstructurally perceived and processed properties. Each type will be considered separately in human males and in human females.

## Coding and Storing Attributes
## on the Basis of the Attributes' Perceived Structure

### Human Males

In many male mammals, the main attribute composing the lovemap is odor, an attribute that is coded and stored on the basis of its structure. In the human male, olfaction plays a lesser role in the composition of the lovemap than does vision. In human adolescent and adult heterosexual males, the main attributes that are coded and stored in the lovemap on the basis of the attributes' perceived structure are the proceptive expressive **movements** and the **shape** of the nubile female. In addition, also coded and stored on the basis of their perceived structure are the ontogenetically made-familiar animate and inanimate objects and contexts that have been conditioned to sexually evocative status early in development.

The reason why adult heterosexual human males are visually attracted to the proceptive expressive behavior (movement) of (any) adult female and the degree to which the attraction is innate or is conditioned through life experience is not completely understood. However, because the attraction is to the structurally perceived proceptive expressive behavior, aspects of which look very similar cross-culturally, there is a strong suggestion that both the behavior in heterosexual females and its reception by the stimulus filter in heterosexual males are under the influence of rather closed genetic programs. There appears to be a reciprocal relationship between the degree to which one is perceptually attracted to these feminine proceptive expressive behaviors in others and the degree to which one exhibits the behaviors oneself.

In addition to the attraction to the perceived structure of feminine proceptive expressive behavioral movement, the adolescent and the adult heterosexual male, as has been mentioned, also are attracted to the shape of the (any) nubile female. The degree to which this attraction is innate or conditioned, too, is not known. However, it takes a very small amount of stimulus discriminative ability for a heterosexual adolescent or adult male to recognize the easily discriminable shape,[24] and once recognized, the shape has high stimulus appetence. (See Figure 1.7a.)

The visual vulnerability of human males to the sexual conditioning of ontogenetically made-familiar animate and inanimate objects and contexts is exploited by the garment industry in the industrialized world. The industry has made lace a sexually dimorphic, female fabric (i.e., an inanimate object) that has been conditioned specifically to sexual arousal by being used almost exclusively on adult female lingerie and bridal gowns. (See Figure 1.7b.) Lace has visually complex, highly discriminable patterns embedded within patterns, and in order to see the inner patterns (requiring high discriminative ability), one has to fix one's gaze. When lace is put on and around animate sexual releasers, it takes on sexual releasing properties itself through conditioning. Lace can be incorporated in the lovemap if encountered early enough in development. There is nothing intrinsically feminine or sexual about lace.

The attraction (initial or through conditioning) of the human male of the industrialized West to the sexually dimorphic smell of female-worn perfume and the feel of female-worn, sexually dimorphic fabrics of silk, nylon, and satin also are further evidence of the male's coding and storing capacities on the basis of the stimuli's perceived structure, using olfactory and tactile senses. The attributes (shape, texture, color, movement, and odor) to which males are attracted (either initially or through conditioning) are not random; rather, such attributes have phylogenetic significance: e.g., genital odors = musk-derived perfumes; smooth skin of youth = silk, nylon, and satin. The difference between normalcy and minor paraphilic fetishes in this regard, among adult heterosexual males, is one of degree (see D'Udine, this volume; Domjan, this volume).

## Human Females

In many birds, the attributes in the female lovemap are coded and stored on the basis of perceived structure in a visual format, which is why the males of so many bird species are brightly colored. In human females, for reasons that will be explained, visual attributes appear to play a lesser role in sexual attraction—and, therefore, in the coding and storing in the lovemap—than they do in human males. What human females, more so

a

b

Figure 1.7. Human heterosexual-male sexual releasing stimuli.
(a) Phylogenetically familiar, low degree of discriminableness, nubile-female shape on the tire mudguard on an 18-wheel, semi-tractor trailer, originally advertising a product name.
(b) Ontogenetically familiar, highly discriminable, frequently conditioned sexual releasing stimulus on adult female lingerie and bridal gowns.

than human males, appear to store on the basis of visual-structural properties within their sensory-perceptual stimulus filters is the nonsexual "infant/child schema," first conceptualized by Lorenz in 1943 (see Lorenz, 1981). The degree to which the attraction to the schema is innate or conditioned is not known. Infants and children have a characteristic shape to the face, with a high forehead and puffy cheeks, and relatively large eyes and a large head relative to the size of the body. The phylogenetically familiar infant/child schema requires a very small amount of stimulus discriminative ability in order that the shape be recognized, and once recognized, the shape has high stimulus appetence. (See Figure 1.8.)

In comparison with males, females look more at (any) infants, have more autonomic arousal when they look at (any) infants, and are more attentive to (any) infants.

Because affiliation to a particular infant on the part of the mother is more important at birth than is affiliation to a particular infant on the part of the father, female affiliation may be influenced by more closed genetic programs than is male affiliation of this kind. This predisposition toward becoming affiliated with one's infant probably works through an innate female attraction to the (any) infant schema, as was just discussed. The actual affiliation process between an adult female and a particular human infant is, of course, a postpartum process that takes place over a variable period of time and involves numerous sensory modalities.

The function (effect) of the female parental attraction to the (any) infant schema is to mother/child affiliation what the function of male sexual attraction to the (any) nubile female is to adult male/female affiliation. Both kinds of attraction predispose one to interact with the individual who possesses the "object of attraction." As a result of this interaction, affiliation with a particular individual can occur.

Coding and Storing Attributes on the Basis of
Nonstructurally Perceived and Processed Properties

As discussed previously, some attributes that cannot be perceived on the basis of the attributes' structure are coded and stored in the lovemap in ways that require processing at a higher level of neural integration. Two such bases by which coding and storing occur have been identified: (1) relative age and relative gender and (2) function (to be discussed). The first basis applies in both males and females, while the second basis applies in females only. Both bases will be discussed as they relate to human males and human females after a brief discussion of the concepts of relative age and relative gender and of function.

**Relative age** and **relative gender** are not coded and stored on the basis of their perceived structure, because the attribute is not the perceived age or gender structure per se but, rather, a comparison of the perceived age and gender structure of another individual with the perceived age and gender structure of self, which is mediated through Money's (1986) concept

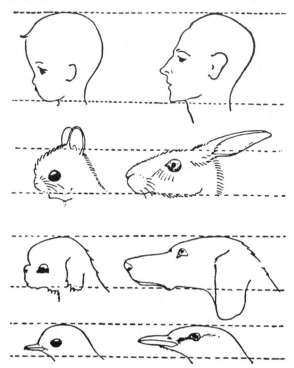

Figure 1.8. "Infant/child schema" of humans. Left: Head proportions that are generally considered to be "cute." Right: Adult forms, which do not activate the drive to care for the young (broodcare). (From Eibl-Eibesfeldt, 1975, p. 491 [originally published by K. Lorenz in Die angeborenen Formen möglicher Erfahrung, *Zeitschrift für Tierpsychologie*, 1943, *5*, 235-409]. Reprinted with the permission of I. Eibl-Eibesfeldt.)

of gender identity role (G-I/R). A higher level of neural-integration processing determines that the other individual is (a) either younger or older than self and (b) either more masculine or more feminine than self (see Figure 1.9). This comparison results in four possibilities, which are seen in the four Attraction Quadrants of Figure 1.9. (For simplicity, the choices are made binary and are limited to "older" and "younger than self." However "older" can be thought of as "same age or older," and "younger" can be thought of as "same age or younger." The same applies to "masculine" and "feminine.")

The concept **"gender,"** as it is used in this chapter, first must be defined from a biosocial point of view and in a meaningful way. An attribute is given a gender designation (masculine or feminine) if its **distribution is skewed between the two sexes but it is not distributed exclusively in one sex or the other.** Attributes that are distributed exclusively in one biological sex or the other are called "male" or

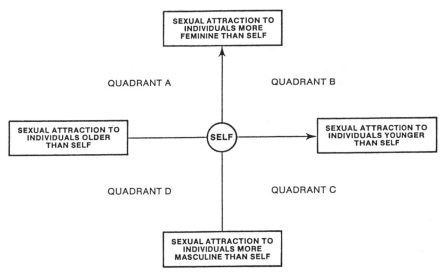

Figure 1.9. The relationship of **relative** age and **relative** gender of individuals toward whom one is sexually attracted—represented by four Attraction Quadrants. (North- and East-pointing arrows are explained in caption to Figure 1.11.)

"female" attributes rather than "masculine" or "feminine" attributes. For example, "small" is a feminine attribute because the average female is smaller than the average male. However, a penis is a male (not a masculine) attribute because only males have a penis. Attributes such as "large," "strong," and "hairy" are considered masculine attributes, and attributes such as "small," (physically) "weak," and "hairless" are considered feminine. The concept of gender, i.e., masculine and feminine, does not depend upon whether genetics ("is strong") or culture ("wears a dress") is responsible for the skewed distribution of the attribute between the two biological sexes.

It is also important to appreciate that among humans, one is not **initially** sexually attracted to another individual's biological sex, inasmuch as one would have to examine an individual's chromosomes to know for certain whether the individual is a biological male (XY) or female (XX). In an initial encounter in clothed societies, one does not see genitals either, perceived structures that usually distinguish biological males from biological females. Rather, one is initially attracted to the individual's perceived shape and movement, to the secondary sexual characteristics, and to the sexually dimorphic (i.e., masculine or feminine) clothing, hairstyle, and adornment. When the sum of the gender attributes is more masculine than feminine, one assumes the individual is a biological male; when the sum of the gender attributes is more feminine than masculine, one assumes the individual is a biological female. However, one male can be more masculine or more feminine than another male, and one female can be more masculine or more feminine than another female.

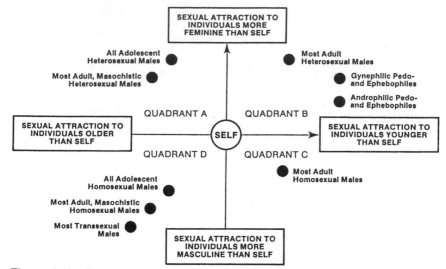

Figure 1.10. Relationship of male androphilic and gynephilic pedophiles and ephebophiles to male individuals with other sexual orientations and to the Attraction Quadrants of relative-age and relative-gender attraction throughout the life span. (North- and East-pointing arrows are explained in caption to Figure 1.11.)

**Function** is another way not based upon perceived structure by which attributes are coded and stored in the lovemap. Functional attributes are explained as follows: The function of a behavior is determined by its effects.[25] Functional attributes are not the perceived structure of behavior per se but, rather, are the consequences, or the effects, of behavior. The human female (but not the human male) lovemap, for reasons that will be explained, is composed of attributes that are coded and stored on the bases of function as well as relative age and relative gender.

*Human Males*

The lovemap of the human male, in addition to its attributes coded and stored on the basis of their perceived structure, also contains attributes coded and stored on the bases of relative age and relative gender. Relative age and relative gender are the bases on which the four Attraction Quadrants for human males in Figures 1.9 and 1.10 were developed. Human males are found in each of the four Attraction Quadrants, depending on their age and sexual orientations as well as their stage in the life span. (See the discussion relating to the Attraction Quadrants in the ensuing greater subsection, which is titled "Who's Who in the Attraction Quadrants.")

*Human Females*

In human females, attributes based on relative age and relative gender are coded and stored on a nonstructural basis in the lovemap throughout the life span. The Attraction Quadrants in which a female resides differ, as in males, throughout the life span and are dependent upon both age and sexual orientations.

Attributes coded and stored on the basis of behavioral function, as a result of processing at higher levels of neural integration, also are in the lovemap of human females. Behaviors that result in functions, such as caring, provisioning, and protecting, would usually be highly desirable components of the female lovemap. Such coding and storing in the human female lovemap of attributes on the basis of their function is most likely a counterstrategy that enables the human female to detect male deception and "false advertising" in the form of visual symbols of reproductive success. However, human males have evolved a counterstrategy to female functional-attribute assessment of them in the form of verbal tales of functional heroism.

### Who's Who in the Attraction Quadrants

Only males will be discussed, since the purpose of this subsection is to show the individual relationships between andro- and gynephilic pedo- and ephebophiles and (male) individuals with other age and sexual orientations throughout the life span.

The following discussion refers to Figure 1.10.

*Quadrant A: Attraction to Individuals*
*Older and More Feminine than Self*

Adolescent heterosexual males' sexuality awakens at puberty to structurally perceived attributes that are fully developed in nubile females who are considerably older and more feminine than self. In modern industrialized societies, sexually evocative adult female models in magazines and actresses in films, voyeurism, and fantasy are the closest means by which most **young** adolescent males can get to the structurally perceived, animate attributes in their lovemap in a sexual context.

Adult male heterosexual masochists often stay in this quadrant throughout their life span. They become fixated on the dominant, fear-inducing role of the female individual in their lovemap more than on her perceived structural attributes.[26] (In general, age correlates positively with dominance.)

*Quadrant B: Attraction to Individuals*
*Younger and More Feminine than Self*

Almost all adult heterosexual males eventually wind up in this quadrant after passing through a transient phase, starting at the end of their second decade of life, of maximum sexual attraction to individuals more feminine than and of the same age as self.

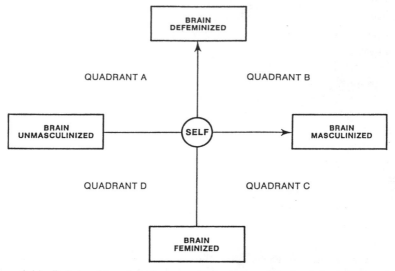

Figure 1.11. Relationship of brain masculinization and brain defeminization in the male to relative-age and relative-gender preferences in the four Attraction Quadrants. Compare to Figure 1.10 and see text. The North- and East-pointing arrows signify that the brains of male (and female) fetuses start out unmasculinized and feminized and that their degree of masculinization and defeminization is primarily responsible for the variance in gender-typical behavior and gender-typical sexual attraction both within and between the two biological sexes.

All (androphilic and gynephilic) pedo- and ephebophiles are in this quadrant throughout their life span. Male as well as female children and adolescents are always younger and more feminine than an adult male pedo- or ephebophile throughout his life span.

### Quadrant C: Attraction to Individuals Younger and More Masculine than Self

Almost all adult homosexual males are in this quadrant after having passed through a transient phase, starting at the end of their second decade of life, of maximal sexual attraction to individuals more masculine than and of the same age as self. It is for this reason that adult homosexual males, more so than adult heterosexual males, value (in themselves and others) the signs and symbols of male youthfulness and masculinity, such as a muscular body and facial hair. Adult homosexual males are not very attracted to the more feminine, smooth, hairless skin and lanky habitus of a pubescent male, which attract the androphilic ephebophile. Adult homosexual males have virtually no sexual attraction to the prepubertal habitus of a male child, which attracts the androphilic pedophile.

*Quadrant D: Attraction to Individuals*
*Older and More Masculine than Self*

Homosexual males' sexuality awakens at adolescence to structurally perceived attributes that are fully developed in males who are older and more masculine than self. In contrast to adolescent heterosexual males, however, adolescent homosexual males have more opportunities for confronting the structurally perceived, animate attributes of their lovemap in person rather than through magazines, films, voyeurism, and fantasy. Almost any older male, with perhaps the exception of an older transsexual male, would be more masculine than self, and there are numerous societally institutionalized opportunities afforded for culturally sanctioned all-male nudity. Adult male androphilic ephebophiles are the obvious individuals whose interests as well as attributes match the relative age and relative gender attractions of adolescent homosexual males.

Adult male homosexual masochists often stay in this quadrant throughout their life span. They are fixated on the dominant, fear-inducing role of the individual in their lovemap more than on the individual's structurally perceived attributes.[27]

Most transsexual males are in this quadrant throughout their life span. The usual definition of a transsexual male is "a male individual whose G-I/R is so feminine that he subjectively feels like a biological female."

## Proximate Mechanisms Underlying Specific Age and Sexual Orientations in Human Males: The Two-Dimensional Model

### Introduction

The data on the sexual differentiation of the male brain and the correlation of this differentiation with behavioral sex differences in childhood, adolescence, and adulthood are best understood using the two-dimensional "organizational" model of embryological hormonalization:

1. The process of masculinization and
2. The process of defeminization.

(See Goy and McEwen, 1980; McEwen, 1987; Pillard and Weinrich, 1987). This model is illustrated in Figure 1.11, overlaid on the already discussed Attraction Quadrants.

The two-dimensional "organizational" model of embryological hormonalization means that **masculinization of the brain is not the same as defeminization.** There is good corroborating, empirical evidence in the rat that masculinization and defeminization are mediated by temporally and hormonally different, although related, processes (Meaney et al., 1983; Hutchison and Hutchison, this volume). However, it should not be assumed that the effects of defeminization and masculinization are completely independent processes in any species, especially in humans, in whom the concept of G-I/R is an important intervening variable (see Money, 1986).

The above-described organizing effects of sex hormones on the sexual differentiation of the brain during embryogenesis must be contrasted with the activating effects of the sex hormones on the development of secondary and tertiary (explained later) sexual characteristics of puberty. For example, Goy and McEwen (1980, pp. 6-7) suggest that there are three basic types of "male-more-frequent" sexually dimorphic behaviors (tertiary sexual characteristics), which are mediated by three different proximate mechanisms:

1. Type I—Those behavioral characteristics that cannot be brought to full expression unless the relevant hormone(s) is (are) present in adequate amounts in the circulation during both the critical (organizational) period of early development and a later (activating) life stage. Examples are
   a. Male intromissive and ejaculatory behavior
   b. Male fighting behavior (some species/strains)
2. Type II—Those behaviors that seemingly require only activation at later ages by appropriate hormones. Examples are
   a. Yawning behavior of rhesus monkeys
   b. Mounting behavior (some species/strains)
3. Type III—Those behaviors that require only the organizational effects of androgens, in which no activational influence is required for their full expression. Examples are
   a. Juvenile play and mounting behavior of rhesus monkeys
   b. Urinary (micturational) patterns of dogs

The relationship of these three types of sexual behavior and their three underlying proximate mechanisms to andro- and gynephilic pedo- and ephebophilia is that the components and correlates of these age orientations in humans can eventually be subjected to a similar typology.

## Sociopolitical Background

The editor of and the contributors to this volume are aware of the socially and politically sensitive topics about which they write. Numerous well-respected social scientists have objected to behavioral-physiology and -biochemistry, mechanistic research on sexual orientation, in that the research implies the presence of an "abnormality" in the medical sense. The same argument could apply to similar research on age orientation. However, the search for mechanistic, physiological and biochemical correlates of behavioral variability concerning both age and gender attractions does not imply that the correlates or the individuals in whom the correlates are found are "medically abnormal."

Also, the relationship between adult male homosexuals and male androphilic pedo- and ephebophiles is both socially and politically very sensitive. Yet, empirical evidence suggests that age preference and gender (sex) preference are not completely independent variables. For example, the majority of adult human males are sexually attracted to individuals younger and more feminine than self; the majority of adult human females are sexually attracted to individuals older and more masculine than self.

Finally, there is a strong voice in the gay social science literature to keep separated conceptually and ideologically the concepts of gender-atypical behavior in self and gender-atypical attraction to others. Nevertheless, correlations between gender-atypical behavior and gender-atypical attraction exist (e.g., Green, 1987), and efforts to understand and characterize these correlations are appropriate endeavors of science.

## The Two-Dimensional Mechanisms

It is well established that during embryogenesis, the internal reproductive organs, the external genitals, and the sexual differentiation of the brain will proceed along female-typical lines unless the embryo is masculinized and defeminized to a varying degree by pre- and perinatal organizing hormones.

In the effort to understand some of the outward manifestations of brain defeminization in humans, it is helpful to use Birdwhistell's concept of **"tertiary sexual characteristics"** as being "sexual characteristics which are patterned social-behavioral in form" (Birdwhistell, 1979, p. 42). Such tertiary sexual characteristics are differentiated from the morphological, secondary sexual characteristics of puberty and from the primary sexual characteristics (male or female genitals) that are present at birth. In this subsection on proximate mechanisms, the female-more-frequent, feminine (often called **"effeminate"** when they occur in a biological male) behaviors to be discussed under "Defeminization" can be thought of as being tertiary sexual characteristics.

The processes of brain masculinization and defeminization will be discussed, especially in reference to their possible relationship to pedo- and ephebophilia. Brain masculinization is discussed first because it occurs first in both phylogeny and ontogeny. All male brains start out unmasculinized on the (horizontal) unmasculinized-masculinized axis and feminized on the (vertical) feminized-defeminized axis in Figure 1.11.

### Masculinization

Masculinization, from a proximate, mechanistic perspective, is the association of social dominance and all that is connected with it (e.g., male/male competitive aggressivity; proceptive, **searching**, appetitive behavior; and mounting behavior[28]) with sexuality. It is also the functional dissociation and distancing of fear from sexuality (see Medicus and Hopf, this volume).

Because the appetitive component of male-more-frequent proceptive sexual behavior involves more locomotor activity than does the female-more-frequent stationary, proceptive expressive display, masculinization of the brain appears to produce an overall increase in nonspecific motor behavior in the male in many different contexts. It is for this reason that even the average prepubertal nonhuman, as well as human, primate male is more active (and generally more aggressive) than the average prepubertal female. Interestingly, human female children whose brains have been organizationally masculinized in utero as a result of adrenogenital syndrome show the level of activity and the rough-and-tumble play that are characteristic of male children (Ehrhard, 1974).

The predisposition of most males to associate social dominance (in themselves) with their own sexuality causes submissive attributes (in others) to become sexually alluring to them. Also, submissive displays by others inhibit aggressivity and allow courtship by self to proceed. As a result of these two factors, many adolescent and adult human females not only dress themselves so that they appear to be submissive and helpless but also behave more submissively and helplessly in the presence of males than in the presence of other females. Submissive attributes, such as "small," "weak," "young," and "helpless," are, of course, attributes of all (male and female) children and adolescents in comparison to adult males. In relation to children and adolescents, all males become more dominant as they move from puberty to adulthood.

To understand the relationship of dominance to male sexuality, one must appreciate the nature of vertebrate social behavior, in which both dominance and submission are relative, relationship- and context-dependent roles in each sex and in each individual. The dual (dominant/submissive) potentiality of all individuals is best seen in human sadomasochism/bondage-dominance (S&M/B&D), a paraphilia in which hierarchal (dominant/submissive) role relationships both predominate and facilitate sexual arousal. Comparing the distribution of the roles between the two sexes, the average adult human female's sexual fantasies and behavior tend to be self-reported as submissive and associated with fear, whereas the average adult male's sexual fantasies and behavior, when compared to the average female's, are self-reported to be more dominant and associated with aggressivity (see Eibl-Eibesfeldt, this volume; Medicus and Hopf, this volume).

Comparing the distribution of role-related sexual behavior among males, one finds, although such studies are plagued by sampling biases, that self-reported heterosexual males may tend to prefer the dominant role somewhat more than do self-reported bisexual and homosexual males, although they are shown graphically as equally masculinized in Figure 1.10. All (androphilic and gynephilic) pedo- and ephebophiles, whose brains are extremely masculinized throughout their life span, are in very dominant roles in their sexual interactions with children and adolescents. Although it is not shown graphically in Figure 1.10, all pedophiles would be more masculinized than all ephebophiles. Transsexual males, whose brains are never masculinized in their life span (i.e., they remain unmasculinized), are most often sexually attracted to power and dominance in very masculinized, older-than-self, heterosexual males.

The same masculine dominance sexuality whose reptilian origins make submissive attributes sexually alluring in a potential mate can also engender feelings of nurturance and caregiving towards individuals with these attributes, partly because of the phylogenetic origins of this response from mammalian parent/offspring relations (see Eibl-Eibesfeldt, this volume). However, dominance sexuality can also be associated with sadism towards a sexual partner, which almost certainly is redirected, functionally proximate aggression that evolved in the service of intraspecific, male/male sexual competition.

However, as previously discussed in the section of this chapter titled "The Lovemap," compared to the structurally perceived, coded, and stored attributes of shape and movement of the proceptive nubile female (Figure 1.7a), the attributes of submissiveness are not coded and stored on the basis of perceived structure, in that they first are processed (to determine relative social rank) at higher levels of neural integration. Therefore, submissiveness per se cannot serve very well as an unconditioned stimulus through which a previously neutral stimulus is transformed into sexually evocative status. For example, the sight of relative smallness per se—all other attributes, including relative age and relative gender, being randomized—itself would not be associated with male sexual arousal.

Because of this relative unconditionability of submissive- (and dominant-) role-related sexual behavior per se, adult male humans who are aroused by dominant- or submissive-role relationships have undergone the conditioning of their sexual arousal to specific paraphernalia (e.g., black leather), which gets paired with and conditioned directly to the sexual arousal associated with their use. Black leather is no more intrinsically dominant or submissive today than lace is intrinsically feminine.

## Defeminization

The defeminization of a male is the process by which the male comes to exhibit less female-more-frequent, proceptive and mount-receiving behavior. Much female-more-frequent behavior, if not inhibited by the defeminizing effects of androgens and their metabolites, appears to be mediated by the female sex hormone estrogen and to be facilitated by the female sex hormone progesterone. In an exquisite example of inductive neurobiology, Pfaff (1980) has shown the relationship of estrogen and progesterone to the most feminine of all rodent behaviors, lordosis, which is the arching of the back and the rotating of the pelvis dorsally (towards the buttocks), a signal of mounting-behavior receptivity and a facilitation of ventral/dorsal (conceptive phase) mating.

Although humans have risen from quadrupedalism to bipedalism (i.e., walking on two rather than four limbs) and are capable, along with bonobos (pygmy chimpanzees), of ventral-ventral mating, evolution is conservative.

As a result, female lordosis remains a preadapted visual releasing stimulus to the heterosexual human male that is part of the proceptive, expressive-behavior repertoire of human females. Lordosis is very evident in sexually evocative "pin-up" photographs of human females, in the sexual selection for steatopygia (fat deposits on the buttocks) in Hottentot females, and in the "bustle dress" worn in the late 19th and early 20th centuries by urbanized Western adult females. (See exaggerated lordosis in nubile female releasing stimuli shape in Figure 1.7a.) Because of human bipedalism and the freeing of the upper extremities, which came to be used in communication, among other activities, there are a variety of other female-more-frequent, proceptive, expressive behavioral motor patterns of both the upper and lower extremities that are attributable to a relative lack of brain defeminization.

The proximate segments of both the upper and lower extremities (i.e., forearms and thighs) are carried closer to the midline of the body by females than by males, resulting in a relatively smaller stride in females. In contrast, in females more so than in males, during sexually evocative displays there is more loose-jointed flexion and extension in the more distal segments of both the upper (wrists and fingers) and the lower (ankles) extremities.

There also are numerous female-more-frequent, preadapted, proceptive, expressive facial and eye behavioral motor patterns, such as tongue thrusting, lip pursing, vertical eye rolling, and increased social smiling and eyebrow flashing. In addition, there are female-more-frequent whole-body movements, social behaviors, and the expressive-behavior component of speech.

Since (a) remaining brain feminized (not being brain defeminized) results in the execution of structurally codable and storable, female-more-frequent, proceptive, expressive behavioral motor patterns in heterosexual females and since (b) brain-defeminized heterosexual males are characterized by a relative lack of such behavioral motor patterns in themselves and (visual) attraction to such behavioral motor patterns in others, then (c) brain defeminization is organizationally associated with the male-more-frequent visual-structural-perceptual configuration of the stimulus filter of the lovemap. That is, the female-more-frequent pattern is the execution of these proceptive expressive behavioral motor patterns, and the male-more-frequent pattern is the proceptive visual search for both the behavior and the individuals exhibiting it.

Defeminization, which organizationally inhibits the expression of female-more-frequent, proceptive expressive behavior as well as biasing the stimulus filter toward visual-structural-perceptual configuration, will now be discussed along with the organizational effects of masculinization in males with differing age and sexual orientations in order that pedo- and ephebophilic males can be seen in perspective.

The Age and Sexual Orientations[29]

*Heterosexuality*

Brain masculinization makes submissive-like diminutive size sexually alluring. Another effect of brain masculinization—which is associated with aggressive, male/male sexual competitiveness over access to nubile females or is replaced by sublimated, less physically violent behaviors in industrialized societies—is resource competition in the marketplace. Adult heterosexual males also still actively search and exclusively show mounting (insertion) behavior.

As a result of brain defeminization, the marked degree to which visual, structurally perceived, coded, and stored attributes compose the lovemap in self-reported heterosexual males also leads to the subsequent, easily conditioned eroticization of an array of animate, inanimate, and contextual, visual, structurally perceived, codable and storable objects. Remember that stimulus potency increases with the degree of stimulus discrimination in individuals who have a high capacity to discriminate stimuli once the phylogenetically familiar stimulus has been found (see top and then right half of the bell-shaped curve in Figure 1.5). Therefore, in heterosexual human males, visual eroticism causes stimulus appetence toward the (**any**) phylogenetically familiar, nubile female shape, the accompanying feminine proceptive, expressive behavior, and the idiosyncratically conditioned, ontogenetically made-familiar, accompanying visual-structural appurtenances such as lace.

Most self-reported heterosexual males exhibit relatively little female-more-frequent, proceptive expressive behavior. The variance in the expression of this behavior probably is accounted for by variance in the degree of male-brain defeminization and by the self-report method of defining this population.

*Pedo- and Ephebophilia*

Brain masculinization is mainly responsible for the very strong eroticization of diminutive, submissive-like attributes characteristic of children and adolescents and forms the major proximate basis for pedophilia and ephebophilia. Although it is not shown graphically in Figure 1.10, pedophiles are more masculinized than ephebophiles. Male/male competitive aggressivity is reflected best in socioeconomic status in stratified societies, but sufficient data to support or refute testable hypotheses relating to the socioeconomic status of pedo- and ephebophiles have not been collected. Searching proceptive behaviors are very evident, but mounting behavior (insertion) is conspicuous by its relative absence with children but by its presence with adolescents.

The defeminized coding and storing of the lovemap on the basis of perceived structure may account, although to a slightly lesser degree than in heterosexual males (see Figures 1.10 and 1.11), for some aspects of pedo- and ephebophiles' visual-structural-perceptual attraction to the infant/child schema as well as their attraction to the visual-structural-perceptual aspects of specific stages of nascent or budding secondary sexual characteristics or attributes. Within pedo- and ephebophiles, androphilic individuals are less defeminized than gynephilic individuals (see Figure 1.10). If the ease of visual sexual conditioning is a function of the degree of brain defeminization, then pedo- and ephebophiles should be slightly less prone to visual conditioned sexual arousal than heterosexual males, with androphilic pedo- and ephebophiles less prone than gynephilic pedo- and ephebophiles.

The relatively high degree of brain defeminization in all pedo- and ephebophiles is also evident in the relative lack of female-more-frequent proceptive expressive behaviors in this population as compared to homosexual and transsexual males.

Freund et al. (1989) present the following unsolved paradox regarding the ratio of gynephilic to androphilic pedo- and ephebophilic males, for which there is now a new biosocial explanation using the two-dimensional model of differential masculinization and defeminization of the brain.

The ratio of female to male children and adolescents reported to have been sexually involved with adults is approximately 2:1, whereas the ratio of heterosexual to homosexual adult males, who are attracted to adults, is approximately 20:1. Yet, self-reported and plethysmograph-verified adult homosexual males are no more sexually aroused plethysmographically by male children and adolescents than adult heterosexual males are sexually aroused plethysmographically by female children and adolescents. Freund et al. conclude, therefore, that androphilic pedo- and ephebophilia are more closely linked to homosexuality than to heterosexuality, a conclusion that will be contested by the alternative, two-dimensional biosocial model. (Freund et al.'s terminology was made compatible with this volume.)

There are two other compatible-with-each-other explanations of this paradox not mentioned by Freund et al.: (1) Abel et al.'s data in the recent literature and (2) the biosocial, two-dimensional model developed in this chapter:

(1) Abel et al.'s (1987) study of self-reported sex crimes of nonincarcerated paraphiliacs found that although the ratio of gynephilic pedo- and ephebophiles to androphilic pedo- and ephebophiles was approximately 1.5:1.0, the ratio of the mean number of paraphilic acts per gynephilic pedo- or ephebophile to androphilic pedo- or ephebophile was approximately 1.0:10.0. The ratio of completed acts per female child or adolescent:male child or adolescent was approximately 1.0:1.5, and the ratio of female children and adolescents to male children and adolescents who are sexually involved with an adult male is calculated to be approximately 1:5. Therefore, estimating the ratio of gynephilic to androphilic pedo- and ephebophiles from the ratio of female to male children who are sexually

involved with adults is a sampling error that overestimates the ratio of androphilic to gynephilic pedo- and ephebophiles and explains the paradox.

(2) The biosocial model herein developed assumes that the central tendency in evolution is to produce heterosexual males by producing an optimal amount of masculinization and defeminization of the male brain in utero. As a first-order approximation, if the points in Figure 1.10 are thought of as representing rectangular cartesian coordinates originating where the two axes bisect, both an X- and a Y-axis normal distribution can be imagined in which the point that represents adult heterosexual males would be in the center of the normal distributions on both the X- and the Y-axes.

The distance on the Y-axis between adult heterosexual males and gynephilic pedo- and ephebophiles is slightly less than the distance between adult heterosexual males and androphilic pedo- and ephebophiles. Therefore, based on an overlying normal distribution on the Y-axis around heterosexual males, the model correctly predicts that there should be slightly more gynephilic than androphilic pedo- and ephebophilic males in the general population.

Again, based on how the points are distributed in the model, the distance between adult heterosexual males and adult homosexual males is significantly less on both the X- and the Y-axes than the distance on these same two axes between adult heterosexual males and transsexual males. If these distances on the X- and the Y-axes reflect frequencies in overlying normal distributions, they correctly predict that there would be several orders of magnitude difference between the population frequencies of adult homosexual and transsexual males.

In contrast to Freund et al.'s interpretation of their data that pedo- and ephebophilia are more closely linked with male homosexuality than with male heterosexuality, the model developed herein comes to exactly the opposite conclusion: All (andro- and gynephilic) adult male pedo- and ephebophiles should be more closely linked to adult male heterosexuals than to adult male homosexuals. Therefore, adult females would (counter-intuitively) be predicted to be sexually preferred over adult males by the majority of both andro- and gynephilic pedo-and ephebophiles.

Likewise, based on how the points are distributed in the model and assuming two normal distributions around heterosexuality, androphilic pedo- and ephebophilic males are (counter-intuitively) predicted to be more common in the general population than homosexual males. Since androphilic pedo- and ephebophilic males are so close to adult heterosexual males in the model, it is suggested that such pedo- and ephebophilic males can facultatively adapt to whatever behavior is culturally accepted.

If the distribution of the points in the model reflects differing degrees of masculinization and defeminization of the male brain, then there is every reason to believe that the distributions would actually be continuous across all males rather than being discontinuous around arbitrary and nonmutually exclusive categories such as "heterosexual" and "androphilic ephebophile." Remember that both heterosexual males and androphilic ephebophiles are capable of being sexually attracted to individuals who are younger and more feminine than themselves, since they both reside very near each other in Quadrant B in Figures 1.9, 1.10, and 1.11.

In certain historical times, such as ancient Greece, males in the lower half of Quadrant B openly interacted sexually with both adult females and adolescent males. In most modern industrialized societies, the majority of such males most likely live out their adult lives as married or single heterosexual males. The ones that do not often come to the attention of the types of professional individuals who would be interested in this volume.

*Homosexuality*

Brain masculinization should produce eroticization of diminutive attributes, but because of a concomitant lack of defeminization (see Figure 1.10), this potential is not realized in attributes stored on the basis of their perceived structure as much as it is in heterosexual males. As a result, brain masculinization is realized most in appetitive searching ("cruising") behavior. Male/male resource-competitive aggressiveness is not under cultural selection pressures from heterosexual females, and as a result, in industrialized societies, homosexual males are drawn towards the human services more than towards highly resource-competitive fields (Feierman, in press). Both brain-masculinization-produced mounting behavior (insertion) and brain-un-defeminized mount-receiving behavior (recipient of insertion) are common.

Compared to adult male heterosexuals and all pedo- and ephebophiles, adult male homosexuals are more commonly un-defeminized (see Figures 1.10 and 1.11), especially in childhood and adolescence (Green, 1987; Saghir and Robins, 1973). In adulthood, there is much more variance in the degree of phenotypic defeminization among self-reported homosexual males, with some individuals behaving as if they were very defeminized; this variance probably is secondary to variance in both the degree of defeminization and social learning.

The relatively un-defeminized homosexual male, compared to heterosexual and (androphilic and gynephilic) pedo- and ephebophilic males, as previously stated, is relatively less dependent on visual-structure coding and storing of the lovemap, and in such a male, therefore, the conditioning of previously neutral stimuli to the intrinsic and primary structure of sexual gratification, the penis, occurs less easily (see Figures 1.10 and 1.11).

*Transsexualism*

A relative lack of brain masculinization and a lack of cultural selection from heterosexual females would be predicted to produce virtually no male/male resource-competitive aggressivity in the marketplace. Instead, similarly to heterosexual females, who would reside in the same Quadrant

D, there would be more of a relationship between fear and sexuality (see Medicus and Hopf, this volume). This relationship is often not realized because of the low sex drive of many transsexuals. Searching appetitive behavior would be predicted to be virtually absent. Low brain de-feminization accompanied by low brain masculinization would make mount-receiving behavior exclusive over mounting behavior.

Transsexual males are usually defined on the basis of G-I/R. However, a definition of a biological male who is sexually attracted to other individuals who are older and more masculine than self throughout the life span will very nearly capture the same individuals who have been defined as transsexual males on the basis of G-I/R. Transsexual males are the least brain-defeminized males (see Figures 1.10 and 1.11). As a result of very low brain defeminization, they also are less sexually attracted to the penis (theirs and others') than are nontranssexual homosexual males, because the penis is very much a perceived structure and a male structure at that. This relatively diminished attraction is perhaps why they are often able to sacrifice their penis (and testicles) to the surgeon's scalpel. It is predicted that in male transsexuals, there would be few if any visual secondary stimuli conditioned to sexually evocative status (i.e., they would have few animate, inanimate, or contextual fetishes). Their attraction to feminine clothes is an attraction to the feminine G-I/R and is not associated with sexual arousal, which would be the case in an animate fetish.

Transsexual males, being the least brain-defeminized of all males, would be expected to exhibit the greatest number of female-more-frequent, proceptive expressive behaviors and to exhibit them to the greatest degree. Indeed, this prediction is borne out. Transsexual males often exhibit more of these behaviors, in an exaggerated way, than adult females do.

## Summary

Both androphilic and gynephilic adult male pedo- and ephebophiles spend their entire life span in Quadrant B of Figure 1.11, where their brains are (a) slightly less defeminized and slightly more masculinized than occurs in adult heterosexual males, (b) much more defeminized and more masculinized than occurs in adult homosexual males, and (c) markedly more defeminized and markedly more masculinized than occurs in adult transsexual males (compare Figure 1.10 to 1.11).

Comfort (1987, p. 8) comes close to the conclusions that are presented in this chapter when he states, "Paedophilia . . . may be a [visual] imprinting disorder aggravated by low dominance." The imprinting seems to be to the visually perceived structural properties of the highly discriminable, developing secondary sexual characteristics of children or adolescents (see D'Udine, this volume). However, instead of "aggravated by low dominance," this chapter suggests, they are "sexually" aroused by the attributes of high (extreme) diminutive submission." Remember that Figures 1.9, 1.10, and 1.11 refer to **sexual attraction** to relative, not absolute, social status. Many pedo- and ephebophiles are of very high social status, but so are their same-age peers (Brongersma, 1986; Silva, this volume).

## Adult/Child and Adult/Adolescent Sexual Behavior Versus Sexual Abuse

To understand the relationship of adult human sexual behavior with children and adolescents to sexual abuse of children and adolescents requires a more thorough consideration of the concept "sexual abuse." The two aspects of sexual abuse that appear to be paramount will be considered: consent and harm.

### Consent

Consent certainly precludes any behavior that is physically "forced" on an individual or done to or with an individual without "explicit authorization." Sexual behavior without consent is one form of sexual abuse. However, consent is extremely difficult to determine while behavior is occurring and almost impossible to determine retrospectively, except where brute force or weapons are used, which is unusual in adult/child and adult/adolescent sexual behavior. Also, in most jurisdictions, there is an age, usually 12 and under, during which children are not even considered to be capable of giving consent.[30]

The reason consent is so difficult to determine is that consent-containing messages are transmitted simultaneously by both verbal and nonverbal means with the nonverbal messages often containing different and sometimes conflicting information. Also, certain proceptive expressive behaviors that are frequently used in courtship, such as coyness, are assumed by many individuals to be displayed with the conscious, ontogenetic **intention** of sending a flirtatious message of consent. Yet, individuals who behave in a coy manner may verbally self-report that they consciously did not intend to send this message. Their self-reported statement may be true in that intent can be embedded in phylogeny as well as in ontogeny.

With children and adolescents, as well as with adults, it is always possible that there is ontogenetic intent—but that the intent pertains to affiliative behavior that is not necessarily of the kind that leads to sexual behavior. Sexual affiliative displays in the form of proceptive expressive behavior usually are distinctly recognizable by their context and consequences (Moore, 1985), but they often are preceded by nonspecific, nonsexual affiliative displays, such as social smiling.

Sexual **seduction** means "the subtle (verbal or nonverbal) coercion, versus outright (verbal or nonverbal) propositioning, of one individual into sexual behavior by another individual." Seduction must be viewed within the context in which it is occurring. The seduction of a child or an adolescent by an adult is an extreme asymmetry of power, skills, ability, and knowledge and is the reason why any adult/child and adult/adolescent sexual behavior is suspect of being sexual abuse.

The age of peak total sexual outlet (orgasms/period of time) is considerably younger for human males than it is for human females (Kinsey et al., 1948, 1953). Peak total sexual outlet occurs during late adolescence and early adulthood in males, and as a result, adolescence is a time of very high male sexual drive. In many societies, adolescent males, more so than adolescent females, have great difficulty in finding opposite-sex sexual partners of any age, which is one reason why adolescence is often an age of male (and, to a lesser degree, female) homosexual behavior.[31] As a result of this difficulty and for other reasons, seduction by an adult male ephebophile is considerably easier when the adolescent is male rather than female.

## Harm

Harm is the second criterion that would make adult human sexual behavior with children and adolescents qualify as being sexual abuse. In the subsection "Inclusive Fitness and Kin Selection," which was presented earlier in this chapter in the section "Adult/Child and Adult/Adolescent Sexual Behavior Within the Context of Reproductive Behavior," there were five hypotheses proposed for discussion and testing:

1. Adult/child and adult/adolescent sexual behavior derive from biological determinants that are or were adaptive, having evolved by kin selection because they increased inclusive fitness.
2. Adult/child and adult/adolescent sexual behavior derive from biological determinants that are products of random, nonselected genetic mutations.
3. Adult/child and adult/adolescent sexual behavior derive from biological determinants that have been produced by nonselected genetic drift as human populations migrated geographically.
4. Adult/child and adult/adolescent sexual behavior derive from biological determinants that are a by-product of selection for other traits, such as heterosexuality, within human populations.
5. Adult/child and adult/adolescent sexual behavior are psychopathological, maladaptive responses to mental derangement or social dysregulation and actually lower the fitness (i.e., are harmful) to both of the interactants.

This subsection on harm addresses the fifth hypothesis.

Harm, on a short-term basis, can be considered from numerous perspectives. However, so little is known about the norms of typical child and adolescent sexual development in humans that deviations from typical development can hardly be defined. From a purely biological perspective, harm of various types can be condensed into a common concept of "cost" as compared to "benefit." Numerous theoretical biologists use cost:benefit ratios as mathematical predictors of whether a trait should or could evolve by natural, sexual, and kin selection. The currency with which cost and benefit are measured is lifetime fitness.

Yet, measures of fitness are very different from the usual measures of outcome in the social sciences. In addition, most published reports on any long-term consequences of adult/child and adult/adolescent sexual behavior, using any outcome measures, are methodologically weak (Kilpatrick, 1987).

Harm will be examined in regard to female and male, child and adolescent, and heterosexual and homosexual sexual relationships with adults. Homosexual sexual relationships between adult females and female children and adolescents are not included because of a lack of sufficient published data. Harm to the adult male is very society dependent, with the same behavior being normative in one society and punishable by long prison sentences in another society. Certainly, public humiliation and incarceration are harmful to anyone's fitness.

To Female Children and Adolescents
from Heterosexual Relations with Adults

As was previously stated, human females appear to have two reproductive strategies by which they transmit their genes to the next generation: (a) reproduce at a young age, thus taking advantage of the mating appeal of their youth and the support of their extended family, i.e., maximizing mating effort; (b) delay their own reproduction and improve their own spousal appeal, usually through their own education, i.e., maximizing parental investment. In a female adolescent pursuing the second strategy, sexual behavior with males of any age, or even a reputation of sexual promiscuity, during adolescence will have a measurable cost to fitness.

Adult males can give adolescent females sexually transmitted diseases, some of which are a threat to future pregnancies and life. Adult males also can injure female children and adolescents by forcibly attempting intercourse with them. Sexual violence and sexual brutality themselves, however, are a separate issue from adult human sexual behavior with children and adolescents, which is not associated with sexual violence and brutality any more than is adult/adult sexual behavior.

Another type of harm that can be experienced by female adolescents who are involved sexually with adult males is the harm associated with prostitution. Some adolescent females do engage in prostitution with adult males, and most adult female prostitutes started prostitution during their adolescence. Adolescent prostitution provides a very-short-term economic gain and invariably will be shown to correlate with harm in terms of decreased lifetime fitness.

To Male Children and Adolescents from
Heterosexual Relations with Adults

If harm is measured simply on the basis of cost to fitness, this author can think of no harm that would result in a noncoercive sexual interaction between an adolescent male and an adult female as long as the adolescent male did not acquire a sexually transmitted disease. Sexual interactions between adolescent males and adult females are common both in human and nonhuman primates (Anderson and Bielert, this volume; Diamond, this volume). From a purely bioenergetics perspective, there is very little cost to the adolescent male. However, the adolescent male could potentially deplete family resources if he, or his family, were made to provision an out-of-wedlock child from an adult female.

To Male Children and Adolescents from
Homosexual Relations with Adults

*Short-Term Effects*

A sexual relationship between a male child or an adolescent and a male androphilic pedo- or ephebophile could have various outcomes. It currently is impossible, because of the lack of systematic follow-up data, to evaluate the probability of harmfulness or lack of harmfulness in a specific individual relationship. Some of the variance must relate to the age and sexual orientations of the child or adolescent and to the nature of the relationship.

There are numerous studies that report neutral or uneventful, nonfitness-related, short-term consequences in an almost testimonial manner. There also is much self-reporting of nonfitness-related harm, but the interpretation of this type of data is problematic, since it almost always is associated with other clinical psychopathology or criminal prosecution or civil lawsuits. There are, of course, contemporary human societies in the world in which this type of behavior is normative (Schiefenhövel, this volume).

Other studies have pointed out that there are adolescent males who are involved in sexual relationships with adult males who self-report that these relationships are positive experiences for them. There also are adolescent males who engage in sexual behavior with male androphilic ephebophiles for purely short-term economic gain. In terms of short-term effects on fitness, with the exception of the very real possibility of acquiring a sexually transmitted disease, the (biological) effect would have to be considered negligible, inasmuch as in adolescent males, sperm is an almost inexhaustible and easily renewable resource.

## Long-Term Effects

The long-term correlates of adolescent male homosexual prostitution with lifetime fitness are unknown, and when they become known, they probably will not progress beyond the simple correlation stage. As with adolescent female prostitution, short-term economic gain, rather than lifetime fitness, appears to be the proximate motivating factor.

There is a myth perpetuated in the clinical literature that a sexual involvement during childhood or adolescence with an adult male will make a male child or adolescent seek out male children and adolescents for sexual gratification when that male child or adolescent becomes an adult male himself. The evidence for this so-called "abused/abuser hypothesis" has been critically reviewed by Garland and Dougher (this volume) and can best be summarized by the statement that such an experience is neither a necessary nor a sufficient cause of future adult sexual behavior with children and adolescents.

Money (this volume) suggests that double-binded entrapment in an **unpleasant** sexual relationship, rather than adult/child or adult/adolescent sexual behavior per se, is the important variable. From a purely biological perspective, even if sexual experience with an adult male in childhood or adolescence were a necessary and a sufficient cause, it would not necessarily mean that an adult male with this kind of erotic orientation would be less reproductively fit than an adult male without such an orientation. It could easily be argued that such a male would want and father **more** children than an adult male who was not so attracted. The final answer to this question is not known, but the question itself is of immense practical and clinical significance and awaits future empirical research.

Harm has been considered from a purely biological perspective, and this perspective does not consider the short- and long-term human suffering and misery to the child or adolescent and his family that can potentially result from many sexual relationships between adult males and male children and adolescents in contemporary societies.

To be complete, however, one also must consider the suffering and misery to the adult male who is discovered to be sexually involved in any such relationship. In most industrialized societies, such behavior is criminal and is severely punished by public humiliation and long prison sentences. It also must be said that many adult males who are involved in such relationships self-report that they did not intend any harm to the male child or adolescent and that what they thought they were giving was love. (See Brongersma, 1986; Silva, this volume.)

## To Male and Female Children and Adolescents from Heterosexual and Homosexual Relations with Adults

In addition to the specific kinds of harm that have been discussed, other kinds of harm to male and female children and adolescents have been attributed in the professional literature to adult human heterosexual and homosexual behavior with young individuals. Like some of the others, these kinds of harm, also, are long term: for example, increased susceptibility to such conditions as chronic pelvic pain in females, prostitution, juvenile delinquency, drug abuse, criminal behavior, running away in adolescent males, memory problems, confusion, impulsive and self-injurious behaviors, hysteria, personality disorders, characterological disorders, and even schizophrenia and other chronic psychoses.

Other studies find about the same rate of psychiatric disorders in women who were sexually involved with adult males when they were children as would be expected of psychiatric-prevalence rates in the general community. The effects of these symptoms and disorders on lifetime fitness are largely unknown.

Because of the natural design by which the data concerning humans are collected (i.e., no random assignment), the relationship between "childhood sexual abuse" and a myriad of adult conditions and situations may never be shown to be more than a simple correlation. When two conditions, such as A and B, are simply correlated (e.g., A—borderline personality disorder and B—self-report of a history of childhood "sexual abuse"), there are four hypotheses that can be entertained:

1.  The correlation is spurious,
2.  A causes B,
3.  B causes A, and
4.  Some unknown factor causes both A and B.

Apart from specific disorders of sexual functioning, the common element that is found in the life histories of persons with many of the previously described conditions is overwhelming **abuse**: physical, sexual, or emotional. Sexual abuse seems equipotent to, or even less potent than, physical and emotional abuse. How to understand what makes certain types of adult/child and adult/adolescent sexual behavior abusive and other types uneventful and inconsequential is the major task awaiting other behavioral scientists who will study adult human sexual behavior with children and adolescents in the future.

## Conclusions

Pedo- and ephebophilia have been discussed in the context of a paraphilia, a socially unacceptable sexual attraction that now is partially understandable within a biosocial perspective through the overview provided in this introductory chapter and the more focused material presented by the other contributors in this volume. There are three features that make pedo- and ephebophilia relatively common paraphilias:[32] (a) the phylogenetically familiar nature of the stimuli in children and adolescents, (b) the propensity of children and adolescents to be sexually alluring to some males because of their diminutive size, and (c) the highly discriminable appearance of rapidly changing, budding secondary sexual characteristics.

The theoretical curves in Figures 1.3, 1.5, and 1.6 and the placement of pedo- and ephebophiles in Attraction Quadrant B in Figure 1.10 are all first-order approximations made to fit the available data, much of which is preliminary. The following statements are qualifications that pertain to what already has been said; there is some benefit to grouping the qualifications together at the end of the chapter so that the issues they raise can be kept in mind as one reads the rest of this volume.

1. All published studies of pedo- and ephebophilia are the products of sampling biases. There is no way of knowing the true prevalence of sexual attraction to children and adolescents among adult males in the general population. Studies of incarcerated pedo- and ephebophiles may say more about the characteristics of individuals who have poor self-control of their impulses or who cannot negotiate their way out of the prison system than they say about pedo- or ephebophilia.

2. Pedo- and ephebophilia are emotionally charged issues, and as a result, even the most objective of scientific researchers are affected at least by the public's reaction to the subject, if not by their own. There are advocacy groups at both ends of the spectrum (stricter laws versus decriminalization) who often use the forum of the scientific literature to covertly argue their own issue.

3. Pedo- and ephebophilia may be quite different phenomena etiologically and may resemble each other only to a degree. In future studies that look for biosocial or demographic correlates, the two should be kept separate. It is also important that the distinction between pedo- and ephebophilia stay rooted in biosocial criteria, such as the onset of puberty, rather than in legalistic criteria, such as a given chronological age.

4. Androphilic and gynephilic pedo- and ephebophilia may be quite different phenomena and, also, should be addressed as separate concepts in future empirical research.

5. The differences between "normal" hetero- and homosexual males and gynephilic and androphilic male ephebophiles may be subtle. As a result, ephebophiles will always be a more difficult group to study than pedophiles.

6. Pedo- and ephebophilia are quite different from pedo- and ephebosexual behavior, conceptually. Despite this difference, the two often are difficult to separate in practice. As a result, pure groups will be difficult to study.

7. Adult females occasionally are involved in sexual behavior with children and adolescents; adolescents of both sexes also can be involved in sexual behavior with children. Since the known central tendency in human populations is toward the sexual behavior of adult males with children and adolescents, it is correct that the major effort should first be in understanding this group. However, the full understanding of the behavior

will not be complete until adult women and adolescents of both sexes, too, are understood conceptually.

8. Proximate mechanisms must be sought within the disciplines of developmental sexology, developmental neurobiology, neuroethology, and psychoneuroendocrinology.

9. Compared to data that are available on the childhood development of heterosexual, homosexual, and transsexual males, there is almost nothing known of the childhood development of male androphilic or gynephilic pedo- and ephebophiles. This gap in knowledge must be filled if understanding is to proceed.

10. Pedo- and ephebophilia will be fully understood only with the addition of history, anthropology, and biology to the very fine work that already has been done in psychology and sociology. No one discipline has the complete answer to this issue, and the complete picture will require a large amount of interdisciplinary collaboration.

## Summary

The biosocial basis of adult human sexual behavior with children and adolescents was related to culture, behavior, motivation, mood, sexual interactants, sexual attraction, and sexual arousal. The concept of the lovemap was related to stimulus discrimination and to stimulus fitness and potency. The relationship of the lovemap to love and to two components of reproductive behavior, i.e., mating effort and parental investment, was discussed. The context in which reproductive behavior, i.e., its mating-effort and parental-investment components, occurs was used to provide an understanding of aspects of nonsexual reproductive behavior as well as nonprocreative sexual behavior. The relationship of pedophiles and ephebophiles to individuals with other erotic orientations was shown. The relationship of adult/child and adult/adolescent sexual behavior versus abuse was covered using the concepts of consent and harm. Speculations were offered as to some possible proximate mechanisms involved in the development of pedo- and ephebophilia using the concepts developed earlier in the chapter. General conclusions were given regarding the need for conceptual and methodological caution as well as clarity in future research in this field.

## Notes

[1]"Behavior" is defined as "a posture or movement produced by the contraction of voluntary (striated) muscles." From the point of view of ethology, behavior is classified as being **intentional** or **expressive**. Intentional behavior produces functional outcomes, such as walking, running,

or throwing. Expressive behavior, often called "affect," signals mood to a conspecific (member of the same species) and may be self-perceived as feelings (see Zivin, 1985). Expressive behaviors can be performed with or without deliberate, cognitive intent or self-reported awareness. Examples of expressive behaviors include smiling, frowning, and flirting.

[2]"Stimulus filter" is an ethological construct that refers to the receptive component of the innate releasing mechanism. After passing through the stimulus filter, a specific stimulus may release a specific behavioral response in the form of a fixed-action pattern (see Lorenz, 1981).

[3]The term "adolescent" is defined in this and other chapters in this volume as "an individual from the time at which secondary sexual characteristics begin to develop to the time at which the development of these characteristics is completed."

[4]"Phylogeny" means "the evolutionary history of the species" (see Medicus and Hopf, this volume).

[5]"Ontogeny" means "the developmental history of the individual" (see Zivin, this volume).

[6]The noun "appetence" derives from the adjective "appetitive" and is used in ethology to mean "a natural appetite" (see Eibl-Eibesfeldt, 1975; Lorenz, 1981). It follows, therefore, that "initial-stimulus appetence" is a property of the perceiver of the initial stimulus, i.e., of the individual's nervous system. "Appetitive" also is used to describe the specific searching behavior that leads to consummatory behavior.

[7]"Stimulus discriminative ability," which is precisely defined later in this section in the subsection titled "Stimulus Discriminative Ability," is a property of the nervous system of the perceiving individual. "Discriminable" is a property of a stimulus. "Degree of stimulus discrimination" is a state that results from the interaction between the nervous system's discriminative ability and the discriminability of the stimulus.

[8]The cumbersome term "sexual-arousal-associated-with stimulus" is necessary because it is not known whether an initial stimulus evokes sexual arousal without prior exposure to it or whether the initial stimulus is conditioned into that status by being present during spontaneous or other-than-initial-stimulus-evoked sexual arousal, as in the sexual arousal that occurs during REM sleep or during mechanical self-masturbation.

[9][L. nubilis, from nubere; to veil oneself, to marry.] marriageable: said of women, with reference to their age or physical development. (Webster's Unabridged Dictionary [2nd ed.]. New York: Ottenheimer Publishers, Inc., 1988.)

[10]It is proposed that a trait called "stimulus discriminative ability" would be closely related to the reciprocal of Clonninger's personality trait "novelty seeking" (Clonninger, 1987). In Clonninger's scheme, individuals who are high in "novelty seeking" would be low in "stimulus discriminative ability," and the reason they seek novelty would be their inability to attend to detail and, therefore, their propensity to experience the resultant early

stimulus habituation. It is not known whether the trait "stimulus discriminative ability" is restricted to sexually relevant stimuli or generalizes to all stimuli. Clonninger's "novelty seeking" trait is not restricted to sexual stimuli.

[11]The difference between the secondary-stimulus appetence for sexually conditioned attributes in the lovemap and the secondary-stimulus appetence for sexually conditioned attributes not in the lovemap is that the former attributes are not contingent upon some schedule of positive reinforcement for continued appetence and the latter are.

[12]"Paraphilic" is the adjectival form of the noun "paraphilia." Money defines "paraphilia" as "a condition occurring in men and women of being compulsively responsive to and obligatively dependent upon an unusual and personally or socially unacceptable stimulus, perceived or in the imagery of fantasy, for optimal initiation and maintenance of erotosexual arousal and the facilitation or attainment of orgasm [from Greek, *para-* + *-philia*]. Paraphilic imagery may be replayed in fantasy during solo masturbation or intercourse with a partner. In legal terminology, a paraphilia is a perversion or deviancy; and in the vernacular it is kinky or bizarre sex" (Money, 1986, p. 267).

[13]The qualifying term "near" is necessary because, if a stimulus or an attribute were exactly optimally-discriminated-for-fitness, it would lie in the exact center of the normal distribution, and its potency value would be zero. Many zeros added together can never equal more than zero.

[14]Because of biological variability and the propensity to stabilize means through balanced polymorphic extremes, there is no reason to assume that all individuals in a population will have a potentially procreative lovemap. Such individuals with nonprocreative lovemaps may reflect the effect of natural, sexual, and kin selection operating on other individuals or on nonlovemap-related traits in the population in which they reside, rather than these selective forces acting on their lovemap directly, as in the spandrels of San Marco (see Gould and Lewontin, 1979).

[15]"Inclusive fitness" is "the successful transfer of one's genes to succeeding generations, including genes that have been transferred by a relative's genitals."

[16]"Kin selection" is "the nepotistic favoritism shown to relatives that facilitates one's inclusive fitness."

[17]A similar sociobiological explanation has been offered for homosexuality (see Wilson, 1978). Robert Trivers is usually credited with having devised the idea.

[18]An "open genetic program" is one in which the propensity to learn a general type of behavioral modification is coded in genetic material but the particular details of the stimulus are left to chance and individual experience (see Lorenz, 1981).

[19]Some anthropologists prefer to define "incest" more broadly as sexual behavior between any culturally disallowed individuals.

[20]Parker and Parker (1986) found that the crucial variable for the lack of erotic interest was not biological fatherhood per se but rather association during a critical period in childhood. Stepfathers who raised children from infancy were no more likely to be sexually involved with them as children or adolescents than were natural fathers. In contrast, natural fathers who were absent during infancy and childhood had as high a risk of sexual involvement with these children and adolescents upon returning to the home as did newly arrived stepfathers.

[21]"Functional proximity" is the concept used to describe two behaviors that can easily be executed simultaneously or in rapid alternation (see Lorenz, 1981).

[22]Multimale species are those species in which the social group to which an individual belongs during activity or during sleep contains more than one adult male.

[23]It is suggested that some paraphilias are, in part, the result of the enormously more complex inanimate and contextual socioecological niche in which the lovemap is acquired in modern industrialized societies as compared to the environment of hunters and gatherers.

[24]The shape of the nubile female is essentially the juxtaposition of a few curves. The neuroethology of the essential elements of the stimuli is revealed in reductionist art, e.g., Picasso. Other, more detailed elements of the stimuli are revealed by less reductionist artists, such as Vargas.

[25]A distinction must be made between "function" and "adaptive function." The former concept encompasses the latter, which has a very specific biological implication (see Dienske, this volume).

[26]It is interesting to speculate that a male child's mother would have the shape of a nubile female but the role of "more dominant than self." The degree to which the male child's brain has been masculinized and defeminized in utero is believed to influence the degree to which shape (stored on the basis of perceived structure) or role (stored on the basis of nonstructurally perceived and processed properties) predominates. The brain of heterosexual male masochists is less masculinized than defeminized in the two-dimensional model to be developed. (See the subsection titled "The Two-Dimensional Mechanisms," which is found later in this section in the greater subsection titled "Proximate Mechanisms Underlying Specific Age and Sexual Orientations in Human Males: The Two-Dimensional Model.")

[27]Compared to adult male heterosexual masochists, within the context of the two-dimensional model, the brain of adult male homosexual masochists is believed to be relatively less defeminized but equally unmasculinized. (See the subsection titled "The Two-Dimensional Mechanisms," which is found later in this section in the greater subsection titled "Proximate Mechanisms Underlying Specific Age and Sexual Orientations in Human Males: The Two-Dimensional Model.") Being less defeminized would make attributes coded and stored on the basis of perceived structure less sexually alluring than attributes coded and stored on

the basis of perceived and possessed role, with the exception of the one structurally perceived attribute with intrinsic and primary sexual gratification, theirs and others' penis.

[28]Mount-receiving behavior is mainly attributable to remaining feminized (with accompanying lordosis) rather than to being unmasculinized. This assignment is most compatible with the available data and with the arrangement of individuals with differing sexual orientations in the two-dimensional model in Figures 1.9, 1.10, and 1.11. The assignment also is compatible with Pillard and Weinrich (1987).

[29]For simplicity and conceptual convenience, the category "bisexual" was not used, and "transsexual," which is usually defined on the basis of G-I/R, is being defined on the basis of age and sexual orientations.

[30]There are social/political lobbies in both the United States and Europe that strive to lower the age of consent. However, the lobbyists appear to be mainly adult male androphilic pedo- and ephebophiles, rather than the children and adolescents or their advocates (see Okami, this volume).

[31]Sexual exploration among same-age and same-sex children and adolescents is often considered a developmental stage in which pedo- and ephebophiles as well as homosexual individuals become "fixated." The two-dimensional biosocial model suggests that age and sexual orientations are largely determined by differing degrees of pre- and perinatal hormonalization with some contribution of life experience during the formation of the lovemap.

[32]The prevalence rate of paraphilias in the general population is unknown. Estimates of relative prevalence can be obtained from the percent of all individuals seeking treatment who have a particular paraphilia (Abel et al., 1987).

## References

Abel, G.G., Becker, J.V., Mittelman, M., Cunningham-Rather, J., Rouleau, J.L., and Murphy, W.D. Self-reported sex crimes of nonincarcerated paraphiliacs. *J. of Interpersonal Violence*, 1987, 2, 3-25.

Bateson, P.E. (Ed.). *Mate choice*. Cambridge: Cambridge University Press, 1983.

Bell, A.P., Weinberg, M.S., and Hammersmith, S.K. *Sexual preference: Its development in men and women*. Bloomington: Indiana University Press, 1981.

Betzig, L., Mulder, M.B., and Turke, P. *Human reproductive behavior: A Darwinian perspective*. Cambridge: Cambridge University Press, 1988.

Birdwhistell, R.L. *Kinesics and context: Essays on body motion communication*. Philadelphia: University of Pennsylvania Press, 1979.

Bowlby, J. *Attachment and loss*, Vol. 1. New York: Basic Books, 1969.

Brongersma, E. *Loving boys*, Vol. 1. Elmhurst, N.Y.: Global Academic Publishers, 1986.

Burgess, A.W., Groth, A.N., Holmstrom, L., and Sgroi, S.M. *Sexual assault of children and adolescents.* Lexington, Mass.: Lexington Books, 1978.

Clonninger, R.C. A systematic method for clinical description and classification of personality variants: A proposal. *Archiv. Gen. Psychiatry,* 1987, *44,* 573-588.

Comfort, A. Deviation and variation. *In* G.D. Wilson (Ed.), *Variant sexuality: Research and theory.* Baltimore: The Johns Hopkins University Press, 1987, pp. 1-20.

Daly, M., and Wilson, M. *Sex, evolution, and behavior.* Boston: Willard Grant Press, 1983.

Draper, P., and Harpending, H. Father absence and reproductive strategy: An evolutionary perspective. *J. Anthropol. Res.,* 1982, *38,* 255-273.

Ehrhard, A.A. Androgens in prenatal development: Behavior changes in nonhuman primates and Man. *Advances in the Biosciences,* 1974, *13,* 154-162.

Eibl-Eibesfeldt, I. *Ethology: The biology of behavior* (2nd ed.). New York: Holt, Rinehart and Winston, Inc., 1975.

Feierman, J.R. Foreword. *In* J. Wolf (Ed.), *Gay priests: Research and commentary.* New York: Harper & Row, in press.

Finkelhor, D. *Child sexual abuse: New theory and research.* New York: The Free Press, 1984.

Freund, K.H., Watson, R., and Rienzo, D. Heterosexuality, homosexuality and erotic age preference. *J. of Sex Research,* 1989, *26,* 107-117.

Gebhard, P.H., Gagnon, J.H., Pomeroy, W.B., and Christenson, C.V. *Sex offenders: An analysis of types.* New York: Harper & Row, 1965.

Gould, S.J., and Lewontin, R.C. The Spandrels of San Marco and the Panglossian paradigm: A critique of the adaptationist program. *Proceedings of the Royal Society of London,* 1979, *205,* 581-598.

Goy, R.W., and McEwen, B.S. *Sexual differentiation of the brain.* Cambridge, Mass.: The MIT Press, 1980.

Green R. *The "Sissy Boy Syndrome" and the development of homosexuality.* New Haven: Yale University Press, 1987.

Hamilton, W.D. The genetical theory of social behavior, I, II. *Journal of Theoretical Biology,* 1964, *7,* 1-52.

Harpending, H., Rogers, A., and Draper, P. Human sociobiology. *Yearbook of Physical Anthropology,* 1987, *30,* 127-150.

Hopf, S. Development of sexual behavior in captive squirrel monkeys (*Saimiri*). *Biologie of Behaviour,* 1979, *4,* 373-382.

Kilpatrick, A.C. Childhood sexual experiences: Problems and issues in studying long-range effects. *The Journal of Sex Research,* 1987, *23,* 173-196.

Kinsey, A.C., Pomeroy, W., and Martin, C.E. (Eds.). *Sexual behavior in the human male.* Philadelphia: W.B. Saunders Company, 1948.

Kinsey, A.C., Pomeroy, W., Martin, C.E., and Gebhard, P.H. (Eds.). *Sexual behavior in the human female*. Philadelphia: W.B. Saunders Company, 1953.

Lancaster, J.B., and Hamburg, B.A. *School-age pregnancy and parenthood: Biosocial dimensions*. New York: Aldine de Gruyter, 1986.

Lancaster, J.B., Altmann, J., Rossi, A.S., and Sherrod, L.R. *Parenting across the life span: Biosocial dimensions*. New York: Aldine de Gruyter, 1987.

Linder, R.M., and Seliger, R.V. (Eds.). *The sex offender in custody: Handbook of correctional psychology*. New York: Philosophical Library, 1947.

Lorenz, K.Z. *The foundations of ethology*. New York: Springer-Verlag, 1981.

Maccoby, E.E., and Jacklin, C.N. *The psychology of sex differences*, Vols. I and II. Stanford, Calif.: Stanford University Press, 1974.

Masters, W.H., and Johnson, V.E. *Human sexual response*. Boston: Little, Brown and Company, 1966.

McEwen, B.S. Observations on brain sexual differentiation: A biochemist's view. *In* J.M. Reinisch, L.A. Rosenblum, and S.A. Sanders (Eds.), *Masculinity/femininity: Basic perspectives*. New York: Oxford University Press, 1987, pp. 68-79.

Meaney, M.J., Stewart, J., Pouliin, P., and McEwen, B.S. Sexual differentiation of social play in rat pups is mediated by the neonatal androgen receptor system. *Neuroendocrinology*, 1983, *37*, 85-90.

Mitchell, G. *Behavioral sex differences in nonhuman primates*. New York: Van Nostrand Reinhold Company, 1979.

Money, J. *Lovemaps*. New York: Irvington Publishers, Inc., 1986.

Moore, M.M. Nonverbal courtship patterns in women: Context and consequence. *Ethology and Sociobiology*, 1985, *6*, 237-248.

Morris, D. *Patterns of reproductive behavior*. New York: McGraw Hill, 1970.

Parker, H., and Parker, S. Father-daughter sexual abuse: An emerging perspective. *Amer. J. Orthopsychiat.*, 1986, *56*, 531-549.

Perper, T. *Sex signals: The biology of love*. Philadelphia: iSi Press, 1985.

Pfaff, D.W. *Estrogens and brain function: Neural analysis of a hormone-controlled mammalian reproductive behavior*. New York: Springer-Verlag, 1980.

Pillard, R.C., and Weinrich, J.D. The Periodic Table model of the gender transpositions: Part I. A theory based on masculinization and defeminization of the brain. *J. of Sex Research*, 1987, *23*, 425-454.

Remoff, H.T. *Sexual choice: Why and how women choose the men they do as sexual partners*. New York: Dutton/Lewis Publishing, 1984.

Saghir, M.T., and Robins, E. *Male & female homosexuality: A comprehensive investigation*. Baltimore: The Williams & Wilkins Company, 1973.

Sandfort, T. *The sexual aspects of pedophile relations.* Amsterdam: Pan/Spartacus, 1981.

Shepher, J. *Incest: A biosocial view.* New York: Academic Press, 1983.

Smith, M.J. Group selection and kin selection. *Nature, Lond.,* 1964, *201,* 1145-1147.

Smith, W.J. *The behavior of communicating: An ethological approach.* Cambridge, Mass.: Harvard University Press, 1977.

Symons, D. *The evolution of human sexuality.* New York: Oxford University Press, 1979.

Tinbergen, N. *The study of instinct.* New York: Oxford University Press, 1951.

Tinbergen, N. *The herring gull's world: A study of the social behavior of birds.* New York: Harper & Row, 1960.

Trivers, R. Parental investment and sexual selection. *In* B. Campbell (Ed.), *Sexual selection and the descent of Man.* Chicago: Aldine-Atherton, 1972, pp. 136-179.

Wickler, W. *The sexual code.* Garden City: Anchor Books, 1973.

Wilson, E.O. *On human nature.* Cambridge, Mass.: Harvard University Press, 1978.

Wolf, A.P., and Huang, C. *Marriage and adoption in China, 1845-1945.* Stanford, Calif.: Stanford University Press, 1980.

Zivin, G. (Ed.). *The development of expressive behavior: Biology-environment interactions.* Orlando, Fl.: Academic Press, 1985.

# 2
# History in Adult Human Sexual Behavior with Children and Adolescents in Western Societies

Vern L. Bullough
*Office of the Dean*
*Faculty of Natural and Social Sciences*
*SUNY College*
*Buffalo, New York 14222*

## Introduction

Though the theme of this book is adult human sexual behavior with children and adolescents, a number of other descriptive terms characterize individual chapters and, perhaps, their respective authors' viewpoints: "pedophilia," "cross-generational sex," "adult/child sexual interactions," "incest," "man/child association," "father/daughter sexual abuse," "childhood sexual abuse." Missing from the preliminary list of terms but present in some of the literature are other terms, such as *"Knabenliebe,"* "boy-love," "pederasty," "Greek love," and "child abuse." Most of the terms in and of themselves are value free, except for the terms "child abuse" and "child sexual abuse," and it is only in the last few decades that these terms entered the lexicon of descriptors. The question the historian has to raise is whether the emergence of these terms reflects a new and changing attitude or new and changing behaviors or both?

The question is not easy to answer because not all the variables are immediately present in any one time period. Moreover, one has to define with greater precision which type of activity constitutes adult human sexual behavior with either children or adolescents. Is it exhibitionism, touching, fondling of genitals above or beneath the clothes, or actual penetration of an appendage in an orifice? This distinction is particularly important in a historical chapter because different societies define these terms differently, and in fact, the sources are often silent about such behaviors as exhibitionism and touching. There also are differences within time periods and among sources in how terms are defined. Even when there are legal definitions that use an individual's age for guidance there are problems, because an individual's chronological age is not easily discernible. Such terms as "pederasty," which literally means "love of a boy," came in many law codes to be synonymous with anal intercourse and even with homosexuality in general and often, therefore, has a broader meaning.

What appears obvious from a historical overview is that adult/child and adult/adolescent sexual behavior has had different meanings at different historical times. These meanings are related to what a particular culture or a society regards as the marriageable age and the desirable difference in age between the spouses. In general, societies have been hostile to adult/child sexual behavior involving penetration and less hostile to other forms of sexual behavior.

If societal attitudes have been somewhat varied in terms of what constitutes prohibited adult/child sexual behavior, there has been almost no confusion in terms of adult/adolescent sexual behavior. In fact, adult/adolescent sexual behavior has not simply been tolerated throughout much of history but, in some time periods, has been the norm. This attitude can be illustrated by a brief, descriptive listing of some famous or near-famous adult individuals in history who were involved in some form of sexual behavior with at least one adolescent or near-adolescent.

A good example to begin with is St. Augustine [354-439], who, perhaps more than any one other individual, set the sexual standards for the Christian Church. Briefly, St. Augustine had converted to Manichaeanism as a young adult, and though he had striven for many years to become one of the Manichaean "Adepts," a person who among other things lived a chaste and celibate life, he had not been able to achieve that status. The difficulty was that though his spirit was willing, his flesh was weak, and Augustine, in spite of his belief system, was unwilling to give up sex, particularly with his mistress. He later reported that his constant prayer during this period in his life was "Give me chastity—but not yet" (Augustine, 1955, VII, vi, 17).

Unable to forego sexual activity, Augustine decided to avoid trying to be an Adept and to regularize his life by marrying. Once this decision was made, he sent his mistress and illegitimate son away and then set out to choose a bride. He selected a young prepubertal girl, and since technically he could not marry her until she came of age (i.e., had her menarche), he was betrothed to her. Unable to give up sex even for this brief period, he took another mistress, and this act, among other things, brought on a personal crisis that led him to convert to Christianity and swear off sex for the rest of his life (Augustine, 1955, IV, ii, VI, xii, VII, i). There is nothing to indicate that marriages to such prepubertal girls were unusual, although custom and law dictated they not be consummated until puberty. Obviously, Augustine was more than twice the age of his bride-to-be (Bullough and Brundage, 1983).

A second figure illustrating the same theme is the prophet Muhammed [570-632], who had married his first wife, Khadijah, when she was around 40 years of age and he was 25. At her death, Muhammed seemed inconsolable, and his friends advised him to marry again so that he might more easily overcome his grief. Although reluctant to agree, the prophet eventually married Ayesha, a young prepubertal girl. It was said that just watching her play with her dolls proved to be a consolation to him. Most Islamic authorities agree the marriage was not consummated until Ayesha began to menstruate, the traditionally acceptable time for intercourse, but there was still a marriage to a girl that many say was only 7 (Bullough, 1973).

The third historical figure is the great Indian mathematical genius, Srinivasa Ramanujan, who was born in 1887 and died some 32 years later. At age 22, he married 9-year-old Srimathia Janki, who brought her mother with her when she moved into his household (Kolata, 1987). Such marriages were not unusual in India, although often the bride and groom were closer to the same age, as was the case with Mahatma Gandhi [1869-1948], the fourth example, who was married at 13. Though he took a vow of sexual abstinence at 37, a vow that he found difficult to observe and that he once described as "walking on the sword's edge," this vow did not stop him from later fondling girls, both pubescent and prepubescent. In his later years, Gandhi took to taking such girls to bed with him to overcome his "shivering fits" in the night. His female companions, who came from his inner circle—all certified virgins or young brides—entered his bed naked in order to warm him with their bodies. Some of them also administered enemas to him. Among the young girls, there was rivalry as to who would sleep with him, and one of his girl disciples reported that his bed companions had a difficult time in restraining themselves and repressing their sexual impulses since he often rubbed against them and touched them (Bullough, 1981). Though his disciples were fearful of public reaction if news of these "pedophilic sexual" interactions was publicized, Gandhi continued to engage in them until his death. Here, there was no sexual intercourse, and most girls were postpubertal, but some were younger. In modern Western society, such activity would be a criminal offense.

The fifth historical figure, Will Durant, was born in the United States in 1865 and died only recently. Durant's future wife, Ariel, had just turned 14 when she entered his classroom in the fall of 1912, and she immediately fell in love with him and set plans to marry him. By March of 1913, he had resigned his position because of his growing interest in her, and they were married October 31, 1913; she was just past 15 and he 28 (Durant and Durant, 1977). The Durant story emphasizes that until recently 14 was the legal age of marriage in most states of the United States, while some states had set younger ages (New Mexico for a time in the 1980's had 13 as the legal age), requiring only the consent of the parents or a judicial official. Some states still have such laws on their books. Quite clearly, in the United States at least, and in many other countries, adult/adolescent sexual behavior, within the context of marriage, was not regarded with horror, although most individuals were not married at such young ages.

It was not only girls who were involved in such relationships but boys, as well. Johann Wolfgang von Goethe wrote of both boys and girls:

> I like boys a lot, but the girls are even nicer. If I tire of her as a girl, she'll play the boy for me as well (Goethe, 1884).

Many famous individuals have formed attachments to adolescent boys, although these attachments were not as socially acceptable as were attachments to girls. George Gordon Byron [1788-1824], or Lord Byron, was attached to Nicolo Giraud, a young French-Greek lad who had been a model for the painter Lusieri before Byron found him. Byron left him 7,000 pounds in his will. When Byron returned to Italy, he became involved with a number of boys in Venice but eventually settled on Loukas Chalandritsanos, age 15, who was with him when he was killed (Crompton, 1985). History, in fact, is full of examples of adult/adolescent sexual relationships. Probably the most cited and the most investigated example is the man/boy relationships in ancient Greece. Since these relationships have been reported by so many writers in such detail, as have the less institutionalized relationships in ancient Rome, they are not recounted here (Buffiere, 1980; Bullough, 1976).

## Adult/Child Sexual Behavior

Adult/child sexual behavior is a more difficult topic to address historically because, as indicated, there are a variety of differing definitions of what might constitute sexual behavior and what constitutes childhood. Even as late as the 19th century, there were a number of "respectable" individuals who today would be classified as "child molesters," including two whose books became classics: Lewis Carroll and J.M. Barrie (see Money, this volume). Carroll was attracted to prepubescent girls and enjoyed photographing them in the nude, among other things (Bullough, 1983), while Barrie's classic Peter Pan seems to have reflected his own sexual needs more than is generally realized (Birkin, 1979). Another writer of children's books, Horatio Alger, was attracted to young boys, and it was this attraction that forced him from the Unitarian ministry into the ranks of full-time authorship (Hoyt, 1974).

The 19th-century examples can be replicated in earlier periods, although usually only extreme cases came to be noted. One such example is the case of the historical Bluebeard, Gilles de Rais (or Retz) [1404-1440], a marshal of France. Among other things, Gilles was appointed protector of Joan of Arc by King Charles VII after she first appeared on the French scene. This effort nearly bankrupted him, and in order to recover, Gilles turned to magic and alchemy, convinced that human sacrifice would save him. He had agents begin scouring the countryside for subjects, particularly young boys, in whom Gilles became interested sexually. Many were sexually assaulted before they died, and allegedly, even after they were dead, he abused their cadavers. Although the disappearance of so many boys around his castle aroused suspicions and rumors, as did Gilles's demands for boy servants, his activities were unchecked until 1440. Then, in a fit of anger, he stormed into a church during mass to seize a minor cleric who had angered him. This act led to a break with his protector and an investigation of his activities. The result was a trial during which he estimated that he had murdered between 150 and 200 boys with whom he had had sex. He was executed on October 26, 1440, at Nantes (Lewis, 1952; Wilson, 1899). When Perrault originally wrote the story of Gilles in 1697, however, Bluebeard's victims were his wives, a nice retelling of history (Perrault, 1697).

Gilles de Rais was a powerful noble, in a hierarchical society in which such persons were in a position to violate both the norms and the laws of society with greater impunity than lesser people, although lesser people also violated them. There was, however, greater enforcement of norms in medieval and early modern European society than there is in modern urban American society. This enforcement existed because, in general, medieval and early modern Europeans were rural people who lived in villages. There was no real concept of privacy until the 18th century, even among the nobility, and in effect, what took place was everybody's business. Though technically the power of the father over the family was very great, there were all kinds of village safeguards that discouraged the abuse of this power. Since there was little privacy and poor sanitation, with the animals and humans in some areas living literally in the same house (for warmth, if nothing else), almost everyone knew about sex and reproduction from an early age. Bawdy talk was frequent, and one need only look at Chaucer, Boccaccio, and Rabelais, among others, to realize this bawdiness extended to the upper classes as well.

Though there were urban centers both in Europe and the United States, until the 19th century few exceeded 100,000 people. Privacy in cities was as difficult to achieve as it was in the countryside, although there was more opportunity for sexual variation in the city than in rural areas; in addition, students of history know of the growing official concern about homosexuality, for example, in cities such as Florence and Venice in the 15th and 16th centuries (Bullough, 1976). As privacy developed as a concept in the 18th century, separate rooms were adopted for special purposes, such as the bedroom or dining room. Cities also began to grow larger, pushed in large part by the growing industrialization that led to rapidly expanding urban centers, at first in England and then elsewhere. Inevitably, social problems that had been relatively minor in the rural countryside were magnified by this increase in population, and initially, government, law, and social institutions were unprepared to cope effectively with the change.

Gradually, there was an increased public awareness of the problem and a demand for greater government intervention. One of the richest sources for documenting this change in public and official attitudes toward adult/child sexual behavior is in the area of prostitution, in which child prostitution was widespread in the 18th and 19th centuries. These new attitudes were particularly evident, again, in England, where the legal code set 12 as the age of sexual consent, unlike most continental countries, which, following the Napoleonic Code, put it much higher. Thus, the laws of England allowed a child of 12 to verbally consent to sexual behavior with a middle-aged adult. Children under 12, though nominally protected, could be seduced with near impunity in privacy, since testamentary evidence from young children could be accepted in English court only if they demonstrated complete understanding of the nature of the oath. Usually children were so frightened by the court proceedings that they were unable to give satisfactory explanations to the judges. As a result, there was no successful prosecution of child/adult sexual behavior in England until the law was changed (Terrot, 1960).

Adding to the complexity of adult/child sexual behavior in England, particularly in the 19th century, was the change in employment conditions for children. These conditions had been totally unregulated at the beginning of the century, and even very young children worked in the emerging factories. In part because of reformers' concern over the welfare of children, legislation protecting children began to be enacted during the century. One of the unfortunate side effects of these otherwise necessary acts was to make children more accessible for sexual services, if only because there were few other alternative ways for them to earn a living, and there were vast numbers of children without any means of support. Dickens discussed some of these problems in his novels, and the picture he portrayed in *Oliver Twist* (1838) was a real one.

This change in working conditions for young children, and the growth in urban areas, coincided with a growing sexual demand for younger children, particularly for young girls, brought about by the growing fear of sexually transmitted diseases. The sequelae of syphilis had been mapped out in the latter part of the 19th century, primarily by Philip Ricord, and were verified by the eventual discovery in 1905 of the spirochete causing the disease. As the horrors of syphilis and consequences of gonorrhea on newborn infants began to be realized, the search for sexual partners who were virgins increased. There also was a popular belief that venereal disease could be cured if the diseased person had intercourse with a young virgin. Whatever the reason, child prostitution increased.

That the individuals who used young girls were not a special class that could be labeled "pedophiles" was indicated by the anonymous memorialist who wrote *My Secret Life*. He also recorded some of the difficulties with having sex with prepubescent girls, although he did not go into the difficulties that are involved in penetration, which would have involved considerable tissue tearing. It was common during this period to chloroform such girls, but the author did not say anything about this practice. Instead, he stated rather matter of factly,

> Verily a gentleman had better fuck them for money, than a butcher boy (fuck them) for nothing. It is the fate of such girls to be fucked young, neither laws social or legal can prevent it. Given opportunities—who has them like the children of the poor—and they will copulate. It is the law of nature which nothing can thwart. A man need have no "compunctions of conscience"—as it is termed—about having such girls first, for assuredly he will had done no harm, and has only been an agent in the inevitable. The consequences to the female being the same, whosoever she may first have been fucked by . . . (*My Secret Life,* 1966, XI, pp. 2191-2192).

He reported that the youngest girl he had ever had sex with was 10 years old, for which he paid her "aunt" 10 pounds. He added that she "was the youngest I ever yet have had, or have wished to have," and complained that she could not give the pleasure "that fully developed women could." Nevertheless, he admitted he had several orgasms with her (*My Secret Life,* 1966, II, p. 206).

Standard prices were paid to procurers for virginal girls willing to engage in sexual relations: 20 pounds plus expenses was paid for a healthy working-class girl between 14 and 18 years of age; a middle-class girl of the same age group cost 100 pounds; and a beautiful child under 12 years of age, preferably from a good background, was said to sell for 400 pounds (Bullough and Bullough, 1987, p. 269).

Benjamin Waugh, an English social worker, reported numerous incidents of young girls being raped and tortured and then thrown out to fend for themselves (Bullough and Bullough, 1987, p. 272). Other reformers, such as Dyer (1880, 1885) and Butler (1881), reported similar cases, but there was a reluctance by large segments of the public to believe them. Boys, also, were used as sexual objects, but even the reformers could not bring themselves to mention this practice. In part because of pressure by the reformers, however, a parliamentary committee began hearing about traffic in young girls in 1881. Though legislation quickly passed through the House of Lords, there was a great reluctance in Commons to deal with this problem.

It was on this scene that the media made their appearance in the person of W.T. Stead, editor of the *Pall Mall Gazette*. Stead had become interested in child prostitution through the efforts of a number of reformers including Josephine Butler and Bramwell Booth of the Salvation Army. To gather the "facts," Stead appointed an investigating committee of both men and women. Two of the women managed to live in a brothel for 10 days, while Stead and some of the men visited brothels to observe what took place there. Stead reported being nauseated when he observed young children, 3-5 years of age, being chloroformed in order to be used as sex partners by adult men. Convinced that reports of observations would not be enough to sway public opinion, Stead decided to demonstrate that he himself could actually buy a child in England to be used for sexual purposes. After some initial efforts at using a professional procurer, he turned to a "reformed" prostitute to act for him. She found him a young girl for which he had to pay 3 pounds; 1 pound went to the child's mother and 2 pounds to an intermediary. Stead had the girl examined by a midwife who specialized in certifying virgins to make sure she was a virgin. The midwife was familiar with the use of such girls as sexual partners, and at her urging, he bought some chloroform from her so that the girl would not suffer too much because she was so young and her vagina so small. Stead then took the girl to a hotel room where he staged a mock seduction, although he was careful to have the girl certified as a virgin afterwards. He then had her "spirited away" to the continent under the protection of the Salvation Army.

Having prepared his case, Stead began publishing it in a six-part series in the *Pall Mall Gazette*. The first article appeared under banner headlines on July 6, 1885, entitled "The Maiden Tribute of Modern Babylon." The shock effect was more than Stead wanted or desired, since, though Parliament quickly passed legislation demanded by an aroused public, Stead himself was indicted, convicted, and sentenced to three months in jail for abducting a child. The main reason for the successful prosecution was that the father, who had apparently agreed to the sale, had never formally given his consent, although the mother had. When Stead, determined to protect the girl, refused to return her to her parents, the father was able to bring suit against Stead. An angry public, perhaps upset at what was going on around them, was only too willing to see Stead punished (Pearson, 1972). He emerged from jail a hero, however, and went on a world tour. Parenthetically, it should be added that Stead did his task too well. Not only was the age of consent raised to 16, but also, added to the original legislation in the rush to get the bill passed was a clause outlawing sexual relations between two consenting adult males; it was this act under which Oscar Wilde later was prosecuted.

The publicity over the English cases of child prostitution led other countries to investigate the problem, which eventually was taken up by the League of Nations. In the United States, there was an outburst of activity as protection of children became a major agenda for the emerging feminist movement and for labor unions (primarily concerned with child labor). It became a key legislative issue for politicians in this "Progressive Era," who held that the government had a major responsibility to protect children. One result of all of this effort was the establishment of the Children's Bureau in the United States in 1912.

It was in the 19th century also that incest became an issue, first among scholars and then among popular writers. Among those scholars who looked at incest were Darwin (1871), Durkheim (1898), Engels (1884), Frazer (1910), Freud (1913), Morgan (1877), Tylor (1889), Westermarck (1925), and many others. This interest in incest, if James Twitchell (1985) is correct, was also the impetus for much of the horror fiction of the 19th century. With the legal power of the father over the family, the lack of independent economic opportunities for women, and the growth of privacy, incest became more difficult to detect just as it became a matter of greater concern. Incest has remained a topic of interest to a variety of scholars (Arens, 1986; Fox, 1980; Parker, 1976).

## Extent of Adult/Child Sexual Behavior

How widespread was sexual behavior between adults and children in the past? The evidence, scanty as it is, would indicate that it was not very widespread and that probably most such behavior took place within the family, although the answer has to be dependent upon how sexual behavior is defined. If a child is defined, on the basis of age, as being under 12 years old, there was a greater incidence of activity than if a child is defined as being under 9 years old; using the latter definition, there are very few historically documented incidents that this author has found. One kind of evidence to be considered from the late 19th and early 20th centuries for the relatively low incidence of adult/child sexual behavior is the fact that authors in this period who wrote about sexuality did not consider it a major problem area. Krafft-Ebing (1912), who defined so many sexual activities, did not deal with adult/child sexual behavior at all in his early editions, and it was only towards the end of his career that he even mentioned it, and then he tended to minimize it. It was Krafft-Ebing, however, who introduced the term "erotic pedophilia" into the technical literature:

> There are cases in which the sexually needed subject is drawn to children not in consequence of degenerated morality or physical impotence, but rather by a morbid disposition, a psychosexual perversion, which may at present be named pedophilia erotica (p. 55).

Even then, Krafft-Ebing did not give more than passing mention to the topic. He did, however, address separately another kind of sex activity, exposure of the genitals to others, including children, which some today classify under "child sexual abuse."

Ellis (1933), too, did not devote any lengthy discussion to the subject:

> Apart from senility, there seems to be no congenital sexual perversion directed towards children. There may exceptionally be a repressed subconscious impulse towards unripe girls, but the chief contingent before old age is furnished by the weak minded (pp. 150-151, note 1).

Hirschfeld more or less ignored the topic (Hirschfeld, 1948), reporting in one place that he had never seen a child violator who was mentally sound (Mohr, Turner, and Jerry, 1964). Perhaps one reason for the failure of these early writers on sexuality to deal with the subject is that they distinguished it from incest and then failed to discuss incest, which they regarded as outside their purview.

Freud, however, specifically addressed incest, particularly father/daughter incest, but after some initial hesitation, he tended to regard most such self-reported incidents by women as a fantasy notion (Peters, 1976). Other, more recent commentators have called Freud's explanation of women's self-report of incest a cover-up or proof of the bankruptcy of psychoanalytic theory (Herman, 1981, p. 9; Rush, 1980, p. 83). This chapter is not the place to enter into this controversy except to point out that prior to the past decade, the main discussions of adult/adolescent and adult/child sexual behavior in the 20th century took place in the literature of psychoanalytical psychiatry and criminology (Mohr, Turner, and Jerry, 1964).

Other than incest, which they regarded as different somehow, it seems clear that neither Krafft-Ebing, nor Hirschfeld, nor Ellis regarded adult/child sexual behavior as a significant sexual outlet in the urban societies about which they wrote. That they held this perspective means that either they defined adult/child sexual behavior differently than it is defined currently (they included exposure of genitals in a different category) or they did not regard it as being widespread. The Kinsey empirical study on the sexual behavior of the human male also had little to say about sexual behavior with adults that was experienced by the male subjects when they were children or early adolescents (Kinsey, Pomeroy, and Martin, 1948), in part because the question was never considered important enough to ask consistently (Gebhard and Johnson, 1979). Kinsey and his co-workers, however, did ask it of his female subjects, and 24% had had prepubertal experiences ("prepubertal" being defined as "age 13 or under") in which an adult male had established sexual contacts with them or appeared to be making a sexual type of approach. The most frequent type of contact made by the male was that of showing his genital organs, which occurred in approximately 52% of the cases reporting contact with adults. In 31% of the cases, the adult patted the child in an intimate way but did not touch the sex organs, and in 22% of the cases, there was contact with the child's sex organs. (The total is more than 100% because some had more than one contact.) Approximately 80% of the women who reported having sexual contacts with adults as children as defined by Kinsey (under 13 and making approaches) had but 1 experience in childhood, 15% had less than 6 experiences, and 5% had 10 or more as preadolescents. Kinsey reported that when repetitions did occur (usually with adult relatives living in the same household), the child was aggressive in seeking the experience. Again, few contacts (only .07% of the total female sample) involved actual penetration (Kinsey et al., 1953, pp. ll6-122).

## Changes in Attitudes

At some time between the Kinsey studies and the present (1987), there was either a change in attitude about adult/child and adult/adolescent sexual behavior or an increase in such sexual behavior. This author believes that the former occurred rather than the latter. An indication of this change is seen in the entries contained in Schlesinger's (1981) annotated bibliography. In this volume, he compiled references made in scholarly and other journals between 1937 and 1980 to "sexual abuse" of children. Schlesinger was not concerned with the adults involved in such sexual behavior (the criminology literature is replete with such individuals), nor did he investigate to any degree the psychoanalytic literature. In his somewhat less than comprehensive search, he found only one article to list that had been published between 1937 and 1948; after 1948, there was a slight increase until the 1970's, when the literature expanded rapidly. (See Table 2.I.)

One probable reason for the rapid expansion of the literature on child and adolescent sexual abuse is a simple one—money. The expansion demonstrates what this author calls "the Bullough research correlation," namely, if there is research money available, the research in the field will escalate. This somewhat cynical explanation of the direction that funded research takes can be illustrated by the history of how and why money became available for the area of child and adolescent sexual abuse. Nelson (1984) has done a detailed analysis of the forces leading to the enactment of Public Law 93-247, the Child Abuse and Treatment Act, which was signed into law by U.S. President Richard Nixon on January 31, 1974. This chapter cannot give the detailed analysis that Nelson did, except to say that the legislation appropriated $86 million to be spent over a 3½-year period, mostly on research and demonstration projects, and that the appropriations have continued since that time.

Among the factors involved in the growing concern that led to the 1974 legislation were changing attitudes toward the position of the child in the family. In examining incidents of both physical "abuse" of children and sexual behavior of children with adults, social workers and others involved with the family traditionally had put the family unit above the child. This orientation meant that they often strove to rehabilitate the family unit, sometimes to the extent of not dealing effectively with the child who was being abused, since if and when they did act, the child would be removed

TABLE 2.I. Epidemic of sex abuse literature (based on Schlesinger, 1980)

| Year | Number of Items in Journals | Year | Number of Items in Journals |
|------|------|------|------|
| 1937 | 1 | 1969 | 3 |
| 1948 | 1 | 1971 | 4 |
| 1952 | 1 | 1972 | 5 |
| 1954 | 1 | 1973 | 2 |
| 1957 | 1 | 1974 | 2 |
| 1961 | 1 | 1975 | 9 |
| 1963 | 1 | 1976 | 5 |
| 1964 | 3 | 1977 | 17 |
| 1966 | 3 | 1978 | 25 |
| 1967 | 4 | 1979 | 28 |
| 1968 | 3 | 1980 | 16 |

from the family setting. Moreover, perhaps because of the caseload demands, social workers usually had to rely upon others to report actual incidents of physical "abuse" or of sexual behavior with an adult. Nurses, teachers, and police were often the reporting source, and only after such reports were made was an investigation carried out, often long after the incident had occurred. Police, who often were involved, were not as sophisticated in dealing with alleged child sexual abuse, no matter how it is defined, as they have become in recent years. The medical profession, too, was not so alert to the problem, and the U.S. Children's Bureau was concerned with other issues.

One indication of the change came in 1962, when Kempe and his associates published their article "The Battered Child Syndrome." In the early 1960's, the "battered" child achieved considerable publicity, and the media began to respond with articles and portrayals emphasizing the physically, mentally, and sexually exploited child. The publicity soon died down, however, in part because of a series of lawsuits brought against the professionals by parents and others for "falsely" alleging child "abuse." Still, the groundwork had been laid, and a growing coalition of children's-advocacy professionals and other concerned citizens began agitating for greater federal support and intervention. Women as a group had adopted child welfare as a major concern from the time they first entered the political arena at the turn of the century, and the rising second wave of the feminist movement gave renewed impetus to their efforts. The feminist movement, in fact, brought renewed attention to a number of issues dealing with violence and personal autonomy, such as rape, domestic violence, incest, and sexual harassment, thus helping prepare a climate for renewed interest in issues concerning the welfare of children. Adding an additional impetus was a new generation of parents, who had fewer children than earlier generations and, often, first became parents when they were older and who also demanded and expected more help from experts than had earlier generations. Since in many of the new families both parents worked, this new generation also was conscious of a break with tradition and felt more insecure as parents. All of these factors coalesced upon the "child abuse" issue, which gained momentum during the 1970's.

Though child/adult sexual behavior had not been a major thrust of the 1974 legislation, "child abuse" soon became, in the eyes of many individuals, a code term for childhood sexuality. This occurrence played into the hands of many political conservatives who were concerned over the "sexual revolution" taking place in the United States in the late 1960's and early 1970's, much as the AIDS epidemic has more recently done. Child abuse to many became the ultimate result of the changing sexual mores, which in their minds were destroying the family. One perpetrator of this destruction of family values was the working mother, and it was her absence from the family that in the mind of these "anti-feminists" led to an increase in the abuse of children. Inevitably, almost any adult/child relationship that had any possible sexual overtones, no matter how farfetched, was labeled "child sexual abuse." Unfortunately, it became an issue in family squabbles as well, and an angry spouse could accuse the other parent not simply of child abuse but of child sexual abuse. A victim of such a ploy was Lawrence D. Spiegel, a New Jersey clinical psychologist, whose wife, during divorce proceedings, accused him of sexually molesting their 2½-year-old daughter as part of her struggle to gain custody of the child. Spiegel was immediately arrested and charged with sexual molestation, and though there was a happy ending to his story, as told in his recent book, *A Question of Innocence* (Spiegel, 1987), there has been a kind of national panic, and few of those who are accused escape their ordeal without a great deal of trauma.

The panic over adult/child sexual behavior is based upon real concerns, but the matter has been enflamed by the media, which have exploited the topic of child sexual "abuse" and "child abuse" into a headline-attention topic in recent years. Some indication of this change can be emphasized by a personal experience of this author.

> In 1949, I was a reporter for a newspaper, anxious always to get a key story that would carry my byline and perhaps be picked up by the wire services. Through contacts in a local hospital, I received information about what I regarded as a sensational story. A 2½-year-old girl had been taken to surgery with a mangled vagina and a damaged urethra; she was battered and bruised all over. She had been raped by her father. Hospital staff members reported it was the worst case they had seen in years. I approached my editor about writing it up, and he indicated that we did not publish such stories because we were a family newspaper, an attitude more or less typical of the "responsible press" at that time. In fact, as a police reporter, I had compiled the facts in a whole series of cases of what I can only call violently abused and battered children; none of these cases were ever publicized.

The media changed, however, and while media attention is good in bringing a problem into focus, it rarely if ever is good in giving perspective. In typical fashion, the media jumped in on the Minnesota and Los Angeles nursery center cases without stopping to do any kind of investigation, and in the long run, by their exaggeration, they tended to disillusion the public. In fact, it seems safe to predict that the media concern with child abuse and child sexual abuse will soon pass as they become more concerned with other things.

## Research Problems

Unfortunately, by using terms such as "abuse," "perpetrator," and "molestation," researchers, including this author, have in effect influenced social policy indirectly through their terminology. As a sex researcher, this author endorses the use of value-neutral descriptive terms rather than terms that imply that any kind of sexual behavior between adults and younger persons is harmful. As a historian, it is easy for this author to point out that such terms as "sexual abuse" and "self-abuse" once referred to masturbation and that the adoption of such terms made it extremely difficult for researchers to examine masturbation in any kind of scientific way. To aid future historians, the historian in this author suggests that at this time researchers address different kinds of adult/child and adult/adolescent sexual behavior separately, since there might be different motivations and different drives involved and any ability to make careful distinctions is lost when these areas are collapsed into one category called "sexual abuse."

A good current illustration of some of the difficulties present in doing research in these areas exists in the area of child pornography. Though this author strongly believes that children who are used to pose for child pornography are victims of adult exploitation and that no children should be used in this way, it is obviously a legitimate research area. But how does one research a forbidden area? One of the least harmful ways is to find out how children are being used and where the photographs are being produced. But how does one even collect such data without violating the law? Such a task has proven difficult. Even at scientific meetings, slides of the photographs that now are technically illegal to possess or collect are themselves illegal to use as illustrative lecture material. David Sonenschein, in Texas, was recently sentenced to 10 years in prison for his efforts to collect data, although his sentence was overturned later by a federal judge (Sonenschein, 1987). In Buffalo, New York, a law school professor, Al Katz, was arrested in 1986 and eventually, in 1987, pleaded guilty to a misdemeanor charge of sending a child pornography photograph through the mail. In order to "do business" with dealers in child pornography, these researchers, each playing the role of collector, had to mail the dealers an example of child pornography in order to demonstrate bonafide interest. Such demands are made by most dealers because they are conscious that they are violating the law. Inevitably, many of these "dealers" are drops for law enforcement officers, who then arrest the person sending the "good faith" photograph. This scenario is the kind in which Al Katz became enmeshed. Gerald Jones, a published researcher (Jones, 1982), was visited by FBI agents in Los Angeles, and several boxes of material, records, and photographs were seized on the grounds that they appealed to pedophiles, even though Jones's stated interest in the material was in research (G. Jones, personal letter). Patrick LaFollette, an independent researcher, was arrested, also in Los Angeles, for exchanging a photograph labeled "child porn" with a detective. Fortunately for him, his case was dismissed, in large part because his arrest seemed to have been based more on the fact that he was a founder of Family Synergy, which advocates group marriage, than on any real evidence of child sexual abuse or even child pornography (Sonenschein, 1987).

Because of the current legal environment, at least in the United States, investigators are more and more limited to doing research on "safe" topics when it comes to adult/child or adult/adolescent sexual behavior. In addition, researchers are constrained to emphasize their own personal motivation for doing their work when the topic of their research is "child sexual abuse." This legal environment gives rise to a biased picture of what actually exists. The individuals who are "safe" to study are those who have already been convicted of a sexual crime with children or adolescents, and here there is a vast literature. Another "safe" group is the children who have been reported to be "sexually abused"; on these individuals, the body of literature is growing. In the past, investigators could also do research on adult individuals who went to therapists for help because of their proclivity to engage in sexual behavior with children or adolescents. Since federal policy now requires that such clients be reported to law enforcement officers, this group of self-selected individuals has been eliminated as a source of data, unless the therapist is willing to report them or somehow manages to get an exemption, which is difficult to accomplish. Since the simple act of reporting brings all kinds of social and law enforcement agencies into action, it has become almost impossible to even treat these individuals, let alone to study them. It still is possible to do retrospective studies of adults who, as children or adolescents, engaged in sexual behavior, but these studies have the same problems as have all retrospective studies. Inevitably, because of the limits now imposed upon researchers by current law, researchers are getting a very biased sample of adult/child and adult/adolescent sexual behavior.

The one group of adults who have engaged in adult/child or adult/adolescent sexual behavior that can safely be studied in detail is the group of adults who currently are in prison. Karpman (1954) reported that pedophiles and exhibitionists (often included under the current term "child sexual molesters") constituted the largest proportion of sex offenders in his prison sample (p. 29). Similarly, Gebhard et al. (1965) have long sections on both heterosexual and homosexual sex offenses against children and minors committed by their prison sample, as do Mohr, Turner, and Jerry (1964). Unfortunately, it is highly unlikely that these prisoners are typical or representative of adults in the general population who have engaged in similar sexual behavior.

Of groups of adults who are sexually attracted to children and adolescents, the most difficult to study, however, are the voyeurs, some of whom are consumers of child pornography; others are interested in and collect what many would regard as relatively innocuous photographs or portrayals of children or adolescents. Rossman (1976) reported that when *Trim Magazine*, in the 1950's, put a nude 13-year-old on its cover, many pedophiles reacted as follows:

> When I first saw that picture on the magazine cover I was excited, not merely because it was erotic to me but also because I realized at once that there must be other persons like me (p. 35).

Publications appealing to pedophiles, and used by researchers such as this author, have had a rather tenuous existence. The scholarly *International Journal of Greek Love,* which began publication after World War II, ceased publishing after only two issues. Some scholarly apologetic works also appeared, such as *Greek Love* by Eglinton (1964), a pseudonym for W.H. Breen, but it quickly went out of print. There also were a number of photo offset newsletters, such as *Better Life, Hermes,* and *Puberty Rites,* but the extent of their appeal is not known, since they circulated rather surreptitiously along with the hard-core child pornography films, all of which have now gone underground. Some indication of the subject matter of these films can be found from the collection of them housed in the Institute for the Advanced Study of Sexuality in San Francisco.

Based on these newsletters and films and on the existence of the René Guyon Society in Los Angeles, which is a group advocating sex between adults and children, law enforcement officials attempted to identify a mass movement of pedophiles. The Guyon Society, a splinter group from the Sexual Freedom League, was centered in Los Angeles in the 1960's and 1970's, and though this author had contact with Tim O'Hare, the pseudonymous "leader" of the Society, it seemed to be more a one-person operation than any widespread movement. Some of the pedophile organizations, for a time, attempted to hook onto the coattails of the gay liberation movement in numerous Western countries, but the gay movement in the United States avoided the pedophiles like a plague, fearful that all homosexual persons would be labeled "child molesters."

The one major exception to this generalization occurred in the Netherlands, where the Netherlands Association for Sexual Reform, which agitated for gay rights, included a Committee on Pedophilia. The Committee sponsored four study conferences in Holland between 1970 and 1974, which homosexuals also attended, and the result has been to make research into pedophilia both more acceptable and somewhat easier to accomplish than it is in the United States (although the age of consent remains 16 in the Netherlands). Among the more prominent studies that have been conducted in the Netherlands are those of Davidson (1969), Sandfort (1982), and Brongersma (1986).

There also have been significant studies conducted in the United States on adult/child and adult/adolescent sexual behavior, such as those by Finkelhor (1979), Mohr, Turner, and Jerry (1964), Quinsey (1977), Howells (1981), Langevin (1983), and Finkelhor and Araji (1986). What has been missing and what it is hoped this book will accomplish is the beginning of an open, interdisciplinary, and scholarly discussion and challenge to existing and perhaps prematurely arrived at views.

History would indicate that adult/adolescent sexual behavior, even behavior involving penetration, has been accepted as the norm throughout much of humankind's documented past. Whether it should continue to be accepted is something that society feels somewhat ambivalent about. Attitudes seem to change over time, and it is this change that causes the ambivalence and contributes to misunderstandings. On the other hand, historical cultures have generally looked with disfavor upon adult/child sexual behavior, particularly for children under 9. Definitions of what constitutes sexual behavior, however, become all important, since many acts classified as sexual behavior today would not have been so classified earlier. What is happening today, and what made the Jemez Springs Symposium so timely, is that public opinion in Western society, at least in the United States, concerning adult/child and adult/adolescent sexual behavior is undergoing a radical shift. The term "child abuse" is symbolic of this shift, but unfortunately, since the very term is so all encompassing and conclusive, it is meaningless for purposes of academic research. What is needed, at least if the historical and cultural insights are pertinent, are better operational definitions of "sexual behavior" and a distinction among types of such behavior. It also is important to know what kinds of behavior have the most deleterious effect, but this question is one that can be answered only by empirical research.

## Conclusion and Summary

Based on an overview of history, this author would state that adult/child and adult/adolescent sexual behavior occur less frequently now than they did in the past. These kinds of behavior are being defined in new and different ways, however. At the same time, children as a group are much more naive about sex than they once were. Most children no longer grow up in rural areas, where sexual activity, at least among animals, was omnipresent. They have fewer brothers and sisters with whom to interact and explore. Children's play in much of the United States, and at least among the middle and upper classes, is much more structured than it once was. In addition, some simple changes that have taken place in the 20th century have affected adults' ideas about sex play. The widespread use first of washable diapers and then of disposable ones has tended to prevent infants and young children from exploring their own bodies as they once did. Traditionally, too, American parents, holdovers from the era of "masturbation-caused insanity," have been fearful of tolerating the kind of genital exploration that is so common in most areas throughout the world and that was so very common in the premodern period in Western culture. The fear and anxiety aroused by media campaigns about child "sexual abuse" have caused nursery school and day care professionals to think twice about even cuddling children or allowing children, while under their care, to sexually explore with other children. All it takes is the insinuation of child sexual abuse to ruin the reputation of a nursery school or day care center as well as the careers and reputations of the individuals involved. Moreover, more and more children are being cared for in nursery schools and day care centers as occupational opportunities for women open up (O'Connell and Bloom, 1987). Obviously, in this period of surrogate child-rearing, it is necessary to find ways of giving developmentally appropriate sex education to children and adolescents to make up for the lack of the knowledge that their counterparts gained in the past as part of the process of growing up.

What professionals should be doing, and encouraging, is objective empirical research. By stressing this approach, professionals can help channel public opinion and policy, so that these foundations of the evolution of society become more helpful in terms of the long-term welfare of children. Until researchers speak from knowledge, however, the public can react from emotion and fear only. One hopes that investigators can end up with definitions, theories, and avenues for research that will provide meaningful answers. To accomplish this goal, professionals have to speak with caution and not exaggerate what actually is known. A recent advertisement for a videotape on "child sexual abuse" (*Child Sexual Abuse,* Guilford, 1987) claimed that one out of three young patients in the care of medical professionals may have been sexually abused and, therefore, that it was imperative that the medical profession know how to diagnose sexual abuse. As though sexual abuse were a disease! Another advertisement, for Guilford's videotape series Response, Child Sexual Abuse (1987), claims that one out of three children will experience sexual abuse at the hand of an adult. This use of the term "sexual abuse" is so broad that it is alarming and exaggerated, and it is this kind of exaggeration that must be avoided. This latter advertisement was printed in a publication aimed at professionals and appears to be part of a growing sexual-abuse-education industry. Society is undergoing a shift in attitude about adult/child and adult/adolescent sexual behavior, but the shift does not necessarily mean that such behavior is more frequent or more devastating than it was before. It simply means that the priorities in the value system in Western society are changing, and the job of empirical researchers is to look at this change, pointing out the benefits as well as the disadvantages. Though the benefits in protecting the rights of young persons to not be exploited by older persons in this author's opinion outweigh the disadvantages of restricting the rights of older persons, the inclusion of adolescents, especially those well into puberty, with prepubertal children in legislation represents an enormous shift in attitudes and policies from those of the past and will distort comparative historical statistics about adult/child and adult/adolescent sexual behavior.

## References

Arens, W. *The original sin: Incest and its meaning.* New York: Oxford University Press, 1986.

Augustine, St. *Confessions.* (A.C. Outler, Ed. and Trans.) London: SCM Press, 1955.

Birkin, A. *J.M. Barrie and the Lost Boys: The love story that gave birth to "Peter Pan".* New York: Clarkson N. Potter, 1979.

Brongersma, E. *Loving boys,* Vol. I. Elmhurst, N.Y.: Global Publishers, 1986.

Buffiere, F. *Eros adolescent: la pederastie dans la Grece antique.* Paris: Société d'Édition "Les Belles Lettres," 1980.

Bullough, V. *The subordinate sex.* Urbana: University of Illinois Press, 1973.

Bullough, V. *Sexual variance in society and history.* Chicago: University of Chicago Press, 1976.

Bullough, V. Mahatma Gandhi. *Medical Aspects of Human Sexuality,* June 1981, *15,* 11-12.

Bullough, V. Lewis Carroll. *Medical Aspects of Human Sexuality*, October 1983, *17*, 134-140.

Bullough, V., and Brundage, J. *Sexual practices and the Medieval Church*. Buffalo: Prometheus Books, 1983.

Bullough, V., and Bullough, B. *Women and prostitution*. Buffalo: Prometheus Books, 1987.

Butler, J. *A letter to the mothers of England*. Liverpool: Brakell, 1881.

*Child sexual abuse*. A videocassette. *Guilford Press 1987 child catalogue*. New York: Guilford Press, 1987, p. 8.

Crompton, L. *Byron and Greek love*. Berkeley: University of California Press, 1985.

Darwin, C. *The descent of man and selection in relation to sex* (original edition: 1871). Princeton: Princeton University Press, 1981.

Davidson, M. *Some boys*. Kingston, N.Y.: Oliver Layton Press, 1969.

Dickens, C. *Oliver Twist*. London: Richard Bentley, 1883.

Durant, W., and Durant, A. *A dual autobiography*. New York: Simon and Schuster, 1977.

Durkheim, E. *Incest: The nature and origin of the taboo* (original edition: 1898). New York: Lyle Stuart, 1963.

Dyer, A. *The European slave trade in English girls*. London: Dyer Brothers, 1880.

Dyer, A. *Six years' labour and sorrow: The fourth report of the London Committee for Suppressing the Traffic in British Girls for the Purposes of Continental Prostitution*. London: Dyer Brothers, 1885.

Eglinton, J.Z. (pseudonym for Breen, W.H.). *Greek love*. Kingston, N.Y.: Oliver Layton Press, 1964.

Ellis, H. *Psychology of sex*. London: Heinemann, 1933.

Engels, F. *The origin of the family, private property, and the state* (original edition: 1884). New York: International Publishers, 1942.

Finkelhor, D. *Sexually victimized children*. New York: Free Press, 1979.

Finkelhor, D., and Araji, S. Explanations of pedophilia. *Journal of Sex Research*, May 1986, 22, 145-146.

Fox, R. *The red lamp of incest*. New York: Dalton, 1980.

Frazer, J. *Totonism and exogamy*, Vol. 4. London: Macmillan, 1910.

Freud, S. *Totem and taboo* (original edition: 1913). New York: W.W. Norton, 1950.

Gebhard, P., and Johnson, A. *The Kinsey data: Marginal tabulations 1938-1963*. Philadelphia: W.B. Saunders, 1979.

Gebhard, P., Gagnon, J.H., Pomeroy, W., and Christenson, C.V. *Sex offenders*. New York: Harper and Row, 1965.

Goethe, J.W. Notizbuch von der Schlesischen Reiss un Jahre 1790. *In* F. Zarukein (Ed.), *Goethes Werke*. Leipzig: Deutsche Verlaganstalt E. Hallberger, 1884, p. 255.

Herman, J.L. *Father-daughter incest*. Cambridge, Mass.: Harvard University Press, 1981.

Hirschfeld, M. *Sexual anomalies and perversions*. London: Alder, 1948.

Howells, K. Adult sexual interest in children: Considerations relevant to theories of actiology. *In* M. Cook and K. Howells (Eds.), *Adult sexual interest in children*. New York: Academic Press, 1981, pp. 55-94.

Hoyt, E.P. *Horatio's boys: The life and works of Horatio Alger, Jr*. Radnor, Penna.: Chilton Books, 1974.

Jones, G. The social study of pederasty: In search of a literature base. *Journal of Homosexuality*, 1982, *8*, 61-95.

Karpman, B. *The sexual offender and his offenses*. New York: Julian Press, 1954.

Kempe, C.H., et al. The battered child syndrome. *The Journal of the American Medical Association*, July 7, 1962, *181*, 17-24.

Kinsey, A., Pomeroy, W., and Martin, C. *Sexual behavior in the human male*. Philadelphia: W.B. Saunders, 1948.

Kinsey, A., Pomeroy, W., Martin, C., and Gebhard, P. *Sexual behavior in the human female*. Philadelphia: W.B. Saunders, 1953.

Kolata, G. Remembering a "Magical Genius." *Science*, June 10, 1987, *236*, 1519-1520.

Krafft-Ebing, R. *Psychopathia sexualis* (12th ed.). New York: Rebman, 1912.

Langevin, R. *Sexual strands: Understanding and treating sexual anomalies in men*. Hillsdale, N.J.: Lawrence Erlbaum, 1983.

Lewis, D.B.W. *The soul of Marshall Gilles*. London: Eyre and Spotswoode, 1952.

Mohr, J.W., Turner, R.E., and Jerry, M.B. *Pedophilia and exhibitionism*. Toronto: University of Toronto Press, 1964.

Morgan, L.H. *Ancient society*. New York: Holt, 1877.

*My secret life* (original edition: no date given). Introduction by G. Legman, 11 vols. New York: Grove Press, 1966.

Nelson, B.J. *Making an issue of child abuse: Political agenda for social problems*. Chicago: University of Chicago Press, 1984.

O'Connell, M., and Bloom, D.E. Juggling jobs and babies: America's child care challenge. *Population Trends and Public Policy*, 1987, *12*, 1-16.

Parker, S. The precultural basis of the incest taboo. *American Anthropologist*, 1976, *78*, 285-305.

Pearson, M. *The 5 pound virgins*. New York: Saturday Review Press, 1972.

Perrault, C. *Histoires ou contes du temps passé*. Paris: Éditions Barbin, 1697.

Peters, J. Children who are victims of sexual assault and the psychology of offenders. *American Journal of Psychotherapy*, 1976, *30*, 398-421.

Quinsey, V.L. The assessment and treatment of child molesters: A review. *Canadian Psychological Review*, 1977, *18*, 204-222.

Response, child sexual abuse. A videotape series. New York: Guilford Press, 1987.

Rossman, P. *Sexual experience between men and boys.* New York: Association Press, 1976.

Rush, F. *The best kept secret.* Englewood Cliffs, N.J.: Prentice-Hall, 1980.

Sandfort, T. *The sexual aspect of paedophile relations.* Amsterdam: Pan/Spartacus, 1982.

Schlesinger, B. *Sexual abuse of children: An annotated bibliography 1937-80.* Toronto: Ministry of Community and Social Services, 1981.

Sonenschein, D. On having one's research seized. *Journal of Sex Research,* 1987, *23,* 408-414.

Spiegel, L.D. *A question of innocence.* New York: Unicorn House, 1987.

Terrot, C. *Traffic in innocents.* New York: Dutton, 1960.

Twitchell, J. *Dreadful pleasures.* New York: Oxford University Press, 1985.

Tylor, E.B. On a method of investigating the development of institutions: Applied to laws of marriage and descent. *Journal of the Royal Anthropological Institute,* 1889, *18,* 245-269.

Westermarck, E. *The history of human marriage* (5th ed., 3 vols.). London: Macmillan, 1925.

Wilson, T. *Bluebeard: A contribution to history and folklore.* New York: Putnam's, 1899.

# 3
# Sociopolitical Biases in the Contemporary Scientific Literature on Adult Human Sexual Behavior with Children and Adolescents[1]

Paul Okami
*Independent Researcher*
*New York, New York 10024*

*"Reality must not be twisted to suit ideological needs."*
—Diana Russell (1986, p. 312)

## Introduction

This chapter explores certain tendencies within that body of victimology-based literature sometimes referred to as the "new research" and writing on the subject of incest and child sexual abuse.[2] The group of professionals associated with these writings—a group that includes researchers and clinicians as well as political activists and popular writers—characteristically employs polemical devices and research methods that blur the line between social science and social criticism.

Most of the writers in question view themselves not only as social scientists but also as social critics. An assumption of moral purpose, sometimes bordering on self-righteousness, repeatedly emerges from a reading of their work. Indeed, these writers typically display many of the attitudes associated with what Becker (1984) terms "moral entrepreneurs."

Highly subjective and untested assumptions regarding childhood experience and human sexuality abound in these writings. Sexual behavior is viewed overall as comprising a particularly "treacherous" sphere of activity from which children in particular, but also adult females, need special protection (Finkelhor, 1984, pp. 19, 188). Male sexuality is condemned for its inherently "predatory" and "exploitive" nature (Russell, 1986, pp. 173, 210, 392; 1984, pp. 262-263; see also Bass, 1983, pp. 25, 58; Herman, 1981, pp. 3, 62-63). Heterosexual relations are characterized as adversarial virtually by definition and analyzed within political paradigms that emphasize the unequal distribution of social power along the lines of biological sex and age.

Somewhat predictably, researchers and writers who favor descriptive, empirical, or phenomenological models and who may wish to establish a relative degree of objectivity in this difficult field and avoid the rhetorical excesses typical of much of the new research often are attacked by victimologists for "contributing to the disinhibition of child molesters," "condoning adult-child sex," "blaming the victims" of abuse, and even, as in the case of Judith Reisman's charges against Alfred Kinsey, engaging in child molestation (see Russell, 1984, pp. 246-248; 1986, pp. 64, 389; Transcript, 1983 [Reisman]; Herman, 1981, pp. 3-4, 22-25; Bass, 1983, pp. 25-26). Through personal attacks, the victimological paradigm is aggressively promoted as the one and only theoretical structure that can explain the "truth" about incest and sexual abuse.

Although a substantial body of research exists whose data contradict the findings and conclusions reported in the new research (see Kilpatrick, 1986, 1987) and although a few short articles have appeared criticizing the philosophical premises underlying victimological approaches to sex research and clinical practice (e.g., Money, 1986; Schultz, 1980a), virtually no in-depth critiques of the victimological paradigm, or of the research and writings supporting it, have appeared to date in the professional literature. While this critical reticence is understandable—few authors look forward to being branded "condoner of child molestation"—it remains that the writings being considered here under the rubric of the new research have had a striking influence on social policy and public consciousness. This influence pervades current professional discourse, education, medical and psychological services, mass media, and general social climate concerning childhood and sexuality. When the potential effects of such influence are considered, it becomes apparent that a critical examination of the "new research" is urgent and timely.

## Origins of the Political Ideology of the "New Research"

During the late 1960's and early 1970's, in response to sex-biased treatment of rape victims at the judicial, enforcement, and treatment levels, many feminists and other activists organized to effect a radical trans-formation of the manner in which rape was understood in its social, psychological, legal, political, and moral aspects (Rose, 1977).

In their analyses, these activists pointed to the frequency with which rape was interpreted—even by many professionals—as more of a sexual "misunderstanding" than the frequently violent sexual crime it actually is. They dissected socially entrenched imagery regarding women that encouraged this trivialization of rape and exposed the complex process by which rape victims came to be blamed for their own victimization.

Victim advocates then enlarged their focus, drawing parallels between rape and other forms of male violence against females. Finally, connections were drawn between these acts of violence and the sexual abuse of children and adolescents (Rush, 1980; Russell, 1984; Brownmiller, 1975). However, virtually all research in this field, including studies conducted by the victimologists under discussion (e.g., Russell, 1986), documents the low incidence of violence or forceful coercion in cases of adult human sexual behavior with children and adolescents. From an empirical point of view, then, it is incongruous to categorize such interactions as violent crimes, to study them as such, and to engage in discourse permeated by vocabulary and imagery appropriate to the study of violence.

Bass (1983), for example, describes the warning about sexual abuse that she issued her 4-year-old daughter: "There are some grown-ups . . . that if they see a child's vagina or penis, they may want to hurt it. That's why I want you to wear underpants when you're on the street alone" (p. 58). Since data suggest that "hurting" does not characterize the large majority of cross-generational sexual interactions, this contextual association of adult human sexual behavior with children and adolescents with violence appears to be based on the subjective moral principle that any sexual interaction between an adult and a child or an adolescent is a fundamental violation of the younger interactant simply because of the sexual nature of the interaction. Underlying this principle is a powerful, sometimes explicitly articulated conviction that a child or an adolescent is incapable of experiencing a genuinely sexual desire or response. This conviction attributes participation in peer sexual behavior to "curiosity" and participation in adult/nonadult sexual behavior to "coercion."

Herman (1981) succinctly advances this position: "Any sexual relationship between [an adult and a child or an adolescent] must necessarily take on some of the coercive characteristics of rape" (p. 27). Psychologist Henry Giaretto (in Crewdson, 1988) puts it even more colorfully: "Adult-child sex is like putting a high school boxer in the ring with Muhammed Ali" (p. 252).

Statements like Giaretto's and Herman's underscore the general view of sexual behavior that characterizes the new research—that sex consists in essence of a power struggle between its interactants, the consequences of which, for adult females in heterosexual interactions and children and adolescents in adult/nonadult sexual interactions, are those consequences that result from their being the less powerful "combatant" in some sort of battle. Such beliefs, characteristic both of victimology and what this author will term "cultural feminism,"[3] tend to discount the subjective experience of individuals for whom sexual activity more often than not serves as an expression of affection and pleasure, rather than of conflict.

## The Social Purity/Feminist Alliance and Its Inheritance

The beliefs and assumptions underlying the new research have sometimes come under attack from sexologists, sexual libertarians, feminists, child psychologists, anthropologists, and radical children's rights activists for representing a form of that particular Western cultural outlook that Rubin (1986) and others have termed "sex negativism" (see also Constantine, 1981a,c; Ramey, 1970; Yates, 1978; Money, 1986; Currier, 1981). Since both victimology and cultural feminism have their roots in the same 1960's radical left and counter-culture movements that also gave birth to "children's liberation" and contemporary sexual libertarianism, the victimologists and cultural feminists under discussion take pains to portray their work as representing a "progressive" stance on sexual matters.

Finkelhor (1984), for example, claims that his position "is not part of a Victorian resurgence. It is compatible with the most progressive attitude toward sexuality currently being voiced" (p. 22). Despite this reassurance, there is evidence to suggest that the current moral crusade against sexual abuse does, in fact, bear a great deal in common with Victorian beliefs, values, and sexual ideology.

As Snitow (1985), Burstyn (1985), Pivar (1973), and others have pointed out, from the powerful feminist voices of the late 1800's, two major currents eventually emerged. The more influential of these, swayed by class interests and the ideology of the social purity movement with which it eventually allied itself, accepted the traditional Victorian view of males and females as utterly disparate beings residing in separate spheres of psychological and social existence. These activists judged adult males' nature as essentially base and violent. Adult females were seen as the standard bearers of a higher, chaster morality. Adult females' sexual life was characterized as consisting virtually in its entirety of danger and victimization, and reforms were sought to protect adult females, adolescents, and children from the bestial nature of the male (DuBois and Gordon, 1984).

Although the fundamentally paternalistic measures advocated by the social purity feminists drew attention to the genuine victimization of adult females and also allowed a small group of privileged adult females to gain economic advantage or political power, these measures had the disadvantage of restricting adult females' mobility and possibilities for true economic liberation or sexual exploration. For example, adult females—particularly during adolescence or young adulthood—who did not conform to the social purity prescriptions for proper sexual behavior were condemned by these feminists with a hostility comparable to that accorded male violators. Such sexual "delinquents" eventually constituted the largest category of female reformatory inmates in late 19th century America.

The second force in feminist activism, lesser in number and influence, emphasized adult females' equality with adult males and sought reforms that would free adult females not only from adult male domination and violence but also from the very paternalism inherent in the platform of the social purity/feminist alliance. Some of these activists involved themselves in sexual freedom movements or socialist politics (Rubin, 1986).

The social purity tradition in feminist activism was well representative of Victorian sexual culture. Both the movement's ideology and its tactics—forming alliances over specific issues with powerful, male-dominated groups themselves opposed to any genuine social or political empowerment of adult females—have been carried forward into the 1980's in the work of the antipornography activists and those feminists for whom the dangerous and exploitive aspects of sexual behavior are the primary areas of focus for discourse and activism (Snitow, 1985; Burstyn, 1985; DuBois and Gordon, 1984). A review of the literature demonstrates a connection between the antipornography movement and that part of the antisexual-abuse movement reflected in the new research that is so strong as to make the two virtually synonymous.

For example, both Diana Russell and Florence Rush (the latter whose work is considered among the earliest and most influential of the new research on sexual abuse) are as well known for their antipornography activism as for their work in the field of sexual abuse. In Russell's writings and lectures, she discusses "pornography-related victimizations" of adult females, adolescents, and children (1986, p. 173) and refers to what she terms the current "pornographic reign of terror" (in Nobile and Nadler 1986, p. 71). Along with Finkelhor (1984, p. 180), she claims that exposing children to pornography itself constitutes child abuse (Russell, 1986, p. 310) and, again with Finkelhor's and also Bass's (1983) concurrence, cites pornography as a probable contributory cause of the sexual abuse of children (1986, p. 82).

In these pronouncements and in the use of slogans such as "Pornography is violence against women," the equation is once again being made between **moral violation** and **physical violence**. This equation, while conceivably defensible as metaphor, has apparently been taken literally both by antipornography activists and antisexual-abuse activists.

Russell's "pornography-related victimizations" are viewed by her as characteristic manifestations of what she terms "predatory" male sexuality. Adult males are said to be "pre-disposed to violence, to rape, to sexual harassment, and to sexually abusing children" (1984, p. 290). Feminist critics of this point of view note that antipornography activists, and others subscribing to this general ideology, portray all adult male sexual behavior as "inherently aggressive" (Ellis et al., 1986, p. 6) and, in fact, display a clear revulsion to heterosexuality—a revulsion that serves as the "thinnest of covers for disgust with sex itself" (Willis, 1986, p. 56). Considering this expressed revulsion, Russell's placement of adult/nonadult sexual interaction in the same category with imprisoning children in basements or abandoning them (1986, p. 9), Finkelhor's portrayal of such interactions as morally analogous to slavery (1984, pp. 16-17), and Herman's claim that incest is as destructive to women as the mutilation of their genitals (in Russell, 1986, p. 3) become more easily comprehensible.

Anthropologist Gayle Rubin (1986) analyzes the writings of the antipornography and associated feminist movements in the following manner:

> This discourse on sexuality is less a sexology than a demonology. It presents most sexual behavior in the worst possible light. Its descriptions of erotic conduct always use the worst available example as if it were representative. It presents the most disgusting pornography, the most exploited forms of prostitution, and the least palatable or most shocking manifestations of sexual variation. This rhetorical tactic consistently misrepresents human sexuality in all its forms. The picture of human sexuality that emerges from this literature is unremittingly ugly (p. 301).

About Robin Morgan, whose work well typifies these writings, Ellis (1986) comments, "A situation in which male sexual arousal, however achieved, might elicit a complementary response in a woman, and be a source of pleasure to her, is to Morgan simply inconceivable" (p. 45). (Morgan has defined rape as existing "any time sexual intercourse occurs when it has not been initiated by the woman.") There is an implicit suggestion here that, on a fundamental level, even gentle and loving, adult/adult heterosexual interactions are considered violent assaults. Andrea Dworkin (1986), a major antipornography activist and also an outspoken antisexual-abuse activist, makes this explicit by stating that "intercourse is punishment."

As a logical complement to the rather pessimistic view of male sexual behavior expressed in the new research, and in accord with Victorian tradition, adult females, adolescents, and children—children in particular—are painted in highly idealized hues. The Victorian idealization of children as sexless innocents is clearly apparent in victimologists' repeated, unsubstantiated assertions that children are by definition incapable either of desiring or voluntarily cooperating in a sexual interaction with an adult (cf. Russell 1986, pp. 392-393; Bass, 1983, pp. 24, 27, 30; Herman, 1981, p. 27; Rush, 1980).

For example, Russell (1986) contends that children are incapable of experiencing incestuous sexual longings themselves, but can only be victims of a (male) relative's projection of his own desires (p. 393). She goes on to discuss the seduction of daughters by their fathers, adding:

> Even the widespread use of the word "seduce" in this context is an offensive misnomer. It assumes a mutuality—if not initially, then once the child has submitted. But the notion that a father could seduce, rather

than violate, his daughter is itself a myth. And the notion that some daughters seduce their fathers is a double myth (pp. 392-393).

While the question of whether or not some daughters seduce their fathers may be arguable, to refer to the seduction of daughters by their fathers as a "myth" is clearly a rhetorical ploy that violates common sense as well as rules of evidence. The use of the term "myth" to refer to phenomena that have been well established is a characteristic rhetorical device both of the new research and political propaganda. While such tactics may be useful and appropriate in the political arena, they are simply out of place in the context of scientific investigation.

Bass (1983) reveals a similar idealism when she claims that "[in every sexual interaction between an adult male and a child or an adolescent] there is coercion" (p. 27) and that, by definition, a child cannot desire a sexual interaction with an adult and therefore cannot be the initiator of such interaction (pp. 24, 30). Indeed, Bass refers to sexual interaction between an adult and a child as the "desecration" of the child, unwittingly stating in literal terms the view both of children and of sex propagated by many of the writers with whom this chapter is concerned.

## Sex and Danger

While these writers' association of sexuality with violent assault is strongest in their discussions of adult/nonadult sex, it is by no means limited to such discussions. Warnings of all sorts highlighting the destructive potential of sex not only for children and adolescents, but also for adult females, pervade the literature.

Moreover, childhood sexual experiences even among peers come under sharp scrutiny by victimologists for signs of potential abuse—a development consistent with this author's impression that it is childhood sexual activity, rather than childhood sexual abuse, that represents the ultimate target of concern of some of those responsible for the new research. Several recent victimological studies, for example, have "identified" a new group of "perpetrators of child sexual abuse": other children. Johnson (1988) includes the following in her criteria for subject inclusion in her sample of 4- to 13-year-old "offenders":

> 1) They had acted in a sexual way with another child; and 2) they had used force or coercion in order to obtain the participation of the other child, or the victim was too young to realize he/she was being violated and did not resist the sexual behavior, or it was an offense such as exhibitionism; and 3) there was an age differential of at least two years; and 4) there was a pattern of sexually overt behavior in their history (p. 221).

Johnson's definitions of **coercion** are vague and include terms such as "verbal cajoling." These definitions are also excessively dependent upon her own interpretation of what may have transpired based on repeated interrogation of "suspected perpetrators" at the Children's Institute International (C.I.I.)—an organization that specializes in "uncovering" "hidden" instances of sexual abuse.[4]

Leaving the question of coercion aside, then, when a small child who has "acted in a sexual way" in the past "acts in a sexual way" in the present with a child two years younger who does not resist because, in Johnson's opinion, the child is "too young" to know he or she is being "violated," then according to Johnson's criteria, the older child becomes a "perpetrator of sexual abuse" and the younger child a "victim." And again, even should no "coercion" be suspected, one is left with instances of "exhibitionism" by a 4-year-old being referred to by Johnson as "offenses." Johnson warns that ". . . . The behavior of these child perpetrators must not be ignored any longer" (p. 219).

Cantwell (1988), also investigating child "perpetrators of sexual abuse," urges parents to "report and investigate incidents of sexual interaction between children," and to encourage children to "tell someone if anyone, even a same-age child, approaches them initiating sexual play." She then challenges what she construes to be a generally benign societal view of childhood sex play by wondering whether engaging in such play is "normal."

Possible consequences of this line of investigation are evident when one looks at the manner in which Johnson's results have been reported in the popular press and the influence such reports may have on the dissemination of information to the public about childhood sexuality. For example, Curtin (1988) opens her *St. Petersburg* (Fla.) *Times* article on Johnson's study with the following:

> For a long time most people wrote it off as just "playing doctor." Now we know better. Children as young as 4 and 5 are sexually abusing other children.

In his widely publicized mass-market book on sexual abuse, Crewdson (1988, p. 207), taking his cue from articles such as Johnson's and Cantwell's, shrilly warns that childhood sex play may be a breeding ground for pedophilia and future sexual abusers and thus should be closely monitored (as though it were not already!). Finkelhor (1979) also seems inclined to issue warnings of the destructive potential of peer sexual experiences in childhood.

Many cultural feminist and victimologist writers in fact seem unable or unwilling to conceptualize heterosexuality itself as including any sort of affectional component at all. They present what they term "non-exploitive" sex as the only context for sexual activity that is relatively free of damaging effects. However, since they define male sexuality itself as "inherently exploitive," it is unclear how this criterion for nonexploitation can possibly be met in any sexual interaction that involves an adult male.

They furthermore assume the existence of a clear line of demarcation between erotic feelings and affectional feelings and without substantiation suggest that, in the case of adult/nonadult relationships, these feelings are mutually exclusive (see Finkelhor, 1984, p. 12; Russell, 1984, p. 236).

Assumptions such as these, and the consequent exclusive use of negatively loaded terminology such as "abuse," "assault," "attack," "molestation," "exploitation," or "victimization" to refer generically to all adult human sexual behavior with children and adolescents, confound attempts to understand such interactions and may reflect, as Kilpatrick (1987) suggests, a serious conflict of interest between scientific inquiry on the one hand and enforcement of social norms or propagation of political ideology on the other.

## Failures of Methodological Integrity

While the preceding material was intended to present an overview of the general discursive tone and ideology of the new research, what follows is an analysis of specific abuses of research methodology that occur as a logical consequence of ideology.

### Structural Bias

Rosenthal (1976) and others have noted the powerful effects of expectancy bias and demand characteristics in research involving human subjects. Such biases are rarely intended, however, and thus may be referred to as methodological "weaknesses." To see how methodological weakness becomes true failure of methodological integrity—that is, where these biases are intentional, structural, and ideologically rationalized—one may turn to several current studies, notably Russell's (1984, 1986) major National Institute of Mental Health (NIMH)-sponsored study of the sexual abuse of female children, adolescents, and adults.

### The Russell "Incest" Study

Throughout her book *The Secret Trauma—Incest in the Lives of Girls and Women* (1986), Russell initiates the claim that her study is the most valid, indeed, perhaps the only truly valid and informative study on the subject of intrafamilial sexual behaviors, which she terms "incest" or "incestuous abuse" (p. 137). (Russell apparently considers all types of sexual behaviors between individuals related even distantly or by marriage to constitute "incest.") She sees her study as the "first opportunity to evaluate some of the contemporary controversies surrounding incest on the basis of a scientifically selected non-clinical population" (p. 10) and asserts that "it is the methodology of our survey that sets it apart from all previous studies" (p. 19).

With the exception of Wyatt (1985), which used a research approach similar to that of Russell and obtained similar results, Russell's reported combined prevalence rates for intra- and extrafamilial sexual abuse greatly exceed those of all other studies reviewed. These studies include nine investigations, reviewed by Peters, Wyatt, and Finkelhor (1986), that used various types of random sampling procedures. Among these nine was the investigation by Lewis (1985), the first, and thus far the only, study of sexual abuse to use a random national sample. To bring the extent of variance between Russell's or Wyatt's work and virtually all other major studies into sharper relief, it should be noted that Russell's and Wyatt's prevalence figures are a full 32-35 percentage points above Lewis's—which are in turn considerably higher than those reported in eight out of the nine studies reviewed by Peters, Wyatt, and Finkelhor, as well as several others reviewed by Russell herself and by this author.[5]

Russell devotes quite a bit of space attempting to unearth the deficiencies in all these studies that might account for the disparity between their results and her own. The idea that there may have been something amiss in her research is not considered. However, problems in her methodology are immediately apparent.

Along with her sampling techniques, Russell's claims to the superiority of her study rest primarily on what she terms the "training" and "sensitization" of her interviewers to the subject of incest and sexual abuse. It is this lack of "sensitization" that she claims is responsible for the supposed inaccuracy of all previous studies. Referring, for instance, to a previous study whose 1% prevalence rate for intrafamilial sexual abuse of females differed sharply from her 19% figure, Russell comments, "Since [the interviewers were] not educated in this fashion, they can therefore be assumed to subscribe to common myths about women who are sexually abused" (p. 25).

According to Russell, her training regimen gave interviewers a "better sense of what questions encourage disclosure" and "what types of resistance to expect" (p. 20). Interviewers were specifically chosen for their "non-victim-blaming attitudes," thus weeding out what she terms the "bigotry" of those who might not view all of the younger interactants in adult/nonadult sex as victims (p. 21). Indeed, she repeats that she used "careful selection of interviewers who did not subscribe to the usual myths about sexual abuse." If one recalls that among these "myths" Russell counts the idea that a child might willingly engage in a sexual interaction with an older individual and later self-report that this interaction was benign—a "myth" that has been established as factual by empirical, cross-cultural, and anecdotal data[6]—it is clear that interviewers were "carefully selected" to include only those who were unwilling to acknowledge the existence of these data.

It may reasonably be concluded from all of the foregoing that Russell equates    "training"    and    "sensitization"    with    passionate    ideological indoctrination of interviewers who have been preselected for their receptivity to the indoctrination. These interviewers are then charged with the duty to collect only certain kinds of data. Such mandated selective disregard of undesirable facts becomes obvious when one looks carefully at several of Russell's interviewing techniques. For example, she declares:

> The widely held notion of the child taking the initiative in sexual liaisons with adults[7] is a classic case of the victim blaming so common in sexual abuse mythology. How can children initiate acts of which they have little or no understanding? To avoid propagating this myth we did not specifically ask who took the initiative (p. 124).

Since it has never been demonstrated that all individuals under age 18 or 16 or even 14 have "little or no understanding" of sexual acts, or that even if they did not, that they would therefore be unable to "initiate" these acts through proceptive expressive behavior, Russell's statement—rather than reflecting a desire to avoid propagating a myth—probably reflects a general disinclination to collect data that might contradict a political or moral position.

In a similar effort to guide response in an approved direction, Russell asked the following to elicit data on the important question of subject affect during and following the sexual interaction:

> Overall, how upset were you by this experience—extremely upset, somewhat upset, or not very upset? (p. 138).

Set off from these choices by parentheses on the interviewer's sheet was the designation "(not at all upset)." Russell explains that it was left up to the "interviewer's discretion" whether to include this parenthetical choice in her interview schedule. The alternatives offered to respondents, then, ran the gamut of the negative, and the one comparatively neutral response (still utilizing the negatively loaded word "upset," however) was in an unspecified number of cases not even presented. Russell defends this practice with the following:

> The reason this final choice was put in parentheses [and only presented at the interviewer's discretion] is to prevent the respondent from experiencing this part of the question as insulting or insensitive (p. 138).

Russell considers it an "insult" to allow for the possibility that a respondent may not have been upset by her experience, and the possibility of overtly positive affect is structurally disallowed. One possible subject response to this kind of interviewer bias is described by Germaine Greer (1975) when she relates the experience of one of her school friends:

> [She] enjoyed sex with her uncle throughout her childhood and never realized that anything was unusual until she went away to school. What disturbed her then was not what her uncle had done, but the attitude of her teachers and psychiatrist. They assumed that she must have been traumatized and disgusted and therefore in need of very special help. In

order to capitulate to their expectations, she began to fake symptoms she did not feel, until at length she began to feel truly guilty for not having felt guilty. She ended up judging herself quite harshly for this innate lechery. (Page number not given.)

In defending such research techniques, writers in Russell's theoretical camp borrow from conflict theory and point to the manner in which mainstream social science methodology has fallaciously been promoted as "objective" while in actuality it reflects prevailing cultural biases and protects the interests of specific groups or classes. Some of these writers indict the very idea of "value-free" research as itself representing an ideological bias.

While there is evidence to support this view, "affirmative action" bias such as is found in much of the new research is hardly a solution. A difference must still be noted between the methods of committed science and those of political persuasion. One may have strongly held values and still use every safeguard available to prevent those values from obscuring an accurate understanding of phenomena. In the case at hand, it would seem that accurate information is primary and essential for the creation of effective strategies not only for the prevention of sexual abuse of children but also for the maintenance of their sexual health.

### Finkelhor

Similar, if less overt, examples of the sort of ideologically based structural bias found in Russell's work can be found in the work of Finkelhor. For example, in the instructions presented to respondents in his study of childhood sexual experiences among a sample of college students (1979), Finkelhor describes the experiences being studied in the following manner: "Some of these [childhood sexual experiences] are very upsetting and painful and some are not." This statement seems to set the stage for the expected negative reports. One might well imagine **Finkelhor's** critical response should some other investigator have instructed her or his respondents, "Some of these experiences are very delightful and pleasurable and some are not." It should be emphasized that Finkelhor's study was ostensibly designed to examine childhood sexual experiences in general, not sexual abuse in particular. The use of "very upsetting and painful" to refer by implication to the larger portion of these experiences is therefore quite revealing of the investigator's bias.

A further inflation of negative reports in this study results from the fact that sexual experiences about which Finkelhor's respondents reported having felt "neutral"—a designation that may include mixed as well as truly neutral feelings—were graded by coders as constituting **negative** experiences if an age discrepancy of more than five years existed between the participants (1981, p. 141). The rationale for this apparent disregard of the subject's sense of her or his own reality is simply the investigator's

**personal moral belief** that any and all sexual contacts between minors and those more than five years older (including older children) are abusive (1984, pp. 14-21).

In Finkelhor's investigation, co-authored with Redfield (Finkelhor and Redfield, 1984), of how the general public defines sexual abuse, the investigators designed a series of vignettes of potentially abusive sexual situations with variables dissociated and crossed in as many patterns as seemed practically feasible. Their idea was to explore the "boundaries of people's definitions of sexual abuse" by proposing even the most "unusual and unlikely" sexual situations involving adults and nonadults to see whether or not respondents considered each incident to be abusive and, if so, to what degree of abusiveness the incident was rated.

Out of the representative list of vignettes reproduced in Finkelhor's report, only 3 (out of 14) are not explicitly described in negative terms, and in these 3, an adolescent male is seen simply "agreeing" to perform a sexual act on an adult female or "asking" an older individual to perform a sexual act. No adjectives are used to describe affect or outcome in these neutral descriptions; a typical one reads: "A 40-year-old woman had intercourse with her 15-year-old son. The boy asked her to do it" (pp. 126-127).

In contrast, the remaining 11 vignettes describe overtly coerced, unpleasant experiences. Unlike the three neutral reports, these vignettes include descriptions of negative outcome and affect. In the appendix to this study, Finkelhor and Redfield list all independent variables related to outcome; that is, they present all the alternatives appearing in the vignettes as descriptions of the effects of the experience on the younger participant/victim. The list consists of the following:

[Note: (V) = victim]
1. Nothing [no effect] (50% of the vignettes)
2. One of the following (50% of the vignettes)
   a. Later (V) had nightmares about it
   b. Later (V) was upset it had happened
   c. (V) was ashamed about it for many years afterward.

Thus, Finkelhor and Redfield's pool of possible outcomes—when outcome is noted at all—consists entirely of negative variables. Not surprisingly, respondents in this study rated all of the vignettes as sexually abusive, providing Finkelhor and Redfield with evidence that the average person agrees with victimological characterizations of adult/nonadult sex as constituting abuse regardless of the degree to which a child appears to voluntarily participate.

This study also serves a second function for the authors, one that is emphasized in the victimological literature: education. The reader, like the respondent, is presented with a circumscribed universe of experiences—a continuum with a severely truncated positive end—while being told that this universe is "inclusive of even the most unusual and unlikely" experiences.

Thus, the reader is educated to the "truth" about adult/nonadult sexual interactions.

When respondents in a retrospective study whose data are under analysis as of this writing (Okami, unpublished data) were asked to describe their responses to childhood and adolescent sexual interactions with adults, they spoke of "fear," "disgust," "anger," "contempt," "confusion," and "hatred." They also spoke of "ecstasy," "gratitude," "warmth," "desire," "tenderness," and "love." Clearly, then, Finkelhor's vignettes are not representative of the full range of possible sexual experiences involving adults and nonadults, inclusive of "even the most unusual or unlikely." Considering the accessibility of data that do describe this full range, it seems unreasonable for social scientists to employ methodologies structured to ignore or suppress these data simply because the phenomena they describe are not compatible with a political paradigm.

## Kilpatrick (1986): A Contrasting Model

So that the potential power of structural bias may be fully appreciated, and a contrasting model of responsible research in this field presented, Kilpatrick's (1986) investigation of the effects on adult females of childhood sexual experiences will be reviewed.

Kilpatrick took deliberate care to avoid structural bias. Experiences being studied were referred to in respondent's instructions simply as "sexual experiences engaged in during childhood years" with no further comment. This description contrasts with Finklelhor's use of "very upsetting and painful," as already described. (Wyatt's [1985] instructions to her subjects were virtually identical to Finkelhor's.) Kilpatrick's protocol also compares favorably, from both scientific and ethical standpoints, with Russell's "foot-in-the-door" explanation to potential respondents that her study was concerned simply with "crime." Russell's interviewers made no mention of sexual abuse until entry was gained into the respondent's home and demographic data already obtained.

Kilpatrick's subjects were offered a wide range of choices with which to rate the positive or negative qualities of their experience, the extent to which it was perceived as voluntary or forced, and the perception of who initiated the interaction. This study also measured written self-report of level of adult functioning using the Hudson scales. Cook and Campbell's (1979) deliberate sampling procedure was employed to assure heterogeneity, and 501 adult females participated.

Kilpatrick found that 68% of her sample had positive self-report responses to their experience, 38% self-reported that it was mostly or entirely pleasant, and 67% of the respondents stated that the contacts were "voluntary." Only 25% of her sample self-reported that their experience was essentially unpleasant, and 33% reported that they were to some degree coerced into participation.

Although this study included peer experiences, and Kilpatrick's initial report (1986) does not specifically isolate adult/nonadult interactions from intragenerational ones, she subsequently conducted sophisticated analyses of variables such as the respondent's age at the time of the experience and the age of the other interactant. These analyses found no significant differences in self-reported outcome according to age differential. While certain types of adult/nonadult experiences were significantly more likely than others to result in self-reported negative outcomes—as were certain types of peer experiences—the adult/nonadult interactions as a whole were no more likely than peer experiences to result in self-report of negative outcomes (Kilpatrick, personal communication).

## Utilization of Legal, Moral, and Political Criteria, Rather Than Empirically Based Criteria, in Establishing Operational Definitions

Terms such as "abuse" and "victimization" appear in the new research in very different senses then they are normally understood. Moreover, victimologists alternate between their own specialized usage and common usage at will as a rhetorical technique. So then, after first defining **sexual victimization** or **abuse** as any sexual experience between an individual under age 18 (or 16) and a person five or more years older—a definition that would indict a large portion of marriages in the majority of human societies throughout history (Frayser, 1985)—victimologists may, in virtually the same paragraph, report catastrophic sequelae of **sexual victimization** or **abuse**, this time implicitly defining such terms in their commonly understood meanings (i.e., force, coercion, physical or emotional brutality). The reader is left with the impression that these catastrophic sequelae are intrinsic to any sexual interaction between an individual under 18 (or 16) and someone five or more years older.

Moreover, "victims" of such "sexual abuse" are often referred to as **survivors**, or even more fancifully in terms such as "the walking wounded" (Blume, 1986). The reader thus concludes that individuals under 18 who experience sexual interaction with someone five or more years older globally suffer psychological or physiological effects normally experienced by those emerging alive from a life-threatening encounter. When one notes that victimological definitions of sexual abuse frequently include activities such as the making of suggestive remarks, even by a peer (e.g., Wyatt, 1985), it becomes even more difficult to defend the use of terms such as **survivor** in this context.

These practices and the analyses underlying them create serious problems in establishing workable operational definitions or even informal definitions. The victimological paradox is exemplified in the following statement from Wyatt (in Crewdson, 1988):

> [Some persons report that their sexual abuse] was done in such a loving
> and warm way, that the child never knew that this was something
> inappropriate until years later when someone labelled it for them. It was
> a pleasurable experience, not traumatic; there was no physical coercion
> involved. But you can look at someone else who had that very same
> experience—being fondled by an uncle every time the uncle came over
> for a holiday—and that woman might say it was one of the most
> horrendous experiences of her life, shaped her attitude toward men,
> created difficulty in her relationships, and on and on (p. 209).

If experiences such as the former described above are to be defined as
**sexual assaults, abuse,** or **victimizations,** as they are in the new research
(including Wyatt's 1985 study), then for Wyatt to describe them as
"loving," "warm," "pleasurable," and "lacking coercion" would seem to
present a contradiction in terms.

But if it is true that some adult/nonadult sexual interactions are
perceived and self-reported as "positive" by the younger interactant in the
manner described by Wyatt, then there is no **empirical** basis, at least, for
automatically and categorically defining them as abuse and victimization;
and if there is no empirical basis for so defining them, then there is no
rationale for doing so that does not originate in the realms of law, sexual
politics, or sexual morality. While law, politics, and morality present
important issues for social debate and activism, they should not pervade
empirical research unless it is made clear that such research is to be judged
as polemic.

While extensive and convincing evidence has been gathered indicating
that unwanted sexual experiences (like many other kinds of unwanted
childhood experiences) can result in serious short- and long-term
consequences for the interactants (Kilpatrick, 1986, 1987; Money, this
volume) and while this evidence presents solid grounds for enacting
effective legislation to protect children and adolescents from such
experiences, the evidence presents no rationale whatever for studying
adult/nonadult sex in a scientific context while utilizing definitions drawn
from such legal, political, or moral constructs. O'Grady (1988) refers to
such practices as "slippage" (p. 360) and notes their "serious" threat to
construct validity.

To use an analogy, simply because alcohol use by children and
adolescents is illegal and is considered by many to be immoral, and because
some young people may not be as competent as some adults to make
decisions regarding their use of alcohol, professionals in the field of
substance abuse would not operationally define "juvenile alcohol abuse" as
"any use of alcohol by juveniles." Powerful empirical evidence would first
have to be presented to demonstrate a structural difference between the
nature of alcohol abuse when the drinker is below the legal drinking age
and when he or she is above that age. Writers such as Finkelhor and
Russell offer no reasonable explanation why such an empirically based

structural difference should not also be demonstrated before one labels as "sexual abuse" a voluntary interaction that would—were the younger interactant age 18 rather than 13, for example—be labeled "sexual experience" or "relationship."

This paradox is resolved in two ways in the new research. The first is to admit that political or moral criteria are being used to establish operational definitions, but to defend this practice as resulting in reduced, rather than increased bias—a technique that can be termed "affirmative action bias." Victimologists taking this approach claim that to study the issue from an empirical rather than an "ethical" viewpoint is itself a form of bias, and a morally unacceptable one (Finkelhor, 1984).

Since these writers use moral and political criteria to define **abuse**—criteria usually drawn from considerations of the problems of informed consent and unequal distribution of social power—they dismiss self-reports of inconsequential adult/nonadult sexual interactions as representing an individual's politically and morally incorrect and invalid interpretation of her or his own experience (e.g., Finkelhor 1984, pp. 16-17).

A second, less philosophical and more psychological tack taken by victimologists to resolve the paradox presented by reports of nonabusive "sexual abuse" is to attribute such reports to distortions of memory resulting from a subject's alleged "denial" or "repression" of what the victimologist claims must have been, in fact, a negative experience with harmful effects (Russell, 1986, pp. 43-44, 53, 138; Blume, 1986; De Mott, 1980).

While repression or confabulation of this sort may well occur in some portion of cases, to assume that any given self-report of a positive experience is the result of distortions of memory, simply because one believes for ideological reasons that such an experience should not be thought possible, is a line of reasoning that hardly merits critique.

Using arguments such as the above to reduce all sexual interactions between adults and children and adolescents to "sexual abuse" also results in frequent contradictory assertions from victimologists. For example, Russell (1986) complains that the extent of harm to the child in adult/nonadult sexual interactions has been greatly underestimated because measurements have been taken only of a child's subsequent levels of impairment, ignoring the harm caused simply by having participated in an "unpleasant experience." "Her [the victim's] feelings must be counted as important," writes Russell. This is a compelling point. However, at the same time, she asserts that any intrafamilial sexual interaction involving children or adolescents should be considered abusive if one of the participants was five or more years older than the other "regardless of whether or not the respondent considered it a neutral or positive experience" (p. 55). Apparently a child's self-reported feelings about a sexual experience are only considered "important" if they are negative.

Another natural consequence of the use of legal, moral, or political criteria for the establishment of definitions for sexual abuse and incest is the increased broadening of such definitions that one can see occurring. For example, Russell's (1986) definition of **incestuous child sexual abuse** would include an incident of tongue kissing between a 13-year-old and her second cousin's 19-year-old husband.

Similarly, Wyatt's (1985) definition of **child sexual abuse** would include the making of suggestive remarks by one 17-year-old to another or the employment of a 17-year-old as a nude model or dancer. While not minimizing the possible unpleasantness of unwanted verbal propositions or the problems that may result for young females working as nude models or dancers, one must seriously question the inclusion of these phenomena within the same definitional category as, for example, the anal rape of a 3-year-old by a parent. One must particularly wonder whether the sexual harassment by peers of sexually mature individuals past the age of consent should be used to help produce the kind of alarming prevalence statistics for "child sexual abuse" reported by Wyatt.

This broadening of definitions in the victimological literature sometimes reaches a point of near absurdity, as when Blume (1986) defines incest as inclusive of sexual interaction between an individual and her dentist. Definitional criteria such as these degrade the experiences of individuals who have suffered actual sexual abuse or incest by diluting the terms **abuse** and **incest** to such an extent that they are rendered virtually meaningless.

## Failures of Integrity in Discourse

While the validity of the methodological practices outlined above may be debated from a scientific point of view, the rhetorical tactic, common to the new research, of misrepresenting the positions taken by nonvictimologists and making character-related accusations against such people is difficult to defend in this author's view.

Proponents of paradigms that are incompatible with the tenets of victimology—paradigms that soon may include the "biosocial" perspective—are condemned in the new research in two ways. First, by implication, as when Russell (1986, p. 3) juxtaposes harrowing accounts of traumatic sexual abuse of female children by their fathers with Wardell Pomeroy's out-of-context quotation acknowledging the "beautiful and mutually satisfying" nature of "many" father/daughter incestuous relationships that have "no harmful effects." The effect of this juxtaposition is to suggest that Pomeroy callously disregards the suffering of children who are genuine victims of sexual victimization or violent rape by a parent. However, Russell neglects to inform the reader that Pomeroy was referring specifically to **consensual relationships in adulthood**.

Although it is true that Pomeroy (1976) has acknowledged that data gathered during the Kinsey investigations suggest that in certain cases adult/child incest can also be "an enriching experience" (p. 10), he emphasizes the relative rarity of such an event and in fact explicitly condemns adult/child incest in a source from which Russell (1984, p. 247) extracts several other quotations but ignores the following: "The trouble with incest isn't incest at all, it's pedophilia. There are real problems with a thirty-five-year-old father having sex with his thirteen or fourteen-year-old daughter because of his one-up position" (Pomeroy in Nobile, 1977). Pomeroy's statement is incompatible with Russell's (1986) claim that he "overlooks the whole issue of children's powerlessness in relation to adults who want to have sex with them" (p. 8).

Researchers are also explicitly indicted, as when Russell (1986) without justification takes Karin Meiselman to task for "belittling—if not condoning—adult-child sexual contact in general" (p. 389). Russell similarly accuses all other professionals who do not accept the victimological analysis of "contributing to the reduction of internal inhibitions against acting out sexual desires directed toward children" (1984, pp. 246-248).

Herman (1981) characterizes commentators who have advocated relaxation of the human-created and culturally transmitted incest taboos as belonging to a group she refers to as "pornographers and others" (p. 4). She describes the Kinsey Institute for Research in Sex, Gender, and Reproduction, for example, as being "closely allied to pornographers," and then, as the ultimate castigation, erroneously refers to it as the "all-male Institute for Sex Research."[8]

Reisman (who recently received a $734,000 U.S. Justice Department grant to study "child-related imagery" in cartoons appearing in magazines such as *Playboy* and *Penthouse*) continues in this fashion when she refers to Alfred Kinsey's research (Kinsey et al., 1948, 1953) as "pedophile-biased," and accuses Kinsey of involvement in "the vicious genital torture of hundreds of children" (Transcript, 1983). She reports that her in-press manuscript describes Kinsey's work as "in the best case falsified data and in the worst case it was inhumane and malevolently harmful child sexuality experimentation" (Transcript, 1983). Reisman has thus far provided no evidence to document her claims.

Finally, de Young (1982) proposes the existence of an "organized" and "powerful" group of researchers who "support" adult/child sex, in effect blaming this group for the continued existence of such abuse (p. 162). However, none of the small group of investigators named by de Young, with one possible exception, has ever written anything that could reasonably be interpreted as promoting adult/child sex. Each has simply noted the empirical fact that some individuals who experience childhood sexual interaction with older children or adults do not consider themselves to have been abused or victimized, do not describe the interaction in terms that would normally warrant the use of words such as **abuse** or **victimization**, and do not appear to have suffered any sort of functional impairment as a result of their experience.

Furthermore, none of these "powerful" researchers has ever obtained substantial funding or support (consider Reisman's $734,000 or Russell's NIMH grant) for research aimed at the study of any positive aspect of childhood sexuality—certainly not for studies designed to "support" adult/child sex.

## Iatrogenic Correlates of the "New Research"

Virtually all researchers and serious commentators in this field, while they may debate the **extent** of harm caused by certain social and institutional responses to sexual abuse, have noted the occurrence of such harm. This statement applies to all of the victimologists under discussion. Parental overreaction or lack of support, insensitive police interrogation, grueling judicial proceedings, and social alienation have all been cited as in some cases contributing to, or possibly even exceeding, the damage caused to the child by the abuse itself (Finkelhor, 1984; Constantine, 1981b).

Schultz (1980a) discusses iatrogenic response by mental health and social work professionals in the following manner:

> Much of the [sexual abuse] literature is couched in acceptable access, where well-meaning emotional noise masks statistical reality. We seem to arbitrarily create "norms" for minors and then justify departures from them as traumatic. Such fabrication is professionally unethical and possibly damaging to minors involved in sexual behaviors with others. What inappropriate trauma ideology does is pit the professional (true believer) against the child or the parents who may feel differently. The risk is that a type of self fulfilling prophecy emerges that manages to produce the problem it claims to abhor, but which it, in fact, must have in order to sustain the ideology it is based upon (p. 40).

Professionals who adopt the ideology reflected in the new research may therefore tend to remain unreceptive to the self-reported subjective realities of individuals who do not define their experience in negative terms. Nelson (1984) cites the following complaint from one respondent in her study of the effects of incest experiences: "My therapist is so opinionated against child molesters that she wouldn't be able to understand if I told her I enjoyed it. I'm sure she'd kill me" (p. 220).

Horror stories related to false allegations of abuse or hysterical response to the threat of abuse also abound (Hentoff, 1984; Nathan, 1987). While many such stories involving wrongful imprisonment, children hastily and traumatically removed from homes and placed in foster care, suicides, financial ruin, and so on may be said to occur sporadically to a limited number of individuals, some of these negative social consequences may have become structural, affecting a larger number of individuals.

This author was somewhat disturbed, for example, to discover that in the wake of the McMartin preschool sexual abuse allegations, the San Francisco Child Development Agency had passed down "suggestions" to (particularly male) child care workers that they (1) not remain alone in a room with a child for any reason and (2) refrain from hugging, kissing, or holding on the lap (as while reading a story) any child over the age of 3.

Moreover, in spite of victimologists' frequent accusations of societal denial to children and adolescents of the right to say "no" to sexual touching, a look at the current (1986) SIECUS (Sex Education Council of the United States) selected bibliography counted more than 80 books and 25 films and videos geared to children and adolescents, with *It's Okay to Say "No!"* being a keynote title. Books such as *Private Zone; Red Flag, Green Flag People; My Body is Private;* and *I Like You to Make Jokes With Me But I Don't Want You to Touch Me* teach children, according to their blurbs, about "good" touches and "bad" (i.e., sexual) touches, "uncomfortable" (i.e., genital) touches, and "private zones" that no one should touch other than "parent or physician" (and one wonders whether, in later editions, the word "parent" will be removed). In a society where the operative word in answer to most sexual requests or desires is "no," the publishing of books such as *It's Okay to Say "No!"* does not seem to constitute a major act of social rebellion.

Other possible consequences of this sort of response to sexual abuse are alluded to by sociologist and incest researcher James R. Ramey (1979):

> There is a huge group of individuals who are being damaged by our drum beating—those who have not been involved in incest. American families have been so imbued with prohibitions against incest that they bend over backward to avoid any possible incestuous involvement or possible accusation that they might become involved. This results ... [among other things] in complete and total abandonment of parent-child physical contact at puberty, just when the child needs its reassurance most (p. 7).

While the paper from which this quote was drawn has been vilified by victimologists over the years, Ramey's point intuitively seems valid at least for a substantial number of families.

Finally, Bullough (this volume) and Schultz (1980b) have commented on the alarming disappearance at the judicial level of concern with the physical abuse of children—a development reflected in popular media where, despite the flurry that accompanies sensationalistic coverage of particularly gruesome cases of death due to physical abuse, the term **child abuse** has passed into usage to signify **child sexual abuse**.

According to Schultz, prosecutors find convictions for sexual abuse much easier to obtain[9] because defendants are generally male, whereas defendants in physical abuse cases are often mothers. Although judges and juries are perfectly willing to award men custody of children in divorce cases, neither wishes to challenge the sanctity of prevailing images of motherhood, and doing so within the context of physical abuse proceedings is often a thankless and unproductive task for all concerned.

Knowing the difficulty of obtaining convictions in these cases and the consequent risk of lawsuits brought by acquitted defendants, medical practitioners have become reticent about reporting physical abuse and have instead focused on sexual abuse—where the professional rewards for disclosure are less ambiguous. Acquitted defendants in sexual abuse cases generally do not bring lawsuits but, rather, attempt to disappear under the nearest rug.

In a related study (Okami, 1988), college students rated sexual abuse of children the most serious crime from a list of 14, significantly more serious than either murder or the physical or emotional abuse of a child. Physical abuse was, in fact, ranked alarmingly low in seriousness.[10]

The new research reflects and encourages such attitudes. Sexual abuse is portrayed by many of the writers with whom this chapter has been concerned as the most devastating experience a child can endure. For example, Russell (1986, p. 231) refers to father/daughter incest as "the supreme betrayal" of the child. On the other hand, at least as destructive and probably more prevalent (Avery-Clarke, 1981), physical abuse of children is, with certain exceptions (e.g., Finkelhor, 1988), virtually ignored.

In accord with the current author's view, Katz (1984) specifically attributes the decline in concern over physical and emotional abuse of children to the "hysteria" surrounding the issue of sexual abuse. However, one must also take into account a general cultural tendency toward greater acceptance of violent feelings and behaviors over sexual ones. For example, children and adolescents are permitted to view graphic media depictions of sadistic murder, torture, and mutilation, but they are not permitted to view realistic depictions even of affectionate sexual interactions.

In summary, policy decisions must evaluate both the damage caused by child sexual abuse and the damage caused by iatrogenic response to actual abuse or to the threat of abuse. While the new research has had the positive effect of making vivid the general political powerlessness of children and the alarming pervasiveness of sexual abuse, it may have had the negative effect of fueling what many observers have characterized as a generally hysterical and counter-productive social climate.

## Conclusions

A careful review of the new victimology-based literature in the field of child sexual abuse provides ample evidence to suggest that a portion of these writings, and a portion of the outrage frequently expressed within them, may be generated by factors not specifically related to concern over the actual effects on children and adolescents of sexual interactions with adults. Indeed, the marked similarities between the writings discussed in this chapter and works of political propaganda suggest that children are being used by some of these writers largely as symbols for rhetorical battles in the theater of sexual politics.

Cultural feminists and victimologists are able to advance with impunity, "under the cover" of considerations of child sexual abuse, fundamentally reactionary and sex-negative propositions—propositions that might meet with sharp critical response were they to be applied to adult sexuality. This impunity is no doubt the result both of Western societies' traditional unwillingness to examine or even acknowledge childhood sexuality (Masters, 1986; Howells and Cook, 1981; Lee, 1980) and the stigmatization within the professional community associated with appearing to be "soft" on the issue of sexual abuse. Finkelhor's assertion that the point of view expressed in the new research is "compatible with the most progressive attitude toward sexuality currently being voiced" must therefore be questioned.

It has not been the intention of this chapter to belittle the suffering caused by the actual sexual abuse of children and adolescents, which, like physical and emotional abuse, is a major social problem. Nor is this chapter implying that adult/nonadult sexual interactions are generally benign. On the contrary, there is strong evidence presented in other chapters in this volume and elsewhere to suggest that a substantial number, possibly a substantial majority, of such interactions in Western societies are at best unpleasant and unhappy and at worst severely traumatic—resulting in short- and long-term impairment on many levels. However, it must also be pointed out that data exist that suggest that a significant number of these interactions appear to be neither unpleasant nor traumatic.

Much of the new research, then, however well meaning, shares the basic flaw of most polemical work: Moral and empirical truths are ignored, suppressed, or distorted in the interests of furthering the cause. In this case, there seems to be a danger of throwing out the baby with the bathwater— the bathwater here being child and adolescent sexual abuse, and the baby, his or her own affectional life, normal sexual curiosity, and erotic impulse. Both the suppression of childhood and adolescent sexuality and the transmission to children and adolescents of fearful and negative messages about sex that is indirectly encouraged in the new research may well constitute a form of sexual abuse affecting a great many more children than are victimized in the traditional sense.

## Summary

This chapter examined the manner in which sociopolitical biases pervade and compromise much of the current victimology-informed research and writing on the subject of adult human sexual interactions with children and adolescents. It was the author's contention that the strong social-activist posture taken by many of the professionals responsible for this new research, combined with their implicit or explicit endorsement of specific sexual-political ideologies, has engendered a body of literature that could more properly be described as social criticism than as social science. Seriously flawed research methods and discursive practices similar to those found in works of political propaganda were analyzed. It was noted that the victimologists' use of legal, moral, and political criteria to supplant the use of empirical or phenomenological criteria in the design and conduct of research on sexual abuse has served to obscure an accurate understanding of the phenomena under investigation. Iatrogenic correlates of the "new research" were also discussed, and a contrasting model (Kilpatrick, 1986) of productive and comparatively bias-free research design and conduct was reviewed.

### Acknowledgments

Several people contributed to whatever may be valuable in this chapter. I must first thank Lawrence Stanley for his theoretical input, hard-nosed editing, research assistance, and assorted tireless efforts. I also gratefully acknowledge the advice and assistance of Barbara Moulton, Hope Carr, Vita Rabinowitz, Michael Wood, Allie Kilpatrick, Nadine Castro, Joan Nelson, Milton Diamond, Jay Feierman, and Charles Parker. I must especially thank Stefanie Kelly and my daughter Masai for bearing with me.

# Notes

[1]A version of this chapter was presented at the annual meeting of the Society for the Scientific Study of Sex (SSSS), which was held November 11-13, 1988, in San Francisco, California.

[2]This chapter does not explore the other end of the sociopolitical spectrum, which advocates lowering or abolishing the age-of-consent laws. The literature is confined to a few out-of-the-mainstream publications (Brongersma, 1986; O'Carroll, 1982; Tsang, 1981), and the point of view is represented by only one organization in the United States, the North American Man-Boy Love Association (NAMBLA), whose membership numbers less than 500, and by several smaller organizations in Europe, among them *Stichting Matijn* in the Netherlands. There is no public funding for research on or advocacy of this position, and simply being on a mailing list to receive information from NAMBLA is politically dangerous in this country. If simply judged by number of publications per year, the "new research" group outpublishes the "age of consent lowering" group by a ratio of approximately 1,000:1. The political tactic of the "age of consent lowering" group, which is composed mainly of pedophiles, ephebophiles, and self-defined sex-radicals, is to argue for the "sexual rights of children and adolescents."

[3]The designation "cultural feminist" is used here to distinguish this group from other feminists, such as those who have been associated with radical politics or sexual libertarianism. These classifications are analogous to those used to describe the major split in black activism during the late 1960's between "cultural nationalists" and radical socialists.

[4]An example of the kinds of interrogation techniques favored by this organization may be found in this portion of an interview conducted by Kee McFarlaine of C.I.I. (quoted in Coleman, 1986, p. 3). Here, McFarlaine is attempting to get a little boy to describe the so-called "naked movie star game" that defendants in the McMartin daycare center sexual abuse trial were alleged to have played with children at the center. The reader should bear in mind that McFarlaine is interviewing a possible victim, not a perpetrator:

KM:  I thought that was a naked game.
Boy:  Not exactly.
KM:  Did somebody take their clothes off?
Boy:  When I was there no one was naked.
KM:  Some of the kids were told they might be killed. It was a trick. Alright, Mr. Alligator [meaning the boy], are you going to be stupid, or are you smart and can tell? Some think you're smart.
Boy:  I'll be smart.
KM:  Mr. Monkey [the puppet the boy had used earlier] is chicken. He can't remember the games, but you know the naked movie star game, or is your memory bad?
Boy:  I haven't seen the naked movie star game.
KM:  You must be dumb.
Boy:  I don't remember.

[5]The one study reviewed by Peters, Wyatt, and Finkelhor that found a higher prevalence rate than Lewis still reported a rate of 25-28 percentage points lower than Russell's and Wyatt's. This study also included unwanted verbal propositions and exhibitionism in its definition of "sexual abuse."

[6]A partial listing of sources supporting a continuum model of adult/nonadult sexual interactions—a continuum whose points range from the involuntary and traumatagenic to the voluntary and benign—would include the following: Bagley, 1969; Bauermann, 1982; Bender and Blau, 1937; Bender and Grugett, 1952; Bernard, 1981; Burton, 1965; Brunhold, 1964; Constantine, 1981a,b,c; Elwin, 1968; Farrell, 1977; Ford and Beach, 1951; Frayser, 1985; Friday, 1975; Gebhard et al., 1965; Geiser, 1987; Geisler, 1959; Henderson, 1976, 1983; Ingram, 1981; Kaplan, 1982; Kinsey et al., 1953; Landis, 1956; Lukianowicz, 1972; Martinson, 1976; Meiselman, 1975; Menninger, 1942; McCaghy, 1985; Mohr et al., 1964; Nelson, 1981; Okami, 1987; Powell and Chalkley, 1981; Revitch and Weiss, 1962; Rascovsky and Rascovsky, 1950; Rogers and Weiss, 1953; Schultz, 1980a; Symonds, Mendoza, and Harrell, 1981; Virkunnen, 1981; Weiss et al., 1955; and Yates, 1978.

[7]Russell presents no evidence to support her contention that this notion is "widely held." Rather, the opposite is clearly the case, as reflected both in the scientific literature and in the popular media and folklore.

[8]June Reinisch is the Director of the Kinsey Institute. Cornelia Christenson was a member of Kinsey's original research team. Sue Hammersmith co-authored the Kinsey report on homosexuality. The percentage of female researchers associated with the Kinsey Institute has steadily increased since its inception to its currently largely female-constituted staff (Kinsey Institute, personal communication).

[9]In 1985, of every 100 persons arrested for sexual offenses against minors, 90% were prosecuted, 65% of those prosecuted were convicted, and 13% of those convicted spent more than one year incarcerated (testimony of Representative Dan Coates, Department of Justice investigation, 1985).

[10]This cultural posture—which characterizes adult/child sex as a crime without equal in hatefulness—is succinctly expressed by Norman Podhoretz (1987), who writes of such sexual behavior: "Nothing in the realm of human abominations seems so self-evidently evil."

## References

Avery-Clarke, C., et al. A comparison of intra-familial sexual abuse and physical abuse. *In* K. Howells and M. Cook (Eds.), *Adult sexual interest in children*. London: Academic Press, 1981.

Bagley, C. Incest behavior and incest taboo. *Social Problems,* 1969, *16.*

Bass, E. Introduction. *In* E. Bass and L. Thornton (Eds.), *I never told anyone: Writings by women survivors of child sexual abuse.* New York: Harper & Row, 1983.

Bauermann, M.C. *Sexualitaet, Gewalt und psychische folden.* Bundeskriminalamt Wiesbaden, 1982. English Summary.

Becker, H.S. Moral entrepreneurs: The creation and enforcement of deviant categories. *In* D. Kelly (Ed.), *Deviant behavior.* New York: St. Martin's Press, 1984.

Bender, L., and Blau, A. The reaction of children to sexual relations with adults. *American Journal of Orthopsychiatry,* 1937, *7,* 500-578.

Bender, L., and Grugett, A. Follow-up report on children who had atypical sexual experience. *American Journal of Orthopsychiatry,* 1952, *22,* 825-837.

Bernard, F. Pedophilia: Psychological consequences for the child. *In* L. Constantine and F. Martinson (Eds.), *Children and sex.* Boston: Little Brown and Co., 1981.

Besharov, D.J. Unfounded allegations—a new child abuse problem. *The Public Interest,* 1986, *83.*

Blume, S. The walking wounded: Post-incest syndrome. *SIECUS Report,* 1986, *15,* 1-3.

Borneman, E. Progress in empirical research on children's sexuality. *SIECUS Report*, 1983, *12*, 2.

Brongersma, E. *Loving boys*, Vol. 1. Elmhurst, N.Y.: Global Academic Publishers, 1986.

Brownmiller, S. *Against our will: Men, women, and rape*. New York: Simon and Schuster, 1986.

Brunold, H. Observations after sexual trauma suffered in childhood. *Excerpta Criminologica (Netherlands)*, 1964, *4*, 5-9.

Burstyn, V. (Ed.). *Women against censorship*. Vancouver: Douglas and McIntyre, 1985.

Burton, L. *Vulnerable children*. London: Routledge and Kegan Paul, 1967.

Cantwell, H. Child sexual abuse: Very young perpetrators. *Child Abuse and Neglect*, 1988, *12*, 579-582.

Coleman, L. Learning from the McMartin hoax. Paper presented to V.O.C.A.L. Convention, October 24-26, 1986, Torrance, Calif.

Constantine, L. Preface. *In* L. Constantine and F. Martinson (Eds.), *Children and sex*. Boston: Little Brown and Co., 1981a.

Constantine, L. The effects of early sexual experiences: A review and synthesis of research. *In* L. Constantine and F. Martinson (Eds.), *Children and sex*. Boston: Little Brown and Co., 1981b.

Constantine, L. The sexual rights of children: Implications of a radical perspective. *In* L. Constantine and F. Martinson (Eds.), *Children and sex*. Boston: Little Brown and Co., 1981c.

Crewdson, J. *By silence betrayed*. Boston: Little Brown and Co., 1988.

Currier, R. Debunking the double-think on juvenile sexuality. *Human Behavior*, September 1977.

Currier, R. Juvenile sexuality in global perspective. *In* L. Constantine and F. Martinson (Eds.), *Children and sex*. Boston: Little Brown and Co., 1981.

Curtin, P. Child abusers may be children. *St. Petersburg* (Fla.) *Times*, October 16, 1988, p. 1.

De Mott, B. The pro-incest lobby. *Psychology Today*, March 1980 (page numbers not given).

de Young, M. *The sexual victimization of children*. London: McFarland and Co., 1982.

DuBois, E.C., and Gordon, L. Seeking ecstacy on the battlefield. *In* C.S. Vance (Ed.), *Pleasure and danger*. Boston: Routeledge and Kegan Paul, 1984.

Ellis, K. I'm black and blue from the Rolling Stones and I'm not sure how I feel about it. *In* K. Ellis, B. O'Dair, and A. Tallmer (Eds.), *Caught looking: Feminism, censorship and pornography*. New York: Caught Looking, Inc., 1986.

Ellis, K., O'Dair, B., and Tallmer, A. (Eds.). Introduction. *In* K. Ellis, B. O'Dair, and A. Tallmer (Eds.), *Caught looking: Feminism, censorship and pornography*. New York: Caught Looking, Inc., 1986.

Elwin, V. *Kingdom of youth*. London: Oxford University Press, 1968.

Finkelhor, D. *Sexually victimized children*. New York: Free Press, 1979.

Finkelhor, D. Sex between siblings: Sex, play, incest, and aggression. *In* L. Constantine and F. Martinson (Eds.), *Children and sex*. Boston: Little Brown and Co., 1981.

Finkelhor, D. *Child sexual abuse: New theory and research*. New York: Free Press, 1984.

Finkelhor, D., and Redfield, D. How the public defines sexual abuse. Co-authored chapter in D. Finkelhor, *Child sexual abuse: New theory and research*. New York: Free Press, 1984 (page numbers not given).

Ford, C., and Beach, F. *Patterns of sexual behavior*. New York: Harper & Row, 1951.

Frayser, S. *Varieties of sexual experience*. New Haven: HRAF, 1985.

Friday, N. *Forbidden flowers*. New York: Pocket Books, 1975.

Gagnon, J. Female child victims of sex offenses. *Social Problems*, 1965, *13*, 176-192.

Gebhard, P., Gagnon, J., Pomeroy, W., and Christenson, C. *Sex offenders: An analysis of types*. New York: Harper & Row, 1965.

Geiser, R. *Hidden victims*. Boston: Beacon Press, 1979.

Geisler, E. *Das sexuell missbrauchte Kind: Beitrag zur sexuellen Entwicklung, iher Gefahrdung und zu forensischen Fragen*. Gottingen: Verlag für medizinische Psychologie, 1959.

Greer, G. *Seduction is a four-letter word*. New York: John Cushman Associates, Inc., 1975.

Henderson, J. Incest. *In* A.M. Freedman et al. (Eds.), *A comprehensive textbook of psychiatry*, Vol. 2 (2nd ed.). Baltimore: Williams and Wilkins, 1975.

Henderson, J. Is incest harmful? *California Journal of Psychiatry*, 1983, *28*, 34-39.

Hentoff, N. This is child porn? *Washington Post*, August 8, 1984, p. 14.

Herman, J. *Father-daughter incest*. Cambridge: Harvard University Press, 1981.

Ingram, M. Participating victims: A study of sexual offenses with boys. *In* L. Constantine and F. Martinson (Eds.), *Children and sex*. Boston: Little Brown and Co., 1981.

Johnson, T.C. Child perpetrators—children who molest other children: Preliminary findings. *Child Abuse and Neglect*, 1988, *12*, 219-229.

Kaplan, G. Sexual exploitation of children: The conspiracy of silence. *Police Magazine*, January 1982, pp. 43-51.

Katz, S.J. Stop the witch-hunt for child molesters. *New York Times*, June 20, 1984 (page number not given).

Kilpatrick, A. Some correlates of women's childhood sexual experiences: A retrospective study. *Journal of Sex Research*, 1986, *22*, 2.

Kilpatrick, A. Childhood sexual experiences: Problems and issues in studying long-range effects. *Journal of Sex Research*, 1987, *23*, 2.

Kinsey, A., et al. *Sexual behavior in the human male.* Philadelphia: Saunders, 1948.

Kinsey, A., et al. *Sexual behavior in the human female.* Philadelphia: Saunders, 1953.

Landis, L. Experiences of 500 children with adult sexual deviation. *Psychiatry Quarterly,* 1956, *30,* supplement.

Lee, J.A. The politics of child sexuality. *Proceedings of the Montreal Symposium on Childhood Sexuality.* Montreal: Éditions Vivantes, 1980.

Lewis, I.A. (Two articles; titles not available.) *Los Angeles Times,* August 25 and August 26, 1985, p. 1.

Lukianowicz, N. Incest. *British Journal of Psychiatry,* 1972, *120,* 301-313.

Martinson, F. Eroticism in infancy and childhood. *Journal of Sex Research,* 1976, *12,* 4.

McCaghy, C. *Deviant behavior: Crime, conflict and interest groups* (2nd ed.). New York: Macmillan, 1985.

Meiselman, K. *Incest.* San Francisco: Jossey-Bass, 1978.

Menninger, K. *Love against hate.* New York: Harcourt, Brace & World, Inc., 1942.

Mohr, J., and Turner, R. Sexual deviations, part IV: Pedophilia. *Applied Therapeutics,* 1967, *9,* 362-365.

Money, J. *Venuses penuses.* Buffalo: Prometheus, 1986.

Nadler, E., and Nobile, P. *The United States of America vs. sex.* New York: Minotaur Press, Ltd., 1986.

Nathan, D. The making of a modern witch trial. *Village Voice,* September 29, 1987, p. 19.

Nelson, J. The impact of incest: Factors in self-evaluation. *In* L. Constantine and F. Martinson (Eds.), *Children and sex.* Boston: Little Brown and Co., 1981.

Nelson, J. Incest. Unpublished doctoral dissertation, Institute for the Advanced Study of Human Sexuality, San Francisco, 1984.

Nelson, J. Incest: Self-report findings from a non-clinical sample. *Journal of Sex Research,* 1986, *22,* 4.

Nobile, P. Incest: The last taboo. *Penthouse,* January 1977, p. 117.

O'Carroll, T. *Paedophilia: The radical case.* Boston: Alyson Publications, 1982.

O'Grady, K.E. Donnerstein, Malamuth, and Mould: The conduct of research and the nature of inquiry. *Journal of Sex Research,* 1988, *24,* 358-362.

Okami, P. Sexual contacts between adults and minors: Points along a continuum. Paper presented at the 15th annual Hunter College Psychology Convention, New York City, N.Y., 1987.

Okami, P. Is child abuse normatively sanctioned? Paper presented at the 16th annual Hunter College Psychology Convention, New York City, N.Y., 1988.

Peters, S.D., Wyatt, G.E., and Finkelhor, D. Prevalence. *In* D. Finkelhor (Ed.), *A sourcebook on child sexual abuse*. Beverly Hills: Sage Publications, 1986.

Pivar, D. *Purity crusades, sexual morality, and social control, 1868-1900*. Westport: Greenwood, 1973.

Podhoretz, N. When horror no longer horrifies. *New York Post*, September 15, 1987 (page number not given).

Pomeroy, W. A new look at incest. *Forum*, November 1976, pp. 9-13.

Powell, G., and Chalkey, A. Effects of pedophile attention on the child. *In* B. Taylor (Ed.), *Perspectives on paedophilia*. London: Batsford Academic, 1981.

Ramey, J. Dealing with the last taboo. *SIECUS Report*, 1979, *VII*(5), 1-2, 6-7.

Rascovsky, M., and Rascovsky, A. On consummated incest. *International Journal of Psychoanalysis*, 1950, *31*, 42.

Revitch, E., and Weiss, R. The pedophile offender. *Diseases of the Nervous System*, 1962, *23*, 73-78.

Rogers, E., and Weiss, R. *A study of sex crimes against children*. Sexual Deviation Research, Department of Mental Hygiene, State of California, 1953.

Rose, V.M. Rape as a social problem: A byproduct of the feminist movement. *Social Problems*, 1977, *25*, 75-89.

Rosenthal, R. *Experimenter effects in behavioral research* (enlarged ed.). New York: Halsted/Wiley, 1976.

Rubin, G. Thinking sex. *In* C.S. Vance (Ed.), *Pleasure and danger*. Boston: Routeledge and Kegan Paul, 1986.

Rush, F. *The best kept secret*. New York: Prentice Hall, 1980.

Russell, D. *Rape, child sexual abuse, and workplace harassment*. Beverly Hills: Sage Publications, 1984.

Russell, D. *The secret trauma: Incest in the lives of girls and women*. New York: Basic Books, 1986.

Sandfort, T. Sex in pedophilic relationships: An empirical investigation among a non-representative group of boys. *Journal of Sex Research*, 1984, *20*(2), 123-142.

Schultz, L. Diagnosis and treatment—An introduction. *In* L. Schultz (Ed.), *The sexual victimology of youth*. New York: Charles C. Thomas, 1980a.

Schultz, L. The sexual abuse of children and minors: A short history of legal control efforts. *In* L. Schultz (Ed.), *The sexual victimology of youth*. New York: Charles C. Thomas, 1980b.

Snitow, A. Retrenchment vs. transformation: The politics of the anti-pornography movement. In V. Burstyn (Ed.), *Women against censorship*. Vancouver: Douglas and McIntyre, 1985.

Symonds, C.L., Mendoza, M.J., and Harrell, W.C. Forbidden sexual behavior among kin: A study of self-selected respondents. *In* L.

Constantine and F. Martinson (Eds.), *Children and sex.* Boston: Little Brown and Co., 1981.

Transcript. Braden-Buchanan Show, May 23, 1983, WRC Radio, Washington, D.C. Reprinted in *Proceedings of the U.S. House,* 1984, pp. 638-649.

Tsang, D. (Ed.). *The age taboo: Gay male sexuality, power and consent.* Boston: Alyson Publications, 1981.

Virkunnen, M. The child as participating victim. *In* K. Howells and M. Cook (Eds.), *Adult sexual interest in children.* London: Academic Press, 1981.

Weiss, J., et al. A study of girl sex victims. *Psychiatric Quarterly,* 1955, *29,* 1-27.

Willis, E. Feminism, morality and pornography. *In* K. Ellis, B. O'Dair, and A. Tallmer (Eds.), *Caught looking: Feminism, censorship and pornography.* New York: Caught Looking, Inc., 1986.

Wyatt, G.E. The sexual abuse of Afro-American and white women in childhood. *Child Abuse and Neglect,* 1985, *9,* 507-519.

Yates, A. *Sex without shame: Encouraging the child's healthy sexual development.* New York: Morrow, 1978.

# 4
# The Phylogeny of Male/Female Differences in Sexual Behavior

Gerhard Medicus
*Forschungsstelle für Humanethologie in der*
*Max-Planck-Gesellschaft*
*D-8138 Andechs*
*Federal Republic of Germany*
  *and*
*Landes-Nervenkrankenhaus Hall in Tirol*
*A-6060 Hall in Tirol*
*Austria*
  *and*
Sigrid Hopf
*Max-Planck-Institut für Psychiatrie*
*D-8000 München 40*
*Federal Republic of Germany*

## Introduction

In order to understand human behavior, including adult human sexual behavior with children and adolescents, one cannot neglect humans' phylogenetic[1] heritage, part of which is the result of the evolution of behavior through natural selection. This chapter examines the phylogenetic bases of differences in sexual behavior between the sexes. Especially in the Introduction, it is intended to familiarize readers from other disciplines with some of the fundamental evolutionary-biology principles of male/female differences in sexual behavior. Also, it is necessary to consider the phylogenetic reciprocal causes of male and of female sexual behavior in order to better understand adult human sexual behavior with children and adolescents, the topic of this edited volume. Many social scientists attribute most behavioral differences between males and females to the differing processes and influences that each sex experiences during socialization (for further references, see, e.g., Maccoby and Jacklin, 1974). Although it is true that males and females are raised differently by their parents and are treated differently by society, certain basic biology-related differences in behavior between the sexes do exist, and these differences can best be understood through a phylogenetic approach.

Behavioral scientists and clinicians find it difficult to decide on the "degree" to which any human trait, such as objectively observable behavior or subjective inner life, is determined either by closed (i.e., innate) genetic programs or by open genetic programs (i.e., mainly[2] learned by the individual). Here, also, a comparative phylogenetic approach can help. Certain behaviors, such as the facial expressions associated with laughing and crying, are seen in all known human cultures (e.g., Eibl-Eibesfeldt, 1967, 1984), and variations of these traits are seen in some nonhuman, higher primates (e.g., van Hoff, 1972; Jolly, 1972). In cases where a behavioral trait is seen in numerous closely related species, it is highly probable that the behavior is regulated by relatively closed genetic programs in the form of fixed-action patterns[3] that can be traced back to similar genetic material acquired from a common archetypal ancestor. Examples of behavior patterns that are controlled by relatively closed genetic programs also are revealed by ethological deprivation experiments and by research on twins and on certain psychiatric disorders within families.

Other behavioral traits may be regulated at an initial level by seemingly closed genetic programs but then can be modified by individual learning (i.e., relatively open genetic programs). These latter learning programs are advantageous because they allow the modification of innate characteristics to occur much more rapidly than occurs through genetic mutation and natural selection.

Under natural and seminatural conditions, the modification of behavior through **learning** almost always results in the adaptive modification of behavior,[4] implying that a large number of genetically based learning programs are present. Simply stated, genetic programs structure what is learned and how easily and where, when, and how learning takes place. These programs can also be called "predispositions," or "tendencies to learn," and must be considered in the context of both normative (species- and sex-typical) and variant (species- and sex-atypical) behavior. For example, anyone who has observed the behavioral development of kittens and puppies can appreciate how different they are as species in spontaneous play and in the ease with which they learn various things. Similar differences, although more subtle, can be found when one compares the development of a male or a female of the same species.

## Natural History

Darwin was the first person to interpret the variation among species as being the result of "natural selection" working on individual "variation" within a species. Modern geneticists have corroborated a part of his theory at the molecular level. A standard sequence of base-pairs of genetic material contains instructions for the morphology and the physiological function of an organism. According to genetics, random mutations in the sequence of base-pairs may cause new variants (mutations) in the morphology and/or the physiological function of the organism. Subsequently, natural selection works on the different individuals. Mutation and selection create variation within a species and finally among species. Mutations also affect the morphology of the nerve tissue itself, as well as the physiological processes within nerve cells and tissues, creating behavioral variation among individuals.

Evolution (both morphological and behavioral) of species thus has two origins: first, random **mutations** and second, natural **selection**. In selection, e.g., by environmental factors, a mutant is furthered or hindered in the population by the relative number of offspring carrying the mutation who survive and reproduce. This principle of mutation and selection holds true for asexual as well as sexual reproduction.

In trying to understand organisms and their behavior, science must heed an important rule in biology: it must take into consideration both the currently perceivable adaptations of organisms and the phylogeny of these adaptations. For example, the legs of insects and of tetrapods (vertebrates with four legs) confer adaptive advantage, i.e., the legs are accommodated (suited) to particular environmental conditions and, therefore, are important factors in the fitness[5] of the individuals. The differences in the construction plans of the legs are understandable only historically (phylogenetically), not functionally. The same holds true for the differences between the eyes of cephalopods (such as the octopus) and of vertebrates. Phylogeny also explains the differences between the locomotion of most fish and the locomotion of dolphins. Most fish move their tail fins from side to side, or horizontally; dolphins move their tails up and down, or vertically. Ancient mammals, ancestors of dolphins, had a "suspension bridge construction" between their fore and hind legs. The musculoskeletal apparatus forming this "bridge" (especially the dorsal muscles of the body) was more likely to produce a vertical movement in swimming mammals such as dolphins. The ancestors of fish, on the other hand, were constructed so that the movement of the tail in organisms that descended from them was more likely to be horizontal.

Preconditions (i.e., older traits) influence phylogenetically more recent behavioral traits of organisms. Once firmly established, traits (e.g., behavioral traits) usually are retained in some form in subsequent branches of the phylogenetic tree (e.g., Riedl, 1975). Relationships among animal species can be recognized and a phylogenetic tree can be established only on the basis of the continuity of morphological and behavioral traits. When similar traits of different animal species are traceable back to a common ancestor (e.g., any vertebral column to a basic vertebrate), one speaks of **homology**.

Similar genetic material is the basis for homologies, i.e., similar traits. Also, homologies have similar morphology or similar behavioral structure. They can be understood independently of their function, which occasionally changes in phylogeny, even among closely related species. Conversely, when similar traits in different species have evolved independently in that they have a similar function, one speaks of **analogy**. For example, camera eyes in vertebrates and cephalopods (e.g., cuttlefish) or the legs of insects and tetrapods developed convergently, or in other words, independently (i.e., analogously). They are not traceable back to a common ancestor.

The common ancestor of mammals and birds (a now-extinct reptile) did not show the trait of brood provisioning. (This conclusion is based on the study of extant reptiles.) Therefore, brood provisioning developed analogously in mammals and birds. Since billing and kissing between adult mates developed from brood provisioning, billing and kissing in birds and mammals also are analogous developments. Analogies can be more important than homologies in the effort by science to derive specific natural laws concerning adaptation to certain conditions (Lorenz, 1974).

## Inference from Animal to Human Behavior

Two pitfalls should be avoided in comparative phylogenetic research: direct inference from animals to humans and anthropomorphism in the investigation of the behavior of animals. Important considerations in comparative phylogenetic research are (a) From which animals and in which respect may one draw conclusions to humans? (b) What changes may have occurred in previous (retained) behavioral traits under selective conditions that were created by new behavioral traits? (c) On the basis of which previous behavioral traits (or phylogenetic preconditions) did which new qualitative behavioral traits of the nervous system emerge? (d) Which traits are traceable back to a common ancestor (i.e., homology), and which developed independently (i.e., analogy)? (See, e.g., von Cranach, 1976.) Inference from one particular species to another one (e.g., from one particular nonhuman primate to humans) should be made only with reservations. If similarities between species can be observed, it is important that science try to understand the phylogenetic as well as the functional causes of these similarities (see Dienske, this volume). In regard to some disciplines, such as human psychology, it is necessary for science to further elucidate the phylogenetic basis of behavior (also called **ultimate** causes) if science is to understand behavior. **Proximate** causes are life events that release a behavior or that cause a modification of a behavior within the phylogenetically caused framework. The distinction between ultimate and proximate cause can be useful for a better understanding of both normal and variant behavior.

## Biology of Reproduction

All species die out if their individuals fail to reproduce, be it sexually or asexually. However, reproduction does more than counter the loss of individuals. Reproduction allows change over generations to occur. It is a prerequisite for phylogenetic development.

Any type of reproduction requires a mechanism for genetic duplication. In the duplication process, mistakes in the genes (i.e., mutations) can occur. As described previously, mutations result in individuals with variations (i.e., mutants). In asexual reproduction, phylogenetic development (i.e., evolution) occurs exclusively by mutation and selection.

Sexual reproduction adds a factor to mutation and selection that furthers phylogenetic development, in that in sexual reproduction, genetic material from two individual parents becomes **recombined** in the offspring; new variations occur by this recombination alone. Natural selection then acts on the new variations caused by mutations and recombination. Each somatic cell (body cell as opposed to egg or sperm) of metazoans (multicellular animals) contains genetic material in duplicate. That is, in every somatic cell, all of the different chromosomes are present in identical pairs (i.e., chromosome pairs—the diploid number of chromosomes). Each metazoan parent's germ cells (eggs or sperm) contain only one-half (one side) of each parent's chromosome pairs, however (i.e., one of each chromosome—the haploid number of chromosomes). In fertilization, the germ cells of the parents combine, producing in the offspring the total amount of genes, the usual diploid number of chromosomes (i.e., a recombination of genetic material).

Mutation and recombination establish more variety in genetic patterns than mutation does alone; and in recombination, genetic material is tested from one generation to the next in various combinations. Then, within the genetic variety that is caused by mutation and recombination, more variants will survive in comparison to a similar amount of variants caused by mutation alone. This is because genes have already been tested in the parents, although in another combination. One can therefore say that the repertoire for (trial and) error, or the field of lethal possibilities, is narrowed within the variety caused by (mutation and) recombination.

Sexual reproduction is advantageous in comparison with asexual reproduction for several reasons. One is that the intrinsic process of sexual reproduction, i.e., the recombination of genetic material, creates variety that survives and reproduces faster than it is created in asexual, nonrecombinant reproduction, in which mutation is the only source of variation (cf. Rechenberg, 1973). More variants, caused by a higher rate of mutation, can endanger, rather than enhance, the survival of a species, since most mutations are deleterious rather than beneficial. Therefore, sexual reproduction allows adaptation to a changing world and phylogenetic development to proceed faster (Bell, 1985; Michod and Levin, 1988), with more safeguards to the integrity of species, than occurs by means of asexual reproduction.

Another advantage of sexual reproduction is "heterozygosity." In homozygous cells, which are produced by inbreeding over several generations, both halves of the chromosome pairs are identical, i.e., the genetic material is the same in each chromosome of a given pair. In heterozygous cells, the halves are not identical. Empirical evidence suggests that the heterozygosity of diploid somatic cells works as a genetic security mechanism, diminishing the effect of potentially disadvantageous recessive mutants (e.g., Lewontin, 1974).

During phylogeny, the benefits of sexual reproduction must outweigh the costs. Otherwise, the species reproducing sexually will not survive. An example of costs to metazoans is the necessary development of the ability to recognize a mating partner who is of the other sex and of the same species. During phylogeny, however, as soon as a species develops brood provisioning, individuals of the species are no longer distributed randomly within a population from birth, and as a result, mother/young affiliative bonds make inbreeding between mother and young, as well as among the offspring, more likely. The potential disadvantages of mother/young affiliative bonds for sexual reproduction, i.e., the potential creation of homozygous somatic cells in the next generation, are overcome by costly inbreeding-avoidance mechanisms that also develop during phylogeny (see Pusey, this volume). These mechanisms become as important to individual survival as is sexual reproduction itself (Bischof, 1975, 1985; Shepher, 1983).

Mutation and recombination are the primary causes of diversification in the animal kingdom. However, **isolation** caused by geographical distance, by adaptation to different ecological niches, and by sexual selection (which will be discussed subsequently) also result in substantial diversity, as evidenced by the many different species and animal groups. In short, the main origins of phylogeny are mutation, recombination, selection, and isolation.

## The Evolution of Mating Effort: Sexual Attraction and Courtship—A Form of Communication

Sexual behavior certainly evolved within the context of reproductive behavior (but is only one facet of reproductive behavior). Reproductive behavior in its biological sense has two components: mating effort and parental investment. This subsection considers the evolutionary mechanisms underlying mating effort. Parental investment is discussed in several other chapters in this volume (see Feierman, this volume, Chapter 1; Mackey, this volume; Taub, this volume).

Selection is affected not only by the environment, which is external to the species, but also by other individuals within the species; the latter phenomenon is called "intraspecific selection" (e.g., Mayr, 1972). Sexual selection is a special case of intraspecific selection. Intraspecific communication is both a means for this intraspecific selection and a product of it.

Intraspecific communication emerged from a phylogenetic process called "ritualization." For example, in geese, when an initiator moved to take flight, the intention movement took on a communicative function for the recipient group members during phylogeny. In this way, a common takeoff among members of a flock became inducible. Behavioral phenomena in an initiator or a signaler take on communicative meaning for a recipient. Wickler (1970) calls this occurrence "semantization by the receiver." Further mutations and selection may then lead to improved communicability, e.g., increased clarity in the initiator's signal. Other examples of ritualized behavior that are derived from sexual gestures became gestures of dominance and submission and vice versa (see Eibl-Eibesfeldt, this volume).

Mood and its outward behavioral expressions (i.e., affect) in an initiator must be phylogenetically tuned to the stimulus filter in the recipient so that the initiator's expression and the recipient's impression conform to each other (Leyhausen, 1968). In this phylogenetic process, expressive behaviors can become modified, and their meaning or function can change (e.g., van Hooff, 1972). One example, which will be developed in detail later in this chapter, is that many human adult females, who are smaller in size than their male counterparts, also are less boastful in their behavior (especially during courtship) than many males. These characteristics of the females are attributes of human children and adolescents, as well. Correspondingly, many courting human males expect such attributes in potential love and sexual partners. These expectations are one reason for the relative ease with which pedo- and ephebophilia can develop in adult males. (It must be noted that the degree of sexual differences in appearance and behavior just mentioned can vary substantially between cultures and even within cultures, depending on status, environment [urban or rural], and other factors.)

Mutations and intraspecific selection may on occasion lead to the evolution of traits that become disadvantageous, sometimes even so extremely disadvantageous that the survival of the species as a whole is endangered because of external selection (e.g., Lorenz, 1978). One example of this phenomenon is seen in the Great Argus's (*Argusianus argus*, a pheasant) courtship behavior, a type of intraspecific communication. The female of the Great Argus prefers to court males with exceptionally large wing feathers. Thus, during phylogeny, these wing feathers have developed to such an extent that the males of the species are almost unable to fly (e.g., Lorenz, 1978).

An example of the interplay between intra- and extraspecific selection can be observed in the male stickleback (*Gasterosteus aculeatus*). Females of this species prefer males that are courting them that have red bellies. In the northwestern United States (Washington State), however, sticklebacks are a prey of the blue dogfish (*Novumbra hubbsi*). A red belly makes the sticklebacks easier for the predator to see. Consequently, the courting male sticklebacks in this region developed a black belly over generations. The development occurred even though the females still prefer red-bellied males five times more than black-bellied males when tested experimentally (McPhail, 1969, cited after Eibl-Eibesfeldt, 1967).

As a general principle, the overall behavioral repertoire of a species is fairly similar in both sexes (Ploog, Hopf, and Winter, 1967). Behavioral dimorphism between the sexes is largely characterized by a differing **frequency, intensity**,[6] and **sequential use** of certain behavior patterns. This circumstance is similar within all vertebrate species (e.g., Wickler, 1969). In humans, the frequency distributions of types of behavior that are demonstrated by both males and females overlap greatly, and there is more variance between the sexes in atypical sexual behavior than there is in typical sexual behavior. Among individuals displaying atypical, or variant, sexual behavior, males are overrepresented (this topic will be discussed later in this chapter).

Male/female differences in sexual behavior in human and nonhuman primates result from (phylo-) genetic predispositions and from cultural modifications and amplifications. The bases of human dimorphism in sexual behavior and generalizations about them are highly controversial, and therefore, the biological evidence of these bases and the sociopolitical implications of this evidence must be considered (cf. Hutt, 1972; Lee and Steward, 1976).

This chapter deals with sexual behavior in humans. It therefore does not concentrate on the intricate manifestations of the large variety of male/female differences in sexual behavior in the animal kingdom, which has been reviewed by others (e.g., Wickler and Seibt, 1983). However, the next part of this chapter discusses the phylogeny of some aspects of nonhuman sexual behavior insofar as that phylogeny could have relevance to humans. This discussion leads into the third part, which addresses certain human sexual behavior patterns and their variations, some of which can be better understood through the consideration of phylogeny.

## On the Phylogeny of Male/Female Dimorphism

Generally, there are two sexes in both plants and animals, and each sex shows sex-specific traits. It will be demonstrated that the differences between the sexes (see Table 4.I) started with the inception of sexual reproduction in metazoans (e.g., Bell, 1982; Hoekstra, 1980; Parker, 1978, 1982; Smith, 1984; Stearns, 1987; Trivers, 1972; Wickler and Seibt, 1983).

In order for two kinds of germ cells, or gametes, to join successfully and flourish, two conditions must be fulfilled:
1. There must be a high probability that the two germ cells will meet, and
2. A certain minimum size must be reached after fertilization to ensure a good chance for further development.

These conditions are best fulfilled when one sex produces a small number of large, nutritious germ cells while the other sex produces large numbers of small, and in some species highly mobile, germ cells. A species with such heterogamy (different-size germ cells) will outreproduce a species with isogamy (same-size germ cells). As a result, heterogamy is ubiquitous in metazoans. The large, nutrient-rich germ cells (i.e., egg cells), produced by the female,[7] secure the chance for life to start. The smaller but numerous germ cells (i.e., sperm), produced by the male, increase the probability of direct joining with the large cells of the female because sperm are produced in surplus and are mobile in many species. If all germ cells were as large as egg cells (i.e., isogamy), an insufficient number would be produced, and therefore, not enough fertilizations could take place. If, on the other hand, all germ cells were as tiny as sperm (also isogamy), the cells, even if they were fertilized, would be lacking in nutrients and would have less chance for further development.

Despite the production of vast numbers of germ cells by the male (which allows, for example, the external fertilization that is characteristic of most fish), the male's expenditure of time and of energy in reproduction usually is many orders of magnitude smaller than are such expenditures by the female. More recently, in phylogenetic terms, additional expenditures such as long gestational periods and suckling of the young have been required of the female placentalia (i.e., vertebrates with placenta).

Because males of most species make relatively small expenditures in time and energy in the effort at reproduction, it follows that a male can mate more often than a female and sire many more offspring than one female can bear. This capacity means that a male can improve his reproductive success by mating with more than one female within a certain period of time, whereas a female, once pregnant, cannot bear more offspring by mating with more males. This basic sex difference in reproductive physiology is the foundation of many of the fundamental differences in male and female sexual behavior. In general, the resources limiting female reproduction are mainly nutrition and time: to produce eggs, to nourish a fetus, to nurse the young. In contrast, almost the only resource limiting male reproduction in many species is the availability of the female.

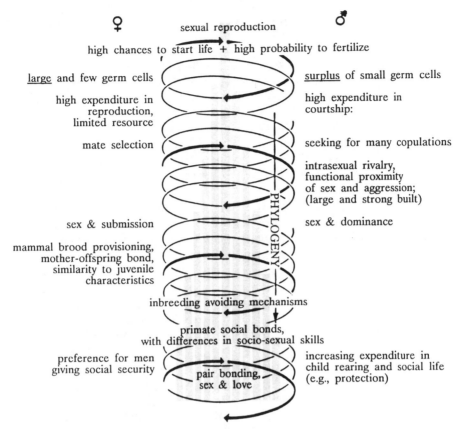

♀    sexual reproduction    ♂

high chances to start life + high probability to fertilize

large and few germ cells

surplus of small germ cells

high expenditure in
reproduction,
limited resource

high expenditure in
courtship:

mate selection

seeking for many copulations

intrasexual rivalry,
functional proximity
of sex and aggression;
(large and strong built)

PHYLOGENY

sex & submission

sex & dominance

mammal brood provisioning,
mother-offspring bond,
similarity to juvenile
characteristics

inbreeding avoiding mechanisms

primate social bonds,
with differences in socio-sexual skills

preference for men
giving social security

increasing expenditure in
child rearing and social life
(e.g., protection)

pair bonding,
sex & love

TABLE 4.I. Idealized diagram of some milestones of the phylogeny of human sexual dimorphism. The broad variety of dimorphic developments in the animal kingdom, caused by different functional/historical conditions, is not considered in this table. Sexual dimorphism can differ substantially in closely related species. Therefore, human sexual dimorphism apparently did not develop in the unilinear fashion that is shown in this idealized table. The phylogenetic spiral line symbolizes the reciprocal causes of dimorphistic developments prompted by both sexes. The shaded stripes symbolize the probability of the maintenance of old phylogenetic characteristics. (In this respect, this diagram is similar to the diagram of a "phylogenetic tree of behavioral capabilities" in Medicus, 1987, which is based upon Lorenz, 1973.) But remaining characteristics can become modified by different functional conditions (or by changes of functions), e.g., they can be prompted by phylogenetically newer characteristics superimposed on the older preconditions. But sometimes, phylogenetically older characteristics may become more apparent in some variants of human sexual behavior. See text and Eibl-Eibesfeldt, this volume, for further explanation.

## The Concept of "Functional Proximity" of Mood and of Behavior

Because the female represents the limiting resource for the male, males are biologically predisposed to search for and court female partners more actively and intensely than females search for and court males. This difference in sexual behavior leads to intense male competition for females (e.g., Symons, 1979; Trivers, 1972; Wickler and Seibt, 1983). In species in which males expend more energy in parental care than do females (e.g., sea horses or such birds as ostriches, hornbills, and lyrebirds), the females court the males more intensely than the males court the females (e.g., Wickler and Seibt, 1983).

As Eibl-Eibesfeldt (this volume) shows, the consequence of males' searching and competing for females is a sexuality based on male dominance and female submission (which only later in evolution was overlaid by an affiliative sexuality). In species where males compete for females, males have an advantage if they are able to switch rapidly from courtship behavior to male intrasexual competitive aggression and vice versa. This ease of behavioral change is reflected in the nominative expression "functionally proximate behavior." As defined in ethology, patterns of functionally proximate behavior occur frequently within relatively short periods of time (cf. Baerends, 1976; Lorenz, 1978; Wiepkema, 1961).

Behavior can be combined in very different ways (i.e., can occur simultaneously or alternatingly) and to very different degrees, depending upon the species, the sex, and the context. Because of the human capacity for self-assessment by introspection and reflection, humans realize that this principle also applies to human "inner life," e.g., the moods (self-perceived as feelings) underlying human behavior. Because of such combining, for example, some functionally proximate moods, such as sex and hostility, can become superimposed somewhat easily in males of many species.

The mood for flight from a predator is relatively distant from the mood for courtship behavior on the continuum between functionally close and functionally distant behavior-inducing moods; therefore, a change from flight to courtship (e.g., Lorenz, 1963), the respective behavior patterns that result from these moods, takes much longer to occur than does the change between functionally more proximate moods or behavior patterns (Lorenz, 1978). Life-threatening shortness of breath is another example of an extreme state that precludes any quick switch to a predisposition such as sex or hunger.

The closely related, sometimes simultaneous aggression and courtship behavior patterns of male intrasexual competition have evolved into differing kinds of behavior in the vertebrate classes. Beatrice Oehlert (1958) was the first to write about this relationship, citing cichlid fish (*Cichlasoma biocellatum* and *Geophagus brasiliensis*) as an example:

Courtship behavior often begins with hostility. When a male is defeated, it immediately loses its interest in courtship behavior and flees. In comparison to this, a submissive female is, despite all readiness to flee, able to perform sexual actions; but the female never shows courtship behavior when she is dominant. If two males meet, they do not pair, because the weaker flees immediately. Two females do not show pairing behavior towards one another . . . [i.e., the dominant one cannot be in a sexual mood at the same time as she is dominant]" (p. 169).

Thus, homosexual pairing is rare, because to engage in courtship behavior, a male, in certain species, must be dominant, and a female must be submissive.

Male/female differences in behavior are especially relevant in species in which the sexes are identical in outward appearance. Certainly, male/female dimorphism in sexual behavior does not show the symmetrical complementariness between the sexes in all vertebrates as is shown in the cichlid fish cited by Oehlert (Table 4.II) and only sometimes functions as a mechanism that prevents homosexual pairings. In many other species, display behavior (an aspect of courtship) is shown almost entirely by the male, from the very beginning of courtship behavior onwards, and this behavior serves both to intimidate other males and to attract females. According to Lorenz (1963), Oehlert's observations can even provide a basis for the understanding of some aspects of gender-based dimorphism in human sexual behavior (see also Bischof, 1979; Eibl-Eibesfeldt, 1967; Medicus, 1987). Lorenz (1963, Chapter VI[8]) wrote: "Two motives, which in one sex scarcely inhibit each other, exclude each other in the other sex in a sharp shunting mechanism." This topic also is discussed in *Human Ethology* by Eibl-Eibesfeldt (1984). (See also Eibl-Eibesfeldt, this volume.) The observations by Oehlert gave the first indication that male/female dimorphism of emotions might better be understood by the considering of phylogeny. A search in this direction in turn may shed light on some variants in human sexual behavior.

In a stable hierarchical relationship, aggression is linked to dominance more than to submission, and fear is linked to submission[9] more than to dominance (see also Eibl-Eibesfeldt, this volume), although many dominance/submission relationships show (almost) no aggression or fear. Also, in many species, even when male courtship and male aggressive competition are not strongly linked with each other, they nevertheless may not inhibit each other.

## Body-Size Dimorphism

Understanding the complex selection mechanisms that regulate size differences between the sexes of a species is a difficult task (Frayer and Wolpoff, 1985). Larger females within a species raise relatively more infants than do the smaller females (cf. Lewin, 1988; Ralls, 1976). This

TABLE 4.II. Effects of certain types of fear and certain types of aggression on male and female sexual behavior of some **animal** species (based on Oehlert, 1958; see also Eibl-Eibesfeldt, 1984; Lorenz, 1963).*

|  | FEAR (of mate) | AGRESSION (hostility toward mate) |
|---|---|---|
| MALES | neutral to inhibit | neutral to facilitate |
| FEMALES | neutral to facilitate | neutral to inhibit |

*In most **human** males and females, sexual arousal usually is **inhibited** by real fear or strong hostile aggression. However, in a relatively few human individuals, sexual arousal can be facilitated by these emotions. Within this population, hostile aggression facilitates sexual arousal almost exclusively in males. In addition, anecdotal evidence indicates that fear can facilitate sexual arousal in more females than in males, although most likely only in a few (sometimes pubescent individuals) (cf. Eibl-Eibesfeldt, this volume). It appears that in humans, the facilitation of sexual arousal by fear or hostile aggression is dependent upon (a) sex, (b) age, (c) situation and context of fear or aggression, and (d) individual differences, e.g., responses learned by the individual within the biological framework. (See text for further explanation.) A phylogenetic heritage might help to explain why, within this population, hostile aggression facilitates sexual arousal more commonly in males and fear most likely has a similar effect more commonly in females.

tendency (i.e., larger females = more offspring) evidently could not counteract the trend of selection for larger males than females in many mammals, however. In polygynous species, though, as a rule,[10] the male is larger. This dimorphism exists because, in the face of marked male competition for females, strong, large, and dominance-seeking males usually develop during phylogeny. One example of unimale-polygyny-induced male largeness is the sea elephant, a species in which the males are up to four times as heavy as the females. Other examples of extreme male/female dimorphism in size are unimale-polygynous hamadryas baboons, orangutans, and gorillas, in which males are approximately twice as heavy as females (Harcourt et al., 1981; Hrdy, 1981; Kummer, 1968; Martin and May, 1981; Mitchell, 1979; Poirier, 1972). Male body size in these mammals appears to be related to the degree of male competition for the female.

Male body size also can be influenced phylogenetically through female sexual selection (Bateson, 1983; O'Donald, 1967; Trivers, 1972, 1985), an intraspecific kind of selection that results from the females' choice of mates. The male descendents of a female who has chosen a large, strong, and dominant male as a mate will have a selective advantage, because large and strong males are more likely to beget large and strong sons capable of intimidating other males. As a result of this intraspecific selection during phylogeny, in many species the male impresses the female by sumptuous and seemingly overenergetic shows of dominance and power (a characteristic that is present, for example, in many mammals and birds). In contrast to the trend of strong males, females of many species (especially polygynous species) have taken on opposite or complementary traits. As mentioned previously, they are smaller and weaker than males and sometimes bear more resemblance to a nonadult than they do to an adult male. As a result of phylogeny, this kind of resemblance also exists in human females, and also based on phylogeny, small size in human females is an attribute that many human males find attractive. It is possible that because of these characteristics of human females, certain traits exhibited by children and adolescents sexually stimulate some adult males. This realization may be important in helping science to understand adult human sexual behavior with children and adolescents.

## Human Male/Female Sexual Dimorphism

As was just noted, the human species is mildly dimorphic sexually. The average human female is smaller in body size than the average human male and has a weaker musculoskeletal build than the male. This dimorphism may have had its origin in polygynous mating systems. Its continuation, however, could be the result of several other factors, one candidate being the division of labor. For example, a strong male, especially one that is of high rank, potentially can provide better protection and resources than a weaker male can. The importance of female sexual selection for these traits is evident. Many adult males try to impress adult females by boasting about their strength and status, whereas the courtship behavior of adult females often invites friendly interaction and is sometimes associated with submission.

Also, in human reproduction as in the reproduction of many other species of animals, most fathers expend less time and energy than do most mothers. This characteristic is one result of selection (but can be modified by culture). However, the characteristic may not be of great significance in terms of the phylogeny of humans, because male/female differences in expenditures of time and energy are relatively more important in species in which fathers do nothing more than sire the children.

Paternal contributions to the care of offspring have increased in humans during more recent phylogeny, a trend that has not occurred in other extant hominoids (apes). Such contributions can vary widely from virtually no investment to almost complete care of the offspring. Paternal investment is manifested by social activities such as sharing food, caring for and protecting the family, and teaching and playing socially with offspring (see Mackey, this volume; cf. Schmidt-Denter, 1984). Offspring receiving biparental care generally are more advantaged than are offspring who lack such care. This comparatively large male contribution to parental investment (relative to other hominoids) may be one reason why certain sexually dimorphic behavioral traits are phylogenetically less distinct in humans than they are in some other primate species. An additional reason may be the previously mentioned compatibility of moods. Male protection of a female and offspring is compatible with externally directed threat, but threat is not appropriate between the protector and the protected. Protection should not be frightening to the protected (cf. text to Table 4.II).

The phylogeny-based capacity to establish long-lasting monogamy appears to be related primarily to biparental care. This capacity is especially relevant under ecological conditions in which brood provisioning cannot be accomplished as well, or even at all, by a single parent. The reproduction-related behavior of many species of birds exemplifies this relationship. In many species, both parents are needed for the successful provisioning of the offspring and are active in the effort, and the parents pairbond. Male mammals lack functional mammary glands and, consequently, cannot contribute to feeding the sucklings during their most dependent period of life. Accordingly, mammals pairbond relatively rarely compared to birds. One example of monogamous mammals is marmosets, New World monkeys the males of which contribute greatly to the raising of the young by carrying the infants (e.g., Welker and Schäfer-Witt, 1987).

From the perspective of sociobiology or socioethology, parental-investment types of behavior make sense only if adult males and adult females raise offspring to whom they are closely related, because the effort will enhance the survival of the genes of the offspring—and consequently, the genes of the adults. Usually, there is no question that females (e.g., female mammals) raise their young. This principle is not always true for males, however, but it can become increasingly so as the paternal certainty of males increases. A male can increase his paternal certainty by monopolizing an individual female for at least one period of estrus, as occurs, for example, in sea elephants and sometimes in chimpanzees. In mammals, both brood provisioning by the female and the sexual monopolization of the female by the male were phylogenetic preconditions for the development of contributions by males to brood provisioning. This behavior then resulted in more permanent male/female bonding and, also, allowed a female to monopolize the paternal investment for her own family. In human societies, adult females and males often direct some of their parental investment beyond their own offspring, contributing toward the rearing of their sisters' and brothers' offspring, with whom they share, on average,

25% of their variant genes. (Concerning avuncular relationships, cf. Chagnon and Irons, 1979; Eibl-Eibesfeldt, 1984.)

As stated previously, adult/adult pairbonding (i.e., affiliation, attachment) is relatively rare in mammals as compared with birds. Yet, as has been shown, adult male/female pairbonding does develop in mammals to varying degrees. This statement applies to humans, in which the degree of such bonding is shown by a variety of expressions from monogamy through polygamy. Attempts to categorize the degree of pairbonding in all humans requires an oversimplification, because there is considerable intersocietal variance in both monogamous and polygamous relationships. For example, even though monogamy is professed through socially sanctioned marriage, it is not necessarily strictly followed. Conversely, in cultures in which polygyny is permitted, it is realized in a relatively small percentage of adult males, who command adequate resources to procure and support several wives. (Polygyny [one male/many females] is found more often than polyandry [one female/many males]). Also, male/female bonds of affection do not necessarily last a lifetime, and as one bond ends and the next begins, a pattern of serial monogamy is produced in some societies.

Some aspects of human mating systems can be understood by means of cross-cultural comparisons (e.g., Ford and Beach, 1951; Symons, 1979). Lifelong and relatively strict monogamy does exist in some cultures (although perhaps somewhat at odds with the nature mainly of human males), and it can be interpreted as being a cultural adaptation that increases cooperation in the rearing of young,[11] facilitates the avoidance of social conflicts among families, or as proposed in more recent literature, helps to prevent the contraction of sexually transmitted diseases.

The significance of ethopsychology to the understanding of adult human sexual behavior with children and adolescents is that ethopsychology shows why even married adult males with relatively regular opportunities for sexual intercourse can be vulnerable to sexual attraction, arousal, and behavior with children and adolescents while adult females are less vulnerable. Ethopsychology demonstrates why many adult males who actually are married and have offspring of their own (Alter-Reid et al., 1986; Daly and Wilson, 1985) can become sexually involved with children and adolescents. Also, ethopsychology can address an interesting question— whether maternal feelings affect sexuality differently than do paternal feelings. Again, it must be emphasized that demonstrating why males are predisposed more than females to such behavior in no way justifies relationships that can be detrimental to any partner. The elucidation of the reasons simply helps to explain the phenomenon.

## Biopsychology of Human Courtship

Male/female dimorphism of sexual behavior is observable in humans. In general, human males search for a partner and court more "ardently" and obviously than do the "reluctant" human females (Symons, 1979). Also, in common with the probabilities that are pertinent to most other mammalian males and females, human males are more likely to initiate obvious and overt sexual actions than are human females (e.g., Ellis, 1986; Goodman, 1976; Goy and McEwen, 1980; Masica, Money, and Ehrhardt, 1971; Michael, 1968; Money and Ehrhardt, 1972; Money and Mathews, 1982; Money, Schwartz, and Lewis, 1984; Symons, 1979). In addition, masturbation is more likely to be self-discovered by young human males after puberty than by young human females. Once the behavior is discovered, young males engage in it more frequently than young females, and more young males practice it than young females (e.g., Kinsey, Pomeroy, and Martin, 1948; Kinsey et al., 1953).

Among humans, males are more[12] easily sexually aroused by visual stimuli of anonymous sexually provocative adult females than are females by similar visual stimuli of anonymous sexually provocative males (see Feierman, this volume, Chapter 1). Also, males are aroused by novelty (e.g., by variety of sexual partners) more than females are. This dimorphism is in accordance with natural selection, because males with such a proclivity have more offspring than males without it. Apart from the fact that human males often are attracted to specific physical or cosmetic attributes in their female counterparts, many males do not appear to be very particular in their choice of sexual partners. This broad-mindedness exists because males do not necessarily expend much time and energy in reproduction. Clearly, a female who mates with many males will not increase her fitness as much as a male who mates with many females (e.g., Freedman, 1979; Smith, 1984), because once a female is pregnant, further matings during her pregnancy will not lead to more offspring. In many tribal societies, as well as in much of the "Third World," human females spend most of their fertile lifetime either pregnant or nursing. The male/female dimorphism in the number of offspring that humans can produce makes it likely that male/female differences in biopsychological skills were selected for.

Differences in the desire for polygamy can also be observed by comparing male and female homosexuals. Most sociosexual affiliative bonds between male homosexuals are not as enduring as are those between most female homosexuals. During their lifetimes, female homosexuals usually have far fewer sexual partners than male homosexuals (Hooker, 1967; Kinsey et al., 1953; Symons, 1979). In the case of heterosexual relations, Symons (1979) emphasized that many human males are likely to establish social bonds (if any) to attain sexual access and that human females are more likely to accept sexual behavior to attain social affiliative bonds. If such an affiliative bond is really established, human males are more likely to contribute in child rearing.[13]

As is true of other vertebrate males during courtship, many courting human males try to impress females by direct and indirect displays of power, status, and resources. The impressive but usually affiliative behavior of human males during the search-and-pursue stage of courtship is a form of ritualized threat that developed phylogenetically from male intrasexual competition. Because of the potential protective ability of males, many females tend to find male strength attractive; they often respond positively to high-status characteristics (e.g., Miller, 1981).

Some body traits of adult human females, such as smooth skin, relative hairlessness, and softness, make them resemble children. Adult males usually have fewer of these kind of body traits or have some of them to a lesser degree. In the human female, traits of smallness, tenderness, and childlike features (cf. "child schema" of Lorenz, 1943; see also Schleidt, 1962) can be exaggerated by aspects of culture, e.g., by fashion, cosmetics, and learned behavior, to the point that females actually appear to be helpless and in need of male protection. It is important to emphasize that by no means all males seek small helpless females and that mate selection in many cultures does not emphasize such qualities, although male attraction to childlike features and behavior in females may be an innate tendency. Another important and contrasting characteristic of attraction in males can be material qualities and attributes of economic competence.

Human female courtship behavior, such as proceptive flirting behavior, is less boastfully threatening than is the behavioral counterpart in some males and sometimes is associated with submission and insecurity (Grammer, paper in preparation) rather than with strong competition or aggression. Combinations of nonthreatening behavior with finely tuned interactive behavior often are characteristic of female courtship behavior (Beckmann, 1977; Buss, 1985; Lockard and Adams, 1980; Moore, 1985; Perper and Weis, 1987; Wilson and Lang, 1981). Despite the previously mentioned male/female behavioral differences in the search-and-pursue aspect of courtship, human females often initiate courtship with a desirable male, e.g., by inconspicuous and brief eye contact, by preening, or by other attention-getting proceptive behaviors (e.g., Beach, 1976; Moore, 1985). There is much cultural variation in female strategies of competition. Nevertheless, in general, even when they are in competition for a high-status male, females may use these inconspicuous (and seemingly passive) methods of seeking contact.

Courtship behavior in adult females actually is similar in some ways to the behavior of children and adolescents (see Eibl-Eibesfeldt, this volume; Feierman, this volume, Chapter 1), and it appears that many pedophiles and ephebophiles misinterpret friendly behavior by children and adolescents as being sexually seductive. Human females frequently control the development of interaction by acknowledging or ignoring male behavior. To exert this control, females use a variety of nonverbal signals (e.g., Givens, 1978; Perper and Weis, 1987). Such subtle and finely tuned interactive behavior is certainly more developed in most adults than it is in children and adolescents.

Coyness,[14] one adult female response to a male's courtship efforts, may lengthen the period of time in which a mutual decision is made. Human females do not value superficial physical qualities and sexual attractiveness in a potential mate as much as males do. In addition to sexual relations, females are more likely to seek affection, as well as the capacity for intimacy, security, and trust and the ability of potential fathers to provide for their offspring (Strassmann, 1981). Because females seek these returns, the length and quality of acquaintance from which a mutual decision can arise is particularly important to the female during the process of pairbonding. But the adaptational causes of a behavior in general and sexual choice in particular are certainly not always conscious in humans (e.g., during courtship).

## Biosocial Consequences

The previously mentioned differences between the sexes in appearance and behavior, caused by mutation and intraspecific selection, have consequences that go beyond courtship and sexual behavior. Because of their nonaggressive, nonthreatening appearance and behavior, human females are usually treated as if they were of lower rank, even if they are of equal rank or status with males (e.g., Rosenblatt and Cunningham, 1976). For example, it is noticeable that both sexes (except a courting male) normally accord all females less attention and status than they accord all males (e.g., Greif, 1980; Thorne and Henley, 1975; Zimmermann and West, 1975).

The male's conflict in courtship consists of his keeping rivals at a distance while he approaches the female. The conflict for the female is that the courting male can be perceived either as being threatening or as offering security. In the eyes of a male in a competitive context, the nonthreatening behavior of adult females and young may appear to be a signal of weakness and, therefore, may be perceived as submission, even if the behavior is not intended as such by an adult female partner. Therefore, there may be a certain phylogenetic basis for the relative lack of status of females and young that is conferred by adult males and females. However, this kind of "submission" can also be seen as a social skill that may be used to de-escalate tendencies toward conflict, to achieve appeasement, and to promote positive social relations.

## Conclusion

So far, this chapter has tried to develop a phylogenetic understanding of why there is a functional relationship between tendencies towards aggression, fear, and sexual behavior between the two sexes and how the relationship operates (e.g., Brown, 1981; Cordoba and Chapel, 1983; Donovan, 1985; Eibl-Eibesfeldt, 1984; Gray, 1971; Lorenz, 1963; Marshall and Christie, 1981; Oehlert, 1958; Revitch, 1980; Rubin, Reinisch, and Haskett, 1981; Spengler, 1979; Spodak, Falck, and Rappeport, 1978; Zillmann, 1984).

As has been pointed out, adult human sexual behavior with children and adolescents can be understood within the context of dimorphism. Male/female differences in sexual behavior result at least in part from the different amounts of energy and time each sex expends for reproduction (see Table 4.I). This initial difference produces a difference in the functional proximity of the moods of fear and aggression to sexual mood (see Table 4.II), as well as a difference in the likelihood for active pursuit of sexual opportunities (Ghesquire, Martin, and Newcombe, 1985).

A biopsychological understanding, derived from the study of the pertinent phylogeny, might be useful in the effort to understand why the seduction of an adult sexual partner may be undertaken, in different forms, by both adult males and adult females but why rape and other forms of sexual violence appear to be committed almost exclusively by a very few males. Ethology helps to provide an understanding of male/female differences in behavior that relate to the frequency of occurrence of variant sexual behavior. By no means does ethology encourage or justify any behavior that harms or takes advantage of a partner (cf. Bischof, 1985).

Like sexual violence, adult human sexual behavior with children and adolescents is almost completely a male phenomenon (e.g., Alter-Reid et al., 1986; Finkelhor, 1979; Lechmann, 1987). One of the most consistent psychological correlates that has been identified is that many adult males who are sexually attracted to children and adolescents show manifestations of (real or self-perceived) social inadequacy with peers. Such males may suffer from feelings of anxiety when they consider sexual behavior with an adult partner (Johnston and Johnston, 1986; Panton, 1979; Segal and Marshall, 1985). Because sex and fear are such functionally distant moods in males, many human adult males cannot perform sexual actions when they feel inferior to their sexual partner or when they feel anxious (e.g., Bancroft, 1985; Eicher, 1980). This explanation is in accordance with the previously mentioned male/female dimorphism in the relationship of mood and behavior (see Table 4.II).

Because of their small size, lack of experience, and sense of insecurity, children and adolescents of either sex do not arouse feelings of inferiority, fear, and anxiety in adult males. Thus, children and adolescents can become "sexual objects" for males who in sociosexual relations with adults feel inferior or anxious. Furthermore, the similarity of appearance between children and adolescents and adult females (cf. "child schema") makes it easier for the male pedophile or ephebophile to substitute a child or an adolescent for an adult female partner. Moreover, as mentioned previously, it is adult males who are more likely to search out and initiate sexual behavior than adult females.

Leaving out the possibility of physical violence, which is very rare, one harmful effect to a child or an adolescent who has experienced sexual activities with an adult might be the absence of the experience of a gradual psychosexual maturation—that is, the absence of the experience of the many stages of falling in love (Kretz, Reichel, and Zöchling, 1987). The degree to which this deficiency may burden a child's or an adolescent's ability to establish meaningful adult relationships is yet to be determined.

The understanding of biopsychological differences between the sexes (in children and adolescents and in adults) provides a biosocial basis of the appreciation of one's own, as well as others', predispositions. However, the realization that comes from this understanding should lead to caution in the attempt to project the understanding of one's own sexuality onto the sexuality of children and adolescents who are developing or onto the sexuality of a partner of the opposite sex. Care also should be taken to avoid extrapolating the male/female differences found in courtship behavior and sexual behavior to other types of interpersonal behavior. Other social relationships should be viewed in their own right.

## Summary

This chapter offered a biology-based contribution toward a better understanding of the male/female dimorphism of human sexual behavior. This dimorphism helps in explaining why adult human sexual behavior with children and adolescents is almost exclusively an adult male phenomenon. However, the views elucidated in this chapter should by no means be misused to excuse or justify socially insensitive behavior toward any adult female, any child, or any adolescent or to reinforce socially unjust male dominance. Rather, biological knowledge that clarifies human behavioral predispositions should encourage the prevention of negative behavior and enhance the personal and social aspects of human relationships.

## Notes

[1]"Phylogenetic" (adjective) or "phylogeny" (noun) means "the change of species by mutation and selection during natural history."

[2]The term "mainly" is an important qualifying term, since no learning program can be **completely** open or closed. Likewise, different species' predispositions for ease of learning the same task show that even simple learning is processed through nerve tissue. The structure of nerve tissue is genetically determined and is under the influence of natural selection.

[3]"Fixed-action patterns" are movements that have an innately constant form and need not be learned, such as a spontaneous smile.

[4]Lorenz (e.g., 1978) defines learning as a modification of behavior that is **almost always** adaptive.

[5]"**Fitness**" means "the sum total of capabilities that give an individual a reproductive advantage over other individuals." **Adaptations** can be considered to be the components of overall fitness.

[6]For example, differences in the intensities of combinable moods. Combinable moods are discussed later in this chapter.

[7]The sex producing the lesser number of the larger germ cells is by definition the female.

[8]In the English version, *On Aggression*, Reprint 1972, p. 89.

[9]Aggression is a behavioral tool used, for example, in gaining dominance. In many species (for example, chimpanzees; for further references, see, e.g., Goodall, 1986), changes in the dominance/submission relationship can occur in relation to estrus; and in many species (e.g., many birds) in which males and females provide brood provisioning, the dominance/submission relationship changes during the period of provisioning.

[10]Here, one exception is the Weddell seal.

[11]Advantages of biparental care for social learning of children can remain as a predominant factor, for example, in some social classes of the industrialized world in which mothers are not predominantly dependent upon paternal economic help.

[12]The word "more" is used to emphasize that human females, too, are aroused by visual erotica (although usually not as much by genital close-ups as human males), even though they do not seek it out on their own to the same degree as males (Masica, Money, and Ehrhardt, 1971; Symons, 1979; and others).

[13]During the phylogenetic development of such a social system with a bond between the parents, a perceivable estrus could have lost importance (cf. Benshoof and Thornhill, 1979). In addition, a concealed ovulation (i.e., a not perceivable estrus) might have improved the possibility for the female to better control the selection of a mate to bond with. This is especially important for the female because a bigger variance of parental contributions is possible in males than in females. Instead of a temporary estrus (which cannot be controlled by the female and therefore can occur at the wrong time), permanent traits of attractiveness by certain distributions of fat (i.e., cheeks, hips, breasts) have developed.

[14]Expressions of coyness, which prolong courtship and are exhibited mainly by the female, have a phylogenetic basis: it is a phylogenetically ritualized form of the female conflict between attraction tendencies and flight tendencies (e.g., Eibl-Eibesfeldt, 1967, 1984). Because of the different expenditures for reproduction in terms of time, energy, materials, and risk (cf. reproductive strategies) between the sexes, coyness in courtship is now understandable in mammals as being adaptive for females.

144    Gerhard Medicus and Sigrid Hopf

## References

Alter-Reid, K., Gibbs, M.S., Lachenmeyer, J.R., Sigal, J., and Massoth, N.A. Sexual abuse of children: A review of the empirical findings. *Clinical Psychology Review*, 1986, *6*, 249-266.

Baerends, G.P. On drive, conflict and instinct, and the functional organization of behavior. *In* M.A. Corner and D.F. Swaab (Eds.), *Perspectives in brain research*. Progress in Brain Research series, 45. Amsterdam: Elsevier, 1976, pp. 427-447.

Bancroft, J. *Grundlagen und Probleme menschlicher Sexualität*. Stuttgart: Ferdinand Enke Verlag, 1985. (Original English version: *Human sexuality and its problems*. Churchill: Longman, 1983.)

Bateson, P. (Ed.). *Mate choice*. Cambridge, England: Cambridge University Press, 1983.

Beach, F.A. Sexual attractivity, proceptivity, and receptivity in female mammals. *Hormones and Behavior*, 1976, *7*, 105-138.

Beckmann, D. Selbst- und Fremdbild der Frau. *Familiendynamik*, 1977, *1*, 35-49.

Bell, G. *The masterpiece of nature, the evolution and genetics of sexuality*. London: Croom Helm, 1982.

Bell, G. Two theories of sex and variation. *Experientia*, 1985, *41*, 1235-1245.

Benshoof, L., and Thornhill, R. The evolution of monogamy and concealed ovulation in humans. *J. of Social and Biological Structures*, 1979, *2*, 95-106.

Bischof, N. Comparative ethology of incest avoidance. *In* R. Fox (Ed.), *Biosocial anthropology*. London: Malaby Press, 1975, pp. 37-67.

Bischof, N. Der biologische Sinn der Zweigeschlechtlichkeit. *In* E. Sullerot (Ed.), *Die Wirklichkeit der Frau*. München: Steinhausen, 1979, pp. 38-60.

Bischof, N. *Das Rätsel Oedipus*. München: Piper, 1985. (English translation in preparation.)

Brown, W.A. Testosterone and human behavior. *International Journal of Mental Health*, 1981, *9*, 45-66.

Buss, D.M. Human mate selection. *American Scientist*, 1985, *73*, 47-51.

Chagnon, N.A., and Irons, W. (Eds.). *Evolutionary biology and human social behavior*. North Scituate, Mass.: Duxbury Press, 1979.

Cordoba, O.A., and Chapel, J.L. Medroxyprogesterone acetate antiandrogen treatment of hypersexuality in a pedophiliac sex offender. *American Journal of Psychiatry*, 1983, *140*, 1036-1039.

Cranach, M. von (Ed.). *Methods of inference from animal to human behavior*. Chicago: Aldine, 1976.

Daly, M., and Wilson, M. Child abuse and other risks of not living with both parents. *Ethology and Sociobiology*, 1985, *6*, 197-210.

Donovan, B.T. *Hormones and human behavior*. Cambridge, England: Cambridge University Press, 1985.

Eibl-Eibesfeldt, I. *Grundriss der vergleichenden Verhaltensforschung*. München: Piper, 1967. (English translation: *Ethology, the biology of behavior*, New York: Holt, Rinehart, and Winston, 1970.)

Eibl-Eibesfeldt, I. *Liebe und Hass*. München: Piper, 1970. (English translation: *Love and hate. The natural history of behavior patterns*. New York: Holt, Rinehart, and Winston, 1972.)

Eibl-Eibesfeldt, I. *Die Biologie des menschlichen Verhaltens: Grundriss der Humanethologie*. München: Piper, 1984. (English translation: *Human ethology*. New York: Aldine de Gruyter, in press.)

Eicher, W. (Ed.). *Sexualmedizin in der Praxis*. Stuttgart, New York: Gustav Fischer Verlag, 1980.

Ellis, L. Evidence of neuroandrogenic etiology of sex roles from a combined analysis of human, nonhuman primate and nonprimate mammalian studies. *Personality and Individual Differences*, 1986, *7*, 519-552.

Finkelhor, D. *Sexually victimized children*. New York: Macmillan, 1979.

Ford, C.S., and Beach, F.A. *Patterns of sexual behavior*. New York: Harper & Row, 1951.

Frayer, D.W., and Wolpoff, M.H. Sexual dimorphism. *Ann. Rev. Anthropol.*, 1985, *14*, 429-473.

Freedman, D.G. *Human sociobiology*. New York: The Free Press, Macmillan, 1979.

Ghesquire, J., Martin, R.D., and Newcombe, F. (Eds.). *Human sexual dimorphism*. London: Taylor and Francis, 1985.

Givens, D.B. The nonverbal basis of attraction: Flirtation, courtship, and seduction. *Psychiatry*, 1978, *41*, 346-359.

Goodall, J. *The chimpanzees of Gombe*. Cambridge, Mass.: Harvard University Press, 1986.

Goodman, J.D. The behavior of hypersexual delinquent girls. *American Journal of Psychiatry*, 1976, *133*, 662-668.

Goy, R.W., and McEwen, B.S. *Sexual differentiation of the brain*. Cambridge Mass.: The MIT Press, 1980.

Grammer, K. Strangers meet: Laughter and non-verbal signals of interest in mixed sex encounters. Paper in preparation.

Gray, J.A. Sex differences in emotional behavior in mammals including Man: Endocrine bases. *Acta Psychologica*, 1971, *35*, 29-46.

Greif, E.B. Sex differences in parent-child conversation. *Women's Studies Int. Quart.*, 1980, *3*, 253-258.

Harcourt, A.H., Harvey, P.H., Larson, S.G., and Short, R.V. Testis weight, body weight and breeding system in primates. *Nature*, 1981, *293*, 55-57.

Hoekstra, R.F. Why do organisms produce gametes of only two different sizes? Some theoretical aspects of the evolution of anisogamy. *Journal of Theoretical Biology*, 1980, *87*, 785-793.

Hooff, J.A. van. A comparative approach to the phylogeny of laughter and smiling. *In* R.A. Hinde (Ed.), *Nonverbal communication*. Cambridge, England: Cambridge University Press, 1972, pp. 209-241.

Hooker, E. The homosexual community. *In* J.H. Gagnon and W. Simon (Eds.), *Sexual deviance*. New York: Harper & Row, 1967, pp. 167-184.

Hrdy, S.B. *The woman that never evolved*. Cambridge, Mass.: Harvard University Press, 1981.

Hutt, C. *Males & females*. Middlesex, England: Penguin, 1972.

Johnston, F.A., and Johnston, S.A. Differences between human figure drawings of child molesters and control groups. *Journal of Clinical Psychology*, 1986, *42*, 638-647.

Jolly, A. The evolution of primate behavior. New York: Macmillan, 1972.

Kinsey, A.C., Pomeroy, W.B., and Martin, C.E. *Sexual behavior in the human male*. Philadelphia: W.B. Saunders, 1948.

Kinsey, A.C., Pomeroy, W.B., Martin, C.E., and Gebhard, P.H. *Sexual behavior in the human female*. Philadelphia: W.B. Saunders, 1953.

Kretz, I., Reichel, R., and Zöchling, M. *Sexueller Missbrauch von Kindern in Österreich*. Wien: Informations-Service des Bundesministeriums für Familie, Jugend und Konsumentenschutz, 1987.

Kummer, H. *Social organization of hamadryas baboons*. Chicago: University of Chicago Press, 1968.

Lechmann, C. Erzwungene Liebe. *Psychologie heute*, 1987, *10*, 63-67.

Lee, P.C., and Steward, R.S. (Eds.). *Sex differences, cultural and developmental dimensions*. New York: Urizen Books, 1976.

Lewin, R. *Why is the world full of large females?* Science, 1988, *240*, 884.

Lewontin, R.C. *The genetic basis of evolutionary change*. No. XXV, Columbia Biological Series. New York: Columbia University Press, 1974.

Leyhausen, P. Biologie von Ausdruck und Eindruck (1967). *In* K. Lorenz and P. Leyhausen (Eds.), *Antriebe tierischen und menschlichen Verhaltens, Gesammelte Abhandlungen*. München: Piper, 1968, pp. 297-407.

Lockard, J.S., and Adams, R.M. Courtship behaviors in public: Different age/sex roles. *Ethology and Sociobiology*, 1980, *1*, 245-253.

Lorenz, K. Die angeborenen Formen möglicher Erfahrung. *Zeitschrift für Tierpsychologie*, 1943, *5*, 235-409.

Lorenz, K. *Das sogenannte Böse. Zur Naturgeschichte der Aggression*. Wien: Borotha-Schoeler, 1963. (English translation: *On aggression*. London: Methuen University Paperback, reprint 1972.)

Lorenz, K. *Die Rückseite des Spiegels. Versuch einer Naturgeschichte menschlichen Erkennens*. Munich: Piper, 1973. (English translation:

*Behind the mirror. A search for a natural history of human knowledge.* London: Methuen, 1977.)

Lorenz, K. Analogy as a source of knowledge. Les Prix Nobel en 1973. The Nobel Foundation, 1974, pp. 185-195. (This talk also was published in *Science*, 1974, *185*, 229-234.)

Lorenz, K. *Vergleichende Verhaltensforschung. Grundlagen der Ethologie.* Wien: Springer, 1978. (English translation: *The foundations of ethology.* New York: Springer, 1983.)

Maccoby, E.E., and Jacklin, C.N. *The psychology of sex differences.* Stanford, Calif.: Stanford University Press, 1974.

Marshall, W.L., and Christie, M.M. Pedophilia and aggression. *Criminal Justice and Behavior*, 1981, *8*, 145-158.

Martin, R.D., and May, R.M. Outward signs of breeding. *Nature*, 1981, *293*, 7-9.

Masica, D.N., Money, J., and Ehrhardt, A.A. Fetal feminization and female gender identity in the testicular feminizing syndrome of androgen insensitivity. *Archives of Sexual Behavior*, 1971, *1*, 131-142.

Mayr, E. Sexual selection and natural selection. *In* B. Campbell (Ed.), *Sexual selection and the descent of Man 1871-1971.* London: Heinemann, 1972, pp. 87-104.

McPhail, J.D. Predation and the evolution of a stickleback (*Gasterosteus*). *J. Fisheries Research Board of Canada*, 1969, *26*, 3183-3208.

Medicus, G. Toward an etho-psychology: A phylogenetic tree of behavioral capabilities proposed as a common basis for communication between current theories in psychology and psychiatry. *In* J.R. Feierman (Guest Ed.), *The Ethology of Psychiatric Populations. Ethology and Sociobiology*, 1987, *8*(3S), 131S-150S, supplement.

Michael, R.P. (Ed.). *Endocrinology and human behavior.* London: Oxford University Press, 1968.

Michod, R.E., and Levin, B.R. (Eds.). *The evolution of sex.* Sunderland, Mass.: Sinauer, 1988.

Miller, C.T. Effects of dominance cues on attributions of sexual behavior. *Journal of Research in Personality*, 1981, *15*, 135-146.

Mitchell, G. *Behavioral sex differences in nonhuman primates.* New York: Van Nostrand Reinhold Company, 1979.

Money, J., and Ehrhardt, A. *Man and woman, boy and girl: The differentiation and dimorphism of gender identity from conception to maturity.* Baltimore: Johns Hopkins Press, 1972.

Money, J., and Mathews, D. Prenatal exposure to virilizing progestins: An adult follow-up study of twelve women. *Archives of Sexual Behavior*, 1982, *11*, 73-83.

Money, J., Schwartz, M., and Lewis, V.G. Adult erotosexual status and fetal hormonal masculinization and demasculinization: 46,XX congenital virilizing adrenal hyperplasia and 46,XY androgen-insensitivity syndrome compared. *Psychoneuroendocrinology*, 1984, *9*, 405-414.

Moore, M.M. Nonverbal courtship patterns in women; context and consequences. *Ethology and Sociobiology*, 1985, *6*, 237-247.

O'Donald, P. A general model of sexual and natural selection. *Heredity*, 1967, *22*, 499-518.

Oehlert, B. Kampf und Paarbildung einiger Cichliden. *Zeitschrift für Tierpsychologie*, 1958, *15*, 141-174.

Panton, J.H. MMPI profile configurations associated with incestuous and non-incestuous child molesting. *Psychological Reports*, 1979, *45*, 335-338.

Parker, G.A. Selection on non-random fusion of gametes during the evolution of anisogamy. *Journal of Theoretical Biology*, 1978, *73*, 1-28.

Parker, G.A. Why are there so many tiny sperm? Sperm competition and the maintenance of two sexes. *Journal of Theoretical Biology*, 1982, *96*, 281-294.

Perper, T., and Weis, D.L. Proceptive and rejective strategies of U.S. and Canadian college women. *The Journal of Sex Research*, 1987, *23*, 455-480.

Ploog, D., Hopf, S., and Winter, P. Ontogenese des Verhaltens von Totenkopfaffen (*Saimiri sciureus*). *Psychol. Forsch.*, 1967, *31*, 1-41.

Poirier, F.E. (Ed.). *Primate socialization*. New York: Random House, 1972.

Ralls, K. Mammals in which females are larger than males. *The Quarterly Review of Biology*, 1976, *51*, 245-276.

Rechenberg, J. *Evolutionsstrategie: Optimierung technischer Systeme nach Prinzipien der biologischen Evolution*. Stuttgart: Frommann, 1973.

Revitch, E. Gynocide and unprovoked attacks on women. *Corrective and Social Psychiatry and Journal of Behavior Technology, Methods and Therapy*, 1980, *26*, 6-11.

Riedl, R. *Die Ordnung des Lebendigen*. Hamburg: Parey, 1975. (English translation: *Order in living organisms*. Chichester: John Wiley, 1978.)

Rosenblatt, P.C., and Cunningham, M.R. Sex differences in cross-cultural perspective. *In* B. Lloyd and J. Archer (Eds.), *Exploring sex differences*. London: Academic Press, 1976, pp. 71-94.

Rubin, R.T., Reinisch, J.M., and Haskett, R.F. Postnatal gonadal steroid effects on human behavior. *Science*, 1981, *211*, 1318-1324.

Schleidt, W.M. Die historische Entwicklung der Begriffe "Angeborenes auslösendes Schema" und "Angeborener Auslösemechanismus." *Zeitschrift für Tierpsychologie*, 1962, *19*, 697-722.

Schmidt-Denter, U. *Die soziale Umwelt des Kindes*. Berlin: Springer, 1984.

Segal, Z.V., and Marshall, W.L. Heterosexual social skills in a population of rapists and child molesters. *Journal of Consulting and Clinical Psychology*, 1985, *53*, 55-63.

Shepher, J. *Incest, a biosocial view*. New York: Academic Press, 1983.

Smith, R.L. (Ed.). *Sperm competition and the evolution of animal mating systems*. Orlando: Academic Press, Inc., 1984.

Spengler, A. *Sadomasochisten und ihre Subkulturen.* Frankfurt, New York: Campus Verlag, 1979.

Spodak, M.K., Falck, Z.A., and Rappeport, J.R. The hormonal treatment of paraphiliacs with depo-provera. *Criminal Justice and Behavior,* 1978, *5,* 304-314.

Stearns, S.C. (Ed.). *The Evolution of Sex and Its Consequences.* (*Experientia* Suppl. Vol. 55.) Basel: Birkhäuser Verlag, 1987.

Strassmann, B.I. Sexual selection, parental care, and concealed ovulation in humans. *Ethology and Sociobiology,* 1981, *2,* 31-40.

Symons, D. *The evolution of human sexuality.* New York: Oxford University Press, 1979.

Thorne, B., and Henley, N. (Eds.). *Language and sex: Difference and dominance.* Rowley, Mass.: Newbury House, 1975.

Trivers, R.L. Parental investment and sexual selection. *In* B. Campbell (Ed.), *Sexual selection and the descent of Man 1871-1971.* London: Heinemann, 1972, pp. 136-179.

Trivers, R.L. *Social evolution.* Menlo Park, Calif.: The Benjamin/Cummings Publishing Company, Inc., 1985.

Welker, C., and Schäfer-Witt, C. On the carrying behaviour of basic South American primates. *Human Evolution,* 1987, *5,* 459-473.

Wickler, W. *Sind wir Sünder? Naturgesetze der Ehe.* München: Droemer Knaur, 1969. (English translation: *The sexual code.* New York: Doubleday, 1972.)

Wickler, W. *Stammesgeschichte und Ritualisierung. Zur Entstehung tierischer und menschlicher Verhaltensmuster.* München: Piper, 1970.

Wickler, W., and Seibt, U. *Männlich weiblich.* München: Piper, 1983.

Wiepkema, P.R. An ethological analysis of the reproductive behavior of the bitterling (*Rhodeus amarus Bloch*). *Extr. des Archives Nèerlaandaises de Zoologie,* 1961, *14,* 103-199.

Wilson, G.D., and Lang, R.J. Sex differences in sexual fantasy patterns. *Personality and Individual Differences,* 1981, *2,* 343-346.

Zillmann, D. *Connections between sex and aggression.* Hillsdale, N.J.: Lawrence Erlbaum Associates Publishers, 1984.

Zimmermann, D.H., and West, C. Sex roles, interruptions and silences in conversation. *In* B. Thorne and N. Henley (Eds.), *Language and sex: Difference and dominance.* Rowley, Mass.: Newbury House, 1975, pp. 105-129.

# 5
# Dominance, Submission, and Love: Sexual Pathologies from the Perspective of Ethology

Irenäus Eibl-Eibesfeldt
*Forschungsstelle für Humanethologie in der*
*Max-Planck-Gesellschaft*
*D-8138 Andechs*
*Federal Republic of Germany*

## Introduction

In attempting to understand adult human sexual behavior with children and adolescents, the researcher must realize that although human beings tend to associate sex with love, sex without love or tenderness also exists in humans as part of the archaic vertebrate heritage of the species. Therefore, an understanding of (a) sex without love, i.e., before love existed, in the human phylogenetic past and (b) the means by which love entered adult/adult sexual relationships during human evolution can shed light on many of the unusual and atypical aspects of sexual behavior that are found in human societies today. This chapter will take a brief look at some of the developments throughout human phylogenetic history that changed sexual relationships from ones characterized primarily by dominance/submission relations to a sexuality characterized by affiliative relations, bonding, and love. The suggestions will be made that vestiges of a sexuality based on dominance-and-submission relations without love are still present in some human sexual behaviors and that, if these sexual behaviors are not under the control of love, this dissociation may predispose some individuals to engage in one type of adult human sexual behavior with children and adolescents.

Another type of adult/child and adult/adolescent sexual behavior is interpreted as being the result of the evolutionary origins of adult/adult romantic or erotic love. Both types of adult human sexual behavior with children and adolescents will be discussed in this chapter.

Throughout the chapter, the terms "affiliation," "bonding," and "love" are used. When two individuals merely come together, their interaction is simply called an "association." There are many types of associations, and many of them are not based on affiliation, bonding, or love. For example, if animals come together because they are attracted by certain features of the environment, such as a common food supply or a protected sleeping place, the word "aggregation" is used to describe the community. Aggregations may also be based on mutual social attraction. Such social aggregations occur as anonymous groups in which individuals do not recognize each other, such as schools of fish. They also occur as social groups in which individuals do recognize each other and in which individual social interactions are structured by relationships of dominance and submission. The latter kind of social aggregation is characterized by what might be called "agonal sociality."

Affiliations differ from aggregations in that the former involve nurturant behavior (or, in humans, "friendly" behavior), such as grooming, kissing, or feeding. Affiliations can be anonymous, as occurs in social insects, or individualized, as occurs in birds and mammals, when personal relations are based on individual recognition. Bonding is the basis and the mechanism of affiliation. Two individuals are said to be bonded if their relationship is a friendship based upon affiliation. The term "bond" denotes a presumed underlying mechanism. In humans, this mechanism works through the emotions, and it may do so in animals, as well, although science can do no more than speculate about this possibility, since it is unknown how or whether animals feel. Recent studies, which are shedding some light on the chemical basis of emotions, eventually may clarify some of the mechanisms behind bonding.

The term "love" implies an association that is of stronger intensity than is the intensity meant by "affiliation." For example, it is usual to have an affiliative relationship with neighbors or co-workers, but most people do not use the term "love" in this context. Love often is divided into types, such as platonic, fraternal, parental, romantic, and erotic. It is beyond the scope of this chapter to address the types of love, although it is most probable that they all have much in common. It is sufficient in this chapter to simply say that love is an intense affiliative relationship based upon an affectual bond between two individuals.

# Sex Before Love Existed

## Reptiles

The absence of love or friendly interactions in lower vertebrates can be observed in the marine iguanas on the Galápagos Islands (I. Eibl-Eibesfeldt, personal observation). Hundreds of these large reptiles bask on the rocky coast, lying side by side apparently in gregarious groups (Figures 5.1 and 5.2). However, to a human observer, something appears to be missing. These animals seem simply incapable of any friendly interactions. Anyone familiar with birds and mammals can observe in representatives of both groups a rich repertory of friendly or nurturant behaviors. Birds groom each other in friendly encounters, such as during courtship. They exchange gifts of nesting material during rituals of greeting and feed each other during courtship.

Marine iguanas, however, do nothing similar. The only social behavior that can be observed consists of threat displays, fights, and submission. Males fight one another during the breeding season in a highly ritualized manner. The interaction starts on a rock, with an introductory display during which a pair of rivals circle each other with a strutting gait, demonstrating their respective profiles to the opponent, nodding their heads, and gaping as if intending to bite. Finally, they take positions opposite each other, rush at the opponent, and clash head-on with lowered heads. A wrestling tournament ensues, with each attempting to push the other from the rock. This contest of strength continues until one is pushed off. An alternative conclusion often occurs in such battles, in that one individual behaves as if he "realizes" he has no chance to win. In such a case, he assumes a submissive posture, lying flat on his belly, thus discouraging further attacks. Then, while the rival waits in threatening posture, the loser scuttles away (Figure 5.3a and 5.3b).

Such ritual fights may not seem extraordinary to the human observer, but the interesting fact is that males also use the intimidation display—and only this display—for courtship. The male approaches the female in full threat display. If she is ready to copulate, she simply assumes the submissive posture, whereupon he grasps her at the nape of her neck with his jaws, pins her down, mounts, and copulates. If she is not ready, she simply runs as he approaches. Direct observation of these lizards, and an examination of the literature, show that the social behavior of reptiles, including their sexual behavior, is based upon dominance-and-submission relationships (Greenberg and MacLean, 1978). One can describe their sexual behavior as an agonal, hierarchal sexuality based on male-dominance and female-submission behaviors.

Figure 5.1

Figure 5.2

Figures 5.1 and 5.2. Marine iguanas (*Amblyrhynchus cristatus*) on the Galápagos Islands, gregarious but unable to interact in an affiliative and/or friendly way. (Photographs by I. Eibl-Eibesfeldt.)

## Fish

In most of the fish in which the courtship of individuals occurs, the situation is similar: males display, females submit. In a number of cichlid fish that lack sexual dimorphism, however, both sexes display, and the male can mate only if he succeeds in dominating the female. In addition to what is learned through behavioral analysis, the motivational analysis of cichlid fish has demonstrated that sexual behavior in the male is inhibited if he is fearful but not if he is aggressive. Conversely, sexual behavior in the female is inhibited if she is aggressive but not if she is fearful (Oehlert, 1958). (Also see Medicus and Hopf, this volume.) There are some variations in the courtship behavior of cichlids, such as in some mouthbreeding cichlids in which the male lures the female to the spawning site, taking advantage of the female's readiness to respond to eggs by presenting the "egg spot" markings that occur on his anal fin as a luring device. In general, however, interactions that seem to be truly affiliative cannot be observed in fish, and the dominance/submission mechanisms play the decisive part.

## Sexual Behavior in the Context of Love in Birds and Mammals: From Parental to Romantic Love

Friendly or nurturant behavior is a relatively late addition to the repertory of vertebrate behavior, and it most likely developed out of parental care provided to infants. With the evolution of parental-care behaviors came the existence of such activities as the feeding, warming, and grooming of young, activities to which the young respond in a positive way by seeking the proximity of the nurturing parent. The young in turn developed signs and signals that trigger caretaking responses. Once these behaviors between parent and child had evolved, they were used in reinforcing parent/child affiliation and also were extended to other relationships. They were a preadaptation, so to speak, enabling adults to form affiliative relationships. Indeed, they are used in this way. If one observes courtship and greeting rituals in birds and mammals, one soon becomes aware that the patterns by which a friendly affiliation is established, upheld, or strengthened are basically derived from maternal behaviors and infantile appeals that trigger these patterns (Eibl-Eibesfeldt, 1966, 1970a; Wickler, 1967a). When European sparrows court, they employ, among other signals, infantile appeals. A courting male may act like a nestling, fluttering his wings and gaping. This behavior attracts the female, who then feeds him. She, in turn, might employ the infantile appeal to trigger his friendly feeding response. Pairs of the African bird *Trachyphonus* sing together in duets. The males incorporate into their part of the song begging    songs    of    the    young.    The    finches    of    the    genus    *Lonchura*

a

b

Figure 5.3. (a) Male marine iguanas on the Galápagos Islands engage in ritualized fights, pushing each other with their heads. (b) This headbutting tournament ends when one individual (left) assumes a submissive posture, lying flat on his belly. (Photographs by I. Eibl-Eibesfeldt.)

demonstrate beak clattering during courtship, a motor pattern derived from feeding the young (Wickler and Uhrig, 1969).

In many birds, as can be seen, broodcare feeding became ritualized into friendly displays, such as courtship feeding with or without the transfer of food (Figures 5.4 and 5.5). Similar developments can be observed in mammals. Chimpanzees greet each other by embrace and by lip-to-lip contact. Sometimes food is transferred, which reveals that this behavior pattern had its origin in maternal kissfeeding. In humans, too, adults kissfeed babies. However, kissfeeding also is an expression of tenderness, and in this function, it is not restricted to the adult/infant relationship. In all of the cultures with which this author is familiar, children are kissed by adults, and adults express affection toward one another in the same way (Figures 5.6-5.10). Kissing occurs among adults in a great variety of societies. In the *Kamasutra*, the Indian book of love, is found the remark that lovers exchange wine mouth to mouth. A Japanese text from pre-European times warns lovers not to stick their tongue into the mouth of a woman during orgasm because she might bite (Eibl-Eibesfeldt, 1970a). Recently, this author noted kissfeeding ceremonies in the designs of pre-Columbian Peruvian pottery. Lovers kissfeed each other in the Wiru, Southern Highlands, in New Guinea. In most societies, kissing does not occur in public, because nonindustrialized societies are less exhibitionistic than are the societies of the industrialized world, particularly of the industrialized West. Researchers do not know, therefore, how widespread kissing and kissfeeding are in intimate relations (Eibl-Eibesfeldt, 1986).

The motor pattern in kissing clearly portrays its origin from kissfeeding, with one partner playing the accepting part by opening the mouth in babyish fashion and the other partner performing tongue movements as if to pass food. In humans, of course, feeding occurs in many culturally elaborated and derived forms, such as in the presentation of gifts of food.

In many mammals, infantile appeals are used to diminish a partner's fear and to buffer aggression. When a male hamster follows a female during courtship, he utters the call by which a baby hamster alerts its mother when it is in distress. A wolf approaches a high-ranking individual of its pack by pushing with its snout against the corners of the mouth of the high-ranking individual. Wolf pups perform this behavior when they beg for food. In submission, a wolf rolls onto its back, offering its belly to the opponent in the way pups do when they offer themselves for cleaning to their mothers. Often, the lower ranking wolf urinates, which releases licking by the dominant one. Thus, a hostile relation can be turned into a friendly one (Figure 5.11) (Schenkel, 1967). These examples should be sufficient to illustrate the point that these parental behaviors, which evolved independently in birds and mammals, constitute a turning point in the evolution of sociality, because the behaviors introduced signals of

Figure 5.4 (a) and (b). Parental feeding in the common tern (a) and in the raven (b). Tthe derived courtship ritual: (a) a male tern courts with a fish in his beak while the female begs in an infantile role; (b) a raven pair during courtship feeding. The terns (left and right) are a; the ravens (left and right) are b. (Drawings by H. Kacher, after photographs by H. Rittinghaus (a) and E. Gwinner (b) in Wickler, 1969.)

Figure 5.5. Courting female black-headed gull begging for food in the infantile manner. (Drawing by H. Kacher, after a photograph by N. Tinbergen in Eibl-Eibesfeldt, 1970a.)

friendliness into vertebrate behavior. Furthermore, these behaviors gave origin to the development of affiliative relationships. In many birds and mammals, there are individual affiliative relationships between mother and infant that function in securing the attachment of the two individuals in a long-lasting relationship. Sometimes, as in sheep, goats, and sea lions, the affiliation takes place in a very short period, immediately after birth, during which mother and newborn are extremely sensitive to each other. Once an affiliation between mother and infant has been established, mothers respond to young that are not their own with rejection. Since the personal affiliation is in essence what characterizes love, it can be said that with maternal care, love came into the world. With the development of maternal care, a decisive step in the evolution of social behavior was taken. Group life based in part upon friendly relations and love could develop. New social potentialities opened up. Even humankind's nation ethos is a derivation and extension of its family ethos.

With the evolution of parental care and the affiliative mechanisms that developed with it, adult/adult sexual relations had the potential to become affiliative. Therefore, researchers can speak of an affiliative sexuality, i.e., one characterized by friendly behavior and in many cases, though not in all, by love. In humans, in whom the maturation and socialization period for children is so long, there probably has been strong selection for the strengthening of affiliative sexuality into love. Such an outcome should keep spouses together and thus assure paternal as well as maternal investment. This dual investment, resulting most likely from the affiliative sexuality and the subsequent capability for love that characterizes humans, is the opposite of the nonnurturing behavior of most reptiles toward their offspring, behavior that is commensurate with the agonal sexuality of the reptiles.

## The Reptilian Brain Within Us: Sex, Dominance, and Aggression

That the archaic reptilian brain is still within humans was emphasized by MacLean (1970). It is located in the human forebrain as an assemblage of ganglia as large as a fist, which in its internal organization and chemistry corresponds to a certain area of the brain of reptiles. Dopamine, which acts as a neurotransmitter, is concentrated here in reptiles, birds, and mammals. Superimposed upon this area in mammals is the limbic cortex, which is the old mammalian brain and upon which, in turn, lies the neocortex of the higher mammals. Human aggression is believed to be rooted in the reptilian brain. Valzelli and Morgese (1981) and Bailey (1987) interpret pathological aggression as a regression to the reptilian level associated with cessation of the cortical control. This regression can happen under the influence of alcohol or by active indoctrination. It is postulated that the archaic reptile stratum plays a significant role in human sexual relations and behavior, as well as in aggression.

That there exists a linkage between male sexual behavior and aggression has been amply documented (Zillman, 1986). Studies in various mammals demonstrate this linkage on the physiological and behavioral levels. In the tree shrew (*Tupaja*), for example, blood-testosterone levels are higher in dominant individuals and lower in subdominant and submissive individuals. This principle seems to hold in general in nonhuman primates as well, in which the subdominant individual seems to be psychologically castrated by the presence of the dominant individual. In humans, too, male sexual behavior and dominance appear to be connected. For example, one can observe a significant increase in the plasma-testosterone level after young males win in a tennis match and a significant decrease after they lose (Mazur and Lamb, 1980). Such changes do not occur only in competitions involving bodily exercise. Medical students show a similar increase in the plasma-testosterone level if they pass their examination and a decrease if they fail (Mazur and Lamb, 1980).

Furthermore, there are remarkable expressive-behavior patterns in primates that link male sexual behavior to dominance. When groups of cercopithecid monkeys forage, some males sit guard with their backs to the group, displaying their brilliantly colored genitals. They sit, so to speak, as living border posts, threatening members of other groups with mounting in case they should come too close. If a member of another group does come too close, the guards have erections.

Dominance between group members is also expressed by ritualized mounting, and submission, in turn, is expressed by female-type presenting. From these kinds of greeting rituals have evolved behaviors such as those of hamadryas baboons, in which males approaching high-ranking individuals present as if they, the presenters, were females. Their buttocks are hairless and red in mimicry of the female buttocks, thus enhancing the signal value of presenting (Wickler, 1966, 1967b). The high-ranking individual may mount or just perform the intention to mount in response to the other's presenting. This use by primates of sexual motor patterns to acknowledge dominance rank order has often been interpreted as being equivalent to human homosexuality. This interpretation is an oversimplification. These sexual motor patterns are derived from copulatory behaviors but, then, have acquired a new function related to social hierarchies: mounting serves as an indication of dominance, and presenting serves as an indication of submission, an agonistic buffer in a greeting context (see Anderson and Bielert, this volume). Wickler (1967b) calls these patterns "socio-sexual signals," but the more exact origin of these signals is dominance sexuality.

Phallic displays are not restricted to nonhuman primates. In fact, such displays are used in a variety of interesting ways in human societies, in which they are less often expressed in overt behavior and more often expressed in artifacts such as sculptures that serve the purpose of warding off spirits or evil. Phallic apotropaic figurines are common on old churches in Europe, mainly of the Romanic and Gothic periods. Such figurines also can be found in other societies and in other contexts as well. For example, Hermes, in the mythology of ancient Greece, served as a guardian marking borders and entrances. Phallic figurines that are found in Africa, the New World, and Indonesia serve similar functions. In modern Japan, phallic amulets are used to provide protection. Many of these various figurines have been interpreted as being fertility demons, but they really function as guardians, which is evident from their threatening expressions (Figure 5.12).

As is the case concerning sculptures, direct phallic displays by the human male likewise can be identified as being displays of dominance, because of the accompanying threatening expression on the individual's face. Such displays are rarely observed, however, because of conventions of modesty that are present in most human societies. Among the Eipo in the western part of New Guinea (which belongs to Indonesia), males cover their penises with conspicuous penis gourds, which are used for display in two ways. When a male mocks an enemy, he loosens the cord that holds the gourd against the body. Then, he jumps up and down in place, causing the gourd to swing up and down in a conspicuous way. When startled or surprised, he makes a clicking sound as a sort of warning by flicking his thumbnail against the gourd. At the same time, he utters sacred words, similar to Western Europeans' exclaiming, "Jesus Christ," thus shielding himself by the sacred against a potential danger (Eibl-Eibesfeldt, 1986).

Human males frequently use phallic curses as dominance displays, such as when the Arabs threaten or mock someone with the utterance, "The phallus in your eye." "Fuck you" seems to be the Anglo-Saxon equivalent. Dominance mounting also occurs among humans. For example, the late French consul assigned to Algiers was ritually raped by insurgents in Algeria during the so-called "Algerian War" of independence from France [1954-1962]. There are other examples of that sort known, such as the orgies of rape performed by winning human military troops, orgies that are a clear manifestation of male-dominance sexuality, lacking the affiliative component.

In an institutionalized and ritualized form, adult male sexual behavior with adolescent males plays an important role in the initiation of males in some societies in Melanesia (Creed, 1984). Creed considers this behavior as being a mechanism of control that operates in order to perpetuate a system of inequality based on sex and age. It supports the status and position of older adult males over and against females and younger males (see Schiefenhövel, this volume). In this context, the initiation rites of French youth gangs, which include the leaders' having anal coitus with the aspirants, are noteworthy (Roumajon, 1960).

It can be speculated that, just as male sexual-dominance behavior exists as a part of the archaic vertebrate heritage of humans, so does male sexual-dominance lust exist, with the female counterpart being the lust of submission. Such lust still plays a significant role in normal human sexual behavior, but it is supplemented and controlled by the phylogenetically newly acquired affiliative sexuality and love. Without this supplementation, the expression of such hierarchal lust by humans often is considered to be atypical, that is, variant, or deviant, sexual behavior. The deviance may take a variety of forms. For example, sadism and domination are very likely hypertrophied expressions of male sexual-dominance lust, and its counterpart could well be masochism and bondage, the exaggerated lusts of submission. Whereas the study of phylogeny suggests that dominance should be associated with maleness and submission with femaleness, there also are submissive males and dominant females. Phylogeny can suggest central tendencies only. The variations of these tendencies are yet to be fully understood (see Feierman, this volume, Chapter 1).

In her investigation of human female sexuality, Kitzinger (1984) describes submissive fantasies of adult females in a sexual context. She interprets these fantasies as being a reflection of social reality, while they also are, at least in part, an expression of an old vertebrate female heritage. Culture, of course, can encourage or suppress the submissive components of female sexuality as well as the newer, affiliative aspects. A female student once confided to this author that several times she experienced orgasm while writing school examinations under the pressure of time, a task she always dreaded. This response is an example of the cultural encouragement of female sexuality that is founded on submission, because the student was required to take the examinations. Conversely, a female may pursue sexual arousal by actively seeking fear, in disregard of the influence of culture. For example, in a number of female kleptomaniacs, who steal things they do not need or could actually afford to buy, self-directed sexual motivation is involved. Interviews have revealed that many of these individuals become sexually aroused during stealing (i.e., they are kleptophiles), and some even experience orgasm while running away (Stoller, 1979).

In studying male exhibitionism, Müsch (1976) found that the motivation behind it was less sexuality than the desire to frighten, which reveals that this behavior certainly may be an old phallic-threat behavior gone astray. Meesters (1984) reports that exhibitionists want to demonstrate their superiority by display, which fits the interpretation of Müsch. In addition, some exhibitionists seek to startle or surprise the onlooker, and others seek admiration (J. Money, personal communication).

It also is possible that a certain type of promiscuous and anonymous adult-male/adult-male homosexual behavior may have originated from the archaic vertebrate dominance-and-submission sexuality. This type of adult male homosexual behavior is characterized by frequent changes in sexual partners and, often, by idiosyncratic preferences on the part of the participants for having the role of dominant inserter or submissive recipient. When children and adolescents are involved in sexual behavior with adults, role-related (adult) dominance and (child and adolescent) submission are inevitable. It must be emphasized, however, that archaic hierarchal sexuality is only one possible root of one type of human homosexual behavior. It does not account for much of male homosexuality, and it accounts for almost none of female homosexuality. Homosexuality, both male and female, has many different expressions, which suggests that it has many different origins. Some homosexual males have a clear love relationship, and this type of homosexuality may have its origin in the variance among males in the degree to which their brains are masculinized or defeminized by hormones in utero (Dörner, 1980; Feierman, this volume, Chapter 1; Pillard and Weinrich, 1987). Also, in some adult male androphilic pedo- and ephebophiles who become sexually involved with children and adolescents, this behavior may be based on the eroticization of parental love, as can happen in adult male gynephilic pedo- and ephebophiles. In other cases, fixation on a partner of the same sex may be the result of life experiences in the form of a type of imprinting (see, in this volume, D'Udine; Garland and Dougher; Money).

## Phylogeny and the Two Types of Adult Human Sexual Behavior with Children and Adolescents

On the basis of the material presented thus far, one can divide adult human sexual behavior with children and adolescents into two types. The first type is associated with the agonal, hierarchal sexuality of dominance and submission and with sexual behavior that is not necessarily characterized by affiliation. This type is paraphilic lust for children or adolescents. The second type is associated with a redirection or a reentrainment (see Money, this volume) of romantic or erotic love onto children and adolescents, who usually evoke parental love from adults. The sexual behavior that can result from pedophilia or ephebophilia is derived from this second type.

Children and adolescents are younger and smaller than adults, so that any adult who interacts with children and adolescents in any manner is automatically in a position of dominance to them. It would appear that, for some adult males who are aroused by the lust of submission in a sexual partner, children and adolescents will invariably have at least some of the necessary characteristics. Because the roles (dominant and submissive) are more important than the individuals who fill the roles, the dominance/submission-related sexual behavior with children and adolescents, i.e., paraphilic lust for children and adolescents, is impersonal and therefore is likely to be engaged in with numerous partners, who may be adults or children and adolescents.

In contrast, adult human sexual behavior with children and adolescents can also grow out of a love relationship. If adult/adult romantic love has its phylogenetic origins in parent/offspring love, it is quite easy to understand how children and adolescents can evoke feelings of love in adults, even when it is a socially unacceptable kind of love. The characteristics of a child release strong affective responses of caretaking, and in this context, it is noteworthy that heterosexual males are attracted by adult females who combine the sexual signals of the mature female with infantile facial characteristics, such as a small mouth and delicate features, i.e., the "Babydoll" appearance (see also Eibl-Eibesfeldt, 1986). Indeed, it seems as if, in some societies, females were selected for pedomorphic traits. In Southeast Asia in particular, females bear pedomorphic features. Childlike behaviors, too, are culturally emphasized, such as in Japan, where women walk in a short-stepped gait that is enforced by a dress that does not allow them to take long strides.

Children and adolescents are protected, to some degree, from feelings of romantic or erotic love towards individuals with whom they associated in early childhood. Parents also seem to be protected from feeling the unacceptable type of love towards their offspring. There are at least two mechanisms involved. One mechanism protects the children, and the other mechanism protects the parents.

The Westermarck effect, which de-eroticizes individuals known to a child when the child grows up to be an adolescent and adult, protects children from eventually falling in love with their own siblings and parents. The Westermarck effect has been studied in humans in the Chinese child-bride marriages (Wolf and Huang, 1980) as well as in the Israeli kibbutzim (Shepher, 1971). It is possible that the Westermarck effect also has some de-eroticizing effect indirectly on parents, since if children and adolescents are not sexually attracted to their parents, they probably would not direct proceptive (flirting) behaviors towards their parents. Since proceptive behaviors initiate courtship, parents may not feel sexually inclined when they interact with a child or an adolescent who is not sending them proceptive signals.

However, there is another mechanism that protects parents from having erotic feelings towards their own offspring. This mechanism is called the Coolidge effect (Symons, 1979, pp. 208-213). Essentially, the effect is that familiarity produces sexual boredom. In humans, for example, a parent who raises a child from infancy to adolescence is so familiar with the child by the time the child is an adolescent that sexual attraction does not occur. It often is not possible to separate the Westermarck effect from the Coolidge effect in a particular individual. However, research into the subject on a population of individuals can separate the two effects, in that the Westermarck effect depends on a somewhat critical period of time, whereas the Coolidge effect depends more on total time. (See Parker and Parker, 1986.) The lack of both the Westermarck effect and the Coolidge effect probably explains why adult males who are in the role of surrogate father with children and adolescents are so vulnerable to sexual interactions with their young charges.

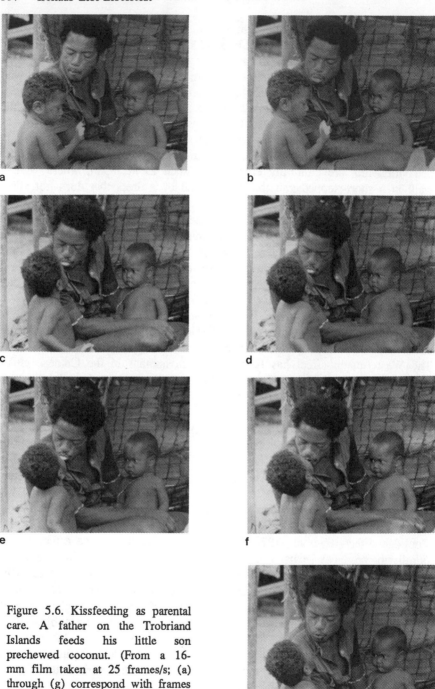

Figure 5.6. Kissfeeding as parental care. A father on the Trobriand Islands feeds his little son prechewed coconut. (From a 16-mm film taken at 25 frames/s; (a) through (g) correspond with frames 1, 53, 57, 59, 61, 65, and 67 of the sequence. Film taken by I. Eibl-Eibesfeldt.)

Figure 5.7. A !Ko-woman of the Bushmen of the Central Kalahari Desert comforts her little sister by kissfeeding. (From a 16-mm film taken by I. Eibl-Eibesfeldt.)

## Rapid Evolution and the Vulnerability of Humans to Behavioral Disorders

Humans, in general, seem particularly prone to behavioral disorders. This state probably exists because human social behavior is safeguarded to a lesser degree by phylogenetic adaptations than is the social behavior of other species. There is an exception in some higher primates that seem similarly vulnerable to behavioral disorders, however. Chimpanzees exemplify this kind of exception. For the past several years, this author has made regular visits to the chimpanzee reserve in the Gombe National Park in Tanzania, Africa, to document chimpanzee behavior on film. It is remarkable how easily and quickly chimps escalate their aggressive behavior. Two males who are friends may start some friendly wrestling, and then suddenly one apparently becomes angry or aggressive. A short clash follows, ending with the flight of one. A couple of minutes later, both may approach carefully with friendly utterances and resume playwrestling—and again an escalation of apparent anger or aggression may be observed. Male chimpanzees, in fits of rage, have wounded and even seriously mauled not only group members of their own sex but also females and their young, who probably are the males' own offspring or close blood relatives. Females turn to cannibalism on infants and on members of their own group (Goodall, 1977, 1986). In male baboons of this area, the escalation of fits of anger having fatal consequences to young and females also was observed. Such dyscontrol seems to indicate that the critical points in the regulation of social behavior are less secured by phylogenetic adaptations in these primates than in other mammals. One might speculate that the rapid evolution of these groups, evolution that affected the growth of the brain in particular, did not allow for all the fine tuning needed for such behavior-influencing safeguards. This lack of instinctual fixation allows for an increased role for learning and permits the development of culture in humans, but it also involves risks in the form of behavioral disorders.

Behavioral disorders, sexual and nonsexual, can have many different origins, including phylogenetic origins (Feierman, 1987). Dienske et al. (1987) suggest that some psychiatric disorders may be the result of too much or too little of some behavioral traits that in moderation are adaptive. Such behavioral traits would lie in the tails of frequency-distribution curves. Hypertrophies or atrophies of a variety of basic biological drives, including the sex drive, could bring about disordered behavior. Dienske et al. (1987) describe compulsive responsibility as being one form of psychiatric disorder in which the patient feels obligated by too much responsibility, while Harpending and Sobus (1987) describe individuals with antisocial personality disorder as exhibiting too little responsibility. In some individuals, too much or too little aggressive motivation (Dienske, 1987), or in other individuals, the lack of control of aggression (McGuire and Troisi, 1987) may underlie behavioral disorders.

Healthy human beings have a strong urge to maintain friendly bonds with others, but a certain ambivalence is always present because humans also fear their fellow humans. If for some reason this intraspecies fear of other humans, i.e., of conspecifics, or members of the same species, predominates, the individual may be handicapped in establishing friendly relations. Some forms of autism may be worsened by such fear. Although the initial cause seems to be internal, intuitively friendly initiatives and responses from caretakers may result in a vicious cycle that often makes things worse (Tinbergen, 1974; see also Dienske et al., 1987). An exaggerated interspecies fear of predators, too, may lead to behavioral disorders, as has been suggested for catatonia, a form of tonic immobility that sometimes is seen in persons with schizophrenia (Feierman, 1982).

In other types of behavioral disturbances, in which behavioral responses are not triggered by innate releasing mechanisms but, rather, by acquired ones, fixation to the wrong object may occur; such fixations may prove to be quite resistant to therapy. Some sexual disturbances, such as the paraphilias, seem to fit this pattern (see Money, this volume; see Domjan, this volume, for an empirical validation in an animal model).

Other behavioral disturbances stem from the fact that the environment in which humans exist changes, and has changed, rapidly. Dispositions, such as aggressivity, that once were adaptive have become maladaptive in the brief course of human history (Eibl-Eibesfeldt, 1972).

All in all, humans are certainly a high-risk species for behavioral disturbances, but this flexibility of behavior, which puts humans at risk, also allows for new and better adaptations, and it is these latter adaptations for which humans should strive.

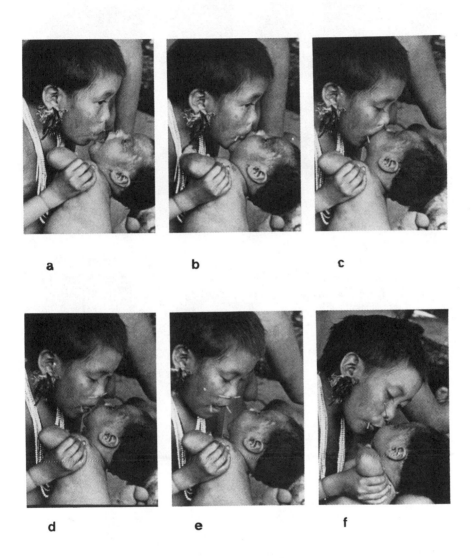

Figure 5.8. Kissfeeding as an expression of affection. A young Yanomami female in the region of the Upper Orinoco River kissfeeds her little sister with saliva and coos to her. (From a 16-mm film taken at 25 frames/s; (a) through (f) correspond with frames 1, 54, 124, 127, 129, and 219. Film taken by I. Eibl-Eibesfeldt.)

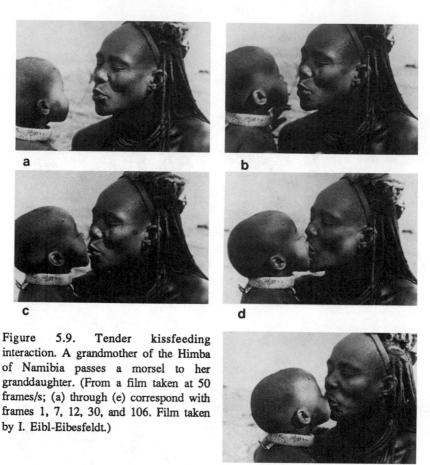

Figure 5.9. Tender kissfeeding interaction. A grandmother of the Himba of Namibia passes a morsel to her granddaughter. (From a film taken at 50 frames/s; (a) through (e) correspond with frames 1, 7, 12, 30, and 106. Film taken by I. Eibl-Eibesfeldt.)

## Discussion

One aspect of adult human sexual behavior with children and adolescents that has not been addressed in this chapter is the predominance of these behaviors in adult human males compared to adult human females. Although the subject is quite speculative, this discrepancy can be considered within the context of the material that has been developed herein.

Based upon both the lust of submission and the phylogenetic origins of romantic love, the size discrepancy between an adult human male and a child or an adolescent can facilitate feelings in the adult male of both sexuality and romantic love. In an adult human female, in contrast, the size discrepancy between her and a child or an adolescent can facilitate feelings of romantic love but not of sexuality. One might speculate that this male/female difference in vulnerability to the eroticizing of their respective relationships with children and adolescents lies in the difference in size between an adult male and a child or an adolescent compared with the

Figure 5.10. Eipo adult female of West New Guinea kisses a baby. (Photograph taken by I. Eibl-Eibesfeldt.)

difference in size between an adult female and a child or an adolescent. This comparative difference is negligible, however, when measured against the difference in size between an adult of either sex and a child or an adolescent. Therefore, the male/female difference in vulnerability seems not to be the result of the comparative difference in size. Diminutive size in a partner facilitates feelings of dominance over that partner by an adult of either sex, but dominance is a part of the phylogeny of male sexual behavior, whereas submission is a part of the phylogeny of female sexual behavior. Therefore, the male/female difference in vulnerability may lie in the differing respective sexual responses to diminutive partners on the part of adult males and adult females. Assuming, then, that both adult males and adult females are capable of forming loving, nonerotic bonds with children, it would be predicted that the bond becomes eroticized and overtly sexual in (some) males only. Indeed, behavior that confirms this prediction is what is found, in that males more than females are involved sexually with children and adolescents, by a ratio of approximately 10:1. The identification of the factors that make certain males vulnerable to this misplaced eroticization is one of the challenges facing behavioral scientists in the future. There are many other, equally plausible evolution-based explanations for the greater prevalence of all types of atypical sexual behaviors among human males compared to human females. For example, there is a difference between the sexes in the cost of reproduction as measured by the respective expenditure of energy. Females, who expend more energy than do males in activities related to reproduction, are more cautious and goal directed in their sexual behavior than are males (Symons, 1979; Daly and Wilson, 1983). On the basis of the expenditure of energy, males can afford to engage in nonprocreative sexual behavior more than females can. At this early stage in the scientific study of adult human sexual behavior with children and adolescents, data that would enable researchers to reject incorrect explanations or to show, for example, that several mechanisms are operative simultaneously and perhaps even additively simply are not available.

There are, of course, exceptions to all generalization, including to many of the generalizations that have formed much of the material in this chapter. Two obvious examples would be (a) sexual behavior between an

Figure 5.11. Appeasement behavior in the wolf. Background—upper pair: A submissive wolf presents to the other by rolling on its back as a young one does when offering itself for cleaning. Foreground—lower pair: A submissive wolf approaches a high-ranking wolf as a young one does when begging for food. (After Schenkel, 1967.)

adult human female and a child or an adolescent and (b) a masochistic human male who seeks out adult human females to dominate and hurt him for his sexual gratification. However, behavior can be understood only if the modal tendency is examined first, even if "modal tendency" refers to a species-atypical behavior, as it does in adult human sexual behavior with children and adolescents.

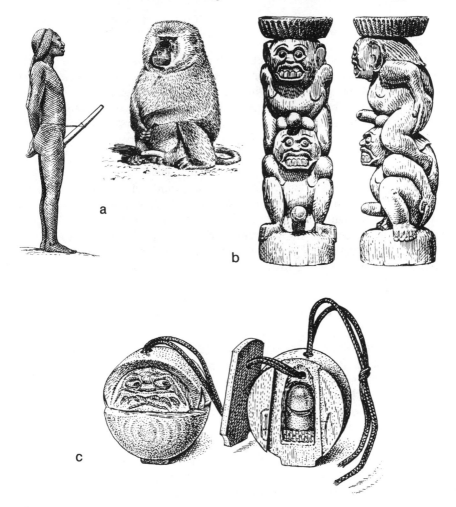

Figure 5.12. (a) Phallic displays in primates. Left: Papuan with penis sheath (gourd); right: hamadryas baboon sitting on guard. (b) Guardian figures with phallic display and threat face from Bali. (c) Phallic protective amulets from Japan. (See also Eibl-Eibesfeldt and Wickler, 1968, and Eibl-Eibesfeldt, 1970b. From Eibl-Eibesfeldt, 1970a.)

The exceptions represent variations on variations, and they, too, can be studied. For example, based upon what has been discussed so far, it could be predicted that adult females who become sexually involved with male children and adolescents would be motivated more by love than by lust. The important point is that both modal deviant tendency and variations of modal deviant tendency can be studied empirically by means of testable hypotheses and can be understood.

## Conclusion

Phylogenetic adaptations determine behavior in a predictable manner, and sexual behavior is not an exception to this rule. Therefore, to understand human sexual behavior, one must conceptualize it within the context of phylogeny as well as of ontogeny. The study of the phylogeny of human sexual behavior reveals two major themes—the agonal, hierarchal origins from reptilian sexual behavior and the independent evolution of sexual behavior in the context of affiliative relationships in birds and mammals. In addition, the rapid evolution that occurred within the primate order may have freed primates from the constraints of instinctual fixations, thereby allowing for an increased role for individual learning and for the development of culture. Such flexibility has not been without a price, however, as evidenced by the vulnerability of primates in general and humans in particular to behavioral extremes and dysregulation that may underlie various behavioral disorders including sexual disorders.

## Summary

In human sexual behavior, strata of different phylogenetic origins can be distinguished. Sexuality based upon the mechanisms of male dominance and female submission, which characterizes the reptiles, also constitutes the basic layer of human sexuality. This reptilian heritage is superimposed, however, by a more recently acquired sexuality characterized by affiliation and love. The new potentiality to act in a friendly manner evolved with the development of parental care independently in birds and in mammals. In normal human sexual behavior, the archaic agonal sexuality is controlled by affiliative sexuality and, therefore, is characterized by love. Agonal sexuality is still with us, however, as indicated, among other features, by the phallic male-dominance displays, by a male hormonal response linked to dominance achievement, and by the sexual fantasies of submission that are experienced by females. Agonal sexuality normally is under the control of affiliative sexuality, and therefore, humans correctly associate sex with love. Certain forms of sexuality, such as sadomasochism and a particular form of male homosexuality, are explained as being a regression to the archaic agonal sexuality.

Pedophilia and pedosexual behavior are explained within the regression context, too. Children have characteristics, such as small size, that facilitate adult males' feeling dominant to them, as occurs in pedosexual behavior. Since human adult/adult romantic love is derived by phylogeny from parental caregiving behavior, it is easily seen how, in some adult humans, the feeling of love toward children has been retained and eroticized, which is the true meaning of the term "pedophilia."

# References

Bailey, K.G. Human paleopsychology. *In* G.G. Neumann (Ed.), *Origins of human aggression.* New York: Human Sciences Press, 1987, pp. 50-63.

Creed, G.W. Sexual subordination: Institutionalized homosexuality and social control in Melanesia. *Ethology,* 1984, *13,* 157-176.

Daly, M., and Wilson, M. *Sex, evolution, and behavior* (2nd ed.). Boston: Willard Grant Press, 1983.

Dienske, H., Sanders-Woudstra, J.A.R., and de Jonge, G. A biologically meaningful classification in child psychiatry that is based upon ethological methods. *In* J.R. Feierman (Guest Ed.), *The Ethology of Psychiatric Populations. Ethology and Sociobiology,* 1987, *8*(3S), 27S-45S, supplement.

Dörner, G. Sexual differentiation of the brain. *Vitamins and Hormones,* 1980, *38,* 325-381.

Eibl-Eibesfeldt, I. Ethologie, die Biologie des Verhaltens. *In* F. Gessner and L. v. Bertalanffy (Eds.), *Handbuch der Biologie,* 2. Frankfurt: Athenaion, 1966, 341-559.

Eibl-Eibesfeldt, I. *Liebe und Hass. Zur Naturgeschichte elementarer Verhaltensweisen.* München: Piper, 1970a.

Eibl-Eibesfeldt, I. Männliche und weibliche Schutzamulette im modernen Japan. *Homo,* 1970b, *21,* 175-188.

Eibl-Eibesfeldt, I. *Love and hate: The natural history of behavior patterns.* New York: Holt, Rinehart and Winston, 1972. (English translation of Eibl-Eibesfeldt, I. *Liebe und Hass. Zur Naturgeschichte elementarer Verhaltensweisen.* München: Piper, 1970.)

Eibl-Eibesfeldt, I. *Die Biologie des menschlichen Verhaltens. Grundriss der Humanethologie.* München: Piper, 1986. (English translation: *Human ethology.* New York: Aldine de Gruyter, in press.)

Eibl-Eibesfeldt, I., and Wickler, W. Die ethologische Deutung einiger Wächterfiguren auf Bali. *Z. Tierpsychol.,* 1968, *25,* 719-726.

Feierman, J.R. Nocturnalism: An ethological theory of schizophrenia. *Medical Hypotheses,* 1982, *9,* 455-479.

Feierman, J.R. The ethology of psychiatric populations: An introduction. *In* J.R. Feierman (Guest Ed.), *The Ethology of Psychiatric Populations. Ethology and Sociobiology,* 1987, *8*(3S),1S-8S, supplement.

Goodall, J. Infant killing and cannibalism in free-living chimpanzees. *Folia Primat.,* 1977, *28,* 259-282.

Goodall, J. *The chimpanzees of Gombe: Patterns of behavior.* Cambridge, Mass.: The Belknap Press of Harvard University Press, 1986.

Greenberg, N., and MacLean, P.D. (Eds.). *Behavior and neurology of lizards: An interdisciplinary colloquium.* Rockville, Md.: U.S. Department of Health, Education, and Welfare (DHEW), U.S. Public Health Service, Drug Abuse and Mental Health Administration,

174    Irenäus Eibl-Eibesfeldt

National Institute of Mental Health, DHEW Publication Number (ADM) 77-491, 1978.

Harpending, H.C., and Sobus, J. Sociopathy as an adaptation. *In* J.R. Feierman (Guest Ed.), *The Ethology of Psychiatric Populations. Ethology and Sociobiology*, 1987, *8*(3S), 63S-72S, supplement.

Kitzinger, S. *Sexualität im Leben der Frau.* München: Biederstein, 1984.

MacLean, P.D. The triune brain, emotion and scientific bias. *In* F.O. Schmitt, G.C. Quarton, Th. Meilnechuk, and G. Adelmann (Eds.), *The neurosciences,* 2nd study program. New York: The Rockefeller University Press, 1970, pp. 336-349.

Mazur, A., and Lamb, Th. A. Testosterone, status, and mood in human males. *Hormones and Behavior,* 1980, *14,* 236-246.

McGuire, M.T., and Troisi, A. Physiological regulation-deregulation and psychiatric disorders. *In* J.R. Feierman (Guest Ed.), *The Ethology of Psychiatric Populations. Ethology and Sociobiology,* 1987, *8*(3S), 9S-25S.

Meesters, H. Zur Phänomenologie und Entstehungsgeschichte des Exhibitionismus. *Fortschr. Neurol. Psychiat.,* 1984, *52,* 237-249.

Müsch, H. Exhibitionismus, Phalluskult und Genitalpräsentieren. *Sexualmedizin,* 1976, *5,* 358-363.

Oehlert, B. Kampf und Paarbildung einiger Cichliden. *Z. Tierpsychol.,* 1958, *15,* 141-174.

Parker, H., and Parker, S. Father-daughter sexual abuse: An emerging perspective. *Amer. J. Orthopsychiat.,* 1986, *56,* 531-549.

Pillard, R.C., and Weinrich, J. The Periodic Table model of the gender transpositions: Part I. A theory based on masculinization and defeminization of the brain. *J. of Sex Research,* 1987, *23,* 425-454.

Roumajon, Y. 3. Kongress der Deutschen Gesellschaft für Psychotherapie und Tiefenpsychologie in Paris, 1960. (Oral report.)

Schenkel, R. Submission, its features and function in the wolf and dog. *Am. Zool.,* 1967, *7,* 319-329.

Shepher, J. Mate selection among second generation kibbutz adolescents and adults: Incest avoidance and negative imprinting. *Arch. Sex Behav.,* 1971, *1,* 293-307.

Stoller, R.J. *Perversion—Die erotische Form von Hass.* Hamburg: Rowohlt, 1979. (German translation of Stoller, R.J. *Perversion: The erotic form of hatred.* New York: Pantheon Books, 1975.)

Symons, D. *The evolution of human sexuality.* New York: Oxford University Press, 1979.

Tinbergen, N. Ethology and stress disease. *Science,* 1974, *185,* 20-27.

Valzelli, I., and Morgese, I. (Eds.). *Aggression and violence: A psycho/biological and clinical approach.* Milano: Editione Saint Vicent, 1981.

Wickler, W. Ursprung und biologische Deutung des Genitalpräsentierens männlicher Primaten. *Z. Tierpsychol.,* 1966, *23,* 422-437.

Wickler, W. Vergleichende Verhaltensforschung und Phylogenetik. *In* G. Heberer (Ed.), *Die Evolution der Organismen*, I., 3rd ed. Stuttgart: Fischer, 1967a, 420-508.

Wickler, W. Socio-sexual signals and their intraspecific imitation among primates. *In* D. Morris (Ed.), *Primate ethology*. London: Weidenfeld and Nicolson, 1967b, 69-147.

Wickler, W. *Sind wir Sünder? Naturgesetze der Ehe*. München: Droemer, 1969.

Wickler, W., and Uhrig, D. Bettelrufe, Antwortszeit und Rassenunterschiede im Begrussungsduett des Schmuckbartvogels *Trachyphonus d'arnaudii*. *Z. Tierpsychol.*, 1969, *26*, 651-661.

Wolf, A.P., and Huang, C. *Marriage and adoption in China, 1845-1945*. Stanford, Calif.: Stanford University Press, 1980.

Zillman, D. *Connections between sex and aggression*. New York: Lawrence NCE Erlbaum, 1986.

# 6
# Adolescent/Adult Copulatory Behavior in Nonhuman Primates

Connie M. Anderson
*Department of Anthropology*
*Hartwick College*
*Oneonta, New York 13820*
  *and*
Craig Bielert
*Department of Psychology*
*SUNY College*
*Oneonta, New York 13820*

## Introduction

Few of the hundreds of studies of nonhuman primate behavior have focused on the sexual behavior of adolescents. Further, of the approximately 200 extant species of primates, only a relatively small number have been the subject of intensive fieldwork, and only a small fraction of these have been studied at more than one locale. In consequence, attempts at comprehensive reviews within the entire order immediately run up against some problems of comparison.

In view of the well-documented extent to which social factors strongly influence the sexual interactions of primates in a group (e.g., Smuts et al., 1987), it seems appropriate to limit the focus of this chapter to that information which has been obtained from wild populations.

More information is available on wild baboons (*Papio* spp.) than on any other primate genus (see Table 6.I). Baboons have been studied for several decades by a small army of researchers from several disciplines.

The several species and/or subspecies included in the genus *Papio* display considerable variation in social organization within and among populations and inhabit a tremendous ecological and geographical range, including deserts, mountains, rain forest, scrub forest, and savanna grassland. Their sexual behavior has been described under both laboratory (e.g., Bachmann and Kummer, 1980; Bielert, 1986; Bielert and Anderson, 1985; Bielert et al., 1986; Gilbert and Gillman, 1960; Kling and Westfahl, 1978; Kummer et al., 1974; Rowell, 1967) and field conditions (e.g., Altmann, 1980; Anderson, 1989; Busse and Hamilton, 1981; Byrne et al., 1987; Collins, 1986; Dunbar, 1984; Kummer, 1968; Ransom, 1981; Rasmussen, 1986; Saayman, 1973; Scott, 1984; Seyfarth, 1978; Smuts, 1985; Strum, 1983). Thus, until such time when adolescent sexual behavior is more widely studied within the primate order, baboons can provide a preliminary illustration of possible sexual interaction patterns between adults and immatures among nonhuman primates, under different natural conditions, within a single genus.

TABLE 6.I. Scientific and common names of the baboon (*Papio*) species referred to in Chapter 6

| Scientific Name | Common Name |
|---|---|
| *Papio cynocephalus anubis* | anubis or olive baboon |
| *Papio cynocephalus cynocephalus* | yellow baboon |
| *Papio cynocephalus ursinus* | chacma baboon |
| *Papio hamadryas* | hamadryas baboon |
| *Theropithecus gelada* | gelada baboon |
| *Papio sphinx* | mandrill |
| *Papio leucophaeus* | drill |

Baboons are also of particular relevance to humans because they live in large, multimale groups, as humans do now and have throughout their evolutionary history; in addition, baboons inhabit those savanna environments that have always been most characteristic of humans. This chapter will concentrate on the behavior changes that characterize the period of adolescence, with specific regard to copulatory behavior, in this well-studied genus. Copulations between adults and adolescents in other species will be briefly mentioned where they fit into typical baboon behaviors, and a category of typical primate adult/adolescent copulatory behavior that does not occur among baboons will be described as well.

"Copulation" consists of mounting, intromission, and ejaculation, which may or may not result in impregnation. Under field conditions, it may be impossible to determine whether mounting is followed by intromission and ejaculation. In this chapter, the authors use the term "copulation" where they are reasonably sure that not only intromission but also ejaculation occurred, based on various visible and/or audible changes in one or both partners. For example, adult female chacma baboons produce a "copulation call" on over

99% of intromissions by adult males when the female's perineum is swollen to any extent. This call is given on approximately 70% of the occasions when swollen adult females receive intromissions from subadult or immature males or when adolescent swollen females receive intromissions from males of any age (Anderson, unpublished field observations; Bielert, unpublished colony observations; Saayman, 1973).

Where the authors use "mounting" instead, they assume that a serious but unsuccessful attempt at intromission and ejaculation has occurred. The authors do not include so-called "dominance" mounts in this category but, rather, refer only to heterosexual pairs in which the male appeared to be seriously trying to achieve intromission based on repeated thrusting and repositioning. These cases usually involved either immatures or females who moved away from the male.

The authors use the term "mating" when they do not intend to make a distinction between the two categories.

The term "immature" here means an individual of either sex who has not yet reached subadulthood. A "subadult" male has completed skeletal growth, but his canine teeth are not yet fully erupted, and he weighs considerably less than a fully adult male, mainly because his musculature is less extensive. For females, subadulthood usually begins at first conception and continues until growth has been completed; in baboons, this stage typically lasts until some time after the first infant has been weaned. General definitions of "immature" and "subadult" are given in Table 6.II, as are definitions of the terms "infant," "juvenile," "adolescent," and "adult." The definition of a nonhuman-primate "juvenile" is comparable to the definition of a human "child."

## Adult/Immature Copulatory Behavior in Baboons

These interactions fall naturally into one or the other of two very widespread types that are also found in many other primate species. The first may be called the "typical," multimale pattern, while the other can be accurately described as the "exclusive," unimale pattern.

## The Typical, or Multimale, Pattern: Description

Adult female baboons displaying the typical pattern have sexual experiences with males of virtually all ages, while adult males direct sexual behavior only to adult females. Adolescent and subadult females engage in sexual behavior only with males of the same age or younger, because of the preference of all males to mate with older females. Adolescent and juvenile males have limited sexual interactions with females of all age classes, but subadult males are limited by their own preference for adult females, on the one hand, and by competition for those adult females from adult males, on

TABLE 6.II. Age classes of baboons, as used in Chapter 6

| Term | Definition |
| --- | --- |
| Immature | An individual from the time of birth until the time of subadulthood, including infant, juvenile (child), and adolescent. |
| Infant | An individual from birth to the time of weaning. |
| Juvenile | An individual from the time of weaning until the beginning of adolescence. |
| Adolescent | An individual from the time when secondary sexual characteristics first appear until adult skeletal growth is complete. |
| Subadult | An individual from the time when skeletal growth is complete until the time when full adult weight and musculature are attained. |
| Adult | An individual whose size is within the range of that of middle-aged individuals. |

the other. Thus, sexual access to members of the opposite sex expands as females mature but narrows as males do. This pattern has been observed in many populations of "savanna" baboons, including the subspecies *Papio cynocephalus anubis* (e.g., Ransom, 1981; Rowell, 1972; Scott, 1984; Smuts, 1985; Strum, 1983); *P. c. cynocephalus* (e.g., Hausfater, 1975; Rasmussen, 1983); and *P. c. ursinus* (e.g., Hall, 1963; Hall and DeVore, 1965; Stoltz and Saayman, 1970; personal observation).

Infants and juveniles, though not yet fertile, begin "practicing" adult sexual behaviors through play. Both sexes present themselves in the sexually inviting postures typical of adult females to other baboons rather indiscriminately, regardless of age or sex, and both sexes mount and are mounted by other infants and juveniles. They are much less competent than adults at such behavior, however, and intromissions apparently never occur, particularly since adult and adolescent males do not mount preadolescent females. Juvenile males do mount adolescent, subadult, and adult females. The age of potential sexual partners is unrestricted for males but is limited to peers for females at this stage.

Adolescent sexual behavior approximates adult behavior much more closely, particularly in males, who have had several years of experience with older partners by the time they begin ejaculating. Adolescent females continue to interact sexually with males of their own age or younger, while older males ignore them, especially during their first few estrous cycles of perineal swelling during the periovulatory period. They may occasionally copulate with subadult males but almost never with adults, despite intense efforts by the adolescent females to interest the older males. For the first six cycles (some eight months), infant, juvenile, and adolescent males are the adolescent females' only partners. Eventually, their sexual swellings will equal or even surpass those of most adult females in size, and adult males will begin to copulate with them, but only during their one or two days of maximum attractiveness per menstrual cycle.

Adolescent males, on the other hand, often become fathers, especially of infants born to subadult females, who remain less popular than fully adult females until after their second pregnancy (Altmann, 1980; Anderson, 1986; Ransom, 1981). Adolescent males copulate regularly with adolescent, subadult, and adult females, although adult males often monopolize females of the latter two ages at the point of peak fertility. Males reproduce, though at a low rate, throughout adolescence, while females will cycle for one to two years before they finally become pregnant for the first time (Anderson, 1986).

Subadult females mate with males of all ages but are slightly less preferred than fully adult females, especially by adult males. Subadult males, on the other hand, usually experience a decline in sexual activity, with much lower rates of copulation between them and adult or subadult females. Although the females are quite willing to mate with subadult males, the adult males begin to challenge younger competitors who have reached subadulthood, and the subadults are still neither heavily muscled nor experienced enough to resist the adults successfully. They mate with adult and subadult females early or late in their cycles or when the adult males cannot see them. They seem to be less attracted to adolescent females than when they were younger, since they mate less frequently with them than do adolescent males, even though adult males do not compete with them for adolescent females. Subadult males are restricted to certain ages of females for the first time, while subadult females have become relatively unrestricted for the first time.

Full adulthood accentuates this trend: adult females interact sexually with males of all ages, while adult males do not interact sexually with immature females. Adult males occasionally mate with subadult females, and much less often with adolescent females who have been cycling for almost a year already. The average adult female probably has an adult male as a partner for not more than 50% of her sexual interactions, with infant through subadult males involved equally often.

Adult males avoid mating with younger females when they have a choice in this same manner in virtually all other reported primate species (Anderson, 1986). In the prosimian *Varecia variegata*, for example, males mate with adolescent females much less often than with adults (Foerg, 1982). The same is true among apes: for gorillas (Harcourt et al., 1980), chimpanzees (Coe et al., 1979; de Waal, 1982), and orangutans (Galdikas, 1981; Schürmann, 1981). Male chimpanzees even chose the older of two adult females in estrus on 27 of 30 occasions (Tutin, 1979), and males do not consort with or behave possessively toward adult females who have not yet had their first infant (Tutin, 1975). Orangutan males also prefer females who have already produced offspring to younger, nulliparous adults (Schürmann, 1981) and very rarely consort with adolescents, usually rejecting them outright (Galdikas, 1981).

The same pattern appears among monkeys, the last of the three major divisions of the Order Primates. In Japanese macaques, only the lowest ranking males ever mate with adolescents, doing so as a last resort when more dominant males exclude them from adults (Takahata, 1982). Rhesus macaques mate with the older of a range of adult females whenever possible, even when the younger one is more dominant (Lindburg, 1971), so that the older the female is, the more partners she has and the higher is the dominance rank of the partners (Conaway and Koford, 1965; Kaufmann, 1965; Lindburg, 1983; Loy, 1971). Both adult and subadult male bonnet macaques very rarely mate with adolescent or subadult females, regardless of rank (Glick, 1980). Among langurs, a male Hanuman langur may actually expel adolescent females from a group that he has newly entered as the sole male (Hrdy, 1977); the same phenomenon occurs in purple-faced (*Presbytis senex*) and Douc (*Pygathrix nemaeus*) langurs (Lippold, 1977; Rudran, 1973).

## The Typical, or Multimale, Pattern: Adaptive Significance

The immature animals benefit in many ways from engaging in sexual activity before full adulthood, since they must learn how to copulate successfully. Both sexes have to learn both the proper mechanical techniques and the proper social techniques. Adolescent males must learn how to establish a consortship with a female nearing ovulation, for example, and adolescent females must learn not to run away before a male has ejaculated, among other things.

The adult male baboon who does not mate with an adolescent female who solicits him is also behaving rationally, as the chance that such a mating will increase his reproductive success is very low. He already has all the practice he needs, and the mechanics of mating with a small female must not be pleasant, since adult male baboons are twice the size of fully grown adult females. An adolescent is still considerably smaller in overall size than an adult female, and she will not be able to conceive until one or two years after she has begun mating with adult males, while an adult female will get pregnant after an average of only four months (e.g., Altmann, 1980; Anderson, 1986; Packer, 1979; Ransom, 1981; Sigg et al., 1982). Adolescents are also less likely to carry a fetus to term, and infant mortality is almost twice as high for first-born infants (e.g., Altmann et al., 1977; Anderson, 1986; Nicolson, 1982). An adult male has little reason to mate with any but adult females.

Adolescent and subadult females similarly had much lower reproductive success than older, fully adult, especially multiparous females in many other primate species (see Table 6.III).

TABLE 6.III. Nonhuman primate species in which female reproductive success has been found to increase with age and parity

| Species | | References |
|---|---|---|
| *Common Name* | *Scientific Name* | |
| bushbaby | *Galago senegalensis* | Butler, 1974 |
| ruffed lemur | *Varecia variegata* | Foerg, 1982 |
| gorilla | *Gorilla gorilla* | Fossey, 1982; Harcourt et al., 1980; Nadler, 1975 |
| chimpanzee | *Pan troglodytes* | Butler, 1974; Coe et al., 1979; Goodall, 1983; Graham, 1970; Lehrman, 1961; Pusey, 1980; Teleki et al., 1976; Tutin, 1975, 1980; de Waal, 1982 |
| orangutan | *Pongo pygmaeus* | Galdikas, 1981; Schürmann, 1981 |
| howler monkey | *Alouatta palliata* | Glander, 1980; Clarke and Glander, 1984 |
| mangabey | *Cercocebus torquatus* | Rowell and Richard, 1979 |
| vervet monkey | *Cercopithecus aethiops* | Butler, 1974; Kusher et al., 1982; Rowell and Richard, 1979 |
| blue monkey | *C. mitis* | Rowell and Richard, 1979 |
| crabeating macaque | *Macaca fascicularis* | Kemps and Timmermans, 1984 |
| Japanese macaque | *M. fuscata* | Mori, 1979 |
| rhesus macaque | *M. mulatta* | Brandt and Mitchell, 1971; Drickamer, 1974; Hird et al., 1975; Lancaster, 1984; Lehrman, 1961; Lindburg, 1983; Loy, 1971; Mitchell et al., 1966; Sade et al., 1976; Silk, 1984; Small, 1984; Symons, 1978; Wilson et al., 1978 |
| pigtailed macaque | *M. nemestrina* | Dazey and Erwin, 1976; Fredrickson and Bowers, 1981; Kuyk et al., 1976; Sackett et al., 1974 |
| bonnet macaque | *M. radiata* | Silk, 1984; Silk et al., 1981 |
| toque macaque | *M. sinica* | Dittus, 1975 |
| Hanuman langur | *Presbytis entellus* | Boggess, 1980; Curtin, 1975; Dolhinow et al., 1979; Hrdy, 1977 |
| squirrel monkey | *Saimiri sciureus* | Taub, 1980; Taub et al., 1978 |

Adult female baboons do allow infants and juveniles to mount them, however, unlike adult males, despite the impossibility of conception. This difference in tolerance of immatures' sexual advances between adult males and adult females probably results from the fact that a female does not decrease her likelihood of eventual conception when she mates with infertile males, as long as fertile males also mate with her. For an adult male, though, his chances of mating with a fertile female may be significantly decreased by mating with an adolescent, for several reasons. First, males fight over females, risking serious wounds that may require withdrawal from all mating activities for some time (e.g., Hausfater, 1975; Busse and Hamilton, 1981). A consorting male uses a great deal of energy meeting the challenges of other males even if they do not physically attack him (Dunbar, 1978; Rasmussen, 1986). Finally, a male with a low sperm count is also less likely to be able to impregnate an adult female (Lindburg, 1983).

Female baboons in at least some populations may harass each other during copulation (e.g., Wasser and Starling, 1986), but an estrous female has never been reported to have been hurt in this way, possibly because the males intervene. A female cannot waste her egg by copulating with an infertile male because her egg remains available to the sperm of fertile males until it begins to disintegrate.

Finally, many of the infant and juvenile sexual partners of an adult female may be related to her (Scott, 1984; personal observation), so that an adult female may also benefit indirectly by increasing her male relatives' future reproductive success by helping them to learn proper copulatory techniques before they become fully fertile. Reproductive behavior includes both mating effort and parental investment (Trivers, 1972). Although most of the copulatory behavior described in this chapter is mating effort, sexual behavior of this type may be analogous to parental investment, if the concept is broadened to include kin more distantly related than one's own offspring.

Wolfe (1986) has also suggested that adult females mate with immature males when there are not many unfamiliar adult males available, at least in Japanese macaques. This behavior has the effect of preventing incest or close inbreeding. Wolfe feels that natural selection has produced female primates who prefer novel sexual partners and that, as a result, immature males may often be chosen if there is a relative shortage of novel mature males. (See Table 6.IV.)

TABLE 6.IV. The two typical nonhuman primate adult/immature sexual interaction patterns seen in wild baboons. (Note that *P. c. ursinus* appears under both patterns, since both have been observed in populations of this species.)

### The Typical, Multimale Pattern

Species:  *Papio cynocephalus anubis, P. c. cynocephalus, P. c. ursinus*
Habitat:  Savanna grassland
Sexual Partners:

|                          |                             |
| ------------------------ | --------------------------- |
| Of immature males:       | Females of all ages         |
| Of immature females:     | Males of same age or younger |
| Of adult males:          | Adult and subadult females  |
| Of adult females:        | Males of all ages           |

Pairbonding:  Rare, nonexclusive, and intense

### The Exclusive, Unimale Pattern

Species:  *Papio cynocephalus ursinus, P. hamadryas, P. papio, Theropithecus gelada*
Habitat:  Arid; high-altitude; or jungle
Sexual Partners:

|                          |                                       |
| ------------------------ | ------------------------------------- |
| Of immature males:       | Females of all ages                   |
| Of immature females:     | Males of all ages                     |
| Of adult males:          | Adult, subadult, and adolescent females |
| Of adult females:        | Adult and subadult males              |

Pairbonding:  Universal, sexually exclusive, less intense

## The Exclusive, or Unimale, Pattern

The "exclusive" pattern occurs in species or populations in which an adult female mates with only one adult male during any given estrous cycle, although her partner may be replaced by another over time. Where a female in a chacma population with the typical pattern may mate with all the available adult males per cycle, limited only by each male's attempts to keep others away, a chacma male in a population with the exclusive pattern succeeds in keeping all the other males away. The typical male almost never attacks a female in estrus, and she can leave to mate with a third male while her original consort and a rival fight, but an exclusive male will attack the female herself regularly if necessary to keep her away from other males, so that she mates with him exclusively at and even several days before ovulation (Abegglen, 1984; Dunbar, 1980, 1984; Kummer, 1968; Sigg and Stolba, 1981; Sigg et al., 1982). The two patterns are summarized in Table 6.IV.

Males maintain exclusive access to one or more females amongst hamadryas baboons, in some populations of chacma baboons, in gelada baboons, and probably in two lesser known species, the mandrill and the drill. In these populations, females live in a harem headed by one adult male all their lives. Their harem joins several others to form a large group or "troop," while the typical population contains no units within a troop except mother/offspring pairs. All populations with the exclusive pattern live in unusual habitats for baboons, and most of the habitats also are unusual for all primate species: dense rain forest floors (drill and mandrill); high altitude (gelada and chacma); or arid, near-desert steppe (hamadryas and some chacma populations) (Anderson, 1983; Stammbach, 1987).

What has to happen to sexual behavior in a population where a single male controls access to each fertile female? Adult males do not interfere with the sexual activities of infant and juvenile males in such cases, and so the mating patterns of immature males do not change significantly. Adolescent, subadult, and adult males are attacked and driven off if they try to mate with a female past puberty, however; so most subadults do not mate at all. Even adults with harems mate with fewer females on average than do males in a typical population, since harems average only two to three females (Dunbar, 1984; Stammbach, 1987). A male who has a harem will not mate with a fully swollen female if she is not a member of his harem (Kummer, 1968; Kummer et al., 1974).

In the exclusive pattern, female sexual activity is less limited by age than in the typical pattern, while male activity is more limited by age because males without harems pursue even infant females. Approximately 30% or more of adult males have no females at any one time (Dunbar, 1984; Kummer, 1968), while most subadults and all adolescents have none. Adult and, much more rarely, subadult males occasionally acquire one or more adult females in a "takeover," when a harem leader loses his females in a fight (Dunbar, 1984; Kummer, 1968). Most adult males obtain a female only by coaxing a juvenile or an infant female out of her father's harem and displaying intense parental behavior towards her while waiting for her to grow up, since all adult and subadult females are already harem members, as are most adolescents (Dunbar, 1984; Kummer, 1968).

Trying to avoid the harem leader, the young adult male will follow a particular 1- or 2-year-old female for months, walking next to her, grooming her, and carrying her, in a parental fashion, until she begins to follow him instead of her mother. The male will care for her for several more years, behaving more solicitously to her than her own father does (Abegglen, 1984; Sigg et al., 1982).

He does not try to copulate with her until her first estrous cycle; then he does immediately begin copulating, even though he is by now a full adult and she is a very small adolescent. Unlike females in a typical population, an exclusive-pattern adolescent female thus has an adult male for her first sexual partner. Since adult males allow adolescent females considerable freedom of movement even during estrus, however, such females circulate through the troop and may mate with juvenile, adolescent, and subadult males who have no harem yet (Dunbar, 1984). Juvenile female hamadryas baboons may begin estrous cycling prematurely in terms of chronological age, of growth stage, and of the length of adolescent sterility: females of other species begin cycling at about 4 years and undergo approximately a year and a half of adolescent sterility before giving birth for the first time at about 6 (Altmann, 1980). Hamadryas females give birth for the first time at about 6 years of age also, but their estrous cycles may begin as young as 3 years (Hamilton, 1984), when they are still considerably smaller than they will be at age 4. Age at first estrus has apparently been lowered, while first birth and completion of growth have not, so that the period of adolescent sterility and mating is almost doubled.

At least two different changes have occurred. First, females enter adolescence, as evidenced by the onset of cyclical periovulatory perineal swellings, at an earlier age. Second, adult males are willing to copulate with adolescents, even ones that are comparatively smaller because of their earlier onset age than are adolescents in other species.

There is no real male/male competition in exclusive populations among harem leaders, as they do not mate with each others' females even when solicited. This characteristic means they have less to lose by mating with adolescents, since by doing so, they are not decreasing their current or future ability to mate with adults. However, where a male has access to females of both ages, a harem leader with both an adult and an adolescent female harem member in estrus simultaneously rarely mates with the adolescent (Kummer, 1968; Sigg et al., 1982). Hamadryas females cycle synchronously within harems, so that the male is essentially still following a strategy similar to that of males in typical populations: he only mates with the adolescent after the adult has conceived and stopped cycling due to her pregnancy.

Among geladas, too, males only mate with females that belong to their harems, which they obtain either by defeating a harem leader or by detaching a young female (Dunbar, 1984). Geladas choose older females to detach, typically adolescents or subadults, and it takes them almost two years instead of one to succeed (Dunbar, 1984). Gelada males apparently do not attempt to influence infant or juvenile females, unlike hamadryas males. They often establish special relationships with male infants and juveniles in the harem containing the target female, however. This sex difference in adult male associations with immatures apparently is attributable to the immatures rather than to the adult male, since male immatures are much more likely to approach an outside adult male, while immature females avoid adult males (Dunbar, 1984).

## Suikerbosrand

Chacma baboons are considered "savanna" baboons and, therefore, might be expected to demonstrate the typical baboon adult/adolescent pattern, but instead, they show an interesting combination of behaviors according to their environment and social conditions. Their range extends from Zimbabwe south to the coast and includes both high-altitude mountain populations in Azania (South Africa) and isolated desert populations in Namibia.

At Suikerbosrand, a nature reserve 50 km south of Johannesburg, the baboon population appears to be in the process of developing the exclusive pattern out of the typical one. This occurrence is tremendously significant, as it shows that the differing degrees of mating exclusiveness and of age preferences must be very plastic traits governed by open genetic programs rather than fixed traits governed by closed genetic programs.

Because of its southern location and altitude of 2,000 meters, the Suikerbosrand Reserve has an average of approximately 120 frost nights per year, with low temperatures of -11°C. Much less food is available to the baboons in winter, as 70% of the rain falls in the three summer months. The population was studied for more than seven years. For the first five, there were no predators, although a leopard entered the Reserve near the end of the fifth year.

The large troops at Suikerbosrand broke up into small units in the winter, reducing feeding and mating competition and shortening the distance each individual had to travel each day. These units became progressively more and more like the harems observed in hamadryas and geladas over seven years, with an average of two adult females per unit. When these units joined to form the large troops in summer, almost all adults mated only with members of their winter unit by the end of the first five years, although initially, no adults of either sex had mated exclusively with only one individual. Adult females occasionally mated with immature males from other units, however. The Reserve and studies there that are relevant to the topic of this chapter have been described more fully in Anderson (e.g., 1980; 1981a,b; 1989).

When observations began in 1978, adult males almost never mated with adolescent females even if no other females had estrous swellings, as in the typical pattern. By 1984 and 1985, however, both adult and subadult males had begun interacting much more often with infants and juveniles than they had in 1978, and adult and subadult males were mating with adolescent and subadult females more frequently. These females now mated with adult males on 15.9% of their days of maximum perineal swelling, compared to 5.1% in 1978. Subadult males did not mate with maximally swollen adolescents and subadults more often, but they did mate with such females before the females had reached their maximum swelling state on 14.8% of their days, instead of on 5% as in 1978. The authors believe that the subadults would have mated much more often with younger females at maximal swelling as well if it had not been that adult males had begun to mate with them, too, and, on the females' days of maximum swelling, were preventing subadults from mating with them. These differences are statistically significant (Table 6.V).

The behavior of adult females has not changed over the seven-year period of observation. Adult males have greatly increased sexual behavior

TABLE 6.V. Changing mating patterns at Suikerbosrand

|  |  | *1978-1979* |
| --- | --- | --- |
| Days observed at maximal swelling with **adult** male copulation partner | Subadult females: | 7.2% (41/572) |
|  | Adolescent females: | 2.9% (15/520) |
|  |  | $\bar{x} = 5.1\%$ |
|  |  | *1984-1985* |
|  | Subadult females: | 19.0% (120/624) |
|  | Adolescent females: | 11.5% (54/468) |
|  |  | $\bar{x} = 15.9\%$ |
|  |  | *1978-1979* |
| Days observed at **less** than maximal swelling with **subadult** male copulation partners | Subadult **and** adolescent females: | 5.0% (165/3307) |
|  |  | *1984-1985* |
|  | Subadult **and** adolescent females: | 13.8% (456/3307) |
|  |  | *1978-1979* |
| Days observed at maximal swelling with **subadult** male copulation partners | Subadult **and** adolescent females: | 2.1% (23/1092) |
|  |  | *1984-1985* |
|  | Subadult **and** adolescent females: | 2.3% (25/1092) |

with adolescent females beginning with the first signs of puberty, and both adult and subadult males display much more parental-like caregiving behavior to infant and juvenile females.

Males who are able to almost-monopolize females because these males lead winter units have also increased parental-like caregiving such as the carrying, grooming, holding, and protecting of male infants and juveniles since the leopard arrived. Infants and juveniles who receive such protection are more likely to survive than are those who do not (Anderson, 1989). This behavior provides females with an incentive to restrict matings to the single male in their unit, who will thereafter care for their infants and increase their reproductive success. Males who do not have such a unit are then forced to try to recruit adolescent females who are not yet following a particular male, producing the gelada-type exclusive pattern.

Although the sample is small, the data suggest that males without winter units also spend a great deal of time in parental-like caring for female infants and juveniles, as in the hamadryas exclusive pattern, while males who already have units invest in both sexes approximately equally. Biological fathers are apparently investing in their own offspring regardless of sex, while males with no females who are not yet fathers are instead investing in young females in order to obtain them as future mating partners and harem members once the females reach puberty.

## Unimale Social Units

Many other primate species have one or the other of the grouping patterns just described, where several adult males live in the same relatively undifferentiated large group (typical) or where the large group is internally differentiated into smaller units (exclusive). There is a third major grouping type that is even more common in primates, although it does not occur among baboons, in which the exclusive-type small units are the **only** units, so that no unit at any level contains more than one adult male.

Adult/adolescent copulations differ according to which type of unimale social unit occurs, whether it be monogamous (one adult male, one adult female), polygynous (one adult male, more than one adult female), or solitary (adults of both sexes live alone or accompanied only by immatures).

In monogamous species such as the gibbon (*Hylobates* spp.) or marmoset (*Callithrix* spp.), each sex usually leaves the natal family during subadulthood, and matings between adults and subadults do not occur. However, if the subadult remains long enough to begin copulating with the adult member of the opposite sex, he or she will be forcibly driven out by the adult of the same sex (e.g., Tilson, 1981). In most marmosets, subadult sexual activity appears to be almost entirely suppressed by the presence of adults of the same sex within the group, so that subadult females do not begin ovulating until they leave, thus also preventing adult/adolescent copulation (e.g., Abbott et al., 1981). However, if the adult of either sex in such a group is killed, the subadult of that sex will immediately begin typical sexual functioning and mate with the remaining adult parent (e.g., Manley, 1986).

A third variant occurs in those very few primate species in which adults are essentially solitary. Here, adolescent and subadult males and females gradually leave their mothers and seek adult sexual partners, usually with little success. Both male and female adults avoid mating with adolescents and subadults among orangutans, for example, so that adolescents copulate only with other adolescents for several years (Galdikas, 1981, 1985; Rijksen, 1978; Schürmann, 1981). Young males often attempt to force adult females to mate with them among orangutans, usually unsuccessfully (Galdikas, 1985), although this coercion has not been reported for other species. Adult males do not attempt forcible copulations, presumably because they are preferred by females of all ages over younger males and also because they have learned to tell the difference between a receptive (periovulatory) and a nonreceptive female.

In those species where polygynous harems are the only social units, male and/or female subadults may leave the group, as in monogamous species, and live as solitaries for a time before joining or forming a new group. A new group forms, apparently, when a young adult male meets a solitary female. More commonly, a male effects a "takeover" of an existing troop, much as males in hamadryas or geladas do with harems. Females join a lone male or work their way into an existing troop (e.g., Marsh, 1979). Immature males do not seem to mate with mature females in these species because the adult male prevents it, and adolescent females are ignored or even driven out by adult males (e.g., Hrdy, 1977; Lippold, 1977; Rudran, 1973).

## Discussion

Adult/immature sexual relations in baboons and other primates are affected by inbreeding avoidance mechanisms, such as avoidance of individuals known in infancy (e.g., Scott, 1984) or dispersal of only one sex at puberty (e.g., Pusey and Packer, 1987). Since siblings interact with their mother and therefore with each other throughout the mother's lifetime, both sexes can easily recognize mothers and siblings and can therefore avoid mating with them, at least after the male partner is capable of producing viable sperm. In all known species of primates in natural or seminatural conditions, most individuals do not mate with siblings, and sons do not typically mate with mothers after the male enters adolescence (e.g., Crockett and Eisenberg, 1987; Gouzoules and Gouzoules, 1987; Leighton, 1987; Melnick and Pearl, 1987; Pusey and Packer, 1987).

It is rarely possible to identify the actual biological father in the typical baboon pattern, since more than one male mates with most females on and before the day of conception. Even under the exclusive pattern, a male fathers infants in a particular harem for only three to five years on average (Dunbar, 1984; Sigg et al., 1982), so that by the time a daughter reaches adolescence, her father will typically have left the harem and joined the pool of males without harems. Males who were resident in a troop or harem when a female was conceived typically avoid mating with all females of the appropriate age when the females reach adolescence and later, while the young females rarely solicit males old enough to be their fathers (Pusey and Packer, 1987; Stewart and Harcourt, 1987). This behavior should ensure that father/daughter inbreeding does not occur inadvertently, given the limited life span of male baboons and the several years necessary for a female to reach reproductive maturity.

Inbreeding avoidance is thus probably a contributing factor in the lack of attraction to adolescent females by adult males under both patterns. The relative infertility of adolescent females coupled with competition among adult males for mates also significantly affects adult/adolescent sexual interactions.

All species of baboons, whether predominantly of the typical or the exclusive pattern, regularly produce at least a few individuals capable of intense association with one heterosexual partner, so that all or most matings occur with that one individual only. A small number (10% or less) of possible pairs in many populations with the typical pattern have relationships lasting for several years in which sexual activity is concentrated on or limited to the other sole partner, and males care for infants born to the females in such a pair situation (Altmann, 1980; Anderson, 1989; Busse, 1985; Collins, 1986; Hamilton, 1984; Scott, 1984; Smuts, 1985; Strum, 1983).

The nature of the bonding mechanism between adult males and adult females in the exclusive populations differs somewhat from one population to the next. Subadult male geladas often develop intense associations with adolescent females that include frequent copulation, but these associations do not usually last into adulthood. When the male becomes an adult, he leaves his natal harem and attaches himself to a distant one, trying to lure away a young female. Alternatively, the female becomes a subadult, and she leaves her natal harem in the company of a strange adult male before her subadult associate has become fully adult (e.g., Dunbar, 1984). Intense associations in these species are thus initially formed in the absence of ongoing sexual activity.

The ability to form an intense association with an individual of the opposite sex is apparently a potential of most baboon individuals, though it forms the basis for long-term reproductive relationships only rarely in the typical pattern. Once some factor such as severe seasonality, cold, aridity, or absence of predation increases the frequency of such intense associations, most males appear to be able to perform the necessary behavior when it is the only way they can acquire a mate. Exclusive associations that form among adolescents are much less likely to last past the female's first pregnancy, as long-term intense associations appear to be restricted to pairs in which at least one of the parties is an adult (Anderson, 1989; Scott, 1984; Smuts, 1985).

The Suikerbosrand data demonstrate that interest in adolescent and juvenile females by adult males is not the result of a genetic difference between the hamadryas and gelada exclusive, unimale species on the one hand and the anubis, chacma, and yellow baboon typical, multimale species on the other. The development of the exclusive pattern from the typical pattern occurred in response to environmental conditions and was much too fast to have involved genetic change.

## Conclusions

The factors affecting adult/immature sexual relations in baboons are as follows: inbreeding avoidance; the potential to form long-lasting, nearly exclusive, intense associations with a member of the opposite sex; the very low fertility of adolescent and slightly lower fertility of subadult as compared with adult females; aggressive competition among males for estrous females, which may become violent and is always relatively energy intensive; and the reduced likelihood of successful impregnation for a male who has recently ejaculated numerous times.

The results are the two basic copulatory patterns here described, the typical, multimale pattern and the exclusive, unimale pattern, one or the other of which is found as a species-wide pattern in many other "unimale" and "multimale" species. The two differ mainly as a result of changes in male behavior. In the typical multimale pattern, adult and subadult females mate with males of all ages; adolescent females mate with males who are subadults and younger; and juvenile females are mounted by infant and juvenile males who do not achieve intromission. Adult males mate with adult females, rarely with subadult females, and only very rarely with females in the latter stages of adolescence; they never even mount juvenile or infant females. Subadult males, though fully fertile, mate less often than any other male class and do so with all age classes older than juveniles. Adolescent males are fertile, although considerably smaller and less muscular than adults, and mate with all female age classes, including, though rarely, juveniles. Juvenile and infant males mount females of all ages but rarely if ever achieve intromission or ejaculation.

In the exclusive, unimale pattern, adult, subadult, and adolescent females mate with males of all ages, and adolescence begins somewhat earlier. Infant and juvenile females do not mate but develop intense nonsexual relationships, resembling those between parent and offspring, with adult or subadult males, and they are mounted by adolescent, juvenile, and infant males. Adult and subadult males mate with adult, subadult, and adolescent females. Adolescent males have much less opportunity to mate with females of any age, because none have harems yet, and all females approaching puberty are guarded by adult or subadult males. However, adolescent males do occasionally mate with, or at least mount, older females at the beginning or end of their estrous cycles (Kummer, 1968).

Among nonhuman primates, then, sexual interaction between adult females and immature males is universal. Adult males do not typically direct copulatory behavior towards immature or even adolescent females, in contrast, except when all females past puberty are monopolized by an individual male who guards them.

## Summary

Among those species of nonhuman primates that have been well-studied, adult males rarely mate with any but fully adult females. Subadult and especially adolescent females, although they exhibit the anatomical and/or behavioral changes typical of estrus for their species, often to an exaggerated extent (Anderson, 1986), are much less likely to conceive, give birth to, or successfully raise healthy offspring. Males conserve their time, energy, fighting ability, and sperm for mating with females who are more likely to enhance the males' reproductive success. Older adult males also avoid mating with females young enough to be their daughters if the males are long-term residents in a group. Inbreeding is rare, as a result, since males do not mate with females born after their entry into a troop. Young females also avoid mating with males old enough to be their fathers.

Adult females do interact sexually with males of all ages, including infants too young to be capable of intromission or ejaculation. Females have little to lose by doing so, since they do not deplete their egg supply by unsuccessful matings and since they are unlikely to be seriously injured in the process. They may also help their immature male relatives by allowing them access to experienced females to practice sexual behavior so that they can perform successfully from the time spermatogenesis begins. Thus, this behavior may represent the parental-investment, rather than the mating-effort, component of sexual or reproductive behavior for adult females.

Where environmental conditions favor unimale harems as part of a larger social group, adult females mate with only one male per cycle, and adult males mate only with the females in their harem if they have one. Adult, subadult, and adolescent females are monopolized by adult male harem-holders, leaving a few adult and all subadult males without adult sexual partners. Under these conditions, males without harems choose a particular juvenile female to follow and display intense parental-like behavior towards her. Eventually, she becomes the first individual in the male's harem, and he begins mating with her at her first estrous swelling. Thus, both parental-like and copulatory motor patterns are directed at the same individual over the course of time and, for a brief period, even simultaneously.

Males and females can adopt the behaviors characteristic of either the typical or the exclusive pattern depending upon circumstances. The differences in behavior between the two types of populations are not the result of genetic differences between them to any significant degree.

*Acknowledgments*

We thank Jay Feierman first and foremost, since without his persistence, we never would have written this chapter, and thinking about these issues has stimulated a whole new line of fruitful inquiry that we might have overlooked otherwise. We thank the Servants of the Paraclete, Susan Weiss, and everyone else involved in executing the Jemez Springs Symposium so beautifully. Last, we extend thanks to all of our fellow contributors for their stimulating ideas and delightful company.

# References

Abbott, D., McNeilly, A., Lunn, S., Hulme, M., and Burden, F. Inhibition of ovarian function in subordinate female marmoset monkeys (*Callithrix jacchus jacchus*). *Journal of Reproduction and Fertility,* 1981, *63*, 335-345.

Abegglen, J.-J. *On socialization in hamadryas baboons.* Cranbury, N.J.: Associated University Presses, 1984.

Altmann, J. *Baboon mothers and infants.* Cambridge, Mass.: Harvard University Press, 1980.

Altmann, J., Altmann, S., Hausfater, G., and McCuskey, S. Life history of yellow baboons. *Primates,* 1977, *18*, 315-330.

Anderson, C. Chacma baboon (*Papio ursinus*) social groups and their interrelationships in the Suikerbosrand Reserve, South Africa. Unpublished Ph.D. dissertation, University of California, Riverside, 1980.

Anderson, C. Intertroop relations of chacma baboons (*Papio ursinus*). *International Journal of Primatology,* 1981a, 2, 285-310.

Anderson, C. Subtrooping in a chacma baboon (*Papio ursinus*) population. *Primates,* 1981b, 22, 445-458.

Anderson, C. Levels of social organization and male-female bonding in the genus *Papio. American Journal of Physical Anthropology,* 1983, *60*, 15-22.

Anderson, C. Female age: Male preference and reproductive success in primates. *International Journal of Primatology,* 1986, *7*, 305-326.

Anderson, C. The spread of exclusive mating in a chacma baboon population. *American Journal of Physical Anthropology,* 1989, *78*, 355-360.

Bachmann, C., and Kummer, H. Male assessment of female choice in hamadryas baboons. *Behavioral Ecology and Sociobiology*, 1980, *6*, 315-321.

Bielert, C. Sexual interactions between captive adult male and female chacma baboons (*Papio ursinus*) as related to the female's menstrual cycle. *Journal of Zoology, London*, 1986, *209*, 521-536.

Bielert, C., and Anderson, C. Baboon sexual swellings and male response. *International Journal of Primatology*, 1985, *6*, 375-391.

Bielert, C., Girolami, L., and Anderson, C. Male chacma baboon (*Papio ursinus*) sexual arousal: Studies with adolescent and adult females as visual stimuli. *Developmental Psychobiology*, 1986, *19*, 369-383.

Boggess, J. Intermale relations and troop male membership changes in langurs (*Presbytis entellus*) in Nepal. *International Journal of Primatology*, 1980, *1*, 233-274.

Brandt, E., and Mitchell, G. Parturition in primates. *In* L. Rosenblum (Ed.), *Primate behavior: Developments in field and laboratory research*, Vol. 2. New York: Academic Press, 1971, pp. 177-223.

Busse, C. Paternity recognition in multi-male primate groups. *American Zoologist*, 1985, *25*, 873-881.

Busse, C., and Hamilton, W.J., III. Infant carrying by male chacma baboons. *Science*, 1981, *212*, 1281-1283.

Butler, H. Evolutionary trends in primate sex cycles. *Contributions to Primatology*, 1974, *2*, 2-35.

Byrne, R., Whiten, A., and Henzi, P. One-male groups and intergroup interactions of mountain baboons. *International Journal of Primatology*, 1987, *8*, 615-633.

Clarke, M., and Glander, K. Female reproductive success in a group of free-ranging howling monkeys (*Alouatta palliata*) in Costa Rica. *In* M. Small (Ed.), *Female primates: Studies by women primatologists*. New York: Alan Liss, 1984, pp. 111-126.

Coe, C., Connolly, C., Kraemer, H., and Le Vine, S. Reproductive development and behavior of captive female chimpanzees. *Primates*, 1979, *20*, 571-582.

Collins, D. Interactions between adult male and infant yellow baboons (*Papio c. cynocephalus*) in Tanzania. *Animal Behaviour*, 1986, *34*, 430-443.

Conaway, C., and Koford, C. Estrous cycles and mating behavior in a free-ranging herd of rhesus monkeys. *Journal of Mammalogy*, 1965, *45*, 579-588.

Crockett, C., and Eisenberg, J. Howlers: Variations in group size and demography. *In* B. Smuts, D. Cheney, R. Seyfarth, R. Wrangham, and T. Struhsaker (Eds.), *Primate societies*. Chicago: University of Chicago Press, 1987, pp. 54-68.

Curtin, R. The socioecology of the common langurs (*Presbytis entellus*) in the Nepal Himalaya. Unpublished Ph.D. dissertation, University of California, Berkeley, 1975.

Dazey, J., and Erwin, J. Infant mortality in *Macaca nemestrina*. *Theriogenology*, 1976, *5*, 267-279.

Dittus, W. Population dynamics of the toque monkey, *Macaca sinica*. *In* R. Tuttle (Ed.), *Socioecology and psychology of primates*. Chicago: Aldine, 1975, pp. 125-152.

Dolhinow, P., McKenna, J., and Vonder Haar Laws, J. Rank and reproduction among female langur monkeys. *Aggressive Behavior*, 1979, *5*, 19-30.

Drickamer, L. A ten-year summary of reproductive data for free-ranging *Macaca mulatta*. *Folia Primatologica*, 1974, *21*, 61-80.

Dunbar, R. Sexual behaviour and social relationships among gelada baboons. *Animal Behaviour*, 1978, *26*, 167-178.

Dunbar, R. Demographic and life history variables of a population of gelada baboons (*Theropithecus gelada*). *Journal of Animal Ecology*, 1980, *49*, 485-506.

Dunbar, R. *Reproductive decisions: An economic analysis of gelada baboon social strategies*. Princeton: Princeton University Press, 1984.

Foerg, R. Reproductive behavior in *Varecia variegata*. *Folia Primatologica*, 1982, *38*, 108-121.

Fossey, D. Reproduction among free-living mountain gorillas. *American Journal of Primatology Supplement*, 1982, *1*, 97-104.

Fredrickson, W., and Bowers, C. Predicting survival of infant pigtailed macaques at 30 days by the assessment of background, maternal, and infant variables. *Developmental Psychobiology*, 1981, *17*, 319-325.

Galdikas, B. Orangutan reproduction in the wild. *In* C. Graham (Ed.), *Reproductive biology of the great apes*. New York: Academic Press, 1981, pp. 281-300.

Galdikas, B. Orangutan social organization at Tanjung Puting Reserve. *American Journal of Primatology*, 1985, *9*, 101-119.

Gilbert, C., and Gillman, J. Puberty in the baboon (*Papio ursinus*) in relation to age and body weight. *South African Journal of Medical Science*, 1960, *25*, 99-103.

Glander, K. Reproduction and population growth in free-ranging mantled howling monkeys. *American Journal of Physical Anthropology*, 1980, *53*, 25-36.

Glick, B. Ontogenetic and psychobiological aspects of the mating activities of male *Macaca radiata*. *In* D. Lindburg (Ed.), *The macaques*. New York: Van Nostrand, 1980, pp. 345-370.

Goodall, J. Population dynamics during a 15-year period in one community of free-living chimpanzees in the Gombe National Park, Tanzania. *Zeitschrift für Tierpsychologie*, 1983, *61*, 1-60.

Gouzoules, S., and Gouzoules, H. Kinship. *In* B. Smuts, D. Cheney, R. Seyfarth, R. Wrangham, and T. Struhsaker (Eds.), *Primate societies*. Chicago: University of Chicago Press, 1987, pp. 299-305.

Graham, C. Reproductive physiology of the chimpanzees. *In* G. Bourne (Ed.), *The chimpanzee*, Vol. 3. Basel: Karger, 1970, pp. 183-220.

Hall, K. Variations in the ecology of the chacma baboon, *Papio ursinus*. *Symposia of the Zoological Society, London*, 1963, *10*, 1-28.

Hall, K., and DeVore, I. Baboon social behavior. *In* I. DeVore (Ed.), *Primate behavior*. New York: Holt, Rinehart and Winston, 1965, pp. 53-110.

Hamilton, W.J., III. Significance of paternal investment by primates to the evolution of adult male-female associations. *In* D. Taub (Ed.), *Primate paternalism*. New York: Van Nostrand, 1984, pp. 309-335.

Harcourt, A., Fossey, D., Stewart, K., and Watts, D. Reproduction in wild gorillas and some comparisons with chimpanzees. *Journal of Reproduction and Fertility*, 1980, *28*, 59-70.

Hausfater, G. *Dominance and reproduction in baboons*. Basel: Karger, 1975.

Hird, D., Hendrickson, R., and Hendrickx, A. Infant mortality in *Macaca mulatta*. *Journal of Medical Primatology*, 1975, *4*, 8-22.

Hrdy, S. *The langurs of Abu*. Cambridge, Mass.: Harvard University Press, 1977.

Kaufmann, J. A three-year study of mating behavior in a free-ranging band of rhesus monkeys. *Ecology*, 1965, *46*, 500-512.

Kemps, A., and Timmermans, P. Effects of social rearing conditions and partus experience on periparturition behaviour in Java macaques (*Macaca fascicularis*). *Behaviour*, 1984, *88*, 200-214.

Kling, O., and Westfahl, P. Steroid changes during the menstrual cycle of the baboon (*Papio cynocephalus*) and human. *Biology of Reproduction*, 1978, *18*, 392-400.

Kummer, H. *Social organization of hamadryas baboons*. Chicago: University of Chicago Press, 1968.

Kummer, H., Goetz, W., and Angst, W. Triadic differentiation: An inhibitory process protecting pair bonds in baboons. *Behaviour*, 1974, *49*, 62-87.

Kusher, H., Kraft-Schreyer, N., Angelakos, E., and Wudarski, E. Analysis of reproductive data in a breeding colony of African green monkeys. *Journal of Medical Primatology*, 1982, *11*, 77-84.

Kuyk, K., Dazey, J., and Erwin, J. Primiparous and multiparous pigtail monkey mothers (*Macaca nemestrina*). *Journal of Biological Psychology*, 1976, *18*, 16-19.

Lancaster, J. Evolutionary perspectives on sex differences in the higher primates. *In* A. Rossi (Ed.), *Gender and the life course*. Hawthorne, N.Y.: Aldine, 1984, pp. 3-27.

Lehrman, D. Hormonal regulation of parental behavior in birds and infrahuman mammals. *In* W. Young (Ed.), *Sex and internal secretions.* Baltimore: Williams and Wilkins, 1961, pp. 1268-1382.

Leighton, D. Gibbons: Territoriality and monogamy. *In* B. Smuts, D. Cheney, R. Seyfarth, R. Wrangham, and T. Struhsaker (Eds.), *Primate societies.* Chicago: University of Chicago Press, 1987, pp. 135-145.

Lindburg, D. The rhesus monkey in North India. *In* L. Rosenblum (Ed.), *Primate behavior,* Vol. 2. New York: Academic Press, 1971, pp. 1-106.

Lindburg, D. Mating behavior and estrus in the Indian rhesus monkey. *In* P. Seth (Ed.), *Perspectives in primate biology.* New Delhi: Today and Tomorrow, 1983, pp. 45-61.

Lippold, L. The Douc langur. *In* H.S.H. Prince Rainier and G. Bourne (Eds.), *Primate conservation.* New York: Academic Press, 1977, pp. 513-538.

Loy, J. Estrous behavior of free-ranging rhesus monkeys. *Primates,* 1971, *12,* 1-31.

Manley, G. Through the territorial barrier: Harem accretion in *Presbytis senex. In* J. Else and P. Lee (Eds.), *Primate ontogeny, cognition and social behaviour.* Cambridge, England: Cambridge University Press, 1986, pp. 363-370.

Marsh, C. Female transference and mate choice among Tana River red colobus. *Nature,* 1979, *281,* 568-569.

Melnick, D., and Pearl, M. Cercopithecines in multimale groups: Genetic diversity and population structure. *In* B. Smuts, D. Cheney, R. Seyfarth, R. Wrangham, and T. Struhsaker (Eds.), *Primate societies.* Chicago: University of Chicago Press, 1987, pp. 121-134.

Mitchell, G., Ruppenthal, G., Raymond, E., and Harlow, H. Long-term effects of multiparous and primiparous monkey mother rearing. *Child Development,* 1966, *37,* 781-791.

Mori, A. Analysis of population changes by measurement of body weight in the Koshima troop of Japanese monkeys. *Primates,* 1979, *20,* 371-399.

Nadler, R. Determinants of variability in maternal behavior of captive female gorillas. *In* S. Kondo, M. Kawai, A. Ehara, and S. Kawamura (Eds.), *Proceedings from the Symposia of the Fifth International Congress of Primatology.* Tokyo: Japan Science Press, 1975, pp. 207-216.

Nicolson, N. Weaning and the development of independence in olive baboons. Unpublished Ph.D. thesis, Harvard University, 1982.

Packer, C. Intertroop transfer and inbreeding avoidance in *Papio anubis. Animal Behaviour,* 1979, *27,* 1-36.

Pusey, A. Inbreeding avoidance in chimpanzees. *Animal Behaviour,* 1980, *28,* 543-552.

Pusey, A., and Packer, C. Dispersal and philopatry. *In* B. Smuts, D. Cheney, R. Seyfarth, R. Wrangham, and T. Struhsaker (Eds.), *Primate societies*. Chicago: University of Chicago Press, 1987, pp. 250-266.

Ransom, T. *Beach troop of the Gombe*. East Brunswick, N.J.: Associated University Presses, 1981.

Rasmussen, K. Age-related variation in the interactions of adult females with adult males in yellow baboons. *In* R. Hinde (Ed.), *Primate social relationships*. Oxford: Blackwell, 1983, pp. 47-53.

Rasmussen, K. Spatial patterns and peripheralisation of yellow baboons (*Papio cynocephalus*) during sexual consortships. *Behaviour*, 1986, *97*, 161-180.

Rijksen, H. *A field study on Sumatran orang utans (Pongo pygmaeus abelii) (Lesson 1827)*. Wageningen: Veenman and Zonen, 1978.

Rowell, T. A quantitative comparison of the behaviour of a wild and caged baboon troop. *Animal Behaviour*, 1967, *15*, 499-509.

Rowell, T. *Social behaviour of monkeys*. Baltimore: Penguin, 1972.

Rowell, T., and Richard, S. Reproductive strategies of some African monkeys. *Journal of Mammalogy*, 1979, *60*, 58-59.

Rudran, R. Adult male replacement in one-male troops of purplefaced langurs (*Presbytis senex senex*) and its effect on population structure. *Folia Primatologica*, 1973, *19*, 166-192.

Saayman, G. Effects of ovarian hormones on the sexual skin and behavior of ovariectomized baboons under free-ranging conditions. *Symposia of the IVth International Congress of Primatology*, 1973, *2*, 64-98.

Sackett, G., Holm, R., Davis, A., and Fahrenbruch, D. Prematurity and low birth weight in pigtail macaques. *Symposia of the Vth Congress of the International Primatological Society*, 1974, pp. 189-205.

Sade, D., Cushing, K., Cushing, P., Dunaif, J., Figuerva, A., Kaplan, J., Lauer, C., Rhodes, D., and Schneider, J. Population dynamics in relation to social structure on Cayo Santiago. *Yearbook of Physical Anthropology*, 1976, *20*, 253-262.

Schürmann, C. Courtship and mating behavior of wild orangutans in Sumatra. *In* A. Chiarelli and R. Corruccini (Eds.), *Primate behavior and sociobiology*. Berlin: Springer-Verlag, 1981, pp. 130-135.

Scott, L. Reproductive behavior of adolescent female baboons (*Papio anubis*) in Kenya. *In* M. Small (Ed.), *Female primates*. New York: Alan Liss, 1984, pp. 77-100.

Seyfarth, R. Social relationships among adult male and female baboons. *Behaviour*, 1978, *64*, 204-247.

Sigg, H., and Stolba, A. Home range and daily march in a hamadryas baboon troop. *Folia Primatologica*, 1981, *36*, 40-75.

Sigg, H., Stolba, A., Abegglen, J.-J., and Dasser, V. Life history of hamadryas baboons. *Primates*, 1982, *23*, 473-487.

Silk, J. Measurement of the relative importance of individual selection and kin selection among females of the genus *Macaca*. *Evolution*, 1984, *38*, 553-559.

Silk, J., Clark-Wheatley, C., Rodman, P., and Samueles, A. Differential reproductive success and facultative adjustment of sex ratios among captive female bonnet macaques (*Macaca radiata*). *Animal Behaviour*, 1981, *29*, 1106-1120.

Small, M. Aging and reproductive success in female *Macaca mulatta*. *In* M. Small (Ed.), *Female primates*. New York: Alan Liss, 1984, pp. 249-260.

Smuts, B. *Sex and friendship in baboons*. Hawthorne, N.Y.: Aldine, 1985.

Smuts, B., Cheney, D., Seyfarth, R., Wrangham, R., and Struhsaker, T. (Eds.), *Primate societies*. Chicago: University of Chicago Press, 1987.

Stammbach, E. Desert, forest, and montane baboons: Multilevel societies. *In* B. Smuts, D. Cheney, R. Seyfarth, R. Wrangham, and T. Struhsaker (Eds.), *Primate societies*. Chicago: University of Chicago Press, 1987, pp. 112-120.

Stewart, K., and Harcourt, A. Gorillas: Variation in female relationships. *In* B. Smuts, D. Cheney, R. Seyfarth, R. Wrangham, and T. Struhsaker (Eds.), *Primate societies*. Chicago: University of Chicago Press, 1987, pp. 155-164.

Stoltz, L., and Saayman, G. Ecology and behaviour of baboons in the northern Transvaal. *Annals of the Transvaal Museum*, 1970, *26*, 99-143.

Strum, S. Use of females by male olive baboons (*Papio anubis*). *American Journal of Primatology*, 1983, *5*, 93-109.

Symons, D. *Play and aggression: A study of rhesus monkeys*. New York: Columbia University Press, 1978.

Takahata, Y. The socio-sexual behavior of Japanese monkeys. *Zeitschrift für Tierpsychologie*, 1982, *59*, 89-108.

Taub, D. Age at first pregnancy and reproductive success among colony-born squirrel monkeys. *Folia Primatologica*, 1980, *33*, 262-272.

Taub, D., Adams, M., and Auerbach, K. Reproductive performance in a breeding colony of Brazilian squirrel monkeys (*Saimiri sciureus*). *Laboratory Animal Science*, 1978, *28*, 562-566.

Teleki, G., Hunt, E., and Pfifferling, J. Demographic observations (1963-1973) on the chimpanzees of Gombe National Park, Tanzania. *Journal of Human Evolution*, 1976, *5*, 559-598.

Tilson, R. Family formation strategies of Kloss's gibbons. *Folia Primatologica*, 1981, *29*, 259-287.

Trivers, R. Parental investment and sexual selection. *In* B. Campbell (Ed.), *Sexual selection and the descent of Man, 1871-1971*. Chicago: Aldine, 1972, pp. 136-179.

200    Connie M. Anderson and Craig Bielert

Tutin, C. Exceptions to promiscuity in a feral chimpanzee community. *In* S. Kondo, K. Kawai, and A. Ehara (Eds.), *Contemporary primatology.* Basel: Karger, 1975, pp. 445-449.

Tutin, C. Mating patterns and reproductive strategies in a community of wild chimpanzees (*Pan troglodytes schweinfurthii*). *Behavioral Ecology and Sociobiology,* 1979, *6,* 29-38.

Tutin, C. Reproductive behavior of wild chimpanzees in the Gombe National Park, Tanzania. *Reproduction and Fertility Supplement,* 1980, *28,* 43-47.

de Waal, F. *Chimpanzee politics.* London: Unwin, 1982.

Wasser, S., and Starling, A. Reproductive competition among female yellow baboons. *In* J. Else and P. Lee (Eds.), *Primate ontogeny, cognition and social behaviour.* Cambridge, England: Cambridge University Press, 1986, pp. 343-354.

Wilson, M., Gordon, T., and Bernstein, I. Timing of births and reproductive success in rhesus monkey social groups. *Journal of Medical Primatology,* 1978, *7,* 202-212.

Wolfe, L. Sexual strategies of female Japanese macaques (*Macaca fuscata*). *Human Evolution,* 1986, *1,* 267-275.

# 7
# Mechanisms of Inbreeding Avoidance in Nonhuman Primates

Anne Pusey
*Department of Ecology and Behavioral Biology*
*University of Minnesota*
*Minneapolis, Minnesota 55455*

## Introduction

Anthropologists have long noted that there is a universal tendency for humans to avoid and to prohibit sexual activity between various categories of relatives. This universal phenomenon of incest avoidance was regarded by some as a uniquely human characteristic that sets humans apart from animals. Recently, however, it has become clear that many animals also avoid mating with their close relatives, and several anthropologists have pointed to a biological basis for human incest taboos (e.g., Bischof, 1975; van den Berghe, 1982; Durham, in press). In this chapter, this author reviews the evidence that nonhuman primates avoid mating with their relatives and almost never breed with them. "Inbreeding" is used as a general term to describe breeding with consanguineous relatives. Close inbreeding is defined as "mating and breeding with first-degree relatives such as parents or siblings" and is synonymous with incest as it is defined in this volume.

There are compelling biological reasons to avoid close inbreeding. There is abundant evidence that mating between close relatives leads to an increase in genetic homozygosity in the resulting offspring, which can cause inbreeding depression: a reduction in the viability and fertility of offspring. Although few data from natural populations of any animal are available, inbreeding depression has been consistently documented in captive studies of a wide variety of animals (Ralls and Ballou, 1983) and in humans (see Cavalli-Sforza and Bodmer, 1971). Another deleterious effect of increased homozygosity is increased susceptibility to pathogens that are more easily able to decimate a population of genetically similar individuals (O'Brien et al., 1985).

In a recent review of the 28 most extensively studied species of birds and mammals, Ralls et al. (1986) found that breeding between parents and offspring or between full siblings occurred at low rates. In only two species did these kinds of unions compose more than 5% of the total, and most species showed rates of close inbreeding that were at or close to zero. How then do animals avoid close inbreeding? Two mechanisms have been documented: physical separation of close relatives, either by death or dispersal, and active behavioral avoidance or suppression of mating between close kin living in the same social group (Ralls et al., 1986; Pusey and Packer, 1987; Blouin and Blouin, 1988). Both mechanisms may operate in the same species.

## Sex-Biased Dispersal

Primates exhibit a variety of social organizations (Smuts et al., 1987). Most species are gregarious and live in permanent social groups containing several breeding females and one to several adult males. In a few species, the adults are solitary, and in some they form monogamous pairs. Although primate social groups used to be thought of as closed social units, it is now clear that there is considerable movement of individuals between social groups (see review by Pusey and Packer, 1987). The most common pattern is for virtually all males to leave their social group or area, while females remain. Males usually leave at puberty and move to new groups or areas before breeding (natal dispersal). In many cases, these males also disperse again as adults to other groups or areas (breeding dispersal) but rarely return to the natal group. A small proportion of species (e.g., chimpanzees, some red colobus populations, hamadryas baboons) show the opposite pattern. In these species, most or all **females** leave at or before adolescence, while males stay, and females may also disperse as adults. Finally, in monogamous species and a few gregarious species, a proportion of both sexes disperses. It is striking that in all well-studied species, most or all individuals of one sex or the other disperse.

Although these dispersal patterns result in the separation of close relatives and a consequent reduction in the opportunity for close inbreeding, there has been considerable debate over the view that sex-biased dispersal has evolved as an inbreeding avoidance mechanism (Harcourt, 1978; Packer, 1979; Greenwood, 1980; Moore and Ali, 1984; Packer, 1985; Dobson and Jones, 1985; Ralls et al., 1986; Pusey and Packer, 1987; Pusey, 1987). Critics of this view argue that dispersal patterns can be more simply explained by other factors, particularly intrasexual competition (Moore and Ali, 1984). There is no doubt that some dispersal results from intrasexual competition (see review by Pusey and Packer, 1987). In polygynous species, one or a few males are often able to maintain exclusive access to a larger number of females, and in some species, males are evicted from social groups by other males. Also, males in some species disperse to groups or areas where they have access to more females, particularly during breeding dispersal. Among monogamous primates such as gibbons, competition with the same-sex parent often hastens the emigration of subadults. In a few species, such as howlers, female/female competition results in female dispersal.

Competition alone, however, appears insufficient to explain the ubiquitous dispersal of one sex or the other. In some species where males disperse, males usually leave regardless of the levels of competition within their natal group and may even leave when no adult males are present (Pusey and Packer, 1987; Sugiyama, 1976). Moreover, individuals dispersing to new social groups often encounter higher levels of aggression there than they did in their natal group—the opposite of what would be expected if they were dispersing to avoid competition (Pusey and Packer, 1987). Finally, a common proximate factor in natal dispersal is greater attraction of dispersing individuals to unfamiliar mates in other groups (see below), a pattern that is more consistent with inbreeding avoidance than with the avoidance of competition (Pusey, 1987).

Comparative evidence both within primates and across all mammals strongly implicates inbreeding avoidance as an important factor determining patterns of sex-biased dispersal. Figure 7.1 shows that across gregarious species of primates, the tendency of females to disperse is negatively correlated with the proportion of males in their natal group that are immigrants. Females are most likely to disperse in species where their male relatives remain as adults in the females' natal group. Similarly, Clutton-Brock (1989) has recently shown that there is a strong relationship between the likelihood of female dispersal and the length of adult male tenure in the female's natal group across all gregarious species of mammals. In most species, average male tenure in a group is shorter than the time it takes females to reach sexual maturity, and females do not disperse; but in species where average male tenure exceeds this period, females do disperse and, thus, avoid mating with their fathers.

These dispersal patterns result in a low likelihood of close relatives residing in the same group. They are a straightforward prediction of the inbreeding-avoidance hypothesis for sex-biased dispersal and are difficult to explain solely on the basis of species differences in levels of intrasexual competition. It therefore seems likely that sex-biased dispersal has evolved at least in part as an inbreeding-avoidance mechanism.

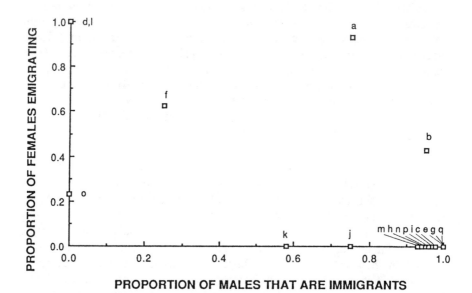

**PROPORTION OF MALES THAT ARE IMMIGRANTS**

Figure 7.1. Female emigration versus availability of unrelated males in natal group. Each letter represents one species. a = *Alouatta palliata*, b = *A. seniculus*, c = *Cercopithecus aethiops*, d = *Colobus badius*, e = *Erythrocebus patas*, f = *Gorilla gorilla*, g = *Macaca fascicularis*, h = *M. fuscata*, i = *M. mulatta*, j = *M. sinica*, k = *M. sylvanus*, l = *Pan troglodytes*, m = *Papio anubis*, n = *P. cynocephalus*, o = *P. hamadryas*, p = *P. ursinus*, q = *Presbytis entellus*. The probability that females emigrate from their natal group is highest where the proportion of immigrant males in that group is lowest (across species: rs = -0.69, n = 17, p < 0.005; across genera: rs = -0.86, n = 10, p < 0.005). Correlations are also calculated from genus averages since most species of *Macaca* and *Papio* showed similar patterns. (Data from Table 21-1 of Pusey and Packer, 1987. Figure redrawn from Figure 12-4 of Pusey and Packer, 1987, with permission from the University of Chicago Press.)

# Avoidance of Mating Between Close Relatives Residing Together in Adulthood

Although dispersal patterns in primates greatly reduce the probability of close relatives of the opposite sex residing together in adulthood, they do not eliminate the condition entirely. In some cases, members of the dispersing sex reach sexual maturity before leaving and reside in the same group as their siblings. Also, in some cases, parents are still present when their offspring of the opposite sex reach reproductive age. When the opportunity to mate with close relatives exists, is it realized? and if not, what mechanisms prevent such mating?

## Avoidance of Mating Between Maternal Relatives

The earliest reports of behavioral avoidance of mating between close relatives involved the avoidance of mating between mother and son in various species of macaques (Imanishi, 1965; Tokuda, 1961-2; Sade, 1968). Later studies of macaques and other species have corroborated these reports and have also demonstrated behavioral avoidance of other maternal relatives.

In macaques, males generally leave their natal groups at puberty, but especially in large, provisioned groups, some males remain for some time as sexually mature individuals. Detailed studies of the sexual behavior of adult male Japanese macaques have shown that sexual behavior is the least common with their closest female relatives. In the large Arashiyama group, sexual activity was significantly less frequent than random in all maternal-kin dyads as closely related as cousins but not significantly different from random in more distantly related dyads (Takahata, 1982). In Shiga A troop, high-ranking natal males copulated less with females of their own matriline than with females of others (Enomoto, 1974), and no sexual activity was observed between a son and his mother, although he mated actively with other females (Enomoto, 1978). Sexual activity was almost nonexistent between three pairs of maternal siblings, rare in one uncle/niece and three aunt/nephew dyads, and common in only three of seven cousin/cousin dyads (Enomoto, 1978). In most cases where any sexual activity was observed between close relatives in either group, the male was more active than the female in initiating the interaction (Enomoto, 1974, 1978; Takahata, 1982).

Similarly, in one group of rhesus macaques on Cayo Santiago, two high-ranking natal adult males never consorted with their mother, maternal sisters, or other female members of their matriline, although they consorted actively with other females (Chapais, 1983).

Among a group of captive stump-tail macaques, mounting of mothers or maternal sisters by adult males occurred significantly less frequently than expected by chance and was observed in only one out of six mother/son pairs (Murray and Smith, 1983). In a detailed study of mating behavior in a captive population of Barbary macaques, where only half of the males had left their natal troop by full size, no matings were observed between 22 mother/son pairs or 45 brother/sister pairs where the male was still in his natal troop at age 4-9 years, and only one copulation was observed in one of eight uncle/niece dyads, whereas the same males mated frequently with unrelated females. Males sometimes inspected their estrous mothers and sisters but never attempted to copulate. Females never formed sexual associations with sons or brothers (Paul and Kuester, 1985).

Most studies have concentrated on the sexual behavior of males after puberty, but a few have described sexual behavior between immature and pubertal males and their female relatives (see Anderson and Bielert, this volume). In a detailed study of the development of sexual behavior in captive Japanese macaques, Hanby and Brown (1974) found that infant males copulated with their mothers but that juvenile and adolescent males rarely did so and never achieved ejaculation.

In the rhesus monkeys of Cayo Santiago, where male puberty occurs in the fourth year (Colvin, 1983), Missakian (1973) found that most males of 3-5 years of age who were still in their natal troop did not show any mating activity, but those that did show such activity mated almost exclusively with their mothers and maternal sisters. Mating was observed between 8 of 26 pairs of mothers and sons and between 6 of 42 brother/sister pairs (in which both male and female were at least 3 years old). In contrast, males older than 5 years that stayed in their natal group mated actively with other females but not with their sisters or mothers. In a study of another troop on Cayo Santiago, Sade et al. (1984) reported mating between 7 of 52 mother/son pairs. From their report, it appears that these seven males were probably also in the 3- to 5-year age group. It seems that in this species, mating with relatives sometimes occurs in pubertal males but disappears by the time the males are fully adult. In both studies in which mother/son mating was observed, the sexual behavior was atypical. Missakian (1973) emphasized that none of the males that mated with their mothers showed typical consort behavior, which consists of following the female, extensive reciprocal grooming, repeated mount series, and copulations. Similarly, Sade et al. (1984) noted that most of the mother/son matings that they observed were "unusual in their behavioral details, suggesting that the motivational and emotional content of the events distinguished them from nonincestuous matings."

Similar findings have been made in other Old World monkeys. Unlike macaques, male baboons generally stay in their natal troops for several years after puberty and transfer to other troops only when they are approximately full sized (Pusey and Packer, 1987). They show some consorting activity prior to transferring (Packer, 1979) and, therefore, have considerable opportunity to mate with their mothers and sisters. However, such matings are rare. In one study, no postpubertal male ever consorted with his mother or sisters during daily recording of consorting activity in three troops over a four-year period (Packer, 1979). During 19 months of focal-animal sampling, three males had mothers or sisters that showed estrous cycles. One male achieved a complete copulation with his pregnant mother. The same male mounted his mother without intromission when she was just postestrus, and another male mounted his lactating mother. On both occasions, the mother made aggressive vocalizations and terminated the mount. Also, one prepubertal juvenile was observed to copulate several times with his cycling sister (Packer, 1979). In another detailed study, no postpubertal male copulated with his mother or maternal sisters around the time of ovulation (Scott, 1984). Finally, in a third study, two known postpubertal sons and four presumed sons showed no sexual interest in their mother when she was in estrus (Smuts, 1985).

In a large group of captive vervets, an inverse relationship was found between sexual activity and the degree of maternal kinship among adult males and females (Bramblett, 1983). Similarly, no cases of mother/son copulations have been observed in a 10-year study of several groups of wild vervet monkeys (Cheney and Seyfarth, personal communication).

Low frequencies of mother/son and sibling matings have also been reported among chimpanzees. Chimpanzees show an unusual social structure. Males remain in their natal groups as adults, while most females transfer at adolescence to other groups (Pusey, 1980; Nishida and Hiraiwa-Hasegawa, 1987). This pattern means that many females reside in the same groups as their adult sons. Some sexual behavior has been described between infant and juvenile males and their mothers and siblings (Tutin, 1979; Pusey, 1978). During weaning, juveniles sometimes get very upset, and mothers sometimes present to them, whereupon juvenile males mount and thrust with intromission (Clark, 1977). As adults, however, males almost never mate with their mothers (Tutin, 1979; Pusey, 1980; Goodall, 1986). At Gombe, six adult males have each been observed with their respective mothers during 2-5 periods of estrus. Four never showed any signs of interest or sexual arousal in her presence, although all readily mated with other females. One once copulated with his mother; she screamed loudly throughout and leaped away prior to ejaculation. The sixth male (Goblin) quite frequently showed sexual interest in his mother and attempted to copulate on seven occasions. His mother always resisted him strenuously, but he pursued and attacked her and succeeded in copulating three times, although she usually jumped away before ejaculation (Goodall, 1986).

Although female chimpanzees often transfer to neighboring groups during adolescence, they experience a two-year period of adolescent sterility and usually spend some of their estrous periods mating with males from their natal group. Pusey (1980) found that juvenile and adolescent females associated at high levels with their older male maternal siblings until their first estrus, at which point the association declined abruptly. Nevertheless, these females were sometimes observed with their brothers when in estrus but almost never copulated with them, although they copulated readily with other males. Brothers showed little sexual interest in their sisters compared to other females, but when they did court or copulate with their sisters, the sisters usually protested and tried to escape. Recently, Goodall (1986) extended this analysis and presented data on another sibling dyad. She showed that one female that remained as an adult in her natal community mated more frequently with her brother following the birth of her second offspring, but he did not father her infant. In the additional dyad, the male (Goblin) copulated with his sister frequently, although she resisted his sexual advances much more frequently than she resisted those of other males. It is interesting that this pair of siblings had had a lower association than the other pairs before the female's first estrus because the male spent unusually little time with his mother and sister after he reached puberty (Pusey, manuscript in preparation).

It is possible that in gibbons sexual behavior between relatives is less inhibited than in other species. Gibbons are monogamous, and subadults of both sexes always leave their natal group if both parents are still alive. However, in one case, a male Kloss's gibbon paired with his widowed mother and mated, and they eventually produced an offspring. In two other cases, subadult males remained with their widowed mothers but had not been observed to mate by the end of the study (Tilson, 1981). Temporary mother/son pairings in one group of siamangs and one group of white-handed gibbons have also been observed, but neither lasted or bred (Leighton, 1987). Although data on family formation in gibbons indicate that incestuous pairs may be common, they probably usually involve mates of widely disparate ages whose pairbond does not last long enough to result in much inbreeding, and the advantages of inheriting the natal territory in a crowded area are likely to outweigh any costs of inbreeding (Tilson, 1981; Leighton, 1987; Pusey and Packer, 1987).

## Avoidance of Mating Between Fathers and Daughters

There are fewer data on the incidence of sexual activity between fathers and daughters because in most cases fathers are hard for observers to identify even if they are still present in the same social group, but there is evidence from some species that such activity is rare. Male baboons usually transfer to other troops before their daughters are old enough to mate, but some remain longer and are still present when females that could be their daughters become sexually active. Packer (1979) found that nine such males consorted less with these females than with other females, whereas some other males who could not have been fathers of the females consorted with these females more, and the difference between the two types of males was significant. Similarly, at another study site, Scott (1984) found that two males that had been present in the group at the birth of several now-adolescent females showed very low rates of sexual activity with them. Packer (1979) found that juvenile female baboons associated more closely with males that had been present in the troop at their birth than with males that had entered the troop after their birth and suggests that this greater familiarity might be the basis upon which these females base later mating patterns. One of these females was eventually observed receiving consortship attention from a male that had been in the troop at her birth, but she avoided this male at unusually high rates. In another population, Smuts (1985) found that females who had had close relationships with particular adult males in immaturity showed no sexual behavior with them when the females reached sexual maturity.

Adolescent female chimpanzees that are still in their natal group sometimes show reluctance to mate with older males. One female, who had a very close relationship with a male old enough to be her father, was never observed in any sexual interaction with him, although she mated readily with younger males (Pusey, 1980). Several other females were observed to scream and avoid the courtship of some males old enough to be their fathers, while mating readily with other males (Tutin, 1979; Pusey, 1980). However, Goodall (1986) recently presented data on two additional females that showed no aversion to mating with their presumed fathers. The latter, however, showed little interest in mating with these young females. Indeed, consortships between males and females young enough to be their daughters were comparatively uncommon, and none resulted in conception by the female (Goodall, 1986).

The social organization of gorillas often results in male relatives being present when females reach maturity (Stewart and Harcourt, 1987). Most social groups consist of one adult male and a small group of adult females and their young, but a few also contain other, younger adult males who usually were born in the group. Male tenure in groups is long, and immigration of males into bisexual groups is very rare. Most females emigrate from their natal group as adolescents or young adults. The timing of female emigration and the sexual behavior of females in their natal group suggest that they are inhibited from mating with the dominant male, who is likely to be their father, but are more likely to mate with younger males, who are often but not always half-brothers. Of seven natal females, four emigrated before breeding and, in all cases, left groups in which the only breeding male was their known or presumed father. In contrast, the other three did not emigrate before breeding. In all these cases, the groups included at least one other, younger adult male. In one case, the female is known to have been unrelated to the male, since he was the only male ever observed to immigrate into a bisexual group. Furthermore, of four young females who were observed to mate (but not necessarily breed) in their natal groups, three copulated only with the younger, subordinate male, who was at most a half-sibling. Only one female was observed to copulate with her presumed father, and she appeared to be much less sexually attracted to him than to the younger male (Stewart and Harcourt, 1987).

There are other species, however, in which sexual behavior between father and daughter may be more common, at least under some circumstances. Among gibbons, fathers have been observed to exhibit sexual interest in and mate with their maturing daughters, but such behavior did not last long and never resulted in breeding, because the mother increased aggression toward her daughter and forced her to the periphery of the group (Tilson, 1981; Leighton, 1987). In a captive group of rhesus macaques, there was frequent mating between father and daughter that did result in conception (Smith, 1982). However, these conditions were highly artificial, because no male dispersal was permitted. In free-living rhesus macaques, adult males leave groups after a few years, and females always have a choice of immigrants with whom to mate.

## Avoidance of Mating with other Members of the Natal Group

Many primate social groups are likely to contain paternal as well as maternal half-siblings and, also, other paternal relatives. Data on whether there is avoidance of mating between paternal siblings are for the most part unavailable because observers usually have no means of identifying such individuals. Mating between paternal siblings was found to be frequent in a captive rhesus group where males were kept in their natal group (Smith, 1982). Mating also occurred between paternal half-sibs in gorillas more frequently than between females and their fathers before females left their natal group (Stewart and Harcourt, 1987).

In some species, there is some evidence of a general lack of sexual activity between individuals born in the same group. In baboons, males form exclusive consortships with estrous females and often fight to keep the female from other males. Although natal males usually stay in their natal group until they are fully grown and sometimes become socially dominant before transferring to other groups, the males of one population only consorted with females at very low levels while in their natal group and avoided competition over females with other males (Packer, 1979). In contrast, when they transferred to a new group, they showed intense interest in females of the new group and competed at high levels to consort with them. Females showing estrous cycles also preferred to interact and consort with immigrant males rather than natal males. In this population, group size was relatively small, and all males emigrated from their natal group as they reached full size (Packer, 1979). Packer suggests that the immediate motivation for transfer in this species was attraction to unfamiliar females. In other populations, a small proportion of natal males have been observed to stay and breed in their natal groups (reviewed in Pusey and Packer, 1987). In one such group, it was said, females did not avoid mating with these males, but no details were given on group size or the degree of relatedness of the males to the females with whom they mated (Bulger and Hamilton, 1988).

Adolescent female chimpanzees generally transfer to new groups when they are in estrus, and two females that were observed both with males of their natal community and those of a neighboring community appeared to be more sexually attracted to the latter (Pusey, 1980). Also, male chimpanzees appear to be more attracted to immigrant than natal females (Goodall, 1986). A general lack of attraction to opposite-sex individuals of the natal group and a greater attraction to those in other groups has also been described in vervets (Henzi and Lucas, 1980; Cheney and Seyfarth, personal communication), toque macaques (Dittus, 1977), and long-tailed macaques (van Noordwijk and van Schaik, 1985).

## Reproductive Suppression by Relatives

The examples of avoidance of mating between relatives, discussed above, involve individuals who are sexually mature and capable of mating with other individuals. However, there are also examples among nonprimate species where sexual maturity in young individuals is delayed or suppressed by the presence of relatives (usually parents) of the opposite sex (reviewed in Blouin and Blouin, 1988). Among primates, reproductive suppression has been demonstrated most clearly in various species of callitrichid monkeys (marmosets and tamarins). In these species, only the dominant pair breed, and ovarian cycling is suppressed in young females as long as they remain in their natal family or are exposed to the group's odor (e.g., Epple and Katz, 1984). However, although Blouin and Blouin (1988) cite the exposure to the group's odor as a possible mechanism for inbreeding avoidance, the evidence suggests that it is odors from the mother that are the most effective in this suppression, and an alternative explanation is that damaging reproductive competition between mother and daughter for limited resources is thereby avoided.

# What Recognition Mechanisms Are Involved in the Avoidance of Mating with Kin?

Avoidance of mating between relatives requires some mechanism of identifying relatives. There are two possible ways that animals might make such an identification. Animals may classify individuals on the basis of some measure of similarity to themselves or their familiar kin and by these means classify even unfamiliar individuals, or they may classify individuals according to their degree of familiarity with them (see review by Holmes and Sherman, 1983). In most mammal species, there is likely to be a high correlation between degree of friendly association and degree of kinship. Experiments to demonstrate the former mechanism involve raising individuals either alone or in groups with some relatives and then testing whether they behave differently to different classes of unfamiliar relatives and nonrelatives. Such experiments have revealed that several species, such as Japanese quail, tadpoles, and ground squirrels, are able to make these discriminations. Similar experiments in primates have been conducted only with paternal and not maternal kin, and the results are equivocal (reviewed by Walters, 1987).

There is a general consensus that the second mechanism is of prime importance in mammals (see review by Walters, 1987). In rodents, evidence that familiarity per se rather than relatedness is important in reduced sexual attraction comes from experiments in which both relatives and nonrelatives raised together delayed reproduction compared to those that were raised apart (reviewed by Blouin and Blouin, 1988). Similar evidence exists for humans and has been termed the Westermarck effect, following Westermarck's early recognition of the phenomenon (Westermarck, 1891). Unrelated children that were raised together in the same kibbutz never marry, although such marriages would be socially sanctioned (Shepher, 1971), and the obsolete Chinese practice of raising bride and groom together from infancy resulted in a reluctance to marry and in more sexual and marital dissatisfaction than results from other forms of arranged marriage (Wolf and Huang, 1980). Also, a recent study of sexual behavior between children and adolescents, on the one hand, and fathers or step-fathers, on the other, showed that familiarity between male parent and child or adolescent during the child's or adolescent's infancy significantly reduced the chances of sexual interactions with male parents of both categories (Parker and Parker, 1986).

In nonhuman primates, there are only a few studies that have distinguished between the effects of familiarity and of kinship. Anecdotal evidence from zoos suggests that unrelated primates raised together often show reduced sexual attraction. In one study of captive chimpanzees, where two social groups of unrelated individuals that had been raised together were mixed shortly before the beginning of the study, it was found that sexual activity was much less frequent between individuals that had been raised together than between those that had recently been introduced. In the case of one familiar pair, it was shown that while the male frequently inspected the estrous swelling of the female, no copulations occurred because the female consistently avoided the male (Coe et al., 1979).

Another study that bears on this question was conducted in Japanese macaques (Itoigawa et al., 1981). An adult male, his mother, an unrelated adult female who was a close associate of the male's mother, an unrelated adult female who was not a close associate of his mother, and another adult male were all taken into captivity from a stable subgroup of the Katsuyama group and housed separately. Then they were paired in cages in different combinations for varying periods. The son was paired with each of these females and with some unfamiliar females, and the females were paired both with the familiar male and with some unfamiliar males. The results were striking. While all these individuals mated readily with the unfamiliar males, mating was least frequent between the most familiar individuals, and there was almost no sexual behavior between the son and either his mother or the unrelated but close female associate of his mother; instead, the son engaged in extensive reciprocal grooming with each of these females.

Finally, there is some evidence from natural populations that long-term familiarity between unrelated adults of the opposite sex leads to reduced sexual activity in some species. In two groups of Japanese macaques, sexual activity was the least frequent between individuals that had strong associations and grooming relationships and the most frequent between male newcomers and females of the group (Enomoto, 1978; Takahata, 1982). In rhesus macaques on Cayo Santiago, males that have held high rank in a group for a long time sometimes show very little sexual activity and appear to be more interested in the females of other groups (Berard, personal communication). In one population of baboons, females appeared to be the most strongly sexually attracted to the newest male immigrants to the group (Packer, 1979), and in langurs, females from groups with long-term resident males were the most likely to seek copulations from extragroup males (Hrdy, 1977).

## Discussion and Conclusion

It is clear that the patterns of sex-biased dispersal found in primates greatly reduce the chances of close relatives residing in the same group as adults. Although these patterns are partly the result of other factors, such as intrasexual competition, evidence from cross-species comparisons and the contexts of dispersal in many species strongly support the hypothesis that inbreeding avoidance is also an important factor in determining these patterns. Dispersal, however, does not completely eliminate the opportunity for close inbreeding. In those cases where close relatives still reside in the same group, there is now considerable evidence for an inhibition of breeding behavior between them. It is less clear to what extent inbreeding is avoided between more distant relatives. In Japanese macaques, where some of the most detailed genealogical data exist, breeding is avoided with relatives as distantly related as first cousins. With the increasing use of DNA-fingerprinting techniques (e.g., Burke et al., 1989), it should be possible to determine more accurately the levels of inbreeding that are avoided in other species.

It should be noted that although breeding with familiar relatives is very rare, sexual behavior between relatives is not completely inhibited in all species. Among some, such as baboons and some macaques, mounts and even complete copulations between sexually mature relatives do occur. However, they almost never occur during periods in which the female is likely to conceive and, therefore, do not result in procreation. In addition, elements of sexual behavior occur between mothers and infant or juvenile sons and between and among immature and mature siblings in some species (e.g., chimpanzees, Japanese macaques, rhesus macaques; see above) (see also Anderson and Bielert, this volume). In captive orangutans, mothers frequently mount the genitals of their infants of both sexes (Maple, 1980). Sexual play between siblings and between cohort mates has also been reported to be more common in humans before than after puberty (reviewed in Bischof, 1975). Sexual behavior of immature individuals has no direct procreative function but, rather, can be regarded as practice. When such practice involves parent and offspring, it may represent a type of parental investment rather than reproductive effort. In some species, sexual behavior has taken on a social communicative function beyond that of procreation (see de Waal, this volume), and in many cases, such behavior between adult relatives should perhaps be interpreted in this light.

An early explanation for the lack of mother/son matings in macaques was that males were inhibited from mating with their mother because their mother ranked higher in social dominance than they did (Sade, 1968). However, this reasoning does not explain the occurrence of early sexual behavior between immature males and their mothers, and subsequent studies of pubertal and postpubertal macaques have failed to demonstrate a relationship between relative rank of mother and son or siblings and the likelihood of sexual behavior (Missakian, 1973; Murray and Smith, 1983). Also, in chimpanzees, adult males rank higher than their mothers and sisters but still do not usually mate with them (Goodall, 1986).

The chief factor that leads to inhibition of breeding behavior among relatives appears to be close familiarity during the immaturity of one or both individuals. Although only a few primate studies have actually demonstrated that familiarity during immaturity, rather than genetic relatedness per se, is responsible for this inhibition (e.g., Coe et al., 1979; Itoigawa et al., 1981), it is likely that primates resemble other mammals in this respect. Among primates, mating appears to be the most strongly inhibited between close maternal kin. In almost all primate species, young individuals associate and interact more with their mother than with any other individual, and in species that live in groups of related females, such as macaques, young individuals associate at higher levels with maternal kin than with other individuals because of their close association with their mother (Gouzoules and Gouzoules, 1987). The differences in the strength of the inhibition of mating between different classes of relatives reported above, with mother/son matings being the most consistently avoided, are therefore consistent with differences in the degree of familiarity of immature individuals with these different classes. Similarly, the inhibition of mating between female baboons and males that were present in the group at their birth appears to be based on differences in familiarity with different types of males.

In several species where any sexual behavior has been observed between closely related adults, males appear to be more eager to mate with their female relatives than vice versa, although the males usually show less interest in their relatives than in other females (e.g., Japanese macaques—Enomoto, 1974, 1978; baboons—Packer, 1979; chimpanzees—Tutin, 1979; Pusey, 1980; Goodall, 1986; Coe et al., 1979). This finding is consistent with the fact that female mammals usually have more to lose from inbred matings than males (see review by Waser et al., 1986). Because female mammals have a more limited reproductive potential than males, each inbred offspring will represent a greater proportion of her total reproductive output than it would for males, and inbreeding will thus be more costly.

It has sometimes been suggested that mechanisms for inhibiting mating between relatives are more strongly developed in species where such relatives are more likely to reside together (Walters, 1987). For example, Paul and Kuester (1985) argue that mating is more strongly inhibited among related Barbary macaques than other species because males do not leave their natal group at puberty with such regularity in Barbary macaques as in other species, and hence, the risk of inbreeding is greater. Walters (1987) suggests that sexual behavior may be less inhibited between relatives in gibbons because the same-sex parent usually drives the subadult out of the group and the opportunity for breeding is thus precluded. Similarly, Smith (1982) suggests a relationship between the fact that inhibitory mechanisms between females and fathers or paternal siblings are lacking in rhesus macaques and the fact that these males usually leave the group before the opportunity of mating with female relatives arises in natural populations. However, it is possible that although female rhesus do not distinguish between familiar males of different degrees of relatedness, they may be able to distinguish between familiar and unfamiliar males as baboons do. In natural populations, where there is extensive male immigration, this level of discernment would be sufficient for them to avoid mating with paternal relatives even if some of the latter remained in the group. More data are needed in order for investigators to determine the nature and extent of species differences in inhibitory mechanisms and to relate these to differences in dispersal patterns.

A final point concerns the effects of captivity on the inhibition of mating between relatives. Many of the studies demonstrating inhibition of mating between maternal relatives cited here were of captive groups. It appears that both in the wild and in captivity, individuals try to mate with less familiar individuals if given the chance. However, where there is no choice, close relatives may mate. For example, twin orangutans raised together in the Seattle Zoo subsequently bred and produced an infant (Maple, 1980). Also, in gibbons, where the costs of dispersal are very high because territories are in short supply, incestuous pairings sometimes occur (see above), as is expected if dispersal costs exceed the costs of inbreeding (Bengtsson, 1978). Data are lacking on whether there are longer latencies to mate or abnormal sexual behavior in these situations, as has been observed in rodents (Blouin and Blouin, 1988).

In conclusion, there is now abundant evidence that primates, like other mammals and birds, consistently avoid close inbreeding. A primary mechanism that reduces close inbreeding is dispersal of one sex or the other before breeding. Before dispersing individuals leave or where close relatives do continue to reside in the same group as adults, there is evidence of reduced sexual attraction between close relatives, particularly maternal relatives. The proximate cause of this phenomenon seems to be close association between these individuals during the early life of one or both.

## Summary

There are two main ways in which nonhuman primates avoid the deleterious effects of close inbreeding. Almost all species show sex-biased dispersal in which most or all of the members of one sex or the other leave their social group before breeding. Although this dispersal results in the separation of close relatives in adulthood, there is debate over whether it has evolved as an inbreeding-avoidance mechanism or whether it results from intrasexual competition. Two kinds of evidence support the former view. First, cross-species comparisons show that when males do not leave their natal group, females do. Second, individuals often appear to join new groups because of sexual attraction to unfamiliar members of the opposite sex and will do so even in the face of intense opposition from same-sex individuals in the new group. In cases where close relatives are not separated by dispersal, a second mechanism operates. Although there is often some sexual activity between immature individuals and their immature or adult relatives, mating is very rare between related adults. Mating appears to be the most strongly inhibited between mothers and sons and between maternal siblings, but it may be inhibited among maternal relatives as distantly related as cousins in some species and even between any members of the natal group in others. Mating between fathers and daughters is also avoided in some species. As in other mammals, this mating inhibition appears to result from the close association of individuals during the early life of one or both. Among primates, associations are usually highest among maternal kin, and the degree of mating inhibition generally parallels the degree of association in immaturity. However, in cases where nonrelatives are reared together, inhibition of mating is also observed, as it is in humans.

## References

Bengtsson, B.O. Avoiding inbreeding: At what cost? *Journal of Theoretical Biology*, 1978, *73*, 439-444.

Bischof, N. Comparative ethology of incest avoidance. *In* R. Fox (Ed.), *Biosocial anthropology*. New York: Wiley, 1975, pp. 37-67.

Blouin, S.F., and Blouin, M. Inbreeding avoidance behaviors. *Trends in Ecology and Evolution*, 1988, *3*, 230-233.

Bramblett, C.A. Incest avoidance in socially living vervet monkeys. *American Journal of Physical Anthropology*, 1983, *63*, 176.

Bulger, J., and Hamilton, W.J., III. Inbreeding and reproductive success in a natural chacma baboon, *Papio cynocephalus ursinus*, population. *Animal Behaviour*, 1988, *36*, 574-578.

Burke, T., Davies, N.B., Bruford, M.W., and Hatchwell, B.J. Parental care and mating behavior of polyandrous dunnocks *Prunella modularis* related to paternity by DNA fingerprinting. *Nature,* 1989, *338,* 249-251.

Cavalli-Sforza, L.L., and Bodmer, W.F. *The genetics of human populations.* San Francisco: W.H. Freeman, 1971.

Chapais, B. Male dominance and reproductive activity in rhesus monkeys. *In* R.A. Hinde (Ed.), *Primate social relationships: An integrated approach.* Oxford: Blackwell, 1983, pp. 267-271.

Clark, C.B. A preliminary report on weaning among chimpanzees of Gombe National Park, Tanzania. *In* S. Chevalier-Skolnikoff and F.E. Poirier (Eds.), *Primate bio-social development.* New York: Garland Press, 1977, pp. 235-260.

Clutton-Brock, T.H. Female transfer and inbreeding avoidance in social mammals. *Nature,* 1989, *337,* 70-72.

Coe, C.L., Conolly, A.C., Kraemer, H.C., and Levine, S. Reproductive development and behavior of captive female chimpanzees. *Primates,* 1979, *20,* 571-582.

Colvin, J. Influences of the social situation on male emigration. *In* R.A. Hinde (Ed.), *Primate social relationships.* Sunderland, Mass.: Sinauer, 1983, pp. 160-171.

Dittus, W. The social regulation of populations density and age-sex distribution in the toque monkey. *Behaviour,* 1977, *63,* 281-322.

Dobson, F.S., and Jones, W.T. Multiple causes of dispersal. *American Naturalist,* 1985, *126,* 855-858.

Durham, W.H. *Coevolution: Genes, culture and human diversity.* Stanford: Stanford University Press, in press.

Enomoto, T. The sexual behavior of Japanese monkeys. *Journal of Human Evolution,* 1974, *3,* 351-372.

Enomoto, T. On social preference in sexual behavior of Japanese monkeys (*Macaca fuscata*). *Journal of Human Evolution,* 1978, *7,* 283-293.

Epple, G., and Katz, Y. Social influences on estrogen excretion and ovarian cyclicity in saddle back tamarins (*Saguinus fuscollis*). *American Journal of Primatology,* 1984, *6,* 215-227.

Goodall, J. *The chimpanzees of Gombe.* Cambridge, Mass.: Belknap Press of Harvard University Press, 1986.

Gouzoules, S., and Gouzoules, H. Group life. *In* B.B. Smuts, D.L. Cheney, R.M. Seyfarth, R.W. Wrangham, and T.T. Struhsaker (Eds.), *Primate societies.* Chicago: University of Chicago Press, 1987, pp. 299-305.

Greenwood, P.T. Mating systems, philopatry, and dispersal in birds and mammals. *Animal Behaviour,* 1980, *28,* 1140-1162.

Hanby, J.P., and Brown, C.E. The development of sociosexual behaviours in Japanese macaques, *Macaca fuscata. Behaviour,* 1974, *49,* 152-196.

Harcourt, A.H. Strategies of emigration and transfer by primates, with particular reference to gorillas. *Zeitschrift für Tierpsychologie,* 1978, *48,* 401-420.

Henzi, S.P., and Lucas, J.W. Observations on the inter-troop movement of adult vervet monkeys (*Cercopithecus aethiops*). *Folia Primatologica,* 1980, *33,* 220-235.

Holmes, W.G., and Sherman, P.W. Kin recognition in animals. *American Scientist,* 1983, *71,* 46-55.

Hrdy, S.B. *The langurs of Abu.* Cambridge, Mass.: Harvard University Press, 1977.

Imanishi, K. The origin of the human family—a primatological approach. *In* K. Imanishi and S.A. Altmann (Eds.), *Japanese monkeys.* Published by the editors, 1965, pp. 113-140.

Itoigawa, N., Negayama, K., and Kondo, K. Experimental study on sexual behavior between mother and son in Japanese monkeys (*Macaca fuscata*). *Primates,* 1981, *22,* 494-502.

Leighton, D.R. Gibbons, territoriality and monogamy. *In* B.B. Smuts, D.L. Cheney, R.M. Seyfarth, R.W. Wrangham, and T.T. Struhsaker (Eds.), *Primate societies.* Chicago: University of Chicago Press, 1987, pp. 135-145.

Maple, T.L. *Orang utan behavior.* New York: Van Nostrand Reinhold, 1980.

Missakian, E.A. Genealogical mating activity in free-ranging groups of rhesus monkeys (*Macaca mulatta*) on Cayo Santiago. *Behaviour,* 1973, *45,* 224-240.

Moore, J., and Ali, R. Are dispersal and inbreeding avoidance related? *Animal Behaviour,* 1984, *32,* 94-112.

Murray, R.D., and Smith, E.O. The role of dominance and intrafamilial bonding in the avoidance of close inbreeding. *Journal of Human Evolution,* 1983, *12,* 481-486.

Nishida, T., and Hiraiwa-Hasegawa, M. Chimpanzees and bonobos: Cooperative relationships among males. *In* B.B. Smuts, D.L. Cheney, R.M. Seyfarth, R.W. Wrangham, and T.T. Struhsaker (Eds.), *Primate societies.* Chicago: University of Chicago Press, 1987, pp. 165-177.

van Noordwijk, M.A., and van Schaik, C.P. Male migration and rank acquisition in wild long-tailed macaques *Macaca fascicularis. Animal Behaviour,* 1985, *33,* 849-861.

O'Brien, S.J., Roelke, M.E., Marker, L., Newman, A., Winkler, C.A., Meltzer, D., Colly, L., Evermann, J.F., Bush, M., and Wildt, D.E. A genetic basis for species vulnerability in the cheetah. *Science,* 1985, *227,* 1428-1434.

Packer, C. Inter-troop transfer and inbreeding avoidance in *Papio anubis. Animal Behaviour,* 1979, *27,* 1-36.

Packer, C. Dispersal and inbreeding avoidance. *Animal Behaviour,* 1985, *33,* 666-668.

Parker, H., and Parker, S. Father-daughter sexual abuse: An emerging perspective. *American Journal of Orthopsychiatry,* 1986, *56,* 531-549.

Paul, A., and Kuester, J. Intergroup transfer and incest avoidance in semi-free-ranging Barbary macaques (*Macaca sylvanus*) at Salem (FRG). *American Journal of Primatology*, 1985, *8*, 317-322.

Pusey, A.E. The physical and social development of wild adolescent chimpanzees (*Pan troglodytes schweinfurtchii*). Ph.D. dissertation, 1978, Stanford University.

Pusey, A.E. Inbreeding avoidance in chimpanzees. *Animal Behaviour*, 1980, *28*, 543-582.

Pusey, A.E. Mother-offspring relationships in chimpanzees after weaning. *Animal Behaviour*, 1983, *31*, 363-377.

Pusey, A.E. Sex-biased dispersal and inbreeding avoidance in birds and mammals. *Trends in Ecology and Evolution*, 1987, *2*, 295-299.

Pusey, A.E., and Packer, C. Dispersal and philopatry. *In* B.B. Smuts, D.L. Cheney, R.M. Seyfarth, R.W. Wrangham, and T.T. Struhsaker (Eds.), *Primate societies*. Chicago: University of Chicago Press, 1987, pp. 250-266.

Ralls, K., and Ballou, J. Extinction: Lessons from zoos. *In* C.M. Schonewald-Cox, S.M. Chambers, B. MacBryde, and L. Thomas (Eds.), *Genetics and conservation: A reference for managing wild animal and plant populations*. Menlo Park, Calif.: Benjamin-Cummings, 1983, pp. 164-184.

Ralls, K., Harvey, P.H., and Lyles, A.M. Inbreeding in natural populations of birds and mammals. *In* M. Soule (Ed.), *Conservation biology: The science of scarcity and diversity*. Sunderland, Mass.: Sinauer Associates Inc., 1986, pp. 35-56.

Sade, D.S. Inhibition of mother-son mating among free-ranging rhesus monkeys. *Science and Psychoanalysis*, 1968, *12*, 18-38.

Sade, D.S., Rhodes, D.L., Loy, J., Hausfater, G., Breuggeman, J.A., Kaplan, J.R., Chepko-Sade, B.D., and Cushing-Kaplan, K. New findings on incest among free-ranging rhesus monkeys. *American Journal of Physical Anthropology*, 1984, *63*, 212-213.

Scott, L.M. Reproductive behavior of adolescent female baboons (*Papio anubis*) in Kenya. *In* M. Small (Ed.), *Female primates: Studies by women primatologists*. New York: Alan R. Liss, Inc., 1984, pp. 77-100.

Shepher, J. Mate selection among second generation kibbutz adolescents and adults: Incest avoidance and negative imprinting. *Archives of Sexual Behavior*, 1971, *1*, 293-307.

Smith, D.G. Inbreeding in three captive groups of rhesus monkeys. *American Journal of Physical Anthropology*, 1982, *58*, 447-451.

Smuts, B.B. *Sex and friendship in baboons*. New York: Aldine, 1985.

Smuts, B.B., Cheney, D.L., Seyfarth, R.M., Wrangham, R.W., and Struhsaker, T.T. (Eds.), *Primate societies*. Chicago: University of Chicago Press, 1987.

Stewart, K.J., and Harcourt, A.H. Gorillas: Variation in female relationships. *In* B.B. Smuts, D.L. Cheney, R.M. Seyfarth, R.W. Wrangham, and T.T. Struhsaker (Eds.), *Primate societies*. Chicago: University of Chicago Press, 1987, pp. 155-164.

Sugiyama, Y. Life history of male Japanese monkeys. *In* J.S. Rosenblatt, R.A. Hinde, E. Shaw, and C. Beer (Eds.), *Advances in the study of behavior*, Vol. 7. New York: Academic Press, 1976, pp. 255-284.

Takahata, Y. The socio-sexual behavior of Japanese monkeys. *Zeitschrift für Tierpsychologie*, 1982, *59*, 89-108.

Tilson, R.L. Family formation strategies of Kloss's gibbon. *Folia Primatologica*, 1981, *35*, 259-287.

Tokuda, K. A study on the sexual behavior in the Japanese monkey troop. *Primates*, 1961-2, *3*, 1-40.

Tutin, C.E.G. Mating patterns and reproductive strategies in a community of wild chimpanzees (*Pan troglodytes schweinfurthii*). *Behavioral Ecology and Sociobiology*, 1979, *6*, 29-38.

van den Berghe, P.L. Human inbreeding avoidance: Culture in nature. *Behavioral and Brain Sciences*, 1982, *6*, 91-124.

Walters, J.R. Kin recognition in nonhuman primates. *In* D.J.C. Fletcher and C.D. Michener (Eds.), *Kin recognition in animals*. New York: John Wiley, 1987, pp. 359-393.

Waser, P.M., Austad, S.N., and Keane, B. When should animals tolerate inbreeding? *American Naturalist*, 1986, *128*, 529-537.

Westermarck, E.A. *The history of human marriage*. 3 vols. London: Macmillan, 1891.

Wolf, A.P., and Huang, C. *Marriage and adoption in China*. Stanford: Stanford University Press, 1980.

# 8
# The Modification of Sexual Behavior Through Imprinting: A Rodent Model

Bruno D'Udine
*Museo di Storia Naturale e Laboratorio*
*Università di Parma*
*I-43100 Parma*
*Italy*

## Introduction

This edited volume addresses the biosocial dimensions of adult human sexual behavior with children and adolescents. Such behavior would seem to have a deleterious effect on genetic fitness in that such behavior, and the assumed underlying sexual attraction that motivates it, seems to have no direct procreative benefit. Although the lack of direct procreative benefit does not preclude yet to be understood long-term fitness gains for the adult, the child, or the adolescent, the basis by which the attraction develops and the behavior ensues requires investigation in its own right.

Rodents are ideal animals in which to study the determinants of sexual attraction and its ensuing sexual behavior, which together can be studied as mate choice. The short life span and small size of rodents allow for easy experimentation on the effects of early life experience on adult behavior. In addition, the variation in maturity at birth (the precocial-altricial axis) in rodents allows for generalities regarding that parameter. (Altricial refers to those species that require appreciable parental care during a shorter or longer period of infancy and precocial to those species in which a newborn can move about and feed itself. Humans are the most altricial of all primates.) Although direct comparisons from rodents to humans must be avoided, some generalities that arise suggest testable hypotheses for both human and nonhuman primates. With these reservations and cautions in mind, the author of this chapter reviews the effects of early experience on mate choice in both altricial and precocial rodents. As will be seen, through experimental manipulation of rearing conditions, it is quite easy to derail sexual attraction and sexual behavior (i.e., mate choice) and turn these phenomena toward a nonprocreative partner.

The growing interest in mating preferences in numerous species has been generated by the renewed vitality of evolutionary biology. A characteristic that successfully attracts a member of the opposite sex might become increasingly common in the population simply because it is likely to be transmitted to offspring, which in turn may be better than others at winning mates. This evolutionary process, which is part of what is called "sexual selection," could be an important source of genetic change. Even though sexual selection is uppermost in many minds, what animals actually do must not be confused with the evolutionary process. When the term "mate selection" is used for what animals do, its use can quickly lead to the assumption that an individual's preference for a particular kind of mate necessarily has implications for sexual selection. This assumption is false. Therefore, the immediate outcome of an individual's mating preference must be referred to as "mate choice," while "sexual selection" is used for the evolutionary process and its effect upon the distribution of characteristics within a population (Bateson, 1983b). The corollary may be more true, however. Previous sexual selection in a population has implications for individual mate choice within that population.

It is commonly assumed that sexual imprinting in early life plays a crucial role in the context of adult mate choice in animals. This assumption will be systematically reviewed among selected species of rodents. Also, adult human sexual behavior with children and adolescents is obviously not the same phenomenon as mate choice; yet, sexual attraction underlies both of these activities, and it is hoped that an understanding of one phenomenon will further science's knowledge of the other. (See Feierman, this volume, Chapter 1, for a discussion of the relationship of mate choice to sexual preference, sexual choice, and sexual attraction.)

## How a Mate Is Chosen

In those species that reproduce sexually, the quality of a mate is a critical determinant of the genetic constitution and future reproductive success of the offspring. Hence, it is not surprising to find that, under natural conditions, individuals seldom mate indiscriminately. Various mechanisms ensure some selectivity in the sexual process, and in many species, this selectivity depends not merely upon the mechanical compatibility of the sexual organs but also upon the perceptual discrimination and selective sexual arousal of the individuals involved. A survey of individuals' mating patterns in numerous species reveals a remarkable variety in the frequency and form of mate choice. While some individuals take but a single mate in their lifetime, others may acquire many, either successively or simultaneously, while others, especially males, acquire none. Polygyny, polyandry, monogamy, and promiscuity are only general labels for the varied mating systems to be found both among and within individual species in the animal kingdom.

Seemingly, mate choice takes place overtly when individuals are ready to engage in reproductive activity, but there are some notable exceptions to this generalization. In fact, in some bird species, heterosexual pairbonding may occur long before reproductive activity commences. For example, in the African violet-eared waxbill (*Uraeginthus granatinus*), monogamous heterosexual pairs are established before the partners are 15 days old. At this time, they are still being fed by their parents and are far from reproductive age.

In some primate species, sexual relationships emerge from juvenile associations that occur when the individuals are themselves not sexually mature. For example, an adult male hamadryas baboon (*Papio hamadryas*) acquires a harem of several females long before he attains adulthood. Often, these associations develop 2-3 years before the females achieve sexual maturity (see Anderson and Bielert, this volume). Therefore, there is, again, no temporal continuity between the time of mate selection and actual sexual interaction.

In those species in which overt mate choice is a direct temporal prelude to sexual behavior, it is not necessarily the case that every breeding cycle is preceded by the selection of a new mate. Many animals, especially birds, retain the same mate from one breeding cycle to another, and in some cases, the pairs remain together for many years. An essential problem in procreation is merely to select the right species and sex. When parents in fact are of different species, the offspring generally are infertile and incapable of adapting to the ecological niche of either parent. Hence, cross-species hybridization in nature is invariably disadvantageous. Therefore, the pressure of natural selection generates mechanisms that increase the probability that the selection of mates will be from among members of the same species. The barriers to hybridization, whether geographic, climatic, mechanical, or behavioral, are known as "reproductive isolating mechanisms."

Mates must be selected according to sex, age, and time (e.g., during estrus) as well as according to species for procreation to occur. While males and females, as well as nonadults and adults, differ in a number of structural and behavioral dimensions in many species, identification as to male or female, juvenile or adult, often depends upon the presence or absence of relatively few features. In most mammalian species (i.e., in rodents, which make up 90% of all mammals), visual and auditory stimulation is generally less effective than olfactory stimulation in arousing sexual attraction in oneself and in others. The odors used in communication are called "pheromones," and their presence and characteristics depend upon the hormonal state of the individuals emitting them. For example, female rats and mice ovulate every few days, and during the hours prior to ovulation, the females become receptive to the sexual advances of males. Moreover, at this time, the odor of the female changes and becomes more attractive to the males. Both the odor and the behavioral receptivity are dependent upon hormones from the female's ovaries. However, even if several individuals may be of the same species, sex, age, and physiological readiness for breeding, their attractiveness as mates often depends upon some associated, extrinsic feature and not upon any behavioral or morphological characteristic intrinsic to the individual itself. For example, the quantity and the quality of resources, such as a territory or social rank, held by a male may be an important determinant of his attractiveness as a mate. Such extrinsic (to self) attributes must be remembered when one evaluates the results of experiments that assess mate choice under artificial, laboratory settings, such as are described in this chapter.

In many species, individuals return to their former mates in each breeding season, and in some species, the same partner is retained for life. This phenomenon suggests that the partners recognize each other as individuals and exhibit a preference for each other as mates. The retention of a partner from one breeding season to another may provide several advantages. For instance, if animals recognize each other as individuals, the time and effort spent in identifying a partner's species and sex can be reduced or eliminated altogether. This result may provide a considerable advantage in terms of breeding efficiency.

An important question is the degree to which each sex selects the mating partner. Darwin (1874) suggested that it is more often the female than the male who selects from among potential mates. Although this generalization appears to be broadly correct in a wide variety of species, it remained unclear for nearly a century why this circumstance should exist. Biologists now seem to have reached some agreement in their explanation, however (see Trivers, 1985). In most species, the costs in time and energy to the female of producing offspring are relatively great compared to the male. Typically, she must provide the embryo with yolk as a nutrient reserve, as occurs in birds, or she must nourish a fetus in utero throughout an extended period of internal gestation, as is the case in mammals. In most mammals and in some birds, the provision of postnatal care (i.e., parental investment) falls on the female alone. One expects, then, that females will commit themselves to such an investment only when conditions are optimal for reproductive success. Since the quality of the male mate may represent a very important condition in this regard, one expects females to be highly discriminating with respect to potential mates. Indeed this situation is exactly what is found.

By comparison, the costs in time and energy of reproduction to the male are usually low. The males of most species can produce millions of sperm cells and can copulate with the females at relatively little expense in terms of time and energy. Males may attempt to increase their production of offspring—i.e., their (reproductive) fitness—if only marginally, by mating with "inferior" individuals. Even such very slight chances of success are likely to warrant their reproductive efforts when the costs of these efforts are low. Dewsbury (1982), however, pointed out that in some species, the costs of sperm depletion are significant. Nevertheless, males will court and copulate with a wide variety of sexual partners including, if given the opportunity, partners of other (not opposite) sexes and ages and even of other species (see Daly and Wilson, 1983). The features of mate choice, which vary widely among and within animal species, invariably reflect the best reproductive strategy for those individuals that exhibit them under natural conditions. In many, if not most, species, the mechanisms of mate selection are only partially understood. Under laboratory conditions, it is possible, however, to manipulate early experience to determine its effect on later mate choice. It is this strategy that is employed in the studies of rodents that are reported in this chapter.

# Imprinting, Early Experience, and Behavioral Plasticity

## Sexual and Filial (Parent/Offspring) Imprinting

From the classic ethology literature, researchers learn that one of the most striking examples of the long-term effects of a young bird's early social life can be the phenomenon of sexual imprinting (Lorenz, 1935, 1937). This kind of learning leads a mature bird in certain species to direct its sexual behavior preferentially towards individuals similar to the birds that it encountered when it was young. Sexual imprinting has now been studied both in birds and mammals. As with filial imprinting, sexual imprinting raises several interesting questions. These two phenomena, when compared, show certain remarkable differences as well as some similarities.

As has been pointed out (Chalmers, 1983), in both phenomena there is a sensitive period during which the animal is predisposed to form an attachment to another individual or class of individuals. The sensitive period for sexual imprinting typically occurs later in development than does the sensitive period for filial imprinting. Usually, filial imprinting occurs within the first days of life, while the sensitive period for sexual imprinting, in geese for example, does not even begin until some weeks after hatching and then may last for several weeks. Another important difference is that in filial imprinting, the individual makes its response, that of following, at the same age at which it is undergoing the imprinting. By contrast, in sexual imprinting, the sexual courtship and copulatory response are not performed until maturity, many weeks, months, or years after the imprinting has taken place. This hiatus can make experiments on sexual imprinting difficult to interpret, because it is difficult to control for the extent to which the animal's experience between the end of the fostering period and the onset of sexual maturity affects its subsequent behavior. (See also Hess, 1973; Scott, 1978.)

The proximate biochemical, physiological, and behavioral mechanisms controlling the beginning and end of the sensitive period of sexual imprinting are poorly understood (see Hutchison and Hutchison, this volume). An obvious suggestion is that the timing of sensitive periods is dependent upon the postpartum differentiation of the brain, which is linked to hormonal changes. However, despite earlier evidence that appeared to support this idea (Immelmann, 1972), it now seems that at least in some species sexual imprinting can take place during a time period that is without the action of postpartum endogenous hormones, such as testosterone. For example, Hutchison and Bateson found that sexual imprinting took place in male Japanese quail that previously had been castrated. As with filial imprinting, the bird's experience during the sensitive period is likely to hasten the end of that period. As one object becomes familiar, so other objects, which are novel, will increasingly be avoided. The end of imprinting correlates with a narrowing of potential characteristics in a potential mate that will be capable of eliciting sexual arousal and behavior.

## Imprinting-Like Processes and Early Experience

The general question, when one speaks of sexual imprinting, is: How do early experiences influence sexual preferences later in life? (See Zivin, this volume, for a discussion of the complexity of this question.) Before one can try to answer this question, one has to go back to some more general concepts and definitions.

In highly complex animals, such as birds and mammals, the ontogenesis (development) of behavior can be considered as being a result of the co-action (Oyama, 1982) of innate predispositions, or tendencies, and life experience. Life experience is the necessary prerequisite for the occurrence of all learning. As the ability to learn may last for the whole lifetime, experiences occurring between birth and weaning possess peculiar properties in influencing future behavioral development, in that they play a fundamental role in the building, determination, and shaping of the basic features of future adult behavior.

Lorenz (1935) described for the first time how the characteristics of a given behavior, observed in an adult animal, depend on the nature of experiences in early life. It was in that article that the term "imprinting" first came into use. Lorenz listed four main criteria for imprinting:

1. It can take place only during a restricted period of an individual's life, the so-called "sensitive period."
2. It is irreversible—that is, the experience cannot be forgotten.
3. It involves the learning of supra-individual, species-specific characters.
4. It may be completed at a time when the appropriate behavioral reaction itself is not yet performed.

Lorenz considered as being one of the main characteristics of imprinting the fact that the capacity for it to occur is phylogenetically preprogrammed. In this view, imprinting occurs only at a certain critical developmental stage, when the immature organism is the most sensitive to a given combination of stimuli that induces an unconditioned response. Association would occur between these unconditioned stimuli and other, concomitant, conditioned stimuli that do not have the capacity to induce any initial response by themselves. In most cases, the teleonomic function ("teleonomic" means "species preserving," as distinct from "teleological," which means "purposeful" in a less restricted way) of this conditioning process, or association, and of the whole process of imprinting, would consist in eventually directing a given sexual behavioral pattern towards the appropriate sexual object for procreation.

Subsequent research has pointed out that imprinting is not such a rigid process as originally depicted. Some imprinted behavior in some species is not always irreversible; under particular experiential conditions, an imprinted behavior can be modified by a process of re-imprinting (Clarke and Clarke, 1976; Salzen and Meyer, 1968). In addition, sensitive periods are not strictly fixed; they can undergo shifts in their occurrence and modifications in their temporal extent (Bateson, 1978). The tendency occurs nowadays to avoid the term "imprinting," which is linked historically to a rather inflexible view of the early determination of behavior, in favor of expressions such as "imprinting-like processes" or "early experience," which refer to less mechanistic processes in behavioral ontogenesis. In this context, "early experience" is defined as "any environmental experience occurring from conception to sexual maturity that contributes to shape adult behavior." As is the case in imprinting, the concept of early experience cannot be detached from the concept of "sensitive period." This latter refers to the fact that there are individual characters—morphological, functional, and behavioral—the development of which is influenced by environmental variables at certain developmental stages more than at others (Bateson, 1979, 1981; Scott, 1962; Sluckin, 1972).

Thus, sensitive periods are critical time periods during which certain environmental cues may prime, orient, or specifically instruct behavioral development more so than at other times.

## Behavioral Plasticity

As a general rule, behavior is more plastic, i.e., more modifiable, in young subjects than in adults. The term "plasticity," as it is used in today's developmental and ethological literature, has been borrowed from neurophysiology. According to neurophysiologists, "plasticity" can be defined as "the property of the nervous system that enables it to undergo and sustain a long-term, functional modification." (Functional modification is defined by its effects, as in a modified response to the same stimulus.) Learning and memory are prime examples of such plastic changes.

The term "plasticity," as it is used by ethologists, was developed and tentatively defined by Oliverio (1980): ". . . rigidity or plasticity: these terms are used to indicate that there are species (or strains) which are characterized by behavioral and neurological precocity at birth, which rely on fixed action patterns and other behaviors that are more structurally determined and therefore may be defined in terms of rigidity or specialization (Mayr, 1974; Oliverio, Castellano, and Puglisi-Allegra, 1979). On the contrary, there are species or strains which are more flexible, depend on individual experience for acquiring useful behavior . . . these species may be defined in terms of plasticity or generalization."

In summary, there is more plasticity in altricial versus precocial species. This generalization takes on added significance because, as was stated previously, humans are the most altricial of all primates.

The greater plasticity of the young central nervous system (CNS) over the aged CNS is demonstrated by the fact that behavioral consequences of brain damage frequently are less severe in young individuals than in adults (Nonneman and Isaacson, 1973). A possible explanation of how behavioral plasticity may be maintained in the adult is given by Bateson (1979): "The characteristics of many behavioral systems are determined at particular stages in development, but . . . the mechanisms generating those characteristics can . . . remain in operation through life . . . ." Alternatively, the working of these mechanisms may be inhibited more under certain circumstances at some stages of development than at others, but the capacity to form preferences can remain latent, rather than disappearing or being made ineffectual.

Under natural conditions, the persistence in adulthood of behavioral plasticity seems to be of major importance in two situations at least: when animals live in societies or when they live in an unpredictably varying environment. In a social or natural habitat that can change rapidly and with unforeseeable outcomes, the ability to adapt behavior to the new conditions, independent of age, would raise the probability of survival and of successful reproduction. In such a case, behavioral plasticity could involve the ability to solve new problems, to adopt different strategies of survival and reproduction, or even to experiment with totally new strategies.

The skill to cope with novelty by means of behavioral changes could be acquired through several forms of learning, ranging from "trial and error learning"—that could occur during experimentation with solutions to new environmental problems—to "insight learning" that could conceivably lead to new strategies. According to Thorpe (1956), insight learning implies a new adaptation, arising as the result of an insight, where "insight" is defined as "the comprehension of connections," such as is seen in the higher primates, including humans (see Medicus, 1987). Thus, if behavioral plasticity is the ability to cope with a changing environment, individual learning (as compared to phylogenetic, i.e., species, learning) can be considered as being one aspect of this ability. Recently, it has been postulated that the plasticity of the behavior of a developing organism, under some conditions in some species, can be re-induced in the adult by mild or severe conditions of stress and related behavioral manipulations (Bateson, 1983a). This aspect of behavioral plasticity will be discussed at the end of this chapter.

# Early Experience and Sociosexual Preferences in Rodents

## General Aspects

The work on rodents shows that certain types of early experience, mainly cross-fostering, can affect sexual preferences and, in some cases, break the reproductive barriers between species. Interspecific cross-fostering is a common experimental procedure used to study the effects of the early adoption of pups of one species by a surrogate mother of a different species on subsequent patterns of behavior. Looking at the existing literature, one sees that there has been a fairly confusing use of the terms "sexual preferences" and "social preferences," and sometimes, no definite measures of actual sexual behavior were recorded. In this context, the term "sexual" will be used even in cases where it was used inappropriately by the original authors, "inappropriately" since the investigators observed that the animals approached or spent some time close to the possible mate but did not observe actual courtship or copulatory behavior. Also, before examining the data describing the effects of early-cross-fostering experiments on sociosexual preferences later in life, this author must remind the reader that rodents have evolved a variety of genetic isolating mechanisms, most of which involve behavior, that have resulted in the maintenance of reproductive barriers **between** species.

On the other hand, **within** a species, behavioral mechanisms leading to genetic recombination have been suggested. Assortative mating (i.e., the tendency to depart from random mating preferences) has been considered to be an important mechanism in the determination of the genetic composition of natural populations of rodents and other species. Negative assortative mating occurs when there is a tendency not to mate with individuals showing a particular characteristic, and positive assortative mating is the opposite tendency. Assortative mating, either negative or positive, has been thought to influence the degree of homozygosity, the total variance of any character, and the similarity between relatives in the population.

In a previous work (D'Udine and Alleva, 1983), studies were listed in which an experimental manipulation at an early stage of life was carried out on precocial (born developmentally mature) species of rodents. Pups were exposed to a variety of stimuli or surrogates, and the influence of early exposure subsequently was tested. These data are listed in Table 8.I.

Table 8.II lists studies in which young of several altricial (born developmentally immature) species were cross-fostered to a different altricial species in order to test the effects of early exposure on later social and sexual preferences. Early exposure resulted mainly in a reduced preference for conspecifics (members of one's own species) and in an enhanced preference for the cross-fostering species.

From all these data, three points can be made.

1. Experimental manipulation of the individuals to whom one is exposed in early life, to include a foster or surrogate species and to exclude one's own species, instead of redirecting the "species awareness" towards a different species (Lorenz, 1937), results in a broadening of the objects of sexual attraction to include the foster or surrogate.

   Lagerspetz and Heino (1970) found that altricial mice, raised by rat mothers, engaged in more sexual behavior with a small rat in premature estrus than did mouse-reared control animals. In other words, sexual behavior directed towards mice was lower in the rat-reared animals. Similarly, male *Mus musculus*, previously cross-fostered to *Baiomys taylori* dams, subsequently mounted *Baiomys* (Quadagno and Banks, 1970). In only one precocial species, the

TABLE 8.I. Effects of early exposure in precocial rodents

| Author(s) | Exposed species | Exposure duration (days) | Stimulus | Age at test (days) | Effect of early exposure |
|---|---|---|---|---|---|
| Kunkel & Kunkel, 1964; Harper, 1970 | ♂ *Cavia porcellus* | 1–21 | Hand | 40–60 | Attempt to copulate with hands[a] |
| Beauchamp & Hess, 1971 | ♂ *Cavia porcellus* | 1–90 | Chicks | 1–21 | Preference for chicks instead of conspecifics[a] |
| Beauchamp & Hess, 1971 | ♀ *Cavia porcellus* | 1–90 | Chicks | 1–49 | Preference for chicks instead of conspecifics |
| Carter, 1972 | ♂ *Cavia porcellus* | 1–21 | Acetophenone or ethyl benzoate | 75 | Enhanced attractiveness of the female in presence of the stimulus |
| Beauchamp & Hess, 1973 | ♂ *Cavia porcellus* | 1–42 | Rat | 70 | Strong interest for the rat[a] |
| Porter & Etscorn, 1974, 1975 | ♂ + ♀ *Acomys cahirinus* | 1–2 | Cinnamon or cumin | 2 | Strong preference for the stimulus |
| Porter *et al.*, 1977, 1978 | ♂ + ♀ *Acomys cahirinus* | 1–3 | Mouse | 3 | Strong preference for mouse odour |

[a] Sexual activity (attempts to mount, etc.).

from D'Udine and Alleva, 1983

TABLE 8.II. Effects of cross-fostering in altricial rodents

| Author(s) | Species | | Fostering period (days) | Age at preference test (days) | Preference for | |
| | Fostered | Fostering | | | Natural species | Cross-fostering species |
| --- | --- | --- | --- | --- | --- | --- |
| Denenberg, Hudgens & Zarrow, 1964 | Mus musculus ♂ | Rattus norvegicus | 3–63 | 64–68 | Almost absent | Greatly enhanced |
| Lagerspetz & Heino, 1970 | Mus musculus ♂ | Rattus norvegicus | 2–21 | 40 | Greatly reduced | Greatly enhanced |
| Quadagno & Banks, 1970 | Baiomys taylori ♂ | Mus musculus | 1–21 | 80–115 | — | Enhanced |
| | Baiomys taylori ♀ | Mus musculus | 1–21 | 80–115 | Greatly reduced | Enhanced |
| | Mus musculus ♂ | Baiomys taylori | 1–21 | 80–115 | Greatly reduced | Enhanced[a] |
| | Mus musculus ♀ | Baiomys taylori | 1–21 | 80–115 | Greatly reduced | Greatly enhanced |
| McCarty & Southwick 1977 | Onychomys torridus ♂ | Peromyscus leucopus | 2–25 | 30–110 | Reduced | Enhanced |
| | Onychomys torridus ♀ | Peromyscus leucopus | 2–25 | 30–110 | Reduced | Enhanced |
| | Peromyscus leucopus ♂ | Onychomys torridus | 2–25 | 30–110 | Reduced | Greatly enhanced |
| | Peromyscus leucopus ♀ | Onychomys torridus | 2–25 | 30–110 | Reduced | Greatly enhanced |
| McDonald & Forslund 1978 | Microtus montanus ♂ | Microtus canicaudus | 1–28 | 80 | Reduced | Greatly enhanced |
| | Microtus montanus ♀ | Microtus canicaudus | 1–28 | 80 | Reduced | Enhanced |
| | Microtus canicaudus ♂ | Microtus montanus | 1–28 | 80 | — | Almost unaffected |
| | Microtus canicaudus ♀ | Microtus montanus | 1–28 | 80 | Reduced | — |
| Kirchhof-Glazier, 1979 | Mus musculus ♀ | Peromyscus maniculatus | 1–18 | 44 | Enhanced | Reduced |
| Murphy, 1980 | Mesocricetus auratus ♂ | Mesocricetus brandti | 2–31 | 210 | Greatly reduced | — |
| | Mesocricetus brandti ♂ | Mesocricetus auratus | 2–31 | 210 | Reduced | — |
| Huck & Banks, 1980a, b | Dicrostonyx groenland ♂ | Lemmus trimucronatus | 1–18 | 60 | Reduced | Greatly enhanced[a] |
| | Dicrostonyx groenland ♀ | Lemmus trimucronatus | 1–18 | 60 | Greatly reduced | Enhanced |
| | Lemmus trimucronatus ♂ | Dicrostonyx groenland | 1–18 | 60 | Reduced | Enhanced |
| | Lemmus trimucronatus ♀ | Dicrostonyx groenland | 1–18 | 60 | Greatly reduced | Enhanced[a] |

Starting from the left of the table, parental species are listed, followed by the cross-fostering species, the age at which cross-fostering was initiated and terminated, and age at later tests.
[a] Sexual activity (attempts to mount, lordosis, etc.).

from D'Udine and Alleva, 1983

guinea pig, has it been reported that some hand-reared males directed precopulatory responses to the experimenter's hand. In the same study, comparisons made of the responses elicited by different stimuli to which animals had been exposed suggested that some of these stimuli were more "adequate" than others (Beauchamp and Hess, 1971, 1973). This differential adequacy probably exists because certain stimuli were more similar to the natural releasing stimuli that the individual would encounter under natural conditions. In summary, early social experience with appropriate conspecifics (i.e., normal rearing) seems to affect the pups differently from experimentally introduced experiences with other stimuli both animate and inanimate.

2. Some behavior patterns, such as allogrooming (grooming of other members of the social group), are labile and easily changeable, while others, such as copulation, are more fixed and less subject to modification. (See Domjan, this volume.) Beach (1976) proposed that the various aspects of reproductive behavior, including association, preference, and copulation, may be controlled by different neural, hormonal, and experiential factors. The same possibility had been considered by Quadagno and Banks (1970) when they argued that certain "social" behavior patterns, e.g., allogrooming and approach, are labile but that sexual behavior is more fixed and less subject to early experimental modification. Indeed, cross-fostering of *Mus musculus* pups to *Baiomys taylori* affected allogrooming, aggressive behavior, and approach/avoidance

behavior more than it affected the ability of the pups to mate with a conspecific. In summary, nonmating social behaviors are affected by cross-fostering more than are mating-related social behaviors.

3. Differences are found between the sexes. Males display weaker sexual preferences (i.e., they are less discriminatory) than do females of the same species (Doty, 1974), the female investment being different for reasons already discussed. The observation of rodent sexual behavior reveals that males, even males raised with their own species, do not show very much discrimination in whom they mount. Males will mount other males of the same and different species, and they will also mount conspecific as well as heterospecific females. This observation is in agreement with the evolutionary theory that, in general, selection for responses important for maintaining sexual isolation, and thereby minimizing hybridization, would be expected to act more strongly on females than on males.

## Genetic Determinants of the Effects of Early Experience on Sociosexual Preferences in Female Mice

It is particularly important to have information on the genetic determinants of mating preferences in house mice, because this species, which gives birth to altricial young, has been the principal laboratory mammal used in behavior genetics. Yet, research on preferential mating in inbred laboratory strains of mice has been comparatively neglected, and work on wild populations even more so. The early work in this field was done by Mainardi and co-workers (Mainardi, 1963a,b; Mainardi, 1964; Mainardi, Marsan, and Pasquali, 1965a,b). More recently, Alleva, D'Udine, and Oliverio (1980), using two inbred laboratory strains, C57BL6/J and SEC1Re/J, that are characterized by several contrasting biochemical, physiological, and behavioral patterns, investigated the effects of early olfactory experience on the sexual preferences of the two strains.

According to Mainardi, female mice (the more discriminating of the two sexes) raised by parents scented with Parma Violet perfume, on reaching adulthood preferred a Parma Violet-scented male to a nonscented male. In experiments performed by the current author, during a 24-hour test, each female was allowed to choose between a Parma Violet-scented male and a nonscented one, each confined separately by a yoke at the two ends of a cage that was divided into three equal compartments. An automatic device recorded the female's presence in each compartment. Experimental females of both strains had been raised by parents that had been artificially scented through the weaning time of pups. Control females had been raised by nonscented parents. From the data, it became evident that experimental C57 females strongly preferred males characterized by the same familiar odor as the father, in this case artificially altered by the Parma Violet. In contrast, experimental SEC females showed no difference vis-a-vis the control group. These experiments established that at least for the C57 strain, an early olfactory experience can strongly redirect the adult preferences of the female.

The significance of this finding is that it demonstrates that there is a genetic influence on the degree to which early experience can affect later sexual preference in female, inbred, laboratory mice.

In general, the experiments on inbred strains of mice seem to produce a confusing picture because of the unstandardized experimental conditions used by different investigators. Also, inbred mice might show very different behavior either within strains or in comparison with wild mice for a number of different reasons. A better approach to the study of normal olfactory and mating preferences would be to use wild house mice. In fact, little work has been done on the relevance of mating preferences of females to wild populations. Mice under natural conditions are known to live in small demes (relatively isolated breeding populations) where the dominant male is assumed to be the sire of most of the offspring, including the offspring of his own daughters and granddaughters (Anderson, 1964; Crowcroft and Rowe, 1963; Reimer and Petras, 1967; see Pusey, this volume).

Under such stable conditions, especially when migration is rare, female preference may not be very significant. However, there is evidence of large deviations from these stable conditions (Bronson, 1979). It is known, for example, that migration of the young may take place when the population becomes overcrowded and that migration of mice of all ages may occur with seasonal changes in food or temperature. Migration also may happen when the mice are too inbred. Mice migrate either to unoccupied areas and establish new populations or, possibly, into established populations (Delong, 1967; Rowe, Taylor, and Chudly, 1963). The latter pattern is possible, since mice tend to accept intruders if they invade in large numbers (Reimer and Petras, 1967). If female preference exists in the wild under natural conditions, it is more likely to be important under such circumstances.

## A Role for Males in Mate Choice in Mice

As previously stated, males of most species are less discriminating in their choice of sexual partners than are females (Daly and Wilson, 1983). Up to recent times, male mice have been considered not to show any significant preference among females within their own or other strains (Mainardi, Marsan, and Pasquali, 1965a; Yanai and McClearn, 1973a,b). However, Yamazaki et al. (1976, 1978) pointed out that mating preferences of male mice do exist and that these preferences are linked to genes in the major histocompatibility complex. Sometimes this link results in a preference for a female with the same genotype as the male being tested, and sometimes for the other genotype, depending upon the particular male and female genotype used. Yamazaki et al. suggested that females of a particular H-2 antigen type may prefer males of similar or of dissimilar H-2 type, depending on which particular H-2 type is offered as the alternative. This possibility suggests a scale of preferences in which the similar H-2 type of the female may rank lower or higher than other H-2 types.

Of the several functions mating preference might serve in nature, the most easily comprehensible is maintenance of the heterozygosity of genes in the proximity of H-2. One obvious advantage of H-2 heterozygosity arises because this region includes immune-response (Ir) genes with dominant alleles conferring strong responsiveness to particular antigens. Where infections are a prominent environmental hazard, hybrids would enjoy the advantage of a wider range of immune defenses. Therefore, genes in the major histocompatibility complex may be involved in male mouse preferences, and further experiments are needed to test the possibility of a tendency of a male to mate with a "self" or a "nonself" as guided by the recognition of the species, the subspecies, the strain, or the H-2 complex.

Bateson (1979) explained the seemingly contradictory evidence obtained from mate choice in mice in terms of the optimal-discrepancy hypothesis. Sexual preferences for both familiar and novel stimuli have been demonstrated depending, it seems, on the choices offered to the mice (e.g., Gilder and Slater, 1978; Mainardi, Marsan, and Pasquali, 1965a,b; Oedberg, 1976). A similar interpretation may apply to the result of Yamazaki et al. (1976), who found that in four sets of crosses out of six, male mice mated significantly more with females differing from themselves in genes determining histocompatibility than with females that were genetically the same. In one set of crosses, the males mated to a significantly greater extent with females with identical genes determining histocompatibility. It can be argued that the genes in the major histocompatibility complex may determine the female smell or the male recognition system or both. However, the males may be influenced by their own smell and prefer to mate with a female whose odor is "optimally" different, according to Bateson's hypothesis.

It should also be pointed out that adaptation-related arguments about behavior in inbred laboratory strains of any species are always very speculative, in that the strains are the product of human rather than natural and sexual selection. This circumstance does not diminish the finding of a genetic correlate to the propensity to form learned preferences, however.

# Early Olfactory Preferences and Behavioral Plasticity in Mice

In the previous section, this author discussed the possible role of genes that are linked to or are part of the major histocompatibility complex in guiding male's mate choice in mice. In a recent work, Hepper (1987) introduced the idea that discrimination of different degrees of relatedness in rats could be based on a genetic identifier. The "kin identifier," according to Hepper, can be defined as "a set of perceptual features that delimit an individual as belonging to a particular kin group" (p. 549). A genetic identifier would greatly reduce the "transient variability of the identifier" (p. 549). An olfaction-related genetic identifier could be more influenced by many contingencies and show a greater degree of variability. It is not known whether olfactory preferences in rodents, once established, are reversible or modifiable.

Olfactory imprinting is assumed to be as established a phenomenon in rodents as visual imprinting is in birds, and according to Lorenz's original view, the irreversibility of imprinting was a defining characteristic. Also, social and sexual preferences of adults traditionally have been thought to originate largely from experiences that occurred early in life (Immelmann, 1972), and little research has been done on whether or not appropriate social stimuli experienced in adult life could influence the choices made by adult animals. (However, see Domjan, this volume.)

As has been stressed, research on a wide variety of birds and mammals has suggested that behavioral ontogeny is best seen in terms of a complex interplay between initial predisposition and life experience. This view is supported by the increasing evidence that the developing organism responds preferentially, or more effectively, to some experiences than to others. The consequences to behavioral development of experiencing a given stimulus appear to be mainly influenced by (a) the nature of the stimulus itself, (b) the length of the exposure to the stimulus, and (c) the ontogenetic phase in which the experience of the stimulus occurs.

To consider house mice again, it can be hypothesized that they possess the ability to evaluate the magnitude of the differences between their own and other strains. Thus, when the alternative is between their own strain and a strain that is "too different," the former is preferred. When the difference is not so great, their own strain is discarded, and the other is preferred. In mice, it is assumed that, mainly through olfaction, sexual behavior under natural conditions is promoted and directed towards an appropriate (i.e., optimally procreative) goal. Chemical cues released with feces and urine, as well as by sebaceous and apocrine glands, seem to mediate courtship and mating in mice (Doty, 1974). A positive correlation has been found between the preference for the scent of a given conspecific for nonsexual social proximity and the preference for the same individual as a sexual partner (Huck and Banks, 1980a,b; Yanai and McClearn, 1973a), and the mechanisms responsible for the ability to select the "right" mate are considered to be determined or at least influenced in part by early experience. In particular, the experience with parents and siblings, lasting from birth or, more likely, from conception to weaning, seems to play a major role in defining mate choice. In addition, influences of intrauterine factors on the postnatal development of behavior have been demonstrated by, among others, Armitage et al. (1980), Blass and Pedersen (1980), and Rudy and Cheattle (1977).

To study the degree to which early experiences are irreversible in mice, Albonetti and D'Udine (1986) analyzed the role of social experience occurring during adult life and its effects on sociosexual olfactory preferences in two inbred strains. Changes, resulting from adult social experience, in the preference of female mice for male scent of their own or of a different strain were studied. Olfactory choices first were tested when the subjects were naive and, then, after they had experienced male cues from either strain. Adult female mice of the inbred strain SEC1Re/J, either individually cross-fostered by the C57BL6/J strain or nonfostered, preferred, when naive, the scent of C57 males to that of SEC males. Following an exposure to males of either strain, which allowed behavioral acoustic and olfactory interactions to take place between the experimental females and the stimulus males, those females that had experienced C57 males' cues strengthened their preference for C57 male scent. By contrast, subjects exposed to SEC males preferred SEC males' scent, thus reversing their previous choice. Therefore, the initial tendency to choose the odor of C57 males appeared to be modified by the effects of experimentally manipulated social experience during adulthood.

Two conclusions can be reached from these findings:

1. Because the experience of cues from conspecific adults of the opposite sex appeared to be effective in influencing sexual choices—probably mediated by olfaction in adulthood, but not before weaning—ontogenetic phases of sensitivity to appropriate social stimulation may be not confined to early developmental stages. Evidence for the influence of postweaning social experience on social choices in mice was also found by Nagy (1965). Accordingly, in mice, sociosexual choices between two different inbred strains can be modulated by specific social experience after the behavioral mechanism leading to the choices themselves has become apparent in the adult animal.

2. There is an apparent superimposition of experience on an initial bias that causes the preferential response to some stimuli more so than to others. In this sense, the original tendency to choose C57 male scent was maintained or even strengthened by exposure to C57 males, while that tendency was made nonsignificant by the occurrence of the opposite tendency after the experience of exposure to SEC males. This behavioral modification suggests that, at least in mice, the interaction between tendencies underlying experience and the experience itself may be effective not merely in early life but through a considerable part, or even the whole, of an individual's life span, giving behavioral plasticity an important role in mate choice.

# Conclusion

The concept of sexual imprinting has been reexamined not only in light of the shaping role of early experiences but also in light of the persistence of behavioral plasticity in animals through life. Rodents and mice in particular, having been extensively studied from the point of view of behavioral ontogeny, provide a very useful instrument in the effort to disentangle and understand the complex interactions between inborn predispositions and the role of experience and individual learning. The emerging patterns from numerous studies in this very rich field of research in rodents could perhaps provide a direction to similar work on other species that has not yet been undertaken.

# Summary

General evolutionary aspects of mate choice and sexual selection were introduced in reference to the overall theme of this volume. The usefulness of rodents, because of their small size and short life span, was discussed. The concepts of and differences among filial and sexual imprinting, early experience, and behavioral plasticity were analyzed. The effects of early experience on sociosexual preferences in a number of altricial and precocial species of rodents were reviewed. The role of early experience with respect to sociosexual preferences in adult mice was discussed particularly within the framework of behavioral plasticity. In general, altricial species are more behaviorally plastic than nonaltricial species, and experiences in adulthood as well as in early life can affect adult sexual preferences.

# References

Albonetti, M.E., and D'Udine, B. Social experience occurring during adult life: Its effects on socio-sexual olfactory preferences in inbred mice, *Mus musculus. Animal Behaviour,* 1986, *34,* 1844-1847.

Alleva, E., D'Udine, B., and Oliverio, A. Effect d'une expérience olfactive précoce sur les préférences sexuelles de deux souches de souris consanguines. *Biology of Behaviour,* 1981, *6,* 73-78.

Anderson, P.K. Lethal alleles in *Mus musculus:* Local distribution and evidence for isolation of deme. *Science,* 1964, *145,* 177-178.

Armitage, S.E., Baldwin, B.A., and Vince, M.A. The fetal sound environment of the sheep. *Science,* 1980, *208,* 1173-1174.

Bateson, P.P.G. Sexual imprinting and optimal outbreeding. *Nature,* 1978, *273,* 259-60.

Bateson, P.P.G. How do sensitive periods arise and what are they for? *Animal Behaviour,* 1979, *27,* 470-486.

Bateson, P.P.G. Ontogeny of behaviour. *British Medical Bulletin*, 1981, *37*(2), 159-164.

Bateson, P.P.G. The interpretation of sensitive periods. *In* A. Oliverio and M. Zappella (Eds.), *The behaviour of human infants*. New York: Plenum, 1983a, pp. 57-70.

Bateson, P.P.G. Introduction. *In* P.P.G. Bateson (Ed.), *Mate choice*. Cambridge, England: Cambridge University Press, 1983b, pp. IX-XV.

Beach, F.A. Sexual attractivity, proceptivity and receptivity in female mammals. *Hormones and Behaviour*, 1976, *7*, 105-138.

Beauchamp, G.K., and Hess, E.H. The effect of cross-species rearing on the social and sexual preferences of Guinea pigs. *Zeitschrift für Tierpsychologie*, 1971, *28*, 69-76.

Beauchamp, G.K., and Hess, E.H. Abnormal early rearing and sexual responsiveness in male Guinea pigs. *Journal of Comparative and Psychological Psychology*, 1973, *85*(2), 383-396.

Blass, E.M., and Pedersen, P.E. Surgical manipulation of the uterine environment of rat foetuses. *Physiology and Behaviour*, 1980, *25*, 993-995.

Bronson, F.H. The reproductive ecology of the house mouse. *Quarterly Review of Biology*, 1979, *54*, 265-299.

Carter, C.S. Effects of olfactory experience on the behaviour of the Guinea pig (*Cavia porcellus*). *Animal Behaviour*, 1972, *20*, 54-60.

Chalmers, N. The development of social relationships. *In* P.J.B. Slater and T.R. Halliday (Eds.), *Animal behaviour: III. Genes, development and learning*. Oxford: Blackwell, 1983, pp. 114-148.

Clarke, A.M., and Clarke, A.D.B. *Early experience: Myth and evidence*. London: Open Books, 1976.

Crowcroft, P., and Rowe, P.F. Social organization and territorial behaviour in the wild house mouse (*Mus musculus*). *Proceedings of the Zoological Society of London*, 1963, *140*, 517-553.

D'Udine, B., and Alleva, E. Early experience and sexual preferences in rodents. *In* P.P.G. Bateson (Ed.), *Mate choice*. Cambridge, England: Cambridge University Press, 1983, pp. 311-327.

Daly, M., and Wilson, M. *Sex, evolution, and behavior* (2nd ed.). Boston: Willard Grant Press, 1983.

Darwin, C. *The descent of Man, and selection in relation to sex* (2nd ed.). New York: A.L. Burt, Publisher, 1874.

Delong, K.T. Population ecology of feral house mice. *Ecology*, 1967, *48*, 611-634.

Denenberg, V.H., Hudgens, G.A., and Zarrow, M.X. Mice reared with rats: Modifications of behaviour by early experience with another species. *Science*, 1964, *143*, 380-381.

Dewsbury, D. Ejaculate cost and male choice. *American Naturalist*, 1982, *119*, 601-610.

Doty, R.L. A cry for the liberation of the female rodent: Courtship and copulation in Rodentia. *Psychological Bulletin*, 1974, *81*, 159-172.

Gilder, P.M., and Slater, P.J.B. Interest of mice in conspecific male odour is influenced by the degree of kinship. *Nature*, 1978, *274*, 364-365.

Hepper, P. The discrimination of different degrees of relatedness in the rat: Evidence for a genetic identifier? *Animal Behaviour*, 1987, *35*, 549-554.

Hess, E.H. *Imprinting*. New York: D. Van Nostrand, 1973.

Huck, U.W., and Banks, E.M. The effects of cross-fostering on the behaviour of two species of North American lemmings, *Dicrostonyx groenlandicus* and *Lemmus trimucronatus*: I. Olfactory preferences. *Animal Behaviour*, 1980a, *28*, 1046-1052.

Huck, U.W., and Banks, E.M. The effects of cross-fostering on the behaviour of two species of North American lemmings, *Dicrostonyx groenlandicus* and *Lemmus trimucronatus*: II. Sexual behaviour. *Animal Behaviour*, 1980b, *28*, 1053-1062.

Immelmann, K. Sexual and other long term aspects of imprinting in birds and other species. *In* D.S. Lehrman, R.A. Hinde, and E. Shaw (Eds.), *Advances in the Study of Behaviour*. New York: Academic Press, 1972, pp. 147-174.

Kirchhof-Glazier, D.A. Absence of sexual imprinting in house mice cross-fostered to deermice. *Physiology and Behaviour*, 1979, *23*, 1073-1080.

Kunkel, P., and Kunkel, I. Beitrage zur Ethologie des Hausmeerschweinschens (*Cavia apera f. porcellus*). *Zeitschrift für Tierpsychologie*, 1964, *21*, 602-641.

Lagerspetz, K., and Heino, T. Changes in social reactions resulting from early experience with another species. *Psychological Reports*, 1970, *27*, 255-262.

Lorenz, K. Der Kumpan in der Umwelt des Vogels. *Journal of Ornithology*, 1935, *83*, 137-213. (English translation: Lorenz, K. Companions as factors in the bird's environment. *In* Lorenz, K. *Studies in animal and human behavior, Vol. I*. Cambridge, Mass.: Harvard University Press, 1970, pp. 101-254.)

Lorenz, K. The companion in the bird's world. *Auk*, 1937, *54*, 245-273.

Mainardi, D. Speciazioni nel topo: Fattori etologici determinanti barriere riproduttive tra *Mus musculus domesticus* e *M. m. bactrianus*. *Istituto Lombardo (Rendiconti Scientifici)*, 1963a, *B97*, 135-142.

Mainardi, D. Eliminazione della barriera etologica all'isolamento riproduttivo tra *Mus musculus domesticus* e *M. m. bactrianus* mediante azione sull'apprendimento infantile. *Istituto Lombardo (Rendiconti Scientifici)*, 1963b, *B97*, 291-299.

Mainardi, D. Relation between early experience and sexual preferences in female mice (a progress report). *Atti Associazione Genetica Italiana*, 1964, *9*, 141-145.

Mainardi, D., Marsan, M., and Pasquali, A. Assenza di preferenze sessuali tra ceppi nel maschio di *Mus musculus domesticus. Istituto Lombardo (Rendiconti Scientifici)*, 1965a, *B99*, 26-34.

Mainardi, D., Marsan, M., and Pasquali, A. Causation of sexual preferences in the house mouse: The behaviour of mice reared by parents whose odour was artificially altered. *Atti Società Italiana di Scienze Naturali Museo Civico Milano*, 1965b, *104*, 325-338.

Mayr, E. Behaviour programs and evolutionary strategies. *American Scientist*, 1974, *62*, 650-659.

McCarty, R., and Southwich, C.H. Cross-species fostering: Effects on the olfactory preference of *Onychomys torridus* and *Peromyscus leucopus. Behavioral Biology*, 1977, *19*, 255-260.

McDonald, D.L., and Forslund, L.G. The development of social preferences in the voles *Microtus montanus* and *Microtus canicaudus:* Effects of cross-fostering. *Behavioral Biology*, 1978, *22*, 457-508.

Medicus, G. Toward an etho-psychology: A phylogenetic tree of behavioral capabilities proposed as a common basis for communication between current theories in psychology and psychiatry. *In* J.R. Feierman (Guest Ed.), *The Ethology of Psychiatric Populations. Ethology and Sociobiology*, 1987, *8*(3S), 131S-150S, supplement.

Murphy, M.R. Sexual preferences of male hamsters: Importance of preweaning and adult experience, vaginal secretion, and olfactory or vomeronasal sensation. *Behavioural and Neural Biology*, 1980, *3*, 323-340.

Nagy, Z.M. Effects of early environment upon later social preference in two species of mice. *Journal Comparative Physiology and Psychology*, 1965, *60*, 98-101.

Nonneman, A.J., and Isaacson, R.L. Task dependent recovery after early brain damage. *Behavioral Biology*, 1973, *8*, 143-172.

Oedberg, F. Failure to demonstrate imprinting on an artificial odour in two strains of mice. *Biology of Behaviour*, 1976, *1*, 309-327.

Oliverio, A. A genetic approach to the functional state of the brain in infancy and adulthood. *In* M. Koukkou, D. Lerman, and J. Augst (Eds.), *Functional states of the brain: Their determinants.* Amsterdam: Elsevier, North Holland Biomedical Press, 1980, pp. 23-38.

Oliverio, A., Castellano, C., and Puglisi-Allegra, S. A genetic approach to behavioural plasticity and rigidity. *In* J.R. Royce and L. Moos (Eds.), *Theoretical advances in behaviour genetics.* Amsterdam: Sijthoff and Noordhoff, 1979, pp. 139-168.

Oyama, S. A reformulation of the idea of maturation. *In* P.P.G. Bateson and P.H. Klopfer (Eds.), *Perspectives in ethology*, Vol. 5. New York: Plenum, 1982, pp. 101-131.

Porter, R.H., and Etscorn, F. Olfactory imprinting resulting from brief exposure in *Acomys cahirinus. Nature*, 1974, *20*, 732-733.

Porter, R.H., and Etscorn, F. A primacy effect for olfactory imprinting in spiny mice. *Behavioral Biology*, 1975, *15*, 511-517.

Porter, R.H., Deni, R., and Doane, H.M. Responses of *Acomys cahirinus* pups to chemical cues produced by a foster species. *Behavioral Biology*, 1977, *20*, 244-251.

Porter, R.H., Wyrick, M., and Pankey, J. Sibling recognition in spiny mice (*Acomys cahirinus*). *Behavioral Ecology and Sociobiology*, 1978, *3*, 61-68.

Quadagno, D.M., and Banks, E.M. The effect of reciprocal cross-fostering on the behaviour of two species of rodents, *Mus musculus* and *Baiomys taylori ater*. *Animal Behaviour*, 1970, *18*, 379-390.

Reimer, J.D., and Petras, M.L. Breeding structure of the house mouse, *Mus musculus*, in a population cage. *Journal of Mammalogy*, 1967, *45*, 88-89.

Rowe, F.P., Taylor, E.J., and Chudly, J.H. The number and movements of house mouse (*Mus musculus*) in the vicinity of four corn ricks. *Journal of Animal Ecology*, 1963, *32*, 87-97.

Rudy, J.W., and Cheattle, M.D. Odor aversion learning in neonatal rats. *Science*, 1977, *198*, 845-847.

Salzen, E.A., and Meyer, C.C. Reversibility of imprinting. *Journal Comparative Physiology and Psychology*, 1968, *66*(2), 269-275.

Scott, J.P. Critical periods in behavioural development. *Science*, 1962, *138*, 949-958.

Scott, J.P. (Ed.). *Critical periods*. Stroudsburg, Penna.: Dowden, Hutchinson & Ross, Inc., 1978.

Sluckin, W. *Imprinting and early learning*. London: Methuen Press, 1972.

Thorpe, W.H. *Learning and instinct in animals*. London: Methuen Press, 1956.

Trivers, R. *Social evolution*. Menlo Park, Calif.: The Benjamin/Cummings Publishing Company, Inc., 1985.

Yamazaki, K., Boyse, E.A., Miké, V., Thaler, H.T., Mathieson, B.J., Abbott, J., Boyse, J., Zayas, Z.A., and Thomas, L. Control of mating preferences in mice by genes in the major histocompatibility complex. *Journal of Experimental Medicine*, 1976, *144*, 1324-1335.

Yamazaki, K., Yamaguchi, M., Andrews, P.W., Peake, B., and Boyse, E.A. Mating preferences of F2 segregants of crosses between MHC-congenic mouse strains. *Immunogenetics*, 1978, *6*, 253-259.

Yanai, J., and McClearn, G.E. Assortative mating in mice: II. Strain differences in female mating preference, male preference, and the question of possible sexual selection. *Behavior Genetics*, 1973a, *3*(1), 65-74.

Yanai, J., and McClearn, G.E. Assortative mating in mice: III. Genetic determination of female mating preference. *Behavior Genetics*, 1973b, *3*(1), 75-84.

# 9
# The Modification of Sexual Behavior Through Conditioning: An Avian Model

Michael Domjan
*Department of Psychology and*
*Institute for Neurological Sciences*
*University of Texas at Austin*
*Austin, Texas 78712*

## Introduction

A critical aspect of the analysis of sexual behavior involves identifying which stimuli are effective in eliciting the behavior and determining how these stimuli acquire their effectiveness. These questions can be addressed with respect both to species-specific stimuli that animals are likely to encounter in their natural environment and to "arbitrary" stimuli that do not occur under natural circumstances.

The current chapter describes studies with male Japanese quail that illustrate how species-specific and arbitrary stimuli that elicit sexual behavior may be identified. The experiments also illustrate some of the routes through which, based on the prior experience of the individual, these stimuli acquire their effectiveness. The influences of prior experience are considered to be instances of learning (Flaherty, 1985; Mazur, 1986). Information about the role of learning in sexual behavior in response to both species-specific and arbitrary stimuli is important for understanding the plasticity of reproductive behavior. Such information also may provide insights into mechanisms of the acquisition of unusual sexual practices.

Domesticated Japanese quail were used in the research because much is already known about the neurohormonal mechanisms of sexual behavior in this species (Adkins et al., 1980; Domjan, 1987; Schumacher and Balthazart, 1983; Wada, 1982) and because the species is convenient (e.g., in terms of size and ease of care of individuals) for laboratory investigation (Kovach, 1974). Japanese quail belong to the order Galliformes and to the family Phasianidae. The quail were domesticated in Japan around the 12th century, although the species still exists in the wild in the Far East and Hawaii. Female Japanese quail ovulate once a day. Males readily engage in sexual behavior provided they are maintained in a state of sexual readiness by either photostimulation or hormone treatment.

The birds that served in the current experiments were obtained from a colony maintained at the University of Texas. They were hatched in the laboratory and maintained in mixed-sex groups in brooders until 4-5 weeks of age, by which time the males and females had developed their sexually dimorphic plumage, although the birds were still sexually immature. The males then were moved to individual wire-mesh cages, and the females were moved to group cages. The colony and test rooms were maintained on a 16-hour-light/8-hour-dark schedule of photostimulation, which is sufficient to prime the neuroendocrine system of the birds. Individuals did not serve in experiments until they were at least 60 days old, by which time they were sexually mature.

# Elicitation of Sexual Behavior by Species-Typical Stimuli in Socially Experienced Quail

Mating behavior may be characterized as consisting of a sequence of activities between individuals, starting with a search for and the identification of a potential sexual partner, followed by approach, courtship, and finally, sexual-contact behaviors. There are some points of overlap and interaction among these activities. Identification and approach, for example, are interactive; as approach proceeds, better identification becomes possible, and as a result, the approach may continue or be broken off. In any event, some components of the behavior sequence clearly occur earlier than others. Early components may be labeled "appetitive," and late components may be labeled "consummatory" (Craig, 1918).

During a sexual encounter, an individual may experience a wide range of stimuli provided by its potential sexual partner. These stimuli include visual, olfactory, auditory, and tactile cues, as well as movement-related stimuli. However, not all of the stimuli are likely to be necessary for the occurrence of sexual behavior. A central idea in the study of species-typical behavior is that behavior elicited by complex natural stimuli is in fact a response to select stimulus components called **sign stimuli**. A powerful technique for isolating the functional stimulus components involves testing animals with models that contain only selected stimulus features. Tinbergen, for example, noted, "It is the dependence of innate behavior on sign stimuli that renders it possible to evoke reactions in an animal by presenting it with dummies. As a matter of fact, when any animal readily responds to a dummy, this is a certain indication that its reaction is dependent on sign stimuli" (Tinbergen, 1951, p. 37).

In the initial studies conducted in this laboratory, taxidermic specimens and models of various types were used to identify the sign stimuli that are sufficient to elicit appetitive and consummatory sexual behavior in adult male Japanese quail. In the tradition of previous laboratory studies with male domesticated fowl (Carbaugh, Schein, and Hale, 1962; Schein and Hale, 1957, 1965; Schoettle and Schein, 1959), these initial studies employed sexually and socially experienced birds. The individuals typically received 15-20 periods of access to female quail (during which copulation invariably occurred) and extensive visual exposure to male and female quail before being tested (for additional details, see Domjan and Hall, 1986; Domjan and Nash, 1988; and Domjan, Greene, and North, 1989). Two of the models that were used in the tests are shown in Figure 9.1.

Figure 9.1. Taxidermic specimens used in tests of the sexual behavior of male Japanese quail. Left panel: A female quail's head and neck, mounted on a vertical dowel. Right panel: A female quail's head and neck, mounted in front of a foam pad that provided supporting stimulation for grab, mount, and cloacal-contact responses. (The taxidermic specimens were about 9 cm tall and were prepared with the assistance of N. Camille North; the sketches were made by Marilyn McDonald.)

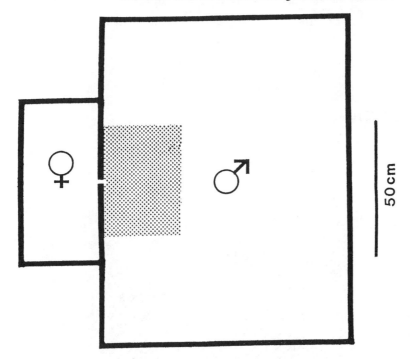

Figure 9.2. Floor plan of the apparatus used in tests of social-proximity behavior. A male quail resided in the larger compartment, and a female quail resided in the adjacent side cage. Visual access between the two compartments was limited to a narrow vertical window. The male bird was considered to be near the window (and, hence, near the female bird) if he was in the stippled area.

## Sign Stimuli that Elicit Appetitive Sexual Behavior

The aspect of appetitive sexual behavior that continues to be investigated in this laboratory is the behavior of approaching and remaining near a conspecific. The apparatus used for the study of approach and social-proximity behavior is illustrated in Figure 9.2. Male birds were housed in the larger side of a two-compartment chamber (122 x 91 x 107 cm), and female quail were housed in the smaller, adjacent enclosure. The two compartments were separated by an opaque sliding door that usually remained closed. The middle of this door had a narrow vertical slit, or "window" (1.3 x 15.2 cm). When the window was open, the male could see the female on the other side if he stood directly in front of the window. Using a time-sampling procedure (see Domjan and Nash, 1988), observers measured social-proximity behavior by recording how often the male was in a designated area near the window to the female's compartment (see Figure 9.2).

Socially experienced male birds spend 70-80% of their time near the window to the female's compartment. However, they do not spend much

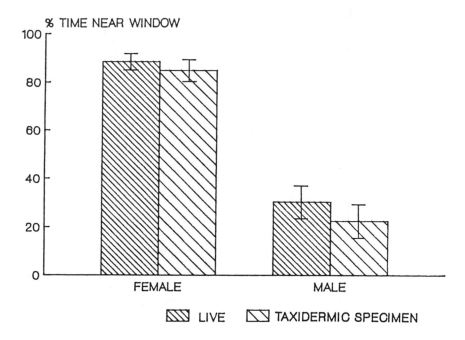

Figure 9.3. Mean percentage of time sexually experienced male Japanese quail spent near the window when the compartment on the other side contained a live female or male conspecific or a taxidermic specimen of a female or a male quail. (Vertical line within each bar represents ± standard error.)

time near the window when the side cage is empty or when it contains a male quail or birds of other species (Domjan and Hall, 1986). A male bird's tendency to remain near female quail is established by sexual experience with females in the test arena. Once the social-proximity behavior has been acquired, it persists in the test situation at the same level throughout daylight hours and for weeks without additional copulatory opportunity (Domjan and Hall, 1986). The behavior is a response to "general" female traits. Novelty, age, reproductive status, and the prior social experience of the female birds have little effect on the proximity behavior of the male quail (Domjan and Hall, 1986). In addition, male social-proximity behavior has been shown to be androgen dependent. Restriction of the photoperiod, which causes involution of the testes and a decline in testosterone production, eliminated the male proximity response. However, the social-proximity behavior could be restored by increasing the photoperiod enough to produce recrudescence of the testes or by administering exogenous testosterone (Domjan, 1987).

Because social-proximity behavior is highly persistent and, in this laboratory's experimental situation, occurs in response to female but not to male conspecifics, the behavior provides a convenient tool for identifying sign stimuli that are involved in eliciting appetitive sexual behavior in male quail. There are a number of salient morphological and behavioral differences between male and female Japanese quail. Females are somewhat larger, they have a different set of vocalizations and postures, and they tend to be less active. In addition, Japanese quail have sexually dimorphic feathers on the head and neck, with females having white spots and gray instead of brown feathers. The researchers in this laboratory decided to explore these morphological male/female differences experimentally and, therefore, tested male birds with taxidermically prepared specimens of male and female quail. The researchers also compared the behavior elicited by these taxidermic specimens to social-proximity behavior elicited by live conspecifics on the other side of the window.

The results of one experiment are summarized in Figure 9.3. Male birds spent significantly more time near female than near male conspecifics, and they responded similarly when they were tested with live conspecifics and with stationary taxidermic specimens of conspecifics. These findings show that static morphological features of female as compared to male quail are sufficient to elicit social-proximity behavior. Auditory, olfactory, and movement-related stimuli did not have a discernible effect on male proximity behavior in this experiment (Domjan and Nash, 1988).

In an effort to identify more precisely the features of female vs. male quail relevant for social-proximity behavior, the researchers partitioned the taxidermic specimens to determine the aspects of them that were the most important. In one study, male birds were presented with test objects consisting of only the head and neck of male and female quail (see Figure 9.1, left panel, for an illustration of a female head+neck taxidermic specimen). The same individuals were also tested with full-body taxidermic specimens of male and female birds for comparison. The results of that experiment are summarized in Figure 9.4. The birds responded to the head+neck specimens in the same way that they responded to the full-body specimens. In other tests, it was found that social-proximity behavior is disrupted significantly when the head and neck of a full-body taxidermic specimen of a female is covered with a brown cloth hood or when a female head+neck taxidermic specimen is presented upside down. These results support the conclusion that the static visual cues of the head and neck of a female bird in an upright orientation provide sufficient sign stimuli for male social-proximity behavior in Japanese quail in the current experimental situation (Domjan and Nash, 1988). Cues from other body parts, from movement, and from vocalization are not necessary for the expression of the behavior.

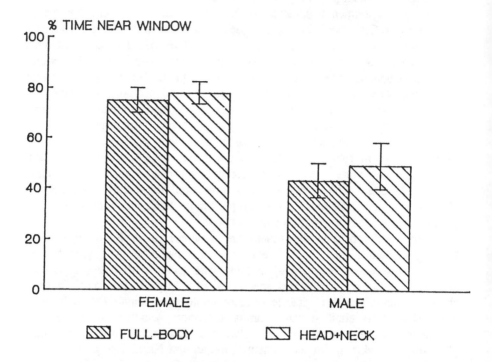

Figure 9.4. Mean percentage of time sexually experienced male Japanese quail spent near the window when the compartment on the other side contained a taxidermic specimen consisting of the entire body or the head+neck of a female or a male conspecific. (Vertical line within each bar represents ± standard error.)

## Sign Stimuli that Elicit Consummatory Sexual Behavior

Sexual-contact behavior in Japanese quail begins with the male's grabbing the back of the female's head with his beak. The male then mounts the female and arches his back, bringing his cloaca in contact with that of the female (Wilson and Bermant, 1972). An investigation was conducted of the cues that are sufficient for eliciting sexual-contact behavior in sexually experienced quail using various types of taxidermic specimens. It was found that head-and-neck stimuli that are sufficient for eliciting appetitive components of sexual behavior also are sufficient for eliciting consummatory aspects of sexual behavior (Domjan, Greene, and North, 1989).

In one test series, researchers in the laboratory compared sexual-contact behaviors in response to a live female bird, a full-body taxidermic specimen of a female quail, and a female head+neck taxidermic specimen.

No more than one test was conducted with each male bird on a given day in order to ensure high levels of sexual motivation. In preliminary work, the investigators found that the head+neck taxidermic specimen did not support mount and cloacal-contact responses unless a mounting platform was provided. Therefore, a piece of hard packing foam was placed behind the head and neck to serve as a mounting platform (see Figure 9.1, right panel).

Male quail copulate vigorously during the first 5 minutes of access to an effective eliciting stimulus and become inactive thereafter (Schein, Diamond, and Carter, 1972). The number of grab responses that were elicited by the live female quail and the taxidermic specimens during the first 5 minutes of access to the stimulus objects is summarized in Figure 9.5. The full-body taxidermic specimen was highly effective in eliciting sexual-contact behavior. In fact, statistically significantly more grab responses occurred during the test with the full-body specimen than during the other tests. The head+neck specimen stimulated responses similar to those that occurred when a live female quail was present.

It is not clear why the full-body taxidermic specimen supported more sexual-contact behavior than did the live female quail or the head+neck taxidermic specimen. More grab responses may have been directed at the full-body taxidermic specimen than at the live female birds because the taxidermic specimen was immobile and did not run away or otherwise resist sexual-contact responses. The fact that the full-body taxidermic specimen was more effective than the head+neck specimen suggests that parts of the torso of a female quail contribute to the elicitation of sexual-contact responses. That contribution notwithstanding, the current results demonstrate that static visual cues of the head and neck of a female bird are sufficient to elicit normal levels of sexual-contact behavior. Therefore, these results serve to identify static visual cues of a female's head and neck as sign stimuli that elicit consummatory sexual behavior in male quail.

## Role of Learning in the Elicitation of Sexual Behavior by Species-Typical Stimuli

The studies described previously draw attention to the head and neck of a female quail as a source of sign stimuli that elicit both appetitive and consummatory quail sexual responses in the current experimental situation. Now, attention can be turned toward mechanisms responsible for the effectiveness of these species-typical cues. Originally, the concept of a sign stimulus was closely related to the concept of "innate releasing mechanisms." Nevertheless, even early investigators recognized that behavior elicited by species-specific sign stimuli may be acquired through common experiences of members of the species. Tinbergen, for example, noted, "In numerous cases the external conditions under which the young grow up are in many respects exactly the same for all" (Tinbergen, 1951, p. 52). This

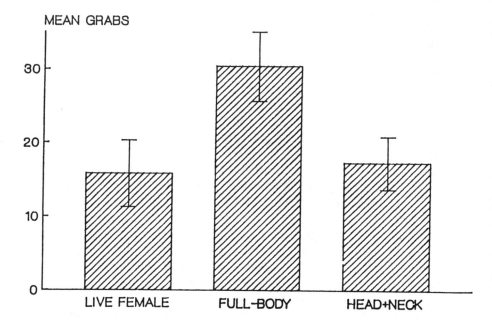

Figure 9.5. Mean number of grab responses subjects made to a live female quail, a taxidermic specimen consisting of the entire body of a female quail, or a taxidermic specimen consisting of the head+neck of a female quail mounted in front of a foam pad. (Vertical line within each bar represents ± standard error.)

sameness allows for the learning of species-typical behavior. With these ideas in mind, the researchers in the laboratory proceeded to search for the aspect of the life history of the experimental birds that might have made the static visual cues of a female quail's head and neck effective in eliciting sexual behavior.

Often when investigators approach a question of this sort, they first search for early-life experiences that may be critical for the acquisition of the behavior. Studies of sexual imprinting have confirmed that social experience before puberty can have a major effect on later mate choice (see D'Udine, this volume). Because all of the laboratory's experiments up to this point had been conducted with sexually and socially experienced male Japanese quail, the investigators decided to study the effects of adult, rather than juvenile, social experience on adult sexual behavior.

## Learning To Discriminate Between Males and Females

As was noted above, the laboratory's studies showed that male Japanese quail are much more likely to approach and remain near female conspecifics than they are to approach and remain near other males (see Figures 9.3 and 9.4). The birds that provided these results previously had extensive sexual experience with female quail and also had received exposure to other male quail. As it turns out, both of these aspects of their prior experience are important regarding the tendency of male quail to spend significantly more time near female than near male conspecifics (Nash, Domjan, and Askins, 1989).

In the first experiment on how Japanese quail learn to discriminate between male and female conspecifics, the researchers varied the amount of sexual experience and the amount of visual exposure to male birds that male subjects received. Two groups of adult male quail (n = 11) served in the experiment. One group (Group 4) received 4 mating trials before a series of test trials, and the other group (Group 20) received 20 mating trials. Each mating trial consisted of access to a receptive adult female bird for 2 hours. Copulation occurred during each of these trials except for the first or second. Mating trials were conducted on successive days, with the trials for Group 4 delayed so that both groups would end the first phase of the experiment at the same time. (Sexually inexperienced individuals were not tested because they show little social-proximity behavior [see Domjan and Hall, 1986].)

Following the mating trials, the subjects received visual exposure to female and to male quail on the other side of a narrow window, and the subjects' social-proximity behavior was measured. No further opportunities for copulation were provided. The test sequence and the results are summarized in Figure 9.6. The first data point shows how much time individuals spent near the window when a live female bird was present on the other side after the different amounts of sexual experience. The two groups showed no statistical differences in their tendencies to remain near the female during this test. Each group then received a series of exposures to male birds in the side cage. During the first test block with males, the individuals of both groups spent nearly as much time near the window as they had during the prior test with female quail. Thus, at this point in the experiment, neither group showed a discrimination between male and female conspecifics. With repeated testing, the level of response to male birds declined substantially in Group 20 but did not decrease much in Group 4.

After 14 test exposures to male quail on the other side of the window, the subjects again were tested with female quail in the side cages. Now the response of Group 20 increased substantially, indicating that a discrimination between male and female quail had been established. Group 4 also showed an increase in response to the females, but their increase was less than was the increase in response of Group 20 and was not statistically significant.

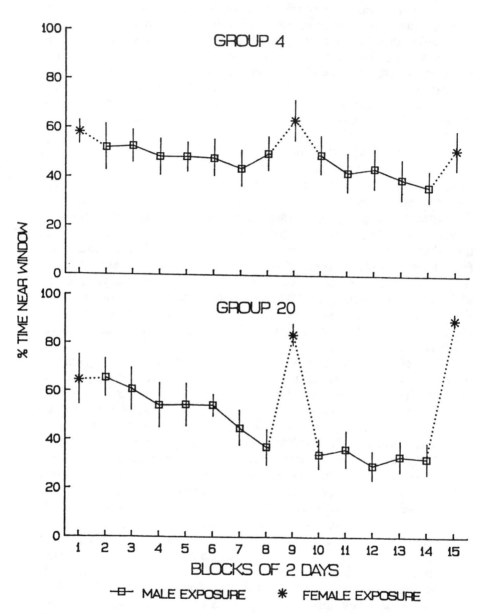

Figure 9.6. Mean percentage of time individuals in Group 4 (top panel) and Group 20 (bottom panel) spent near the window during successive 2-day blocks of tests. Data for tests with male quail on the other side of the window are depicted with open squares. Data for tests with female quail on the other side of the window are depicted with asterisks. (Vertical line through each symbol represents ± standard error.)

Hence, Group 4 did not evidence a discrimination between males and females at this point.

The next phase of the experiment involved another series of exposures to male birds, followed by another test with female quail. A comparison of the data gathered from the last test with females with the data gathered from the immediately preceding test with males demonstrated again that Group 20 discriminated much more strongly between males and females than did Group 4. Another interesting aspect of the data is that the response of Group 20 to female quail increased as a result of exposure to males. Notice that each data point for tests with female quail is higher than the preceding point. In contrast, the response to females did not change much in Group 4.

The results of this experiment show that Japanese quail learn to discriminate between male and female conspecifics and that this learning can take place in adulthood. These results also show that in this experimental situation, the discrimination is facilitated by prior sexual experience. Prior sexual experience contributed to the discrimination in two ways: it facilitated the decline of responding to males, and it resulted in a contrast type of increase of responding to females.

Since male/female discrimination learning was facilitated by sexual experience in this experiment, male individuals in all of the subsequent studies on this problem also received 20 mating trials. These trials were followed by various types of exposure to conspecifics over 16 trials. Finally, individuals were tested for differential responding to male and female quail (Nash, Domjan, and Askins, 1989). The investigators found that if individuals are exposed to male and female quail in alternating blocks of trials, their discrimination develops gradually. Exposure only to female quail in the viewing box following sexual experience does not produce a male/female discrimination in proximity behavior but facilitates discrimination learning when exposures to male and to female quail subsequently are alternated. Having individuals simply spend time in the experimental chamber without exposure to any conspecifics does not produce a discrimination.

This last finding suggested that a critical factor in the development of a discrimination between male and female conspecifics in the experimental situation may be the amount of prior exposure individuals received to male birds following repeated mating trials with female quail. The more an individual is exposed to males, the more likely that individual is to respond subsequently to female than to male quail. To evaluate this idea, the researchers conducted a meta-analysis across all of the experiments that had employed the standard protocol of 20 mating trials followed by 16 stimulus-exposure trials and, finally, tests with male and female conspecifics. Figure 9.7 shows the results of this analysis. Each point in this display represents the mean of a group of individuals (n = 4-8). For each group, the investigators obtained a measure of exposure to males by calculating the mean time individuals spent in front of the window to the side compartment when male birds were located there. (If individuals did not receive exposure to males, they got a score of zero on this measure.) The investigators then calculated a discrimination score by subtracting the degree of response to male quail from the degree of response to female quail during the first block of male and female tests at the end of the experiment. Higher scores on this measure reflect a better discrimination between male and female quail. Discrimination performance turned out to be closely related to the amount of exposure to males. The correlation between these measures was .75.

What mechanisms might have produced the discrimination learning effects described above? One possibility is that quail have some sort of a template of male vs. female conspecifics that has to be activated or refined by ontogenetic experience. As it turns out, the data do not require the assuming of such a learning predisposition. Rather, all of the findings are consistent with principles that have been discovered in studies of how animals learn discriminations between arbitrary stimuli with positive reinforcement.

To translate the paradigm into a conventional discrimination learning procedure, one has to assume that female visual cues constitute a stimulus (S+) in the presence of which approach behavior is reinforced, that male visual cues constitute a stimulus (S-) in the presence of which approach behavior is not reinforced, and that copulation is a positive reinforcer. Copulation with a female quail constitutes pairings of the S+ with the reinforcer.

In conventional discriminations, as a general principle, prior pairings of the S+ with the reinforcer facilitate the decline in response to S- (Amsel, 1962). This relationship is analogous to the finding by the current researchers that male/female discrimination learning is facilitated by prior sexual experience (see Figure 9.6). In conventional discriminations, the decline in response to S-, and hence the development of the discrimination, is a function of the amount of S- exposure (Lachman, 1961). This relationship is analogous to the current researchers' finding that discrimination learning was a function of a male's exposure to other males (S-) (see Figure 9.7). In conventional learning studies, overtraining on S+ does not produce a discrimination but facilitates its development (Amsel, 1962). In an analogous fashion, the current investigators found that repeated exposure to female quail on the other side of the window does not produce a discrimination but facilitates its later development. Finally, in conventional learning studies, after the discrimination has been well learned, a contrast effect is observed whereby the response to S+ is higher following exposure to S- (Boneau and Axelrod, 1962; Mellgren, Wrather, and Dyck, 1972). Analogously, the current researchers found that a male bird's tendency to remain near a female conspecific is higher after exposure to other males (see Figure 9.6).

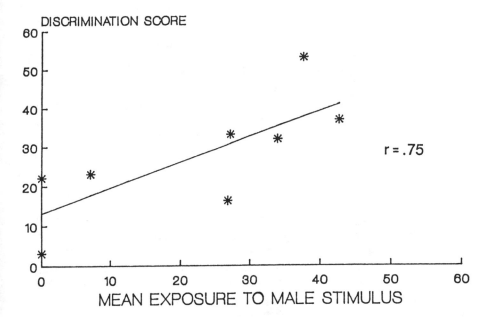

Figure 9.7. Relationship between degree of discrimination between male and female quail and amount of previous exposure to male birds. Each point represents the mean of a group of subjects. (See text for details.)

The current studies permit the conclusion that in this experimental situation appetitive components of the reproductive behavior of Japanese quail are elicited by species-specific static visual cues, which acquire their differential effectiveness largely through conventional discrimination learning mechanisms. Clearly, simply because a behavior is species typical and controlled by species-specific stimuli does not necessarily mean that the behavior is the product of a closed genetic program. To this point may be added that such a behavior is not necessarily the product of highly specialized learning processes either.

## Learning and the Elicitation of Consummatory Sexual Behavior

The researchers in this laboratory next turned their attention to mechanisms of learning involved in the elicitation of consummatory components of sexual behavior by visual stimuli of a female quail's head and neck. This laboratory's initial studies of copulatory behavior elicited by taxidermic specimens were conducted with sexually experienced individuals. Each episode of copulation may be viewed as a conditioning trial in which visual cues of a female quail, or other cues involving the copulatory episode, are paired with sexual satisfaction. Therefore, in the previous studies, copulatory behavior elicited by the static visual cues of a female's head and neck may have reflected what the male birds had learned during earlier opportunities to copulate with live female quail. The female head-and-neck cues may have become conditioned stimuli.

To evaluate what male birds may have learned during opportunities to copulate with female quail, the investigators first compared two groups of individuals (Domjan, Greene, and North, 1989). One group did not receive sexual experience prior to the test sessions but was habituated to the test cages. The other group received 15 mating trials, conducted one per day, with an adult female in the test cages. Then two tests were conducted, one on each of 2 successive days. Individuals first were tested for copulation with a head+neck taxidermic specimen (see Figure 9.1, right panel). They then were tested with a live adult female bird to be sure that they would copulate in response to the normal eliciting stimuli provided by a live female.

Figure 9.8 summarizes the number of grab responses each group made during the test sessions. (Similar results were obtained with the mount response.) Sexually naive birds responded less during the test with the head+neck taxidermic specimen than did sexually experienced birds. However, during the test with the live female quail, the sexually naive birds responded more than the sexually experienced individuals. A difference between the two groups also was evident in the number of individuals that exhibited at least one cloacal-contact response when tested with the head+neck taxidermic specimen. All of the sexually experienced birds (n = 16) were observed to make at least one cloacal-contact response to the taxidermic specimen. In contrast, only 10 of 16 sexually naive individuals copulated with the taxidermic specimen. These differences, which are statistically significant, clearly demonstrate that in this experimental situation adult sexual experience facilitates the occurrence of copulatory behavior in response to static visual cues of a female quail's head and neck.

The attention of the investigators turned next to the kind of learning that might be involved in this facilitation effect. Two prominent hypotheses were considered: the object-learning hypothesis and the contextual-conditioning hypothesis.

### The Object-Learning Hypothesis

This hypothesis assumes that just as the male quail had to learn to discriminate between their male and female conspecifics so did the birds have to learn something about the nature of the stimulus to which they directed their sexual behavior. Static visual cues of a female quail's head and neck may have become effective in eliciting copulatory behavior through association with sexual satisfaction. Initially, copulatory behavior may have been elicited by a combination of the features of a live female bird, possibly including visual cues involving her torso, tactile cues, locomotion, posture, and/or vocalizations. Once sexual-contact responses occurred and the consummatory-response sequence was completed, isolated stimulus features such as static visual cues of the head and neck could,

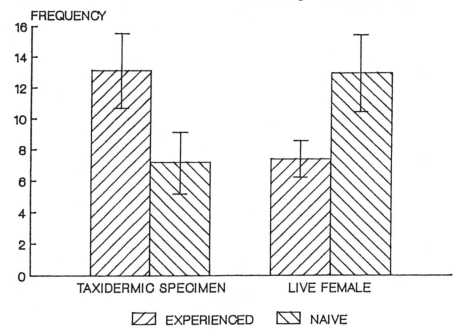

Figure 9.8. Mean frequency of grab responses by sexually experienced and sexually naive male quail in tests with a head+neck taxidermic specimen and a live female bird. (Vertical line within each bar represents ± standard error.)

through conditioning, become associated with sexual satisfaction and thereby become capable of eliciting copulatory behavior.

This scenario is a form of object learning. The birds are assumed to associate certain features of a female bird (e.g., the sight of her head and neck) with other features (e.g., satisfaction from copulation). Presumably, such object learning can occur no matter where male birds are permitted to copulate with a live quail hen. Thus, the object-learning interpretation assumes that the place where sexual experience occurs should not affect what is learned.

This prediction was tested in the next experiment by the comparing of two groups of birds (Domjan, Greene, and North, 1989). All of the individuals were housed in the laboratory's large, wooden test cages on some days and in much smaller, wire-mesh home cages on other days. One group received 15 mating trials with an adult female bird when that group was in the test cages; the other group received its mating trials when it was in the wire-mesh holding cages. Both groups then were tested for response to the head+neck taxidermic specimen and to a live female bird in the test cages.

The results of this experiment are summarized in Figure 9.9. Individuals given sexual experience in the test cages responded about three times as often to the head+neck taxidermic specimen as did individuals given sexual experience in the home cages. However, the response of both

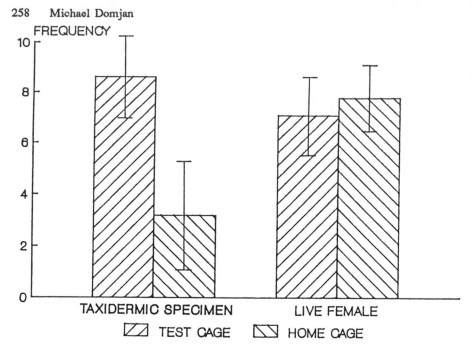

Figure 9.9. Mean frequency of grab responses during tests with a head+neck taxidermic specimen and a live female bird. The tested individuals previously received sexual experience either in the test cages or in the home cages. (Vertical line within each bar represents ± standard error.)

groups of individuals to a live female quail was very similar. The difference in response to the taxidermic specimen also was dramatically evident in the number of individuals that made sexual contact with the taxidermic specimen. Among birds that received sexual pretraining in the test cages, 72% mated with the taxidermic specimen and 28% did not. In contrast, among birds that received sexual pretraining in the home cages, only 18% mated with the taxidermic specimen and 82% did not, a statistically significant difference.

Another interesting aspect of the results was that copulatory experience in the wire-mesh home cages did not seem to afford any advantage to the individuals in their reaction to the taxidermic specimen. Birds in this experiment that received sexual experience in the home cages were no more likely to copulate with the taxidermic specimen than were sexually inexperienced birds in the previous study (compare the left panels of Figures 9.8 and 9.9).

The results of this experiment demonstrate that the place of sexual experience makes a statistically significant difference in the response of individuals to the head-and-neck visual cues. Sexual experience was not enough for the occurrence of sexual-contact behavior directed at the taxidermic specimen. Rather, the sexual experience had to be in the same place where responding to the taxidermic specimen was assessed. This outcome is inconsistent with the object-learning hypothesis that sexual experience facilitates copulation with a head+neck taxidermic specimen by enabling individuals to associate the head-and-neck cues with sexual satisfaction.

### The Contextual-Conditioning Hypothesis

These data are consistent with the hypothesis that sexual experience in the test cages resulted in the conditioning of sexual arousal to contextual cues associated with those cages. Given the sexual arousal elicited by the contextual cues, the head+neck taxidermic specimen provided sufficient additional stimulation for the elicitation of sexual behavior. However, the head+neck visual cues were not sufficient to elicit sexual-contact behavior in individuals that were not already sexually aroused by the conditioned contextual cues.

This form of learning involved in the elicitation of consummatory sexual behavior is different from that which was involved in the control of appetitive sexual behavior. In the case of appetitive behavior, individuals learned which stimuli to approach and remain near and which stimuli to not approach. Learning to approach and remain near a female but not a male conspecific involved learning something about the stimuli that elicited the approach and proximity behaviors. In the case of consummatory sexual behavior, individuals learned something about the place where they were likely to have a chance to copulate with a female bird. Learning about the place where copulation was likely was more important than learning something about features of a female quail.

# Learning and the Elicitation of Sexual Behavior by Arbitrary Stimuli

The studies described thus far have concerned the involvement of learning in the elicitation of various components of sexual behavior by species-specific stimuli. These studies serve to illustrate the plasticity of the stimulus mediation of sexual behavior. One way to test the limits of this plasticity is to investigate the extent to which components of sexual behavior can come to be elicited by nonbiological, arbitrary stimuli—stimuli that the species would never encounter in its natural habitat. The researchers investigated this question by attempting to condition appetitive and consummatory components of quail sexual behavior to arbitrary stimuli (Domjan, O'Vary, and Greene, 1988).

## Sexual Conditioning to an Embellished Female Quail

The arbitrary stimulus used in the first experiment consisted of two chicken feathers (9 cm long) dyed fluorescent orange. Orange was selected because it is a color very different from the color of quail feathers. Thus, it constitutes an "arbitrary" stimulus for this species. To make sure that the orange feathers were presented in a manner that provided supporting stimulation for sexual-contact responses, the investigators attached the feathers to a live adult female quail. The feathers were secured with Velcro® (Velcro U.S.A., Inc.) tabs, one near each shoulder, and were positioned to extend back at about 45°. Female quail embellished with the orange feathers looked very different from normal quail in both color and shape. However, to the degree that it was possible to tell, the females did not behave in an unusual manner. The feathers were light and mounted in such a way that the birds seemed to tolerate them well.

The object of the study was to see whether the orange feathers could become conditioned to elicit sexual arousal by serving as a signal for sexual opportunity. In pilot work, the effort was made to get male birds to copulate directly with an embellished female quail, but success was inconsistent. The method finally used was a variation of one introduced by Timberlake and Grant (1975) for a different purpose. In this procedure, exposure to a conspecific is used as a conditioned stimulus signaling the presentation of another event. In the current adaptation of the procedure, the researchers used exposure to the embellished female quail as the conditioned stimulus signaling opportunity to copulate with a normal, unembellished female bird.

The standard test arenas were modified slightly for the experiment, as illustrated in Figure 9.10. Before the start of a conditioning trial, the stimulus compartment containing the embellished bird was lined up with the doorway to the test arena. The door was then raised, providing exposure to the embellished bird for 30 seconds. At the end of this stimulus exposure, for individuals in the experimental group the stimulus compartments were shifted, bringing the unrestrained normal female quail's compartment in line with the doorway. The male bird then was allowed to copulate with the normal female quail for 5 minutes. The door was then closed, and the female bird taking part in that specific trial was returned to her home cage for the rest of the day.

Individuals in a control group received the same type of exposure to an embellished female quail as did the experimental group, except that following each such exposure, the control group did not get access to a normal female bird. Instead, the normal unrestrained female was introduced into the test cage through the hinged front cage door, so that the male bird had access to her, about 2 hours before each exposure to an embellished quail. Thus, for the control group, exposure to an embellished bird was not followed by access to a normal female bird, the sequence necessary for excitatory classical conditioning to occur.

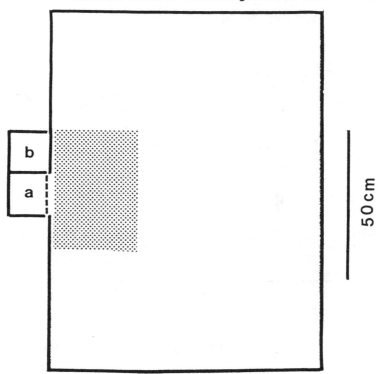

Figure 9.10. Apparatus used in experiments involving the conditioning of sexual behavior to arbitrary stimuli. A small doorway (14 x 15.5 cm) was centered along one side wall of the test cage. Access through this doorway was controlled by a vertically sliding opaque panel. The doorway opened to a two-compartment stimulus chamber that could be rolled back and forth on casters along the outside wall of the test arena. Each stimulus compartment was 11.5 cm deep and had the same width and height as the doorway, so that only one compartment could be lined up with the doorway at a time. The first stimulus compartment (a) was enclosed by a wire screen and contained an adult female quail embellished with bright orange chicken feathers. The second stimulus compartment (b) contained a normal, unrestrained, sexually receptive adult female quail. When the second compartment was lined up with the doorway to the test arena, no barrier existed between the normal female quail and the male bird.

The investigators assessed conditioning of the appetitive approach component of sexual behavior by measuring how much time individuals spent in a designated area near the embellished female bird during each conditioning trial. The criterial zone was the same as in the studies of social-proximity behavior (see Figure 9.2). The results of the experiment are summarized in Figure 9.11. Within a few conditioning trials, individuals in the experimental group came to spend nearly all of their time near the embellished female when she was visible. This behavior reflected approach to the embellished female, since the individuals went to the embellished female from other parts of the test cage when the female became visible. In

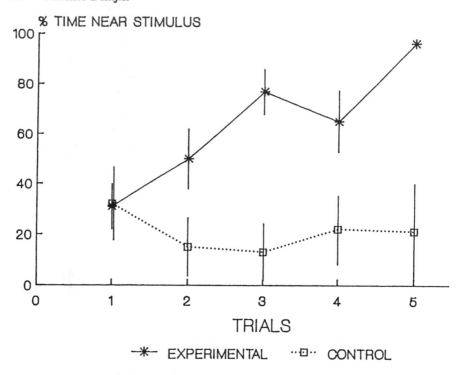

Figure 9.11. Mean percentage of time male birds spent near a female quail embellished with bright orange feathers during successive conditioning trials. For the experimental group but not for the control group, exposure to the embellished female was paired with opportunity to copulate with a normal female quail. (Vertical line through each symbol represents ± standard error.)

contrast, approach or proximity behavior did not develop in the control group. The experimental group acquired the conditioned approach behavior quickly, demonstrating how easily appetitive components of reproductive behavior can be experimentally modified by a conditioning procedure (for other examples of sexual conditioning of approach behavior, see Domjan et al., 1986).

A day or two after the conditioning trials, the investigators measured the extent to which the conditioning procedure had made the embellished female bird an effective conditioned stimulus for eliciting consummatory components of reproductive behavior in the same male individuals. For this test, an embellished female quail was released into the test arena for a 5-minute period, and the frequency of grab, mount, and cloacal-contact responses was observed. The results of that test are shown in Figure 9.12. The experimental group performed significantly more grab, mount, and cloacal-contact responses directed at the embellished bird than did the control group. Thus, the conditioning procedure increased the sexual attractiveness of the embellished female bird sufficiently to stimulate all

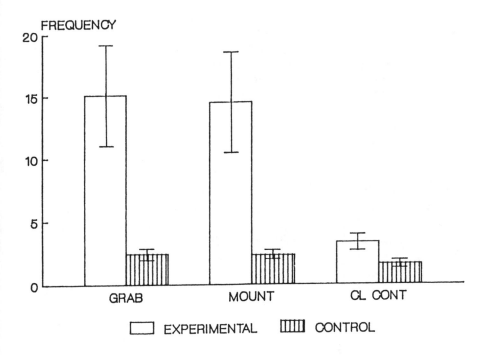

Figure 9.12. Mean frequency of grab, mount, and cloacal-contact responses male birds made to a female quail embellished with bright orange feathers. The experimental group but not the control group previously received exposure to the embellished female bird paired with opportunity to copulate with a normal female. (Vertical line within each bar represents ± standard error.)

three components of sexual-contact behavior. This outcome illustrates that consummatory sexual responses are to some extent subject to conditioning.

## A Counterconditioning Hypothesis

The embellished quail used as the conditioned-stimulus object in the study of course had many stimulus components in addition to the orange feathers. Most important, the orange feathers were on a female quail, and the visual features of the female's head and neck (previously shown to be releasing stimuli) were present. The fact that individuals in the control group did not show much approach or copulatory behavior in response to the embellished bird demonstrates that the head-and-neck cues were not sufficient to stimulate sexual behavior in the presence of the orange feathers. Since head-and-neck cues alone supported normal levels of sexual behavior in previous studies, one may conclude that the orange feathers disrupted the usual sexual behavior elicited by a female quail's head and neck. The disruptive effects of the "repulsive" orange feathers were gradually overcome in the experimental group as a result of the pairing of the embellished female with copulatory opportunity. Thus, the conditioning procedure, which paired "repulsive" orange feathers with copulatory opportunity, may have resulted in counterconditioning of the disruptive effects of the orange feathers. According to this interpretation, individuals in the experimental group did not learn to associate sexual satisfaction with the orange feathers. Rather, they did not allow the "repulsive" orange feathers to distract them from paying attention to the attractive features of the embellished female quail, namely, her head and neck.

One prediction of the counterconditioning interpretation is that the conditioned orange feathers will not stimulate sexual behavior if they are presented in the absence of a female quail's head and neck. The investigators tested this prediction by presenting the orange feathers on a block of wood. Only individuals from the experimental group (who had engaged in sexual behavior with an embellished female) served in these tests. During one test, the embellished block of wood was presented alone in the same stimulus compartment that had been used to present an embellished female during conditioning trials. In another test, the embellished block of wood was presented with a taxidermic specimen of a female quail's head and neck in front of it. Individuals spent a mean of 37% of their time near the embellished wood block without the head+neck specimen, which was not statistically significantly different from the amount of time they spent near the stimulus compartment when the compartment was empty (mean = 36%). In contrast, they spent 82% of their time near the stimulus compartment when it contained the embellished wood block with the head+neck specimen in front of it. Thus, the orange feathers did not significantly stimulate approach behavior in the absence of cues of a female quail's head and neck. These results support the counterconditioning interpretation.

## Sexual Conditioning to a Toy Dog

Perhaps the orange feathers had not come to elicit sexual arousal in the study because, during conditioning trials, the feathers had been presented in the company of more powerful species-specific stimuli exhibited by a female quail. An arbitrary stimulus presented in the absence of competing species-specific cues might be more likely to become conditioned to elicit sexual arousal and copulation. To test this idea, the investigators chose an object that had no quail-like features. The object was a stuffed toy dog, a Pound Puppy™ (Tonka Corporation, Pound Puppies, Inc.), measuring about 14 cm long. It had a bright yellow terry cloth surface, a thin black collar, a black nose button, and white eyes with small black pupils. Prior to the conditioning trials, the dog's neck was propped up with 5.5 cm of stiff wire, so that its head was about the height of a resting female quail's head.

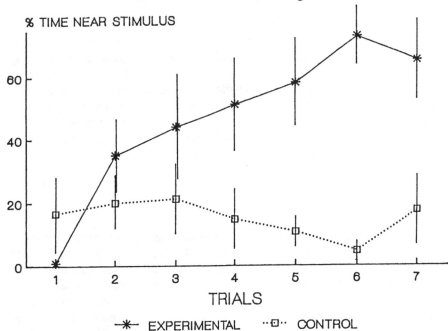

Figure 9.13. Mean percentage of time male birds spent near a toy dog during successive conditioning trials. For the experimental group but not for the control group, exposure to the toy dog was paired with opportunity to copulate with a normal female quail. (Vertical line through each symbol represents ± standard error.)

The conditioning procedure was the same as had been employed with the embellished female quail. For the experimental group, each exposure to the toy dog for 30 seconds was followed without delay by opportunity to copulate with a receptive adult female quail for 5 minutes. For the control group, exposure to the toy dog occurred about 2 hours after each copulatory opportunity.

The development of conditioned approach to the toy dog is illustrated in Figure 9.13. The experimental group gradually came to spend about 70% of its time near the toy dog when the toy was visible. In contrast, such proximity behavior did not develop in the control group. Acquisition of the conditioned-approach behavior was not as rapid in this experiment as it had been to the embellished female quail (compare Figures 9.11 and 9.13). However, a clear difference between the experimental and control groups emerged.

After seven conditioning trials, the investigators placed the toy dog in the center of the test arena to see whether the male birds would direct sexual-contact responses towards it. No grab, mount, or cloacal-contact responses occurred during this test. To increase the chances of observing some kind of activity directed at the toy dog, the researchers tested the individuals a second time, after discrimination training. Discrimination training consisted of the standard conditioning trials alternated with blank trials, in which the door to the respective stimulus compartments was opened but the toy dog was not presented and the individuals did not receive access to a normal female quail. Following discrimination training, the male birds in the experimental group showed significantly more approach toward the stimulus compartment when it contained the toy dog than when it was empty. Thus, the discrimination-training procedure successfully limited the conditioned-approach behavior to the presence of the toy dog. However, despite the additional training, no sexual-contact responses came to be directed at the toy dog.

## Sources of Constraints on the Conditioning of Sexual-Contact Responses

In these experiments, sexual conditioned-approach behavior developed readily when an embellished female quail and when a toy dog served as the conditioned stimulus. However, only the embellished quail came to elicit sexual-contact behavior as a result of the conditioning trials. These findings are consistent with previous suggestions that appetitive components of a behavioral sequence are more easily modified by experience than are consummatory components (e.g., Tinbergen, 1951, p. 105). Thus, there seems to be some sort of a constraint on the conditioning of consummatory sexual behavior. What is the source of this constraint?

Perhaps the most obvious answer is that the constraint on the conditioning of consummatory behavior resides in the nature of the stimuli that are necessary for the elicitation of sexual-contact responses. Quail may require the species-specific features of the head and neck of a female conspecific as supporting stimulation for copulation. Perhaps stimuli lacking these features cannot become conditioned to elicit sexual-contact responses. Although this idea might be plausible, there are other prominent possibilities.

One possibility focuses on commonalities between the objects that served as the conditioned and the unconditioned stimuli in these experiments. In the embellished-female experiment, the conditioned- and the unconditioned-stimulus objects had numerous common features since both were adult female quail. Probably the most important of these common features were visual cues of the head and neck of the females. The presence of these salient common features could have facilitated conditioning through associative mediation. The orange feathers could have become associated with the head and neck of the embellished female; those head-and-neck stimuli in turn could have become associated with sexual satisfaction during subsequent copulation with the normal female quail. Since the toy dog had far fewer stimulus features in common with a female quail (the unconditioned stimulus), such associative mediation was much less likely in the toy dog experiments.

The second line of argument focuses on the fact that the embellished female was a moving stimulus whereas the toy dog was immobile and was presented in the same orientation on every conditioning trial. Movement of the conditioned stimulus may have been important because it increased attention to the stimulus. Movement also may have facilitated the transfer of the conditioned behavior for the test session. During the test session, the conditioned-stimulus object was placed in the center of the test arena so the male quail would have enough room to grab and mount it. Movement may have facilitated the transfer of conditioned properties in two ways. First, it may have facilitated the perceptual integration of the conditioned stimulus as an object so that the embellished bird was seen as the same thing when viewed from different orientations. Second, movement may have facilitated the perceptual differentiation of the conditioned-stimulus object from background cues. With the immobile toy dog, conditioning may have accrued to a configuration of the toy together with background cues. If the toy became conditioned as part of such a stimulus configuration, changes in that configuration resulting from relocating the toy to the center of the test cage for testing would have resulted in the loss of the conditioned behavior.

## Conditioning of Sexual Behavior to Arbitrary Stimuli in Mammals

A few provocative examples of the conditioning of sexual behavior to arbitrary stimuli in mammals also are available. Dizinno, Whitney, and Nyby (1978), for example, found that sexual experience with female conspecifics induces inbred male mice to emit ultrasound vocalizations in response to the odor of female urine. Such ultrasound vocalizations can also come to be elicited by a musk odor if that odor is sprayed on the female mice with whom the males then are allowed to copulate. Thus, the odor of musk can come to elicit ultrasound vocalizations by association with copulation. However, tests with the odor of ethanol were not successful (Nyby et al., 1978; see also Nyby et al., 1983).

Sexual conditioning also has been investigated in domesticated rats. Zamble et al. (1985) placed male rats in a plastic tub with wood shavings for 10 minutes as the conditioned stimulus preceding exposure for 20 minutes to a female rat behind a wire screen. For male rats in a control group, placement in the plastic tub occurred at random times relative to exposure to the female rat. Eight conditioning trials were conducted, followed by a test trial. The test trial was designed to identify the effects exposure to the conditioned stimulus has on male copulatory behavior. For the test trial, each male rat was exposed to the conditioned stimulus and was then placed in a cage with a female rat. Individuals in the experimental group ejaculated with much shorter latencies during the postconditioning test than did individuals in the control group. In subsequent experiments,

Zamble et al. (1985) demonstrated that a flashing light and a small toy fish can also be successfully used as conditioned stimuli in this paradigm. After conditioning, these stimuli also came to facilitate the copulatory behavior of male rats, as evidenced in shorter latencies to ejaculation when the males were permitted to copulate with a female rat (see also Zamble, Mitchell, and Findlay, 1986).

In a related experiment, Graham and Desjardins (1980) investigated classical conditioning of the release of luteinizing hormone and testosterone in male rats. The conditioned stimulus consisted of placing the males in a cage containing vapors of methyl salicylate for 7 minutes. Rats in the experimental group received access to a sexually receptive female rat immediately afterward. For rats in a control group, access to the receptive female was provided 6 hours later. After 14 conditioning trials, placement in the cage containing the methyl salicylate odor was found to increase serum levels of luteinizing hormone and of testosterone in rats in the experimental group compared to rats in the control group. This study provides suggestive evidence that sexual conditioned-behavior responses may be mediated by conditioned modifications of neuroendocrine systems involved in sexual behavior.

## Conclusion

The current studies illustrate that considerable plasticity exists in the mechanisms whereby stimuli elicit reproductive behavior. The elicitation of appetitive and consummatory components of sexual behavior by arbitrary and species-specific stimuli was found to depend on the prior experience of the individual male Japanese quail. The current studies demonstrate that as many as four different forms of learning are involved.

One type of learning involves the **acquisition of sexual responses to previously ineffective stimuli**. This type of learning was clearly evident in the fact that appetitive components of reproductive behavior in male Japanese quail (approach and proximity) came to be elicited by nonbiological, arbitrary stimuli (e.g., a toy dog) as a result of a conditioning procedure in which visual exposure to that stimulus occurred just before the opportunity to copulate with a female conspecific (see also Domjan et al., 1986). When exposure to the stimulus was presented unpaired with sexual opportunity, approach behavior did not develop. Thus, the toy dog came to elicit approach behavior through association with sexual opportunity. In regard to procedure, the type of conditioning involved was similar to other forms of Pavlovian approach conditioning (cf. Hearst and Jenkins, 1974). However, similarities among the underlying mechanisms involved remain to be documented.

A second form of learning identified in the current studies involves **learning to respond differentially to sexually relevant stimuli**. This type of learning was evident in how male Japanese quail came to discriminate between male and female conspecifics. The static visual cues of the head and neck of male and female quail were found to be sufficient to elicit differential approach and social-proximity behavior in male Japanese quail. Socially experienced male birds were more likely to approach and spend time near a taxidermic specimen consisting of the head and neck of a female quail than a taxidermic specimen consisting of the head and neck of a male quail. This differential responding depended on prior experience. The individuals initially spent similar amounts of time near female and male birds but learned to suppress their approach to male conspecifics with repeated exposure to the male cues. Thus, differential responding to male vs. female conspecifics required that the males learn to suppress approach cues exhibited by a male conspecific. The learning involved in the acquisition of this discrimination had many features in common with conventional discrimination learning processes.

A third type of learning identified in the current studies involves **contextual conditioning**. This type of learning was important in the elicitation of consummatory sexual behavior by sign stimuli. Male Japanese quail will copulate with a taxidermic specimen consisting of the head and neck of a female quail mounted in front of a foam pad. However, such a simple stimulus elicited sexual-contact responses only if the individuals were tested in the same place (i.e., context) where they had been allowed to copulate with a normal live female quail previously. Thus, sexual conditioning of the contextual cues of the test arena was important for the elicitation of sexual-contact behavior by sign stimuli contained in the head+neck taxidermic specimen.

The fourth type of learning implicated in the current studies is **counterconditioning of disruptive effects of unusual stimuli**. This type of learning is implicated in the response of male Japanese quail to a female conspecific whose colors and shape had been radically altered by the addition of fluorescent-orange chicken feathers. Individual male birds that received exposures to such an embellished female quail shortly before opportunities to copulate with a normal female learned not to be disrupted by the unusual embellishments and came to copulate with the embellished bird. Individuals that received exposures to the embellished bird unpaired with copulatory opportunity were much less likely to make sexual contact with the embellished bird subsequently. Thus, through pairings with copulation, the bright orange feathers were counterconditioned so that they no longer disrupted copulatory behavior.

This summary shows that some forms of learning were clearly evident in studies of appetitive sexual behavior and other forms of learning were evident in studies of consummatory sexual behavior. The idea that different types of learning are involved in different components of the sexual behavior sequence is intriguing. However, it is premature to accept such an hypothesis. With some yet to be discovered procedures, research may be able to demonstrate that sexual-contact behavior can become conditioned to biologically arbitrary stimuli. Future research also may reveal that discriminative conditioning is necessary in order for male birds to show a greater likelihood of copulating with female as compared with male conspecifics (Sachs, 1966; Wilson and Bermant, 1972). Thus, acquiring sexual responses to previously ineffective stimuli and learning to respond differentially to sexually relevant stimuli may turn out not to be limited to the appetitive components of sexual behavior. Conversely, contextual conditioning and sexual counterconditioning may not be limited to the consummatory components of reproductive behavior.

Finally, the four types of learning identified in the current studies should not be regarded as the only types that are of potential importance in sexual behavior (see Domjan and Hollis, 1988). The current studies focused on postpubertal learning experiences. The importance of early-life learning experiences was not considered (see D'Udine, this volume). Furthermore, the types of learning emphasized here constitute a small fraction of the known learning processes (see Domjan and Burkhard, 1986). Therefore, even within the domain of adult learning, future studies are likely to identify additional influences on learning that are important in the regulation and expression of sexual behavior.

## Summary

Experiments served to identify stimuli that elicit appetitive and consummatory components of the reproductive behavior of adult male Japanese quail and the mechanisms whereby these stimuli acquire their effectiveness. Appetitive sexual behavior was measured as approach and social-proximity behavior. Consummatory sexual behavior was measured in terms of the occurrence of grab, mount, and cloacal-contact responses. Sexually and socially experienced male quail were more likely to approach and remain near female than near male conspecifics. Tests with whole and parts of taxidermic specimens led to the conclusion that static visual cues of the head and neck of female quail contain sufficient sign stimuli to elicit male approach and social-proximity behavior. The differential approach to female vs. male conspecifics depended on learning processes similar to those involved in the learning of discriminations between arbitrary stimuli.

Consummatory sexual behavior, too, occurred in male birds in response to a taxidermic specimen containing only the head and neck of female conspecifics. However, the elicitation of sexual-contact responses by such a taxidermic specimen depended on sexual conditioning of the contextual cues of the test arena. Individual male birds were more likely to copulate with the taxidermic specimen if they previously had sexual experience with a normal female conspecific in the test arena than if their prior sexual experience occurred in a different environment.

The mechanisms of sexual learning were explored further in studies of sexual behavior conditioned to arbitrary stimuli. Appetitive components of sexual behavior readily developed in response to arbitrary stimuli, such as a small toy dog, that served as a signal for sexual opportunity. However, consummatory sexual behavior was observed in the presence of arbitrary stimuli only if species-specific cues of a female quail's head and neck were also present. The implications of these findings for the existence of a possible constraint on the conditioning of consummatory sexual behavior were discussed.

The current studies focused attention on four different types of learning that occur in adulthood and are of potential importance in sexual behavior: acquisition of sexual responses to previously ineffective stimuli, learning to respond differentially to sexually relevant stimuli, contextual conditioning, and counterconditioning of the disruptive effects of unusual stimuli.

*Acknowledgments*

The research described in this chapter was supported by grant MH 39940 from the U.S. Public Health Service.

# References

Adkins, E.K., Koutnik, D.L., Morris, J.B., Pniewski, E.E., and Boop, J.J. Further evidence that androgen aromatization is essential for the activation of copulation in male quail. *Physiology and Behavior,* 1980, *24,* 441-446.

Amsel, A. Frustrative nonreward in partial reinforcement and discrimination learning: Some recent history and a theoretical extension. *Psychological Review,* 1962, *69,* 306-328.

Boneau, C.A., and Axelrod, S. Work decrement and reminiscence in pigeon operant responding. *Journal of Experimental Psychology,* 1962, *64,* 352-354.

Carbaugh, B.T., Schein, M.W., and Hale, E.B. Effects of morphological variations of chicken models on sexual responses of cocks. *Animal Behaviour,* 1962, *10,* 235-238.

Craig, W. Appetites and aversions as constituents of instincts. *Biological Bulletin,* Woods Hole, 1918, *34,* 91-107.

Dizinno, G., Whitney, G., and Nyby, J. Ultrasonic vocalizations by male mice (*Mus musculus*) to female sex pheromone: Experiential determinants. *Behavioral Biology,* 1978, *22,* 104-113.

Domjan, M. Photoperiodic and endocrine control of social proximity behavior in male Japanese quail (*Coturnix coturnix japonica*). *Behavioral Neuroscience,* 1987, *101,* 385-392.

Domjan, M., and Burkhard, B. *Principles of learning and behavior* (2nd ed.). Monterey, Calif.: Brooks/Cole, 1986.

Domjan, M., and Hall, S. Determinants of social proximity behavior in Japanese quail (*Coturnix coturnix japonica*): Male behavior. *Journal of Comparative Psychology*, 1986, *100*, 59-67.

Domjan, M., and Hollis, K.L. Reproductive behavior: A potential model system for adaptive specializations in learning. *In* R.C. Bolles and M.D. Beecher (Eds.), *Evolution and learning*. Hillsdale, N.J.: Lawrence Erlbaum Associates, 1988, pp. 213-237.

Domjan, M., and Nash, S. Stimulus control of social behavior in male Japanese quail (*Coturnix coturnix japonica*). *Animal Behaviour*, 1988, *36*, 1006-1015.

Domjan, M., Lyons, R., North, N.C., and Bruell, J. Sexual Pavlovian conditioned approach behavior in male Japanese quail (*Coturnix coturnix japonica*). *Journal of Comparative Psychology*, 1986, *100*, 413-421.

Domjan, M., O'Vary, D., and Greene, P. Conditioning of appetitive and consummatory sexual behavior in male Japanese quail. *Journal of the Experimental Analysis of Behavior*, 1988, *50*, 505-519.

Domjan, M., Greene, P., and North, N.C. Contextual conditioning and the control of copulatory behavior by species-specific stimuli in male Japanese quail. *Journal of Experimental Psychology: Animal Behavior Processes*, 1989, *15*, 147-153.

Flaherty, C.F. *Animal learning and cognition*. New York: Knopf, 1985.

Graham, J.M., and Desjardins, C. Classical conditioning: Induction of luteinizing hormone and testosterone secretion in anticipation of sexual activity. *Science*, 1980, *210*, 1039-1041.

Hearst, E., and Jenkins, H.M. *Sign tracking: The stimulus-reinforcer relation and directed action*. Austin, Tx.: Psychonomic Society, 1974.

Kovach, J.K. The behaviour of Japanese quail: Review of the literature from a bioethological perspective. *Applied Animal Ethology*, 1974, *1*, 77-102.

Lachman, R. The influence of thirst and schedules of reinforcement-nonreinforcement ratios upon brightness discrimination. *Journal of Experimental Psychology*, 1961, *62*, 80-87.

Mazur, J.E. *Learning and behavior*. Englewood Cliffs, N.J.: Prentice-Hall, 1986.

Mellgren, R.L., Wrather, D.M., and Dyck, D.G. Differential conditioning and contrast effects in rats. *Journal of Comparative and Physiological Psychology*, 1972, *80*, 478-483.

Nash, S., Domjan, M., and Askins, M. Sexual discrimination learning in male Japanese quail (*Coturnix coturnix japonica*). *Journal of Comparative Psychology*, 1989, *103*, 347-358.

Nyby, J., Whitney, G., Schmitz, S., and Dizinno, G. Post-pubertal experience establishes signal value of mammalian sex odor. *Behavioral Biology*, 1978, *22*, 545-552.

Nyby, J., Bigelow, J., Kerchner, M., and Barbehenn, F. Male mouse (*Mus musculus*) ultrasonic vocalizations to female urine: Why is heterosexual experience necessary? *Behavioral and Neural Biology*, 1983, *38*, 32-46.

Sachs, B. Sexual-aggressive interactions among pairs of quail (*Coturnix coturnix japonica*). *American Zoologist*, 1966, *6*, 559.

Schein, M.W., and Hale, E.B. The head as a stimulus for orientation and arousal of sexual behavior in male turkeys. *Anatomical Record*, 1957, *128*, 617-618.

Schein, M.W., and Hale, E.B. Stimuli eliciting sexual behavior. *In* F. Beach (Ed.), *Sex and behavior*. New York: Robert E. Krieger, 1965, pp. 440-482.

Schein, M.W., Diamond, M., and Carter, C.S. Sexual performance levels of male Japanese quail (*Coturnix coturnix japonica*). *Animal Behaviour*, 1972, *20*, 61-66.

Schoettle, H.E.T., and Schein, M.W. Sexual reactions of male turkeys to deviations from a normal female head model. *Anatomical Record*, 1959, *134*, 635.

Schumacher, M., and Balthazart, J. The effects of testosterone and its metabolites on sexual behavior and morphology in male and female Japanese quail. *Physiology and Behavior*, 1983, *30*, 335-339.

Timberlake, W., and Grant, D.L. Auto-shaping in rats to the presentation of another rat predicting food. *Science*, 1975, *190*, 690-692.

Tinbergen, N. *The study of instinct*. London: Oxford University Press, 1951.

Wada, M. Effects of sex steroids on calling, locomotor activity, and sexual behavior in castrated male Japanese quail. *Hormones and Behavior*, 1982, *16*, 147-157.

Wilson, M.I., and Bermant, G. An analysis of social interaction in Japanese quail (*Coturnix coturnix japonica*). *Animal Behaviour*, 1972, *20*, 252-258.

Zamble, E., Hadad, G.M., Mitchell, J.B., and Cutmore, T.R.H. Pavlovian conditioning of sexual arousal: First- and second-order effects. *Journal of Experimental Psychology: Animal Behavior Processes*, 1985, *11*, 598-610.

Zamble, E., Mitchell, J.B., and Findlay, H. Pavlovian conditioning of sexual arousal: Parametric and background manipulations. *Journal of Experimental Psychology: Animal Behavior Processes*, 1986, *12*, 403-411.

# 10
# Hormones and Neuroendocrine Factors in Atypical Human Sexual Behavior

Brian A. Gladue
*Department of Psychology*
*North Dakota State University*
*Fargo, North Dakota 58103*

## Introduction

Exactly 100 years ago, Brown-Sequard reported apparent physiological and behavioral consequences of self-injection of animal testicular extracts (Brown-Sequard, 1889). Such self-experimentation among scientists and physicians was not uncommon during those "frontier days" of endocrinology and medicine. What was unusual was Brown-Sequard's descriptive report of astonishing and fast-acting (within days) rejuvenating effects of guinea pig and dog testicular fluids on human affect, physiology, and behavior. He claimed that his appetite, energy level, mood, demeanor, intellectual capacities, muscular strength, and digestive and excretory systems were all improved. He also claimed that stopping the injections resulted in a gradual but complete return to his preexperimental condition. Brown-Sequard concluded that some "great dynamogenic power is possessed by some substance or substances which our blood owes to the testicles" (Brown-Sequard, 1889, p. 105).

Researchers know now, as some suspected even then, that Brown-Sequard probably was reporting a placebo effect, since his preparations of aqueous extracts of animal testes were almost certainly devoid of water-insoluble, gonadal steroid hormones. However, the notion that even something as complex as motivation and sexual behavior might be influenced by the gonads, an idea "known" anecdotally for centuries, now is held to be acceptable. All told, Brown-Sequard's thesis, like those of many scientists before and since, can be held to be "right, but for the wrong reasons." Clearer and more convincing evidence for testicular influences on mammalian male sexual behavior came later (Steinach, 1894).

The idea that human sexual behavior is biologically organized or modified (at least in part) by hormones has gained considerable attention in the past 20 years, largely because of advances in the technology with which hormones are measured. Additionally, a change in perspective allowing that human behavior is not simply the result of learning and culture and, therefore, somehow is exempt from biological influences, has boosted recent investigator interest in the relationships between hormones and human sexual behavior. It now is known that hormones definitely play a mediating role in human sexual behavior, although the extent to which and mechanisms by which this role is accomplished still is being elucidated.

Among the many fundamental questions being asked are, Do hormones play a role in the development and expression of **atypical** sexual behavior? If they do play a role, what is that role, and to what extent do they influence the development and expression of the behavior under discussion? If typical human sexual behavior (consensual adult heterosexual interactions) has hormonal correlates, are there comparable correlates for atypical human sexual behavior? In particular, are there endocrine and neuroendocrine correlates of sexual object choice? Additionally, are there hormonal correlates of paraphilic sexuality such as pedophilia, rape, and sexual aggression? The goal of this chapter is to explore the endocrinology of typical and selected atypical human male sexual behaviors.

## Testosterone Levels and Typical Sexual Behavior

In general, hormone levels in males are associated with sexual mood (readiness for sexual behavior), arousal (erection), and behavior (courtship and copulatory motor patterns). (See Bancroft, 1980, 1983, and Donovan, 1984, for extensive reviews on this subject.)

A positive correlation between resting plasma testosterone (T) levels and human sexual behavior has been demonstrated by Kraemer and co-workers (1976). Persky and colleagues (1978) found that husbands' average T levels were highly correlated with their initiation of sexual behavior and subsequent female responsivity. More recently, Knussman, Christiansen, and Couwenbergs (1986), based on self-report diaries, reported a significant correlation between plasma T levels and sexual fantasizing, copulations, masturbation, and arousal in adult human males over a 13-day period.

In other approaches, plasma T levels have been correlated with varying degrees of sexual arousal in human males as measured by penile responsiveness (plethysmography) to erotic stimuli (Lange et al., 1980). Higher levels of T (mean = 1,090 ng/dl) were correlated with shorter time periods to achieve full erectile tumescence when compared to males with lower (mean = 460 ng/dl) levels of T (normal range for plasma T in adult males is 300-1,000 ng/dl). Elsewhere, a comparison of sexually functional with sexually dysfunctional adult males (reporting primary and secondary erectile failure or impotence) found no differences in plasma T levels (Schwartz, Kolodny, and Masters, 1980). However, Davidson, Camargo, and Smith (1979) found that in hypogonadal males, administration of exogenous androgen (A) elicited increases in nocturnal erections, coital attempts, masturbation frequency, and self-reported sexual desire. Later work involving 41- to 93-year-old males confirmed that sexual **activity** per se was less correlated with plasma T levels than was self-reported sexual desire (Davidson, Kwan, and Greenleaf, 1982). Bancroft (1980, 1983) has shown over the years that plasma T levels, resulting from endogenous T or exogenous T (administered to hypogonadal adult males), had more effect on sexual arousability through central (brain and spinal cord) than through peripheral (parasympathetic and sympathetic nervous system) avenues (Bancroft and Wu, 1983).

Beyond a certain, somewhat variable theoretical "threshold" level, plasma T may have less effect on peripheral, end-organ arousal than on the central nervous system (CNS) tissue that mediates sexual thoughts, feelings, and behavior. Data from Davidson, Kwan, and Greenleaf (1982) suggest that the pleasurable awareness of genital sexual feelings and functional responses modifies subsequent thresholds of sexual arousability. Within this threshold, T may enhance the sensitivity of genital sensory receptors, thereby increasing sexual desire (Donovan, 1984). Beyond threshold needs for erectile capability, T may lower the threshold of sexual motivation in general, more than having a direct effect on actual genital functioning. This effect of T on CNS tissues, i.e., affecting the threshold of sexually motivated thoughts, feelings, and behaviors, emerges consistently across many studies.

## Testosterone and Aggressive Behavior

Since T affects species-typical male sexual behavior, it also may affect species-atypical male sexual behavior, such as occurs in rape, pedosexual behavior, or sadomasochistic behavior. The relationship between T and aggression will be reviewed, and the review will be followed by a presentation of studies of neuroendocrine correlates between aggressive and sexually motivated behavior.

The functional relationship between male sexual and aggressive behavior was described first by Oehlert (1958) in fish. In her studies, she showed that sexual behavior and aggressive behavior were capable of combining in males because of the functional proximity of sexual and aggressive motivational states. In contrast, sexual motivation and fear motivation are incompatible in males. In females, sexual and fear motivation can coexist, but sexual motivation and aggressive motivation cannot. Medicus and Hopf (this volume) relate these findings to pedophilia.

Attempts to correlate plasma T levels to human aggression have produced mixed results. While some workers found significant correlations between T measures and various pencil-and-paper measures of hostility or aggression (typically the Buss-Durkee Hostility Inventory) (Persky, Smith, and Basu, 1971), others either failed to directly replicate such findings (Meyer-Bahlburg et al., 1974) or reported inconclusive results from similarly designed studies (Doering et al., 1974; Doering et al., 1975; Monti, Brown, and Corriveau, 1977). Efforts to relate T levels to overt aggressive behavior in athletes (hockey players—Scaramella and Brown, 1978; wrestlers—Elias, 1981) have failed. Studies of male criminals are equally unconvincing (Ehrenkranz, Bliss, and Sheard, 1974; Kreuz and Rose, 1972). Bain et al. (1987), for example, found no difference in plasma T and A levels between adult males charged with murder and attempted murder and, in contrast, adult males charged with nonviolent crimes (property offenses). Christiansen and Knussman (1987) reported significant correlations between various androgens (total T, free T, and dihydrotestosterone [DHT]) and self-ratings of spontaneous aggression in 20- to 30-year-old males. However, self-report of interest in sexual aggression was only weakly correlated with plasma levels of free T. The current author's laboratory, too, found in 20- to 30-year-old males a similar, positive correlation ($r = 0.35$) of circulating plasma T to a paper-and-pencil measure of aggression (Gladue, journal article in preparation).

In 10-year-old adolescent, compared to adult, males, Olweus and colleagues (Olweus, 1979; Olweus et al., 1980) found positive correlations between T plasma levels and self-report measures of aggressivity. Olweus (1979) has argued that such aggressive reaction patterns are remarkably stable in males, manifesting themselves early in life. Other workers (Sussman et al., 1987), using comparable self-report questionnaire measures of aggressivity in pubertal children (ages 9-14 years), found that high levels of plasma androgens correlated positively with aggressivity.

Overall, efforts to relate plasma T levels to psychological measures of hostility and aggression are equivocal at best. Evidence correlating measures of aggressive behavior and plasma androgens are weaker in adults than in children and adolescents. All such studies are weak in sample selection and in the assessment of aggressive behavior (for a longer critique, see Meyer-Bahlburg, 1981).

# Atypical Sexual Behavior and Hormones

Sexually aggressive behavior is sexual behavior occurring either simultaneously or in rapid alternation with aggressive behavior, where aggressive behavior is defined as "threat display or actual infliction of bodily harm." Three parameters are studied in the effort to relate endocrine factors to sexually aggressive behavior: (a) the level of circulating hormone, (b) the production, mechanism of action, and effect of antiandrogens, and (c) the response of a neuroendocrine subsystem.

## Hormone Studies in Sex Offenders

Rada, Laws, and Kellner (1976) originally reported and then failed to replicate (Rada et al., 1983) that plasma T is significantly higher in sadistic than in nonsadistic rapists. Bradford and McLean (1984) and Langevin et al. (1985) also found negative results, although Langevin et al. (1985) found dehydroepiandrosterone sulphate (DHEA-S) significantly elevated in rapists compared to controls.

## Antiandrogens as Therapy for Sex Offenders

The antiandrogenic agents cyproterone acetate (CPA) and medroxy-progesterone acetate (MPA; e.g., Depo-Provera®) sometimes are used to treat sex offenders. Both drugs inhibit T production through the suppression of the secretion by the pituitary of luteinizing hormone (LH) and follicle-stimulating hormone (FSH), and each drug has a separate secondary effect on androgens: CPA is a competitive inhibitor of androgens at the receptor site (Brotherton and Bernard, 1974; Stern and Eisenfeld, 1969), while MPA appears to interfere directly with T biosynthesis (Gordon et al., 1970).

Early studies suggested that CPA reduced self-reports of erectile frequency, sexual fantasies, restlessness, and agitation and decreased plasma T levels (Laschet and Laschet, 1969). Davies (1974) reported a 5-year prospective study in which CPA was given to adult males convicted of sexual assault or indecent exposure, with no further sexual offense reported. Cooper (1981), in a placebo-controlled study, reported decreases in several measures of sexual activity with a corresponding "tranquilizer-like" effect on self-reported general anxiety and arousal.

Other studies report the effectiveness of Depo-Provera® as a chemical means of modifying sexual behavior (Berlin, 1983; Berlin and Meinecke, 1981; Cooper, 1987; Gagne, 1981; Money, 1970, 1972, 1987b; Money et al., 1975).

The most commonly claimed mechanism of action of Depo-Provera® is the reduction of T levels to around 150 ng/dl. Because of the correlation between a decline in T blood levels with an apparent corresponding decrease in self-reported sexual imagery or "desire to commit paraphilic sex offenses" (Money, 1987b), some researchers have argued that the drop in T causes the change in self-reported imagery and desire (Berlin and Meinecke, 1981). Alternatively, because MPA accumulates in the primate hypothalamus and other brain areas (Rees, Bonsall, and Michael, 1986), the possibility exists that the steroid drug also acts directly on brain cells that may be involved in sexual behavior.

Finally, MPA may be acting not primarily as an antiandrogen through decreased T production or by directly affecting neural target sites associated with sexual behavior but, rather, indirectly as an antianxiety agent (Berlin, 1983). It is important to appreciate that both of these drugs, CPA and MPA, are associated with an overall reduction of self-reported sex drive or sexually motivated thoughts, feelings, and behaviors. The drugs are **not specific** as to one's sexual object choice or concomitant sexual scenario, and they have been shown to have the same effects on sex drive when given to males whose sexual object choice is an appropriate-age adult female (Berlin, 1983).

## Neuroendocrine Response Studies in Sex Offenders

Because T production is under the control of the hypothalamic-pituitary-gonadal (HPG) axis, an evaluation of the responsiveness of this axis in sex offenders has been investigated. Gaffney and Berlin (1984) evaluated HPG functioning in three groups of adult males by using an infusion of exogenous luteinizing hormone-releasing hormone (LH-RH), a hypothalamic peptide hormone that triggers the release of LH from the pituitary. An expected typical response pattern in physically healthy males following LH-RH infusion would be an immediate elevation of LH with a rapid return to preinfusion levels. When three groups of subjects (pedophiles, nonpedophilic paraphiles, and heterosexual controls) were studied, only the pedophiles showed an aberrant hormone response pattern (see Figure 10.1).

Pedophilic subjects responded to LH-RH infusion with a marked elevation of LH at greater amplitude and of longer temporal persistence than occurred in nonpedophilic paraphiles or controls. These unreplicated results must be considered preliminary.

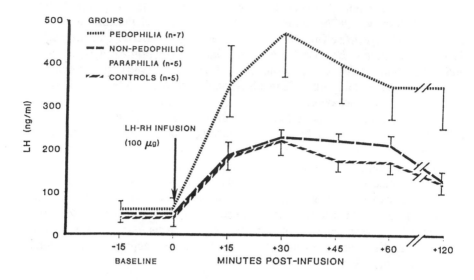

Figure 10.1. Neuroendocrine response to LH-RH infusion in male paraphilic individuals compared to controls. Note that LH values in pedophilic individuals are enhanced and prolonged compared to nonpedophiles and to nonparaphilic controls. (Figure drawn from data reported by Gaffney and Berlin, 1984, and presented in graph form with the permission of F. Berlin.)

## Hormonal and Neuroendocrine Response Patterns in Adult Human Males Who Vary in Sexual Object Choice

Traditionally, efforts to understand the development of atypical sexual behavior, particularly regarding biological factors involved in such psychosexual variations as homosexuality and bisexuality, assume that such atypicalities need "explaining" and that heterosexuality, the typical "norm," needs none. This chapter reflects the viewpoint that there is, as yet, no generally accepted model regarding the role of biological factors in the development of sexual object choice, no matter whether the choice defines heterosexuality, bisexuality, or homosexuality. It may be believed by some individuals that because heterosexuality is predominant among humans it needs no explanation, since heterosexuals are following an obvious (to some) procreative drive. Such a belief implies that bi-and homosexuality defy biological understanding, since it implies a failure to follow this simple reproductive dictum. Yet, if the main function (effect) of heterosexuality is essentially reproduction and therefore is biologically determined, variations in this behavior also need biological explanations.

If age-appropriate heterosexual behavior is the choosing of the typical, biologically determined sexual object, then homosexuality and bisexuality might be able to be correlated with other measures of biological variability. Evidence for biological, especially hormonal correlates of atypical sexual behavior is meager at this time, because the majority of the work has been done only since the early to middle 1970's. Yet, since then, the study of the psychoendocrinology of human sexuality has begun to yield a body of evidence that suggests that hormonal factors are influential in the development and expression of sexual orientation and sexual object choice.

## Hormonal Studies of Homosexual Behavior

Behavioral responses to sex hormones in adulthood often depend upon the organizing effects of perinatal hormonal exposure during sexual differentiation in the fetus. This view of the dependency of dimorphic (male different from female) sexual behavior upon pre- and postnatal hormones in nonhuman mammals has stimulated interest in the possibility of a similar hormonal component to human sexual behavior. While hormonal correlates of human sexual behavior may not be as easily demonstrable as are such correlates of the sexual behavior of nonhuman species, similar correlations between endocrine factors and sexual behavior in humans have been shown.

Two main elements are necessary if hormones are to act: (a) a critical level of active (free or unbound) hormone must be present and (b) the hormone must effectively interact with a particular target tissue. This end-organ sensitivity is a consequence of a particular cell's genetic instructions, metabolic capabilities, and receptor/hormone interactions (Martin and Reichlin, 1987). The same hormone has different effects on different end-organ tissues in the same body.

With regard to sexual object choice, a central question is: Do hormones "cause" homosexuality or bisexuality? That hormones **do** cause these orientations is, historically, the most commonly held notion about biological influences on the development of sexual object choice. Many studies, with equivocal and conflicting results, have examined the relationship of hormone **levels** to sexual orientation in men.

## Male Homosexual Behavior

Nearly two decades of endocrine research in this area suggest no convincing relationship between baseline circulating **levels** of hormones and sexual object choice. As shown in Table 10.I, the vast majority of studies have found no differences between homosexual and heterosexual males on measures of blood levels of androgenic steroids. (The relationship between hormones and sexual orientation was reviewed by Meyer-Bahlburg, 1984, and by Sanders, Bain, and Langevin, 1985.) Diet, drug intake, age, and time

TABLE 10.I. Survey of studies relating hormone levels with sexual object choice: Comparisons between heterosexual and homosexual adult males

|  | Hormone | | |
|---|---|---|---|
|  | Testosterone | Androstenedione | Estrogens |
| Number of Studies in Which Levels of the Hormone Were Significantly **Higher** in | | | |
| Heterosexuals (Kinsey 0-1)* | 3 | 0 | 0 |
| Homosexuals (Kinsey 2-6)* | 3 | 1 | 3 |
| Number of Studies in Which There Was No Difference Between Heterosexuals and Homosexuals | 23 | 5 | 7 |

Note: Not every research group investigated all hormones indicated.
*On a 7-point scale, from 0 to 6, Kinsey and colleagues (1948) categorized sexual orientation as follows:

  Kinsey 0-1: Self-report of exclusive or nearly exclusive heterosexuality.
  Kinsey 2-6: Self-report of more-than-incidental to exclusive homosexuality.

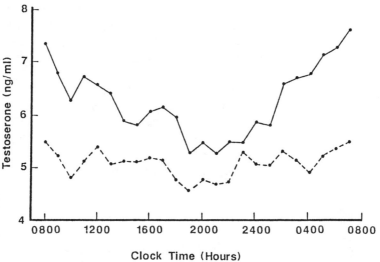

Clock Time (Hours)

Figure 10.2. Serum testosterone levels across a 24-hour period in young (23-28 years of age [solid line]) and older (58-82 years of age [dashed line]) healthy males. Peak values for the young males are at 0800 hours with a nadir at 1900-2400 hours. Note that the circadian cycle is not present in older males. (Figure after Bremner, Vitiello, and Prinz, 1983. Printed with the permission of The Endocrine Society. Copyright by The Endocrine Society.)

of day, i.e., circadian fluctuations (Bremner, Vitiello, and Prinz, 1983) (see Figure 10.2), can all affect results.

However, relationships between baseline levels of hormones and sexual behavior may be a conceptual matter—of "degree" rather than of "kind." Recent data suggest that in physically healthy adult males there is a correlation, albeit a weak one, between self-reports of the frequency of sexual behavior and the amount of free or of bound T present in the bloodstream (Knussman, Christiansen, and Couwenbergs, 1986). Yet, no such relationship seems to exist between the level of T and typical versus atypical preference in sexual partner (i.e., sexual object choice). It appears that within the normal range of blood levels of T, such levels are correlated with frequency of sex **drive** rather than **object** of male sexual behavior.

## Hormone/Brain Interactions: The Perinatal Hormone Theory

While it is unlikely that adult sex hormone **levels** have any correlation with adult sexual object choice, there is considerable evidence that perinatal hormone levels have an **organizing** effect upon the developing nervous system, with the result that the nervous system may have later behavioral predispositions (reviewed in Durden-Smith and Desimone, 1983; Schumacher, Legros, and Balthazart, 1987). The exposure of the fetal brain to particular hormones during a critical or sensitive developmental period can have far-ranging and lasting consequences regarding the functioning of the adult brain and the related behavioral repertoire. During specific critical periods of development, A masculinizes (and defeminizes) the CNS (McEwen, 1983). The absence of androgenic hormones results in a feminized CNS in biological male and biological female fetuses (Feder, 1981; McEwen, 1983). For humans, evidence of this perinatal hormone theory is weaker because of the obvious ethical prohibitions of the experimental design and, also, because of a reliance on data from naturally disordered fetuses and adults (Hines, 1982). Yet, these so-called "experiments of nature data" implicate prenatal hormones in the development of gender-identity/role behaviors and verbally reported sexual object choice (Ehrhardt et al., 1985; Money and Dalery, 1976; Money and Lewis, 1982; Money and Ogunro, 1974; Money, Schwartz, and Lewis, 1984; Schwartz and Money, 1983).

Three categories of human sex research that address the perinatal hormone theory are (a) studies of neuroendocrine hormone patterns in adults, (b) studies of congenital endocrine disorders, and (c) studies of offspring of females who were treated with hormones during pregnancy. Only the first category is covered in this chapter. For more information on the latter two categories, the interested reader is directed to Gladue (1987), Ellis and Ames (1987), and Money (1987a).

## Neuroendocrine Studies

Testing the perinatal hormone theory requires a measure in adults of some parameter that reflects the consequences of differential neural development caused by differences in perinatal hormonal exposure. The pattern of adult estrogen sensitivity and LH secretion is believed to meet this criterion. This pattern of LH secretion depends upon the amount of perinatal A that was present during the sexual differentiation of the brain. The existence of such a perinatal critical period is supported by work in nonhuman animals (Gorski, 1984). Males exposed to A during this critical period show patterns of LH secretion as adults that do not fluctuate throughout the month. Normal females, on the other hand, who ordinarily are not exposed to A during fetal development, secrete LH in a cyclic pattern that is related to the ovulatory cycle. Hence, the pattern of secretion of LH is alleged to be a rough indicator of the degree to which perinatal hormones differentiated this neuroendocrine function and, presumably, differentiated behaviorally relevant regions and functions of the brain, as well.

LH secretion patterns also depend, in part, upon adult neural responsiveness to estrogen. During part of the female menstrual cycle, a rising level of estrogen (of either an endogenous or exogenous source) causes a rapid decline in the LH level (the "negative-feedback effect"), which is followed by a sharp increase in LH (Loriaux et al., 1977; Knobil, 1980; Krey, 1984). This pattern appears to be dependent upon the sensitivity of the hypothalamus to estrogen (Keye and Jaffe, 1975). The ability of a rising level of circulating estrogen to ultimately enhance the release of LH, termed the "positive-feedback estrogen phenomenon," is thought to have been determined by the aforementioned developmental, hormone-mediated, sexual differentiation process (Gorski, 1984; McEwen, 1983). This response, typically seen in females, reflects the "feminized" brain. The typical absence of this response in males reflects the degree to which their brains have been defeminized and/or masculinized. This positive-feedback estrogen phenomenon has been found in rhesus monkeys (Karsch, Dierschke, and Knobil, 1973; Yamada et al., 1971) and human beings (Monroe, Jaffe, and Midgley, 1972). Human males usually do not show the positive-feedback response pattern (Kulin and Reiter, 1976), although considerable variation has been reported (Barbarino and De Marinis, 1980; Barbarino, De Marinis, and Mancini, 1983; and Barbarino et al., 1982). Figure 10.3 shows that as estrogen levels in castrated adult human males increase (artificially, by means of treatments with estradiol), there is a rapid increase in subsequent LH levels; yet, FSH, another pituitary gonadotrophin, does not show such a change.

This sex-dimorphic neuroendocrine response pattern has been used to explore biosocial correlates of human sexual behavior. Since the mid-1970's, Dörner and colleagues (Dörner, 1976, 1983, 1986; Dörner, Rohde, and

Schnorr, 1975; Dörner et al., 1975, 1976, 1983b) have reported that a single intravenous injection of an estrogen compound can elevate the circulating level of LH above initial values in homosexual but not in heterosexual adult males (see Figure 10.4, lower panel). They concluded that the positive-feedback response to estrogen seen in homosexual males reflects a predominantly female-differentiated brain, which, they believe, is the result of the natural biological variation in perinatal A levels that occurs during a critical period in fetal development. Further, Dörner and his colleagues argue that this female-differentiated brain would, among other things, mediate sexual attraction to and arousal by males (which the authors consider to be a typically female response).

Dörner's findings (for a review, see Dörner, 1983; also, see Meyer-Bahlburg, 1982, for a critique of these studies) prompted other workers to reexamine neuroendocrinological parameters of sexual object

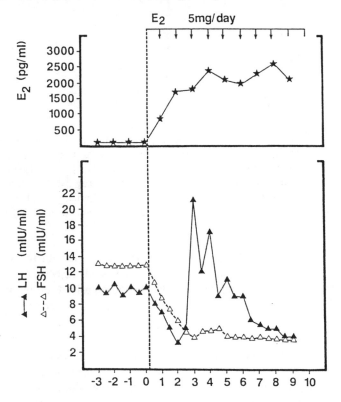

Figure 10.3. Serum estradiol ($E_2$), LH, and FSH in castrated adult males before and spanning daily administration of 5 mg of estradiol. Arrows indicate estrogen treatment days. Note that estradiol treatment initially decreases then increases LH levels in these castrated males. (Figure after data presented by Barbarino and De Marinis, 1980. Printed with the permission of The Endocrine Society. Copyright by The Endocrine Society.)

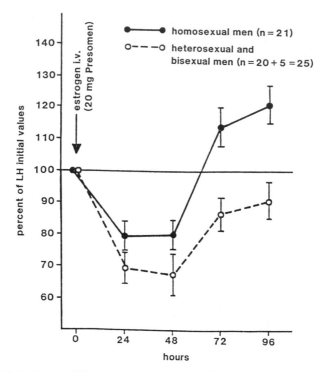

Figure 10.4. Serum LH response to a single intravenous injection of conjugated estrogen (Presomèn®, 20 mg) expressed as percentage of baseline levels of LH in two groups of human males—heterosexuals (Kinsey 0-1*) and bisexuals (Kinsey 2-4*)—and in a group of homosexual human males (Kinsey 5-6*). Values shown are mean ± standard error of the mean. (* = Kinsey, Pomeroy, and Martin, 1948, 7-point scale of sexual orientation.) (From Dörner, 1988, with permission of the author and Plenum Publishing Corp.)

choice. The current author's laboratory confirmed that there were neuro-endocrine differences related to self-reported sexual object choice (Gladue, Green, and Hellman, 1984). The results are summarized in Figure 10.5 by the two lower curves. Most, but not all, of the self-reported homosexual adult males showed an LH response pattern intermediate between that of most heterosexual adult males and heterosexual adult females, whereas none of the self-reported heterosexual males showed such a response pattern.

Furthermore, T secretion following this estrogen injection differed in adult males according to self-reported sexual orientation: serum T levels in these homosexual males were significantly depressed for longer periods of time when compared with these levels in the group of heterosexual males (Gladue, Green, and Hellman, 1984). (See Figure 10.6, lower panel.) None of the homosexual males showed a typically female response pattern. Responses in the adult females were earlier and of greater magnitude than

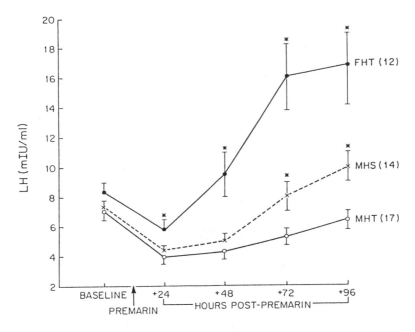

Figure 10.5. Change in LH response to a single 25-mg injection of Premarin® in groups of heterosexual females (FHT), heterosexual males (MHT), and homosexual males (MHS). Values are means ± standard errors (vertical bars). Group comparisons: (*) FHT significantly different from MHT and MHS at all time points post-Premarin® (p < 0.05); MHS significantly different from MHT at 72 hours and 96 hours post-Premarin® (p < 0.05). Both groups of males are comparable at baseline but differ following Premarin® injection. Number of individuals per group indicated in parentheses. (Gladue, Green, and Hellman, 1984. Copyright **1984** by the AAAS.)

were those in the males. There were no detectable changes in T levels in the heterosexual females in that study.

In another study, the neuroendocrine response to estrogen was studied in two groups of adult males who self-reported similar, earlier histories of at least 10 years of bisexual behavior and fantasies since puberty but who differed in their current self-reported sexual object choices and behavior. Baseline levels of T, LH, or cortisol did not differ between the two groups; however, their LH response to estrogen (Premarin®) did. LH levels 72 and 96 hours post-Premarin® were substantially elevated in the six subjects with a self-reported current, exclusively homosexual object choice and lifestyle, whereas the three subjects self-reporting a current heterosexual object choice responded with a different pattern of LH level, a pattern similar to the one found in self-reported lifelong heterosexual males (Figure 10.7). Both groups of subjects were comparable on a variety of physical and demographic measures including age, weight, education, years of sexual activity, and general physical and mental health.

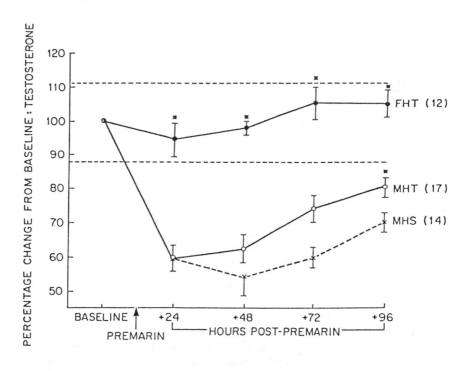

Figure 10.6. Change in testosterone (T) in response to Premarin®. Results are depicted as percentage of change from baseline values in order to allow comparison of both groups of males with the response pattern seen in females. Asterisks (*) indicate significant differences between groups at certain time points following injection. Dashed lines indicate 95% confidence interval for baseline values. Note that only the male groups show a decrease in T in response to Premarin®. (Gladue, Green, and Hellman, 1984. Copyright **1984** by the AAAS.)

These results must be interpreted cautiously. Recent research on some primate species attributes estrogen-induced LH responsiveness to a testicular factor that is not T or DHT (Steiner et al., 1976; Westfahl et al., 1984). Differences in the response of LH to estrogen in homosexual or heterosexual adult human males also might be the result of differential steroid responsiveness of testis cells to LH and/or estrogen stimulation rather than differential responsiveness to estrogen by the brain (Gooren, 1986a,b) or possible effects of the acquired immune deficiency syndrome (AIDS) and other immunological disorders affecting neural tissue that might impact the HPG system (Croxson et al., 1986).

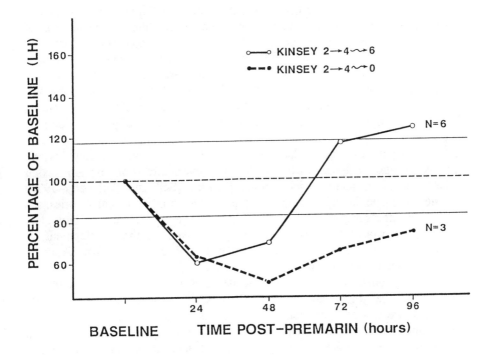

Figure 10.7. Change in LH in response to Premarin®, depicted as percentage of change from baseline values. Solid line depicts response pattern in currently exclusively homosexual adult males who report a prior history as bisexuals (n = 6); dashed line depicts response pattern in currently exclusively heterosexual adult males reporting prior bisexual activity and fantasy (n = 3). Dashed lines indicate 95% confidence interval for baseline values. Note that in both groups LH levels decrease immediately following Premarin®, yet only the exclusively homosexual group exhibits a surge in LH similar to that reported for homosexual adult males elsewhere.

## Conclusion

In *Sexual Behavior in the Human Male*, Kinsey, Pomeroy, and Martin (1948) considered factors that might account for atypical (specifically homosexual) behavior. Because variation in sexual object choice exists across a continuum (and is not merely "all-or-none"), biological explanations must consider this variance. Since Kinsey's challenge was posed, several lines of evidence suggest biological measures that may correlate with an individual, particular, sexual object choice. While no definitive set of studies has met Kinsey's strict criteria for identifying biological bases of homosexuality or heterosexuality, an emerging body of evidence suggests that the development of sexual object choice must be viewed within a biosocial context (Money, 1987a).

Yet, it should be noted, too, that there may be limitations to biological explanations of psychosexuality, especially regarding atypical sexual expression. Males may arrive at an adult sexual object choice through different routes. Indeed, the variance in neuroendocrine-hormone response among adult homosexual males, along with the variability of the outcome of treatment reported in studies of sex offenders, all argue against obvious, simple biological correlates for atypical sexual behavior. Atypical sexuality, like typical aspects of heterosexuality, may not be readily understood or explained through theories of singular mechanisms or origins. For some males, the path to a particular sexual identity and orientation may involve mainly genetic or biochemical factors. However, efforts to explain sexual orientation based upon social-learning theories (Bell and Weinberg, 1978) are no more convincing than are simplistic genetic or hormonal theories. As is the case regarding much of human behavior, a combination of biological and psychosocial factors is most likely involved in the development of sexuality; therefore, a biosocial approach is the approach most likely to yield a better understanding.

In any biosocial inquiry into sexual object choice, the idea must be kept clear that most human adult homosexual males, like heterosexual males, desire a sexual partner of adult status. It is a subset of andro- and gynephilic, pedo- and ephebophilic males who prefer (are compelled toward?) young children or pre-/peripubertal individuals for sexual desire and gratification. The biosocial approach to understanding atypical gender object choice (as in homosexuality) must distinguish between age of partners. Homosexual and bisexual adult human males are **not** likely to share genetic and biochemical factors with androphilic pedophiles. Little is known, however, of biochemical, neuroendocrine, or even genetic factors that distinguish gynephilic pedophiles from androphilic pedophiles. This area is clearly and essentially one that requires further investigation.

## Summary

Various endocrine explanations and theories have been sought and offered to account for variations in human sexual behavior, especially endocrine correlates of homosexuality. Substantial research efforts from numerous laboratories indicate that simple hormonal correlates for differences in sexual object choice preference do not exist. Alternative approaches to understanding brain/hormone/behavior relationships suggest, with some degree of caution, that dynamic neuroendocrine differences between heterosexual and homosexual adult males might exist. It is doubtful that idiosyncratic and paraphilic sexual object choice can be completely correlated to neuroendocrine parameters alone, which means that associational learning also plays a part. The real challenge for the next decade is two-fold: first, neural/endocrine features of typical sexual behavior must be better characterized and classified; second, based on a fundamental understanding of the psychoneuroendocrinology of what is typical, neural/endocrine factors associated with the development and adult expression of atypical sexual behavior, especially the behaviors associated with the paraphilias, also must be characterized and classified.

NOTE IN PRESS: Recent data from this laboratory suggest that a relationship in the LH response to estrogen in adult human males may be based upon differences in gonadal functioning. Therefore, the probability of an enhanced LH response to estrogen may not be directly associated with sexual partner preferences.

## References

Bain, J., Langevin, R., Dickey, R., and Ben-Aron, M. Sex hormones in murderers and assaulters. *Behavioral Science and the Law*, 1987, *5*(1), 95-101.

Bancroft, J. Endocrinology of sexual function. *Clinics in Obstetrics and Gynaecology*, 1980, *7*, 253-281.

Bancroft, J. *Human sexuality and its problems*. Edinburgh: Churchill Livingstone, 1983.

Bancroft, J., and Wu, F.C.W. Changes in erectile responsiveness during androgen therapy. *Archives of Sexual Behavior*, 1983, *12*, 59-66.

Bancroft, J., Tennent, T., Loncas, K., and Cass, J. Control of deviant sexual behavior by drugs: Behavioral effects of estrogens and antiandrogens. *British Journal of Psychiatry*, 1974, *125*, 310-315.

Barbarino, A., and De Marinis, L. Estrogen induction of luteinizing hormone release in castrated adult males. *Journal of Clinical Endocrinology and Metabolism*, 1980, *51*(2), 280-286.

Barbarino, A., De Marinis, L., and Mancini, A. Estradiol modulation of basal and gonadotropin-releasing hormone-induced gonadotropin release in intact and castrated men. *Neuroendocrinology*, 1983, *36*, 105-111.

Barbarino, A., De Marinis, L., Mancini, A., Giustacchini, M., and Alcini, A.E. Biphasic effect of estradiol on luteinizing hormone response to gonadotropin-releasing hormone in castrated men. *Metabolism*, 1982, *31*, 755-758.

Bell, A.P., and Weinberg, M.S. *Homosexualities: A study of diversity among men and women*. New York: Simon and Schuster, 1978.

Berlin, F. Sex offenders: A biomedical perspective and a status report on biomedical treatment. *In* J. Greer and I. Stuart (Eds.), *The sexual aggressor*. New York: Van Nostrand Reinhold, 1983, pp. 83-123.

Berlin, F., and Meinecke, C. Treatment of sex offenders with antiandrogenic medication: Conceptualization, review of treatment modalities, and preliminary findings. *American Journal of Psychiatry*, 1981, *138*, 601-607.

Bradford, J., and Bourget, D. Sexually aggressive men. *Psychiatric J. Univ. Ottawa*, 1987, *12*(3), 169-175.

Bradford, J., and McLean, D. Sexual offenders, violence and testosterone: A clinical study. *Canadian Journal of Psychiatry*, 1984, *29*, 335-343.

Bremner, W.J., Vitiello, M.V., and Prinz, P.N. Loss of circadian rhythmicity in blood testosterone levels with aging in normal men. *Journal of Clinical Endocrinology and Metabolism*, 1983, *56*(6), 1278-1281.

Brotherton, J., and Bernard, G. Some aspects of the effect of cyproterone acetate on levels of other steroid hormones in Man. *Journal of Reproduction and Fertility*, 1974, *36*, 373-385.

Brown-Sequard, J. The effects produced on Man by subcutaneous injections of a liquid obtained from the testicles of animals. *Lancet*, July 20, 1889, pp. 105-107.

Christiansen, K., and Knussman, R. Androgen levels and components of aggressive behavior in men. *Hormones and Behavior*, 1987, *21*, 170-180.

Cooper, A. A placebo controlled trial of the antiandrogen cyproterone acetate in deviant hypersexuality. *Compr. Psychiatry*, 1981, 22, 458.

Cooper, A. Medroxyprogesterone acetate (MPA) treatment of sexual acting out in men suffering from dementia. *Journal of Clinical Psychiatry*, 1987, *48*(9), 368-370.

Croxson, T.S., Miller, L.K., Mildvan, D., and Zumoff, B. The impact of HTLV-III/LAV infection on psychosexual functioning. Abstracts of the meeting of the International Academy of Sex Research, September 16-20, 1986, Amsterdam, Netherlands.

Davidson, J., Camargo, C., and Smith, E. Effects of androgen on sexual behavior in hypogonadal men. *Journal of Clinical Endocrinology and Metabolism*, 1979, *48*(6), 955-958.

Davidson, J., Kwan, M., and Greenleaf, W. Hormonal replacement and sexuality in men. *Clinics in Endocrinology and Metabolism*, 1982, *11*, 599-623.

Davies, T. Cyproterone acetate for male hypersexuality. *Journal of Int. Med. Res.*, 1974, *2*, 159.

Doering, C.H., Brodie, H.K.H., Kraemer, H.C., Becker, H.B., and Hamburg, D.A. Plasma testosterone levels and psychologic measures in men over a 2-month period. *In* R.C. Friedman, R.L. Richart, and R.L. Van de Wiele (Eds.), *Sex differences in behavior*. New York: Wiley, 1974.

Doering, C.H., Brodie, H.K.H., Kraemer, H.C., Moos, R.H., Becker, H.B., and Hamburg, D.A. Negative affect and plasma testosterone: A longitudinal human study. *Psychosom. Med.*, 1975, *37*, 484-491.

Donovan, B.T. *Hormones and human behaviour*. London: Cambridge University Press, 1984.

Dörner, G. *Hormones and brain differentiation*. Amsterdam: Elsevier, 1976.

Dörner, G. Hormone-dependent brain development. *Psychoneuroendocrinology*, 1983, *8*, 205-212.

Dörner, G. Sex-specific gonadotrophin secretion, sexual orientation and gender role behaviour. *Experimental and Clinical Endocrinology*, 1986, *86*(1), 1-6.

Dörner, G. Neuroendocrine response to estrogen and brain differentiation in heterosexuals, homosexuals, and transsexuals. *Archives of Sexual Behavior*, 1988, *17*, 57-75.

Dörner, G., Rohde, W., and Schnorr, D. Evocability of a slight positive oestrogen feedback action on LH secretion in castrated and oestrogen-primed men. *Endokrinologie*, 1975, *66*, 373-376.

Dörner, G., Rohde, W., Stahl, F., Krell, L., and Masius, W.G. A neuroendocrine predisposition for homosexuality in men. *Archives of Sexual Behavior*, 1975, *4*, 1-8.

Dörner, G., Rohde, W., Siedel, K., Haas, W., and Schott, G. On the evocability of a positive estrogen feedback action on LH secretion in transsexual men and women. *Endokrinologie*, 1976, *67*, 20-25.

Dörner, G., Rohde, W., Schott, G., and Schnabl, C. On the LH response to estrogen and LH-RH in transsexual men. *Experimental and Clinical Endocrinology*, 1983a, *82*, 257-267.

Dörner, G., Schenk, B., Schmiedel, B., and Ahrens, L. Stressful events in prenatal life of bi- and homosexual men. *Experimental and Clinical Endocrinology*, 1983b, *81*, 83-87.

Durden-Smith, J., and Desimone, D. *Sex and the brain*. New York: Arbor House, 1983.

Ehrenkranz, J., Bliss, D., and Sheard, M.H. Plasma testosterone: Correlation with aggressive behavior and social dominance in man. *Psychosomatic Medicine*, 1974, *36*, 469-475.

Ehrhardt, A.A., Meyer-Bahlburg, H.F.L., Rosen, L.R., Feldman, J.F., Veridiano, N.P., Zimmerman, I., and McEwen, B.S. Sexual orientation after prenatal exposure to exogenous estrogen. *Archives of Sexual Behavior*, 1985, *14*, 57-78.

Elias, M. Serum cortisol, testosterone, and testosterone-binding globulin responses to competitive fighting in human males. *Aggressive Behavior*, 1981, *7*, 215-224.

Ellis, L., and Ames, M.A. Neurohormonal functioning and sexual orientation: A theory of homosexuality-heterosexuality. *Psychological Bulletin*, 1987, *10*(2), 233-258.

Feder, H.H. Perinatal hormones and their role in the development of sexually dimorphic behaviors. *In* N.T. Adler (Ed.), *Neuroendocrinology of reproduction*. New York: Plenum Press, 1981, pp. 127-158.

Gaffney, G., and Berlin, F. Is there hypothalamic-pituitary-gonadal dysfunction in paedophilia? A pilot study. *British Journal of Psychiatry*, 1984, *145*, 657-660.

Gagne, P. Treatment of sex offenders with medroxyprogesterone acetate. *American Journal of Psychiatry*, 1981, *138*, 644-646.

Gladue, B.A. Psychobiological contributions. *In* L. Diamant (Ed.), *Male and female homosexuality: Psychological approaches*. Washington, D.C.: Hemisphere, 1987, pp. 129-154.

Gladue, B.A. Gender differences in hormonal correlates of aggression (tentative title). Journal article in preparation.

Gladue, B.A., Green, R., and Hellman, R.E. Neuroendocrine response to estrogen and sexual orientation. *Science*, 1984, *225*, 1496-1499.

Gooren, L. The neuroendocrine response of luteinizing hormone to estrogen administration in heterosexual, homosexual, and transsexual subjects. *Journal of Clinical Endocrinology and Metabolism*, 1986a, *63*, 583-588.

Gooren, L. The neuroendocrine response of luteinizing hormone to estrogen administration in the human is not sex specific but dependent on the hormonal environment. *Journal of Clinical Endocrinology and Metabolism*, 1986b, *63*, 589-593.

Gordon, G., Southern, A., Tochimoto, S., Olivo, J., Altman, K., Rand, J., and Lemberger, L. Effect of medroxyprogesterone acetate (Provera) on the metabolism and biological activity of testosterone. *Journal of Clinical Endocrinology*, 1970, *30*, 449-456.

Gorski, R.A. Critical role for the medial preoptic area in the sexual differentiation of the brain. *In* G.J. De Vries, J.P.C. De Bruin, H.B.M. Uylings, and M.A. Corner (Eds.), *Sex differences in the brain*. Progress in Brain Research series, Vol. 61. New York: Elsevier Press, 1984, pp. 129-146.

Hines, M. Prenatal gonadal hormones and sex differences in human behavior. *Psychological Bulletin*, 1982, *92*, 56-80.

Karsch, F.J., Dierschke, D.J., and Knobil, E. Sexual differentiation of pituitary function: Apparent difference between primates and rodents. *Science*, 1973, *179*, 484-486.

Keye, W.R., and Jaffe, R.B. Strength-duration characteristics of estrogen effects on gonadotropin response to gonadotropin-releasing hormone in women. I. Effects of varying duration of estradiol administration. *Journal of Clinical Endocrinology and Metabolism*, 1975, *41*, 1003-1008.

Kinsey, A.C., Pomeroy, W.B., and Martin, C.E. *Sexual behavior in the human male*. Philadelphia: W.B. Saunders Co., 1948, pp. 606-651.

Knobil, E. The neuroendocrine control of the menstrual cycle. *Recent Progress in Hormone Research*, 1980, *36*, 53-88.

Knussman, R., Christiansen, K., and Couwenbergs, C. Relations between sex hormone levels and sexual behavior in men. *Archives of Sexual Behavior*, 1986, *15*(5), 429-445.

Kraemer, H.C., Becker, H.B., Brodie, H.K.H., Doering, C.H., Moos, R.H., and Hamburg, D.A. Orgasmic frequency and plasma testosterone levels in normal human males. *Archives of Sexual Behavior*, 1976, *5*(2), 125-132.

Kreuz, L.E., and Rose, R.M. Assessment of aggressive behavior and plasma testosterone in a young criminal population. *Psychosomatic Medicine*, 1972, *34*, 321-332.

Krey, L.C. Neuronal and endocrine mechanisms involved in the control of gonadotropin secretion. *In* G.M. Brown, S.H. Koslow, and S. Reichlin (Eds.), *Neuroendocrinology and psychiatric disorder*. New York: Raven Press, 1984, pp. 325-338.

Kulin, H.E., and Reiter, E.O. Gonadotropin and testosterone measurements after estrogen administration to adult men, prepubertal and pubertal boys and men with hypogonadotropism: Evidence for maturation of positive feedback in the male. *Pediatric Research*, 1976, *10*, 46-51.

Lange, J., Brown, W., Wincze, J., and Zwicks, W. Serum testosterone concentration and penile tumescence changes in men. *Hormones and Behavior*, 1980, *14*, 267-270.

Langevin, R., Bain, J., Ben-Aron, M.H., Coulthard, R., Day, D., Handy, L., Heasman, G., Hucker, S.J., Purins, J.E., Roper, V., Russon, A.E., Webster, C.D., and Wortzman, G. Sexual aggression: Constructing a predictive equation. A controlled pilot study. *In* R. Langevin (Ed.), *Erotic preference, gender identity and aggression in men*. Hillsdale, N.J.: Lawrence Erlbaum Associates, 1985, pp. 39-76.

Laschet, V., and Laschet, L. Three years' clinical results with cyproterone-acetate in the inhibiting regulation of male sexuality. *Acta Endocrinologica Suppl.*, 1969, *138*, 103.

Laschet, V., and Laschet, L. Antiandrogens in the treatment of sexual deviations in men. *Journal of Steroid Biochemistry*, 1975, *6*, 821-826.

Loriaux, D.L.L., Vigersky, R.A., Marynick, S.P., Janick, J.J., and Sherons, R. Androgen and estrogen effects in the regulation of LH in Man. *In* P. Troen and H.R. Nankin (Eds.), *The testis in normal and infertile men*. New York: Raven Press, 1977, pp. 213-225.

Martin, J.B., and Reichlin, S. Effects of hormones on the brain and behavior. *In* J.B. Martin and S. Reichlin (Eds.), *Clinical neuroendocrinology* (2nd ed.). Contemporary Neurology series, No. 28. Philadelphia: F.A. Davis Company, 1987, pp. 639-667.

McEwen, B.S. Gonadal steroid influences on brain development and sexual differentiation. *In* R.O. Greep (Ed.), *Reproductive Physiology IV, International Review of Physiology*, Vol. 27. Baltimore: University Park Press, 1983, pp. 99-145.

Meyer-Bahlburg, H.F.L. Androgens and human aggression. *In* P.F. Brain and D. Benton (Eds.), *The biology of aggression*. Alphen aan den Rijn: Sijthoff and Noordhoff, 1981, pp. 263-290.

Meyer-Bahlburg, H.F.L. Hormones and psychosexual differentiation: Implications for the management of intersexuality, homosexuality and transsexuality. *Clinics in Endocrinology and Metabolism*, 1982, *11*, 681-701.

Meyer-Bahlburg, H.F.L. Psychoendocrine research on sexual orientation. Current status and future options. *In* G.J. De Vries, J.P.C. De Bruin, H.B.M. Uylings, and M.A. Corner (Eds.), *Sex differences in the brain*. Progress in Brain Research series, Vol. 61. New York: Elsevier Press, 1984, pp. 375-398.

Meyer-Bahlburg, H.F.L., Nat, R., Boon, D., Sharma, M., and Edwards, J. Aggressiveness and testosterone measures in Man. *Psychosomatic Medicine*, 1974, *36*(3), 269-274.

Money, J. Use of an androgen depleting hormone in the treatment of male sex offenders. *J. Sex Res.*, 1970, *6*, 165-172.

Money, J. The therapeutic use of androgen depleting hormone. *Int. Psychiatry Clin.*, 1972, *8*(4), 165-174.

Money, J. Sin, sickness, or status? Homosexual gender identity and psychoneuroendocrinology. *American Psychologist*, 1987a, *42*, 384-399.

Money, J. Treatment guidelines: Antiandrogen and counseling of paraphilic sex offenders. *Journal of Sex and Marital Therapy*, 1987b, *13*(3), 219-223.

Money, J., and Dalery, J. Iatrogenic homosexuality: Gender identity in seven 46,XX chromosomal females with hyperadreno-cortical hermaphroditism born with a penis, three reared as boys, four reared as girls. *Journal of Homosexuality*, 1976, *1*, 357-371.

Money, J., and Lewis, V.G. Homosexual/heterosexual status in boys at puberty: Idiopathic adolescent gynecomastia and congenital virilizing adrenocorticism compared. *Psychoneuroendocrinology*, 1982, *7*, 339-345.

Money, J., and Ogunro, C. Behavioral sexology: Ten cases of genetic male intersexuality with impaired prenatal and pubertal androgenization. *Archives of Sexual Behavior*, 1974, *3*, 181-205.

Money, J., Schwartz, M., and Lewis, V.G. Adult erotosexual status and fetal hormonal masculinization and demasculinization: 46,XX congenital virilizing adrenal hyperplasia (CVAH) and 46,XY androgen insensitivity syndrome (AIS) compared. *Psychoneuroendocrinology*, 1984, *9*, 405-414.

Money, J., Wiedeking, C., Walker, P., Migeon, C., Meyer, W., and Borgoankar, D. 47,XYY and 46,XY males with antisocial and/or sex-offending behavior: Antiandrogen therapy plus counselling. *Psychoneuroendocrinology*, 1975, *1*, 165-178.

Monroe, S.E., Jaffe, R.B., and Midgley, A.R., Jr. Regulation of human gonadotropins. XII. Increase in serum gonadotropins in response to estradiol. *Journal of Clinical Endocrinology*, 1972, *34*, 342.

Monti, P.M., Brown, W.A., and Corriveau, D.P. Testosterone and components of aggressive and sexual behavior in Man. *American J. Psychiat.*, 1977, *134*, 692-694.

Oehlert, B. Kampf und Paarbildung einiger Cichliden. *Zeitschrift für Tierpsychologie*, 1958, *15*(2), 141-174.

Olweus, D. Stability of aggressive reaction patterns in males: A review. *Psychological Bulletin*, 1979, *86*(4), 852-875.

Olweus, D., Mattsson, A., Schalling, D., and Low, H. Testosterone, aggression, physical, and personality dimensions in normal adolescent males. *Psychosom. Med.*, 1980, *42*(2), 253-269.

Persky, H., Smith, K.D., and Basu, G.K. Relation of psychological measures of aggression and hostility to testosterone production in Man. *Psychosom. Med.*, 1971, *33*, 265-277.

Persky, H., Lief, H., Strauss, D., Miller, W., and O'Brien, C. Plasma testosterone level and sexual behavior of couples. *Archives of Sexual Behavior*, 1978, *7*(3), 157-173.

Rada, R.T., Laws, D.R., and Kellner, R. Plasma testosterone in the rapist. *Psychosom. Med.*, 1976, *38*, 257-268.

Rada, R.T., Laws, D.R., Kellner, R., Stivastava, L., and Peake, G. Plasma androgens in violent and non-violent sex offenders. *Bull. Am. Acad. Psychiatry and Law*, 1983, *11*, 149-158.

Rees, H., Bonsall, R., and Michael, R. Preoptic and hypothalamic neurons accumulate (3H) medroxyprogesterone acetate in male *Cynomolgus* monkeys. *Life Science*, 1986, *39*, 1353-1359.

Sanders, R.M., Bain, J., and Langevin, R. Peripheral sex hormones, homosexuality, and gender identity. *In* R. Langevin (Ed.), *Erotic preference, gender identity, and aggression in men*. Hillsdale, N.J.: Lawrence Erlbaum Associates, 1985, pp. 227-247.

Scaramella, T., and Brown, W. Serum testosterone and aggressiveness in hockey players. *Psychosom. Med.*, 1978, *40*(3), 262-265.

Schumacher, M., Legros, J.J., and Balthazart, J. Steroid hormones, behavior and sexual dimorphism in animals and men: The nature-nurture controversy. *Experimental and Clinical Endocrinology*, 1987, *90*, 129-156.

Schwartz, M.F., and Money, J. Dating, romance and sexuality in young adult adrenogenital females. *Neuroendocrinology Letters*, 1983, *5*, 132.

Schwartz, M., Kolodny, R., and Masters, W. Plasma testosterone levels of sexually functional and dysfunctional men. *Archives of Sexual Behavior*, 1980, *9*(5), 355-366.

Steinach, E. Investigations into the comparative physiology of the male sexual organs with particular reference to the accessory sexual glands. Translated from *Pfluegers Archive Ges. Physiol.*, 1894, *56*, 304-338.

Steiner, R.A., Clifton, D.K., Spies, H.G., and Resko, J.A. Sexual differentiation and feedback control of luteinizing hormone in the rhesus monkey. *Biology of Reproduction,* 1976, *15,* 206-212.

Stern, J., and Eisenfeld, A. Androgen accumulation and binding to macromolecules in seminal vesicles: Inhibition by cyproterone. *Science,* 1969, *166,* 233-235.

Sussman, E., Inoff-Germain, G., Nottelmann, E., Loriaux, D., Cutler, G., and Chrousos, G. Hormones, emotional dispositions, and aggressive attributes in young adolescents. *Child Development,* 1987, *58,* 1114-1134.

Westfahl, P.K., Stadelman, H.L., Horton, L.E., and Resko, J.A. Experimental induction of estradiol positive feedback in intact male monkeys: Absence of inhibition by physiologic concentrations of testosterone. *Biology of Reproduction,* 1984, *31,* 856-862.

Yamada, T., Dierschke, D.J., Hotchkiss, J., Bhattacharya, A.N., Surve, A.H., and Knobil, E. Estrogen induction of LH release in the rhesus monkey. *Endocrinology,* 1971, *89,* 1034.

# 11
# Adult-Male/Juvenile Association as a Species-Characteristic Human Trait: A Comparative Field Approach

Wade C. Mackey
*Division of Humanities*
*El Paso Community College*
*El Paso, Texas 79998*

## Introduction

The adult-male/juvenile[1] relationship reflects patterns of behavior that have been found in all human societies that have been studied. The systematic availability of a stable adult male to the offspring of mothers appears to be a universal event (Barry and Paxson, 1971; Levinson and Malone, 1980; Mackey, 1985; Murdock, 1957; Murdock, 1967; Murdock and Provost, 1973; Stephens, 1963). The biological father is usually the adult male who is readily available to his offspring, but occasionally the mother's brother fulfills this role (Alexander and Noonan, 1979; Schlegel, 1972; Van den Berghe, 1979). The purpose of this chapter is to explore, in a systematic manner, the character, trends, and variations of the association between adult males and juveniles across a wide array of societies.

Although the father figure (in America) seems an obvious topic for study by behavioral scientists, the actual data on fatherlike behavior are sparse.[2] The data that do exist can be divided into two time frames: data published before the mid-1970's and data published after the mid-1970's. Until the 1970's, virtually no empirical data on fatherlike behavior were available. There were interviews with fathers (e.g., Tasch, 1952) and mothers' reports (Pedersen and Robson, 1969), but in the main, speculations, untested assumptions, and culture-wide myths subtended the literature on fatherlike behavior. (For an early example, see Gardner, 1947. See Benson, 1968, Nash, 1965, 1976, and Price-Bonham, 1976, for then-current reviews of the literature.)

Three sources of and reflections of the prevailing views of fatherlike behavior came from (a) a cultural anthropologist, Margaret Mead; (b) a psychologist, John Bowlby; and (c) a primatologist, Harry Harlow. Mead (1949) popularized the notion that fatherhood was a biological necessity but that fatherlike behaviors were a social accident. Bowlby (1952, 1958) intensified the focus upon the mother as being the primary source of nurturance of an infant (monotropy) (cf. Shaffer and Emerson, 1964). Harlow (1971) generalized from his pioneering work on rhesus macaques to humans and indicated that there was no independent adult-male/juvenile bond but that adult males associated with juveniles because adult males liked to associate with adult females and adult females liked to associate with juveniles: thus, the adult-male/juvenile association was a derivative effect (see Adams, 1960, for a similar argument). In general, theorists did not consider the father figure as being very important in the overall social, emotional, and cognitive development of the juvenile.

By the mid-1970's, a clear shift had occurred in the notion of what constituted a proper American father. Lamb's landmark book *The Role of the Father in Child Development* (1976) and Levine's *Who Will Raise the Children?* (1976) (answer: men and women in an equal partnership) helped set the agenda on what fathers were expected to be and to do. Fathering was redefined along the lines of the traditional mother template. As a consequence of this realignment, fathers were considered to be important but, also, to be underachieving in the actual execution of their parenting responsibilities.

Both the earlier imagery and the more current expectations of fathering were constructed without reference to data gathered systematically from actual adult-male/juvenile interactions. In complement to these symbolic and mythical structures of fathering, the study presented in this chapter was organized and conducted in order to gather systematically data pertaining to the actual behavior between the adult males and the juveniles of a society. Two main patterns of behavior were sought: (a) the central tendency of the magnitude of associations between adult males and juveniles across a diverse set of societies and (b) the predictable variations, if any, that could be expected to be found as a result of societies' ecological adaptations to the particular environments in which they are situated.

As it is with any facet of human behavior, because of the added dimension of culture, there are two bases of the maintenance and transmission of adult-male/juvenile behavior:

1. A genetic basis and
2. A cultural basis. Included in the cultural basis are
   a. Those behaviors that represent seemingly arbitrary traditions, that are not a direct result of ecological imperatives, and
   b. The societies' linguistic symbolic/folklore traditions.

Although it is clear that the genetic and cultural bases overlap considerably and are interdependent, it is possible to study them separately.

## The Genetic Basis

If any behavior, in this instance adult-male/juvenile association, is biased by genetic information and if this genetic information was acquired early in human evolution, then the behavior ought to exist and be found in a recognizable form in geographically and culturally diverse human societies. This notion reflects similarity by homology, or by common orgin. The same genotypic information shared by individuals in the various societies could be generating the behavioral consistencies. (See Ekman, 1973, and Eibl-Eibesfeldt, 1975, for examples of this strategy; cf. Freedman, 1974.)

## The Cultural Basis

Operating within the context of the intergenerational transmission of behavioral central tendencies through imitation or reinforced learning, societies, which have functioned independently from one another over the millennia, might be expected to generate independently similar cultural solutions to similar ecological problems in maintaining societal viability. This notion reflects similarity by analogy (see Brown, 1970; Divale and Harris, 1976; Maclachlan, 1983; White, Burton, and Brudner, 1977; White, Burton, and Dow, 1981). (For theoretical discussions on cultural evolution, see Harris, 1979, and Burton and Reitz, 1981.)

It should be noted that articulated belief systems (folklore) can strongly affect behavior in a variety of ways. However, although myth systems can clarify or buttress actual behavioral patterns, they also can just as well hide or camouflage them (Arens, 1979; Harris, 1974a,b; cf. Freeman, 1983). Because of the problematic linkage between actual behaviors and the belief systems that surround and immerse them, this chapter will not examine any society's folklore or myth system. Instead, the chapter will focus on the behaviors per se of the societies' individuals and examine the way in which certain types of behaviors, behaviors that occur between adult males and juveniles, are maintained and transmitted across generations.

## Background of the Human Adult-Male/Juvenile Association: The Genetic Basis of the Behavioral Central Tendency of the Relationship

There are two possible origins of any genetic contribution to adult-male/juvenile association behavior. These origins include (a) a phylogenetic heritage that *Homo* shares with some subset of the order Primate and (b) a uniquely human heritage that became selected for **after** the divergence of (early) *Homo* from Pongids 5-10 million years ago.

### Primate Phylogeny

Although primate paternalism, across species, covers a wide range of behaviors, high levels of interaction within the perimeter of the troop's territory are relatively rare, with exceptions such as occur in some macaques, and are virtually nonexistent outside the perimeter of the troop's territory when no adult female is present (Higley and Suomi, 1986; Mitchell, 1979; Redican and Taub, 1981; Taub, 1984; see Taub, this volume). Most of humans' nearest phylogenetic relatives, the apes (e.g., the chimpanzees, gorillas, and orangutans), have relatively low levels of adult-male/young interaction (Galdikas, 1986; van Lawick-Goodall, 1971; Mackinnon, 1971, 1974; Schaller, 1964). Exceptions among the apes include the arboreal gibbons and siamangs and among the monkeys include the equally arboreal marmosets of South America (Mendoza and Mason, 1986), both exceptions having "monogamous" family structures and relatively high levels of adult-male/young contact. However, the exclusive association of adult males and young in the absence of the adult female outside of their territory has not been reported in any nonhuman primate to this author's knowledge. Consequently, predictions about humans based on the behavior of terrestrial monkeys and apes would include very low levels of association outside of the domicile, especially in the absence of adult females.[3]

### Ecological Heritage of *Homo* as a Social Omnivore

The second candidate as the source of the central tendency of the adult-male/juvenile association is the combined ecological heritage and selective history of *Homo* that developed after the Pongid/*Homo* divergence.

It is suggested here that the onset of systematic hunting and scavenging as being a progressively important subsistence strategy exerted correspondingly stronger selective pressures upon early *Homo*. One characteristic of these selective pressures would favor the tendency of adult males to bring back and actively share meat with the adult females and young of the social group. This trait of systematically returning to a camp and actively sharing food with young is not a primate trait, but it is a trait of some social omnivores, e.g., the wolf, coyote, jackal, hunting dog, and fox, whose males return to a camp and regurgitate food to the pups. The adult males in the above-mentioned species also have been reported to "play" with their pups (Isaac, 1978; Mowat, 1963; Rasa, 1986; Schaller and Lowther, 1969; cf. Bunn, 1981; Bunn and Kroll, 1986). These canid adult males, which actively share food and play with their young, can be contrasted with other social omnivores and carnivores, e.g., the lion and the hyena, whose adult males neither return to their young to share food nor play with their young. In fact, these adult males are occasionally a clear danger to the young of the social group even to the point of infanticide (Guggisberg, 1963; Hausfater and Hrdy, 1984; Rasa, 1986; Rudnai, 1973; Schaller, 1972).

Based on what is known of extant hunter-gatherers, one can speculate that the pressures on the early *Homo* adult males to share food would be intensified if, as is quite likely, the early *Homo* adult females did **not** hunt. Although other carnivore females hunt and scavenge as a matter of course, inferential evidence suggests that subsistence hunting and scavenging progressively was, primarily or exclusively, a males-only prerogative (Murdock, 1937; Murdock and Provost, 1973; cf. Brown, 1970).

# Systematic Study of the Human Adult-Male/Juvenile Association Among Diverse Societies

## Method

### Introduction

There are three places where human behavior can be observed and recorded: in (a) the laboratory, (b) the home, and (c) the field. Each of the three has advantages and disadvantages. The laboratory allows maximal control of the subject's environment and is therefore an ideal place in which to study behavioral capacities and thresholds. However, it also is the least suitable place in which to study the frequencies or distributions of behavior as a function of the subjects' priorities. Naturalistic observation of humans in the field allows the researcher to learn more about the actual behavior and effective priorities of the subjects, but control of important variables is quite minimal. Studies in individuals' homes often are awkward in their intrusiveness, and therefore, the home is intermediate in suitability between the laboratory and the field as a location in which to study behavior that is based on priorities. Because the object of this project was to discover naturalistic patterns of adult-male/juvenile associations, the field was chosen as the site for data collection.

## Selection of the Sample of Societies

Over a period of approximately a dozen years, 19 societies in 15 countries on five continents were surveyed. A list of the societies is presented in Table 11.I. Criteria for the selecting of societies are found in Mackey (1981a, 1985).[4]

## Observation Sites

In each society, at least four sites were used for observing adults and juveniles interacting with each other. One site was a place where children were playing. One site was a place of commerce. At least two additional and separate sites were selected by the fieldworker *ad libitum*.

All observation sites were located in public places that provided equal access for males and females. All observations were made during daylight hours. Strict anonymity of the fieldworker and his or her assignment was attempted in order to minimize the influence of the coder on the coded. Ideally, the only influence that the coder did have upon the adults and juveniles was to be the effect a sedentary stranger would have upon the groups of individuals in public places (cf. Robinson, Lockard, and Adams, 1979).

## Coding Intervals

The observations that are relevant here are those coded during time intervals in which adult males were expected to be available to juveniles, for example, sabbaths, festival days, afterwork hours, weekends, and holidays. These adult males were able to be with juveniles but did not have to be. That is, the diagnostic intervals were "adult-males-not-precluded" intervals, which are not the same as "adult-males-are-present" intervals or "adult-males-must-be-present" intervals.[5] These times were periods of great discretion and latitude for adult males during which they could spend their time in a variety of mutually exclusive ways.

## Coded Items

Fieldworkers coded the biological-sex composition of each adult/ juvenile group. The workers also coded the number of juveniles in each group on the basis of age ranges; thus, youngest = birth - 4 years; middle = 5 - 7 years; oldest = 8 years - onset of puberty. Any one group of adults and juveniles was coded only once per day per site. (See Mackey, 1985, for a complete discussion of the method.) The actual sampling itself consisted either of a complete survey of (sparsely) populated places or a randomized sampling procedure in (more densely) populated places.

The fieldworkers coded each juvenile who was associated with at least one adult into one of three types of adult groups:

TABLE 11.I. Communities within the (sub)cultures that were the sites of adult/juvenile association

| Culture (Total Number of Juveniles) | Communities |
|---|---|
| Mexico (2,212) | Saltillo, Sabinas, Piedras Negras, Allende, Morelos (all in Coahuila state) |
| Spain (1,738) | Madrid, Guadalajara, Lerida, Zeura |
| Virginia, U.S.A. (14,499) | 132 sites throughout this state |
| Ireland (3,213) | Dublin, Tralee, Cashel, Athlone, Sligo |
| The Karaja of Brazil (840) | The Villages of Sao Felix, Fontoura, Tapirape, MaCauba |
| Iowa, U.S.A. (711) | Mt. Pleasant, Burlington, New London |
| Ivory Coast (2,658) | Korhogo, Bouake, Dimbokro, Ferkessedougou, Abidjan |
| Morocco (2,265) | Marrakech, Ouirgane, Casablanca, Azrou, Fes |
| Lima, Peru (573) | Greater Lima area |
| Japan (2,578) | Okayama, Ogi-Megi, Seto, Takamatsu, Nagoya |
| India (1,336) | New Delhi, Madras, Khajuraho, Allahabad, Bombay |
| Israel (3,018) | The kibbutzim of Givat Brenner, K'far Monahs, K'far Blum, Givat Hay'yin, Sde Nitzan, Moshen Tsofet |
| Reykjavik, Iceland (2,587) | Greater Reykjavik area |
| Sri Lanka (2,538) | Colombo, Kandy, Nagambo, Rathapura, Hatton, Polanurawa, Chilow |
| Hong Kong (164) | Hong Kong Island |
| Taiwan (4,336) | Lu Kang, Ma Kung, Da Yuan, Lung Tan, Chu Nan, Tung Hsiao, Ching Shui |
| Brazil—Rural (722) | Bom Jardim, Silvania, Vianopolis |
| Brazil—Urbanizing (562) | Monte Mor |
| The Senufo of the Ivory Coast (3,320) | Ferkessedougou, Dabakala, Gbon, Boundial, Siempurgo, Dikogougou, Niakaramandougou |

1. An "adult-males-only" group (one or more adult males, but no adult females present),
2. An "adult-females-only" group (one or more adult females, but no adult males present), or
3. An "adult-males/adult-females" group (at least one adult male and at least one adult female present).

Three interactive indices from the adult to the juvenile also were coded:

1. Touch,
2. Personal distance, and
3. Visual inclusion (See/Nonsee).

Each fieldworker was given pretests and passed reliability tests (90%+) for the coding of age, biological sex, and interaction prior to going into the field.

## Results

### Measurement of the Behavioral Central Tendency

The distribution of juveniles in the three adult groups is presented in Figure 11.1. Note that the summed percentage of juveniles in "adult-males/ adult-females" groups (i.e., "men-and-women" groups) **plus** the same calculation for "adult-males-only" groups (i.e., "men-only" groups) was 52.8%. Consequently, if a juvenile was with at least one adult, for more than half of the occasions the juvenile was with an adult male.

### Major Variables Considered: Age and Biological Sex

The age of the juvenile was important in terms of whether or not the juvenile would be observed to be associating with an adult. In general, younger juveniles were overrepresented and older juveniles were under-represented (compared to demographic data). This trend was true in **all** 19 cultures for "adult-males/adult-females" groups and in 15 and 18 cultures, respectively, for "adult-males-only" and "adult-females-only" groups.[6]

The biological sex of the juvenile was important solely for "adult-males-only" groups; in 15 of 19 cultures, juvenile males were over-represented in these groups. As a contrast, the "adult-males/adult-females" groups in 15 of 19 cultures illustrated **no** biological-sex preferences. "Adult-females-only" groups illustrated a preference for juvenile females in only 9 of 19 cultures but no biological-sex preference in the remaining 10 cultures. (The referent numbers were compared to demographic data, e.g., United Nations, 1985.)

Although "adult-males-only" groups did illustrate a preference for juvenile males, it should be mentioned that more than a third of the juveniles observed with adult males were juvenile females, and as will be discussed in the next section, ecological factors can account for the biological-sex-preference differentials.

### Interaction Between Age and Biological Sex

Of special pertinence to this volume is the distribution of older juveniles (8 years to onset of puberty) among the three adult groups. Of the

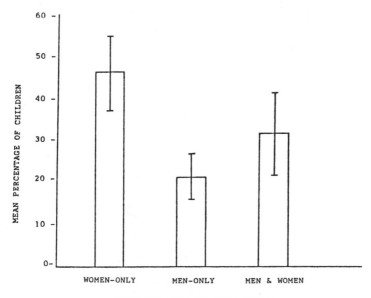

Figure 11.1. Distribution of mean percentage of juveniles associating with adult groups across cultures by biological-sex composition of the adult groups. (Diagnostic time intervals only.)

six combinations that occurred based on the biological sex of the juvenile and the biological-sex mix of the three adult groups, the adult-male/ older-juvenile- (peripubescent- ) male dyad was uniquely elevated across societies. (See Figure 11.2.) In addition, compared to the adult-male/older-juvenile- (peripubescent- ) female dyad, the adult-male/older-juvenile-male dyad was elevated in 15 of 17 societies.[7] The remaining two cultures (Hong Kong and the Karaja of Brazil) had too few cases for analysis.

Variation Among Societies: The "Teeter-Totter Effect"

An additional point of interest was the relationship between the percentage of juveniles in "adult-males/adult-females" groups versus the percentage of juveniles in the "adult-males-only" groups. Specifically, the question was asked: When the percentage of juveniles in "adult-males-only" groups **decreased**, did the juveniles tend to gravitate towards "adult-females-only" groups or towards "adult-males/adult-females" groups or was the redistribution equally divided between both of the alternative adult groups? The answer is clear: the juveniles systematically **increased** their association with the "adult-males/adult-females" groups. (See Figure 11.3.) A teeter-totter effect is in evidence. A strong negative correlation exists between the percentage of juveniles in "adult-males/adult-females" groups

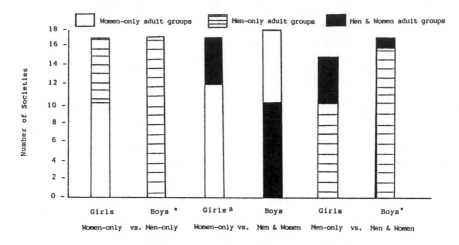

COMPARED ADULT GROUPS ASSOCIATING WITH PERI- PUBESCENT CHILDREN

Figure 11.2. Comparison among adult groups of higher percentage association with peripubescent juveniles in 18 societies. (See Note.)

\*p < .001; Sign test

\*Tie in Ireland

Note: Hong Kong's sample was not large enough for inclusion. The Karaja sample had an insufficient number of cases in the men-only group for analysis. The Brazil-Rural and the Brazil-Urbanizing samples had insufficient numbers for analysis of girls in the men-only versus men & women comparison.

and the percentage in "adult-males-only" groups. In contrast, there is no significant correlation—either positive or negative—between "adult-females-only" groups and "adult-males-only" groups.

These data are compatible with a hypothesis propounding that there is a genetically transmitted threshold of adult-male/juvenile association **below** which societies do not go. In other words, in those societies in which the association between "adult-males/adult-females" groups and juveniles is culturally inhibited, adult males will associate with juveniles in the absence of adult females. Again, it is useful to reemphasize that the diagnostic time intervals examined here are periods during which adult males have discretionary time when they can follow their priorities and their preferences. At the culmination of the decision-making process, the end result is the union of juveniles with adult males.

As Figure 11.4 illustrates, the teeter-totter effect occurs for the "all-juveniles" (i.e., the "all-children") category and especially for the "juvenile-males-only" ("boys-only") category. When juvenile females are examined separately, the correlation is in the predicted direction, but it is weak.[8] The

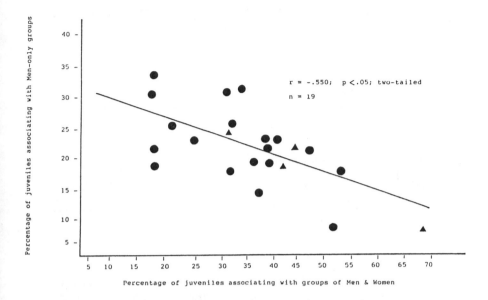

Figure 11.3. Percentage of juveniles (associating with adults) who are associating with "adult-males-only" ("men-only") groups and with "adult-males/adult-females" ("men-and-women") groups: 19 societies. The four new, "predicted" cultures are signified by triangles. (Diagnostic time intervals only.)

correlation is negative for the "infants—gender-unknown" category but, similarly, does not reach significance.

### Interaction: Adults to Juveniles

There are 110 comparisons available between adult males and adult females in the level of their interaction with juveniles during three separate categories of interaction: touch, personal distance, and visual inclusion.[9] Fifty-five of the comparisons are between adult males and adult females in single-biological-sex groups of adults, and 55 comparisons are between the adult males and the adult females in the "adult-males/adult-females" groups. Of these 110 comparisons, the adult males and the adult females have an equal level of interaction in more than 70% of the cases.[10] In addition, when the adult males' interaction toward juvenile males versus juvenile females was examined, nearly 90% of the comparisons indicated the same level of interaction. The remaining comparisons that did reveal differentials were equally divided between juvenile males and juvenile females receiving higher levels of activity from the adult males.

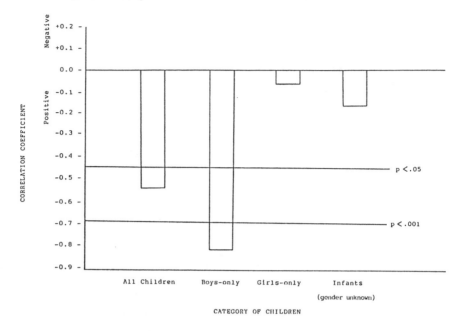

Figure 11.4. Correlations between the percentages of adult/juvenile dyads that were in "adult-male/juvenile" groups and "adult-male/adult-female/juvenile" groups: 19 cultures. (Diagnostic time intervals only.) Note: Similarly computed data for "adult-females-only" ("women-only") groups included "all-juveniles" ("all-children"), -0.833; "juvenile-males-only" ("boys only"), -0.627; "juvenile-females-only" ("girls-only"), -0.796; and "infants—gender-unknown," -0.943. Even though the negative correlations are all significant, an analogous interpretation to the adult-male/juvenile teeter-totter dynamics is not easily available. Because of the requirement for suckling and because of the universality of females' being the primary caretakers of the young, a strong argument for a cultural imperative is available to explain the data patterns quite completely (Barry and Paxson, 1971; Weisner and Gallimore, 1977).

Therefore, there were two behavioral trends, that is, central tendencies, that emerged from these interactive data:

1. Once adult males were with juveniles, they interacted with those juveniles in a manner very similar to the way adult females interacted with juveniles and

2. The biological sex of the juveniles had little relevance to the way adult males interacted with them.

In terms of variation among the societies, the relevant independent variable examined in this study was the Plowman-Protector Index. This index tapped the relative reliance of each society upon the adult males' superior brute strength to perform important selected societal tasks. The two tasks studied here were working with large domesticated animals, e.g., (plow) agriculture, and "policeman/soldier," both of which tend to be given to adult males exclusively across societies. (See Whyte, 1978, and Mackey, 1981a, 1985, 1988, for a discussion.)

Accordingly, a heavily agrarian society with high probabilities of strife was on one polarity on the Plowman-Protector Index, while a pacific, service-oriented society represented the other polarity on the index. (See Table 11.II.)

TABLE 11.II. Ranking of the 19 core-sample cultures in relation to the Plowman-Protector Index (1 = highest rank; 19 = lowest rank)

| Culture | Rank | Culture | Rank |
|---|---|---|---|
| Israeli Kibbutzim | 1 | Lima, Peru | 10 |
| Ivory Coast | 2 | Brazil—Urbanizing | 11 |
| Sri Lanka | 3 | Virginia, U.S.A. | 12 |
| India | 4 | Iowa, U.S.A. | 13 |
| Morocco | 5 | Spain | 14 |
| Mexico | 6 | Ireland | 15 |
| Brazil—Rural | 7 | Hong Kong | 16 |
| Taiwan | 8 | Reykjavik, Iceland | 17 |
| Senufo of the Ivory | | Japan | 18 |
| Coast | 9 | Karaja of Brazil | 19 |

When plotted along the Plowman-Protector Index, the sample of societies revealed the following results.

The **more** that the sample's societies relied on the adult male's superior brute strength (i.e., scored high on the Plowman-Protector Index), (a) the **more** that adult males were increasingly segregated from females, both adult and juvenile, and (b) the **more** that adult/juvenile dyads, isolated from cross-biological-sex adults, were increasingly found in the company of same-biological-sex adults. That is, adult-male/juvenile dyads were increasingly joined by other adult males, and adult-female/juvenile dyads were increasingly joined by other adult females.

Conversely, the **less** that a society relied on adult males' strength (i.e., scored low on the index), (a) the **more** that adult males associated with females (adult and juvenile) and (b) the **more** that a nuclear-family template (i.e., adult-male/adult-female/juvenile triad) displaced triads of adult-male/adult-male/juvenile and adult-female/adult-female/juvenile.

## The Predictive Potency of the Model as
## Tested on Four Additional Societies

Using the same definitions and procedures that were employed for the original core sample of 19 societies, 4 additional societies were surveyed—London (United Kingdom), suburban Paris (France), Vienna and Greiz (Austria), and villages in Kenya.

The hypothesis to be tested was that, across societies and during discretionary times for adult males, the percentages of all "adult/juvenile" groups that were composed of adult-male/adult-female/juvenile traids would be predictably (negatively) correlated with the percentage of all "adult" groups that were composed of adult-male/juvenile dyads. In other words, if societies, for whatever stated cultural reason, inhibited adult males from associating with adult females and juveniles or otherwise failed to encourage this behavior, then the societies systematically opened up channels whereby adult males could associate with juveniles in the absence of adult females. The channels are viewed here as being, simultaneously, **effects** that stem in part from genetic material and, also, proximate **causes** of behavior.

Pertinent to the 19-society core sample, three correlations were of interest:

1. The percentage of "adult-males-only" groups associating with "**all juveniles**" (juvenile males + juvenile females) versus the percentage of "adult-males/adult-females" groups associating with "**all juveniles**,"
2. The percentage of "adult-males-only" groups associating with "**juvenile-males-only**" versus the percentage of "adult-males/adult-females" groups associating with "**juvenile-males-only**," and
3. The percentage of "adult-males-only" groups associating with "**juvenile-females-only**" versus the percentage of "adult-males/adult-females" groups associating with "**juvenile-females-only**."

Three criteria for judging the accuracy of predicting the percentage of adult-male/juvenile dyads (from knowledge of the percentage of adult-male/adult-female/juvenile triads) included

1. Changes in the correlation coefficients developed from the core sample,
2. The absolute differences between predicted percentages that were generated by the resulting regression equation and the observed percentages of adult-male/juvenile dyads, and
3. Whether the predicted percentage of adult-male/juvenile dyads fell within a confidence interval of the score at a standard level of significance.

# Results

Changes in the correlation coefficients produced by the addition of the four new societies were generally small and in the predicted direction. For "all-juveniles" and for "juvenile-males-only," the differences between observed and predicted percentages were of low magnitude, falling within the confidence intervals of the predicted scores (details are presented in Mackey and Day, article in preparation). It is suggested that the predictive potency of the teeter-totter effect supports the concept of a biological threshold of association between adult males and juveniles and thereby lends empirical support to the notion of some degree of genetic determinance of adult-male/juvenile association among humans.

The negative correlation, i.e., the teeter-totter effect, for "all juveniles" was influenced primarily by the adult-male/juvenile-male dyads, which generated strong predictability. (See Figure 11.5.) That is, as associations between juveniles (especially males) and "adult-males-only" groups decreased in individual societies, the juveniles were systematically and predictably found in "adult-males/adult-females" groups. Accordingly, the juveniles and adult males were found in each others' presence at predicted frequencies whether or not adult females were present. It is important to emphasize that these adult-male/juvenile associations were occurring during those times and in those places where adult males had ample opportunity **not** to associate with juveniles.

# Proximate Mechanisms Underlying Behavioral Association Between Adult Males and Juveniles

Given that (a) a substantial percentage of juveniles were in association with adult males, (b) the level of association between "adult-males-only" groups and juveniles can be predicted on the basis of the level of association between "adult-males/adult-females" groups and juveniles, and (c) adult males' interactions with juveniles paralleled the interactions of adult females with juveniles, there must be proximate mechanisms involved in the association of adult males with juveniles.

Two candidates for a proximate mechanism that would mediate such an association are (a) an affiliative bond and (b) alliance formation.

## Affiliative Bond

As pointed out earlier, human adult males share food/provisions with their young, and this sharing by adult males is relatively rare across the zoological kingdom.

It is reasonable that the sharing of a most valuable commodity—food—is much easier emotionally for the provisioner if the provisioner

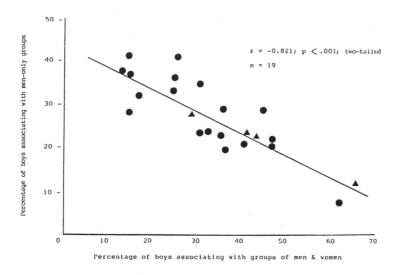

Figure 11.5. Percentage of juvenile males (associating with adults) who were associating with "adult-males-only" ("men-only") groups and "adult-males/adult-females" ("men-and-women") groups: 19 cultures. The four new, "predicted" cultures are signified by triangles. (Diagnostic time intervals only.)

"likes" the recipient, and conversely, a recipient tends to like someone who feeds him or her, especially during the dependency of preadulthood. Accordingly, the behavioral enhancement of any neurohormonal mechanisms (subtended by the relevant genetic material) that resulted in greater affiliative feelings, toward juveniles, for example, would facilitate food sharing. The facilitation might be further sensitized by the stimulus of those young who are provisioned showing outward signs of affiliation towards the provisioner. Across generations, the increased provisioning of juveniles by adult males would marginally increase those juveniles' viability, thereby increasing those adult males' chances of having descendants.

Thus, the alleles in adult males and juveniles that canalized reciprocal adult-male/juvenile affiliative behavior, in general, and the resultant specific adult-male/juvenile association, in particular, would gradually and systematically displace competing alleles that did **not** facilitate the development of affiliation between adult males and juveniles. In the 20th century, food sharing from human adult males to juveniles has been found to be a universal practice (Human Relations Area Files numbers 22-26, 1949).

## Alliance Formation

The prevalence of armed conflict between human adult males is a clearly documented fact across the world's community of societies (e.g., Carneiro, 1970; Divale and Harris, 1976). As a corollary to the theorem of combative males, a larger supply of warriors, *ceteris paribus*, is a better deterrent or a better source of conquest than is a smaller supply. Hence, it would behoove an adult male or a group of adult males to be in a position to recruit **more** juvenile males who are soon to be adults into as expansive a network of reciprocal alliances as possible. Lineages are a good example of how the networks develop. It also is worth noting that, because political alliances and coalitions among kin and nonkin alike have been found in nonhuman primates (see de Waal, this volume) as well as in all human societies that have been studied, the phenomenon is likely to be quite old indeed.

The warrior alliance is one kind of alliance. A second type is one that is formed between an adult male and the offspring of an eligible adult female (e.g., a divorced or widowed mother) as a means of demonstrating the outward signs of paternal investment. Such a demonstration could be used to enhance the adult male's opportunities to gain sexual access to the adult female. As a variant of this strategy, adult males who are pedophiles or hebephiles (in the sexual or erotic sense) could use the socially acceptable adult-male/adult-female relationship to gain intimate access to the adult female's offspring: a less acceptable relationship.

The key difference between affiliation and alliance formation is the motivation that underlies the behavior. "Affiliation" is motivated more by the immediacy of experiential feelings, while "alliance formation" is motivated more by calculated (cognitive) planning geared toward future investments. The two motivations are, of course, not mutually exclusive, and both can result in behaviors that look the same and that are contained in the concept of behavioral association.

## Conclusion

The data presented herein are offered as evidence that adult-male/ juvenile association is a species-characteristic human trait. Although very diverse societies were sampled and although ecological variables clearly affected the composition of groups of adult males with juveniles in public places (teeter-totter effect), there was surprisingly little variability across societies in the percentage of juveniles who were with adult males (sample mean = 20.7%, s.d. = 5.9%; n = 23) or with adult males **and** adult females (sample mean = 33.8%, s.d. = 13.6%; n = 23) during those times when adult males were available to be with juveniles.

The particular character of the proximate mechanisms that act as a base for these data currently is unknown. Nonetheless, an **affiliative bond**—enjoying the juvenile—and **alliance formation**—which, as an associative strategy, fosters a valuable political commodity (perhaps to camouflage a sexual strategy)—are two likely candidates.

A shift in the level of analysis from proximate to distal/ultimate also can be made. A distal/ultimate analysis favors an ecological (analogous) understanding over a phylogenetic (homologous) one. Adult males' associating with juveniles in the absence of adult females and outside of hearth and domicile, a consistent finding since circa 1980, is a behavior that is different from the behavior of nonhuman primates, in degree if not in kind. The basis of this unique adult-male/juvenile association cannot be found in a survey of the nonhuman-primate literature. The relatively high incidence of adult-male/juvenile association (a) with no adult females present and (b) away from the domicile (analogous to the concept of "territory" as it is used in much of the primate literature) would **not** be predicted from science's knowledge of the behavior of nonhuman primates—neither the behavior of any one species nor of any nonhuman subset of the taxon Primate. Accordingly, the more likely basis of adult-male/juvenile association would be the ecological heritage and selective history of *Homo* that occurred after the Pongid/*Homo* divergence of some 5-10 million years ago. Said a little differently, the patterns of adult-male/juvenile association seem to be more analogous to the associations expressed by the behavior of the canid social omnivores, such as wolves, coyotes, and hunting dogs, than to homologous patterns of behavior of any nonhuman primate. There is a small amount of irony in this notion, in that the exclusively male prerogative of communal hunting selected for adult males who also had increased tendencies toward behavior patterns useful for parental nurturing.

The finding (Figure 11.2) that illustrates the atypical elevation of adult-male/older-juvenile-male dyads is suggested to reflect the primordial pattern in which older males recruit peripubescent males into all-male (e.g., hunting and scavenging) groups. (See Mackey, 1981b, and Tiger, 1969, for a discussion.) This latter finding may be an important determinant in science's understanding of the biosocial roots of sexual behavior that occasionally occurs between adult-male and prepubescent-male humans.

## Summary

There are three key points that have been presented in this chapter.

1. Social expectations are configured in such a way that when adult-male humans have free access to juvenile humans, adult males associate with juveniles. When compared to adult-female humans in the same society, adult males associate with juveniles in rather respectable

proportions and do so across an otherwise wide and diverse array of societies.

In public places well away from the domicile, adult males arrange their priorities and options in such a manner that they associate with juveniles, both male and female. This central tendency is argued to reflect some yet to be specified genetic information that biases adult males towards association behavior with juveniles. The genetic information appears to predispose adult males to **like** juveniles (affiliation) or to motivate the adult males to become political allies with them (alliance formation).

2. The association of adult males and young beyond the perimeter of the troop's territory with no adult females present is not a trait typical of mammals in general or of nonhuman primates (whatever the subset being considered) in particular; it is, however, analogous to behaviors found in some social omnivores. The association patterns between adult males and juveniles with no adult females present in the newly studied societies were predictable. These predictions were generated by inductive research on previously studied societies, and the data collected regarding these patterns resulted in the phenomenon known as the "teeter-totter effect."

Given the realities of the much more powerful political status of adult males compared with juveniles, adult males could easily avoid the joint association with juveniles. However, the joint association does occur. It is argued here that it occurs because adult males either **like** juveniles or because they find such association politically advantageous.

3. Of the six adult/juvenile dyads studied, the adult-male/peripubescent-male dyad was uniquely elevated. This unique elevation is suggested to be based on the need of adult males to recruit peripubescent males into all-male hunting/scavenging/warring groups.

*Acknowledgments*

This project was supported by grants from the National Science Foundation and the Harry Frank Guggenheim Foundation. Their generous aid is very gratefully acknowledged. I also thank the fieldworkers, whose efforts and enthusiasm were well beyond the call of duty: George Donahue (Virginia, U.S.A.; the Karaja, Brazil); D. Bruce Carter (Japan); Roger Griffith (Peru; India; Sri Lanka); H. James Martin (Taiwan); Dirk Odland (Hong Kong); Abigail Sills (Israel, kibbutzim); Ellen Suthers (Ivory Coast; Morocco); the Senufo, Ivory Coast); Steven Swensen (Ivory Coast; Morocco); R.D. Day (London, U.K.; Paris, France); Sherrill Richarz (Kenya; Austria).

# Notes

[1]In this chapter, the terms "juvenile" and "juveniles" refer to human infants, children, and adolescents unless nonhuman taxa are specified.

[2]The term "fatherlike behavior" is used to describe the behavioral relationships and associations between adult males and juveniles where such relationships and associations cannot demonstrate actual biological paternity under observational research of behavior in public places.

[3]The concept of "territory" has been used by various authors with shades of meaning in relation to nonhuman animals (Jolly, 1972; Marler and Hamilton, 1966; Wilson, 1975). Generally, if an area is defended, is used with exclusivity, and grants dominance to its inhabitants, the area is defined as being those inhabitants' "territory." Across cultures, the domicile fits the definition when the human "family" is the focus of inquiry. Accordingly, "domicile," as used here, is equated with primate territory.

[4]It should be made clear that these cultures are not completely separate, independent entities. Accordingly, "Galton's Problem," the term given to the dilemma of divining independent invention (functional relationships) from cultural diffusion (historical relationships) does not become problematic but, rather, is a guarantee. As a result of Galton's intrusion with his problem, interpretations are based more on the weight and direction of the data than on any one decisive litmus test or newtonian proof. (See Ford, 1961, for a discussion.)

[5]Observations also were coded during time intervals in which adult males normally would be expected to be precluded from association with juveniles because of cultural norms, for example, while the adult males were tilling fields, tending herds, being at work, or attending special ritual events. The individual times for the "adult-males-precluded" and the "adult-males-not-precluded" periods varied considerably within the same culture at different sites as well as between cultures. The boundaries separating "adult-males-precluded" from "adult-males-not-precluded" intervals were developed by the judgement of each field researcher at each site.

For any given culture, if the total percentage of adult-male/juvenile association was significantly different between the "adult-males-precluded" intervals and the "adult-males-not-precluded" intervals, thereby indicating two populations, then the diagnostic intervals, for subsequent analysis, would be only the "adult-males-not-precluded" intervals ("the adult-males-precluded" intervals generated the expected frequencies).

If the percentage of adult-male/juvenile association was not significantly different between the "adult-males-not-precluded" intervals and the "adult-males-precluded" intervals, thus indicating one population, then the diagnostic intervals for subsequent analysis would be the totals ("adult-males-precluded" plus "adult-males-not-precluded" intervals). In all of the surveyed cultures, there did occur a difference in the levels of adult-male/juvenile association between "adult-males-precluded" and "adult-males-not-precluded" intervals. In **each** instance, the percentage of adult males with juveniles in the "adult-males-not-precluded" intervals was higher than the percentage of adult-male/juvenile association during "adult-males-precluded" intervals. What all of this means is that when adult males can be available to be with juveniles, they are with juveniles.

[6]For "adult-males-only" groups, the exceptions were Mexico, Spain, Sri Lanka, and Brazil—Rural. For "adult-females-only" groups, the sole exception was Sri Lanka.

[7]The two exceptions were Lima, Peru, and the Senufo of the Ivory Coast.

[8]Although the (negative) correlation of the "juvenile-females-only" category failed to reach the criterion on this index, it does not follow that the adult-male/juvenile-female relationship is without patterns. For example, across cultures, the relative degree of adult-male/juvenile-female association was correlated with the lack of availability or the lack of desirability of other adult females joining an adult-female/juvenile dyad for both the 19-culture sample and the 23-culture sample.

[9]The remaining four categories (114 - 110 = 4) could not be analyzed because of the lack of "n."

[10]On 14 occasions, there were **different** levels of interaction in the comparisons between adult males in "adult-males-only" groups versus adult females in "adult-females-only" groups. Of these 14, **adult males** had the higher level of interaction in 71% of the cases. On 18 occasions, there were different levels of interaction when adult males in "adult-males/adult-females" groups were compared to adult females who were also in "adult-males/adult-females" groups. Of these 18, **adult females** were more active in 89% of the comparisons.

# References

Adams, R.N. An inquiry into the nature of the family. *In* G.E. Dole and R.L. Carneiro (Eds.), *Essays in the science of culture in honor of Leslie A. White*. New York: Thomas Y. Crowell, 1960, pp. 30-49.

Alexander, E.D., and Noonan, K.M. Concealment of ovulation, parental care, and human social evolution. *In* N.A. Chagnon and W. Irons (Eds.), *Evolutionary biology and human social behavior: An anthropological perspective*. North Scituate, Mass.: Duxbury Press, 1979, pp. 436-453.

Arens, W. *The man eating myth: Anthropology and anthropophagy*. New York: Oxford University Press, 1979.

Barry, H., and Paxson, L. Infancy and early childhood: Cross-cultural codes 2. *Ethnology*, 1971, *10*, 466-508.

Benson, L. *Fatherhood: A sociological perspective*. New York: Random House, 1968.

Bowlby, J. *Maternal care and mental health*. Geneva: World Health Organization, 1952.

Bowlby, J. The nature of the child's tie to his mother. *International Journal of Psychoanalysis*, 1958, *39*, 350-375.

Brown, J.K. A note on the division of labor. *American Anthropologist,* 1970, *72,* 1073-1078.

Bunn, H.T. Archaeological evidence for meat-eating by Plio-Pleistocene Hominids from Koobi Fora and Olduvai Gorge. *Nature,* 1981, *291,* 574-575.

Bunn, H.T., and Kroll, E.M. Systematic butchery by Plio/Pleistocene Hominids at Olduvai Gorge, Tanzania. *Current Anthropology,* 1986, *27,* 431-452.

Burton, M.L., and Reitz, K. The plow, female contribution to agricultural subsistence and polygyny: A log-linear analysis. *Behavior Science Research,* 1981, *16,* 275-306.

Carneiro, R.L. A theory of the origin of the state. *Science,* 1970, *169,* 733-738.

Divale, W., and Harris, M. Population, warfare, and the male supremacist complex. *American Anthropologist,* 1976, *78,* 521-538.

Eibl-Eibesfeldt, I. *Ethology: The biology of behavior* (2nd ed.). New York: Holt, Rinehart and Winston, 1975.

Ekman, P. Darwin and cross-cultural studies of facial expression. *In* P. Ekman (Ed.), *Darwin and facial expression: A century of research in review.* New York: Academic Press, 1973, pp. 1-83.

Ford, C.S. (Ed.). *Readings in cross-cultural methodology.* New Haven: HRAF Press, 1961.

Freedman, D.G. *Human infancy: An evolutionary perspective.* Hillsdale, N.J.: Lawrence Erlbaum and Associates, 1974.

Freeman, D. *Margaret Mead and Samoa.* Cambridge, Mass.: Harvard University Press, 1983.

Galdikas, B.M.F. Adult male sociality and reproductive tactics among orangutans at Tanjung Puting. *Folia Primatol.,* 1985, *45,* 9-24.

Gardner, L.P. An analysis of children's attitudes towards fathers. *Journal of Genetic Psychology,* 1947, *70,* 3-28.

Guggisberg, C.A.W. *Simba: The life of the lion.* Philadelphia: Chilton, 1963.

Harlow, H.F. *Learning to love.* San Francisco: Albion, 1971, pp. 63-64.

Harris, M. *Cows, pigs, wars, and witches.* New York: Random House, 1974a.

Harris, M. Why a perfect knowledge of all the rules one must know to act like a native cannot lead to the knowledge of how natives act. *Journal of Anthropological Research,* 1974b, *30,* 242-251.

Harris, M. *Cultural materialism.* New York: Random House, 1979.

Hausfater, G., and Hrdy, S.B. (Eds.). *Infanticide.* New York: Aldine, 1984.

Higley, J.D., and Suomi, S.J. Parental behavior in non-human primates. *In* W. Sluckin and M. Herbert (Eds.), *Parental behavior.* Oxford: Basel, 1986.

Human Relations Area Files. New Haven: HRAF Press, 1949.

Isaac, G. Food sharing and human evolution: Archaeological evidence from the Plio-Pleistocene of East Africa. *Journal of Anthropological Research*, 1978, *34*, 311-325.

Jolly, A. *The evolution of primate behavior*. New York: Macmillan, 1972.

Lamb, M.E. (Ed.). *The role of the father in child development*. New York: Wiley, 1976.

van Lawick-Goodall, J. *In the shadow of man*. Boston: Houghton Mifflin Co., 1971, p. 34.

Levine, J. *Who will raise the children? New options for fathers (and mothers)*. Philadelphia: Lippincott, 1976.

Levinson, D., and Malone, M.J. *Toward explaining human culture: A critical review of the findings of worldwide cross-cultural research*. New Haven: HRAF Press, 1980.

Mackey, W.C. A cross-cultural analysis of adult-child proxemic in relation to the Plowman-Protector complex: A preliminary study. *Behavior Science Research*, 1981a, *16*, 187-223.

Mackey, W.C. A cross-cultural analysis of recruitment into all male groups: An ethological perspective. *Journal of Human Evolution*, 1981b, *10*, 281-292.

Mackey, W.C. *Fathering behaviors: The dynamics of the man-child bond*. New York: Plenum Press, 1985.

Mackey, W.C. Patterns of adult-child associations in 18 cultures: An index of the "nuclear family." *Journal of Contemporary Family Studies*, 1988, *19*, 69-84.

Mackey, W.C., and Day, R.D. A test of the man-child bond: A re-evaluation of the U.S. father-figure a decade after the transfiguration. Article in preparation.

Mackinnon, J.R. The orang-utans in Sabah today. *Orynx*, 1971, *11*, 135-141.

Mackinnon, J.R. The behaviour and ecology of wild orang-utans (*Pongo pygmaeus*). *Animal Behavior*, 1974, *22*, 3-74.

Maclachlan, M.D. *Why they did not starve*. Philadelphia: Ishi, 1983.

Marler, P., and Hamilton, W.J. *Mechanisms of animal behavior*. New York: Wiley, 1966.

Mead, M. *Male and female*. New York: Morrow, 1949, pp. 185-190.

Mendoza, S.P., and Mason, W.A. Parental division of labour and differentiation of attachments in a monogamous primate (*Callicebus moloch*). *Animal Behavior*, 1986, *34*, 1336-1347.

Mitchell, G. *Behavior sex differences in non-human primates*. New York: Van Nostrand Reinhold, 1979.

Mowat, F. *Never cry wolf*. Boston: Little Brown and Co., 1963, pp. 96-108.

Murdock, G.P. Comparative data on the division of labor by sex. *Social Forces*, 1937, *15*, 552.

Murdock, G.P. World ethnographic sample. *American Anthropologist*, 1957, *59*, 664-687.

Murdock, G.P. Ethnographic atlas. *Ethnology*, 1967, *6*, 109-236.

Murdock, G.P., and Provost, C. Factors in the division of labor by sex: A cross-cultural analysis. *Ethnology,* 1973, *12,* 203-225.

Nash, J. The father in contemporary culture and current psychological literature. *Child Development,* 1965, *36,* 260-297.

Nash, J. Historical and social changes in the perception of the role of the father. *In* M.E. Lamb (Ed.), *The role of the father in child development.* New York: Wiley, 1976.

Pedersen, F.A., and Robson, H.S. Father participation in infancy. *American Journal of Orthopsychiatry,* 1969, *39,* 466-472.

Price-Bonham, S. Bibliography of literature related to roles of fathers. *Family Coordinator,* 1976, *25,* 489-512.

Rasa, O.A.E. Parental care in carnivores. *In* W. Sluckin and H. Martin (Eds.), *Parental behaviour.* Oxford: Basil Blackwell Ltd., 1986, pp. 117-151.

Redican, W.K., and Taub, D.M. Male parental care in monkeys and apes. *In* M.E. Lamb (Ed.), *The role of the father in child development* (2nd ed.). New York: Wiley, 1981.

Robinson, C.L., Lockard, J.S., and Adams, R.M. Who looks at a baby in public. *Ethology and Sociobiology,* 1979, *1,* 87-91.

Rudnai, J.A. *The social life of the lion.* Wallingford, Penna: Washington Square East, 1973.

Schaller, G.B. *The year of the gorilla.* New York: Ballantine Books, 1964.

Schaller, G.B. *The Serengeti lion.* Chicago: University of Chicago Press, 1972.

Schaller, G.B., and Lowther, G.R. The relevance of carnivore behavior to the study of early Hominids. *Southwestern Journal of Anthropology,* 1969, *25,* 307-336.

Schlegel, A. *Male dominance and female autonomy.* New Haven: HRAF Press, 1972.

Shaffer, H.R., and Emerson, P.E. *The development of social attachments in infancy.* Monographs of the Society for Research in Child Development, 1964, *29*(94, entire issue).

Stephens, W.N. *The family in cross-cultural perspective.* New York: Holt, Rinehart and Winston, 1963.

Tasch, R.J. The role of the father in the family. *Journal of Experimental Education,* 1952, *20,* 319-361.

Taub, D.M. (Ed.). *Primate paternalism.* New York: Van Nostrand Reinhold Co., 1984.

Tiger, L. *Men in groups.* New York: Random House, 1969.

United Nations. *Demographic yearbook.* New York: United Nations, 1985.

Van den Berghe, P.L. *Human family systems.* New York: Elsevier, 1979.

Weisner, T.S., and Gallimore, R. My brother's keeper: Child and sibling caretaking. *Current Anthropology,* 1977, *18,* 169-190.

White, D.R., Burton, M.L., and Brudner, L.A. Entailment theory and method: A cross-cultural analysis of the sexual division of labor. *Behavior Science Research*, 1977, *12*, 1-24.

White, D.R., Burton, M.L., and Dow, M.M. Sexual division of labor of African agriculture: A network autocorrelational analysis. *American Anthropologist*, 1981, *83*, 824-847.

Whyte, M.K. Cross-cultural codes dealing with the relative status of women. *Ethnology*, 1978, *12*, 211-237.

Wilson, E.O. *Sociobiology*. Cambridge, Mass.: Harvard University Press, 1975.

# 12
# The Concept of Function in the Behavioral Sciences with Specific Reference to Pedophilia and Pedosexual Behavior: A Biophilosophical Perspective

Herman Dienske
*TNO Primate Center*
*2280 HV Rijswijk*
*The Netherlands*

## Introduction

In the behavioral sciences, the term function refers to effects that range from those that occur immediately to those that occur over many generations. Long-term functions differ most in meaning from the everyday usage of the concept function. In evolutionary biology, **functions** of behavior refer to contributions made both to the survival of an individual and to reproductive success and, even more ultimately, to a relatively large contribution made to future populations of a species.

Behavior that is obviously functional, such as the feeding and protecting of young offspring, has the connotations good, acceptable, and "natural." Social control in human societies almost universally favors such "natural" behavior.

It is not unusual for individuals to turn this view around and disapprove of and reject behavior that is considered to be and is labeled "unnatural." Pedophilia, or more accurately, its acting out as pedosexual behavior, and homosexual behavior are among the kinds of behavior that frequently are disapproved of for this reason. Many individuals who are opposed to both pedosexual and homosexual behavior think that the only function of sexual behavior is reproduction and the procreation of children; hence, essentially nonprocreative sexual behavior is assumed to be "unnatural" and is rejected. This view is wrong for two reasons.

First, sexual behavior is not synonymous with reproductive behavior. In nature, sexual motor patterns (which are part of sexual behavior) have social and evolutionary functions beyond mere reproduction (see de Waal, this volume). Several functions of the sexual behavior of humans will be described in this chapter. If it can be demonstrated that a characteristic was favored by natural selection (i.e., had **adaptive functions**), the characteristic cannot be rejected on the grounds of being unnatural.[1] The word "unnatural" cannot be translated satisfactorily into scientific language. How can phenomena found in nature, whether common or rare, be unnatural? Furthermore, social norms, values, and traditions in the form of culture, as well as theological "discernment," also are subject to natural selection; they are not constant and, therefore, cannot be immutable criteria against which to judge behavior. The motives that underlie social disapproval and rejection of pedophilia and pedosexual behavior will be considered herein, along with the possible functions of such social disapproval and rejection.

Second, even if a type of behavior is widespread—i.e., seemingly is natural—and has apparent beneficial functions for the actor, many societies may reject it. "Natural" does not necessarily mean "nice." Theft, rape, torture, murder, and warfare can be advantageous at some level for the actor, typically in the absence of effective punishment, and, hence, can be functional and be maintained by natural selection. However, the victims of these selfish crimes, or the advocates for the victims, will attempt prevention and remedy. In a judicious society, transgression and punishment are well balanced.

That even crimes can be functional at some level implies that the consideration of functionality in relation to pedophilia and pedosexual behavior is absolutely irrelevant to the question of their acceptability. In the realm of acceptance, the relevant issues are social injustice and harm, not function. And not only possible harm done by an adult pedophile to a child but, equally, the social injustice done to an adult by societies that excessively punish the pedophile.

The study of evolutionary function is relevant in the understanding of the balance between selfishness (by transgressor or punisher) and cooperation. In addition, such studies may shed light on the question of why particular statistically uncommon kinds of behavior, such as pedosexual behavior, exist. After a consideration of function in general and of functions of sexual behavior in particular, the possible functions of the social rejection of pedosexual behavior will be explored.

# The Concept of Function in Evolutionary Biology

The concept "**adaptive function**" primarily provides insight into the mechanisms of evolutionary change. Great theoretical advantages have been identified through the study of population dynamics, which is the science of the spread of variants of characteristics within and among populations. The degree of functionality of a trait is, in reality, based on comparison. The simplest form of measurement concerns the comparison of two classes of individuals that differ with respect to a particular phenotypical characteristic. Individuals with a variant that contributes more to future generations are by definition better adapted to, and therefore more functional in, the circumstances. It has been demonstrated that, if the environment continues to be favorable, the more functional variant quickly replaces alternative variants. In this way, evolutionary change is achieved.

An example of the usefulness of this theory is provided by the explanation of why so many species have two sexes (Maynard Smith, 1978; Trivers, 1985). The typical process of reasoning is to compare the success of two classes of individuals of a hypothetical species. One class, which reproduces "asexually," has offspring that are genetically identical to the single parent. The other class, which reproduces "sexually," recombines genetic material with the material from another individual. The advantage of the first class over the second is that twice as many individuals produce eggs; no individual is "wasted" as a male that is in need of a female for his reproduction. Hence, the initial number of offspring, in principle, is twofold. The second class has offspring that are not identical to either of the two parents. This outcome has two advantages: (a) the consequence of variation in offspring is that they are more likely to survive in a frequently varying environment and (b) it is more likely that recombination gives rise to individuals having new characteristics that enable individuals to compete better with conspecifics (members of the same species) and, hence, replace them. The widespread (though not universal) occurrence of sexual reproduction indicates that the advantages of the second class usually have been greater. It should be noted that this assessment is post hoc. Such post hoc assessments often apply to explanations based on function.

Although such theoretical considerations are lucid and straightforward, there are many cases in which insights and predictions are hard to establish. Specifically, the empirical demonstration of the functionality of a particular variety of a characteristic can be very difficult or impossible (see Hinde, 1975).

# Adaptive Functions of Human Sexual Behavior

The attempt can be made to classify the adaptive functions of human sexual behavior, but first, "sexual behavior" must be defined (see Feierman, this volume, Chapter 1). "Sexual behavior" can be defined as the motor patterns that occur during copulation, or the motor patterns that occur during periods of sexual arousal, or the motor patterns that are used to stimulate one's own or another's genitals. The following classification of adaptive functions of human sexual behavior is, as is usual in life science, neither mutually exclusive nor comprehensive. The primary aim is to show that sexual behavior, like many other behavioral or anatomical structures, has a variety of functions.

## Fertilization

Fertilization is of course the most obvious function of sexual behavior. Humans have been aware of this effect (function) of copulation for ages. As it seems likely that this awareness does not apply to most, if not all, animal species, awareness per se is not necessary for effective reproduction. Humans as well as a number of other species copulate much more frequently than is necessary for fertilization. According to the typical reasoning that pertains to evolution—that a frequent and energy-requiring act will be selected against if its cost is not outweighed by benefits—the abundance of copulations alone indicates that there are other functions of sexual behavior than fertilization.

## Affiliation

In Morris's famous, provocative oversimplification (1967), it was pointed out that the continuous sexual activity of humans promotes the coherence of the adult-male/adult-female pair and that it encourages the male parent to participate in rearing his offspring. This assumption requires (1) that sex induces affiliation (i.e., the maintenance of proximity and the extension of favors) and (2) that this affiliation is continued after offspring are born and (3) is accompanied by male paternal care. The associations among sex, affiliation, and paternal care seem to be common in humans. This situation does not imply, however, a simple causal relationship. Infrequent or absent sex may precede divorce. It cannot be decided whether infrequent sex reduces affiliation or whether the decreased affiliation reduces sex. It is likely that sex and affiliation mutually enhance each other and that the absence of one of the two leads to a declining spiral that eventually results in separation or disinterest. The associations among sex, affiliation, and paternal care are not invariably present, as indicted by the following examples.

A study in the northeastern United States (Stern and Leiblum, 1986) demonstrated a marked reduction in female sexual inclination after birth, an inclination that was further reduced by lactation. This disinclination would appear to threaten the adult-male/adult-female affiliation exactly during a period of time when staying together is of marked importance. Since frequent breast-feeding suppresses ovulation (see Konner and Worthman, 1980) and, hence, often postpones a next pregnancy, the function of the reduced sexual desire in a female parent is obscure. The phenomenon suggests that affiliative mechanisms other than sexual intercourse exist.

Support for this idea can be seen through Diamond's description (this volume) of how promiscuous sex can exist, such as in traditional Hawaiian society, if the relatives of a female give sufficient care to her offspring. The presence of this kind of tradition shows that there are means other than adult human male/female sexual behavior by which affiliation is maintained and offspring are nurtured. In human societies, the degree to which paternity is uncertain correlates positively with the incidence at which adult males direct their paternal investment towards the offspring of their female siblings. This correlation is well known in anthropology, and it supports the notion that the survival of offspring is more fundamental than is a connection between sex and the affiliation between human males and females.

Among humans, male-parent/offspring affiliation and care often continue after divorce and the termination of sexual interactions between parents (see Mackey, this volume).[2] This fact provides additional evidence that paternal care does not necessarily require frequent copulation between the parents and that such care can be extended after the discontinuation of sexual interactions.

These examples indicate that the associations among sex, affiliation, and paternal care are not compelling in that alternative functional solutions exist. Nevertheless, the affiliation-promoting effect of sex seems apparent. This effect is clearly indicated by the continuous willingness of human females to engage in sexual activity. In many mammalian species, females are willing to copulate only just before and during ovulation. They signal this readiness by odors, behavior, and, sometimes, conspicuous visual stimuli. Human females, in contrast, lack such signals and thus have what is called "concealed ovulation" (Alexander and Noonan, 1979); in fact, the timing of human ovulation was not known until recently. Uncertainty concerning the time at which ovulation occurs would promote frequent copulations. It is possible that continuous sexual behavior in human females is their affiliation-promoting strategy, since it can induce more consistent male proximity (Daniels, 1983). It is important to realize that such an effect (or function), which is a result of a "strategy" in the perspective of evolutionary biology, does not imply conscious awareness (Wilson, 1978; Trivers, 1985).

Proximity and sex, the core ingredients of the establishment and maintenance of affiliation, which includes favors, in adult human hetero-sexual relationships, also apply to many pedophilic and homosexual relationships among humans. That is, relationships between adult males and young females can be affectionate (Dodgson, 1872), and adult female-homosexual pairs generally are described as being strongly affiliative (reviewed by Symons, 1979). Adult male-homosexual interactions, in contrast, often are more superficial and promiscuous, with multiple changes of partners (reviewed by Symons, 1979). It has been suggested that this frequent change of partners and superficiality prevents affiliation, an outcome that confirms the usual, affiliation-fostering effect of sex. However, it seems probable that the incidence of stable male-homosexual pairs has been underemphasized in the literature (Weinrich, 1987b). Sandfort (1987), based upon interview data, wrote that human male-adult/male-juvenile sexual relationships usually were accompanied by playing games, going out, and having lengthy conversations. In addition, affiliation-inducing homosexual behavior has been described for nonhuman primates under natural conditions. Yamagiwa (1987) reported field observations of homosexual relationships among six male adult and subadult virunga mountain gorillas, the least sexually active of the three African-ape species. He described how the homosexual behavior in this all-male group was embedded in the whole network of coherent relationships. The tension-reducing pedo-, homo-, and heterosexual interactions among bonobos (pygmy chimpanzees), described by de Waal (this volume), confirms the affiliation-inducing effects (functions) of a wide variety of sexual activities.

There are no grounds on which to deny that at least some of the previously described pedophilic and homosexual nonprocreative sexual contacts could be considered functional, since favors resulting from the affiliation, which is maintained in part by sexual behavior, can be considerable.

## Promotion of Self-Esteem and Well-Being

The possible adaptive functions (effects) of incidental sexual contact among humans that does not result in the cooperative rearing of offspring, in contrast to sexual contact that occurs between parents, could at least be considered capable of promoting self-esteem and overall personal well-being. The increased self-esteem and overall personal well-being subsequently could result in improved achievement in the many nonsexual tasks of life. The benefits should, of course, be balanced against the risks of sexually transmitted diseases, pregnancy in the absence of sufficient resources to bring up offspring (typically, in the absence of the male parent), and the potential for tension and guilt, shame, and the conflict of values induced in committed stable partners, as in the special case of humans. In addition, incidental sexual contact could serve as preliminary exploration resulting in affiliation.

The frequency of incidental sexual contact varies greatly among individuals.

It seems likely that one of the suggested possible functions of incidental sexual contact, namely improved achievement in other areas as a result of increased self-esteem and well-being, is not confined to adult human male/female sexual contact. This idea will be elaborated on subsequently.

## Reciprocal Altruism Through Exchange of Resources for Services

Among humans, the exchange of resources for sexual services is called "paid prostitution." If interactions are strictly confined to brief copulation, this function (effect) of sexual behavior is purely economic. In the typical exchange of this sort, no personal relationship is formed. As an adaptive function of sexual behavior, the exchange of resources for services, among humans, is distinctly separate from the three previously described sets of functions. The "bed for bread" exchange exemplifies the separation. Among nonhuman animals, in contrast, the distinction between the exchange of resources for services and the other functions is not rigid. Payment, of course, whether by human or nonhuman animal, requires an excess of resources (e.g., money), such an excess being atypical for nonhuman animals. (See Thornhill and Alcock, 1983, for an interesting variation on the theme of payment among insects in the form of food.)

## Positive and Negative Evolutionary Selection in Humans in Relation to Pedophilia and Pedosexual Behavior

As has been shown previously, sexual behavior in humans and in nonhumans can have functions other than direct reproduction. Therefore, some aspects of pedophilia and pedosexual behavior **may** in principle be functional, even though pedosexual behavior does not result in offspring either because the juvenile partner has not reached reproductive maturity or because the participants are of the same sex (see Feierman, this volume, Chapter 1). Although the harmful consequences appear to be more conspicuous than the beneficial effects in many of the publicized cases (Burgess et al., 1978), it is both scientifically and morally correct to ask the question, "Do pedophilia and pedosexual behavior serve a biological function?" if the goal of asking is to understand.

Functionality will be considered under the condition that procreative alternatives either are not available or are avoided, as in voluntary celibacy, for example. The existence and selective biological disadvantage of avoiding procreative relationships will be discussed in the next section. Here, for the time being, the avoidance is regarded as if it were a fact.

Adults who prefer pedophilic/pedosexual relationships potentially could benefit from these relationships through the advantages that occur in other life areas as a result of increased well-being and self-esteem. This situation is especially applicable if other types of love or sexual relationships are not an alternative for a particular individual. Pedophilia and pedosexual behavior are expected to be selected against, however, if social control condemns and punishes such love or sexual relationships. In small societies, which were common in the past, social control can be strong, since behavior hardly can be concealed. Large cities, on the other hand, provide more anonymity as well as less effective social control and, therefore, have attracted individuals who wish to avoid the social norms. Anonymity also may play a role in incest, in that this kind of sexual behavior seems to be more common in isolated families, where it is more likely to remain concealed from outsiders.

In juveniles, possible disadvantages and advantages of sexual relationships with adults obviously are contingent upon whether there is a family relationship between the actors, as well as depending on the sexes and ages involved. The potential harm of both physical violence and strong psychological pressure is obvious; in the following discussion, such pressures are assumed to be absent.

It seems hard to ever imagine any advantages of incestuous pedosexual behavior for a juvenile. The offspring of incestuous relationships have an increased incidence of deleterious recessive homozygous characteristics; this fact is one of the reasons why incest (inbreeding) avoidance is widespread among animals and plants. However, instances of the failure of incest-avoidance mechanisms in animals may be underestimated, because many biologists look for rules rather than exceptions. Goodall (1986), who did not fail to notice the dark side of individuals, described various kinds of incestuous behavior in wild chimpanzees. In human juveniles especially, receiving parental care seems incompatible with a role as the sexual partner of individuals providing that care; halted or deteriorated maturation and vulnerability to traumatic experiences that occur following the pedophilic incestuous experiences are common outcomes that are seen in juveniles who are cast in such a role (see Garland and Dougher, this volume). However, incest (typically not pedophilic) has been described as advantageous when it keeps the advantages of a rich dynasty within the family (Ford and Beach, 1951; Diamond, this volume). In addition, incestual reproduction by individuals for whom nonrelatives are not available must be functional if extinction is the only alternative.

The positive and negative effects of androphilic pedophilia probably are similar to the effects of homosexuality in general. The disadvantages are greatest in societies having an adverse attitude towards homosexuality. The degree to which androphilic pedophilia leads to homosexuality during adulthood, an outcome that could be considered a disadvantage, is not known (Money, 1988). An inducing effect certainly is not universal. In some societies, in fact, temporary male adult/juvenile sexual relationships are common and overt (Ford and Beach, 1951; Herdt, 1981; Schiefenhövel, this volume), and they have been in the past as well—in Western society, for example, during the Greek and Roman eras (see Bullough, this volume).

The relationship between harm or benefit and age is a highly controversial issue (provided that violence is absent). It is clear that some degree of sexual interest is present long before the age at which actual reproduction can occur. This statement also applies to nonhuman primates. Humans incorporate more experience into their individual development than any other species, and this fact is expected to apply to sexual experiences as well. Unfortunately, discussions about age and pedosexual behavior are dominated by the question of the ability to determine the age at which uncoerced consent by the juvenile can be given and not by the actual harm or benefit of the relationship and/or behavior. It seems that the harm brought to the juvenile by the actual pedophilic sexual contact often can be much less evident than the harm of the process of social control, especially when juveniles are witnesses in court trials (Landwirth, 1987). The possibility that there might be any benefits from some early experience related to sexual interactions with other juveniles or with adults has not been sufficiently studied, if for no other reason than that for some adults even entertaining the question is abhorrent.

In large urban areas of industrialized societies, with some cities being more notorious than others, there often are places where juvenile "street hustlers" can be found. Juvenile prostitution is an aspect of the fourth function of sex, described in the previous subsection, the exchange of resources for services. This kind of sexual behavior provides the most blatant illustration of the discrepancy between the functional and the desirable. Hypothetically, it could be more functional to expose a juvenile to prostitution than to face the certainty of the starvation of a whole family. In fact, there are instances where resources generated by juvenile prostitution are used to provision the entire family of the juvenile (Reeves, 1981; Phongpaichit, 1982). However, in many cases of juvenile prostitution, a better, although possibly less lucrative, solution to the income problems of families seems available.

## Functionality and the Evolution of Nonprocreative Sexual Behavior in Humans

If an adult human male is having procreative sexual relationships while also having nonprocreative, i.e., pedosexual or homosexual, sexual relationships, the number of offspring such an individual can produce may not be affected. Weinrich (1987a) has even suggested that in societies with universal male marriage, homosexual extramarital behavior may be more adaptive in terms of evolution than heterosexual extramarital behavior, in that the former behavior does not result in the production of offspring who could deplete and divert resources from legitimate offspring. In individuals who combine nonprocreative and procreative sexual relationships, the nonprocreative sexual behavior may not be afunctional in its own right, for reasons described previously in this chapter under Adaptive Functions of Human Sexual Behavior. Exclusively nonprocreative sexual behavior is much less common. However, exclusive homosexuality is so common, having an incidence of several percent of general populations, that it could not be a trait that was strongly selected **against** in the past. Often, traits that were selected against have an incidence of only one out of a million. The question can be asked, Has a trait with a prevalence of several percent necessarily been selected **for**? This issue is more complex from the standpoint of biology, and a detailed discussion of the topic is beyond the scope of this chapter.

**Non**functional characteristics may be relatively common after drastic changes in the environment have occurred, because natural selection has shaped traits in the past and has no prospective aim. Since many characteristics, and certainly the social ones, have only moderate genetic predispositions, a change in life circumstances, which may be equivalent to a change in the environment, also can easily result in an increase in the incidence of nonfunctional behavior. However, even under rather constant environmental conditions, some nonfunctional characteristics may be relatively prevalent. Such prevalence may exist because humans as a species are specialized in a flexible **early** development. The advantages of a general flexibility in, for example, the attributes to which one is sexually attracted may be so great for so many individuals that these advantages outweigh the disadvantages to the relatively small number of other individuals who develop nonprocreative sexual attractions under particular or unusual environmental circumstances. Only when the latter type of individuals becomes too numerous will selection against flexible development dominate.

It is not necessary (though it is reasonable) to suggest that nonprocreative sexual behavior is functional or even genetically determined, which is what Wilson (1978) suggested in regard to homosexual behavior. **The functionality of a flexible sexual development, which is effective in the majority of individuals, suffices to show how nonprocreative sexual behavior could have evolved by natural selection.**

How this argument relates to the ontogeny of pedophilia and pedosexual behavior and whether environmental circumstances have increased the prevalence of these preferences can be only a matter of interesting speculation at this time. However, the scientific method can eventually find an answer. To date, few scientists have even considered the question.

## Adaptive Function, Social Control, and Pedophilia and Pedosexual Behavior

The norms by which a human society controls members of its "group" are markedly different from the norms that are applied to the outgroup. Slavery, torture, plunder, war, and genocide typically are directed to other societies or to distinct subgroups within a community. As long as the loss resulting from control-generated repercussions (from the outgroup) is less than the gain to the main group, these gruesome actions are functional in the context of evolution. Human history clearly shows that an appalling number of individuals in the main group participate in damaging the outgroup if such behavior is tolerated. On the other hand, ingroup/outgroup tendencies within a single society are less severe but still are directed towards potential gain. (See Eibl-Eibesfeldt, 1979.)

Some of the negative attitude against atypical, or variant, sexual behavior probably is based on ingroup/outgroup discrimination. That is, irrespective of the question of damage or harm, individuals engaging in atypical, or variant, behavior, sexual or otherwise, may be rejected and treated cruelly. This fact applies particularly to male homosexuality, because it is much more visible, in urbanized societies, than is pedophilia or pedosexual behavior. Positive social control should suppress such selfish ingroup/outgroup discrimination within a single society for the same reason that it should suppress the gruesome atrocities humans are so capable of inflicting upon other (outgroup) societies: this kind of suppression results in the well-being of the greater number of individuals. It has long been argued by human ethologists (and misunderstood by many other individuals) that to be aware of a biological predisposition is the first step to be taken toward not being controlled by it. Suppression is better than oppression.

Social-control actions against pedophilia and pedosexual behavior are particularly strong, however, since, in contrast to the partners in adult/adult homosexuality, juveniles are so vulnerable and so easily influenced by adults. For these reasons, there is an inclination to play it safe by being categorically opposed to pedophilia and pedosexual behavior. Playing it safe, however, is neither sophisticated nor invariably harmless. Improved sophistication is particularly necessary with respect to the long-term effects of a juvenile's sexual interactions with an adult, especially in light of the information that is accruing through the investigation of some nonhuman primates (see Hopf, 1979). These effects should be studied, and it also should be kept in mind that **some** of the adverse long-term effects on the participants in adult/juvenile sexual behavior **may** be due to social-control measures and not to the actual sexual actions or the relationship.

All human behavior is subject to natural selection, including behavior that is considered to be culturally transmitted, such as both the measures and the results of social control. Choices about social-control measures are by necessity based primarily on intuitive or, sometimes, explicit standards rooted in humankind's belief about evolutionary function. These standards are not invariably correct and comprehensive. In the case of pedophilia and pedosexual behavior, the essential knowledge about the short- and long-term costs and benefits for the juvenile and the adult is fragmentary. A priori categorical rejection of pedophilia and pedosexual behavior is certainly harmful for the adult for whom, through circumstances beyond his or her control, alternatives seem out of reach. For the juvenile, if the historical, anthropological, and biopsychological evidence is considered, functions **may** range from a degree of potentially beneficial sexual and social development, through neutral effects, to adverse functions in the sense of psychic morbidity and fewer offspring. In the absence of solid knowledge about possible functions of pedophilia and pedosexual behavior in humans, **reasonable** standards of social control are both necessary and required.

## Notes

[1]It can be argued that this sentence is a tautology in that **adaptively functional** characteristics are defined as "characteristics that have been favored by natural selection." The crucial question, therefore, is **whether or not** a characteristic has been favored (selected) by natural selection. If the characteristic can be shown to have been favored (selected), then an argument can be made that the characteristic is functional. However, it is not simple to prove empirically that a characteristic has been favored by natural selection. Both random events and genetic linkage can produce genetic changes in populations that resemble natural selection (Lewontin, 1974).

[2]The converse also is true, especially in modern technological societies. That is, fathers often detach and abandon their children before or after divorce, as in failure to pay child support. Trivers (1985) argues that sociobiological theory predicts that either parent will abandon his or her children when it is more likely than not that the children can be reared by the other parent alone. The social welfare state's support to aid dependent children in some degree may be setting a condition that enables abandonment. It is unlikely that urban fathers who abandon children would do so if they knew the children faced certain death by such abandonment.

## References

Alexander, R.D., and Noonan, K.M. Concealment of ovulation, parental care, and human social evolution. *In* N.A. Chagnon and W.G. Irons (Eds.), *Evolutionary biology and human social organization.* North Scituate, Mass.: Duxbury, 1979.

Burgess, A.W., Groth, A.N., Holmstrom, L., and Sgroi, S.M. *Sexual assault of children and adolescents.* Lexington, Mass.: Lexington Books, 1978.

Daniels, D. The evolution of concealed ovulation and self deception. *Ethology and Sociobiology*, 1983, *4*, 69-87.

Dodgson, C.L. *Through the looking glass, and what Alice found there.* London: Macmillan, 1872.

Eibl-Eibesfeldt, I. *The biology of peace and war.* London: Thames and Hudson, 1979.

Ford, C.S., and Beach, F.A. *Patterns of sexual behavior.* New York: Harper & Row, 1951.

Goodall, J. *The chimpanzees of Gombe: Patterns of behavior.* Cambridge, Mass.: The Belknap Press of Harvard University Press, 1986.

Herdt, G.H. *Guardians of the flutes: Idioms of masculinity.* New York: McGraw Hill, 1981.

Hinde, R.A. The concept of function. *In* G.P. Baerends, C. Beer, and A. Manning (Eds.), *Function and evolution in behaviour.* Oxford: Clarendon Press, 1975, pp. 3-15.

Hopf, S. Development of sexual behavior in captive squirrel monkeys (*Saimiri*). *Biology of Behaviour*, 1979, *4*, 373-382.

Konner, M., and Worthman, C. Nursing frequency, gonadal function and birth spacing among !Kung hunter-gatherers. *Science*, 1980, *207*, 788-791.

Landwirth, J. Children as witnesses in child sexual abuse trials. *Pediatrics*, 1987, *80*, 585-589.

Lewontin, R.C. *The genetic basis of evolutionary change.* New York: Columbia University Press, 1974.

Maynard Smith, J. The ecology of sex. *In* J.R. Krebs and N.B. Davies (Eds.), *Behavioural ecology.* Oxford: Blackwell, 1978, pp. 159-179.

Money, J. *Gay, straight, and in-between: The sexology of erotic orientation.* New York: Oxford University Press, 1988.

Morris, D. *The naked ape.* London: Cape, 1967.

Phongpaichit, P. *From peasant girls to Bangkok masseuses.* Geneva: International Labor Organization, 1982.

Reeves, T. Loving boys. *In* D. Tsang (Ed.), *The age taboo.* Boston: Alyson Publications, 1981.

Sandfort, T. *Boys on their contacts with men: A study of sexually expressed friendships.* New York: Global Academic Publishers, 1987.

Stern, J.M., and Leiblum, S. Postpartum resumption of sexual activity in American women: Effects of absence or frequency of breastfeeding. *In* P.C. Lee and J.G. Else (Eds.), *Ontogeny, cognition and social behaviour of primates.* Cambridge, England: Cambridge University Press, 1986.

Symons, D. *The evolution of human sexuality.* New York: Oxford University Press, 1979.

Thornhill, R., and Alcock, J. *The evolution of insect mating systems.* Cambridge, Mass.: Harvard University Press, 1983.

Trivers, R. *Social evolution.* Menlo Park, Calif.: Benjamin/Cummings, 1985.

Weinrich, J.D. A new sociobiological theory of homosexuality applicable to societies with universal marriage. *Ethology and Sociobiology*, 1987a, *8*, 37-48.

Weinrich, J.D. *Sexual landscapes*. New York: Charles Scribner's Sons, 1987b.

Wilson, E.O. *On human nature*. Cambridge, Mass.: Harvard University Press, 1978.

Yamagiwa, J. Intra- and inter-group interactions in an all-male group of virunga mountain gorillas (*Gorilla gorilla beringei*). *Primates*, 1987, *28*, 1-30.

# 13
# The Functions of Primate Paternalism: A Cross-Species Review

David M. Taub
*Department of Psychiatry and Behavioral Sciences*
*Medical University of South Carolina*
*Charleston, South Carolina 29425*
  *and*
*Laboratory Animal Breeders & Services (LABS)*
*Yemassee, South Carolina 29945*

## Introduction

Intrauterine gestation and the physiological adaptations of females that have allowed them to nourish neonates characterize the class Mammalia, and these characteristics have had revolutionary consequences on the evolution of social organization and mating patterns (Trivers, 1972; Brown, 1975; Maynard Smith, 1977; Wittenberger and Tilson, 1980; Williams, 1966; Gubernick and Klopfer, 1981). This physiological mechanism that allowed a female to solely and directly support her offspring also had dramatic effects on parent/offspring bonds (Trivers, 1972), such that the relationships between mother and child are cardinal to all mammalian social systems. An evolutionary consequence of this female capacity has been the diminution of the role of males in parental duties; indeed, so pervasive is the bond between mammalian mother and child that the term "parental behavior" has become equated with mothering. So reduced has been the role of males that the term "biparental" care has been coined to denote explicitly some parenting role for them. For example, in more than 90% of bird species, the male plays an equal role to the female in offspring nurturing, but only a very small percentage of mammals show analogous parenting behavior (Brown, 1985). However maternocentric investigations of mammalian social structure may have been historically, a new focus on the male's role was inaugurated with the publication of Trivers's (1972) provocative analysis of parental investment and sexual selection.

Recent studies have shown that paternal behaviors vary greatly among mammals, including humans (Lamb, 2nd ed., 1981). This rejuvenation of a generalized interest in mammalian "paternal" behavior has been mirrored in increased attention to the behavior of male nonhuman primates and their role in the care and rearing of offspring (Taub, 1985; Snowdon and Suomi, 1982). During the past 2½ decades of primate studies, interactions between males of all ages and infants have been reported for many species. Far from representing a homogeneous subsystem of parenting interactions, male/infant interactions among these species can be characterized by fundamental differences in structure, in contexts of occurrence, in the frequencies and rates of exhibition, in the distribution among the interacting males and the infants, in various biosocial characteristics of the interacting males (such as rank, age, tenure of group residence, kinship), in the form of the mating system characterizing the species, and in the social structure manifested by the species. For example, male/infant interactions have ranged from, at one extreme, the predominant role male callithrichids play in carrying neonates and the extensive and well-developed system of caretaking characterizing monogamous primates, through the triadic, or "agonistic buffering," system alleged to be common among polygamously mating baboons (Taub and Redican, 1984; Taub, 1985), to, at the other extreme, infanticidal attacks upon infants in a variety of species (Hausfater and Hrdy, 1984). These reports have generated intense interest and controversy over the functional and evolutionary significance of adult-male/nonadult interactions, precisely because, among mammals, males generally have tended to be minor actors in the neonatal-support network.

Among the objectives of this volume is the gaining of a greater understanding of the biosocial underpinnings of a complex set of adult human sexual behaviors with children and adolescents. The goal of this chapter is to provide an overview of the distribution, structure, and function of interactions between adult males and infants among humans' closest phylogenetic relatives in the mammalian world. A comparative, cross-taxa perspective may be helpful in allowing researchers to understand the evolutionary basis of human pedophilia.

## Form and Function

As the data on male/infant interactions among primates began to accumulate in the late 1960's, the first attempts to summarize and synthesize these data appeared (Mitchell, 1969). Since then, a number of summary papers have appeared (Hrdy, 1976; Redican and Taub, 1981; Taub and Redican, 1984; Whitten, 1987). All of the classifications of the types (and functions) of these behaviors have been a combination (perhaps of necessity) of structural criteria and functional interpretations (e.g., Kleiman and Malcolm's [1981] classification for New World primates).

By the late 1970's, as more empirical data became available, it seemed as though the distribution of primate paternalistic behavior divided itself nicely (too nicely to be true) into two essentially separate functional categories that correlated with the mating system and kinship: (a) caretaking, i.e., true paternal investment, and (b) exploitation and using. It is clear today, however, that the distribution of both structure and function of primate paternalism does not lend itself to so straightforward a functional analysis. In many ways, all classifications of the function of male/infant interactions are subjective, artificial, and not mutually exclusive. For example, in the categorization used in this chapter, the structure of infanticidal behaviors of some langur species is at the same time a form of male reproductive strategy (Hrdy, 1977), and langurs could be listed under either category. Nevertheless, the schema proposed here attempts to broadly segregate the diverse types of "paternal" behavior shown by nonhuman primates into some basic functional categories. The categories used in this review are

I.      Caretaking, or True Paternal Investment
II.     Affiliation
III.    Using and Exploitation
IV.     Abuse and Infanticide
V.      Mating and Reproductive Strategies
VI.     None (Tolerance and Ignoring)

In Table 13.I, some species are listed by the type of mating system characteristic of the taxa and the functional type of adult-male/infant behavior shown by these taxa. As can be seen, members of the same taxon may exhibit several functionally different "types" of male/infant interactions.

## Category I: Caretaking, or True Paternal Investment

Theories of kinship investment (Trivers, 1972; Kurland and Gaulin, 1984) predict a close, positive correlation between paternity certainty and male investment. Consequently, it is not too surprising to find some degree of male investment in offspring among virtually all monogamously (and also polyandrously, see below) mating New World primates (Vogt, 1984). This phenomenon is particularly well developed among the four genera of marmosets and tamarins (*Callithrix, Saguinus, Cebuella,* and *Leontopithecus*) and the cebid monkeys *Callicebus* and *Aotus.* Indeed, monogamous New World primates are unsurpassed among primates in the extent of male

TABLE 13.I. Distribution of "Primate Paternalism" by Social Structure and Mating System

| Social Structure/Mating System and Species | Type of Paternalism |
|---|---|
| 1. Monogamy: 1 Male/1 Female | |
| Tamarins (*Saguinus*) | I |
| Marmosets (*Callithrix*) | I |
| Aotus | I |
| Callicebus | I |
| Siamangs (*Syndactalus*) | I |
| Alouatta | II, IV |
| Pithecinae (*Saki* and *Uakari*) | VI |
| 2. Polygyny: 1 Male/Multifemale | |
| Hamadryas baboons | II, V |
| Gelada baboons (*Theropithecus*) | II, V |
| Colobines (Langurs and *Colobus*) | IV |
| Patas | VI |
| Alouatta | VI |
| Guenons (*Cercopithecus*) | IV, VI |
| 3. Polygyny: Multimale/Multifemale | |
| Baboons (*Papio* spp.) | II, III, IV |
| Macaques | I, II, III, VI |
| Apes (*Pan* and *Gorilla*) | II, IV, VI |
| Cebids | II, VI |
| Colobines | VI |
| 4. Polyandry: Multimale/1 Female | |
| Tamarins (*S. fuscicollis*, *S. mystax*, *S. labiatus*, etc.) | I, V |
| Marmosets (*C. humeralifer*) | I, V |

involvement with infants, and the family Callitrichidae is cardinal among all of them in the amount and quality of direct care provided by males. All of these monogamously mating species are truly biparental, as males share all caring duties except nursing and are a major (and, in some species, **the** major) caregiver.

Several reviews of parental care in monogamous New World primate species found that in almost all species studied, males make a significant contribution to infant care (Higley and Suomi, 1986; Vogt, 1984; Kleiman, 1985). Examples of these species are *Callimico goeldi* (Pook, 1978; Heltne et al., 1973; Lorenz, 1972), *Leontopithecus rosalia* (Hoage, 1978), *Callithrix jacchus* (Box, 1975, 1977; Locke-Haydon and Chalmers, 1983; Ingram, 1977, 1978; Epple and Katz, 1983, 1984; Cebul and Epple, 1984), *Saguinus fuscicollis* (Epple, 1975; Epple and Katz, 1983; Goldizen, 1987; Terborgh and Goldizen, 1985; Goldizen and Terborgh, 1986), *Saguinus o. oedipus* (Wolters, 1978; Cleveland and Snowdon, 1982; McGrew, 1988), *Callicebus moloch* (Fragaszy et al., 1982), *Aotus trivirgatus* (Dixson and Fleming, 1981; Dixson, 1983; Robinson et al., 1987; Wright, 1984).

The results of several studies of three species of wild and captive callithrichids indicate that males did substantially more infant carrying than the mothers did (*S. fuscicollis*, Epple, 1975; Vogt et al., 1978; Goldizen and Terborgh, 1986; Ingram, 1978; *L. rosalia*, Hoage, 1978; *C. jacchus*, Box, 1975), while in other studies the opposite was found (Box, 1975; Izawa, 1978). In most species, adult males share food with infants (Brown and Mack, 1978; Goldizen, 1987), carry infants, groom infants, promote the infants' emerging independence (Dixson, 1983) because they provide a secure base from which the infant may explore its environment, and protect infants from other group members and potential predators (Wolters, 1978).

A major source of variability in male caretaking activities among these species seems to revolve around the timing of the onset of these activities. In some species, males actually are reported to begin caretaking at parturition, licking off birth fluids to clean the infant (Epple and Katz, 1983, 1984; Stevenson, 1970, 1978). In other species, male care may not begin for several days or even weeks (Pook, 1978; Hoage, 1978; Vogt, 1984). For example, Hoage (1978) found that among four *L. rosalia* groups, only the female carried the infant in the first weeks of life, but after the fourth week, males became the principal caretaker. Both the number of potential caregivers (see below) and the extent to which the mother promotes (i.e., begins to push the infant off herself) or permits (i.e., allows other caregivers to approach and obtain the infant [Stevenson, 1978; Fragaszy et al., 1982]) strongly affect the timing and extent of male and/or allomaternal caregiving.

The degree of male participation in paternal behavior varies both between species and among different groups of the same species. Besides the degree of maternal restrictiveness/permissiveness, this variation seems to be strongly correlated with group size and the phenomenon of "helpers at the nest." In all of these species, juveniles and subadults appear to be retained within the group (= family) until they reach sexual maturity. In all cases, nonbreeding relatives are available within the group and often act as "helpers" in that they assume caretaking duties (particularly carrying) in addition to the mother and father. Although males are major caretakers, the norm is that all group members, especially older, sexually immature siblings still living in the group, share the infant-caretaking duties with the "father." For example, in eight captive groups of *S. fuscicollis* (Cebul and Epple, 1984), the dominant male accounted for 95% of all carrying with two male helpers in the group, but in another group, also with two helpers, the male accounted for 38%. So strong was the tendency of male *S. fuscicollis* in this study to caretake infants that nonrelated "step-fathers" (males introduced into the groups prior to parturition) were among the most active and vigorous caretakers.

In a study specifically aimed at testing the influence of "helpers" on the amount of both maternal and paternal behavior in cotton-top marmosets (*S. o. oedipus*), McGrew (1988) found that the more helpers available, the less "babysitting" (broadly defined to include all types of infant care) was done by the father. Paternal contribution to infant care thus varied directly with the family's composition. In some other studies of marmoset and tamarin groups, siblings or other allomaternal caregivers make a greater contribution to infant care (Epple, 1975; Cebul and Epple, 1984; Ingram, 1977; Vogt et al., 1978; Cleveland and Snowdon, 1982). "Helping" by these relatives may be at least partly explained by a combination of nepotistic gains and the benefits of becoming experienced at infant care themselves. Infants are more likely to be left alone and unprotected, or even be subjected to aggression, when both the male and the female are inexperienced at caretaking (Epple, 1975). Ingram (1978) found that the probability of a male's showing care for infants who had been abandoned by their mothers was directly related to whether the male had had prior experience with infants. Thus, allomaternal care given by these "helpers" not only provides additional support for the infant but also apparently is critical in the development of adequate parental behavior when these "helpers" become mature and themselves reproduce.

Among the monogamously mating cebid monkeys, *Callicebus* and *Aotus* show extensive male care (Dixson and Fleming, 1981; Fragaszy et al., 1982; Wright, 1984; Robinson et al., 1987; Kinzey, 1977; Mason, 1966, 1968; Robinson, 1977). In captivity, *Aotus* males are the primary carrier of the infant, even from the first day of life (Dixson and Fleming, 1981; Taub, unpublished observations) and may account for upwards of 80% of carrying in the first month of life. Indeed, Taub found that in a captive breeding colony, if a male did not carry the infant after birth, the female rejected it (Taub, unpublished observations). Wright's study of wild *Aotus* has confirmed that the "father" accounts for a majority of carrying duties for the first six months of life or until weaning. In both species, males not only carry the infant but, also, will share food with it, play with it, and groom it. While "helping" by siblings is not as well developed in these cebid species as it is in marmosets and tamarins, sibling "helpers" will carry infants, but only for the first few months of an infant's life (Wright, 1984; Dixson and Fleming, 1981).

The "lesser apes," the gibbons and siamangs, are monogamously mating, arboreal, and territorial (Chivers, 1974; Chivers and Raemaekers, 1980; Tenaza, 1975; Tilson, 1981). Male investment in infant caretaking is extensive among only the siamang (Chivers, 1974); it is most curious (and a general exception to the rule showing a correlation between monogamy and male care) that males in other species of the genus *Hylobates* do not engage in "paternalistic" behavior. Unlike the New World species, however, siamang males generally only carry, groom, and sleep with their offspring and do so only after the offspring are older, typically juveniles and adolescents. The differential degree of male involvement between siamang males and infants and their monogamous callithrichid counterparts in the New World appears to be related to the reproductive burden on the mother (Leutenegger, 1980): hylobatids bear singleton young, while callithrichids bear twins routinely; the callithrichid maternal-to-offspring-weight ratio is five times greater than for hylobatid mothers; the interbirth interval is considerably longer for hylobatids. Thus, the mother is the primary caregiver in the first year to year-and-a-half (although on occasion males may carry infants as young as 6-8 months of age [Chivers, 1974]). Thereafter, there is a shift to the male in the second year, so that during this time, the father becomes the primary caregiver until the offspring are weaned and independent (year 3) (Chivers and Raemaekers, 1980). Males may spend up to three-fourths of their social activity in carrying and grooming infants during this time, but typically, they do so considerably less (Chivers, 1974). Standing in sharp contrast to the "helpers at the nest" phenomenon of the New World monogamous species, maturing hylobatids are actively peripheralized from their natal group, sometimes very aggressively so (Tilson, 1981; Fox, 1972), and it is the father that takes the most active role.

There are one or two nonmonogamously mating primates that can be classified as truly paternal in their patterns of infant socialization, more by virtue of the extensiveness, regularity, and substance of the behavior, if not in fact on biological relatedness. A most remarkable species is the Barbary macaque (Taub, 1978, 1984). Barbary macaques (*Macaca sylvanus*) are polygynously mating, multimale/multifemale, Old World monkeys—the only macaque to exist outside of Asia—living in high montane forests of Morocco and Algeria. Adult and subadult males interact with infants intensively and regularly in every conceivable way, from birth through the first year of life (Taub, 1984). For example, during 559 observation hours, more than 2,231 episodes of male/infant interactions were recorded in a group containing 7 adult, 4 subadult, and 5 juvenile males. Among the most pertinent features of this species' system of paternalism are the following:

1. All males show highly specific preferences for a particular infant or several infants (among all available) for interaction; e.g., among the adult males, 5 had one "primary" infant, 1 had two, and 1 had three, whereas all 4 subadult males preferred only one "primary" infant.

2. There are significant differences among males in the degree to which each is involved with infants in general and with specific infants in particular; e.g., subadult male 4SA accounted for 18% of all male/infant interactions (the highest), while a typical adult male, WN, accounted for 5%.

3. Subadult males, as a class, were generally the most intensively involved with infants, as the 4 in Taub's study group accounted for

44% of all male/infant interaction versus 46% for the 7 adult males.

All males show essentially the same types of behaviors in their interactions with infants. However, while these associations are structurally identical, functionally, they are operating at multiple levels. Taub (1980, 1984) has argued, for example, that subadult males may well be investing in younger siblings (although data are unavailable from his study to test this proposition). Some adult males are investing in both their actual and probable offspring, some in offspring of their relatives, and some in nonrelatives. Males also may be interacting with infants to induce females to copulate with them during the mating season (see in this section the subsection titled "Category V: Mating and Reproductive Strategies"). During the mating season, females mate successively with all the males of the group. They form brief and transient "consociations," breaking off one and forming another, until they mate with virtually all the males many times during their estrous period. Taub (1980) has suggested that this female strategy of allowing each and every male some mathematical probability of actually siring offspring is a mechanism that induces all males to invest in infants in general and in a given female's in particular.

## Category II: Affiliation

Many male/infant affiliative interactions among species catalogued here are similar to true caretaking investment. Affiliative interactions, however, are less frequent and may not be regular components of the social repertory; the examples classified here tend to be more individually idiosyncratic, irregular, and opportunistic in their occurrence, and the biological relationship between males and infants is typically unknown. In many cases, however, there is strong circumstantial evidence that the participants are genetically related. In the absence of definitive genealogical data, frequency of occurrence and regularity of expression serve as a convenient tool for classification in this chapter. To underscore this notion of regularity and consistency, it may be instructive to contrast the frequency of infant interaction between some macaque and baboons species for which quantitative data are available. Rates for all types of baboon male/infant interaction ranged from a low of one interaction (triadic) every 53 observation hours (Packer, 1980) to a high of one episode every 5 observation hours (Busse, 1984). In between these two limits, there are Gilmore's study (Gilmore, 1977) yielding one episode per 26 hours, Strum's (1984) with one per 13 hours, and Smuts's (1982) with one every 22 hours. When these gross rates are adjusted for the number of males in the groups who could possibly engage in infant use, the rates range from one every 1,250 to one every 100 observation hours. For all baboon studies, the pooled, simple average rate of male/infant interactions is about one episode every 19 observation hours; likewise, when this rate is adjusted for the number of possible male actors, the simple, pooled average is about one episode every 344 hours. In contrast, among stumptail macaques (*M. arctoides*), Estrada and Sandoval (1977) found males interacting with infants at a rate of 1.4 interactions per hour (total) and 2.7 interactions per hour adjusted for number of males. Taub (1980, 1984) found the rate of dyadic interactions for Barbary macaques (*M. sylvanus*) to be one every 23 minutes (one per hour for triadic interactions), while Deag (1980) found the rate for Barbary macaques in his study to be one every hour (one every 1½ hours for triadic interactions).

Typically, rates of affiliative interaction tend to be low (with the possible exception of stumptail and perhaps Japanese macaques), but intensive and long-term affiliations may persist between specific male/infant pairs. Such positive affiliative interactions between males and infants have been reported for many primate species.

Although early studies of stumptail macaques suggested that males were uninterested in infants (Bertrand, 1969), in fact among the multimale/multifemale species of polygynously mating cercopithecine primates, they rank second to the Barbary macaque in the extent of their interactions with infants. Gouzoules (1975) found that adult and subadult males ". . . showed interest in, and interacted with infants almost as much as females did." In several captive groups, two adult and two subadult males accumulated more than 1,000 episodes of "social interaction" with six infants during the infants' first six months of life, including holding, carrying, touching, retrieving, and protecting. Male and maternal social rank appeared to be most important in influencing the patterns of male/infant interactions; adult males interacted most frequently, and subadult males preferred older infants of low-ranking females. Hendy-Neely and Rhine (1977) and Rhine and Hendy-Neely (1978) found that five categories of momentary touching accounted for a large majority of all interactions between males and infants, and there were significant differences between the two adult males of each group in the distribution of their interactions.

As with Gouzoules, these differences tended to correlate positively with both male age and social status, as the dominant male tended to be the most actively involved with infants (although each tended to focus the majority of his attention on a few specific infants). Smith and Peffer-Smith (1984) found that adult males accounted for 17% of all interactions with immatures, and as with other studies, social rank correlated strongest with degree of involvement; interestingly, males interacted at a higher rate with immatures to whom they were known to be related than with nonrelated individuals.

That stumptail males probably make true paternal investments in offspring is strongly suggested by a long-term study of a free-ranging island colony (Estrada et al., 1977; Estrada and Sandoval, 1977; Estrada, 1984). In this study, males showed ". . . substantial amounts of care behavior to their infant siblings; . . ." (Estrada and Sandoval, 1977), e.g., three juvenile males with sibling infants showed a significant preference for interactions with them over other infants (67% and 52%). Males of all ages were extensively involved with infants, but infants less than 6 months of age received significantly more male interest generally and male care of a higher quality (e.g., tactile stimulation through grooming, carrying, and so forth) than did older infants. There was, moreover, a strong infant-sex bias in the distribution of male care, as 76% of all contact behaviors and 88% of all proximity and vocalization scores were directed to the two male (versus the five female) infants. In contrast to other studies, however, juvenile males were more active than adult males (518 episodes for all infants pooled versus 289), although this distribution is strongly influenced by the fact that there were striking individual male differences in infant interest (e.g., one juvenile male accounted for more than one-third of all male/infant interactions).

For stumptail macaques, it appears that the salient features of male/ infant associations are as follows:

1. All males show interest in and interact positively with infants.
2. Juvenile males show the most intensive interest.
3. Males display preferences for specific infants, although this specificity may be strongly influenced by both male and maternal social rank and maternal proximity.
4. Male/infant preferences may also be strongly influenced by the degree of genetic relatedness between participants.

It was from studies of Japanese macaques (*Macaca fuscata*) that the first observations of male interactions with infants were derived. Itani (1959) described male care of infants as being extensive, including carrying, hugging, holding, grooming, and playing (although he noted that these male/infant associations did not occur in all troops); other studies in Japan (e.g., Kurland, 1977) have failed to observe any significant distribution of male/infant interactions. Intensive male caretaking was directed almost exclusively to 1- and 2-year-old individuals (yearlings accounted for 74%) and only during the onset of the birth season; Itani suggested that the burden of caretaking was shifted to fully mature males at a time crucial for infant survival, as only fully mature "leader" and "subleader" males exhibited this seasonally intense interest in immatures.

Subsequent studies of the Takasakiyama populations (Hasegawa and Hiraiwa, 1980; Hiraiwa, 1981) have substantiated these patterns of male care. In regard to Itani's functional interpretation of male care being critical to infant survival, Hasegawa and Hiraiwa (1980) noted cases of "adoption" of orphaned infants. They found that adult males showed intensive interest in and carried, groomed, and defended infants whose mothers had died. These adult males became the primary caretakers of these orphaned infants, surpassing the care given to them by siblings, other relatives, nonkin peers, and adult females; the orphans themselves preferred these adult males to other alloparents (note, also, cases of adoption of orphans among rhesus monkeys, a species typically uninvolved with infants; see in this section the subsection titled "Category VI: None (Tolerance and Ignoring)").

Alexander (1970) has reported similar adult male behavior in a corralled troop of Japanese macaques. Seventy-five percent of all sexually mature males showed an increase in affiliative behaviors directed toward immatures (1-4 years old), and although seasonally dependent, these interactions occurred both prior to and during the birth season. The younger adult males, however, interacted with juveniles more than the older males did, and subordinate males were equally as likely to be involved as were high-ranking males. Although the cumulative amount of affiliation and care received by immatures from adult males was small in comparison with such behavior received from other group members, Alexander believed that these males contributed significantly to the socialization of the maturing young.

Patterns of male/infant interest among a free-ranging troop in Texas show some fundamental differences. Gouzoules (1984) found that males did not exhibit the "babysitting" of juveniles when their siblings were born, as previously described for this species. However, fully one-third of all the adult males (n = 9) did develop long-term, persistent patterns of caretaking and affiliation with particular infants. As with other reports, these males interacted with the infants in a diversity of affiliative ways, such as carrying, clutching, holding, grooming, and being in close proximity. Dominance rank and maternal kinship relatedness were among the most important variables accounting for the distribution of these long-term male/infant relationships.

Several forms of male/infant interactions have been reported for many groups of savannah baboons (discussed in more detail in the subsection titled "Category III: Using and Exploitation," which is found within this section). A review of these studies indicates that males may both affiliatively caretake and exploit infants (for use in ameliorating intermale conflict) at the same time and, in some cases, may do so with the same infant (Collins, 1986; Ransom and Ransom, 1971; Altmann, 1980; Stein, 1984; Smuts, 1982, 1985; Strum, 1984; Packer, 1980; Popp, 1978). Clearly, males can form strong, affiliative, mutually preferred attachments to infants (Stein, 1984; Taub, unpublished observations at Gilgil, Kenya, 1983).

In many instances, there is strong evidence of a close genealogical relationship between the males and the infants; e.g., in Packer's study (1980), subadult males preferentially carried their siblings, and males who could have been a particular infant's father showed more male/infant behavior than did males considered unlikely to be related. Similar circumstantial evidence suggesting a closer kinship relationship between "affiliated" males and infants has been noted in many of the baboon studies (see Taub, 1985, for a critique). Strum and Smuts have emphasized the importance of special relationships between these caretaking males, infants, and their mothers over kinship. Indeed, they view these special relationships as critical to the establishment and maintenance of these bonds. The exact mechanisms that are operating notwithstanding, male baboons do form, albeit at low rates of interaction, some intense and quite specific bonds with certain infants.

Some other footnotes to the primatology literature regarding sporadic but positive/affiliative occurrences of male/infant interactions include the following:

1. Adult and immature-sibling sooty mangabey (*Cercocebus atys*) males sometimes carry infants (Bernstein, 1976; Chalmers, 1968), although in a captive group, one adult male in particular ("M"), who was not the dominant male, was observed to carry nine different infants at one time or another (but this behavior was not judged to be a form of agonistic buffering) (Bernstein, 1976).

2. Young "follower" gelada baboon males, in an attempt to establish their own "one male units" (OMUs), may sometimes groom and carry an infant in order to establish a relationship with the infant's mother in order to coopt her into his breeding unit (Mori, 1979).

3. If a deposed hamadryas male remains associated with his former OMU, he may become very solicitous of offspring (presumably his own) if they are threatened by the new leader male (Dunbar and Dunbar, 1975; Dunbar, 1984).

4. Silverback male gorillas are very solicitous of infants, and they may groom, cuddle, and nest with 3- and 4-year-olds, allowing them to play, climb, and tumble over them with impunity (Fossey, 1979, 1983); since it is generally these dominant males that do the mating, these males are quite possibly caretaking their own offspring.

5. Adult male black howler monkeys (which are monogamous) may develop strong bonds with infants, although the adult males rarely actually carry the infants (Bolin, 1981).

6. Captive crab-eating macaques may sometimes carry infants (Auerbach and Taub, 1979), and male squirrel monkeys (a species notorious for their lack of male interest in infants) may huddle, play, and sleep with infants if their mothers are artificially removed from the group (Viatl, 1977).

7. "Adoption" of orphaned infants, sometimes by siblings and sometimes by unrelated males, has been reported for several species, including rhesus monkeys (Berman, 1983; Vessey and Meikle, 1984), Japanese monkeys (Hiraiwa, 1981), hamadryas baboons (Kummer, 1967), and gibbons (Carpenter, 1940). In these cases, very intense, albeit typically brief, associations develop, and these males assume such otherwise maternal duties as holding, cuddling, comforting, grooming, carrying, and protecting these very vulnerable infants.

## Category III: Using and Exploitation

It was a study of wild Japanese macaques (*M. fuscata*) that provided the first systematic, albeit qualitative, account of social relationships between males and infants among a cercopithecine species. Itani (1959) described male caretaking and originally proposed (among other functions) that males used infants to raise their social rank or status in the group. In 1971, Deag and Crook presented qualitative data on an extensive array of social interactions between Barbary macaque males and infants and distinguished two major types of interactions: male care and "agonistic buffering." As the name implies, "agonistic buffering" was viewed as a system whereby males used babies to regulate and otherwise ameliorate their relationships with other males so that low-ranking males could reduce the likelihood of aggression from higher ranking animals. Both the term and its functional explanation were readily adopted among primatologists, and within the next decade, there appeared numerous reports of similar triadic male/infant/male behavior among many species and populations of baboons and macaques (Taub, 1984).

There have been about as many functional explanations of these interactions as there have been reported instances of their occurrence (Taub, 1984; Whitten, 1987). Interactions involving two males and an infant have been referred to as "agonistic buffering" (Deag and Crook, 1971), "kidnapping" (Popp, 1978), "infant use" (Strum, 1984), "passports" (Itani, 1959), "infant carrying" (Busse and Hamilton, 1981), "countercarrying" (Hamilton, 1984), "tripartite relations" (Kummer, 1967), and "triadic male-infant interactions" (Taub, 1980).

When Deag and Crook (1971) first studied the Barbary macaque in its natural habitat (Deag and Crook, 1971; Deag, 1974, 1980), they were immediately struck by the magnitude, intensity, and diversity of male/infant relationships. They were particularly fascinated with a peculiar form of male/infant/male interaction in which, they suggested, a male used babies to regulate his social relationships with other males. Termed "agonistic buffering," its function was said to be a means of enabling a subordinate male to approach and remain near a dominant male with a reduced likelihood of attack. Quantified data from this study (Deag, 1974, 1980) almost exclusively concerned this type of interaction and supported their interpretation of a buffering function. For example, there were larger clusterings of animals in general, and of other males in particular, around a male that had a baby in his possession than when he did not; males made a greater number of friendly approaches to one another when in the presence of infants; and in general, subordinate males carried infants to males higher than themselves in social rank. Frequent close contact between males mediated by a baby's presence resulted in the males' being relatively nonaggressive towards each other, and the handling of babies or infants during fights reduced the likelihood of the handling male's being attacked.

A very brief study of Riffian (northern Morocco) populations of Barbary macaques (Whiten and Rumsey, 1973) classed seven observations as being "agonistic buffering," and an in-depth study of Riffian populations noted that among the frequent male/infant interactions, a very small number could be considered to buffer male aggression (Mehlman, 1986).

Taub's study of Middle Atlas populations of Barbary macaques (Taub, 1978, 1980) confirmed many of Deag's observations, but Taub found cause both to reject the dichotomy between male care and "agonistic buffering" and to reevaluate the function of these peculiar male/infant/male triadic interactions. Social rank did correlate in some general ways with the pattern of triadic interactions, but for the most part, Taub's data could not adequately accommodate the major parameters of Deag and Crook's hypothesis that these interactions functioned to regulate dominant/subordinate relationships among males.

Males did not choose other males equally often to interact with, but rather, each male had a different and limited set of males (of all males available) that he preferred to interact with vis-à-vis infants. Each male showed striking preferences for certain infants in triadic encounters, and these infants were the same ones preferred by that male in dyadic interactions. Finally, males that preferred each other for a triadic interaction showed a mutual preference for the same infants. Taub (1980) concluded that "males choose to participate in triadic encounters by means of a shared, common and special caretaking relationship with the same infant," thus shifting the focus of interpretation away from social status regulation to a shared caretaking network. A later, short-term study of male aggression (Taub and Kurland, 1988) showed that male aggression was not ameliorated by having infants in one's possession. In addition, Mehlman (1986) reported that when infants were present, either in the possession of the male who was being aggressive or the male who was receiving the aggression, rates of intermale agonism were as high as or higher than they were when infants were not present.

Taub's general interpretation of Barbary macaque male/infant interactions (dyadic and triadic), which, he suggests, are based on a kinship network, has been challenged by work on a captive, semifree-ranging population in a European theme park (Kuester and Paul, 1986). The data from this group failed to support the notion that males based their interactions with infants on their genetic relationships. As with data from wild groups, adult and subadult males formed strong relationships with infants. While their data showed that subadult males did prefer kin for interaction, adult males did not show a preference for closely related infants or for the infants of females from their own matriline. Kuester and Paul concluded that interactions with males were the prime source of infant death (a finding totally at variance with data on wild populations). Their interpretation was that males "used" infants for their own benefit (though they failed to identify or quantify what these benefits were), and these investigators believe that the data from their study supported the "agonistic buffering" interpretation originally put forth by Deag.

Finally, a brief study by Smith and Peffer-Smith (1982) failed to find any incidents of "agonistic buffering" among Barbary macaques: lower ranking animals approached higher ranking animals for triadic interactions in 77% of the cases, but in 11%, the initiator was higher ranking (a contradiction to the predictions of "agonistic buffering" also found, but to an even higher degree, by Taub [1980]). They found no difference in the frequency of nonagonistic interactions between juvenile, subadult, and adult males with and without infants present.

The most significant quantified and compelling work on an "agonistic buffering" interpretation of male/infant interactions has come from a number of studies on baboons. Among these baboon studies of male/infant interactions, at least three common and cardinal features stand out in all explanations: (1) the biological relationship (or lack thereof) between the males and infants, (2) the ("special") relationship between the caretaking male and the mother of the infant, and as a corollary, the specificity with which males direct their attention to a particular infant (= "affiliation"), and (3) the social context within which the male actually interacts with the infant.

The baboon studies all fall into three distinct groups as they relate to the degree of relatedness between the "caretaking" male, the infant, and the "opponent." At one end, Popp (1978) has asserted that the actor, or in his parlance, the "kidnapper," is unlikely to have sired the infant he carries (= the "kidnapped" infant) but that the male to whom the kidnapper directs his interactions (= the "opponent") has a higher probability of being the infant's father. Aggression by the opponent toward the kidnapper is thereby inhibited because the opponent would not risk possible injury to his probable offspring. This more extreme exploitative explanation, therefore, argues that males hold one another hostage over their offspring; it is pure exploitation, or classic "agonistic buffering."

At the other extreme, Busse (Busse and Hamilton, 1981; Busse, 1984) has asserted that males who carry infants against other males are protecting their own infants against the possibility of injury by a nonrelated opponent. For example, in 111 of 112 triadic interactions, the actor had a high probability of being the sire of the offspring he interacted with, but the recipient could not have been the sire because he was not a resident in the social group at the time of the infant's conception. In each of two groups, only a few males accounted for the overwhelming majority of male/infant interactions, and males were quite specific in their preference for interactions with a particular few infants. Therefore, it was thought that instead of being a mechanism by which a male uses an infant to "buffer" his relations with other males, interactions by a male with infants were a mechanism whereby probable fathers protected their probable offspring against injury or possible infanticide from unrelated male immigrants.

The remaining baboon studies fall in between the two previous, contrasting interpretations, with all of them asserting some form of exploitation, using, or "agonistic buffering" (Ransom and Ransom, 1971; Altmann, 1980; Packer, 1980; Smuts, 1982; Strum, 1983; Nicholson, 1982; Collins, 1981; Klein, 1983; Gilmore, 1977; Stein, 1981; Stein and Stacey, 1981). For example, Packer (1980) asserts that ". . . there is no evidence that males biased their behaviour further towards those infants born after their entry which were judged to be their offspring by their consorting activity with the mother." But no infant was carried by a male who immigrated after its birth (nonfather), and in fact, possible fathers showed more male/infant behavior than did males who could not have been fathers. In part because there was no clear or consistent pattern relative to probable paternity between actor and infant (although natal, subadult males did statistically bias their interactions toward their siblings), Packer interpreted the male/infant system as exploitative, terming it a case of "mutualism" or "delayed return altruism" in which both the male giving care and the infant receiving care ultimately benefitted more or less equally.

Studying the same population of anubis baboons, Smuts (1982) and Strum (1984) suggest that because actors sometimes could and sometimes could not have been sires, "special relationships," or "affiliations," between the males and the infants through special associations with the infant's mother were more important than probable kinship. In terms of function, each researcher sees a form of buffering in operation. Specific to Strum's study, males of long-term residency (LTR males, and also of lower social rank) most often interacted with infants, using them against males who were of shorter tenure and higher social rank. As with other studies, the most active LTR males had developed special relationships with specific, preferred infants, and Strum (1984) believes that a male's choice of an infant was influenced mainly by whether or not they were "affiliated," i.e., with whom each had a special relationship.

Strum is cautious about assessing the probabilities of paternity between affiliated male/infant pairs but does allow that some affiliated males were the infants' fathers, while there were some that could not have been. Strum concludes that relatedness is neither a primary nor a necessary component and, therefore, rules out the "infant protection" or kinship investment function of male/infant interactions, believing instead that these relationships are part of a larger system of social strategies in which "agonistic buffering" plays a role.

Smuts (1982) has proposed an argument concordant with that of Strum, that is, that "affiliation" with a female is more important than kinship in driving the male/infant system. The primary characteristic of most male/infant interactions is to modulate relations between male troop members, so that the focus of attention is less the infant than it is another male and infants are objects for males to use whether or not they are related to them.

Stein (1981, 1984) distinguished two types of male/infant interactional dyads on the basis of their intensity: those that were classified as "preferred" (in which the adult male accounted for more than 20% of the infant's total time in proximity) and those classified as "nonpreferred" (less than 20%). Most male/infant interactions were accounted for by one or two adult males, who attended to specific, preferred infants with whom each had a preferred relationship; nonpreferred dyads accounted for a minimum amount of attention received by infants. Adult males in preferred dyads had a higher likelihood of having sired infants than did adult males in nonpreferred dyads; however, some preferred dyads contained males who did not monopolize the female during estrus and who, therefore, were estimated to have had a low probability of being the sire of the preferred infants. Yet, 11 males who did sexually monopolize a female did have preferred dyads with infants that they were judged likely to have sired. Thus, some actors, especially the most active males, were more probably sires of infants they interacted with, while others—those usually the least involved—were probably not sires of the infants they interacted with. Stein does not interpret this pattern as a case of kinship investment or infant protection; rather, he views the male/infant interactional system as a classic example of "agonistic buffering," with infants cooperating with specific males who use them as buffers "in exchange" for benefits received through their special, or preferred relationship (= mutualism, or reciprocal altruism) (Stein and Stacey, 1981).

The results of a study on male/infant interactions by Klein (1983) indicate a strong relationship between behavior and kinship, i.e., adult males acted more affiliatively toward mates and toward infants they were likely to have fathered than toward other infants and nonmates. Conversely, adult females and their infants acted more affiliatively toward those males that were likely to be the fathers of the females' offspring than toward other males. Data on four immigrant males and their activities with infants conceived **after**, versus infants born prior to, their entrance into the troop give further evidence of a strong relationship between probable paternity and social attraction to and interactions with probable offspring. Although males were attracted to young infants they were likely to have fathered, actual contact was infrequent. As was found by other studies, this strong preference for particular infants in affiliative contexts also was evident during the selection of infants for use in potentially dangerous encounters with other males. Collins (1981, 1986), too, found that because interactions between males and infants took place only with resident and subadult males, the associations were restricted to possible fathers. The two immigrant males in this study never interacted with infants. Also concordant with other baboon studies, each male appeared to focus his interest and interactions on a limited set of one or more particular infants. Collins observed that only a small portion of the interactions could be explained by the notion that males carried their offspring to protect them from infanticidal males. In fact,

Collins found that, as in previous studies, males both protect and exploit the same infant at different times.

The issue of kinship between the actor male and the infant is critical to the evaluation of the function of male/infant interactions among baboons (and macaques, as well). As yet, there are no definitive, independent data available on paternity certainty among those populations where males interact with infants. Nevertheless, among the baboon studies, it does seem likely that in many instances an actor male has a low probability of having sired the infant he carries. On the other hand, even though most investigators reject the kinship investment interpretation, a large number of instances seem to cluster among specific males and particular infants between whom the probability of being related is quite high. With the exception of the Busse and the Popp studies, all these studies support the finding that the same male (possible father) that showed affiliative behavior to a specific infant was also the exploiter of that infant. Given the strong relationship between male/infant associations and probable paternity in many of these studies, it is probable that many adult male baboons exploit offspring who could be their own. Taub (1984) has noted elsewhere that the theme of kinship is tantalizingly common to most of these studies (see, for example, the Klein and the Collins studies noted above). There is no reason to assume that a single interpretation of this phenomenon of male/infant interactions among baboons will accommodate all occurrences; however, if it turns out that the Busse and Hamilton interpretation is correct, then it may be the case that at least some instances of male/infant interactions among baboons might be more correctly listed as true paternal investment.

There are a number of brief, nonquantified studies that indicate that in several other species, an "agonistic buffering" type of phenomenon may be operating among males that interact with infants. Dunbar (1984) reports that among geladas (*Theropithecus gelada*), males use infants for three purposes. They may engage in classic "agonistic buffering," wherein males carry infants of higher ranking opponents in order to deflect aggression waged by the latter. They may in fact carry their own infants as a warning to opponents that they will defend their own offspring against attack. They also may use a given infant in soliciting support from a third party, usually the infant's mother; this use may also be involved with harem acquisition and, hence, may be a subset of reproductive strategies peculiar to this species' form of social structure (one-male/multiple-female harems); Mori (1979) found similar patterns.

Silk and Samuels (1984) studied a captive group of bonnet macaques (*M. radiata*) and observed triadic interactions among males and infants, and although these interactions were infrequent, they occurred in a variety of circumstances. A male had possession of an infant when he approached or was approached by other males in 43 episodes, was involved in agonistic interactions in 15 episodes, or was near other fighting males in 10 episodes. Adult and subadult males who had possession of infants rarely received aggressive activity. The fact that males were less likely to be displaced, threatened, or attacked while in contact with infants suggested to Silk and Samuels that the triadic interaction with infants served to buffer aggression and that males used infants to that end.

## Category IV: Abuse and Infanticide

In the Preface of their comprehensive and influential volume on infanticide, Hausfater and Hrdy (1984) note: "Over the past decade, the intellectual pendulum in behavioral biology and related disciplines has swung from an earlier view that infanticide could not possibly represent anything other than abnormal and maladaptive behavior to the current view that in many populations infanticide is a normal and individually adaptive activity." Until the publication of this volume, all episodes of infant killing among primates (or, for that matter, any behavior involving injury to infants) was considered by definition to be "abnormal," "dysfunctional," and "maladaptive." Their volume clearly demonstrated the empirical occurrence of primate infanticide, documented and quantified its exhibition (for some species of colobine primates, at least), and offered cogent, compelling arguments and evidence to show that this behavior could function as an adaptive and successful social strategy (at least for some members of the social unit).

To be sure, infanticide is not common; only 24 actual cases of observed infanticide by males encompass 10 species, 3 families, and 4 subfamilies. If one adds to this list of empirically documented cases those additional cases of suspected infanticide (usually inferred from chases by males against mothers and their infants, observed wounding of infants, and disappearances of infants soon after male replacement), then there are another 112 or so additional episodes that could be listed (Struhsaker and Leland, 1987), bringing the total to less than 150 cases.

Among primates, infanticide was first described in a natural population for the gray langur (*Presbytis entellus*) (Sugiyama, 1965). Further evidence of infanticide among gray langurs has come from three areas in India, with some 38 instances of infant killing being attributed to infanticidal males (Sugiyama, 1965, 1966; Mohnot, 1971; Hrdy, 1974, 1977), although only 7 of these events were observed directly (the others were deduced from circumstantial evidence). The following narrative by Vogel and Loch (1984) describes a "typical" case of male replacement/infanticide among gray langurs: "At the end of May, Troop KI consisted of 23 animals: one adult male, 11 adult females, 8 juvenile males and females, and 3 infants all still in their black natal coat. The ... takeover occurred in June ... and by early July ... the new resident male had already established his position. At that time, two juvenile males had left their natal troop. The new resident male was observed to attack all three infants in the troop, all of whom were under 4 months of age. The first infant ... was severely wounded on

July 9 and died the following day. The second infant was badly injured . . . and disappeared 7 days later. The third infant was also threatened by the new male, but the mother (sometimes with the help of other females) was successful in protecting her infant, who in fact survived . . . . The mother of the first infant showed estrous behavior 13 days after the death of her infant. Several copulations between the mother and the infanticidal male were observed. The mother of the second infant resumed estrus 16 days after its disappearance . . . . This female, too, mated with the infanticidal male."

Five other cases have been established in two other colobine species: *P. cristata* (Wolf, 1980, one confirmed case) and *C. badius* (Struhsaker and Leland, 1987, one confirmed case). Infanticide (though not directly observed) has been deduced to occur in three other colobine primates: *P. senex* (Rudran, 1973), *C. guereza* (Oates, 1977), and *C.b. rufomitratus* (Marsh, 1979). Among noncolobine Old World monkeys, several instances of infanticide have been observed directly in two species of guenons: *Cercopithecus ascanius* (Struhsaker, 1977) and *C. mitis* (Butynski, 1982). For example, in a redtail monkey (*C. ascanius*) one-male "harem" of about 10 females with their infants, Leland et al. (1984) observed a new male displace the harem male; the new male subsequently killed two newborn infants in the group within 2½ months of his takeover. In the same study area, in a one-male group of blue monkeys, an invading male drove out the original harem male and killed one infant and was suspected of killing a second only a few hours later.

Also among noncolobine Old World monkeys, several cases of infanticide have been documented among two species of baboons, *Papio cynocephalus* and *P. anubis* (Collins et al., 1984), with many more instances being strongly indicated by cases of fights and wounding. Infanticide is also strongly suspected to have occurred among several groups of chacma baboons (*P. ursinus*) (Busse and Hamilton, 1981; Collins et al., 1984).

Among New World monkeys, only red howler monkey males (*Alouatta seniculus*) have been observed to engage in infant killing (Rudran, 1973; Crockett and Sekulic, 1984). Crockett and Sekulic maintain that infant killing among these howlers in Venezuela occurs frequently, coincident with many changes in adult male group membership, as well as with changes in the breeding status of co-resident males (Sekulic, 1983). During a one-year study, Sekulic observed directly one case of infanticide and 26 cases of infant disappearance or severe injury without disappearance. Of the latter 26 cases, she considered 14 cases of disappearance and 3 injuries only to be "very probably" infanticide or attempted infanticide. The remaining cases could very possibly have been caused by infanticidal male attacks. She found that infanticidal males were successful in subsequently mating with the mothers of the killed infants; in at least 10 cases, the known or presumed infanticidal male mated with the victim's mother. The next recorded infant births were sired by new or newly dominant males in at least nine case, and probably so in three more (Crockett and Sekulic, 1984).

Among the anthropoid apes, infant killing has been documented to occur among gorillas (Fossey, 1979, 1984) and among chimpanzees (Goodall, 1977).

The first serious theoretical attempt to evaluate the function and, hence, the evolution of such a controversial and unexpected social happenstance as infanticide among primates was done by Hrdy (1979), who proposed five categories of function: (1) exploitation of infants as a food resource, usually through cannibalism; (2) resource competition where the death of the infant increases resources available to the perpetrator or his/her relatives; (3) sexual selection where individuals (usually males) improve their own opportunities to breed by eliminating the dependent progeny of a potential mate; (4) parental manipulation of progeny where parents can increase their own lifetime reproductive success or that of other offspring by eliminating some of their offspring; and (5) social pathology where cases of infanticide reduce the fitness of all individuals involved and is conditioned by external factors creating a breakdown in social structure.

Neither parental manipulation nor exploitation as a food resource has been proposed to explain the occurrence of infanticide among nonhuman primates. The principal arguments revolve around the sexual selection (reproductive advantage) versus social pathology interpretations, with some few investigators invoking a resource competition model. For example, as infanticide became widely accepted to occur in several species of langurs, three "competing" explanations (often more vitriolic than enlightening in nature) were proffered, at least as these explanations related to the colobine primates. The most compelling argument, proposed first by Hrdy (1974) and subsequently refined by Hausfater (1984), was based on the sexual selection model. It held that on average, a male gains a reproductive advantage by killing unrelated infants, thereby bringing the female into estrus, whereupon the infanticidal male copulates and impregnates her so she will bear his offspring. In response to this interpretation, other langur researchers maintained this behavior was aberrant and abnormal and was the result of overcrowding in areas in which poor habitat quality had been produced primarily by human disturbances (Dolhinow, 1977; Curtin and Dolhinow, 1978; Boggess, 1979, 1984). A third, partly derivative explanation, proposed by Rudran (1973) for the purple-faced langur (*P. senex*), holds that competition over limited resources was the causative agent.

## Category V: Mating and Reproductive Strategies

Investment in one's own offspring is, of course, a form of reproductive strategy, aimed at maximizing individual male reproductive success (in the Darwinian sense) through enhanced infant survival. Consequently, it is stating the obvious to say that all the species discussed in the subsection titled "Category I: Caretaking, or True Paternal Investment" could also be considered to invest in offspring as a reproductive strategy. If nothing else, this overlap points to the dilemma inherent in the attempt to establish a clear-cut, unambiguous, and exclusive typology for categorizing male care among primates.

Many species of birds have evolved communal rearing of and investment in offspring as a reproductive strategy; perhaps some species of primates have done so, as well. Most callithrichids have been considered to be truly and exclusively monogamous in their mating patterns and social structure. However, recent work by Goldizen and others has shown that in fact some callithrichid species have polyandrous mating systems and that others have had even more complex social systems with multiple breeding females (Goldizen and Terborgh, 1987; Dawson, 1978; Soini, 1982; Rylands, 1981; Garber et al., 1984; Goldizen, 1987). For example, studies of marked groups of saddle-back tamarins (*S. fuscicollis*) in Peru over five years show marked changes in group composition, with frequent intergroup transfers of individuals: only 17% of all groups observed were monogamous groups of one male and one female, whereas 62% of all groups observed contained one female and more than one adult male; 12% of all groups observed contained two females and more than one male; also seen were two females and one male—6% of all groups observed—and only males— 3% of all groups observed. Furthermore, a single group might change composition over time, being monogamous at one time only to become polyandrous sometime later.

Remarkable as this flexible social system among some marmosets and tamarins now appears to be, even more remarkable is the fact that in every case all adult group members participated in all aspects of infant care. Specifically, among the polyandrous groups, nonbreeding adult males (presumably not related) are involved in infant caretaking, and significantly so. As studies of monogamous callithrichids show, "helpers" are critical for the successful rearing of infants, this need being the result primarily of the fact that twins are common in these species and the weights of these neonates represent upwards of 25% of maternal weight (increasing to 50% by the time of weaning) (Leutenegger, 1980).

Since individuals who carry the infants do not feed them, and of course, lactation places significant nutritional demands on the female, more than a single caregiver (especially maternal) appears to be necessary for successful reproduction. It is not coincidental that in the five years of study, no single pair (without helpers) has been seen to produce young in wild saddle-back tamarins. Marmosets and tamarins have solved this reproductive dilemma of multiple births and large infants with a flexible social and mating system that recruits additional caretakers, both monogamously (by using immature siblings) and polyandrously (by incorporating additional potential fathers). Groups without nonreproductive helpers (at least among saddle-back tamarins, but probably among other species as well) typically accept another male as a second breeder and helper. By sharing the probability of siring infants and then helping to care for them cooperatively, males enhance their mutual reproductive success.

Perhaps the most curious notion about the use of infants to increase individual reproductive success comes from the extreme cases of infanticide just discussed. The "sexual selection" interpretation proposes that killing an infant is an adaptive strategy for the infanticidal male whereby he eliminates the progeny of a competitor, while at the same time, he induces the female into reproductive receptivity so he may copulate with and inseminate her. This form of infanticide is most prevalent among polygynously mating primates where breeding is nonseasonal and male tenure and access to females is relatively short. Therefore, for infant killing to function in the sexual selection scheme, it is expected that several conditions should be met: (1) the infanticidal male should be unrelated to the infant he kills or to its close relatives; (2) infants should be unweaned (i.e., young), and the interval should be short between infant loss and postlactation estrus for the mother; (3) the mother should become sexually receptive and the male should gain sexual access to her as a consequence of killing her infant; (4) the social structure should be such that only one resident male sexually monopolizes estrous females or such that one or two dominant males sexually monopolize females and exclude subordinate group males from sexual access; and (5) females should develop counter-strategies to blunt the propensity of males to kill the females' offspring.

The degree to which one may interpret this phenomenon of using infants as part of a larger set of reproductive strategies depends on how well the data from the documented cases of infanticide fit these predictions. In point of fact, for those cases where the data are best, the data fit well indeed (Hausfater and Hrdy, 1984). A detailed theoretical treatment of these competing explanations, which is outside the scope of this review, is provided in the seminal volume edited by Hausfater and Hrdy (1984), and readers are strongly encouraged to refer to this work for what is today the definitive view of this phenomenon. For the purpose of this chapter, it is useful to note that in their brief but cogent review of the relevant parameters of the two dozen cases of known nonhuman primate infanticide, Struhsaker and Leland (1987) list several strong (causative?) correlations: (1) in the overwhelming majority of cases, the perpetrator male was a recent immigrant or one that did not live in the infant's social group (and therefore was unlikely to have been related to the infant), (2) most cases occurred in species characterized by a one-male/multiple-female type of social structure, (3) most cases followed recent male replacement or an immigrant male's rise in social rank over a resident male, and (4) in a large number of cases, the infanticidal male copulated with the mother of the killed infant. The available data seem to fit the sexual selection hypothesis best, for it is found that infanticide (a) occurs more often in one-male breeding groups, (b) has led to counter-strategies by females (e.g., postconception copulations that confuse paternity), and (c) leads to sexual/reproductive access by the infanticidal male to the mother of the killed infant; in addition, neither males (nor females, for that matter) kill their relatives.

Hamadryas (*Papio hamadryas*) and gelada (*Theropithecus gelada*) baboons are characterized by a multilevel social structure. The basic social and reproductive unit is the "harem," or OMU, composed of a single adult male and several adult females with immature offspring (and, sometimes, includes immature male "followers") (see Anderson and Bielert, this volume). Several hamadryas OMUs may become strongly and consistently associated with one another (especially during foraging forays) and form into units referred to as "clans" (Abegglen, 1984). Among geladas (where membership is less consistent), these clusterings are called "bands" (Dunbar and Dunbar, 1975). Among both species, bands/clans congregate into larger, but temporary, associations (usually at restricted resources such as water or cliff sleeping sites) called "herds." While the social structure of these two species is quite remarkable in itself, it is the process of the formation of the basic social unit, the OMU, that draws one's attention.

There are several strategies by which a male establishes his own OMU. One approach involves "using" immatures (not infants in the strict chronological sense). For example, it is not uncommon for a "floater," or "follower," male (usually a subadult) to "kidnap" or "adopt" or otherwise establish a strong relationship with a juvenile female who belongs to an established OMU. Among hamadryas, this kind of event usually occurs between a male and a female of two different OMUs belonging to the same clan, i.e., between individuals that most likely have known each other for a period of time. The male becomes most solicitous of this female, e.g., carrying her across difficult terrain, grooming, and sitting close, and thereby establishes a strong bond with this female. Among geladas, this approach may be an evolutionary offshoot of males' exploitation of infants in a more classic "agonistic buffering" situation (Dunbar, 1984).

A common and cardinal explanatory thread among most of the baboon studies examining male/infant relationships has been the notion of "special affiliations" between the infant, the caretaking male, and the mother of the infant. Smuts (1982, 1985) and Strum (1984) have been particularly vigorous in their exposition of this point of view, arguing convincingly that the "special relationship," or "affiliation," between a male and an infant is more important than probable kinship. Positive male/infant interactions promote infant survival and fitness through protection, carrying, and other affiliative behaviors. These authors reject the kinship investment interpretation because in many cases these males are judged unlikely to be the father of these infants: "... for a male the existence of a special relationship with the mother is a necessary and sufficient condition for the existence of an affiliative relationship between him and the female's infant; being a probable father is likely to result in an affiliative relationship with the infant only if the male also has a special relationship with the mother" (Smuts, 1982, p. 108).

Why then are these unrelated males forming special affiliations with and investing in these infants? Proponents of this view suggest that males form special relationships with infants as a means whereby they may develop a closer and stronger affiliative relationship with the infant's mother. This enhanced, or special, relationship with the mother, in turn, enhances the male's chances of mating with this female in the future. Rasmussen (1983) has shown, for example, that a preferential relationship between male and female baboons outside the sexual consortship influences the females to be more cooperative sexual consort partners during estrus.

Taub has identified three male mating strategies among wild Barbary macaques (Taub, 1980). One of these, the "peripheralize and attract strategy" (PAS), is utilized by the lower ranking males and involves indirect approaches, at a distance, to females and attracting the females' attention by "displaying" to them. These displays take many forms, the most common being the noisy shaking of branches. However, males utilizing display as a sexual gambit often retrieve infants and deliberately carry them in full view of an estrous female. It is probably not coincidental that all subadult males, who are the males that are the most heavily involved in male/infant interactions, use the PAS tactic. Taub has postulated that by carrying any infant (not necessarily that of the estrous female), a male signals both his willingness and ability to take care of infants. The sight of this male carrying an infant and the message it sends to the female regarding future "paternal" resources functions to induce that female to join the PAS male carrying an infant and to copulate with him. This using of infants as a "flag" to attract the attention of a female is likely to be a modification, serving special communication purposes, of the extensive male/infant system characteristic of this species, and the behavior is tied to the more general phenomenon of paternal investment (see in this section the subsection titled "Category I: Caretaking, or True Paternal Investment"). In turn, the peculiar form of female choice of all group males for mating in this species (Taub, 1980) is believed to be a female stratagem for inducing greater male participation in the babysitting of infants.

## Category VI: None (Tolerance and Ignoring)

If there is a general rule regarding the role of adult males in associations with infants, it would be this: Most males of most primate species most often ignore infants and do not interact directly with them. To be sure, males play a very important part in infant survival and fitness, but it is predominantly passive and indirect in most species. For example, male roles in most species are described as follows: protectors of the social unit from predators; guardians of group integrity from contact with intergroup conspecifics; protectors from competition from extragroup, sympatric, nonconspecific primates; and peacekeepers to insure against destructive intragroup aggression. One should not conclude prematurely, however, that males of such typically uninterested species as rhesus monkeys cannot or will not interact positively with infants. Indeed, the potential (= genetic underpinning) for some quite remarkable male/infant relationships appears to exist among some cercopithecine primates who otherwise typically ignore infants, and, perhaps, possessing this potentiality is common to all primates. What it seems to require for its explicit expression is a necessary and sufficient set of environmental and social circumstances not usually characteristic of that species.

The literature on rhesus monkeys is most illuminating on this point. Most studies of rhesus monkeys, whether of wild populations (Lindburg, 1971), of provisioned, free-ranging colonies (Vessey and Meikle, 1984; Berman, 1982), or of captive groups (Rowell, 1974; Spencer-Booth, 1968) indicate that adult males rarely show interest in or interact with infants. Vessey and Meikle (1984), for example, found that less than 1% of all adult male interactions were with infants, and indeed, no adult male was observed to interact with infants during extensive focal male-observation sessions over a two-year period. Yet, under the catalytic stimulus of appropriate social conditions, rhesus males may show remarkably intense relationships with infants. Postulating that the lack of male interest in infants stemmed more from maternal restrictiveness and few opportunities than it did from a lack of innate motivation, Redican (1976) and Redican and Mitchell (1974) removed mothers and allowed a series of single male/ infant pairs to live together in single cages. Not only were males tolerant of these infants (as their wild counterparts would be), but they also became quite accomplished surrogate "mothers." These males exhibited high levels of carrying and grooming to the same extent that mothers would, and they actively protected the infants from sources of danger. Play between these pairs was far more intense and reciprocal than that between mother/infant control pairs.

Suomi (1977, 1979), in a series of similar investigations, allowed infants to be raised in "nuclear" families. Infants raised under such conditions preferred their mothers to other adult females but their fathers to other adult males. The adult males showed quite stable behavioral profiles relative to their positive interactions with infants over time, in contrast to the females (Suomi, 1979). Suomi has interpreted this finding as consistent with Redican's view that maternal restrictiveness holds male/infant associations in check. Lack of opportunity and/or maternal restrictiveness may not explain all cases of male uninterest in infants, however, and there seem to be fundamental species differences in this potentiality or at least in the variables that promote or discourage its exhibition. For example, it seems to be a species-typical phenomenon that langur females are extremely nonrestrictive concerning access to neonates, but male langurs are nevertheless characteristically uninvolved with infants.

Also, it has been noted elsewhere that males may show an extreme form of caretaking by adopting orphaned infants; apparently, a vulnerable, abandoned infant in the absence of its mother is a sufficient stimulus for eliciting the expression of this "paternal" potentiality, at least on a short-term basis.

## General Discussion and Conclusion

This review suggests several fairly fundamental and important ideas regarding the biological and phylogenetic foundations of male interest in and interaction with infants and immatures among primates.

As an ordinal phenomenon, the interaction between males and immatures among primates is a relatively infrequent phenomenon. If one uses as the yardstick of measure such indices as the number of taxa in which such interactions occur, the number of males among all potential actors who actually engage in some form of infant interaction, and the rate or frequency at which those few participating males actually do associate with infants, then one is forced to this conclusion.

On the other hand, males of many primate species, including humans, interact with immature conspecifics in a widely diverse and an enormously complex number of ways (in this volume, see Bullough; Diamond; Mackey; Schiefenhövel; Silva). Perhaps the most characteristic feature of these interactions is the structural and functional heterogeny of their occurrence. This heterogeny makes two-dimensional typological classifications, such as the one used in this chapter, more heuristic than factual; such categorizations are in many ways artificial and subjective, and the reader should always keep a healthy cynicism about this and any other attempt at a definitive classification. It does serve, however, to demonstrate the substantial variability in structure, function, and distribution of male/infant interactions in the Order.

The appearance of male/infant interactions among primates is probably an ancient characteristic. In his comprehensive opus, Hershkovitz (1977) notes that callithrichid anatomy, feeding adaptations, and locomotor systems probably were established early and probably have changed little since the Cenozoic. If one presumes, as seems plausible, that their small size dictated monogamy/polyandry and male investment in offspring (see Leutenegger, 1980, for a detailed discussion of the evolution of callithrichid social structure, mating systems, and male investment), the genetic basis for primate paternalism may be 25 million years old.

Interestingly, it is among the oldest (callithrichids) and the youngest (siamangs and hominids) groups of primates that one finds the most intensive and extensive investment in offspring. Thus, both the potential for elaborate male/infant bonds and its actual expression may have developed very early in primate evolution. Whether male/infant interaction has been an evolutionary variation on the basic theme of true paternal investment, which can account for the appearance of functionally diverse male/infant behaviors in Old World cercopithecines, or whether such interaction evolved independently is not possible to ascertain with the status of current technology. However, the fact that male/infant interactions among some of the macaques are structurally very stereotypic (e.g., Barbary macaques, Taub, 1984) suggests a strong genetic component, which in turn suggests that these interactions may be phylogenetically very old phenomena. Species that typically do not exhibit male/infant interactions can become remarkably "paternalistic" under suitably stimulating conditions, again suggesting that the underlying genetic potentiality for the development of strong male/infant bonds is an old primate characteristic.

As this survey of the Order has shown, the interaction of males with infants is multifunctional. Some of these interactions function as important, nay, critical contributions to infant survival and fitness: males may contribute significantly to the rearing of their own infants, and they may form strong affiliative bonds with infants that are not related to them. Other functions put the infant in grave danger: males exploit them for use in intermale rivalries and may kill infants so as to breed with their mothers; the enhancement of an individual male's fitness (in the Darwinian sense) has outweighed the loss to the infant's fitness in the latter cases. It appears clear, then, that a structurally similar set of "paternalistic" behaviors can operate in a multiplicity of functional contexts depending on what the selective advantage is and to whom it accrues. For this reason, this heterogeneous distribution of male/infant behaviors in the Order can appear to be so contradictory.

Two sets of structurally similar behaviors (males interacting with infants) may differ in a number of fundamental, especially functional, ways, often depending on the context and the value of the resource being competed for. Several different interpretations of superficially similar behaviors are not mutually incompatible; evidence for the existence of one does not *ipso facto* exclude the possible occurrence of the other. This point becomes manifestly clear when one recognizes that among baboons a male may both caretake **and** exploit an infant, even his own. There is no *a priori* reason to expect a single, monolithic explanatory model to accommodate the occurrence of "paternal" behavior among primates.

There is a well-developed system of direct use and exploitation of infants by males to assuage relations between themselves and other competing males. Infants have become "objects" that are means to another end; they are successful in promoting those ends because of the strong sign stimuli they represent for primates. This using has been taken to an extreme form among some colobine primates where infants are sacrificed to enhance an individual male's own reproductive fitness, obviously at the expense of the infant, its biological father, and possibly its mother (depending on her ultimate reproductive output with other males).

Is it possible that this potentiality for using, which is so clearly evident among some nonhuman primate males, has become perturbated over time through social evolutionary forces into the potential for exploitation (of whatever means) among hominids? Is it possible that the proclivity among some human males for pedophilic relationships evolved from a system where a baboon or macaque male used infants to ameliorate his relations with other males? The answers to these questions currently are unknown (see Feierman, this volume, Chapter 1). What seems certain is this: male primates can and do harmfully exploit infants, including their own offspring, with tactics that put the infant at risk, for the selfish purpose of enhancing the male's social and competitive position. This capability of a male to use an infant as an object is phylogenetically old. Whether this behavioral complex represents the biological matrix upon which hominid infant exploitation developed is a critical link in the understanding of the biosocial dimensions of pedophilia.

Caution in extrapolating the findings about nonhuman-primate paternalism to humans must be exercised, because in the strictest sense, male/infant interactions as surveyed here are essentially asexual. (However, see de Waal, this volume.) Males do indeed exploit infants, but it is not sexual exploitation (for a discussion of mating behavior among primates, see Anderson and Bielert, this volume; Pusey, this volume). To emphasize this notion, it is perhaps necessary to clarify what may be misperceived upon casual examination as sexual manipulation of infants by males in some Old World species.

Among most primates, tactile stimulation is a potent social glue, and mutual grooming is the most common of social behaviors. It is not uncommon during intensive grooming bouts, especially in the anogenital area, that males of all ages have erections. Male macaque and baboon caretakers may on occasion inspect, manipulate, and groom the anogenital areas of the infants they caretake, and infants may also investigate their caretaking males' genital areas as they play about on them. This behavior is a subset of a more general social/tactile phenomenon of grooming, and sometimes the infants will have erections (especially among baboons [Taub, personal observation]). Such tactile stimuli function as social facilitators among Old World primates, with sexual arousal as a by-product. Such behavior clearly is **not** sexual exploitation.

There are no behaviors or constellations of sociobehavioral relationships among nonhuman primate males and infants that are clearly analogous, either in structure or function, to human pedophilia, in which the primary motivation, at least for the adult, appears to be sexuoerotic gratification (see Silva, this volume; Money, this volume). Whether there are biological or phylogenetic underpinnings among nonhuman primate males to the evolution and expression of human pedophilia in modern human society is an altogether different question (see Feierman, this volume, Chapter 1). However, there appears to be no nonhuman primate "model" for human pedophilia.

## Summary

This chapter reviewed and synthesized what is known about primate paternalism, which was classified into the following categories of function: I. Caretaking, or True Paternal Investment; II. Affiliation; III. Using and Exploitation; IV. Abuse and Infanticide; V. Mating and Reproductive Strategies; and VI. None (Tolerating and Ignoring). The types of primate paternalism were discussed on the basis of their distribution in different social structures and mating systems. If the number of taxa in which primate paternalism is found is considered along with the actual number of males involved and the relatively low frequency of occurrence, then such associations must be considered to be relatively infrequent. Nevertheless, humans are a species in which this relatively infrequent association is found. Although the origin of adult-male/infant interactions among primates probably exists as an ancient characteristic, great caution must be exercised in looking for the homologs and analogs of human pedophilia in primate paternalism in nonhuman species. Sexual arousal in the context of nonhuman adult-male/infant social grooming appears to be a relatively minor and rare by-product of a more general tactile stimulation in the service of affiliation.

## References

Abegglen, J.J. *On socialization in hamadryas baboons.* Cranbury, N.J.: Associated University Presses, 1984.

Alexander, B.K. Parental behavior of adult male Japanese monkeys. *Behaviour*, 1970, *36*, 270-285.

Altmann, J. *Baboon mothers and infants.* Cambridge, Mass.: Harvard University Press, 1980.

Auerbach, K.G., and Taub, D.M. Paternal behavior in a captive "harem" group of cynomolgus macaques (*Macaca fascicularis*). *Laboratory Primate Newsletter*, 1979, *18*(2), 7-11.

Berman, C. The ontogeny of social relationships with group companions among free-ranging infant rhesus monkeys, 1: Social networks and differentiation. *Animal Behaviour*, 1982, *30*, 149-162.

Berman, C. Effects of being orphaned: A detailed case study of an infant rhesus. *In* R.A. Hinde (Ed.), *Primate social relationships: An integrated approach.* Oxford: Blackwell, 1983, pp. 79-81.

Bernstein, I. Activity patterns in a sooty mangabey group. *Folia Primatologica*, 1976, *26*, 185-206.

Bertrand, M. The behavioral repertoire of the stumptail macaque. *Bibliotheca Primatologica*, 1969, *11*, 1-273.

Boggess, J. Troop male membership changes and infant killing in langurs (*Presbytis entellus*). *Folia Primatologica*, 1979, *32*, 65-107.

Boggess, J. Infant killing and male reproductive strategies in langurs (*Presbytis entellus*). *In* G. Hausfater and S.B. Hrdy (Eds.), *Infanticide: Comparative and evolutionary perspectives*. Hawthorne, N.Y.: Aldine, 1984, pp. 283-310.

Bolin, I. Male parental behavior in black howler monkeys (*Alouatta palliata pigra*) in Belize and Guatemala. *Primates*, 1981, *22*, 349-360.

Box, H.O. A social developmental study of young monkeys (*Callithrix jacchus*) within a captive family group. *Primates*, 1975, *16*, 419-435.

Box, H.O. Quantitative data on the carrying of young monkeys (*Callithrix jacchus*) by other members of their family groups. *Primates*, 1977, *18*, 475-484.

Brown, J.L. *The evolution of behavior*. New York: Norton, 1975.

Brown, K., and Mack, D.S. Food sharing among captive *Leontopithecus rosalia*. *Folia Primatologica*, 1978, *29*, 268-290.

Brown, R.E. Introduction to the symposium: Paternal behavior. *American Zoologist*, 1985, *25*, 781-783.

Busse, C.B. Triadic interactions among male and infant chacma baboons. *In* D.M. Taub (Ed.), *Primate paternalism*. New York: Van Nostrand Reinhold, 1984, pp. 186-212.

Busse, C.B., and Hamilton, W.J. Infant carrying by male chacma baboons. *Science*, 1981, *212*, 1282-1283.

Butynski, T.M. Harem-male replacement and infanticide in the blue monkey (*Cercopithecus mitis stuhlmanii*) in the Kibale Forest, Uganda. *American Journal of Primatology*, 1982, *3*, 1-22.

Carpenter, C.R. A field study in Siam of the behavior and social relations of the gibbon (*Hylobates lar*). *Comparative Psychology Monographs*, 1940, *16*, 1-212.

Cebul, M.S., and Epple, G. Father-offspring relationships in laboratory families of saddle-back tamarins (*Saguinus fuscicollis*). *In* D.M. Taub (Ed.), *Primate paternalism*. New York: Van Nostrand Reinhold, 1984, pp. 1-19.

Chalmers, N. The social behavior of free-living mangabeys in Uganda. *Folia Primatologica*, 1968, *8*, 263-281.

Chivers, D.J. *The siamang in Malaya*. Contributions to primatology, Vol. 4. Basel: S. Karger, 1974.

Chivers, D.J., and Raemaekers, J.J. Long-term changes in behavior. *In* D.J. Chivers (Ed.), *Malayan forest primates: Ten years' study in a tropical rain forest*. New York: Plenum Press, 1980.

Cleveland, J., and Snowdon, C.T. The complex vocal repertoire of the adult cotton-top tamarin (*Saguinus oedipus oedipus*). *Zeitschrift für Tierpsychologie*, 1982, *58*, 231-270.

Collins, D.A. Social behavior and patterns of mating among adult yellow baboons (*Papio c. cynocephalus* L. 1766). Unpublished Ph.D. dissertation, 1981, Cambridge University.

Collins, D.A. Relations between adult male and infant baboons. *In* J.G. Else and P.C. Lee (Eds.), *Primate ontogeny, cognition and social behaviour.* Cambridge, England: Cambridge University Press, 1986, pp. 205-218.

Collins, D.A., Busse, C.D., and Goodall, J. Infanticide in two populations of savannah baboons. *In* G. Hausfater and S.B. Hrdy (Eds.), *Infanticide: Comparative and evolutionary perspectives.* Hawthorne, N.Y.: Aldine, 1984, pp. 193-216.

Crockett, C.M., and Sekulic, R. Infanticide in red howler monkeys (*Alouatta seniculus*). *In* G. Hausfater and S.B. Hrdy (Eds.), *Infanticide: Comparative and evolutionary perspectives.* Hawthorne, N.Y.: Aldine, 1984, pp. 173-192.

Curtin, R., and Dolhinow, P. Primate social behavior in a changing world. *American Scientist,* 1978, *66,* 468-475.

Dawson, G.A. Composition and stability of social groups of the tamarin, *Saguinus oedipus geoffroyi,* in Panama: Ecological and behavioral implications. *In* D.G. Kleiman (Ed.), *The biology and conservation of the Callitrichidae.* Washington, D.C.: Smithsonian Institution Press, 1978, pp. 23-28.

Deag, J.M. A study of the social behaviour and ecology of the wild Barbary macaque *Macaca sylvanus.* Unpublished Ph.D. dissertation, 1974, University of Bristol.

Deag, J.M. Interactions between males and unweaned Barbary macaque: Testing the agonistic buffering hypothesis. *Behaviour,* 1980, *75,* 54-81.

Deag, J.M., and Crook, J. Social behaviour and "agonistic buffering" in the wild Barbary macaque *Macaca sylvana* L. *Folia Primatologica,* 1971, *15,* 183-200.

Dixson, A.F. Observations on the evolution and significance of "sexual skin" in female primates. *In* J.D. Rosenblatt, R.A. Hinde, C. Beer, and M.C. Busnel (Eds.), *Advances in the study of behavior,* Vol. 13. New York: Academic Press, 1983, pp. 63-106.

Dixson, A.F., and Fleming, D. Parental behavior and infant development in owl monkeys (*Aotus trivirgatus griseimembra*). *Journal of Zoology, London,* 1981, *194,* 25-39.

Dolhinow, P. Normal monkeys? *American Scientist,* 1977, *65,* 266.

Dunbar, R.I.M. Infant use by male gelada in agonistic contexts: Agonistic buffering, progeny protection, or soliciting support? *Primates,* 1984, *25,* 28-35.

Dunbar, R., and Dunbar, E. *Social dynamics of gelada baboons.* Basel: S. Karger, 1975.

Epple, G. Parental behavior in *Saguinus fuscicollis* spp. (Callitrichidae). *Folia Primatologica,* 1975, *24,* 221-238.

Epple, G., and Katz, Y. The saddle back tamarin and other tamarins. *In* J. Hearn (Ed.), *Reproduction in New World primates.* Boston: MTP Press Limited, 1983.

Epple, G., and Katz, Y. Social influences on estrogen secretion and ovarian cyclicity in saddle back tamarins (*Saguinus fuscicollis*). *In* C.T. Snowdon, C.H. Brown, and M.R. Peterson (Eds.), *Primate communication.* Cambridge, England: Cambridge University Press, 1984.

Estrada, A. Male-infant interactions among free-ranging stumptail macaques. *In* D.M. Taub (Ed.), *Primate paternalism.* New York: Van Nostrand Reinhold, 1984, pp. 56-87.

Estrada, A., Estrada, R., and Ervin, R. Establishment of a free-ranging troop of stumptail macaques (*Macaca arctoides*): Social relations I. *Primates,* 1977, *18,* 647-676.

Estrada, A., and Sandoval, J. Social relations in a free-ranging group of stumptail macaques (*Macaca arctoides*): Male care behavior I. *Primates,* 1977, *18,* 793-813.

Fossey, D. Development of the mountain gorilla (*Gorilla gorilla beringei*): The first thirty-six months. *In* D.A. Hamburg and E.R. McCowen (Eds.), *The great apes.* Menlo Park, Calif.: Benjamin/Cummings, 1979.

Fossey, D. *Gorillas in the mist.* Boston, Mass.: Houghton Mifflin, 1983.

Fossey, D. Infanticide in mountain gorillas (*Gorilla gorilla beringei*) with comparative notes on chimpanzees. *In* G. Hausfater and S.B. Hrdy (Eds.), *Infanticide: Comparative and evolutionary perspectives.* Hawthorne, N.Y.: Aldine, 1984, pp. 217-236.

Fox, G. Some comparisons between siamang and gibbon behavior. *Folia Primatologica,* 1972, *18,* 122-139.

Fragaszy, D.M., Schwartz, S., and Schinosaka, D. Longitudinal observation of care and development of infant titi monkeys (*Callicebus moloch*). *American Journal of Primatology,* 1982, *2,* 191-200.

Garber, P.A., Moya, L., and Malaga, C. A preliminary field study of the moustached tamarin monkey (*Saguinus mystax*) in northeastern Peru: Questions concerned with the evolution of a communal breeding system. *Folia Primatologica,* 1984, *42,* 17-32.

Gilmore, H.B. The evolution of agonistic buffering in baboons and macaques. Unpublished paper presented at the 46th Annual Meeting of the American Association of Physical Anthropologists, Seattle, Washington, April 1977. *Cited in* S.C. Strum, Why males use infants. *In* D.M. Taub (Ed.), *Primate paternalism.* New York: Van Nostrand Reinhold, 1984, pp. 146-185.

Goldizen, A.W. Tamarins and marmosets: Communal care of offspring. *In* B.B. Smuts, D.L. Cheney, R.M. Seyfarth, R.W. Wrangham, and T.T. Struhsaker (Eds.), *Primate societies.* Chicago: University of Chicago Press, 1987, pp. 34-43.

Goldizen, A.W., and Terborgh, J. Cooperative polyandry and helping behavior in saddle-backed tamarins (*Saguinus fuscicollis*). *In* J.G. Else and P.C. Lee (Eds.), *Primate ecology and conservation*, Vol. 2. Cambridge, England: Cambridge University Press, 1986, pp. 191-198.

Goodall, J. Infant killing and cannibalism in free-living chimpanzees. *Folia Primatologica*, 1977, *28*, 259-282.

Gouzoules, H. Maternal rank and early social interactions of stumptail macaques, *Macaca arctoides*. *Primates*, 1975, *16*, 405-418.

Gouzoules, H. Social relations of males and infants in a troop of Japanese monkeys: A consideration of causal mechanisms. *In* D.M. Taub (Ed.), *Primate paternalism*. New York: Van Nostrand Reinhold, 1984, pp. 127-145.

Gubernick, D.J., and Klopfer, P.H. (Eds.). *Parental care in mammals*. New York: Plenum Press, 1981.

Hamilton, W.J. Significance of paternal investment by primates to the evolution of male-female associations. *In* D.M. Taub (Ed.), *Primate paternalism*. New York: Van Nostrand Reinhold, 1984.

Hasegawa, T., and Hiraiwa, M. Social interactions of orphans observed in a free-ranging troop of Japanese monkeys. *Folia Primatologica*, 1980, *33*, 129-158.

Hausfater, G. Infanticide in langurs: Strategies, counterstrategies, and parameter values. *In* G. Hausfater and S.B. Hrdy (Eds.), *Infanticide: Comparative and evolutionary perspectives*. Hawthorne, N.Y.: Aldine, 1984, pp. 257-282.

Hausfater, G., and Hrdy, S.B. (Eds.). *Infanticide: Comparative and evolutionary perspectives*. Hawthorne, N.Y.: Aldine, 1984.

Heltne, P.G., Turner, D.L., and Wolhandler, J. Maternal and paternal periods in the development of infant *Callimico goeldii*. *American Journal of Physical Anthropology*, 1973, *38*, 555-560.

Hendy-Neely, H., and Rhine, R. Social development of stumptail macaques (*Macaca arctoides*): Momentary touching and other interactions with adult males during the infant's first 60 days of life. *Primates*, 1977, *18*, 589-600.

Hershkovitz, P. *The living New World monkeys, Volume 1*. Chicago: University of Chicago Press, 1977.

Higley, J.D., and Suomi, S.J. Parental behavior in non-human primates. *In* W. Sluckin and M. Herbert (Eds.), *Parental behavior*. London: Basil Blackwell, 1986, pp. 153-207.

Hiraiwa, M. Maternal and alloparental care in a troop of free-ranging Japanese monkeys. *Primates*, 1981, 22(3), pp. 309-329.

Hoage, R.J. Parental care in *Leontopithecus rosalia rosalia*: Sex and age difference in carrying behavior and the role of prior experience. *In* D.G. Kleiman (Ed.), *The biology and conservation of the Callitrichidae*. Washington, D.C.: Smithsonian Institution Press, 1978, pp. 293-306.

Hrdy, S.B. Male-male competition and infanticide among the langurs (*Presbytis entellus*) of Abu, Rajasthan. *Folia Primatologica*, 1974, *22*, 19-58.

Hrdy, S.B. The care and exploitation of nonhuman primate infants by individuals other than the mother. *Advances in the Study of Behavior*, 1976, *6*, 101-158.

Hrdy, S.B. *The langurs of Abu.* Cambridge, Mass.: Harvard University Press, 1977.

Hrdy, S.B. Infanticide among animals: A review, classification, and examination of the implications for the reproductive strategies of females. *Ethology and Sociobiology*, 1979, *1*, 13-40.

Ingram, J.C. Interactions between parents and infants, and the development of independence in the common marmoset. *Animal Behaviour*, 1977, *25*, 811-827.

Ingram, J.C. Parent-infant interactions in the common marmoset (*Callithrix jacchus*). In D.G. Kleiman (Ed.), *The biology and conservation of the Callitrichidae.* Washington, D.C.: Smithsonian Institution Press, 1978, pp. 281-292.

Itani, J. Paternal care in the wild Japanese monkey, *Macaca fuscata fuscata.* *Primates*, 1959, *2*, 61-93.

Izawa, K. A field study of the black-mantle tamarin. *Primates*, 1978, *19*, 241-274.

Kinzey, W.G. Diet and feeding behavior of *Callicebus torquatus.* In T.H. Clutton-Brock (Ed.), *Primate ecology.* London: Academic Press, 1977.

Kleiman, D.G. Parental care in New World primates. *American Zoologist*, 1985, *25*, 857-859.

Kleiman, D.G., and Malcolm, J.R. The evolution of male parental investment in mammals. In D.J. Gubernick and P.H. Klopfer (Eds.), *Parental care in mammals.* New York: Plenum Press, 1981, pp. 347-388.

Klein, H.D. Paternal care and kin selection in yellow baboons, *Papio cynocephalus.* Unpublished Ph.D. dissertation, 1983, University of Washington.

Kuester, J., and Paul, A. Male-infant relationships in semi-free ranging Barbary macaques (*Macaca sylvanus*) of Affenberg Salem/FRG: Testing the "male care" hypothesis. *American Journal of Primatology*, 1986, *10*(4), 315-328.

Kummer, H. Tripartite relations in hamadryas baboons. In S. Altmann (Ed.), *Social communication among primates.* Chicago: University of Chicago Press, 1967.

Kurland, J.A. *Kin selection in the Japanese monkey. Contributions to Primatology, Vol. 12.* Basel: S. Karger, 1977.

Kurland, J.A., and Gaulin, S.J.C. The evolution of male paternal investment: Effects of genetic relatedness and feeding ecology on the allocation of reproductive effort. *In* D.M. Taub (Ed.), *Primate paternalism.* New York: Van Nostrand Reinhold, 1984, pp. 259-308.

Lamb, M.E. (Ed.). *The role of the father in child development* (2nd ed.). New York: Wiley, 1981.

Leland, L., Struhsaker, T., and Butynski, T.M. Infanticide by adult males of three primate species of the Kibale Forest, Uganda: A test of hypotheses. *In* G. Hausfater and S.B. Hrdy (Eds.), *Infanticide: Comparative and evolutionary perspectives.* Hawthorne, N.Y.: Aldine, 1984, pp. 151-172.

Leutenegger, W. Monogamy in callithricids: A consequence of phyletic dwarfism? *International Journal of Primatology,* 1980, *1,* 45-98.

Lindburg, D.G. The rhesus monkey in North India: An ecological and behavioral study. *In* L. Rosenblum (Ed.), *Primate behavior: Developments in field and laboratory research, Vol. 2.* New York: Academic Press, 1971, pp. 1-106.

Locke-Haydon, J., and Chalmers, N.R. The development of infant-caregiver relationships in captive common marmosets (*Callithrix jacchus*). *International Journal of Primatology,* 1983, *4,* 63-81.

Lorenz, R. Management and reproduction of the Goeldi's monkey, *Callimico goeldi* (Thomas 1904) Callimiconidae, Primates. *In* D. Bridgewater (Ed.), *Saving the lion tamarin.* Oglebay Park, W. Va.: The Wild Animal Propagation Trust, 1972, pp. 92-110.

Marsh, C.W. Comparative aspects of social organization in the Tana River red colobus, *Colobus badius rufomitratus. Zeitschrift für Tierpsychologie,* 1979, *51,* 337-362.

Mason, W.A. Social organization of the South American monkey, *Callicebus moloch*: A preliminary report. *Tulane Studies in Zoology,* 1966, *13,* 23-28.

Mason, W.A. Use of space by callicebus groups. *In* P. Jay (Ed.), *Primates: Studies in adaptation and variability.* New York: Holt, Rhinehart, and Winston, 1968, pp. 200-216.

Maynard Smith, J. Parental investment: A prospective analysis. *Animal Behaviour,* 1977, *25,* 1-9.

McGrew, W.C. Parental division of infant caretaking varies with family composition in cotton-top tamarins. *Animal Behaviour,* 1988, *36*(1), 285-286.

Mehlman, P.T. Population ecology of the Barbary macaque (*Macaca sylvanus*) in fir forests of the Ghomara, Moroccan Rif mountains. Unpublished Ph.D. dissertation, 1986, University of Toronto.

Mitchell, G. Paternalistic behavior in primates. *Psychological Bulletin,* 1969, *71,* 399-417.

Mohnot, S.M. Some aspects of social changes and infant-killing in the hanuman langur (*Presbytis entellus*) (Primates: Cercopithecidae) in western India. *Mammalia,* 1971, *35,* 175-198.

Mori, U. Development of sociality and social status. *In* M. Kawai (Ed.), *Ecological and sociological studies of gelada baboons. Contributions to Primatology, Vol. 16.* Basel: S. Karger, 1979, pp. 125-154.

Nicholson, N. Weaning and the development of independence in olive baboons. Unpublished Ph.D. dissertation, 1982, Harvard University.

Oates, J.F. The social life of a black-and-white colobus monkey (*Colobus guereza*). *Zeitschrift für Tierpsychologie*, 1977, *45*, 1-60.

Packer, C. Male care and exploitation of infants in *Papio anubis*. *Animal Behaviour*, 1980, *28*, 512-520.

Pook, A.G. A comparison between the reproduction and parental behavior of the Goeldi's monkey (*Callimico*), and of the true marmosets (*Callitrichidae*). *In* H. Rothe, H.J. Wolters, and J.P. Hearn (Eds.), *Biology and behavior of marmosets*. Göttingen, West Germany: Eignenverlag Hartmut Rothe, 1978, pp. 1-14.

Popp, J.L. Male baboons and evolutionary principles. Unpublished Ph.D. dissertation, 1978, Harvard University.

Ransom, T.W., and Ransom, B.S. Adult male-infant relations among baboons (*Papio anubis*). *Folia Primatologica*, 1971, *16*, 179-195.

Rasmussen, K.L. Influences of affiliative preferences upon the behaviour of male and female baboons during consortships. *In* R.A. Hinde (Ed.), *Primate social relationships: An integrated approach*. Oxford: Blackwell, 1983, pp. 116-120.

Redican, W.K. Adult male-infant interactions in nonhuman primates. *In* M. Lamb (Ed.), *The role of the father in child development*. New York: John Wiley and Sons, 1976, pp. 345-385.

Redican, W.K., and Mitchell, G. Play between adult male and infant rhesus monkeys. *American Zoologist*, 1974, *14*, 295-302.

Redican, W.K., and Taub, D.M. Adult male-infant interactions in nonhuman primates. *In* M.E. Lamb (Ed.), *The role of the father in child development* (2nd ed.). New York: Wiley, 1981, pp. 203-258.

Rhine, R., and Hendy-Neely, H. Social development of stumptail macaques (*Macaca arctoides*): Momentary touching, play and other interactions with aunts and immatures during the infants' first 60 days of life. *Primates*, 1978, *19*, 115-123.

Robinson, J.G. Vocal regulation of spacing in the titi monkey (*Callicebus moloch*). Unpublished Ph.D. dissertation, 1977, University of North Carolina.

Robinson, J.G., Wright, P.C., and Kinzey, W.G. Monogamous cebids and their relatives: Intergroup calls and spacing. *In* B.B. Smuts, D.L. Cheney, R.M. Seyfarth, R.W. Wrangham, and T.T. Struhsaker (Eds.), *Primate societies*. Chicago: University of Chicago Press, 1987, pp. 44-53.

Rowell, T. Contrasting adult male roles in different species of nonhuman primates. *Archives of Sexual Behavior*, 1974, *3*, 143-149.

Rudran, R. Adult male replacement in one-male troops of purple langurs (*Presbytis senex senex*) and its effect on population structure. *Folia Primatologica*, 1973, *19*, 166-192.

Rylands, A.B. Preliminary field observations on the marmoset, *Callithrix humeralifer intermedius* (Hershkovitz, 1977) at Dadanelos, Rio Aripuana, Mato Grosso. *Primates*, 1981, *22*, 46-59.

Sekulic, R. Male relationships and infant deaths in red howler monkeys (*Alouatta seniculus*). *Zeitschrift für Tierpsychologie*, 1983, *61*, 185-202.

Silk, J.B., and Samuels, A. Triadic interactions among *Macaca radiata:* Passports and buffers. *American Journal of Primatology*, 1984, *6*, 373-376.

Smith, E.O., and Peffer-Smith, P.G. Triadic interaction in captive Barbary macaques (*Macaca sylvanus* Linnaeus 1758): "Agonistic buffering"? *American Journal of Primatology*, 1982, 2(1), 99-108.

Smith, E.O., and Peffer-Smith, P.G. Adult male-immature interactions in captive stumptail macaques (*Macaca arctoides*). *In* D.M. Taub (Ed.), *Primate paternalism*. New York: Van Nostrand Reinhold, 1984, pp. 88-112.

Smuts, B. Special relationships between adult male and female olive baboons (*Papio anubis*). Unpublished Ph.D. dissertation, 1982, Stanford University.

Smuts, B. *Sex and friendship in baboons*. Hawthorne, N.Y.: Aldine, 1985.

Snowdon, C.T., and Suomi, S.J. Parental behavior in primates. *In* H. Fitzgerald, J. Mullins, and P. Gage (Eds.), *Child nurturance: Studies of development in nonhuman primates*, Vol. 3. New York: Plenum Press, 1982.

Soini, P. Ecology and population dynamics of the pygmy marmoset, *Cebuella pygmaea*. *Folia Primatologica*, 1982, *39*, 1-21.

Spencer-Booth, Y. The behavior of group companions towards rhesus monkey infants. *Animal Behaviour*, 1968, *16*, 541-557.

Stein, D.M. The nature and function of social interactions between infant and adult male yellow baboons (*Papio cynocephalus*). Unpublished Ph.D. dissertation, 1981, University of Chicago.

Stein, D.M. Ontogeny of infant-adult male relationships during the first year of life for yellow baboons (*Papio cynocephalus*). *In* D.M. Taub (Ed.), *Primate paternalism*. New York: Van Nostrand Reinhold, 1984, pp. 213-243.

Stein, D.M., and Stacey, P.B. A comparison of infant-adult male relations in a one-male group with those in a multi-male group for yellow baboons (*Papio cynocephalus*). *Folia Primatologica*, 1981, *36*, 264-276.

Stevenson, M.F. Birth and perinatal behavior in family groups of the common marmoset (*Callithrix jacchus jacchus*) as compared to other primates. *Journal of Human Evolution*, 1970, *5*, 265-281.

Stevenson, M.F. The behavior and ecology of the common marmoset (*Callithrix jacchus jacchus*) in its natural environment. *In* H. Rothe,

H.J. Wolters, and J.P. Hearn (Eds.), *Biology and behavior of marmosets.* Göttingen, West Germany: Eigenverlag Hartmut Rothe, 1978, p. 298.

Struhsaker, T.T. Infanticide and social organization in the redtail monkey (*Cercopithecus ascanius schmidti*) in the Kibale Forest, Uganda. *Zeitschrift für Tierpsychologie,* 1977, *45,* 75-84.

Struhsaker, T.T., and Leland, L. Infanticide in a patrilineal society of red colobus monkeys. *Zeitschrift für Tierpsychologie,* 1987, *69,* 89-132.

Strum, S.C. Use of females by male olive baboons (*Papio anubis*). *American Journal of Primatology,* 1983, *5,* 93-109.

Strum, S.C. Why males use infants. *In* D.M. Taub (Ed.), *Primate paternalism.* New York: Van Nostrand Reinhold, 1984, pp. 146-185.

Sugiyama, Y. On the social change of hanuman langurs (*Presbytis entellus*) in their natural conditions. *Primates,* 1965, *6,* 213-247.

Sugiyama, Y. An artificial social change in a hanuman langur troop (*Presbytis entellus*). *Primates,* 1966, *7,* 41-72.

Suomi, S. Adult male-infant interactions among monkeys living in nuclear families. *Child Development,* 1977, *48,* 1255-1270.

Suomi, S. Differential development of various social relationships by rhesus monkey infants. *In* M. Lewis and L. Rosenblum (Eds.), *Genesis of behavior, Vol. 2, the child and its family.* New York: Plenum Press, 1979.

Taub, D.M. Aspects of the biology of the wild Barbary macaque (Primates, Cercopithecinae, *Macaca sylvanus* L. 1758): Biogeography, the mating system, and male-infant interactions. Unpublished Ph.D. dissertation, 1978, University of California, Davis.

Taub, D.M. Testing the agonistic buffering hypothesis I. The dynamics of participation in the triadic interaction. *Behavioral Ecology and Sociobiology,* 1980, *6,* 187-197.

Taub, D.M. Male caretaking behavior among wild Barbary macaques (*Macaca sylvanus*). *In* D.M. Taub (Ed.), *Primate paternalism.* New York: Van Nostrand Reinhold, 1984, pp. 337-406.

Taub, D.M. Male-infant interactions in baboons and macaques: A critique and evaluation. *American Zoologist,* 1985, *25,* 861-871.

Taub, D.M., and Kurland, J. Does agonistic buffering buffer agonism? Paper presented at Duke University, March 1988.

Taub, D.M., and Redican, W.K. Adult male-infant interactions in Old World monkeys and apes. *In* D.M. Taub (Ed.), *Primate paternalism.* New York: Van Nostrand Reinhold, 1984, pp. 377-406.

Tenaza, R.R. Territory and monogamy among Kloss' gibbons (*Hylobates klossi*) in Siberut Island, Indonesia. *Zeitschrift für Tierpsychologie,* 1975, *40,* 37-52.

Terborgh, J., and Goldizen, A.W. On the mating system of cooperatively breeding saddle-backed tamarins (*Saguinus fuscicollis*). *Behavioral Ecology and Sociobiology,* 1985, *16,* 293-296.

Tilson, R. Family formation strategies of Kloss' gibbons. *Folia Primatologica*, 1981, *35*, 259-287.

Trivers, R.L. Parental investment and sexual selection. *In* B. Campbell (Ed.), *Sexual selection and the descent of man 1871-1971*. Chicago: Aldine, 1972, pp. 136-179.

Vessey, S., and Meikle, D. Free living rhesus monkeys: Adult male interactions with infants and juveniles. *In* D.M. Taub (Ed.), *Primate paternalism*. New York: Van Nostrand Reinhold, 1984, pp. 113-126.

Viatl, E.A. Social context as a structuring mechanism in captive groups of squirrel monkeys (*Saimiri sciureus*). *Primates*, 1977, *18*, 861-874.

Vogel, C., and Loch, H. Reproductive parameters, adult-male replacements and infanticide among free-ranging langurs (*Presbytis entellus*) at Jodphur (Rajasthan), India. *In* G. Hausfater and S.B. Hrdy (Eds.), *Infanticide: Comparative and evolutionary perspectives*. Hawthorne, N.Y.: Aldine, 1984, pp. 237-256.

Vogt, J.L. Interactions between adult males and infants in prosimians and New World monkeys. *In* D.M. Taub (Ed.), *Primate paternalism*. New York: Van Nostrand Reinhold, 1984, pp. 346-376.

Vogt, J.L., Carlson, H., and Menzel, E. Social behavior of a marmoset (*Saguinus fuscicollis*) group, 1: Parental care and infant development. *Primates*, 1978, *19*, 715-726.

Whiten, A., and Rumsey, T.J. "Agonistic buffering" in the wild Barbary macaque, *Macaca sylvana* L. *Primates*, 1973, *14*, 421-425.

Whitten, P.L. Infants and adult males. *In* B.B. Smuts, D.L. Cheney, R.M. Seyfarth, R.W. Wrangham, and T.T. Struhsaker (Eds.), *Primate societies*. Chicago: University of Chicago Press, 1987, pp. 343-357.

Williams, G.C. *Adaptation and natural selection: A critique of some current evolutionary thought*. Princeton: Princeton University Press, 1966.

Wittenberger, J.F., and Tilson, R.L. The evolution of monogamy: Hypotheses and evidence. *Annual Review of Ecology and Systematics*, 1980, 197-232.

Wolf, K. Social change and male reproductive strategy in silvered leaf-monkeys, *Presbytis cristata*, in Kuala Selangor, Peninsular Malaysia. *American Journal of Physical Anthropology*, 1980, *52*, 294.

Wolters, J. Some aspects of role-taking behavior in captive family groups of the cotton-top tamarin (*Saguinus oedipus oedipus*). *In* H. Rothe, H.J. Wolters, and J.P. Hearn (Eds.), *Biology and behavior of marmosets*. Göttingen, West Germany: Eigenverlag Hartmut Rothe, 1978, pp. 259-278.

Wright, P.C. Biparental care in *Aotus trivirgatus* and *Callicebus moloch*. *In* M.F. Small (Ed.), *Female primates: Studies by women primatologists*. New York: Alan R. Liss, 1984.

# 14
# Sociosexual Behavior Used for Tension Regulation in All Age and Sex Combinations Among Bonobos

Frans B.M. de Waal
*Wisconsin Regional Primate Research Center*
*University of Wisconsin*
*Madison, Wisconsin 53715-1299*

## Introduction

In biology, sexual behavior generally is investigated from the perspective of reproduction. Although the nonreproductive use of the same behavior patterns is common to many species, this use is considered of secondary importance. From an evolutionary perspective, the primary function of sexual behavior, that is, the function most directly relevant for natural selection, is its capacity of producing a zygote. But what if fertile and infertile partner combinations were to engage in sexual behavior with equal intensity and equal frequency? In such a case, it would seem that the reproductive function had decreased in relative importance. This author encountered such a situation during his studies of bonobos (*Pan paniscus*), and it is of particular interest because this little-known ape species, together with the chimpanzee (*P. troglodytes*), is the closest relative of humans.

Before a partial divorce between sexual behavior and its fertilization function is accepted, two conditions must be met. First, sexual contact in infertile partner combinations—such as between individuals of the same sex or between adults and juveniles—should not be a mere substitute for heterosexual contact between adults. In other words, given a choice, the animals should not necessarily give priority to the second type of contact. The frequent isosexual mounts that Yamagiwa (1987) observed within an all-male band of wild gorillas (*Gorilla gorilla beringei*) probably are examples of redirected sex. The dominant silverback males of this band treated the younger males as a "harem," competing over ownership by the same means known of bisexual units. Yamagiwa suggested that the formation of this special male band may have been related to an increased male/female ratio in the population, i.e., to a relative lack of females.

Second, infertile sexual contact would be considered deviant behavior unless such contact is functionally integrated into the species's natural social life. To give an extreme example: a sexual motor pattern that is observed exclusively in individuals reared in isolation would not meet the requirement because it is not possible that sexual behavior evolved under this condition.

In short, it would be accepted that sexual motor patterns serve functions other than fertilization if their infertile use occurs both by choice and in a naturally adaptive context. Both criteria must be kept in mind, because the current study concerns captive bonobos.

The following descriptions are given from an unusual perspective, because the main research focus of this author is not primate sex per se but, rather, aggression and aggression control. Many primate species have evolved special reassurance gestures that maintain peaceful relationships. Calming behavior occurs in response to social tensions (i.e., when there exists a high probability of interindividual conflict) and in the aftermath of fights. Reunions between former adversaries are known as *reconciliations* (de Waal and van Roosmalen, 1979). Whereas reconciliations in the chimpanzee are characterized by kissing and embracing, reconciliations in its congener, the bonobo, often involve genital contact. Intergenerational sex will not be treated separately here, as it is part of this general pattern in bonobo sexuality. For a more detailed presentation of the results, see de Waal (1987, 1988).

## Sociosexual Behavior

The first reports on the bonobo's remarkable sexual behavior resulted from observations of captive animals in German zoos and at the Yerkes Primate Center (Atlanta, Georgia, U.S.A.), followed by field research by a Japanese team at Wamba and a European/American team at Lomako Forest, both in Zaire (Tratz and Heck, 1954; Rempe, 1961; Kirchshofer, 1962; Hübsch, 1970; Jordan, 1977; Savage and Bakeman, 1978; Savage-Rumbaugh and Wilkerson, 1978; Kano, 1980; Kuroda, 1980, 1984; Thompson-Handler, Malenky, and Badrian, 1984; Dahl, 1985, 1986, 1987). These reports agree on the following peculiarities of the species:

1. Compared to the chimpanzee, and to most other primates, the period of sexual receptivity of bonobo females is dramatically extended.
2. Because the vulva is ventrally directed, the genital anatomy seems adapted for face-to-face copulation, a frequently adopted position.
3. Characteristic of the species are lateral genito-genital rubbing movements between females mounted in a ventro-ventral position, one female carrying the other. This pattern is known as *GG-rubbing* (an abbreviation of genito-genital rubbing) (Kuroda, 1980).

These three characteristics also apply to the world's largest captive collection of bonobos, at the San Diego Zoological Garden, which this author studied. Ten of these rare apes were kept in three separate subgroups. One subgroup included an adult male/female pair and an adolescent male. Another subgroup consisted of a mother/infant pair and another adolescent male. The third subgroup included four juveniles, two of each sex. The first two subgroups were merged in the course of the study, allowing the observation of interactions between two adult females and between a fully adult male and two adolescent males. The adolescents were 7 and 8½ years of age, respectively, roughly corresponding in physical and social development with human males of, respectively, 12 and 15 years. The merged group also included a 2-year-old female infant, still being nursed, who frequently interacted with all the others.

The bonobos were observed for nearly 300 hours by the author standing outside the front of their enclosure. Oral accounts of the bonobos' social behavior were recorded either on a cassette audiotape recorder or on the audio channel of a videotape recorder. Video was added at moments of great social activity, such as at feeding time or during the introduction of new group members. Table 14.I provides the distribution of six behavior patterns over 42 dyadic directions (2 directions per pair of individuals) and the combined frequency of sociosexual interaction per dyadic direction per hour of observation. Dyadic directions have been arranged according to the rate with which sociosexual behavior was initiated (the actor is defined as the individual making the first invitational gesture or approach, which individual is not necessarily the sexually most active party). For convenience, the six different behavior patterns will be taken together as "sociosexual" behavior, although this label may be questioned for some of the patterns.

By far the most common pattern was the ventro-ventral mount, observed in no less than 33 different dyadic directions. There is no dyadic category in which this behavior did not occur, except for the one female/female relationship among juveniles. Between the two adult females, the pattern took the form of GG-rubbing, as described previously. This carrying posture—with one female being lifted off the ground, while she clings to her partner much like an infant clings to its mother—allows both

TABLE 14.I. Frequency of six sociosexual interaction patterns among different partner categories of bonobos at the San Diego Zoo. Adults are indicated as Male and Female; adolescents as Adol.; juveniles as Juv.; and the 2-year-old infant as Infant. Each of 42 dyadic directions between individuals is represented separately. Dyadic directions are ordered according to the rate of sociosexual contacts initiated per hour of observation (observation time is not the same for all dyads). Marked with an asterisk are potentially fertile partner combinations.

Table 1: Frequency of six sociosexual interaction patterns among different partner categories of bonobos at the San Diego Zoo. Adults are indicated as Male and Female; adolescents as Adol.; juveniles as Juv., and the two-year-old infant as Infant. Each of 42 dyadic directions between individuals is represented separately. Dyadic directions are ordered according to the rate of sociosexual contacts initiated per hour of observation (observation time is not the same for all dyads). Marked with an asterisk are potentially fertile partner combinations.

| ACTOR | PARTNER | | MOUNTING | | | ORAL & MANUAL | | | Total | Per Hour |
|---|---|---|---|---|---|---|---|---|---|---|
| | | | Ventro-ventral | Ventro-dorsal | Opposite | Genital massage | Oral sex | Mouth-kiss | | |
| Adol. Male | Infant | | 49 | 65 | | | | | 114 | 1.642 |
| Adol. Male | Female | * | 63 | 18 | | | | | 81 | 1.167 |
| Infant | Adol. Male | | 47 | 2 | 3 | | | 1 | 53 | 0.764 |
| Male | Adol. Male | | 5 | 7 | | 23 | | 1 | 36 | 0.642 |
| Female | Female | | 37 | | 4 | | | 1 | 42 | 0.625 |
| Adol. Male | Female | * | 33 | 1 | | | | | 34 | 0.506 |
| Male | Infant | | 19 | 8 | | | | | 27 | 0.490 |
| Infant | Male | | 15 | 5 | | | | | 20 | 0.363 |
| Female | Female | | 10 | 1 | 11 | | | 1 | 23 | 0.342 |
| Juv. Male | Juv. Male | | | 9 | | | 3 | 14 | 26 | 0.320 |
| Adol. Male | Female | * | 25 | 8 | | 1 | | | 34 | 0.311 |
| Male | Adol. Male | | 11 | 7 | 1 | 10 | | 2 | 31 | 0.275 |
| Juv. Male | Juv. Male | | 7 | 1 | | 1 | 5 | 6 | 20 | 0.246 |
| Adol. Male | Adol. Male | | 12 | 3 | | | | | 15 | 0.216 |
| Adol. Male | Male | | 2 | 8 | | 1 | | | 11 | 0.196 |
| Adol. Male | Infant | | 16 | 4 | 1 | | | | 21 | 0.192 |
| Male | Female | * | 9 | | | | | | 9 | 0.163 |
| Male | Female | * | 17 | | | | | | 17 | 0.151 |
| Juv. Female | Juv. Male | | | | | 1 | 4 | 3 | 8 | 0.098 |
| Female | Infant | | 4 | 2 | | | | | 6 | 0.089 |
| Female | Adol. Male | * | 2 | 3 | | | | | 5 | 0.074 |
| Infant | Adol. Male | | 8 | | | | | | 8 | 0.073 |
| Adol. Male | Male | | 3 | | 2 | | 1 | 2 | 8 | 0.071 |
| Juv. Female | Juv. Male | | 2 | | | | 3 | | 5 | 0.061 |
| Female | Male | * | 2 | 1 | | | | | 3 | 0.054 |
| Adol. Male | Female | * | 5 | | | 1 | | | 6 | 0.048 |
| Female | Adol. Male | * | 3 | | | | | | 3 | 0.043 |
| Juv. Female | Juv. Male | | 3 | | | | | | 3 | 0.037 |
| Juv. Male | Juv. Female | | | | | | | 3 | 3 | 0.037 |
| Juv. Female | Juv. Male | | | | | | | 3 | 3 | 0.037 |
| Juv. Male | Juv. Female | | 1 | | | | 1 | 1 | 3 | 0.037 |
| Juv. Male | Juv. Female | | 1 | | | | | 2 | 3 | 0.037 |
| Infant | Female | | | 1 | 1 | | | | 2 | 0.030 |
| Adol. Male | Adol. Male | | 2 | | | | | | 2 | 0.029 |
| Female | Infant | | 3 | | | | | | 3 | 0.027 |
| Female | Adol. Male | * | 2 | 1 | | | | | 3 | 0.024 |
| Female | Adol. Male | * | 1 | | | | | 1 | 2 | 0.018 |
| Female | Male | * | | 1 | | 1 | | | 2 | 0.018 |
| Juv. Male | Juv. Female | | | | | | | 1 | 1 | 0.012 |
| Juv. Female | Juv. Female | | | | | | | 1 | 1 | 0.012 |
| Infant | Female | | 1 | | | | | | 1 | 0.009 |
| Juv. Female | Juv. Female | | | | | | | | 0 | 0.000 |
| Total | | | 420 | 156 | 23 | 39 | 17 | 43 | 698 | |

Figure 14.1. A young adolescent male bonobo (7 years old) is mounted ventro-ventrally by a 2-year-old infant. The infant presses her vulva against the male's erect penis (no intromission occurs) while he performs a series of rapid upward pelvic thrusts.

females to make sideways rubbing movements. In contrast, the posture during so-called "mutual penis rubbing" resembles that of a heterosexual mating, with one male (usually the younger) passively on his back, the other male thrusting on him. Because both males have an erection and because intromission does not occur, their penises rub together. Not even attempts to achieve intromission were observed, and ejaculation never resulted.

A frequent posture involving the female infant was one in which she climbed on the belly of an adolescent male and pressed her vulva against his genitals, whereupon the male—either in a sitting or a recumbent position—made a series of pelvic movements (Figure 14.1). On other occasions, the infant presented for a ventro-dorsal mount, similar to the posture in Figure 14.2 between an adult male and an infant male (this photograph was taken years after the current study). Mounts with the female infant never resulted in intromission or ejaculation. As can be gathered from Table 14.I, sociosexual contacts of adults and adolescents with the infant frequently were initiated by the infant herself (i.e., 32.9%).

Ventro-dorsal mounting positions are typical of most primates. Chimpanzees, for instance, mate in this position almost exclusively (McGinnis, 1973; Savage-Rumbaugh and Wilkerson, 1978; de Waal, personal observations). The low frequency of ventro-dorsal relative to ventro-ventral mounts in the San Diego bonobo colony may not be typical of the species; according to most reports on other populations, both captive and wild, the ventro-dorsal mounting position is the more common one in this species, employed between 62% and 74% of the time (e.g., Jordan, 1977; Kano, 1980; Thompson-Handler, Malenky, and Badrian, 1984). The important point, though, is that thus far all investigators have reported the regular use of both positions, which means that *both* can be considered species-typical.

A rare mounting pattern was observed between the adult females, with the partners facing in opposite directions. While one female lay on her back, the other stood over her, with her back turned, rubbing her genitals against her recumbent partner's. A similar posture occurred a few times between males, with both males standing quadrupedally back-to-back, rubbing their scrota together.

Two oral sociosexual patterns occurred almost exclusively in the group of juveniles (i.e., 83.3%; see Table 14.I). One pattern is the mouth-to-mouth kiss, which in the bonobo has a strikingly sensual character because of prolonged tongue-tongue interaction (Figure 14.3). The second pattern is fellatio, that is, one partner taking the penis of another in the mouth. These two sociosexual patterns frequently occurred in the context of rough-and-tumble play. A bout of chasing and wrestling would be interrupted by sociosexual games in which all four juveniles might participate, some of them mounting, others engaging in the two just-described oral patterns. Play would resume within a few minutes.

The sixth sociosexual behavior pattern is manual massage of another individual's genitals. The large majority of instances (i.e., 84.6%) was directed by the adult male to one of the adolescent males (Figure 14.4). The younger male, with back straight and legs apart, would present his erect penis to the adult male, who would loosely close his hand around the shaft, making caressing up-and-down movements. This pattern is the social equivalent of masturbation, in which males also engaged. Neither genital massage nor masturbation was observed to result in ejaculation.

## Partner Choice

Assuming that the two adolescent males were fertile (both were capable of semen production), 12 dyadic directions concern potentially fertile partner combinations (Table 14.I). The mean ($\pm$SE) hourly rate of sociosexual initiatives in these directions was $0.22\pm0.10$, compared to $0.23\pm0.06$ in infertile directions. The difference between these two means is nonsignificant (t-test, $t = 0.16$, $df = 40$). If the analysis is limited to mounting behavior or if the data are combined for both directions per dyad, the same conclusion applies, that is, fertile and infertile partner combinations show virtually identical frequencies of sociosexual behavior.

Figure 14.2. A 2-year-old male infant presents to an adult male during a ventro-dorsal mount without intromission.

Another way of summarizing the data is to calculate the rate of sociosexual initiatives dependent on two factors: (a) relative age of the partner and (b) sex combination. Four age classes were distinguished: adult (10 years and older); adolescent (7-9 years); juvenile (3-6 years); and infant (0-3 years). Partners can belong to the same age class as actors or to an older or a younger class. Three intersex directions were distinguished: male toward female; female toward male; and same-sex combinations. Figure 14.5 gives the mean rate of sociosexual behavior (±SE) per category. The figure illustrates a relatively high level of heterosexual initiatives toward older partners both by males and by females. Males more often initiated contact with younger partners of the opposite sex than did females. Heterosexual contacts were relatively uncommon between partners of the same age class.

Isosexual initiatives, finally, were mainly directed at partners of the actor's own or a younger age class.

Although this analysis corrects for subgroup composition and observation time, partner choice was not unlimited at the San Diego Zoo. The two juvenile females, for example, exhibited relatively low rates of sexual initiative, yet might have been more active in the presence of an adolescent or adult male. All that can be concluded is that given the conditions under which the bonobos lived—allowing all individuals a choice of partner sex and most individuals a choice of several partner age classes—no evidence was found that potentially fertile partner combinations engaged in sociosexual behavior more often than did infertile combinations.

Moreover, it must be emphasized that heterosexual intercourse between sexually mature individuals is only *potentially* fertile: first, because not every copulation involves ejaculation and second, because females are only fertile during a few days of their menstrual cycle. As an external sign of receptivity, they develop a conspicuous genital swelling, but this sign is unreliable as an indicator of fertility; the swelling phase far exceeds the period of ovulation, and swellings also may be shown by pregnant or lactating, and hence noncycling, females (Dahl, 1986).

Whereas it is virtually impossible to know with certainty which copulations involve an ejaculating male with an ovulating female, it is not difficult to distinguish, on the basis of behavior, infertile mounts. These are mounts without intromission; mounts broken off well before the male partner slowed down for the final, deeper thrusts indicative of ejaculation; and/or mounts involving a female with detumescent genitals. Because the dominant male tended to interfere with the heterosexual intercourse of the adolescent males and because the females mated throughout all cycle phases (cf. Savage-Rumbaugh and Wilkerson, 1978; Thompson-Handler, Malenky, and Badrian, 1984; Dahl, 1987), fertilization could be excluded for a considerable number of mounts in partner combinations marked as potentially fertile in Table 14.I.

## Context of Sociosexual Behavior

Seven conditions were distinguished in the continuous records of bonobo social behavior. These conditions concerned feeding time (i.e., 15 minutes prior to feeding time, during feeding time, and 15 minutes following the daily food provision); spontaneous aggressive incidents in the absence of food (i.e., 15 minutes preceding and following the incident and a subsequent 15-minute block); and the so-called baseline (i.e., remaining observation time). Hourly behavioral rates under these conditions were compared for each pair of individuals. The following changes occurred in a significant majority of dyads (de Waal, 1987):

1. An increase in aggression following food provision.

Figure 14.3. Mouth-to-mouth kissing, with tongue-tongue interaction, between two juvenile males (3½ and 4 years old).

2. A decrease in social grooming following food provision.
3. An increase in nongrooming contact, including sociosexual behavior, following both food provision and aggressive incidents unrelated to food.

Hence, food provision stimulated the bonobos' affiliative and sociosexual behavior (with the exception of grooming behavior, which was suppressed). In theory, this effect can be caused either directly, by the presence of food (e.g., excitement over food is transformed into sexual arousal), or indirectly, by the competitive tendencies created by this resource. The second hypothesis is better supported, because affiliative and sociosexual behavior also increased following aggression that was not food related. In other words, the presence of food was no prerequisite for sociosexual behavior, and the causal factor most elegantly explaining both measured increases is interindividual tension.

Typically, upon the introduction of food, the bonobos would become very active, engaging in aggressive competition but also inviting one another for sociosexual contact. These contacts appeared to reduce the tension and to allow for food sharing. Thus, it could be demonstrated that subordinate group members more often asserted themselves toward dominant food possessors following a sociosexual contact than without such prior contact (de Waal, 1987). The interaction could even take the form of an exchange, e.g., a female presents to a male who is holding a large bundle of branches and leaves and takes the entire bundle out of his hands immediately following sexual intercourse. On other occasions, sociosexual behavior was used as a reconciliation. The majority of instances of genital massage, for instance, followed aggressive incidents in which the adult male had chased one of the adolescent males. After a couple of minutes, the younger male would return to the aggressor to present his genitals.

In short, the bonobo's sociosexual behavior serves important tension-regulating functions. These functions explain why the behavior occurs with high frequency in all partner combinations possible. It is instructive to compare the results arrived at through these observations with the behavior of chimpanzees. This species regulates social tension by means of nongenital contact forms; in various studies of the chimpanzee colony of Arnhem Zoo (the Netherlands), mounting and mating never reached a position among the 10 most frequent modes of reconciliation (de Waal and van Roosmalen, 1979).

Recently, this author observed a colony of chimpanzees at the Yerkes Primate Center in a study modeled after the bonobo study. Sociosexual behavior among the chimpanzees was extremely rare at feeding time, and also, the general frequency of this behavior was significantly lower than among the bonobos. This difference existed in spite of a greater choice of partners for the chimpanzees, which lived in a group of 19 individuals. The average individual bonobo in the San Diego study initiated 0.63 sociosexual contacts per hour, and one adolescent male reached a score of 1.69 initiatives per hour. In contrast, the average chimpanzee in the Yerkes group initiated 0.14 sociosexual contacts per hour, with two young males, a juvenile and an adolescent, tying the top score of 0.41 initiatives per hour.

## Discussion

The bonobo is by no means unique among nonhuman primates for its use of sociosexual behavior. For example, de Waal and Ren (1988) reported a significant increase in "hold-bottom" gestures among stumptail macaques (*Macaca arctoides*) during reconciliations following fights. These monkeys

Figure 14.4. An adolescent male (8½ years old) presents his erect penis to an adult male (left) following an aggressive incident between them. The adult male performs a genital massage.

even occasionally show their so-called "orgasm face" during such postconflict reunions, a particular facial display demonstrably associated with physiological measures of sexual climax (Goldfoot et al., 1980). These behavior patterns are normally part of copulation sequences in this species (Nieuwenhuijsen, 1985).

For scientists to understand human social evolution, however, chimpanzees and bonobos are more relevant than macaques; these monkeys diverged from the human/ape branch of evolution approximately 30 million years ago, whereas humans and the two *Pan* species are estimated to have diverged a "mere" 8 million years ago (Sibley and Ahlquist, 1984). It is rather surprising how much humankind's two closest relatives differ with regard to the use of sociosexual behavior. Based on his extensive observations of captive chimpanzees, this author believes that most sociosexual activity in this species either serves reproduction directly or serves as a preparation for reproductive sex. Thus, juvenile male chimpanzees are attracted to females in estrus, and pubertal females begin to explore sexual contact with older males as soon as their genital swellings develop (van der Weel, 1978; de Waal, 1982; Goodall, 1986). Such intergenerational experience undoubtedly contributes to the development of adequate sexual skills.

The incorporation of sexual elements into reassurance behavior is rather limited in chimpanzees. Although this species shows mouth-to-mouth kissing and although adult males may mount one another during or following aggressive incidents (de Waal and van Hooff, 1981), these contacts lack the intensity and sexual arousal obvious during kissing and isosexual mounts among bonobos. Thus, neither GG-rubbing between females nor tongue-kissing (i.e., tongue-tongue interaction) has ever been reported for chimpanzees. All in all, bonobos seem to do with a variety of sociosexual behavior patterns what chimpanzees do with embracing and relatively "platonic" kissing. It is a difference in degree, but an important one.

This difference cannot be explained as a product of the conditions at the San Diego Zoo. Although a few of the observations have not been reported before—such as the use of mounting postures during reconciliation—this omission probably is due to the detail in which captive animals can be studied rather than to fundamental differences with wild conspecifics. The Japanese team of field workers in particular has reported a remarkable variety of sociosexual behavior patterns in wild bonobos; these largely qualitative descriptions and interpretations are consistent with this author's quantitative data. Here follow two pertinent quotations:

> Coexistence of plural males and females without agonistic competition in mating could be guaranteed by changing the character of sexual behavior into affiliative behavior in which all individuals can participate, and by decreasing the reproductive meaning (Mori, 1984, p. 277).

and

> A young female approached a male, who was eating sugar cane. They copulated in short order, whereupon she took one of the two canes held by him and left. In another case a young female persistently presented to a male possessor, who ignored her at first, but then copulated with her and shared his sugar cane (Kuroda, 1984, p. 317).

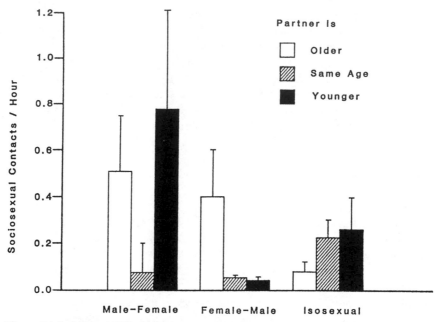

Figure 14.5. Mean (±SE) frequency of sociosexual behavior per hour of observation per dyadic direction. Dyadic directions have been categorized according to (a) sex combination and (b) partner's age relative to the actor's. For further explanation, see text.

In a previous writing, this author has argued that the most logical pathway by which sexual behavior evolved into a general reassurance mechanism is that this mechanism was first established in the adult male/female relationship, after which it was adopted in other age and sex combinations. In other words, the widespread application of sexual behavior patterns in the bonobo's social life has its origin in an emphasis on heterosexual bonding (de Waal, 1987). Field research supports this view in that male/female relationships seem closer and more tolerant in bonobos than in chimpanzees. Chimpanzee foraging parties typically consist either of adult males (sometimes accompanied by females in estrus) or mother/offspring units, whereas bonobos tend toward larger, mixed-sex parties (Badrian and Badrian, 1984; Badrian and Malenky, 1984; Kano and Mulavwa, 1984; Wrangham, 1986). This possible evolutionary background of the phenomena observed in bonobos is of relevance in connection with human sexuality, both because of the shared biological ancestry and the fact that heterosexual bonding is characteristic of the human species as well.

# Conclusion

Humans' close primate relative, the bonobo, shows a large amount of intergenerational sexual behavior. As in other primates, this behavior can partly be explained as an exploration and preparation for adult reproductive sex. Yet, the specific context in which intergenerational sex occurs among captive bonobos suggests an important additional function, which also applies to this species' intragenerational sex. Sociosexual behavior occurs in all possible age and sex combinations as a mechanism of reassurance and appeasement. This function of sexual behavior patterns does not interfere with the fertilization function of these patterns, because males appear to limit penetration and ejaculation to contacts with mature females.

# Summary

Both in the wild and in captivity, the bonobo (*Pan paniscus*) exhibits a surprising variety of sexual and erotic behavior patterns. A quantitative study of 10 captive members of the species kept at the San Diego Zoo investigated the role of sexual and affiliative behavior patterns in the regulation of social tension. These behavior patterns increased in frequency at moments of competition, such as at feeding time, and following aggressive incidents in the colony. Sociosexual behavior occurred with equal frequency and equal intensity in all age and sex combinations possible. Intergenerational sex was part of this general pattern.

The bonobo's sexual reconciliation and reassurance patterns were described and contrasted with the behavior of the chimpanzee, which virtually lacks this nonreproductive function of sexual behavior. The evolutionary origin of this difference was sought in heterosexual bonding among bonobos in their natural habitat.

*Acknowledgments*

The author thanks Katherine Offutt for assistance with data analysis, Bob Dodsworth for the printing of photographs, Juli Bowman for drawing the figure, and Mary Schatz and Jackie Kinney for typing the manuscript. The bonobo study was made possible by the San Diego Zoological Society and a grant from the National Geographic Society. Research at the Yerkes Regional Primate Research Center was made possible by grants from the H.F. Guggenheim Foundation and the National Institutes of Health (RR00165). Research and writing was further supported by a National Institutes of Health grant (RR00167) to the Wisconsin Regional Primate Research Center (WRPRC). This publication is No. 27-034 of the WRPRC.

# References

Badrian, A., and Badrian, N. Social organization of *Pan paniscus* in the Lomako Forest, Zaire. *In* R. Susman (Ed.), *The pygmy chimpanzee*. New York: Plenum Press, 1984, pp. 325-346.

Badrian, N., and Malenky, R. Feeding ecology of *Pan paniscus* in the Lomako Forest, Zaire. *In* R. Susman (Ed.), *The pygmy chimpanzee*. New York: Plenum Press, 1984, pp. 275-299.

Dahl, J. The external genitalia of female pygmy chimpanzees. *The Anatomical Record*, 1985, *211*, 24-28.

Dahl, J. Cyclic perineal swelling during the intermenstrual intervals of captive female pygmy chimpanzees (*Pan paniscus*). *Journal of Human Evolution*, 1986, *15*, 369-385.

Dahl, J. Sexual initiation in a captive group of pygmy chimpanzees (*Pan paniscus*). *Primate Report*, 1987, *16*, 43-53.

Goldfoot, D.A., Westerborg-van Loon, H., Groeneveld, W., and Slob, A.K. Behavioral and physiological evidence of sexual climax in the female stump-tailed macaque (*Macaca arctoides*). *Science*, 1980, *208*, 1477-1479.

Goodall, J. *The chimpanzees of Gombe: Patterns of behavior*. Cambridge, Mass.: The Belknap Press of Harvard University Press, 1986.

Hübsch, I. Einiges zum Verhalten der Zwergschimpansen (*Pan paniscus*) und der Schimpanzen (*Pan troglodytes*) im Frankfurter Zoo. *Zoologische Garten*, 1970, *38*, 107-132.

Jordan, C. Das Verhalten Zoolebender Zwergschimpansen. Unpublished Ph.D. dissertation, 1977, Goethe University, Frankfurt.

Kano, T. Social behavior of wild pygmy chimpanzees (*Pan paniscus*) of Wamba: A preliminary report. *Journal of Human Evolution*, 1980, *9*, 243-260.

Kano, T., and Mulavwa, M. Feeding ecology of the pygmy chimpanzees (*Pan paniscus*) of Wamba. *In* R. Susman (Ed.), *The pygmy chimpanzee*. New York: Plenum Press, 1984, pp. 233-274.

Kirchshofer, R. Beobachtungen bei der Geburt eines Zwergschimpansen (*Pan paniscus* Schwarz 1929) und einige Bemerkungen zum Paarungsverhalten. *Zeitschrift für Tierpsychologie*, 1962, *19*, 597-606.

Kuroda, S. Social behavior of the pygmy chimpanzees. *Primates*, 1980, *21*, 181-197.

Kuroda, S. Interaction over food among pygmy chimpanzees. *In* R. Susman (Ed.), *The pygmy chimpanzee*. New York: Plenum Press, 1984, pp. 301-324.

McGinnis, P. Patterns of sexual behavior in a community of free-living chimpanzees. Unpublished Ph.D. dissertation, 1973, Cambridge University.

Mori, A. An ethological study of pygmy chimpanzees in Wamba, Zaire: A comparison with chimpanzees. *Primates*, 1984, *25*, 255-278.

Nieuwenhuijsen, K. Geslachtshormonen en gedrag bij de beermakaak (*Macaca arctoides*). Unpublished Ph.D. dissertation, 1985, Erasmus University, Rotterdam.

Rempe, U. Einige Beobachtungen an Bonobos (*Pan paniscus*, Schwarz 1929). *Zeitschrift für Wissenschaftliche Zoologie*, 1961, *165*, 81-87.

Savage, S., and Bakeman, R. Sexual morphology and behavior in *Pan paniscus*. *Proceedings of the Sixth International Congress of Primatology*. New York: Academic Press, 1978, pp. 613-616.

Savage-Rumbaugh, S., and Wilkerson, B. Socio-sexual behavior in *Pan paniscus* and *Pan troglodytes:* A comparative study. *Journal of Human Evolution*, 1978, *7*, 327-344.

Sibley, C., and Ahlquist, J. The phylogeny of the Hominoid primates, as indicated by DNA-DNA hybridization. *Journal of Molecular Evolution*, 1984, *20*, 2-15.

Thompson-Handler, N., Malenky, R., and Badrian, N. Sexual behavior of *Pan paniscus* under natural conditions in the Lomako Forest, Equateur, Zaire. *In* R. Susman (Ed.), *The pygmy chimpanzee*. New York: Plenum Press, 1984, pp. 347-368.

Tratz, E., and Heck, H. Der afrikanische Anthropoide "Bonobo," eine neue Menschenaffengattung. *Saugetierkundige Mitteilungen*, 1954, *2*, 97-101.

de Waal, F. *Chimpanzee politics*. London: Jonathan Cape, 1982.

de Waal, F. Tension regulation and nonreproductive functions of sex in captive bonobos (*Pan paniscus*). *National Geographic Research*, 1987, *3*, 318-335.

de Waal, F. The communicative repertoire of captive bonobos (*Pan paniscus*), compared to that of chimpanzees. *Behaviour*, 1988, *106*, 183-251.

de Waal, F., and van Hooff, J. Side-directed communication and agonistic interactions in chimpanzees. *Behaviour*, 1981, *77*, 164-198.

de Waal, F., and Ren, R. Comparison of the reconciliation behavior of stumptail and rhesus macaques. *Ethology*, 1988, *78*, 129-142.

de Waal, F., and van Roosmalen, A. Reconciliation and consolation among chimpanzees. *Behavioral Ecology and Sociobiology*, 1979, *5*, 55-66.

van der Weel, M. Sexuele interacties en relaties tussen chimpansees. Unpublished research report, 1978, University of Utrecht.

Wrangham, R. Ecology and social relationships in two species of chimpanzee. *In* D. Rubenstein and R. Wrangham (Eds.), *Ecological aspects of social evolution: Birds and mammals*. Princeton: Princeton University Press, 1986, pp. 352-378.

Yamagiwa, J. Intra- and inter-group interactions in an all-male group of Virunga mountain gorillas (*Gorilla gorilla beringei*). *Primates*, 1987, *28*, 1-30.

# 15
# Ritualized Adult-Male/ Adolescent-Male Sexual Behavior in Melanesia: An Anthropological and Ethological Perspective

Wulf Schiefenhövel
*Forschungsstelle für Humanethologie*
*in der Max-Planck-Gesellschaft*
*D-8138 Andechs*
  *and*
*Wissenschaftskolleg zu Berlin*
*D-1000 Berlin 33*
*Federal Republic of Germany*

## Introduction

Sexuality rests, even more than hunger or thirst, on the crossroad between biology and culture, being obvious, inevitable, and rather well developed in humans as compared to other mammals. (A possible exception regarding this comparison is the bonobo; see de Waal, this volume.) At the same time (and possibly as a result), sexuality is subject to the transforming powers of cultural tradition.

When individuals who are part of Western tradition are trying to understand the functions, in their own societies, of adult human sexual behavior with children and adolescents, it seems a promising enterprise that they look at sexual behavior among peoples who are living in very different contexts. New Guinea and its surrounding islands have been, since Malinowski's famous but rather cursory account of Trobriand sexuality (1929), one of these areas in which anthropologists and others have studied human sexuality. Also studied in that locale have been certain types of adult-male/adolescent-male sexual behavior, which lately have been the focus of attention of Herdt (e.g., 1984a) and other authors. One could say, *cum grano salis*, that modern, and at the same time still almost stone-age, New Guinea has become what ancient Greece used to be for the discussion of sexual behavior between adult and adolescent males.

Of the large capacity that sexuality, including certain types of homosexuality, has for structuring a society—e.g., assigning gender roles, regulating fertility and population growth (cf. Schiefenhövel, 1984, 1988)—just a few aspects will be covered in this chapter.

Before discussing the subject proper of this volume, adult/child and adult/adolescent sexual behavior, this author will look at some of the wider spread, heterosexual practices occurring in many of the Papuan societies.

At this point, a brief historic and cultural overview seems necessary in order to provide an understanding of some of the findings that will be presented herein. The Papuan population, which probably came from the hinterland of Southeast Asia, arrived at the shores of New Guinea some 50,000 years ago (Swadling, 1981). Today, in the late 1980's, the Papuans live in the interior of the large island and along several of its coasts; other parts of the island, as well as most of the islands surrounding New Guinea, are the home of Austronesian or Melanesian peoples, who migrated along the same route, through Indonesia, but at a much later date, probably some 4,000-5,000 years ago. Racial, linguistic, and cultural traits of those two groups of immigrants are quite different. Roughly 4 million Papuans speak several hundred languages—an obvious sign of their prolonged geographic and cultural isolation; the languages of the Austronesians are much more homogeneous and are spread over wider areas. Subsistence strategies, expertise in navigation, social structure (nonstratified versus stratified), and other features, too, are quite different among these two groups. It is, therefore, rather difficult for one to make statements that apply to all peoples in Melanesia. Because ritualized adult-male/adolescent-male sexual behavior seems to have occurred almost exclusively in only some groups of Papuan origin, the focus of this chapter is primarily on these populations.

This author will refer frequently to the Eipo, a typical, isolated Papuan group living in the Highlands of West New Guinea, where he spent two years doing anthropological and human ethological fieldwork, and to the Trobriand Islanders, with whom the author has been involved, as a result of conducting interdisciplinary research, since 1982. Since 1965, the author has returned repeatedly to live and work among Papuans and Melanesians in Papua New Guinea and in Irian Jaya.

## Dichotomy of Male and Female Worlds

Among the Papuans, the dichotomy of the male and female worlds is very marked, as is culturally enhanced sexual dimorphism. In a number of Highland groups, adult males wear conspicuous penis gourds (a cultural expression of male aggressiveness and dominance rather than sexual signals, cf. Eibl-Eibesfeldt and Wickler, 1968), whereas adult females wear genital aprons of various plant materials (see Figure 15.1). It is quite interesting that among Austronesian peoples, there seems to be less cultural stress on such dimorphism: Trobriand Islanders, for example, when dressed for the typical *milamala* dances, look very similar ("unisex"), with both adult males and adult females wearing grass skirts and similar body decoration (see Figure 15.2).

Among the Papuan groups, adult males usually work, form political alliances, and fight together when they belong to the same "men's house" community. They spend considerable time, during both day and night, in these "clubs." All females are barred from access to the men's houses, which are considered by the community to be sacred. Adult females live in the family houses, nurse their children for two to three years, and are in charge of the everyday work in the gardens, the pigs, and the gathering of small reptiles and insects and their eggs, which are valuable but minimal sources of protein. In some areas, the menstruation/birth houses, situated at the fringe of the village, are nonsacred equivalents of the men's houses.

The temporal and spatial segregation of adult males and adult females is more pronounced in the Papuan than in the Melanesian groups; in the villages of the latter, there usually are no men's houses, and husbands as well as most bachelors sleep in the same family houses as do adult females. Papuan societies also require stricter separation of the sexes in public. Among the Eipo, for instance, one never sees an adolescent or adult female looking for lice in the hair of an adolescent or adult male; social grooming is restricted to one's own sex, as is body contact, such as holding hands and embracing, except in greeting situations.

Among the Trobrianders and other Melanesian groups, rules for conduct in public are much less stringent regarding body contact; e.g., social skin care may be carried out openly by lovers. However, as in Papuan societies, there is definitely no overt sexual behavior among adult males and adult females in the presence of others.

The separation and segregation of male and female spheres are rooted in culturally propagated mythology and strengthened by religious rites. Many authors speak of the "sexual antagonism" of Papuan cultures. While this phrase is a good description of the conceptual, theoretical framework of assigning gender roles, for example, it has much less meaning in the behavior of everyday life. Adult males and adult females are viewed as basically and necessarily belonging to different spheres, in the economic, procreative, and religious senses, to ensure the propagation of human life.

Figure 15.1. Typical female and male genital dress of the Ok Mountain Papua. In some neighboring groups, the (specially grown) penis calabashes are much longer. See Figure 15.5a and 15.5b.

Yet, both the male and the female spheres are considered to be vitally important.

Heterosexual intercourse, although spoken about often and openly, typically is carried out in intimacy and seclusion, as is universally true for *Homo sapiens* (cf. Schiefenhövel, 1982). Heterosexual intercourse constitutes not only the unification of male and female bodies but also is the place where two different worlds, with their conceptually most important but also vulnerable incarnations, meet and where the genital organs partially resolve the culturally transmitted antagonism between the sexes.

## Males' Expressed Fear of Becoming Contaminated Through Sex with Females

One of the most powerful and persistent culturally transmitted beliefs in Papuan societies is that of male contamination through contact with the female sexual organs and their fluids, especially menstrual blood. This author and his wife Grete met unexpected problems among the Eipo (Schiefenhövel, 1976) while conducting a dental survey, for which the volunteers were supposed to sit on a wooden bench nailed to the back of the author's hut. Male individuals firmly declined to sit on the place where an adolescent or adult female previously had sat. Their reluctance was overcome easily with the use of an empty rice bag (strictly reserved for males) as a cover, neutralizing what they believed to be the dangerous forces. The culturally transmitted behavioral response to the culturally transmitted male rhetoric—that from vulva and vagina (*kwat*) as well as from the inner organs of females harmful powers emanate—is a specific style of sitting. Adult females always sit on one of their legs, with the tiny grass skirt tightly tucked underneath, when sitting on stones or similar objects that might also be used by adult males. In this way, the females prevent any of their genital fluids from coming into contact with the seat and then with male individuals.

Sperm, as it is ejaculated during orgasm, and vaginal secretion, as it is discharged during female sexual arousal, are identical, or at least very similar, in concept. The sperm is called *den ala* (*den* = penis; *ala* = slimy fluid); the vaginal secretion is called *kwat ala*. When one considers these linguistic similarities, one finds male vocalized and nonverbal expressions of fear and behavioral avoidance to be even more surprising. Hogbin (1970) reports similar beliefs on the part of the inhabitants of Wogeo, the "island of menstruating men":

> The established doctrine is that the members of each sex group would be safe and invulnerable, healthy and prosperous, if only they were to keep to themselves and refrain from mixing with members of the other sex group. Clearly this is a counsel of perfection . . . everyone past the early adult stage is at the mercy of the drive to copulate, an impulse that can be stifled only for brief interludes, and then with difficulty. The result is that the entire population is perpetually weakened, liable to

Figure 15.2. "Unisex" appearance of male (far right) and female *milamala* dancers during harvest feast on the Trobriand Islands.

disease and misadventure—males because of their association with females, females because of their association with males. The females, however, are the more fortunate in that they are regularly freed from contamination by the normal physiological process of menstruation, when the alien elements flow away of their own accord. The males, on the other hand, are obliged to take positive measures to ensure such a periodic disinfection. Therefore, the elders have the job of taking a boy who is on the brink of puberty and scarifying his tongue, thus ridding him of influences absorbed during childhood; and later, after attaining maturity, all men have to make a practice of gashing the penis to induce profuse bleeding .... That is to say, females regain their purity by natural menstruation, and men regain theirs by artificial menstruation ... (pp. 87-88).

Hogbin (1970) also reports similar beliefs from a typical Highland culture in Papua New Guinea:

From adolescence onwards [Mae Enga] males are taught to shun the company of the opposite sex, and they go into periodical seclusion to purify themselves from chance contacts. Only a husband can risk sexual intercourse because the remedies for protecting virility are available solely to those who are married. But even in wedlock men [speak and behave as though they] fear coitus and reduce the occasions to the minimum necessary for procreation. Above all, they are terrified of menstrual blood (p. 97).

## Some Aspects of Adult Heterosexual Behavior

One may wonder whether these expressed and propagated male attitudes of great fear toward adolescent and adult females—ancient Mediterranean concepts like *vagina dentata* and *baubo* (Dereveux, 1981) come to mind—would allow sexual intercourse at all. Well, they do, rather unsurprisingly! In everyday life, there is more leeway than there is in official vocalized beliefs and societal regulations, a fact that may have remained unaccounted for in Hogbin's (1970) report on the Mae Enga. **Older adult males** say they have little to fear provided they obey the strict sexual taboo during menstruation and some other rules, except if females were to clandestinely use their partners' sperm as "personal leaving" in the widespread *pars-pro-toto* magic to inflict disease or death on them.

Under normal circumstances, then, sexual intercourse is something to be enjoyed thoroughly by older adult males—and perhaps even more so because of all the culturally transmitted, restricting and restraining controlling mechanisms that are applied to adolescent and younger adult males.

The author estimates the average frequency of (exclusively heterosexual) intercourse among adult Eipo males to be about 1-2 occurrences per week, which is within the frequency range experienced by adult males in other societies. It usually is carried out during the daytime in the gardens or thereabouts. To have sex in the family house, that is, in the village, is seen as being rather odd; this pragmatic viewpoint is convenient because of the crowded conditions and the lack of privacy in the Eipo's small dwellings. In contrast, Trobrianders, as typical Melanesians, "sleep," in the literal and figurative senses, with their sexual/marital partners.

Because puberty is rather late (menarche occurs at 16-18 years of age), actual sexual intercourse usually does not start much before that age. Young males, in virtually all Papuan groups, may well be 20 years of age or older before they have their first sexual encounter with an adolescent or adult female.

The concept of and beliefs about sexuality, or rather that concern the powers set free during intercourse, are well illustrated by the following incident that took place among the Eipo. A man called Mangat was seriously injured by enemies during an ambush. He barely survived the attack and was aided by modern medical treatment provided by the author. In a weakened but convalescent state, Mangat was brought into a friend's house. This author observed one of his male friends planting a leafy branch (*bata*), a common taboo sign, into the ground of the path beside the house. Asked why he was planting the branch, the friend replied, "Mangat is still sick and in danger of his soul escaping from him. That's why we must plant the taboo sign, to forbid everyone who has had sexual intercourse today from passing by this road!" As the friend's explanation demonstrates, sexual arousal, orgasm, the intense social encounter, and the elated spirit connected to the sexual act are seen as materially present, powerful, and dangerous for individuals whose health is impaired.

It may have become apparent by now that in many respects New Guinean sexual behavior that actually is performed by adult males is rather similar to sexual behavior performed in Western industrialized societies. Among the Eipo, eroticism often takes the form of beautiful love poems, usually composed and then sung by adult females, in which powerful metaphors for falling and being in love and for the sexual act itself are employed (Hiepko and Schiefenhövel, 1987, pp. 20-21). Jealousy is by no means uncommon. In the rather few polygynous marriages, the two, rarely more, wives of one husband may come to some kind of agreement and be good friends, but the opposite also occurs.

Eipo individuals told this author about rapes. Most of the victims were adult females from valleys farther away, either traveling alone (which was seen as more or less inviting that sort of response) or in a group that included adult males who were attacked and wounded or killed. The latter actions seem to be rather rare, however. One of the adult females in the village in which this author lived had been raped by a group of adult males who afterward decided that one of them should marry her: "We all had intercourse with you," they said; "now we will take care that you can live in our village." The event, which had taken place several years before this author's arrival, was vividly remembered. The adult female, still married and now the mother of children, did not appear to be discriminated against.

Although an older wife, possibly beyond her reproductive life, may be an acceptable marriage partner for an adult Eipo man, even for his first marriage, there is a clear male preference for younger, nubile females. One of the adult males of Munggona village, about 40 years of age, expressed this preference rather emphatically: *"Monob kwat na song, muruk kwat na gil-gil!"* or, "An old vagina I dislike, a half ripe vagina makes me happy!" *Muruk* is a term usually applied to edible fruits that have not yet reached their full stage of maturity. Adult females, too, appear to prefer sexual partners who are young adults, attractive and vigorous. The significance of this preference will become evident later in this chapter.

As a general rule, both in Papuan and Austronesian societies, married partners are *de iure* expected to have no extramarital affairs; *de facto*, however, this principle often is violated. It is difficult to imagine any society in which marital fidelity is followed perfectly, no matter how severe the sanctions for breaking this norm may be. This author believes that the initiative for such unlawful love affairs is quite often taken by adult females, who prefer to "seduce" younger, unmarried adult males. The author and his wife observed this pattern while they lived among the Eipo. They also observed married, older adult males having love affairs with young-adult females and young-adult males falling in love and eventually eloping with females of their own age, not uncommonly the second wife of an older adult male. Of course, these latter actions spark violent outbreaks of jealousy and attempts to regain the lost partner—and they also cause the deprived adult male to lose face. Most intracommunity fights and killings are on these bases (Schiefenhövel, 1984).

In a number of Papuan populations, certain festive periods that are connected to fertility rites ensuring, for example, the growth of garden crops, allowed, even required, the breaking of the official principle of marital fidelity. These ritually meaningful, heterosexual "orgies" were of course quickly exterminated by early missionaries. Williams (1930), writing on the Orokaiva, quotes Chinnery and Beaver:

> In ordinary circumstances an initiation is a time of somewhat general licence, promiscuous intercourse being permitted between any initiated man and woman. Witnesses have assured me that such promiscuity is confined to the initiation ceremonies. The initiates bear no part in it, but between their elders it is unrestricted. No husband might object if another man made free with his wife, for, it was said, he would fear retaliation by sorcery if he interfered. Needless to say I have no more than verbal evidence for this licence, but there is little doubt that at these times it does occur (p. 192).

Adolescents and young adults not yet married were given, in a number of Highland societies like that of the Eipo, temporal and spacial opportunities to have premarital heterosexual intercourse. To the knowledge of this author, this opportunity has not led to much **noticeable** premarital promiscuity. Young-adult males and females may have any number of short-lived relationships, but because of strictly followed exogamous rules of marriage, the number of sexual partners who are eligible to be marriage partners as well is rather limited, and one is happy to eventually find a suitable partner and finally stay with her or him.

Among the Trobriand Islanders, a young-adult male may have his own house (*bwala bukumatula*) in which, from time to time, he will be visited by an unmarried, adolescent or young-adult female once an accord has been reached that the two will spend the night together. The preliminaries of arranging the date in secrecy are an important element of the love affair: messages are delivered, usually by go-betweens, and letters are written (Bell-Krannhals, unpublished manuscript).

## Childhood Sexuality and Heterosexual Behavior Between Adults and Children

Among the Eipo in the Highlands of West New Guinea, female children, from the time they are about 4 years old, are expected to wear a tiny grass skirt, a mini-model of the type worn by adult females. The male children, in contrast, remain completely naked until the age of about 16, when the penis grows and the first pubic hair appears.

Cultural tradition with regard to sexual behavior follows the same line. This author and his colleagues never observed female children playing with their genitals, whereas such behavior was rather common for male children; the latter, in a half mocking, half sexual way, drew back the prepuce while pushing their pelvis forward, exhibiting their genitals in this way (see Figure 15.3), or playfully put on fragments of calebasses (a kind of gourd) in imitation of the penis gourd of the adult males (see Figure 15.4). Everyone, including adults, laughed about these comical acts, which were performed while the male children played in the village. Erections in male children who did not yet wear a penis gourd sometimes occurred, e.g., while they did handicraft work in a squatting posture. Nobody, including female children, openly reacted to the occurrence, and no comments were made. The author and his colleagues also saw male children put long, flowering grass stalks into their anus and then mock dance in the typical way of ridiculing the enemy in warfare. The dancing included pelvic thrusts, i.e., phallic presentation.

This behavior, a mixture of sexual and aggressive moods, also was observed during an "unofficial" dance that was started on a flat rock in a river outside the village by male children and subsequently attracted male adolescents (see Figure 15.5a). The latter individuals loosened the waist strings that held the tip of their respective penis gourds in the usual upward angle, thereby allowing them to swing up and down during the pelvic thrusts (see Figure 15.5b). Everyone, including some adult males of high standing who also had joined the dance, laughed about this obscene

Figure 15.3. An Eipo male child, Highlands of West New Guinea, playfully and publicly pulling back the foreskin and exhibiting his penis. An example of the sexual freedom children, especially male children, enjoy before the onset of puberty.

performance, which would not have been acceptable under normal, i.e., village, contexts.

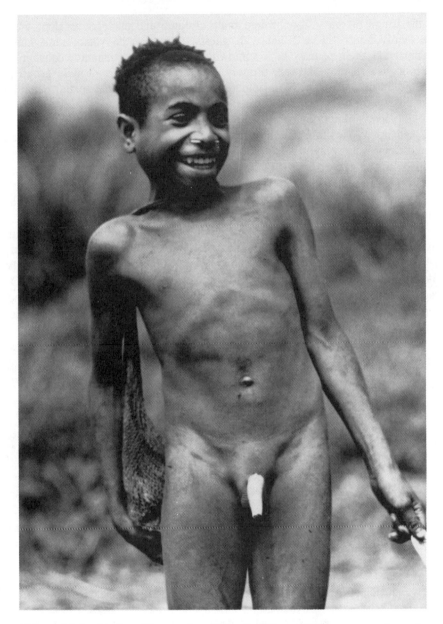

Figure 15.4. Another Eipo male child playfully exhibiting a mock penis gourd.

One of the author's colleagues, Paul Blum (personal communication), observed some young-adult males taking off their penis gourds in a house at the fringe of the village, where male children and adolescents slept when the family houses were filled with guests. Some of the young-adult males manipulated their penises in a somewhat demonstrative manner, causing an erection, which they showed, proudly as it seemed, to the all-male group of youngsters around them. No ejaculation and no interpersonal sexual behavior was observed during this incident.

In many interviews with informants in which sexual topics were touched upon, the information provided led the interviewers to believe that homosexual acts, playful or "serious," among male children, adolescents, or adults do not occur. On the other hand, this author did hear of male and female children "having had intercourse" in the grassland beside the village. Everyone laughed with good humor about this behavior; the children involved were neither reprimanded nor punished in any way.

Small children of both sexes and males until the onset of puberty thus live in an atmosphere of sexual tolerance (Schiefenhövel, 1982). It is only when the latter have grown up, show beard growth, and are thought to be old enough to wear the *mum*, a back ornament typical of the Mek and Ok regions of the Central Highlands of New Guinea (in itself a sexual symbol representing the penis), that one expects from them the decent behavior typical of adult males.

Malinowski (1929) described attitudes toward the sexuality of children and adolescents living in Omarakana on the main Trobriand island, Kiriwina, in the second decade of the 20th century, attitudes that are quite similar to the ones this author found in the West New Guinea Highlands:

> The child's freedom and independence extend also to sexual matters . . . . Young children are allowed to listen to baldly sexual talk, and they understand perfectly well what is being discussed. They are also themselves tolerably expert in swearing and the use of obscene language. Because of their early mental development some quite tiny children are able to make smutty jokes, and these their elders will greet with laughter.
>
> Small girls follow their fathers on fishing expeditions, during which the men remove their pubic ["public" in the original] leaf. Nakedness under these conditions is regarded as natural, since it is necessary. There is no lubricity or ribaldry associated with it . . . .
>
> There are plenty of opportunities for both boys and girls to receive instruction in erotic matters from their companions. The children initiate each other in the mysteries of sexual life in a directly practical manner at a very early age. A premature amorous existence begins among them long before they are able really to carry out the act of sex (pp. 46-48).

The current author's own anthropological and human ethological fieldwork on one of the smaller Trobriand islands essentially confirms this picture; except for the ages Malinowski attributed to children and adolescents, they grow, as Bell-Krannhals and Schiefenhövel (1986) have shown, much more slowly than their European cohorts. It is interesting to note that 70 years of work by Christian missionaries has not had much influence on the sexual behavior of this proud and self-assured Austronesian society. The reason may be that, in contrast to occurrences in other areas of Melanesia, this missionary work fortunately was carried out in a rather mild and nonaggressive way, allowing a slow, syncretistic incorporation of Christian beliefs.

Whereas it is not uncommon that New Guinean mothers fondle the genitals of their infants, possibly causing an erection, and make humorous remarks about children's genitals, in none of the various Papuan and Austronesian groups with which the author has lived in the course of the past 24 years has he ever seen any sign or heard of adults engaging in sexual intercourse with children.

This observation coincides with Malinowski's experience with the Trobrianders. He wrote:

> It is important to note that there is no interference by older persons in the sexual life of children. On rare occasions some old man or woman is suspected of taking a strong sexual interest in the children, and even of having intercourse with some of them. But I never found such suspicions supported even by a general consensus of opinion, and it was always considered both improper and silly for an older man or woman to have sexual dealings with a child (Malinowski, 1929, pp. 50-51).

It seems, then, that in these two, and by far the majority of all, traditional societies on and around New Guinea, the delicate balance between paternal and sexual behavior is maintained, and outright genital intercourse with children and young adolescents is avoided.

The next section will deal with some Papuan groups in which things are quite strikingly different.

## Ritualized Adult-Male/Adolescent-Male Sexual Behavior

As mentioned in the foregoing section, occasional homoerotic or homosexual play or encounters may occur among male children and male adolescents, as is probably common for most human societies. Nevertheless, it is widely believed that, as a result of personal decisions, there is very little male/male sexual behavior among adults in Papuan and Melanesian groups. Among the Eipo and the Trobriand Islanders, there were no publicly known adult/adult homosexual relationships that occurred either during this author's stay there or in the remembered past. The villagers said that adult males would feel "ashamed" (*alye* in the Eipo language; *mwasila* in the Trobriand language) to engage in sexual behavior with another male. Tomalala, a Trobriand informant, explained that if it were known that an adult male showed homosexual tendencies by openly approaching a male adolescent or another adult male, he would be subject to so much gossip and ridicule that he would stop openly behaving in a homosexual way.

Figure 15.5a. Young Eipo males during an "unofficial" dance.

This remark, clearly reflecting the exclusively heterosexual expressed ideal of the Trobriand culture, comes as a bit of a surprise to the foreign visitor because some, mostly younger, adult males have a slightly effeminate air about them, which often is associated with male homosexuality in

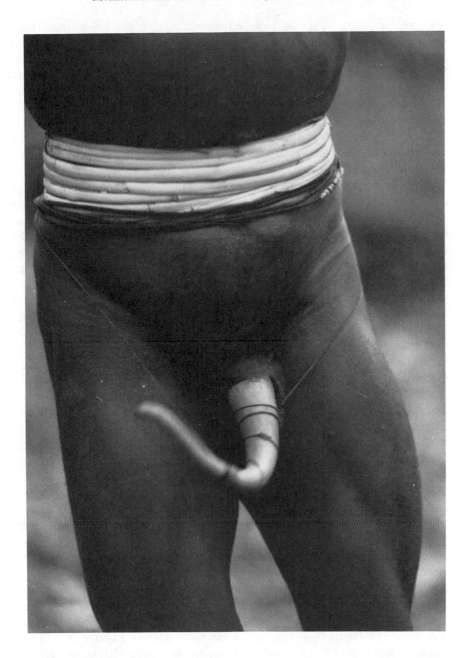

Figure 15.5b. Some of the "dancers" loosen the string of their penis gourd to allow the penis to swing visibly up and down—indecent behavior under normal conditions. In this culture, ritualized adult-male/adolescent-male sexual behavior is absent, and casual homosexuality probably is very rare.

Western societies. Yet, the older effeminate adult males are married, have children, and as far as one can judge, are outwardly happy with their heterosexual relationships. One explanation of their overtly effeminate behavior patterns could be that in this matrilineal society, as has been mentioned, there is little stress on sexual dimorphism, a fact that becomes particularly apparent in the almost "unisex" appearance of female and male dancers.

Of the Papua New Guinea population now living in the big urban centers like the capital, Port Moresby, it is commonly known that some adult and, probably, adolescent males engage in homosexual activities, at least with members of the white expatriate community, who pay or otherwise compensate them for their being available as active or passive sexual partners. To this author's knowledge, no study has yet been carried out on this phenomenon. It would be most interesting to find out about the motives of the Papuans who are involved and whether adult males from areas with ritualized adult-male/adolescent-male sexual behavior are involved to a greater or a lesser degree than would be statistically expected.

While, as will become apparent, there is an impressive body of knowledge on Melanesian male homosexuality, female homosexual behavior is hardly ever mentioned in the literature. Eipo friends of the author quite openly told him about some adult females of the village community who were alleged to engage in mutual sexual stimulation (kwat mamun = vagina close together) apparently by rubbing the vulva against some parts of the partner's body. The essence of the explanation was, "They are horny and that's why they are doing that." No reproachful or otherwise discriminative attitude could be detected with regard to these adult females, whose names were known to everyone. Rather, one spoke of them with definite humorous amusement and with some form of respect for the strength of their sexual desire.

Since the ethnographic work of missionaries and early professional anthropologists was published around the late 19th and early 20th centuries, ritualized homosexual behavior has been described for a number of Papuan groups (see the comprehensive bibliography in Herdt, 1984a). There are some reports on the same phenomenon on Fiji, New Caledonia, the New Hebrides, New Britain, and some other islands. Yet, by far the majority of ethnic groups among which ritualized homosexuality was, and in some cases probably still is, practiced live in various parts of mainland New Guinea, especially along the southern coast on both sides of the border between Irian Jaya and Papua New Guinea; in the Great Papuan Plateau; in just one language group of the comparatively densely populated Highlands and two isolated areas in the Northern Province of Papua New Guinea; and in Irian Jaya (Herdt, 1984b; see Figure 15.6).

Herdt (1984b, p. 12) provided a list of 29 "social units" (some geographical areas, some language and culture groups), i.e., 29 ethnic groups, out of an estimated overall figure of perhaps 1,000 such units in mainland and insular New Guinea in which ritualized homosexuality was or is the accepted rule. According to this estimate, approximately 3% of all ethnic groups would exhibit the cultural trait of ritualized homosexuality. As there has never been a comprehensive record made of all culture and language groups in New Guinea, especially on this sort of topic, one can assume that the "real" percentage may have been twice, perhaps three times as high. It becomes clear from this perspective that ritualized homosexuality has always been a nonuniversal practice, one that did not spread to the majority of Papuan populations.

Having worked in the Gulf of Papua and among some groups along the Fly River, this author is puzzled by the fact that ritualized homosexuality did not spread to the Gulf of Papua proper, whose population, in other aspects, has much in common with the population of the delta of the Fly. This situation is even more surprising when one looks at the map (Figure 15.6) and follows the conjectured, historical "diffusionist" (Herdt, 1984b, p. 53) spread of ritualized homosexuality. Through this process of spreading, there could have existed ("10,000 years ago or less," according to Herdt, 1984b, p. 5) a more or less continuous nexus of societies practicing the behavior; and it is interesting to note that the Purari River, which flows into the Gulf of Papua and is navigable upstream by paddled canoes, would have given access to the only Highland area in which the custom is found. Nevertheless, no matter how the historic development may have taken place (more likely by diffusion than by being established regionally and independently) and no matter which ecological and other factors may have favored ritualized homosexuality, the more interesting aspects within the framework of this volume are the structure and function of this behavior.

F.E. Williams, a British government anthropologist who usually got the information for his substantial monographs on various cultural and language groups through interviews with informants, described the Keraki of the so-called "Trans-Fly area" (Williams, 1936). After the informants made some effort to conceal the practice from him, he learned:

> . . . every male adult in the Morehead district has in his time constantly played both parts in this perversion. The boy is initiated to it at the bull-roarer ceremony and not earlier, for he could not then be trusted to keep the secret from his mother. When he becomes adolescent his part is reversed and he may then sodomize his juniors, the new initiates, to the bull-roarer. I am told that some boys are more attractive and consequently receive more attention of this kind than do others; but all must pass through it, since it is regarded as essential to their bodily growth. There is indeed no question as to the universality of the practice. It is commonly asserted that the early practice of sodomy does nothing to inhibit a man's natural desires when later on he marries; and it is a fact that while the older men are not debarred from indulging, and actually do so at the bull-roarer ceremony, sodomy is virtually restricted as a habit to the *setiriva* [bachelors] (pp. 158-159).

Present-day authors who for a number of reasons are interested in homosexual behavior in cross-cultural perspective criticize Williams and other early anthropologists for using value-laden terms like "unnatural practice" and "sodomy" (cf. Creed, 1984, p. 157). However, who knows which authors possess the pearls of ultimate knowledge and wisdom? Williams, in his one-page description of Keraki "sodomy," has passed on what still can be considered the essentials of ritualized homosexuality:

1. Its occurrence within socioreligious ceremonies connected to male initiation, which thereby limits it to certain age periods and provides an ideological frame of reference.

2. The culturally propagated belief (perhaps rationalization) that male adolescents must be brought into close bodily contact with the semen of adult males so that the adolescents will be transformed into "real" male members of the society.

3. The reversal of roles with increasing chronological age, when the former recipient of semen becomes the "donor."

4. The seeming lack of long-lasting effects of this behavior on the preference for heterosexual intercourse, marriage, and becoming a father, at least for the majority of males who have gone through the rites in both roles.

The Keraki informants told Williams a mythical legend that seems to have served as a justification (rationalization, perhaps) for what otherwise would have been seen as nonnormal behavior:

> Gufa, despite good feeding and attention, was a wretched under-sized little boy, described as pot-bellied and constipated. He was the despair of his father until one day, ostensibly with the sole idea of promoting his growth, he conceived the idea of sodomizing him. He took him apart from his mother during the night and put his idea into effect, rubbing semen over the child's body. The result was a miraculous increase in growth. The boy was instructed to keep this a dead secret from his mother, and when she next saw him she was delighted at the change but attributed it wrongly to the good food which [his father] must have given him . . . . It is to be noted that nowadays boys are not sodomized by their own fathers. The restriction of moiety exogamy is observed in sodomy as it is in marriage (Williams, 1936, pp. 308-309).

Various forms of the transferring of semen into the male children were used: oral intercourse (fellatio) among the Etoro, anal intercourse (sodomy) among the Kaluli, and masturbation and smearing semen on the body surface among the Onobasulu. All three ethnic groups live in a rather confined geographical area close to Mt. Bosavi in the Southern Highlands Province of Papua New Guinea (Kelly, 1980). (See Figure 15.6.)

These different sexual practices are rather striking, in that they show that culture-specific traits are superimposed on an underlying, basic concept of semen transferral—a phenomenon that is typical of the Papuan groups, who often show marked differences between populations that otherwise are rather close and similar. The process that creates these differences, known in evolutionary biology as the process, and the principle, of **character displacement**, operates inherently in the Papuan cultures and, with other processes, has led to the development of the enormous number of very small ethnic groups that are distinct, above all, with regard to their languages.

The interesting question, why the very intricate system of ritualized homosexuality, which involves much more than sexuality itself, should have evolved in some Papuan cultures but not others, is very difficult to answer. Some aspects of this question will be addressed momentarily. At this time, some other sides of the puzzling customs will be examined. Knauft (1985) studied the Gebusi, one of the ethnic groups in the foothills of the Great Papuan Plateau, among whom ritualized homosexuality is practiced. In his work, Knauft stressed the spontaneous character of many of the male homosexual "trysts":

> In general, men do not fear—indeed, they actively seek out— heterosexual liaisons. At the same time, men's sexuality is directed toward other males as well as toward women. Like most societies of the Strickland-Bosavi area, Gebusi believe that insemination of boys is crucial to male growth and development . . . . Homosexual liaisons among Gebusi are most frequent between young men and adolescent boys, or between youths in their late teens. Middle-aged and older men joke about homosexuality, but their actual participation in (or control over) male sexual liaisons is minimal. In terms of kinship, Gebusi homosexual partners should be . . . unrelated or only distantly related to each other . . . . Homosexual trysts are matters of personal excitement and hyperbolic joking (Knauft, 1985, p. 32).

This sexual joking is an integral part of ritualized feats and of the telling of narratives, narratives that are wildly and intensely performed openly in the village and "are often filled with creative pornography" (Knauft, 1985, p. 298).

> Older men relive in their joking the celebrated bisexual vitality believed so characteristic of bachelors and young men. The younger men, likewise, become aroused by the allure of the dance and the songs, and by the generally ribald male orientation. While less bold in their joking, these young men are more apt to depart discretely for sexual trysts with each other (though this is in no sense inevitable). In symbolic/analytic terms, these are complementary solutions to the central problem embodied in the dance: how men can confront their sexual desires without destroying their good company with other men (Knauft, 1985, p. 266).

Does this combination of spontaneous and ritualized homosexuality provide an answer to the questions, How and in achieving what function did ritualized homosexuality evolve in these cultures? Male homoerotic fantasies and drives seem to be aroused rather easily, once a cultural carpet has been laid out.

Still, some adolescent males have difficulty fulfilling the traditionally prescribed roles:

> All males pass through both erotic stages, being first fellators, then fellateds: there are no exceptions since all Sambia males are initiated and pressured to engage in homosexual fellatio.
>
> The symbolism of the first homosexual teachings in initiation is elaborate and rich; the meaning of fellatio is related to secret bamboo flutes, and ritual equations are made between flutes, penis, and mother's breast, and between semen and breast milk .... Boys must drink semen to grow big and strong. At third-stage initiation, bachelors may experience personal difficulty in making the erotic switch in roles. Thereafter they may continue having oral sex with boys until they father children. Essentially, youths pass from an exclusively homosexual behavioral period to a briefer bisexual period, during which they may have both homosexual and heterosexual contacts in secret, and finally to exclusive heterosexual relationships. Social and sexual failures in masculine personhood may be defined as the failure to achieve these transitions (Herdt, 1984c, pp. 173-174).

Among the Kimam on Prince Hendrik Island on the southern coast of Irian Jaya (West New Guinea), it was reported, adolescent male initiates sometimes had anal intercourse with 7-8 adult males during the same night (Serpenti, 1984, p. 306). It seems quite possible that this kind of sexual behavior occurred against the adolescents' will. Probably the initiates know beforehand that a lot of physical hardship and psychological strain is connected to the *rites de passage*, and this knowledge, it is likely, enables them to tolerate and emotionally survive such practices. Serpenti (1984, p. 305) states, on the other hand, that this form of homosexuality can lead to lifelong emotional relationships.

On the Irian Jaya mainland, north of Prince Hendrik Island, live the Jaquai, of whom Boelaars (1981) reported:

> A father can order his son to go and sleep during the night with a certain man who will commit pederasty with him. The father will receive compensation for this. If this happens regularly between a man and the same boy, a stable relationship arises, comparable to that between a father and son ... or anus father and ... anus son .... Such a boy is allowed to consider that man's daughter as his sister and she will be "awarded" to him as his exchange sister for his future marriage (p. 84).

Again, sociopsychological pressure and coercion appear to be part of institutionalized adult-male/adolescent-male sexual behavior. This time, the pressure and coercion seem to be employed in a rather instrumental way by the father to enable him to collect material wealth. As is typical in New Guinean societies, he probably will spend much of it for his family and his clan to fulfill the debts of reciprocal obligations; yet, it is obvious that male children and adolescents in these societies have much less freedom in the important and very personal matters of sexual preference and general autonomy than such individuals have in the majority of other societies, in which ritualized adult-male/adolescent-male sexual behavior is absent.

If Herdt, who is an anthropologist and undoubtedly the leading authority on this matter, was correct when he wrote that ". . . women are more prized as sexual outlets than are boys" (1984c, pp. 189-190), why, then, did the system of adult-male/adolescent-male sexual behavior evolve at all? What is its adaptive function?

# Conclusion: An Attempt To Understand the Institution of Ritualized Adult-Male/Adolescent-Male Sexual Behavior

Many of the climatic, geographic, ecological, socioeconomic, and other factors that are pertinent to the ethnic groups that demonstrate ritualized adult-male/adolescent-male sexual behavior are found in other, quite similar locales in which this behavior does not exist. Therefore, researchers must look for other bases on which to understand the function of this behavior. There are two such bases that can be considered: (1) a culture-inherent, ideological basis and (2) a biosocial basis.

## Culture-Inherent, Ideological Basis of Understanding

It seems that the groups in question are characterized by being mentally and socially preoccupied with semen. In these "sperm cultures," the seminal fluid is a kind of cure-all: young males, and often young females as well (!), are believed to be unable to grow without taking in sperm in one form or other. Adult females do so through normal genital intercourse. Sperm is transferred into the body of young males, applied to the posts of houses, used in rituals to ensure the fertility of the gardens, and the like. Semen is a "scarce resource" (Herdt, 1984c, p. 176). The underlying rationale of this culturally propagated belief is not too difficult to understand, even though Westerners probably would weigh things differently, as do other Papuan and Austronesian societies, and say not that the ejaculate is scarce and therefore "costly" but, rather, that access to a suitable, fertile, female sexual partner is scarce.

This scarcity of adult females is pressingly true, for example, for most adult Eipo males. As can be seen from Figures 15.7 and 15.8, the sex ratio is heavily male biased; that is to say, there are considerably fewer females below approximately 40 years of age than there are males, a condition that is the result of female-biased infanticide. This skewed sex ratio is aggravated further by the existence of facultative polygyny (see Figures 15.8, 15.9). Yet, the Eipo, and very many other groups in Melanesia, have

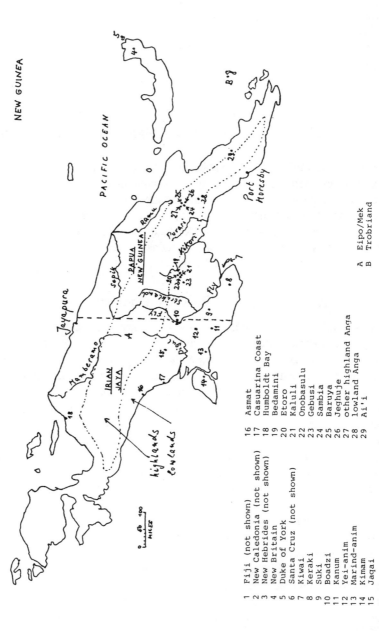

Figure 15.6. Map of the island of New Guinea and surrounding islands showing area in which reside specific ethnic groups that practice ritualized male/male homosexuality. (After Herdt 1984b.)

1  Fiji (not shown)
2  New Caledonia (not shown)
3  New Hebrides (not shown)
4  New Britain
5  Duke of York
6  Santa Cruz (not shown)
7  Kiwai
8  Keraki
9  Suki
10 Boadzi
11 Kanum
12 Yei-anim
13 Marind-anim
14 Kimam
15 Jaqai

16 Asmat
17 Casuarina Coast
18 Humboldt Bay
19 Bedamini
20 Etoro
21 Kaluli
22 Onobasulu
23 Gebusi
24 Sambia
25 Baruya
26 Jeghuje
27 other highland Anga
28 lowland Anga
29 Ai'i

A  Eipo/Mek
B  Trobriand

not developed institutionalized homosexuality as a way out of this apparent and explicitly stated male sexual dilemma. One could argue, however, that the scarcity of female sex partners, which would have existed, as one consequence of preferential female infanticide, in a number of traditional Papuan societies, has led to the cultural institution of homosexuality, through which males in their early years of adulthood and strong sexual drive "spend" their sperm on younger male initiates, thereby being excluded as competitors for procreative sexual intercourse with females.

It seems that, within the framework of emic epistemology, the religion-founded belief in the overriding powers of semen is a *conditio sine qua non* for male homoeroticism and homosexuality to be awakened from its twilight sleep and be used as an apparently very powerful, sociocultural motor of influence in so many spheres of everyday and festive behavior. By reinterpreting the shortage of suitable sexual partners (one must bear in mind exogamy rules, incest taboos, and male/female antagonism in New Guinean societies) as essentially being a shortage of semen that **must be** overcome if the society is to flourish further, these societies actually solve part of the difficulty in finding an "outlet" for the sexual drive. A specific, mythically sanctioned ideology functions in enabling their young-adult male members to utilize the sexual reservoir of adolescents who are their own biological sex.

To test this hypothesis, of course, one would have to have quantitative data that are very difficult to come by, namely, the frequency of overall sexual intercourse of males at different ages in some of the "sperm

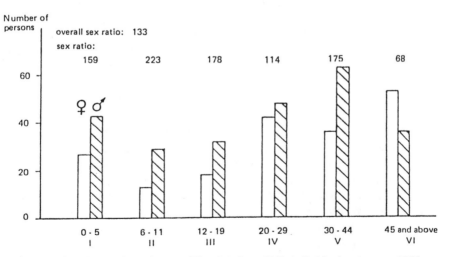

Figure 15.7. Sex ratios of some Eipo hamlets (440 individuals; August 1975 census).

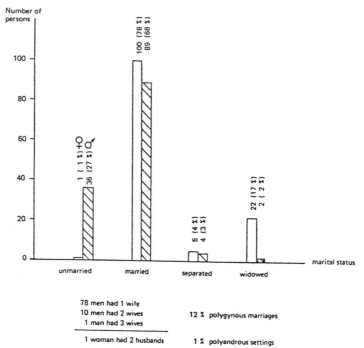

Figure 15.8. Marital status of 128 Eipo adult females and 131 Eipo adult males (259 individuals; August 1975 census).

cultures" and in some controls. One thinks of the adult males of the Dani, who are much more vigorous and better fed than the male members of most groups with ritualized homosexuality. According to Heider (1976), the Dani have a strict postpartum coitus taboo for up to 7 years (!) that includes a taboo against extramarital sex with female or male partners. With this information in mind, one wonders how much variability there is in actual, experienced sexual behavior among the inhabitants of this enigmatic island.

## Biosocial Basis of Understanding

Creed (1984) links ritualized adult-male/adolescent-male sexual behavior to the perpetuation of social order: by sexual subordination, older adult males control the sexual behavior of adolescent and younger adult males. This subordination is accomplished by the older males' imposed draining of the sexual drive and procreative capabilities of the young individuals. Irrespective of the rhetoric, the older adult males seem to fulfill their own social obligations—to impregnate the fertile females.

Another possible biosocial function of the behavior is that it tightly weaves the social fabric of the all-male men's-house alliances and other subgroups of males who eventually will work and fight together. Although

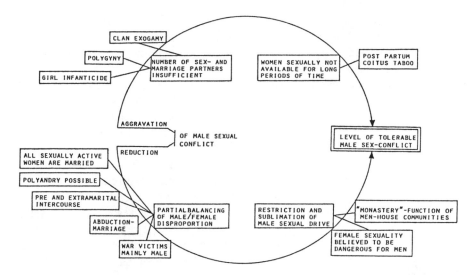

Figure 15.9. Mechanisms of aggravation and reduction of male sexual conflict.

this function constitutes perhaps the best single explanatory stone in the mosaic of ritualized adult-male/adolescent-male sexual behavior, it must be stressed that most societies with all-male men's-house alliances do not have ritualized adult-male/adolescent-male sexual behavior. On the other hand, very similar mechanisms of male/male affiliation have existed in premodern Japan (A. Sibatani, personal communication) and currently operate in Western all-male boarding schools, monasteries, armies, and prisons and in some violent, male urban street gangs.

There definitely is no single and no easy basis for the understanding of ritualized adult-male/adolescent-male sexual behavior in Melanesia, and above all, this behavior cannot serve as a justification for or legitimization of nonritualized androphilic pedo- and ephebophilia in Western industrialized countries.

## Summary

Ritualized adult-male/adolescent-male sexual behavior in Melanesia was discussed from an anthropological and a human-ethology perspective. To provide an understanding of the biosocial function of this behavior, other aspects of sexual behavior in Melanesia were discussed in the context of the culturally transmitted dichotomy of the male and female worlds with the resultant male fear of female genitals and menstrual blood. In the biosocial realm, the approximately 3:2 male-skewed sex ratio during adolescence and early adulthood, as a result of preferential female infanticide existing, for example, among the Eipo of Irian Jaya, has not led to casual or to institutionalized homosexuality. One could argue, however, that in those societies where institutionalized adult-male/adolescent-male sexual behavior was and is found, such a surplus of males might have given rise to the tradition that older, more dominant males somehow control the heterosexual behavior of adolescent and young-adult males. The older males may exert this control through the cultural transmission of the fear-related mythology in conjunction with the socially mandated acting out of adult-male/adolescent-male sexual behavior. The younger, less sexually threatening adolescent males frequently drain off the sexual energies and procreative capacities of the more threatening young-adult males. The strong male/male bond that is created through these and other, less ritualized forms of male homosexual behavior is probably another important factor in the cultural evolution of ritualized homosexuality in some Papuan societies. Men are expected to plan, work, fight, and sometimes, die together. The necessary altruistic behavior and effective cooperation of the warriors as well as the acceptance of a male hierarchy would have been fostered by the institution of prescribed homosexuality. Cautions were given in using such ritualized behavior as a model for understanding pedo- and ephebophilia in Western industrialized societies.

# References

Bell-Krannhals, I.N. Was sich liebt, versteckt sich—Interaktionen zwischen Liebenden auf Kaileuna, Trobriand Inseln. Unpublished manuscript.

Bell-Krannhals, I.N., and Schiefenhövel, W. Repu et de bonne reputation. Système de partage du Yam aux îles de Trobriand, Nouvelle Guinée, Papou. *Bulletin d'Ecologie et Ethologie Humaines*, 1986, *1/2*, 128-140.

Boelaars, J.H.M.C. *Head hunters about themselves.* Verhandelingen van het Koninklijk Instituut voor Taal-, Land- en Volkenkunde series, 92. Den Haag: M. Nijhoff, 1981.

Creed, G.W. Sexual subordination: Institutionalized homosexuality and social control in Melanesia. *Ethnology*, 1984, *3*, 157-176.

Dereveux, G. *Baubo—Die mythische Vulva.* Frankfurt: Syndikat, 1981.

Eibl-Eibesfeldt, I., and Wickler, W. Die ethologische Bedeutung einiger Wächterfiguren auf Bali. *Zeitschrift für Tierpsychologie*, 1968, *25*, 719-726.

Heider, K.G. Dani sexuality: A low energy system. *Man*, 1976, *11*, 188-201.

Herdt, G.H. (Ed.). *Ritualized homosexuality in Melanesia.* Berkeley: University of California Press, 1984a.

Herdt, G.H. Ritualized homosexual behavior in the male cults of Melanesia, 1862-1983: An introduction. *In* G.H. Herdt (Ed.), *Ritualized homosexuality in Melanesia.* Berkeley: University of California Press, 1984b, pp. 1-82.

Herdt, G.H. Semen transaction in Sambia culture. *In* G.H. Herdt (Ed.), *Ritualized homosexuality in Melanesia.* Berkeley: University of California Press, 1984c, pp. 167-210.

Hiepko, P., and Schiefenhövel, W. *Mensch und Pflanze. Ergebnisse ethnotaxonomischer und ethnobotanischer Untersuchungen bei den Eipo, zentrales Bergland von Irian Jaya (West-Neuguinea), Indonesien.* Berlin: Reimer, 1987.

Hogbin, I. *The island of menstruating men. Religion in Wogeo, New Guinea.* Scranton, Penna.: Chandler, 1970.

Kelly, R.C. *Etoro social structure. A study in structural contradiction.* Ann Arbor: The University of Michigan Press, 1980.

Knauft, B. *Good company and violence—Sorcery and social action in a lowland New Guinea society.* Berkeley: University of California Press, 1985.

Malinowski, B. *The sexual life of savages.* London: Lowe & Brydone, 1929.

Schiefenhövel, W. Die Eipo-Leute des Berglands von Indonesisch-Neuguinea. *Homo,* 1976, *4,* 263-275.

Schiefenhövel, W. Kindliche Sexualität, Tabu und Schamgefühl bei "primitiven" Völkern. *In* Th. Hellbrügge (Ed.), *Die Entwicklung der kindlichen Sexualität.* München: Urban & Schwarzenberg, 1982, pp. 145-163.

Schiefenhövel, W. Preferential female infanticide and other mechanisms regulating population size among the Eipo. *In* N. Keyfitz (Ed.), *Population and biology.* Liège: Ordina, 1984.

Schiefenhövel, W. *Geburtsverhalten und reproduktive Strategien der Eipo. Ergebnisse humanethologischer und ethnomedizinischer Untersuchungen im zentralen Bergland von Irian Jaya (West-Neuguinea), Indonesien.* Berlin: Reimer, 1988.

Serpenti, L. The ritual meaning of homosexuality and pedophilia among the Kimam-Papuans of South Irian Jaya. *In* G.H. Herdt (Ed.), *Ritualized homosexuality in Melanesia.* Berkeley: University of California Press, 1984, pp. 292-317.

Swadling, P. *Papua New Guinea's prehistory.* Boroko, Papua New Guinea: National Museum and Art Gallery, 1981.

Williams, F.E. *Orokaiva society.* London: Oxford University Press, 1930.

Williams, F.E. *Papuans of the Trans-Fly.* Oxford, England: Clarendon, 1936.

# 16
# Selected Cross-Generational Sexual Behavior in Traditional Hawai'i: A Sexological Ethnography

Milton Diamond
*Department of Anatomy and Reproductive Biology*
*John A. Burns School of Medicine*
*University of Hawai'i*
*Honolulu, Hawai'i 96822*

## Introduction

Anthropological studies of human sexual behavior traditionally are difficult to conduct and to interpret because so much of any sexual behavior is private and must be understood through reporting by others rather than through direct observation. Sexual behavior between adults and nonadults is especially difficult to study, but an understanding can be facilitated if one looks at that behavior across time, species, and societies. Hawai'i[1] has several characteristics that make it a useful society in which to view such behavior.

Hawai'i was one of the first South Pacific societies to be visited and written about by Westerners (Cook, 1773). What it currently lacks in cultural purity, as a consequence of long association with foreigners, is partly compensated for by 200 years of contact and observation. Furthermore, over the years since Cook's visit, published comparisons have been drawn between Hawai'i and lesser known societies in other parts of Oceania and Polynesia (e.g., Marshall and Suggs, 1971).

This author has spent more than 20 years living and working in Hawai'i as an academic sexologist. This chapter is written mainly for readers who will benefit from seeing aspects of selected cross-generational sexual behavior in the context of a non-Judeo-Christian and non-Western society.

Two introductory notes of caution must be given. The first concerns the research methods. Many of the findings reported in this chapter are derived from historical/anthropological records that were written after the late 18th century, when contact between the Hawaiian Islands and the outside world was established. In addition, some of the information presented was obtained through interviews with Hawaiians, including *kupuna*[2] (elders), who pass down what they know as traditional. Contradictions that arose between research sources, i.e., the written ethnographic records and interviews, were integrated during the preparation of this chapter or are noted herein.

The second caution is about the term "traditional." Traditional behavior patterns are the behavior patterns of the Hawai'i described by Captain Cook and others in the late 1700's. Some of these practices continue to some degree into the 20th century, while others have been lost. The behavior patterns that were the most quickly lost were the ones that were part of the *kapu* (taboo) system, an elaborate cultural pattern of rules, restrictions, and punishments regulating interpersonal actions and relationships to the gods, the chiefs of varying stature (*ali'i*), and the *'aina* (land or homeland) (Kuykendall, 1938, Vol. 1, pp. 7-9; Valeri, 1985, pp. 90-95). The *kapu* system was officially abolished in November 1819 (Kuykendall, 1938, Vol. 1, pp. 65-70; Kamakau, 1961, pp. 219-228).

Under the *kapu* system, there were forms of bondage, human sacrifice (Valeri, 1985), and infanticide (Malo, 1951, p. 70; Kamakau, 1961, p. 234). While adult females were afforded many rights and some had great status, it was *kapu* for them to eat certain foods; they could be put to death for eating pork, certain kinds of bananas or coconuts, and certain fish (Malo, 1951, p. 29). *Poi* and *taro* (basic staples of the Hawaiian diet) were not to be eaten from the same dish by males and females. Furthermore, in certain circumstances upon threat of death, adult males and adult females were not allowed to eat together, although they could have sex together. Religious laws controlled eating more than they controlled sex.

The Western concept of marriage did not exist in Hawai'i (Sahlins, 1985, pp. 22-25), and even if a common definition of marriage is applied (Malinowski, 1962, p. 252; Ford and Beach, 1951, pp. 187-192), sexual/genital interactions were socially accepted in many "nonmarital" situations. The concepts of premarital and extramarital sexual activities were absent, and it was probably true of Hawai'i, as it was said to have been true of much of Polynesia, that "there are no people in the world who indulge themselves more in their sensual appetites than these: . . ." (Ellis, 1782, Vol. 2, p. 153).

Within the framework just presented, this chapter will place human adult/nonadult sexual behavior in Hawai'i in a broader cultural context. (For more in-depth ethnography, see Davenport, 1976; Diamond, 1985; Ford and Beach, 1951; Gregersen, 1982; Handy and Pukui, 1958; Handy et al., 1965; Kamakau, 1961, 1964; Kuykendall, 1938; Malo, 1951; Marshall and Suggs, 1971; Pukui, Haertig, and Lee, 1972, Vols. 1 and 2; Suggs, 1966; and Valeri, 1985.)

## Nudity

In traditional Hawai'i, nudity was not seen primarily as being sexual. Warm climate often dictates less clothing. The basic dress was a *malo* (loin

Figure 16.1. Contemporary male *kupuna* pounding *poi* from *taro* while wearing only a *malo*. (Photograph taken by M. Diamond.)

Figure 16.2. The idols were uncovered during the daytime but wore *malo* in the evening. The expression used to describe such uncovered idols was "*ua ku lewalewa ka laau*" ("the wood stands with its nakedness pendant") (Malo, 1951, p. 169). (Photograph taken by M. Diamond.)

cloth) for adult males (Figure 16.1) and a leaf or *tapa* (bark) skirt for adult females. The female breasts were not covered. A young male was permitted to wear a *malo* only after he began to live in the *hale mua* ("men's house"), usually between the ages of 4 and 6 (Handy and Pukui, 1958, p. 9). Once the pubic hair began to grow, the genitals were covered, reportedly out of respect for the *piko ma'i* (genitals) and to protect the organs that gave progeny. A *tapa* robe might be added for protection against the cold or sun (Handy, 1930, p. 10), not for modesty.

Adult males and adult females engaged in all water sports without clothes. They dared not wear wet clothes on land, because to do so in the presence of royalty was a capital crime (Malo, 1951, p. 56; see Fornander, 1916/1917-1920, Vol. 5, p. 110). (The missionaries banned surfing because the surfers stood unashamedly naked on their boards.)

Nudity among adults had important nonsexual significance, such as being a symbol of death or punishment (Fornander, 1916/1917-1920, Vol. 5, p. 324) or of lamentation and anguish (Kamakau, 1964, pp. 34-35). Individuals who were slated for sacrifice or who were banished were stripped naked. A dream of nudity, it was claimed, was a portent of death.

Nudity as a ceremonial condition could be a sign of submission or of resignation, or it could be an appeal for forgiveness. One who had wronged or angered another might disrobe and follow the injured individual, asking forgiveness. When approached by "night marchers" (souls of the departed) or in the presence of spirits, one might disrobe and lie flat, face up, until they passed (Pukui, Haertig, and Lee, 1972, p. 107).

Nudity also was a sign of respect. Consider this quotation from Kamakau (1961, pp. 208-209) writing in the 1860's of Kamehameha the Great: "Kamehameha did not ordinarily take Keopuolani [his first coital partner] as his sleeping companion. She was his niece and of so high a tabu that he had to take off his *malo* before he came into her presence, but he desired above everything to have children of the highest rank."

Ceremonial nudity also could be a sign of respect extended not merely to the Highest Chief or Chiefess but even to their bearers or possessions. "Whoever happened to meet the King's calabash of water as it was brought from the spring . . . was required to unrobe and lie down upon the earth, till the bearer of the vessel had gone by" (Tyerman and Bennet, 1832, Vol. 2, p. 69).

Ceremonial nudity with prayer was also used to avert sorcery. Hawaiians had a ceremony called "*manewanewa*." At high noon or midnight, families attempting to avert evil disrobed. One person stayed at the doorway to the *hale* (house) and prayed. The others prayed while they walked around the house. After the fifth time around, the one at the door poured water over the heads of the others, and the ceremony ended (Pukui, Haertig, and Lee, 1972, p. 107).

The attitude of traditional Hawaiians toward familial nudity was different from their attitude toward societal nudity. It was common for whole families to bathe and swim together nude in a formalized but also sociable manner, and often, baths or swims occurred several times a day.

On the basis of these examples, therefore, it can be seen that nudity was ritualized in many aspects of society. In fact, an individual seen nude out of a ritualized context was considered to be *pupule* (crazed) with grief, not lustful (Pukui, Haertig, and Lee, 1972, pp. 107, 183).

Mary Kawena Pukui, a highly respected *kupuna*, claimed that "genital exposure was not an indecent, or even sexually-tinged action . . . . To expose oneself was never perversion; it was frequently a protection" (Pukui, Haertig, and Lee, 1972, p. 107). (See Eibl-Eibesfeldt, this volume.)

## Genitals

The genitals were considered holy and were appreciated as being good. They were treated with respect and worship, and ostensibly, they were covered for protection, not shame (Sahlins, 1985, p. 15). Also, it was believed that the genitals possessed *mana* (spiritual power), and this belief was expressed with clarity in the traditional woodcarvings of the powerful gods, whose genitals were shown to be prominent (Figure 16.2).

The positive attitudes held by the traditional Hawaiians toward the genitals also were conveyed in part through some of the stone carvings still present in the Hawaiian Islands, the most noted of the major carvings being the phallic rocks of the Island of Moloka'i. These carvings are of the penis, representing the male god Kane, and the vulva, representing the female deity. Throughout the islands, rocks configured into the shape of male and female genitals or identified as being male or female rocks were not uncommon (Pukui, Haertig, and Lee, 1972, p. 103). (See Figures 16.3 and 16.4.)

On the "Big Island" of Hawai'i, in addition, there is a cave with a rock vagina some 20 feet in length. All of these kinds of formations, possessed of great *mana*, were used to enhance fertility and sexual ability. As can be judged by contemporary offerings seen at these formations, they still are visited reverently in Hawai'i.

## Genital Chant

Within the culture, genitals were addressed in song and story. Traditional Hawaiians had public names for their private parts, and they were proud of their endowments. Hawaiian royalty, and commoners as well, had their own *mele ma'i*, a genital chant (Handy and Pukui, 1958, p. 93; Pukui, Haertig, and Lee, 1972, p. 76). These chants described, sometimes figuratively and sometimes literally and openly, the individual's sexual organs.

Figure 16.3. Phallic rock of Moloka'i showing a subincision mark. This rock is in a cleared area and is marked by a tourist sign. (Photograph taken by M. Diamond.)

Queen Lili'uokulani's *mele ma'i* told of *Anapau* (Frisky), her frolicking genitals that went up and down. King Kalakaua's *mele ma'i* described the large size of his penis (Pukui, Haertig, and Lee, 1972, p. 85).

Figure 16.4. Vulva rock of Moloka'i. The clitoris is prominent. As elsewhere in the Hawaiian Islands, male and female rocks usually were paired. This female rock is some 50 yards distant from the male phallic rock and is among trees and unmarked. (Photograph taken by M. Diamond.)

These *mele ma'i* were composed with respect and affection. Typically, the genitals of *ali'i* were named in infancy, and the songs were written when the individuals were young so they might be predictive or set role expectations. During the celebration of a young *ali'i*'s first birthday, and often a young commoner's, poets, chanters, and dancers composed dances, chants, and songs to that individual. Among these songs and poems were *mele ma'i* describing the genitals as being valuable for begetting future generations (Pukui, Haertig, and Lee, 1972, p. 76; Sahlins, 1985, pp. 15-16).

## Genital Preparation

### Penis

Subincision of the foreskin (Figure 16.2) was practiced, and ostensibly, to prepare for this practice, the penis was blown into daily starting from birth (Handy and Pukui, 1958, p. 94; Pukui, Haertig, and Lee, 1972, p. 75). The blowing was said to loosen and balloon the foreskin and separate it from the glans, so that when the time of subincision came, the skin was quickly and easily slit. The blowing continued daily until the infant was old enough to urinate in an arch, wetting the blower; then it was done less often, perhaps three times a week until the young male was 6 or 7.[3]

A *makua hine* ("aunt") or *kupuna wahine* ("grandmother") did the blowing (Pukui, Haertig, and Lee, 1972, p. 80). Any number of adult females were qualified to be the blower for a particular young male, because traditionally in Hawai'i, all age mates of an offspring's parents were considered to be "parents" in some way, and all individuals of grandparental age were considered to be *kupuna* (grandparent or elder). Therefore, the same term might refer to a blood relative, a nonrelative, or a neighbor.

The penis-blowing procedure was said to guarantee health and efficient coitus (Pukui, Haertig, and Lee, 1972, p. 75). This procedure, and the vulva treatment to be mentioned, was said to make the genitals more beautiful and to be a form of "blessings with which loving relatives desired to endow the firstborn throughout life . . . . What was true for the firstborn was true for subsequent children, to a lesser degree" (Handy and Pukui, 1958, p. 94).

This penis-blowing procedure was reported by several informants as having been experienced personally; one Hawaiian male received this attention as an infant, and one Hawaiian female performed it on her grandchildren; one Caucasian male reported that his Hawaiian mother-in-law had performed the procedure on his own infant. The Hawaiian-male informant placed the procedure in its cultural context and saw it neither as being a sexual activity nor as potentially creating a problem. The Caucasian informant, who had been unaware of the practice, was disturbed when he discovered what his baby-sitting Hawaiian mother-in-law was doing to his young son. Even after his wife and mother-in-law put the procedure in its cultural context, he was not placated. He did convince his mother-in-law to cease the activity, but she did not appreciate his reasoning and remained concerned for her grandson's health.

When a young male was 6 or 7, penile subincision was performed by a specially trained *kahuna* (priest). Whereas the procedure was a puberty initiation rite in the Mangaia Islands (Marshall, 1971), in traditional Hawai'i, it was a religious rite and de facto acceptance of the young male's having reached a certain stage of life (Malo, 1951, pp. 93-94).

## Vulva

While a female was still an infant, mother's breast milk was squirted into her vagina, and the labia were pressed together (Handy and Pukui, 1958, p. 94). The mons was rubbed with *kukui* (candlenut) oil and pressed with the palm of the hand to flatten it and make it less prominent. The molding continued until the labia did not separate. This chore usually was done by the mother or by an "aunt" or a *tutu wahine* ("grandmother": a colloquial, less traditional Hawaiian term than *kupuna wahine*).

Among the Marquesas Islanders, similar attention was given to the vulva, but in addition, the young female's labia minor were stretched to make them longer. This practice often was done orally by the caretaking adult females (Suggs, 1966, p. 42). Danielsson (1986, p. 74) reported similar lengthening of the clitoris of young females in the Society and Austral Islands.

## Buttocks

In the perspective of traditional Hawaiians, the buttocks were related to sexuality and the genitals. The buttocks of infants, males more than females, were molded so that they became rounded and not flat (Handy and Pukui, 1958, p. 91). This practice and all of the practices discussed in relation to the preparation of the genitals exemplified adult/nonadult behavior that was not seen as being erotic, sexual, or abusive. It was seen as being an appropriate aspect of adult care of nonadults, a necessary chore.

## Sex Education in General[4]

Until the age of 4-6, young males and females played together. Between 4 and 6, young males went to live in the *hale mua*, where, through observation, they learned sex roles and sex-related expectations from adult males. Unlike traditions that were present in some other parts of Oceania (see Schiefenhövel, this volume), there is no evidence that ritualized adult-male/adolescent-male sexual activities were practiced in traditional Hawai'i.

Similarly, young females learned from the older women, with whom they remained. They were taught to look forward to sex and appreciate its pleasures. Both sexes heard the sex-positive conversations, songs, and stories of their elders and learned accordingly. Sexual exploration with same-sex age mates was actively encouraged by the age of puberty.

Young males learned to fish, plant, cook, and fight and to honor the *ali'i*, the gods and spirits, and work. Young females, too, learned of the *ali'i*, the gods and spirits, and sex-typed tasks, such as mat weaving, feather-garment and fiber crafts, hula, attending to births, and so on (Kuykendall, 1938, p. 6). In regard to sex, Valeri (1985, p. 123), in a manner some consider highly overdrawn, stated that "the occupation of a young woman is to procreate, which in the Hawaiian culture implies all that relates to seduction, in which it is said that women play a more active role than men ... properly feminine activities are ... chanting, dancing, and other activities that promote eroticism. It is the women who often compose and chant the *'mele inoa'* 'name chants' with their deliberately erotic content, and even the *'mele ma'i'* chants praising the genitals." Actually, these sex-role stereotypes do not reflect the complexity of the situation (see Linnekin, in press).

Sex training was direct and firsthand. Young individuals learned of coitus and sex play from instruction, direct observation, and practice. As they slept in the family house (*hale noa*), they observed their parents having coitus. "Public privacy" among the Mangaian Islanders, as it was described by Marshall (1971, p. 108), probably is similar to the "privacy" that was found in Hawai'i and elsewhere in Polynesia: "[A Mangaian may copulate], at any age, in the single room of a hut that contains from five to fifteen family members of all ages—as have his ancestors before him. His daughter may receive and make love with each of her varied nightly suitors in the same room .... But under most conditions, all of this takes place without social notice; everyone seems to be looking in another direction."

The young observed dogs, pigs, and other animals mating, and these activities were discussed openly with parents or other adults. Parturition was not a secret event and was well attended by the young and by adults, all of whom observed traditions that included the washing and burying of the placenta and, usually, the disposing of the umbilical cord (Pukui, Haertig, and Lee, 1972, p. 16; Handy and Pukui, 1958, p. 78).

The Hawaiian young also acquired sex education in day-by-day exposure to precepts, practices, and attitudes concerning sex. Traditionally, "... childish curiosity about sex was satisfied, with neither guilt nor shame instilled" (Pukui, Haertig, and Lee, 1972, p. 249). With variations depending upon rank, region, and social circumstances, the young individual learned the lore of *kapus*, social restraints and preferences, and attitudes toward both sex for procreation or love and sex for fun and pleasure. Each kind of sex was appreciated for its own value (Pukui, Haertig, and Lee, 1972, p. 79).

## Age and Preparation for First Coitus

Individuals of both sexes were expected to initiate and participate in coitus at puberty, although sexual activity, play, instruction, and so forth occurred much earlier. For instance, as part of exploratory play, the young investigated each other's genitals, and young males and females might masturbate each other heterosexually or homosexually. This activity occurred without adult disapproval, and it was considered to be an introduction to adulthood. Casual intercourse before adolescence was not an uncommon experience both for males (Handy and Pukui, 1958, p. 95) and females (Pukui, Haertig, and Lee, 1972, p. 78).

Ellis (1782, Vol. 2, p. 153) wrote of sexual expression in Oceania: "The ladies are very lavish of their favors ... and some of their attachments seemed purely the effects of affection. They are initiated into this way of life at a very early period; we saw some, who could not be more than ten years old."

The time considered "right" to start coitus was not so much based on chronological age as on ability or maturity (Pukui, Haertig, and Lee, 1972, p. 78). A male doing adult work or holding adult responsibilities was considered to be "old enough." A young male who could grow *taro* or catch many fish was considered mature. A female's first menses usually signaled she was ready for coitus if she had not already experienced it. Kamehameha the Great, who unified all the Hawaiian Islands, took his first "wife," Ka'ahu-manu, when she was 13 (Pukui, Haertig, and Lee, 1972, p. 78); he probably was several years older than she (Judd, 1976, p. 71).

As physical signs of maturity appeared, the young Hawaiian received more formal sex education. Among commoners, this education was traditionally and usually the responsibility of the *tutu wahine* for the females and the *tutu kane* ("grandfather") for the males. Suggs (1966) elaborated on the early sexual experiences of pubertal males with married females in their 30's and 40's in the Marquesas Islands, who "take special pains to be pleasing and patient with them ... a source of enjoyment for many Marquesan women" (p. 61). For young females of the Marquesas Islands, the first coital experience reportedly is earlier than it is for young males— before menarche—and occurs unplanned with an adult male (Suggs, 1966, p. 63).

Among *ali'i*, an experienced chiefess, usually a blood "aunt," instructed and trained the young males. Similarly, young females were trained by their "aunt," by another experienced woman, or by a *tutu kane*. The training concerned not only what to expect and what to do but also how to increase or maximize pleasure. Less formal but similar training was afforded to commoners. There was practice as well as theory. A young male was taught "timing" and how to please a female in order to help her attain orgasm (Pukui, Haertig, and Lee, 1972, p. 79). A young female was taught how to touch and caress a male and move her body to please them both. She was taught how to constrict and rhythmically contract her vaginal muscles (Pukui, Haertig, and Lee, 1972, p. 79). Several of the informants who were interviewed remember being so instructed. One adult female told of being instructed on how to get her vagina to "wink."

These adult/nonadult sexual interactions were socially approved behavior. Kamehameha the Great again can be used as an example. Before he aligned himself with Ka'ahu-manu, he had an infant, while "still a beardless youth," by Chiefess Kanekapoli, a wife of Kalani'opuu (Judd, 1976, p. 71). The infant was welcome and was accepted without stigma, as was any pregnancy resulting from such unions (Handy and Pukui, 1958, p. 110). For adults not to have given such education would have been unthinkable—a dereliction of duty.

Most important for Hawaiian society, the young learned of sexual humor. Among the Hawaiians, sex was a rich source of humor and enjoyment. In everyday conversation and in song and story, it was considered to be an "art form" to speak using sexual double entendres (*kaona*). One well-known folk song, still sung, uses the vowels as erotic expressions; their elongated sounds are highly sexual: aaaaaaa, eeeeeee, iiiiiii, ooooooo, uuuuuuu (Johnson, 1983). Erotic imagery was, and remains, common in speech, poetry, and songs: coconut tree bending over a female; a digging stick spreading a female's legs.

Suggs (1966, p. 39) considered the early manifestations of infantile and childhood sexual behavior, including sexual behavior with adults, to be among the most distinguishing features of Marquesan sexual behavior. Many of the activities he described, however, are similar to activities that were present in Hawai'i and elsewhere in Oceania. Oliver (1974, pp. 458-459), for example, reported on adult/nonadult sexual behavior in Tahiti and quoted the missionary Orsmond from 1832: "In all Tahitians as well as officers who come in ships there is a cry for little girls," and older females, when in a position to choose, preferred younger males. Marshall (1971, p. 126) described the routine early sexual encounters of young males and females in Mangaia as being with older, experienced males and females.

## Rules for Intercourse

As long as the individuals involved were of the appropriate social class, just about any type of sexual behavior between them was sanctioned. If a pregnancy resulted, it was welcome. If a socially inferior male had sex with a female of royalty, however, her family might demand his death or exile, and if a baby was born, it might be killed immediately (Malo, 1951,

p. 70). A higher class male's having sex with a lower class female was seen as being good, on the other hand, in that it added to her status. However, if the two participants were too far apart in class, any offspring was killed or sent into exile (Handy and Pukui, 1958, p. 79).

Neither physical appearance nor age mattered where coitus-for-genealogy was involved. The main concern in such instances was to preserve the highest level of *mana* and rank and to not dilute the family prestige (Kamakau, 1961, p. 208). If no offspring resulted, the sexual behavior itself was considered to be inconsequential.

The word for orgasm, *le'a*, also means "fun" and "joy" (Pukui, Haertig, and Lee, 1972, p. 83), an appropriate term in the Hawaiian language because the object of sexual interactions was mutual happiness and pleasure. There were no restrictions regarding any positions for intercourse. The appellation probably is undeserved, but the position in which the male squats between the supine female's legs has been called the "Oceanic position" since its description by Malinowski (Gregersen, 1982, p. 61).

Sexual positions rarely are mentioned in ethnographies of Hawai'i, while other potentially curious or "uncouth" matters are. For example, oral, anal, masturbatory, and other kinds of sexual behavior were documented practices. Types of homosexual behavior were accepted and, reportedly, were unstigmatized; many of the royalty were known for their ambisexual activities (Kamakau, 1961, pp. 234-235; Malo, 1951, p. 256).

According to the reports of Westerners, extensive foreplay was not a standard part of coitus. Many reports and stories tell of an adult male and an adult female meeting on a trail, in the bush, or on a secluded beach and engaging in coitus immediately, with little conversation and few preliminaries. This kind of behavior also has been reported as having been the norm elsewhere in Oceania, e.g., among Mangaian Islanders (Marshall, 1971, pp. 118-121) and Marquesas Islanders (Suggs, 1966, p. 98). Noteworthy in regard to such behavior is that orgasm for both the female and the male was not reported to be a problem despite the briefness of the encounter. Both males and females reportedly climaxed easily and frequently in traditional societies of Oceania.

Some of the reports of seemingly promiscuous and nonrelational sex that occurred in Oceania might reflect sampling and Western-oriented biases. This possibility has to be considered, because such interactions are not consistent with traditional songs, which speak of erotic and sensual courtship and foreplay (Kekuni Blaisdell, personal communication).

## Virginity, Promiscuity, and Monogamy

Aside from restrictions of class and family, there were few sex *kapu* for common people. Masturbation, sex between uncommitted individuals, paired individuals having lovers, liaisons, polyandry, polygyny, homosexual patterns of behavior, and such were all accepted practices (Malo, 1951, p. 74). Sex was considered to be good and healthy for all, young and old included.

Virginity was considered to be a virtue for female chiefs only, where genealogy was crucial. With this point in mind, *ali'i*—particularly the firstborn of either sex, with special status rights—often were betrothed while they were quite young. Sometimes the age difference between the betrothed was significant. Handy (1952, p. 272) reported the acceptance of pairings in which the female was hardly of walking age and the male was old enough to be her grandfather, as well as pairings in which tiny males were betrothed to elderly matrons. Such young individuals obviously did not have to restrain themselves as their libido matured, but it also is possible that mechanisms, such as the Westermarck effect, dampened eroticism if the individual was betrothed at a very young age (see Shepher, 1971; Wolf and Huang, 1980).

Once paired with a chief, the chiefess, like the commoners she ruled over, could have as many lovers or additional permanent sexual partners as she desired. One missionary, Reverend Thurston, described a secondary wife of Kalaniopu'u, Ruling Chief of the Island of Hawai'i in Cook's time. By her own admission, she had not fewer than 40 sexual partners and usually several concurrently (Thurston, December 10, 1828, Kailua). King Kamehameha had 21 known "wives" (Judd, 1976, pp. 290-292). Regarding age disparity, it was noted: "When he was an old man well on in years ... he took two young chiefesses to warm Kamehameha's old age" (Kamakau, 1961, p. 208).

Peripubertal females, in many cultures of Oceania, were noted to often be publicly sexually active with adults (Oliver, 1974, p. 362). Cook (1773, Vol. 1, p. 128) reported copulation in public in Hawai'i between an adult male and a female estimated to be 11 or 12 "without the least sense of it being indecent or improper." The disapproval implicit in Cook's report probably was caused as much by the public nature of the activity as by the age-related aspects. In Tahiti, one missionary noted in his diary that the High Priest Manimani, "... though nearly blind with age, is as libidinous now as when thirty years younger; ... [he] has frequently upwards of a dozen females with him, some of them apparently not above twelve or thirteen years of age" (cited in Danielsson, 1986, p. 57). Gauguin credited the inspiration for his famous painting "Manao tupapau" ("The Specter Watches Over Her"), completed in 1892, to his 13-year-old Tahitian "wife" Teha'amana (Hobhouse, 1988).

Suggs (1966, pp. 51-53) cited many cases of full heterosexual intercourse in public between adults and prepubertal individuals in Polynesia. The crews of the visiting ships showed no compunction against the activities, and the natives assisted in the efforts. Cunnilingus with young females was recorded without accompanying remarks that this kind of behavior was unusual or disapproved of for the participants. Occasions were recorded of elders assisting youngsters in having sex with other elders. Among the Marquesas Islanders in particular, Suggs (1966, p. 119) reported, extramarital relations were frequent and often involved older males with young virginal females and older females with young virginal males.

Until fairly recently, the birth of an infant to an unmarried female in Hawai'i, as elsewhere in Polynesia, was not a problem for her or society. Her fertility was proven, and the infant was wanted and taken care of by the extended *ohana* (family). Illegitimacy, in the Western sense, is inapplicable in regard to traditional Hawai'i (Pukui, Haertig, and Lee, 1972, p. 96).

While betrothals occurred, occasionally arranged by parents of chiefs or by other prominent persons, such formalized relationships were uncommon (Kamakau, 1964, pp. 25-26). Specific words for "husband" and "wife" did not exist; he was simply called *kane* (man) and she *wahine* (woman) (Handy and Pukui, 1958, p. 51; Sahlins, 1985, p. 23).

Individuals stayed together or not by choice rather than by commitment or obligation. One member of a pair could be monogamous while the other was polygamous. While public announcements of intentions to stay together among *ali'i* were noteworthy and often elaborate affairs, they were uncommon. David Malo, an advisor to King Kalakaua III and an Hawaiian convert to Christianity, wrote in 1839: "Of the people about court there were few who lived in marriage. The number of those who had no legitimate relations with women was greatly in the majority. Sodomy and other unnatural vices in which men were the correspondents, fornication and hired prostitution were practiced about court" (Malo, 1951, p. 65).[5]

A "pairing" ceremony among commoners was even more rare (Sahlins, 1985, p. 23). Couples that wanted to sleep and live together just did so (Sahlins, 1985, p. 23). Typically, no contract was expressed openly, although there probably was a vague set of expectations that linked the couple. Sahlins (1985, p. 23) expressed the situation thus: "For the people as for the chiefs, the effect of sex was society: a shifting set of liaisons that gradually became sorted out and weighted down by the practical considerations attached to them."

Monogamy, polygyny, and polyandry coexisted among *ali'i* and among commoners. Often, polygamy involved siblings (Morgan, 1964, p. 361).[6] Taking another sexual partner usually was acceptable if the first mate knew about the relationship and sanctioned it. Secret relationships were not approved of, however, although the discovery of such a relationship usually was disruptive only temporarily. Such sexual license greatly disturbed the early Christian missionaries. The "crimes" most commonly reported by the *haole* (foreigner, now refers to Caucasians) to occur among the Hawaiians, recorded as being 4-5 times more common than theft or property crimes, were fornication and adultery (Sahlins, 1985, p. 24); these terms, of course, had no meaning to the Hawaiians. "Adultery" came to be defined by the Hawaiians as "sexual activity with a nonregular partner within the *hale*." If the coitus occurred outside the house in private, it was not a problem to the Hawaiians, since it did not disrupt the status quo.

Sexual exclusivity was not associated with "marriage." Such an idea would have been unusual to Polynesian society (Danielsson, 1986, p. 115). Gregersen (1982, p. 250) reported monogamy in only 30 of 127 Pacific island cultures studied, the rest of the cultures being polygamous. Worldwide, Ford and Beach (1951, p. 108) found multiple mateships permitted in 84% of the 185 societies in their sample.

Relationships were dissolved at the desire of one or both partners. Sex with others was not seen as a cause for separation. Jealousy was considered unwarranted. Handy and Pukui (1958, pp. 57-58) wrote: ". . . where love of one man by two women were involved [and vice versa], it was considered bad manners (*maikai ole*, "not good") for a *punalua* (lover) to hold spite or malice in their hearts towards each other. The very existence of the formal [*punalua*] relationship . . . worked against ill feeling . . . ."

If one left a first mate for a second, the relationship to the first was not necessarily broken. Certainly, the ties were kept to the children (Johnson, 1983), and often, the sexual relationship between old partners continued.[7] In this context, the Western concentration on things "premarital," "marital," and "postmarital" did not have comparable meaning to traditional Hawaiians. In fact, it is only within the last 40 years or so that a majority of native Hawaiians have looked to the state licensing board to legitimize their marriages. Cohabitation without legal marriage was and is so frequent that, to encourage formal marriage, "common-law" marriages are not recognized by Hawai'i state law.

Considering that *ali'i* had much *mana*, commoner parents of a young female often wanted her to be impregnated by an *ali'i* male or to be taken as his mistress. The privilege of **jus primae noctis** for chiefs was often observed and was viewed with favor by a young female's parents (Pukui, Haertig, and Lee, 1972, p. 91; Sahlins, 1985, p. 24). If she were lucky, she might conceive his offspring and be allowed to keep it. This wish for high-*mana* descendants and relatives prompted Hawaiian families to send their daughters and wives to sleep with crewmen of early visiting ships. They thought these strange newcomers—with their large vessels and weapons that could kill immediately and at a distance—were indeed gods (Pukui, Haertig, and Lee, 1972, p. 92).

Promiscuity as a concept was not related to the number of sexual partners but rather to an improper concern with the lineage of potential offspring. Invitations to or direct acceptance of sex from the right strangers, on the part of males and females, were seen by the Hawaiians as good fun, good politics, good "*mana*" and cross-fertilization, or just good socialization (Pukui, Haertig, and Lee, 1972, p. 98). To be "propositioned" was considered a compliment, not an insult.

To have sex at the request of another was seen more as being passion than compassion. To want sex with another was seen as being natural. As one respondent put it: "Women didn't say no because it would have been considered "bad form," a rudeness. Also, they took the invitation as a compliment and often also wanted the sex themselves . . . ."

Prostitution, as it now would be defined, was nonexistent in pre-Western-contact Hawai'i, because sexual partners were readily available for mutual enjoyment. After Western contact occurred, the females continued to want sex openly, now with the *mana*-loaded sailors and traders. These males advocated bartering for sex, and with no religious or social restrictions against prostitution, the natives had no hesitancy about profiting from the newcomers' desires.

Females in traditional Hawai'i did experience intercourse that was forced upon them. While Westerners would interpret the forcing of intercourse on an individual as being criminal rape, the Hawaiians supposedly saw a romantic abduction or passionate lust (Johnson, 1983). There also were practices known as "wife-capture" and "husband-capture" (Sahlins, 1985, p. 10). Abductions and imposed sex supposedly were more commonly practiced by the *ali'i*. In one well-known instance, a chief who forced himself sexually upon an unwilling "married" female rewarded her by offering to make an *ali'i* of any possible male offspring, and this arrangement, it was said, was satisfactory to her and her "husband" (Malo, 1951, pp. 258-259).

There are tales of love that was unrequited—for any number of reasons: because one individual was promised to another, because one partner was jealous, because of feuds, for example. Also, sex was rejected—if the other was thought to be extremely unattractive, if one was promised to another, if it was solicited in an inappropriate place or with an inappropriate partner. Suicide because of unrequited love was known (Johnson, 1983).

## Inbreeding and Incest

An Hawaiian legend may be instructive here. *Poi*, the staple food of Hawai'i, is made from the root of the *taro* plant. *Taro* was itself considered sacred, supposedly the heavenly gift of an incestuous union. The god Wakea, the Sky-father, mated with the god Papa, the Earth-mother, to have their first offspring, a daughter, Ho'ohokukalani (night-sky and stars). Wakea later mated with his daughter, and their first offspring was the *taro* root, Haloa. A second incestuous union brought forth a son, Taro. *Taro* is propagated by cuttings; thus, the basic *taro* is considered ageless and godlike. The *taro* stalk, *ha* (ancient one; breath of life), is the symbol of the primary male god, Kane. The image of sacred offspring coming from a central stalk is considered by some to be a positive, folklore model that rationalizes incest, at least for chiefs.[8]

Some types of inbreeding were **preferred** for *ali'i*, and sometimes inbreeding was their obligation. An offspring of a royal full-brother/full-sister incestuous mating was considered to have the highest *mana* and, thus, to be the most sacred. "The children born of these two were gods, fire, heat and raging blazes" (Kamakau, 1964, p. 4). Their dynasty would be strengthened by the union. The chief born of such a union, a *ni'aupi'o*, was so divine he often did not travel during the day, since all who saw him had to prostrate themselves until he left (Malo, 1951, p. 54). To prevent a lust-inspired first mating from occurring between a member of royalty and one of the *kauwa* (despised) cast, young high-born male or female chiefs might be paired "prophylactically" with an older brother or sister or another member of the family (Malo, 1951, p. 71). *Ali'i* were forbidden to defile themselves by mating with members of the outcast *kauwa* group (Pukui, Haertig, and Lee, 1972, p. 86).

Among chiefs, the value of a relationship was measured more by its political and genealogical significance than purely by its consanguinity. Nephew/aunt or niece/uncle pairings were not uncommon and were approved of. It was expected that an older chiefess would sexually train one or more of her nephews, and any offspring of the two were warmly received into the household. Mother/son and father/daughter incestuous unions, however, were not approved of (Pukui, Haertig, and Lee, 1972, p. 86). Father/step-daughter matings also were generally disapproved of, but exceptions were known and occasionally accepted. The same attitude was held regarding matings between "father-in-law" and "daughter-in-law."

The inbreeding and incestuous pairings mentioned for *ali'i* were forbidden to commoners. There was a preference for exogamous matings of both male and female commoners with individuals who were members of a higher social class (hypergamy) (Pukui, Haertig, and Lee, 1972, p. 87), since traditional Hawai'i had several classes or castes (Pukui, Haertig, and Lee, 1972, pp. 286-287).

Within a given caste, first-cousin pairings were common. However, there was cultural disapproval of the mating of an adult female with a young male whom she had taken care of as an infant. Such behavior was not an offense against the gods but, rather, a social faux pas, and the thinking seems to have been, "Why couldn't she find someone more appropriate?" In keeping with the culture's collective attitudes, the punishment was not severe; it was characterized by ridicule and expressions of disgust (Pukui, Haertig, and Lee, 1972, p. 87). Suggs (1966, p. 128) reached a similar conclusion regarding incest in traditional Marquesan society—that it was disapproved of, but not seriously.

# Summary

Traditional Hawaiian society was culturally complex. Sex was seen as being positive and pleasurable, and although many cultural precepts existed concerning nonsexual aspects of life, the attitude toward sex was comparatively open and permissive. Sexual needs and desires were seen as being as basic as the need to eat, and the young were instructed in matters of sex. Adults attended physically to the sexual development of the young, including the preparation of their genitals. These sexual interactions between adults and the young, from the society's perspective, were seen as benefitting the young individual rather than as gratifying the adult. The sexual desire of an adult for a nonadult, heterosexual or homosexual, was accepted (Pukui, Haertig, and Lee, 1972, p. 111), and the regular erotic preference by an adult for a young individual probably was viewed more as being unusual than as being intrinsically bad. As Sahlins (1985, p. 29) put it, the Hawaiian "social system [was] constructed out of passion, structured out of sentiment." Even the basic Hawaiian creation story, "The *Kumulipo*," is highly sexual. It starts with the mating of the male god Wakea and the female god Papa and, throughout, turns to many sexual encounters.[9]

This approach to sex and sex education seemed to be fruitful in many ways. Sexual dysfunctions such as impotence and inhibitions of desire or lack of orgasm among males or females, common enough in Western society today, reportedly were unknown or at least rare (Pukui, Haertig, and Lee, 1972, pp. 84, 97). Sex was a salve and a glue for the total society.

The absence of concern with sexually transmitted disease (this affliction arrived with the first sailors from Europe in 1778), the lack of concern with illegitimacy, a permissive attitude toward multiple sex partners, and a feeling of obligation to sexually instruct in deed as well as in theory freed the traditional Hawaiians from most of contemporary Western society's great fears associated with sexual expression. To the Hawaiians, sex was definitely not a subject nor a set of behaviors to be avoided or reserved only for adults.

To know about sexual interactions between adults and the young in traditional Hawai'i is most instructive, because these interactions illustrate the power that cultural tradition wields not only in contributing to the organization of behavior but also in shaping humans' self-reported attitudes toward behavior patterns.

I believe that if you really **feel** Hawaiian—if in your bones you're Hawaiian—then you'll enjoy intercourse without constraint and with fulfillment. You'll know *le'a* as your ancestors did. It's natural. It's beautiful and satisfying. And it's just lots of fun!

Mary Kawena Pukui
(Pukui, Haertig, and Lee, 1972, p. 98)

*Acknowledgments*

For this work, I am indebted to many persons. My primary thanks go to the informants who shared their confidences and histories with me. Additionally, I would like to thank the following Hawai'i scholars of the University of Hawai'i-Manoa for reviewing this chapter and contributing their insights and advice: Professor Richard Kekuni Blaisdell, Acting Chairman, Hawaii Studies Department; Professor Rubellite Kawena Johnson, Department of Indo-Pacific Languages; Assistant Professor Jocelyn S. Linnekin, Department of Anthropology; Professor Joel Michael Hanna, Professor of Anthropology and Physiology; and Karen Peacock, Hawaii and Pacific Collection Curator. Special thanks go to "Auntie" Emma DeFries for the hours we visited and "talked story." Connie Brinton deserves thanks for her library work and perspective.

# Notes

[1]The apostrophe (') denotes a glottal stop in the pronunciation of Hawaiian words.

[2]Italicized words in this chapter are Hawaiian-language words.

[3]In contemporary times, pediatricians advise mothers to retract the foreskin and wash the glans several times a week, usually during the bath. This action prevents phimosis and serves a hygienic function similar to blowing.

[4]Much of the information presented in this section was modified from Pukui, Haertig, and Lee (1972) and Handy and Pukui (1958).

[5]Terms such as "sodomy," "fornication," and "adultery" were introduced pejoratively by the missionaries and are used pejoratively in these quotations. Among traditional Hawaiians, however, such nuances were absent.

[6]In Hawaiian tradition, lineage rights were transmitted by females, not by males. Thus, a male could have several wives, and each wife maintained her individual inheritance. The inheritance of prime importance was a specific genealogy, not material wealth. Private property was not a feature of traditional Hawaiian life.

[7]Having one or many sexual partners had no necessary correlation with the love of one's primary partner. Intense love was known, and the loss of a dear one was not just lamented but might be evidenced by self-inflicted pain and mutilation (e.g., Whitman, 1979, p. 26) in the form of burning by fire, breaking of teeth, or even blinding. One might take bones or body parts of a dead lover to sleep with (Malo, 1951, p. 99) or as keepsakes (Kamakau, 1964, p. 35).

[8]These gods, too, had multiple sexual partners. Wakea had at least three mates, and Papa had at least eight (Kamakau, 1964, p. 25).

⁹Contrast this story with the biblical concept of Creation, which is completely asexual. The Judeo-Christian God desired the formation of the world, and it came about by His will.

## References

Cook, J. *An account of a voyage round the world.* Vols. I and II. London: Hawkesworth Edition, 1773.

Danielsson, B. *Love in the South Seas.* Honolulu: Mutual Publishing, 1986.

Davenport, W.H. Sex in cross-cultural perspective. *In* F.A. Beach (Ed.), *Human sexuality in four perspectives.* Baltimore: The Johns Hopkins University Press, 1976, pp. 115-163.

Diamond, M. *The world of sexual behavior: Sexwatching.* New York: Gallery Press, 1985.

Ellis, W. *An authentic narrative of a voyage performed by Captain Cook and Captain Clerke ...,* 2 vols. in 1. London: Robinson, 1782. (Reprinted edition: Bibliotheca Australiana #55/56. New York: Da Capo Press, 1969.)

Ford, C.S., and Beach, F.A. *Patterns of sexual behavior.* New York: Harper & Row, 1951.

Fornander, A. *Collection of Hawaiian antiquities and folklore,* 3 vols. Honolulu: Bernice P. Bishop Museum, 1916/1917-1920. (Also published as *Memoirs of the Bishop Museum,* Vols. 4, 5, and 6.)

Gregersen, E. *Sexual practices: The story of human sexuality.* London: Mitchell Beazley, 1982.

Handy, E.S.C. *History and culture in the Society Islands.* Honolulu: Bernice P. Bishop Museum, 1930.

Handy, E.S.C. The Polynesian family system in Ka-u Hawaii. *J. of the Polynesian Society,* 1952, *61*(3,4), 243-282.

Handy, E.S.C., and Pukui, M.K. *The Polynesian family system in Ka-'u Hawaii.* Wellington, New Zealand: The Polynesian Society, 1958.

Handy, E.S.C., et al. *Ancient Hawaiian civilization: A series of lectures delivered at The Kamehameha Schools* (rev. ed.). Rutland, Vt.: Charles E. Tuttle, 1965.

Hobhouse, J. Civilized man, savage artist. *Newsweek,* May 16, 1988, pp. 78-80.

Johnson, R.K. Old Hawaiian sexual indoctrination. Lecture presented at a meeting of the American Association of Sex Educators, Counselors and Therapists, Honolulu, Hi., 1983. Audiotape.

Judd, W.F. *Kamehameha: A biography.* Honolulu: Island Heritage, 1976.

Kamakau, S.M. *Ruling chiefs of Hawaii.* Honolulu: Kamehameha School Press, 1961.

Kamakau, S.M. *Ka Po'e Kahiko: The people of old.* Honolulu: Bernice P. Bishop Museum Press, 1964.

Kuykendall, R.S. *Hawaiian kingdom 1778-1854: Vol. 1. Foundation and transformation.* Honolulu: University of Hawaii, 1938.

Linnekin, J. *Sacred queens and women of consequence: Rank, gender and colonialism in the Hawaiian Islands.* Ann Arbor, University of Michigan Press, in press.

Malinowski, B. *Sex, culture and myth.* New York: Harcourt, Brace & World, 1962.

Malo, D. *Hawaiian antiquities* (2nd ed.). Honolulu: Bernice P. Bishop Museum, 1951.

Marshall, D.S. Sexual behavior on Mangaia. *In* D.S. Marshall and R.C. Suggs (Eds.), *Human sexual behavior.* New York: Basic Books, 1971, pp. 103-162.

Marshall, D.S., and Suggs, R.C. (Eds.). *Human sexual behavior.* New York, Basic Books, 1971.

Morgan, L.H. *Ancient society.* Cambridge, Mass.: Belknap Press of Harvard University Press, 1964.

Oliver, D.L. *Ancient Tahitian society. Vol. 1, ethnography* (2nd ed.). Honolulu: The University Press of Hawaii, 1974.

Pukui, M.K., Haertig, E.W., and Lee, C.A. *Nana I Ke Kumu,* Vols. 1 and 2. Honolulu: Queen Lili'uokalani Children's Center, 1972.

Sahlins, M. *Islands of history.* Chicago: University of Chicago Press, 1985.

Shepher, J. Mate selection among second generation kibbutz adolescents and adults: Incest avoidance and negative imprinting. *Arch. Sex Behav.,* 1971, *1,* 293-307.

Suggs, R.C. *Marquesan sexual behavior.* New York: Harcourt, Brace & World, 1966.

Thurston, A. Missionary letters, 1828. In the collection of the Hawaiian Mission Children's Society Library, Honolulu, Hi.

Tyerman, D., and Bennet, G. *Journal of voyages and travels ... in the South Sea Islands, China, India, etc., between the years 1821 and 1829,* Vol. 2. Boston: Crocker & Brewster, 1832.

Valeri, V. *Kingship and sacrifice: Ritual and society in ancient Hawaii.* Chicago: University of Chicago Press, 1985.

Whitman, J.B. *An account of the Sandwich Islands: The Hawaiian journal of John B. Whitman 1813-1815.* (J.D. Holt, Ed.). Honolulu: Topgallant, 1979.

Wolf, A.P., and Huang, C. *Marriage and adoption in China, 1845-1945.* Stanford, Calif.: Stanford University Press, 1980.

# 17
# Pedophilia: A Specific Instance of New Phylism Theory as Applied to Paraphilic Lovemaps

John Money
*Johns Hopkins University and Hospital*
*Baltimore, Maryland 21205*

## Introduction: Phylism and Pairbonding

In many species, pairbonding between the neonate and one or each parent is necessary for the survival of the dependent young. In mammals, pairbonding of the infant with the mother, or a mother substitute, is a *sine qua non* of nutrition and survival. In terms of the evolutionary neurobiology of behavior, parent/offspring pairbonding is a primordial characteristic of mammalian phylogeny. Thus, the capability for pairbonding between a human parent and his or her baby is phylogenetically programmed into the species. That is to say, pairbonding is a species-determined unit of human existence, predetermined to occur, other things being equal, simply because humans are members of their species. There has been no satisfactory name suggested that includes all phylogenetic, or species-determined, units of human existence. Some, though not all, of them have been rather loosely categorized as instincts and as reflexes. The generic term **"phylism"*** that this author has adopted is derived from "phylogeny."[1] A phylism is defined as "a unit or building block of human existence that belongs to human beings, as individuals, through their heritage as members of their species."

---

*Denotes words or close variations thereof that are defined in the Glossary to this chapter.

Some phylisms have everyday, vernacular names, such as "breathing," "coughing," "sneezing," "hiccupping," "drinking," "swallowing," "biting," "chewing," "pissing," "shitting," "fucking," "laughing," "crying," "walking," "grasping," "holding," "sweating," "touching," "hurting," "tasting," "smelling," "hearing," and "seeing." The complete list has not been counted. Other phylisms have Latinate names, like "thermoregulation," "salt regulation," and "immunoregulation." Still others exist that have yet to be named, or that have been named only recently, for example, "pairbonding" and "troopbonding" (Money, 1983).

In the human species, the phylism of pairbonding applies to the sensuous relationship of parent and child and to the sensual relationship of lovers and of breeding partners. Although the pairs of individuals differ between one kind of pairbonding and the other, these two manifestations share some features in common (see Eibl-Eibesfeldt, this volume). In nature's design of things, the pairbonding of infancy serves a dual developmental role. As it does with other mammals, it ensures the survival of the individual, and as a precursor of later sexuoerotic pairbonding, it also ensures the survival of the species. Both manifestations of pairbonding are intimately related to the skin senses through the acts of holding, cuddling, hugging, rubbing, patting, rocking, and kissing. They are both related to sucking of the nipples and to the possibility of an orgastic climax (which delights some breast-feeding mothers and morally terrorizes others) that is induced by the stimulation of the nipple. In addition, both manifestations of pairbonding may be intimately related to genital arousal. Whereas the signs of genital arousal in female infants at the breast are inconspicuous, in naked male infants they are conspicuously displayed as erection of the penis (personal observation). The male infant's erection during breast-feeding is a developmental phenomenon in the same category as a fetus's erection, which at times is accompanied by manual manipulation as observed by sequential ultrasound imaging in utero (Meizner, 1987). It is also in the same category as sleep erections, which occur off and on for an average of 2 to 3 hours a night in earliest infancy and continue, generally at the same rate, until advanced senescence (Karacan et al., 1972, 1975).

## Entrainment of Sexuoerotic Phylisms

Despite nature's economy in the overlapping sexological aspects of pairbonding between parent and child and lover and lover, the majority of adults require no particular effort to keep the love of a child separate and different from the love of a sexual partner. It is precisely this differentiation that fails in the case of **pedophilia*** (pedo- + -philia*). For the **pedophile**, male or female, gynephilic or androphilic, the phylism of the sexuoeroticism of lover/lover bonding becomes entrained with the caretaking of the phylism of parent/child bonding.

Among the **paraphilias***, the phenomenon of entrainment is not unique to pedophilia. On the contrary, there is a corresponding entrainment of a phylism that can be identified in each of the paraphilias. In the case of **coprophilia*** and of **urophilia***, for example, the phylism that becomes entrained in the service of sexuoerotic arousal is the one, observed in many primate species, according to which the mother keeps her infant clean of excrement by licking it clean (Money, 1986, pp. 87-88). There is also the phylism investigated in rats (Moltz and Lee, 1983; Moltz, 1984) according to which a pheromone in the mother's fecal pellets induces the weanling to eat them, whereby the weanling gains a degree of immunological competence to resist infection.

The neurobiology of the entrainment of one phylism to another, as in the case of the paraphilias, constitutes a scientific problem still awaiting a solution. It is possible, of course, that the crossover may have its origin in an apparently minor error in the genome. It is also possible that its origin is not genomic but, rather, is a product of an error in the neurochemistries responsible for the prenatal or neonatal differentiation of sexual pathways in the developing brain (reviewed in Money, 1987a). Alternatively, the timing may be later in postnatal life, in which case the error would presumably be introduced into the brain during a critical period of development when the differentiation of its **lovemap*** (Money, 1986) is responsive to information received through the eyes, ears, and skin senses—in other words, through social learning, in a manner analogous to the acquisition of native language.

In syndromes of paraphilia, the biographies of sexological development that are retrieved retrospectively do, in some cases, include sufficient detail to implicate developmental learning as playing some role in the crossover, or entrainment, of phylisms. For example, in **klismaphilia*** (the enema paraphilia), the biographical information retrieved often reveals excessive perineal and genital stimulation that occurred in early childhood from the administration of enemas. In addition to information retrieved retrospectively, either from personal memory or from the testimony of others, there is now the promise of anterospectively recorded information, from which the content of developmental experiences progressively recorded throughout childhood can be related to the content of the paraphilic ideation and imagery (Money and Lamacz, 1989). In one published case (Money, 1986, Ch. 21), a paraphilic strategy through which one homosexual courted his own murder by soliciting a "straight" man (homosexual **autassassino-philia***) could be related in concept to biographical experiences, including multiple genital operations, consequent on having been born with an intersexual abnormality (genital ambiguity) and, as a result, having had an early history of ambivalent sex assignment.

The sexuoerotic entrainment of phylisms creates another characteristic that is common to all paraphilias, including pedophilia. Like the other paraphilias, pedophilia is not voluntarily chosen, nor can it be shed by voluntary decision. It is not a preference but a sexuoerotic orientation or status. It may be viewed as analogous to left-handedness or color blindness.

## Juvenile Sexual Rehearsal Play

In the human species, as in other primates for which observations have been recorded, there is in the development of the juveniles a period of sexual rehearsal play that prepares them for maturity (reviewed in Money, 1988). Rhesus monkeys deprived of juvenile sexual rehearsal play by being raised in isolation do not become competent in copulatory presenting and mounting as adults and do not reproduce their species. Juveniles that are released to play with age mates for as briefly as half an hour a day may become capable of copulation but only after a delay from the expected age of 6-9 months to 18-24 months and only in about one-third of cases. These latter juveniles, even though they do copulate, have a low birth rate.

As a species, human beings who are heirs to Western civilization have a long cultural heritage of negative strategies for dealing with juvenile sexual rehearsal play. These are strategies of vandalism that thwart, warp, and distort the normally developing lovemap and make it pathological. The interventions that induce the creation of this pathology include indifference and neglect instead of the active promotion of normophilic development; humiliation, prohibition, and abusive punishment of sexual rehearsal play; and coercive traumatization, wrong timing, and wrong matching of ages in sexual rehearsal play. The malignancy shared by all of these sources of lovemap pathology is the Catch-22 dilemma,[2] or entrapment, inherent in any type of taboo activity, namely, that you're damned if you do reveal it, and damned if you don't. Therefore, no help is available.

When the Catch-22 dilemma prevails, a juvenile involved in a relationship with an older pedophile has no way to escape without being traumatized by the penalties of disclosure and no way to remain without experiencing the penalties of not escaping. A history of this type of entrapment can sometimes be retrieved from adults who were thus entrapped as juveniles and became pedophiles upon reaching maturity. (See The Opponent-Process Principle, later in this chapter.) By contrast, the juvenile who is in a pedophile relationship but is not entrapped in it and is not at risk of retributive punishment if he or she stays in it is not at risk of becoming a pedophile in adulthood (Money and Weinrich, 1983). An example of this latter proposition may be found in certain localities of some big cities. In these localities, by tradition, boys have been sponsored by older pedophiles for three, four, or five generations (unpublished Baltimore data; Reeves, 1981). Since they are following in the footsteps of older male relatives, these boys are not threatened by the outcome of discovery. In addition, they are able to predict that their period of sponsorship will extend from around age 11 to age 15 and that at the latter age, they will begin heterosexual, age-mate dating.

The cultural tradition of pedophilia may belong not just to a small enclave of a population but also to an entire community, as in the case of various tribal peoples scattered across the Pacific in Melanesia and New Guinea (Herdt, 1984). The Sambia of the New Guinea Highlands (Herdt, 1981) are such a tribe. Their ancient customs as fierce head-hunting warriors survived European contact until after World War II. According to their folklore concerning their children, a boy could not become a warrior if he stayed living with women and children after age 8. So, he was taken into the men's longhouse to remain in the company of males only, there to be subjected to the rituals of indoctrination and initiation. As a baby, he had been nourished by woman's milk. As a juvenile, he would have to be nourished with men's milk so that his body would mature in the way that maturation occurs during puberty. It was an obligation of youths still too young to be married not to waste their semen but to have it sucked out of their penises by the prepubertal boys who, once able to ejaculate themselves, would nourish those still younger. At age 19, the age of marriage, their two-way experience of androphilic pedophilia would cease, and their lives would become heterosexual with an adult partner.

## The Vulnerability Factor

The universal male/male pedophilia of the Sambia demonstrates the sexological plasticity of the human organism and the making of pedophilia into the social norm. In a society in which pedophilia is not the social norm, however, postnatal social experiences responsible for the development of lifelong pedophilia that exists in defiance of the social norm cannot, in the present state of knowledge, be specified definitely. At best, such experiences can be specified only as necessary causes, but not as sufficient causes of the development of a pedophile. Conceptually, it is still necessary to postulate that there exists at least one intervening variable or vulnerability factor that is extant between the prenatal and the adult life of a pedophile, the precise nature of which remains to be ascertained. There are some cases of pedophilia, as well as of the other syndromes of paraphilia, in which there is evidence of a vulnerability factor that may be related to actual brain injury, or so-called "minimal brain damage" (Lehne, 1986; Money, 1986, Ch. 16), whereas there are other cases that suggest a vulnerability factor related to eidetic imagery and schizoid hallucinosis (Money, 1986, Ch. 16, Ch. 21) and still other cases suggestive of the cyclicity of manic-depressive illness (unpublished data). The preponderance of evidence, however, points to a vulnerability factor that is epileptiform and akin to temporal-lobe psychomotor epilepsy (Money, 1986, Ch. 16).

There are some cases of pedophilia, as well as cases of all paraphilias, in which there is definite clinical evidence of an altered state of consciousness for which an appropriate name is **"paraphilic fugue\* state"** (Money, 1986, Ch. 16). While in this fugue state, the patient may have an alternative name and an alternative juvenile wardrobe, as well as a juvenile appearance, bearing, and personality. His or her behavior gives the impression of a juvenile social age and of a juvenile sexuoerotic age. The pedophile in this state relates to the younger partner in the manner of a child engaging in sexual rehearsal play with another child. However, the pedophile is likely to have undergone the experience of limerence, that is, of sexuoerotic pairbonding and falling in love. It is doomed to be love unrequited, for the juvenile does not fall in love but, rather, responds with parent/child pairbonding and maybe a touch of hero worship. The latter is greatly enhanced by the juvenile's being treated indulgently and as an equal by the sponsor, without disciplinary moralizing. For the juvenile, engaging in sexual activity is a trade-off, not something that is spontaneously yearned for. The analogy is with a marriage as an arrangement rather than as a consummation of romantic passion. The juvenile's pairbonding to the pedophile is as to a parent or to a charismatic leader and not sexuoerotically as to a lover.

The pedophile's lovemap dictates that, for him or her, sexuoerotic attraction will be able to occur only if the partner is a member of a specified age group. In pedophilia, the age is juvenile and prepubertal. When the younger partner matures and enters a higher age group, then the glue of sexuoerotic attachment fails, and the relationship, if it continues, becomes one of friendship, mutually devoid of erotic passion.

## The Opponent-Process Principle

Participation in a pedophilic act is not synonymous with having the syndrome of pedophilia—the Sambia headhunters bear witness to this truth. For pedophilia to become permanently lodged in the lovemap, some pertinent mechanism has to operate during the course of development. Such a mechanism may be similar to the one that creates addictions. Among the principles of learning, there is only one that fits the data and makes reasonable sense, namely, the principle of opponent-process learning (Solomon, 1980). According to the opponent-process principle, that which at the outset is aversive subsequently reverses and becomes addictive. For example, the terror that accompanies the first free-fall parachute jumps of some learners may transmogrify into euphoria that gets the jumper "hooked" and addicted to parachuting as either a career or a sport. It is possible, though not yet proven, that the change is mediated by a brain-released flood of the body's own opiates or endorphins.

It is sometimes possible in a case of pedophilia to retrieve biographical information consistent with the principle of opponent process. One such example is the case history of a juvenile who was separated from his mother by death and then from his father and his familiar environment by being sent overseas to be taken care of by an aunt and uncle. These latter relatives promptly consigned him to a boys' boarding school. Grief-stricken and devoid of attachments, he was befriended by a pedophilic teacher—and entrapped in a Catch-22 dilemma that decreed that he would lose his only friend if he reported the relationship and would lose his honor if he did not.

A resolution of the dilemma lay in a spontaneous reversal from aversion to attraction with respect to the illicit genital activity. It was an attraction that became an addiction. After the maturation of puberty, he continued to be represented in his own lovemap as a juvenile engaging in juvenile sexual rehearsal play, and like his erstwhile pedophilic lover, he was himself addicted sexuoerotically to male juveniles exclusively. The mother of one of his juvenile partners fell in love with him and tried to convert him to having sex with her, but the conversion did not take.

## Chronophilias: Their Age Ranges

Pedophilia belongs in the category of the **chronophilias\***, which are part of a still larger category of paraphilias, namely, those of the eligibilic and/or stigmatic types. (The categories of paraphilia are described later in this chapter.) These types are the paraphilias in which the paraphile's partner must meet a particular criterion of eligibility, such as being an amputee (**acrotomophilia\***, one of the **morphophilias\***) or a member of another racial stock (an as yet unnamed morphophilia) or another age group (one of the chronophilias).

The chronophilias are named according to the developmental age of the eligible partner, which approximates the sexuoerotic age of the chronologically adult chronophile. If the eligible partner is an infant, **"infantophilia"\*** is the diagnostic term. If it is essential that the infant be wearing diapers, however, the Greek-derived term for the diapered infant, **"nepiophilia"\***, applies. (Look twice at those who come to a masquerade party in diapers!)

In the sequence of the chronophilias, infantophilia is followed by pedophilia, pertaining to the ages between infancy and puberty. For the exclusive pedophile, the maturational changes of puberty introduce not only pubic hair but also, in particular, the odors of the axillary and crotch exocrine glands, all of which nullify the sexuoerotic attractiveness of the juvenile partner.

The sequence of the chronophilias continues with **ephebophilia***, in which the eligible partner is in chronological adolescence. In the United States, federal legislation that was passed in 1984 raised the legal age of childhood to 18 years in order to expand the age range within which sexual contact is applicable for prosecution as "pedophilia" (Public Law 98-292, the Child Protection Act). Therefore, if one week before his 18th birthday a youth of 17 has sexual contact with a male or female friend aged 18, then the 18-year-old qualifies, in the technicality of the law, as a "pedophile." The discrepancy regarding age is not of days, however, but of years if the older partner has a fixation on adolescents exclusively, because the correct term for the chronophilia would be not "pedophilia" but "ephebophilia."

It would be feasible to have additional terms, like "twentyophilia" and so on, for describing the diagnosis of the person whose idealized partner, as represented in the lovemap, has no birthdays but instead remains forever at a particular stage of youthful maturity. In the current nosology, however, there is no terminology for chronophilias that may exist between ephebophilia and **gerontophilia***, the final diagnosis in the chronological sequence. In gerontophilia, the idealized partner represented in the lovemap of an adolescent or a young adult is one who belongs in age to the parental generation or, in some cases, to the grandparental generation. Such a partnership, though not illegal, may be stigmatized in some social circles.

## Pedophilic Genius

There are two 19th-century geniuses in children's literature who, if they lived today, would risk imprisonment, possibly for a lifetime, on accusations of ostensible sexual child abuse as pedophiles. One is the Oxford University mathematician Reverend Charles Dodgson [1832-1898], better known as Lewis Carroll, the author of *Alice's Adventures in Wonderland* and *Through the Looking Glass*. Both books were written for one of the young girls to whom he was attached. The other genius is Sir James Barrie [1860-1937], the author of *Peter Pan*.

Lewis Carroll's devotion was to prepubertal girls. From 1856, when he purchased his first camera, until he gave up photography in 1880, he befriended the mothers of several young girls and charmed the women into giving him permission to obtain an image of their daughters' naked innocence—this was an era when young children might be seen naked at the seaside. Though he was one of the earliest portrait photographers of adults as well as children, his reputation was local, not international, like his fame as an author (Cohen, 1978).

Before he died, he destroyed his own copies of nude portraits of young girls. The surviving copies are those that he had given to the girls' mothers. Four of them, to which Carroll had had oil-painted color and scenery added, are reproduced in Cohen (1978). There is no known evidence as to whether his devoted fondness for his little girl friends was or was not ever expressed in physical caresses.

Of Sir James Barrie it is known that, as a boy of 6, he was indelibly affected by his mother's prolonged mourning for her favorite son, David, who had died in a skating accident at age 13. Barrie became the boy who never grew up and who became intensely attached to young boys. As a writer in London, on his way to literary fame at the end of the 19th century, he became accepted in the household of the Llewelyn-Davies family in the role of an honorary uncle of the five sons. At the outset, he adored in particular the oldest son, George, aged 5, and subsequently, Michael, the fourth son. While still young, each parent became mysteriously stricken with a lethal illness, ostensibly cancer but possibly poisoning. The father died first and, three years later, the mother. After her death, Barrie mistranscribed one word in her will, substituting his own name, Jimmy, for Jenny, so as to ensure for himself legal guardianship of the five sons. George was killed in battle in France in 1915. Michael was drowned with a fellow student at Oxford in 1921 in what was presumed to be a lovers' suicide pact (Birkin, 1979).

In 1901, Barrie invented the character Peter Pan as a projection of himself. The character would achieve instantaneous fame on opening night, December 27, 1904, in the dramatic play that bore his name. In 1901, however, the character was part of a game named The Boy Castaways, the stage setting was Black Lake, a large and shallow pond on Barrie's summer estate, and the character's supporting cast was three young boys, the oldest of the Llewelyn-Davieses' sons (Birkin, 1979).

The genius of Sir James Barrie, like that of Lewis Carroll a generation before him, confronts society with a question for which it as yet has no answer: How great is too great a price to pay for the literary works of pedophilic genius? The appearance of such works, though unpredictable, is contingent upon nature's unfathomable scheme of things whereby, in some people, the phylism of parent/child bonding attaches to the phylism of lover/lover bonding. In the era of Carroll and Barrie, the wisdom of nature's scheme of things was tolerated, whereas today it is not. In the current era of nuclear physics, space flight, and microchip computers, pedophilic attachment has become a crime.

# Six Categories of Paraphilia and Their Associated Grand Stratagems

As was explained previously, pedophilia and ephebophilia are among the eligibilic/stigmatic paraphilias, within which category they are classified as chronophilias. The eligibilic/stigmatic category is one of six categories of paraphilia, each of which incorporates a grand stratagem whereby lust and carnality are dissociated from love and romantic affection. Each of these six grand stratagems has a sexuoerotic application in the paraphilias and, also, an application in the nonsexuoerotic cultural heritage of Western society. Thus sacrifice and expiation apply to religion; marauding and predation to warfare; mercantilism and venality to commerce; fetishes and talismans to magic; eligibility and stigmata to kinship; and solicitation and allure to fashion. Whereas these stratagems are acceptable in the nonsexuoerotic aspects of Western society, they are not acceptable where sex and eroticism are involved. However, they become acceptable to the paraphile, and they allow him or her to partake of sexuoerotic experiences of lust, even while failing to include love.

The significance to paraphilia of each of the six grand stratagems is as follows.

The **sacrificial/expiatory stratagem** requires reparation or atonement for the sin of lust by way of penance and sacrifice. The extreme sacrifice is lust murder—**erotophonophilia\*** when the partner is sacrificed and autassassinophilia when one stage-manages the sacrifice of oneself. Excluding death, there are varying degrees, from major to minor, of sadomasochistic sacrifice and penance for the sin of lust.

The **marauding/predation stratagem** requires that, because saintly lovers do not consent to the sin of lust, a partner in lust must be stolen, abducted, or coerced by force. The extreme case of this stratagem is the syndrome of assaultive and violent paraphilic rape (**raptophilia\*** or **biastophilia\***). The spectrum of coercion ranges from major to minor. In statutory rape, there may be no coercion, but a consensual and pairbonded love affair, one of the partners being below the legal age of consent.

The **mercantile/venal stratagem** requires that sinful lust be traded, bartered, or purchased and paid for, because saintly lovers do not engage consensually in its free exchange. The very existence of this stratagem gets masked by reason of its place in the orgasm trade. Nonetheless, there are some hustlers and prostitutes, as well as their customers, who are paraphiles whose paraphilia is **chrematistophilia\***—marketing and purchasing sex. Some chrematistophiles who are not in the commercial orgasm trade pretend with play money or have the partner impersonate a whore or a hustler and watch while the partner interacts with a third person. Some set themselves up to be victims of blackmail or robbery, and some are blackmailers or robbers.

The **fetishistic/talismanic stratagem** spares the saintly lover from the sin of lust by substituting a token, fetish, or talisman for the lover. Fetishes are predominantly either smelly (in **olfactophilia\***) or touchy-feely (in **hyphephilia\***), and both kinds are derived from the similarity in smell and feel to parts of the human body. Devotion to the fetish may be all-consuming or minor.

The **eligibilic/stigmatic stratagem** requires that the partner in lust be, metaphorically, a pagan infidel—disparate in religion, race, color, nationality, social class, or age from the saintly lovers of one's own social group. The disparity in morphophilia pertains to disparity of bodily appearance, and as explained previously, the disparity in chronophilia relates to age. An exceptional example of morphophilia is acrotomophilia, in which the partner must have an amputation stump. The age-range limits of chronophilia are infantophilia/nepiophilia and gerontophilia, respectively.

The **solicitational/allurative stratagem** protects the saint by displacing lust from the act of copulation in the acceptive phase to an invitational gesture or overture of the proceptive phase. This behavior might be called in the vernacular "the paraphilia of the cockteaser" or, in gay argot, "of the loving queen." Among primates, exhibiting the genitals and inspecting them are prototypic invitations to copulate. In paraphilic exhibitionism of the penis (**peodeiktophilia***) and in **voyeurism*** (being a Peeping Tom), the preliminary overture displaces the main act in lustful importance. Displacement in this stratagem is the counterpart of inclusion of something in the other five stratagems.

In addition to these six grand stratagems of paraphilia, there is a satellite stratagem that may function within the orbit of any one of the other six. In the vocabulary of the theater, it is the stratagem of "the understudy," the one who, in case of emergency, is prepared to replace the leading actor and play the actor's role.

In the course of growing up, children who have no direct experience of the theater know about taking the role of the other, for it is an intrinsic aspect of childhood play. In addition, they hear stories of people who heroically substitute themselves and die to rescue another. They also become acquainted with this theme as a basic tenet of Christianity.

As a stratagem of paraphilia, the **subrogation/understudy stratagem** is one in which someone who represents saintly love is rescued from the defilement of lust by being replaced by an understudy, or subrogate, who becomes defiled instead. The understudy is oneself.

The subrogation/understudy stratagem has different manifestations. It applies to some highly specific cases of paraphilic adultery. To illustrate, Joe, the adulterer, saves his own lust from extinction, but only on the condition that, by having adulterous sex with Jill, he is a stand-in for her abstinent husband, who recoils from being defiled by lust. As another example, there are some highly specific cases of paraphilic incest in adolescent girls in which the only condition whereby such a girl is entitled to her own lust is that she become a stand-in for her mother, who, otherwise, would suffer unwanted defilement by the lust of the man, the girl's father or stepfather, whose lust her mother has renounced. This same girl eventually may run away from home to become a prostitute. She may also become pairbonded as a lesbian while earning her living by sexual service to men.

It may not be a daughter but a son who is the stand-in, saving his mother from the defilement of his father's lust by diverting it to himself in a relationship that is both incestuous and homosexual. In that case, the subrogation/understudy stratagem entails a degree of gender crosscoding, or transposition, in the son that may be full-fledged **transsexualism\*** or **gynemimesis\*** at one extreme, or episodic **transvestophilia\***, or entirely noneffeminated male/male bonding at the other extreme. Homosexual incest between a son and his father or stepfather protects the boy's mother from the lust of only one man. However, insofar as the son becomes the recipient of the lust of other males, he diverts their lust away from other women, as well. In addition, he himself does not defile the saintly love of a woman, because his own lust is directed toward males. The logical counterpart may apply to female homosexuality.

## Conclusion

In society and in the criminal justice system, there are the prevalent assumptions that pedophilia is a voluntary orientation and a product of jaded depravity and that the next step will be sadistic assault and molestation ending up in lust murder. These assumptions are faulty and are based on rare and sporadic cases in which there is an overlapping of pedophilia, which is a paraphilia of the eligibilic/stigmatic type, with a paraphilia of the sacrificial/expiatory type. Pedophilia, both androphilic and gynephilic, is its own syndrome, unaccompanied by sacrificial or expiatory cruelty.

One makes these kinds of distinctions regarding pedophilia first by examining this syndrome in relation to several concepts, such as the lovemap, the phylism, pairbonding, and paraphilia. Then, one broadens the perspective by enumerating the characteristics of each paraphilia, by using these characteristics to devise categories of paraphilia, of which there currently are six, and finally, by determining the category in which pedophilia seems to lie. Thus, one can attempt to show the relationship of pedophilia to other paraphilias and to the behavior that is normative in the eyes of Western society. These efforts, however, are only minimal in the scheme of what is needed if science is to understand and treat the pedophilia syndrome—and all paraphilias. (See Money, 1987b, for a review of the author's treatment guidelines). Indeed, if the levels of social tolerance and funding for research into pedophilia and the other paraphilias remain as low as they are at present, scientific knowledge will remain as it is now—rudimentary—and science's approach and perspective will continue to be narrow.

## Summary

The prevalent legal and public conceptions that a paraphilia is a morally depraved and degenerate sexual preference and that it is voluntarily chosen and, therefore, is deserving of disciplinary action are erroneous.

Because the respective levels of social tolerance and funding of research into the origins of paraphilia are very low, sexology is still at the prescientific stage of debating whether paraphilias are biologically or socially acquired—another version of the oversimplified and discredited nature-versus-nurture debate.

This author's way of circumventing the debate is to say that there are in the human species phylogenetic building blocks, or phylisms, that in the course of individual sexuoerotic development are capable of being diverted from their usual expression, so as to become entrained to sexuoerotic arousal. In the case of pedophilia, the phylism of parent/child pairbonding becomes diverted and entrained to sexuoerotic, lover/lover pairbonding. The pedophile's attachment to a child represents a merger of parental and erotic love.

This merger originates, at least in part, in the childhood of the future pedophile during the developmental period when the lovemap is differentiating. In the human species, this period is the stage of juvenile sexual rehearsal play, a stage that is normal in primate development. If sexual rehearsal play is subject to being thwarted or warped, then the outcome may be a permanent thwarting or warping of the lovemap and, possibly, the subsequent appearance of pedophilia or some other paraphilia.

The full catalogue of interventions that may create the lovemap of a pedophile has yet to be ascertained. Though it is highly likely that the lovemap development of some children is more resistant, and of other children, less resistant, to alteration, it still must be confirmed that some children, perhaps at a critical life phase, are more vulnerable than others to developing as pedophiles. In some, though not all, instances of pedophilia, it is possible to retrieve a juvenile history of a Catch-22 entrapment in a dramatically intense, conspirational, or traumatizing sexual affair with an older partner. If the development of the lovemap subsequently fails to progress in synchrony with chronological age, then the individual remains erotosexually juvenile and is attracted to juveniles. The sex of the original older partner most likely determines whether the subsequent pedophilic attraction will be gynephilic or androphilic. However, a history of being the juvenile partner of a pedophile does not automatically dictate a future history of pedophilia in adulthood. Being entrapped as a juvenile by a pedophile is what jeopardizes the outcome. Among the tribal Sambia of New Guinea (discussed previously in this chapter), where there is no entrapment, a period of pedophilic experience in childhood may be fully compatible with **normophilia\*** in adulthood.

Based on its roots in the Greek language, "pedophilia" means "child love." Two meanings of love are telescoped into the one word. One meaning is love as in parental love and pairbonding between parent and child. The other meaning is love as in making love and the sexual bonding of two partners, one of which is a juvenile. The two meanings share in common the reciprocality of bonding between two people.

## Notes

[1]Editor's Note:   A "phylism" also is compatible with the ethological definition "a unit of adaptive functioning." This definition would make the relationship of a phylism to function similar to the relationship of a fixed-action pattern to (behavioral) structure. Fixed-action patterns change in function phylogenetically but maintain structural integrity, whereas phylisms change in structure phylogenetically but maintain functional integrity. Although it is likely that fixed-action patterns are under the control of the same or similar DNA on homologous chromosomes in closely related species, this mechanism is unknown and unlikely for phylisms. The mechanism of genetic transmission through phylogeny for a trait that is defined on the basis of function is yet to be fully understood. Nevertheless, the concept of a phylism seems to fill a certain need at this time inasmuch as there is no other term that means the same thing.

[2]"Catch-22": An American colloquialism invented by Joseph Heller and introduced in his novel *Catch-22* (New York: Simon and Schuster, 1961).

## Glossary

**acrotomophilia:** a paraphilia of the eligibilic/stigmatic type in which sexuoerotic arousal and facilitation or attainment of orgasm are responsive to and dependent upon having a partner who is an amputee (from the Greek, *akron*, extremity + *tomē*, a cutting + -philia). An acrotomophile is erotically excited by the stump(s) of the amputee partner. The reciprocal paraphilic condition, namely, self-amputation, is **apotemnophilia.**

**autassassinophilia:** a paraphilia of the sacrificial/expiatory type in which sexuoerotic arousal and facilitation or attainment of orgasm are responsive to and dependent upon stage-managing the possibility of one's own masochistic death by murder (from the Greek, *autos*, self + assassin + -philia). The reciprocal condition is **lust murder,** or **erotophonophilia.**

**biastophilia:** a paraphilia of the sacrificial/expiatory type in which sexuoerotic arousal and facilitation or attainment of orgasm are responsive to and dependent upon the surprise attack and continued violent assault of a nonconsenting, terrified, and struggling stranger (from the Greek, *biastes*, rape or forced violation + -philia). Acquiescence on the part of the partner induces a fresh round of threat and violence from the biastophile. Biastophilia may be homosexual as well as heterosexual but is predominantly the latter, whether the biastophile is male or female. There is no term for the reciprocal paraphilic condition, namely, stage-managing one's own brutal rape by a stranger, which probably exists only in attenuated form and rarely gets transmuted from fantasy into actuality. Synonym: **raptophilia**.

**chrematistophilia:** a paraphilia of the mercantile/venal type in which sexuoerotic arousal and facilitation or attainment of orgasm are responsive to and dependent upon being charged or forced to pay, or being robbed by the sexual partner for sexual services (from the Greek, *chremistes*, moneydealer + -philia). There is no technical term for the reciprocal paraphilic condition of forced charging or robbing.

**chronophilia:** one of a group of paraphilias of the eligibilic/stigmatic type in which the paraphile's sexuoerotic age is discordant with his or her actual chronological age and is concordant with the chronological age of the partner, as in, respectively, **infantilism** and **nepiophilia; juvenilism** and **pedophilia; adolescentilism** and **ephebophilia;** and **gerontilism** and **gerontophilia** (from the Greek, *chronos*, time + -philia).

**coprophilia:** a paraphilia of the fetishistic/talismanic type in which sexuoerotic arousal and facilitation or attainment of orgasm are responsive to and dependent upon being smeared with and/or ingesting feces (from the Greek, *kopros*, dung + -philia). There is no technical term for the reciprocal paraphilic conditions of defecating in the mouth or over the body of the partner. See also **urophilia**. Synonym: **coprolagnia** (from the Greek *kopros*, dung + *lagneia*, lust).

**ephebophilia:** a paraphilia of the eligibilic/stigmatic type in which sexuoerotic arousal and facilitation or attainment of orgasm in an adult male or female are responsive to and dependent upon having a partner who is postpubertal and adolescent (from the Greek, *ephebos*, a postpubertal young person + -philia). The age of the younger partner distinguishes ephebophilia from **infantophilia/nepiophilia** and **pedophilia**. The technical term for the reciprocal paraphilic condition in which an older person impersonates an adolescent is **paraphilic adolescentilism**. See also **gerontophilia**.

**erotophonophilia:** a paraphilia of the sacrificial/expiatory type in which sexuoerotic arousal and facilitation or attainment of orgasm are responsive to and dependent upon stage-managing and carrying out the murder of an unsuspecting sexual partner (from the Greek, *eros*, love + *phonein*, to murder + -philia). The erotophonophile's orgasm coincides with the expiration of the partner. The reciprocal paraphilic condition is **autassassinophila**. Synonym: **lust murder**.

**fugue:** an altered state of consciousness in which what is happening now is unrelated to or dissociated from what had happened then, in the preceding phase of existence; as, for example, in the alternating manifestations of dual or multiple personality (from the Latin, *fuga*, a flight).

**gerontophilia:** a paraphilia of the eligibilic/stigmatic type in which sexuoerotic arousal and facilitation or attainment of orgasm are responsive to and dependent upon having a partner who is parental or grandparental in age (from the Greek, *gerās*, old age + -philia). Its parallels are **infantophilia/nepiophilia, pedophilia,** and **ephebophilia.** The technical term for the reciprocal paraphilic condition in which a younger person must impersonate a parent or grandparent is **paraphilic gerontilism.**

**gynemimesis:** a syndrome of female impersonation in a natal male who is able to relate sexuoerotically exclusively with men and who may be hormonally but not surgically sex reassigned. It is a syndrome of gender transposition, not a paraphilia.

**hyphephilia:** one of the paraphilias of the fetishistic/talismanic type in which the sexuoerotic stimulus is associated with the touching or rubbing or the feel of skin, hair, leather, fur, and fabric, especially if worn in proximity to erotically significant parts of the body (from the Greek, *hyphē*, web + -philia).

**infantophilia:** a paraphilia of the eligibilic/stigmatic type in which sexuoerotic arousal and the facilitation or attainment of orgasm in a postpubertal adolescent or adult male or female are responsive to and dependent upon having an infant as a partner. The reciprocal paraphilic condition is **paraphilic infantilism.** See **nepiophilia.**

**klismaphilia:** a paraphilia of the fetishistic/talismanic type in which sexuoerotic arousal and facilitation or attainment of orgasm are responsive to and dependent upon being given an enema by the partner (from the Greek, *klusma*, enema + -philia). There is no technical term for the reciprocal paraphilic condition, namely, of being the enema giver. Klismaphilia may be adjunctive to rubber fetishism or to bondage and discipline.

**lovemap:** a developmental representation, or template, in the mind and in the brain depicting the idealized lover and the idealized program of sexuoerotic activity projected in imagery or actually engaged in with that lover.

**morphophilia:** a paraphilia of the eligibilic/stigmatic type in which sexuoerotic arousal and facilitation or attainment of orgasm are responsive to and dependent upon having a partner whose body characteristics are selectively particularized, prominent, or different from one's own (from the Greek, *morphē*, form + -philia).

**nepiophilia:** a paraphilia of the eligibilic/stigmatic type in which sexuoerotic arousal and the facilitation or attainment of orgasm in a postpubertal adolescent or adult male or female are responsive to and dependent upon having as a partner an infant wearing diapers (from the Greek, *nepon*, infant + -philia). The reciprocal paraphilic condition is **autonepiophilia,** or **paraphilic infantilism,** impersonating a baby. The parallel paraphilias are **ephebophilia, gerontophilia,** and **pedophilia.**

**normophilia:** a condition of being erotosexually in conformity with the standard as dictated by customary, religious, or legal authority (from the Latin, *norma*, carpenter's square + -philia).

**olfactophilia:** a paraphilia of the fetishistic/talismanic type in which the sexuoerotic stimulus is associated with smell and with odors emanating from parts of the body, especially the sexual and adjacent parts (from the Latin, *olfacere*, to smell + -philia).

**paraphilia:** a condition occurring in men and women of being compulsively responsive to and obligatively dependent on an unusual and personally or socially unacceptable stimulus, perceived or in the ideation and imagery of fantasy, for the optimal initiation and maintenance of erotosexual arousal and the facilitation or attainment of orgasm (from the Greek, *para-*, altered + -philia). Paraphilic imagery may be replayed in fantasy during solo masturbation or during intercourse with a partner. In legal terminology, a paraphilia is a perversion or deviancy; and in the vernacular, it is kinky or bizarre sex. Antonym: **normophilia**.

**pedophilia:** a paraphilia of the eligibilic/stigmatic type in which sexuoerotic arousal and the facilitation or attainment of orgasm in a postpubertal adolescent or adult male or female are responsive to and dependent upon having a juvenile partner of prepubertal or peripubertal developmental status (from the Greek, *paidos*, child + -philia). Pedophile relationships may be heterosexual or homosexual or, more rarely, bisexual. They may take place in imagery or actuality or both. The technical term for the reciprocal paraphilic condition in which an older person impersonates a juvenile is **paraphilic juvenilism**. The age and developmental status of the partner distinguishes pedophilia from **infantophilia/nepiophilia** and **ephebophilia**.

**peodeiktophilia:** a paraphilia of the solicitational/allurative type in which sexuoerotic arousal and facilitation or attainment of orgasm are responsive to and dependent upon evoking surprise, dismay, shock, or panic from a stranger by illicitly exhibiting the penis, either flaccid or erect, with orgasm induced or postponed (from the Greek, *peos*, penis + *deiknunain*, to show + -philia). There is no technical term for the reciprocal paraphilic condition, namely, staring at a penis, which is subsumed under the broader concept of **voyeurism**. Voyeurism is the reciprocal condition of **exhibitionism**, which is a paraphilia that is similar to peodeiktophilia in that any erotic part of the body, including the genitalia, is exhibited by either a male or a female.

**-philia:** a word ending meaning love or erotic and sexual love of a person, thing, or activity (from the Greek, *philos*, loving, dear).

**phylism:** a newly coined term (Money, 1983) used to refer to an element or unit of response or behavior of an organism that belongs to an individual through its phylogenetic heritage as a member of its species.

**raptophilia:** (from the Latin, *rapere*, to seize + -philia). See **biastophilia**.

**transsexualism:** the condition of crossing over to live full time in the role of the other sex, with hormonal and surgical sex reassignment (from the Latin, *trans*, across + *sexual*). The term signifies a method of treatment and rehabilitation rather than a diagnostic entity. There are different biographical antecedents to sex reassignment, one of which may be **paraphilic transvestism (transvestophilia** [see next entry]). Transsexualism itself is not a paraphilia.

**transvestophilia:** a paraphilia of the fetishistic/talismanic type in which sexuoerotic arousal and facilitation or attainment of orgasm are responsive to and dependent upon wearing clothes, especially underwear, of the other sex (from the Latin, *trans*, across + *vestis*, garment + -*philia*). The syndrome is believed to occur predominantly in men and seldom, if ever, in women. There is no technical term for the reciprocal paraphilic condition, namely, being sexuoerotically dependent on a cross-dressed partner. **Transvestism** is a synonym for this paraphilic syndrome, but it also refers to the act of cross-dressing.

**urophilia:** a paraphilia of the fetishistic/talismanic type in which sexuoerotic arousal and facilitation or attainment of orgasm are responsive to and dependent upon being urinated upon and/or swallowing urine (from the Greek, *ouron*, urine + -*philia*). There is no technical term for the reciprocal condition of urinating on or in the mouth of the partner. See also **coprophilia.**

**voyeurism:** a paraphilia of the solicitational/allurative type in which sexuoerotic arousal and facilitation or attainment of orgasm are responsive to and dependent upon the risk of being discovered while covertly or illicitly watching a stranger disrobing or engaging in sexual activity (from the French, *voir*, to look at). The reciprocal paraphilic condition is **exhibitionism.** See also **peodeiktophilia.**

## References

Birkin, A. *J.M. Barrie and the Lost Boys: The love story that gave birth to "Peter Pan".* New York: Clarkson N. Potter and Crown Publishers, 1979.

Cohen, M.N. *Lewis Carroll, photographer of children: Four nude studies.* New York: Clarkson N. Potter and Crown Publishers, 1978.

Herdt, G.H. *Guardians of the flutes: Idioms of masculinity.* New York: McGraw-Hill, 1981.

Herdt, G.H. (Ed.). *Ritualized homosexuality in Melanesia.* Berkeley: University of California Press, 1984.

Karacan, I., Hursch, C.J., Williams, R.L., and Littell, R.C. Some characteristics of nocturnal penile tumescence during puberty. *Pediatric Research*, 1972, *6*, 529-537.

Karacan, I., Williams, R.L., Thornby, J.I., and Salis, P.J. Sleep-related penile tumescence as a function of age. *American J. of Psychiatry*, 1975, *132*, 932-937.

Lehne, G.K. Brain damage and paraphilia: Treated with medroxy-progesterone acetate. *Sexuality and Disability*, 1986, *7*, 145-158.

Meizner, I. Sonographic observation of in utero fetal "masturbation." *J. of Ultrasound in Medicine*, 1987, *6*, 111.

Moltz, H. Of rats and infants and necrotizing enterocolitis. *Perspectives in Biology and Medicine*, 1984, *27*, 327-335.

Moltz, H., and Lee, T.M. The coordinate roles of mother and young in establishing and maintaining pheromonal symbiosis in the rat. *In* L.A. Rosenblum and H. Moltz (Eds.), *Symbiosis in parent-offspring interactions*. New York: Plenum Press, 1983.

Money, J. New phylism theory and autism: Pathognomonic impairment of troopbonding. *Medical Hypotheses*, 1983, *11*, 245-250.

Money, J. *Lovemaps: Clinical concepts of sexual/erotic health and pathology, paraphilia, and gender transposition in childhood, adolescence, and maturity*. New York: Irvington Publishers, Inc., 1986.

Money, J. Sin, sickness, or status: Homosexual gender identity and psychoneuroendocrinology. *American Psychologist*, 1987a, *42*, 384-399.

Money, J. Treatment guidelines: Antiandrogen and counseling of paraphilic sex offenders. *J. of Sex and Marital Therapy*, 1987b, *13*, 219-223.

Money, J. *Gay, straight, and in-between: The sexology of erotic orientation*. New York: Oxford University Press, 1988.

Money, J., and Lamacz, M. *Vandalized lovemaps: Paraphilic outcome of seven cases in pediatric sexology*. Buffalo: Prometheus Books, 1989.

Money, J., and Weinrich, J.D. Juvenile, pedophile, heterophile: Hermeneutics of science, medicine and law in two outcome studies. *Medicine and Law*, 1983, *2*, 39-54.

Reeves, T. Loving boys. *In* D. Tsang (Ed.), *The age taboo*. Boston: Alyson Publications, 1981.

Solomon, R.L. The opponent-process theory of acquired motivation. *American Psychologist*, 1980, *35*, 691-712.

# 18
# Pedophilia: An Autobiography

Donald C. Silva
*Institutional Affiliation*
*Withheld at the Request of the Author*

## Introduction

I believe that I was born a pedophile, because I have had feelings of sexual attraction toward children and love for them for as long as I can remember. I was not traumatized into this age orientation (the violently mutilating genital assault I sustained at birth called "circumcision" notwithstanding), nor, certainly, did I ever make a conscious decision to be attracted in this way. Just as homosexuals and heterosexuals discover their sexual orientation, I discovered my age orientation as I grew, and I have been aware of it from a young age.

The popular conception of pedophiles both in the lay media and in much of the clinical literature is seriously and sometimes fatally flawed. As a result of this misconception, I agreed to write this chapter. It has taken quite an effort, both of time and emotion, to reflect on and put these intimate and sometimes painful experiences down on paper. However, if this personal account serves to dispel some of the prevailing myths and increase the understanding of pedophilia, the effort will have been well worthwhile.

In this account, I have tried to avoid appealing to the prurient interests of anyone. Descriptions are rarely graphic and become so only when I feel it necessary to ensure clarity. I am writing from prison under a pseudonym so as to protect the privacy of the many children with whom I have been involved and, also, because my case is still under legal appeal and civil lawsuits are possible. Names and places, too, have been changed for the same reasons. I have given the editor of this volume authorization to make additional changes in names, dates, locations, and other minor details in order to avoid incriminating myself or revealing the identity of the children by what I disclose. (Editor's note: Dr. Silva's original manuscript has been altered deliberately during the editing process.)

## Social and Family Background

I grew up in a middle-class neighborhood of a large city in Western Europe. I am the youngest child of three, and we lived in a private house in a residential area. We were always well provided for and felt loved and well cared for. Both sides of my family were very close to us emotionally, but I was more influenced by the relatives on my mother's side, all of whom lived in neighboring houses.

One of my earliest memories is from when I was about 4½ years of age, when my mother left home for one or two months to obtain her trade license. She began to work upon her return, eventually buying the shop in which she worked. She ran it successfully and, over the years, acquired other businesses along with a partner. My father left his municipal job because of an injury and entered the retail business, giving me my first employment later, in my early teens.

With both parents working, we enjoyed a new-found prosperity, which prompted them to install a small swimming pool in our backyard. This pool became a double-edged sword throughout my childhood; as I soon learned, there were children who were friendly with me in the summer and indifferent to me in the winter. I was especially sensitive to this inconsistency in my early teens.

Although neither of my parents had finished high school, the value of education was stressed. I was blessed with the gift of intelligence, which was recognized and encouraged from an early age. I attended a Catholic grammar school, followed by an all-male, Catholic secondary school. I was provided with ample books to read and even had a private tutor, a local junior high school teacher who came to our home for one hour per week to instruct me in any subject of my choice at an advanced level.

A special gift for dealing with young people was something I shared with and may have inherited from my mother. I remember that 7-year-olds came to her whenever they had a loose tooth because of her reputation as a painless toothpuller. Many adolescent friends of my siblings allowed only her to cut their hair. They were also comfortable discussing their problems with her, and they often took her advice. When a girl of 14 who had many problems began spending time in her shop, she took the girl under her wing for an extended period of time. Of all the people who tried to help a cousin who was dependent on drugs from her teens to her 20's, my mother had the greatest amount of success. She provided much support for a young man of about 20 whom she helped to get off drugs after many years of addiction. She did all of these things in addition to providing for the needs of her own three children.

While my father may not have made a specific contribution beyond providing a wholesome, loving home environment, it should be noted that he was 30 years old when he married my mother, who was 17. His parents' ages also differed by 13 years.

## Childhood

I remember being fascinated by children even during my own childhood. I can clearly remember, from before the age of 10, being at a popular gathering spot on my street and enjoying watching the younger children as they played and had a good time. I contributed to their fun by playing with them as well. Older children and teens tickled and rough-housed with me, also. I had plenty of peer friends with whom I spent much time, or I could be content to be alone in my room where I entertained myself reading, listening to music, or being involved in some other project.

My "girlfriend," 1½ years younger than I, with whom I "went steady" from about the ages of 6-12, lived on my street. I would not say we were in love; rather, we were merely imitating our older siblings. We did not experiment sexually, being ignorant of such matters. Her mother once refused me permission to sleep at her house, the reason being that I was her boyfriend. At 12, having become more curious about matters sexual, I once attempted with the utmost of my persuasive powers to convince her to let me touch her vagina. She refused to a degree that even then I thought unusual, at least compared to other children with whom I had played; she seemed to lack a natural curiosity or to be just too guilt ridden. Many years later, she acknowledged having a homosexual orientation. With other children of both sexes I did play "doctor" or "Show me yours and I'll show you mine," but we did little beyond looking.

I was about 9 when I shared a bed with a female cousin who was two years older than I. I remember that, when we took our clothes off, I got an erection. I was pressing my penis against her during our feeble attempt at intercourse, but being so inexperienced, we did not achieve lubrication, penetration, or orgasm.

My brother was three years older than I, and we shared a bed until I was 10. A couple of times, he asked if he could put his leg on top of me and rub, but I resisted, sometimes calling my parents if he would not stop bothering me. Soon afterwards, we had our own rooms.

Before the age of 12, I did not know how to masturbate to orgasm. I had enjoyed the sensation of erection and sometimes stimulated myself in order to achieve one. I sometimes did so before going outside. Once outside, I tried to maintain an erection with my hand in my pocket, but invariably, I lost it quickly, as soon as my attention wandered.

At 12, my two best friends were brothers, ages 11 and 13. The elder taught me to masturbate to orgasm. I remember the first time I achieved that unusual feeling. The shudder it sent through my body made me a bit uncomfortable. I had no desire to achieve that feeling again for a short while afterward, but soon, the feeling became very enjoyable, and we frequently indulged ourselves.

If it had not been for these two friends, I might have experienced my first intercourse at 11 or 12. I was in my basement with a girl about a year older than I. Both of us still were prepubertal. We had taken our clothes off, and I was lying on top of her. I had an erection, and she told me to "put it in." Inexperienced, I was fumbling around when I heard someone outside the room. We were frightened that my father was coming in, and we quickly got up and dressed, but it was only my two friends.

Semenarche, the onset of ejaculation, occurred just prior to my 13th birthday in the form of a nocturnal emission. I soon had my first experience of ejaculation with a partner, when a peer female allowed me to lie on her and rub my exposed penis against her covered crotch. By now, it was commonplace for me to masturbate. Once, while in my 8th grade class, I placed the head of my erect penis through a hole in my pocket and asked the boy sitting next to me to put his hand in. He did so, and immediately withdrew it, saying, "That's your penis!" Although I knew what that word meant, it was the first time I heard it spoken.

My first "crush" was on a girl in that same class. Smartest of the girls, she had blond hair and blue eyes. I was regarded as the smartest boy and also had blond hair and blue eyes. The role of narcissism here is debatable, but what definitely attracted me to her was that she represented something slightly different from myself. She was female, and I remember being attracted to her budding breasts. Attributes such as intelligence and pubescence still attract me. I was crushed when she did not take seriously my offer to carry her books after I finally got the courage to ask her.

That summer, when I was 13 years old, a 21-year-old female friend of the family moved onto our street, and I spent much time with her. Once, I was at her house while she was asleep, and I remember being stimulated at the sight of her half-bare breast. She did not mind as I sat on the bed and then crawled in bed with her. I will always remember the tingling sensation that went through my body when I touched her breast. I was lying on top of her, clothed, when she took my hand in hers and placed it on her panties for me to see how wet she was there. I wanted to feel that place more, but she removed my hand. I was enjoying just lying there and expected her to instruct me in what to do. Instead, she complained that I was not excited, even though I had an erection. Then, from what must have been a combination of frustration and guilt on her part, she stopped the encounter and told me to try again when I was 15. I deeply regretted the lost opportunity and thought about it frequently for the next two years, but I never repeated that attempt with her.

## Adolescence

I entered the all-male secondary school in the center of the city, to which I commuted by means of public transportation. There, I noted that I was attracted to some of my schoolmates, especially the younger appearing ones. These feelings were confusing initially, and I tried to deny them. After all, in my peer group, "homosexual" was just about the worst epithet that could be hurled.

While I was trying to deny these feelings, I also became fascinated by the workings of the mind. I was keenly interested in the work of Sigmund Freud and of modern psychoanalysts, who, as had Freud, were reporting that a common cause of adult neuroses was guilt induced by sexual repression in childhood. I resolved to try to eliminate any guilt about sex that inhibited me and to develop a positive attitude toward sex.

I felt relieved and proud of myself when I lost my virginity that winter, and I will never forget the experience. It was New Year's Eve. My family had gone out, but I had stayed home because I had injured my knee in a skiing accident a week earlier. I was walking on crutches with my leg in a full-length cast and had been left in the care of our tenant, who just happened to be responsible for her 14-year-old niece, too, that evening. The niece and I were each served a highball at midnight and then given permission to go downstairs, ostensibly to listen to music for a while. We already knew and did like each other and were feeling few inhibitions as we began to kiss. We moved into the bedroom and removed the necessary clothing. We were both very excited as I mounted her, cast and all, and there was no trouble with penetration. I can still vividly remember the thought that ran through my mind: "I can't believe how soft it is in here!" I remained erect following ejaculation and wanted immediately to do it again. She said, "No, next time," and got up to leave. Perhaps my cast had been uncomfortable against her leg. Still in a state of exhilaration, I masturbated to a most strong orgasm. Much to my dismay, our next time did not occur until 14 years later! But I was very satisfied to get this boost to my self-esteem and to have the reassurance that I greatly enjoyed sex with females.

My local peer group was expanding during this time. Sometimes the boys congregated and masturbated. If two of us were alone, we might experiment sexually; oral sex was rare, and even rarer were attempts at anal sex, which invariably were unsuccessful.

My developing experience with sex was occurring when I was 14 and 15 years old, and it was during this time that we in my peer group were befriended by a neighborhood man, about 25, who was known to "like boys." He drove us around and treated us to snacks and movies. Some of my peers experimented with recreational drugs with him or on their own. At times, we went to his apartment, in pairs or as a group, where he took us individually into his bedroom to fellate us. I once spent the night with him. His mother and sister, with whom he lived, barely reacted to my presence there in the morning, as if it were not unusual for him to appear in the morning with a boy. While I enjoyed the oral sex he performed on me, the overall experience was unfulfilling. I was disappointed that he did not feel the emotional bond for me that I expected after such an intimate encounter. I felt satisfied physically but used. Subsequent experiences with him became acceptable once I adjusted my expectations and sought only sexual gratification.

My emotions were maturing. It was during my 14th winter that I felt an unusual emotion for a peer female, virtually from the moment I met her. I was in love but too shy and awkward to express my feelings to her directly. I enjoyed the time I spent with her, but soon she became the girlfriend of someone else.

I was 15 when I attended a large music and arts festival. The atmosphere of peace and love could be felt there, and it impressed me. I was skinnydipping (swimming nude) in a lake near the festival when I saw many nude couples sitting on the side of a gently sloping hill. Feelings of unity, friendship, and freedom were pervasive. The music was very energizing, and the entire experience contributed to my becoming less repressed and more open to other lifestyles.

It was in the ensuing year that a close friendship with a classmate became sexual. He, but not I, knew that he was homosexual. Despite confirmation that I was heterosexually attracted, I was still struggling with my own sexual identity. After our first night together, I felt revolted by the idea that I and another male had "made love," i.e., that this was clearly a homosexual experience. It was different from earlier sex I had had with male peers, who were not homosexual, in which the purpose was merely to "get our rocks off," with little emotional bonding occurring beyond that of friendships typical of that age. That feeling of disgust lasted less than 24 hours, and we spent our next night together. My sense of guilt had diminished greatly, and almost all negative reactions disappeared as our relationship developed. However, I never thought of myself as homosexual; rather, I considered this relationship temporary, until one could be established with a female. It lasted for many years, however, even after we went off to different universities and saw each other only infrequently, and it endured through several of my heterosexual relationships. It is the only adult homosexual relationship I have ever been involved in.

In my junior year in secondary school, I fell in love with a local girl who was a few years older than I. We spent time together in public places but little time alone. The only day I ever purposely stayed out of school was for her. She was very sweet, but an erotic relationship never developed. I felt too awkward to initiate it and was happy just to be in her company. We drifted apart for reasons I do not remember; perhaps she got bored with me, but even to this day, when we meet, we greet each other very warmly.

When I was a senior, there was a freshman I was very fond of. I got to know him at a social, where he was acting a bit silly, not too differently from the way I previously behaved. I spoke to him a few more times during the year, once asking him to accompany a group of seniors I had invited for a weekend ski trip. It was rather unusual for a freshman to mingle with seniors. He declined my invitation, and I failed in my further efforts to see him. I had a very great desire to be his mentor. I did once meet him outside of school by chance, but I was too inhibited at that point to aggressively pursue our friendship; I worried about what he would think of me. I even looked for him at a school reunion many years later but could not find him. To this day, I remember his name.

During these teen years, I continued to enjoy the company of children. Sometimes, when roughhousing with them, I noticed myself getting an erection. It did not occur to me that I was experiencing a sexual attraction, and I did not act upon it.

## University

After I was graduated from secondary school, I entered a university in another city, where I lived in a coed dormitory. There, I finally experienced intercourse again after what seemed like an eternity, since for four years, I had known what I was missing. Throughout this period, I had been masturbating, initially without fantasies, then to fantasies involving adult women.

In my freshman year at the university, I had significant relationships with two women, Fay and Loni, but I still did not feel especially successful with women. Fay did not seem to be in great demand from the point of view of other men, although I liked her well enough to suit me. As our relationship grew, I felt for the first time that I had someone to call my own. I attended that university for one year only, and we broke up two months before I left and before I learned that she was pregnant. Unprepared for fatherhood at 19, I sent her money to terminate the pregnancy, even though I already had returned home. I made this decision on my own, although now I wish I had had some counseling. I do not know what Fay did about the pregnancy, because I never heard from her again.

In my last few weeks at the university, I began to date Loni, or rather, she began to date me. I felt that I was chosen by her. The girls whom I wanted to ask out always seemed to already have boyfriends.

I transferred to a larger urban university in my own city, where I felt like I was back in secondary school because I was commuting daily again. That is where the similarity ended, however. The university was huge, with many buildings and thousands of students, none of whom I knew. I did date several of the students whom I was courageous enough to ask out, but I still felt inhibited concerning some to whom I was especially attracted. I felt I had much competition and feared rejection. It took me several more years to overcome these insecurities and my lack of aggression, which I accomplished when I realized that one rejection was not such a great tragedy.

During my senior year at the university and the year that followed, when I was 22 and 23 years of age, I dated a series of four 26-year-old women, and a pattern emerged of attraction to older women.

It was then that I was applying to medical school. Initially unsuccessful, I enrolled in additional university courses and volunteered to work in the pediatrics department of a municipal hospital in an attempt to strengthen my application. My enjoyment of this work was greatly increased when I switched from the outpatient/emergency department to the inpatient ward. There I was able to develop friendships with children who were on the unit daily for weeks to months. The ward adjoined an outside patio. Paul was 13 and at the beginning of a 12-week stay for a broken leg. On nice days, I wheeled him outside in his bed, traction and all, and stayed with him while supervising other patients who were permitted to go out. My effort was appreciated, because few people took the inpatients outside. Paul and I struck up a friendship, and he was comfortable discussing anything with me, including his mother's use of marijuana and the fact that her smoking previously had made him angry. His attitude had changed as he realized she did love him—and after he began to use marijuana himself. She demonstrated that she cared for him by coming almost daily to visit. Also, she was grateful for the attention I paid her son, particularly because his father, from whom she was separated, was not very involved with the family.

Paul also spoke to me about sex. He told me that another young male inpatient, an 8-year-old dark-skinned boy, would "suck dick." He called the boy over, and the boy placed his mouth on Paul's penis for a few seconds and then on mine for just a second. Paul laughed as he quickly said to the boy, "Don't do that or you'll grow up to be gay." What I permitted was purely out of curiosity. I had no attraction to that boy, and my penis was flaccid. Neither was there any such attraction to Paul. I just enjoyed our friendship. I was mildly attracted to an 11-year-old in the room, but nothing came of that. I became fond of a 9-year-old dark-haired boy who shared that room, and I even visited him a few times at home after discharge, but again, there was no sexual element.

## Adulthood

As the summer approached, I was finally accepted into medical school, in another city. For the first year, I rented a house with other students. Once, an unfortunate-appearing boy was outside, and I invited him in for a sandwich. The next day, a policeman came to the house to falsely accuse me of harboring drugs. Although my roommate resolved the problem with a small payoff to the police officer, I immediately learned that not all children are as sweet and innocent as we like to believe.

In my second semester in medical school, I befriended Peter, a fellow medical student whose family lived in a nearby town. He invited me to meet his family and see the town. Not one to pass up such an opportunity, I accepted. His family was very kind. I will never forget the first time I met his brother Allen, who was 11 or 12 at the time. We were at his mother's office, where we had gone to greet her just after arriving in town. In walked Allen. I was struck by the affection he showed his brother, whom he had not seen for a couple of months. In the families I had known, I was used to seeing sibling relationships more characterized by jealousy and rivalry than by displays of affection. This sight was very pleasing to behold. That affection plus Allen's strikingly cute appearance in his white shorts immediately endeared him to me. I loved the whole family, but what I felt for Allen was stronger than anything I had ever known before. In addition, my classmate Peter was to become my closest friend in a nonsexual relationship, in whom I could confide all. I could not hold back the tears when, after only my second weekend at his house, the time came to leave Allen.

Fortunately, there were to be many more visits to Peter's family. During one of the earliest, I had the opportunity to share a single bed with Allen. The closeness of our bodies as we lay there excited me so much that I was unable to sleep. Indeed, I experienced an intense orgasm as I held him close to me, thinking he was asleep. He left the bed in order to sleep on the floor, because, he told me later, he thought I had urinated in the bed. In future encounters, he was wide awake and actively participated in our sexual relationship, which went on during the next two years and even later whenever I returned to visit. When he was 17, I took him and two friends to a prostitute for their first sexual intercourse; these friends were brothers, close in age to Allen, both of whom worked at his house; I had been sexually involved with one of them. I always looked forward to my visits to Allen's home, which averaged about once a month. My relationship with him was my first true pedophilic/pedosexual relationship. After our sexual activity ceased, we maintained a close friendship that endures to this day. He is in graduate school now and is aware of my incarceration. In our last communication, he told me he wanted to help me get out of prison!

It was at a party during my third semester in medical school that I met Evelyn, who was 6 years my elder. She was a dark-haired, foreign-born woman whom I found refreshingly different from the overly demanding, materialistic women I had come to know. I dated her continuously from then on and married her several years later.

In my fourth semester of medical school, I moved out of the house I shared with classmates and into a boarding house. Other students lived there with the host family, which consisted of a mother and three sons, ages 11, 12, and 13; the boys certainly were a factor in my choice. I lived there for two semesters, during the first of which 13-year-old John lived elsewhere. I was friendly with the boys, especially Robert, 11, who frequently sought out my company. In play, we horsed around, or I tickled him in the ribs or legs. During our fully clothed bodily contact, I experienced erection and orgasm on occasion, but there was no indication that he was ever aware of it.

At the beginning of the following semester, John moved back home. He showed much interest in me, and on my first night back from vacation, we engaged in extended conversation as he helped me unpack. His curiosity was piqued by the issues of *Playboy* he came across, and we began to look at them. We became excited, and it was not long before we removed our clothes and began fondling each other. Similar scenes were repeated over the next several nights, and we had an active, frequent sexual relationship during the ensuing three or four months. Our sexual activity consisted of my fellating or masturbating him or of mutual genital juxtaposition and friction. With a single exception to be described in a moment, never did I penetrate with my penis any of the boys with whom I was involved. On the single occasions that I attempted this behavior with John, once orally and once anally, he declined, and so I immediately desisted.

I treated all my boys well. I took them places or paid them for doing small chores. I gave John driving lessons. Eventually, his mother became suspicious of us, and just before my year with them was up, she announced that for the following semester she would be taking in girls "because they eat less."

By now, it was clear to me that I loved children, especially boys, and was happiest when I was in their company. What I took pleasure in most was seeing them happy and developing healthily in mind and body. So, I encouraged their interests if I felt these interests were healthy, or I exposed them to experiences that I thought would contribute to their educational or cultural edification.

Even in sex, producing pleasure in the children was the most gratifying aspect to me. Only after assuring their pleasure did I concern myself with my own pleasure. What often occurred was that they reciprocated or even initiated activity without any cues from me. I rarely, if ever, attempted anal penetration of my young lovers, mostly out of fear of hurting them, although there was a 13-year-old who regularly demanded this behavior.

I went home for a month during Christmas vacation. While I have always been a true fan of video games, the subconscious fantasy of meeting a new young friend probably was a factor in my frequent visits to arcades, even though my fantasy was rarely realized.

Dennis was 13 when I met him at such an arcade. We both liked to play the same machine, and it turned out that we had a friend in common and similar, uncommon, tastes in music. He asked for a ride home, which I gave him gladly. He fancied himself a musician, and I was struck by his dedication and discipline in practicing on his drumset for several hours daily. He told me that he lived with his mother and sister and that his father had died when he was 8. We began a long, close friendship. I saw him several times in that first month. Each time, we were happier to see each other and quickly became very comfortable together. We were very disappointed when I had to leave at the end of my vacation, but we kept in touch. When I returned again for summer vacation, we sometimes spent upwards of 12 hours a day together, during which we went to the arcade or listened to or played music. We knew all the local arcades and often took a 30-minute bus ride to the other end of town to visit our favorite because of its futuristic atmosphere. Once, upon our arriving at that arcade, he remarked, "This is true love!" While ostensibly he may have been describing how we felt about video games, he was actually describing how we felt about each other. For that entire, intense first year, I did not act on a strong sexual attraction to him. I valued our friendship so much on the level that it was that I did not want to jeopardize it by a sexual advance that might be rejected.

I had a dilemma, for I wanted to express to him how I felt and to take our relationship to a deeper level. After all, we were very honest with each other in all other areas, and I thought he could understand. I had no one with whom I could discuss this wish, Peter being out of the country and I not being in psychotherapy at the time. There was a group I had heard of that was sympathetic to such concerns, and I went to speak to a member. He encouraged me to honestly express my feelings to Dennis who, if he then rejected me, perhaps was not so great a friend as I had thought. I was not very comfortable with that option, but neither was I comfortable with the way things were going. As it was the only advice I had gotten, I took it. The attempt failed miserably, and Dennis was indignant, even though all I did was place my hand on his thigh, saying, "I'd like our relationship to progress." He knew what I meant. He would not speak to me for the next two weeks, during which time I was in touch with a mutual friend in whom he had confided. Through this friend's efforts at mediation, Dennis and I got together to discuss what had happened. He explained that he was not "into that," I accepted that decision, and our friendship resumed. A good, solid friendship continues to this day, many years later, although the level of intensity of our first year has not been matched.

In my last three semesters of medical school, I was kept very busy with long hours of clinical rotations, opting for psychiatry or pediatrics whenever possible. I spent the year following my graduation from medical school studying to pass the comprehensive examinations that would permit me to enter medical-specialty training. I studied for eight hours each day, and because I was living at my parents' home and not working, I had a lot of free time.

It was in this period that I became friends with Eric, just about to turn 9, whose family recently had moved onto our street. I actually met his 6-year-old brother first, who was letting the air out of the tires of parked cars, and I accepted his invitation to play in his house. His mother was, understandably, quite surprised when she saw me. Eric was at home, and he invited me to see some *Playboy* magazines he had stashed away in a hideout. Nothing happened between us physically at that time, but our having met was the start of a long, intense love affair. His proximity made it possible for us to spend much time together. I became a friend of his whole family, which included both parents and a 14-year-old sister. I once took her to a classical music concert when I had an extra ticket. I did not ask Eric to accompany me because I did not think he could appreciate that type of music yet. That was a mistake. He was very hurt that **his** friend had taken his sister instead of him. Actually, I would not have hesitated had I not been inhibited by what others might think and by my own sense of guilt. I believe his family viewed ours as a natural friendship, albeit one that was a bit unusual; in any event, their reaction was not marked by a paranoid hysteria.

When I had returned to my parents' home after being graduated from medical school, I had left Evelyn, my future wife. She and I kept in touch, however, and visited each other on vacations. I began to date Cathy, a foreign-born peer female who lived in my city and worked near our house. I was attracted to her distinct ethnicity as well as to the "class" she showed. I found myself turned off by most of the neighborhood women, who I thought were plastic, i.e., superficial, materialistic, and lacking in class. Cathy seemed more human and down to earth and closer to the values to which I aspired. I enjoyed a good relationship, sexual and otherwise, with Cathy for about six months. Before we broke up, my relationship with Eric had become sexual and more pleasing than that with Cathy, and also, she and I had been growing apart emotionally. I began to feel that I was maintaining our relationship for the sake of appearances and that young males were my true love—especially Eric.

Eric and I had become increasingly close. We spent a full year as friends before our relationship became sexual. This change occurred just after his 10th birthday. We napped together, moving closer each time. This kind of physical closeness became gratifying enough, because I achieved orgasms just from our clothed bodies lying against each other. What made that relationship so beautiful and precious was the way in which it developed, so gradually and naturally.

The relationship became overtly sexual during a weekend ski trip. We had not been sure his father would permit him to go, and I will never forget that ecstatic expression on his blond-hair-crowned, blue-eyed, little round face as he jumped for joy when his father said, "Okay," an emotion I shared completely. In bed during that trip, he said it was "all right" to feel his skin against mine. We were naked, and I was feeling indescribably joyous emotion as I gently caressed and fondled him while he just lay back enjoying the experience. I lost count of the number of orgasms I had each night we slept together. Even after he fell asleep, I had an orgasm every hour or two just from embracing him! I don't believe I ever slept during our nights together. A month later, we went on a second ski trip. Our sex was not heavy, intense, and mutual (although our emotions were); it mostly consisted of naked embraces and, later, my performance of oral sex on him, during which he eventually learned to thrust. That achievement soon was followed by his first orgasm (dry, of course) as each step followed in an orderly fashion during that entire second, sexual year, his 10th. He told me of boys of 8 he knew who had anal sex with each other, but we never attempted that.

Those two weekends, chances to sleep with him all through the night, were precious rarities I will never forget. Most of the time, he just came over to my house and lay down with me for a few moments. One special time was a morning that he was on his way to school. He climbed into my room through my window, as he frequently did, removed his bookbag, and lay down next to me. We embraced for a few moments until we were satisfied and it was time for him to get to school. Not a word was spoken; all of our communication was physical on that occasion. He later gave me a picture of himself, which I still cherish, on the back of which he spontaneously inscribed: "To Donald, you are my friend and the best thing that ever happened to me." Indeed, the feeling was mutual. Clearly, it was not sex that attracted me to him but, rather, our great emotional bond, which made sex so intensely gratifying. Physically, our relationship could not compare to heterosexual intercourse, but that difference was more than compensated for by our feelings for each other. Sex was a small but incredibly beautiful part of our relationship. The vast majority of the time we engaged in many other recreational and constructive activities.

The demise of our relationship began when his mother suspected some friends of mine were using marijuana in his presence. Eric was told we could no longer be friends. When he came to tell me, he cried harder than any other child I had ever seen cry before. I empathized with him completely, because I felt equally devastated, although I am not sure whether I felt worse for myself or for him. I promised to speak to his father, and this beautiful man found it in his heart to forgive me after I assured him that such a thing would not happen again. Needless to say, Eric and I were greatly relieved.

I had recently broken up with Cathy when Evelyn, my future wife, arrived for a visit. In that month, Evelyn met Eric's family, and she and his mother became good friends. Evelyn stayed with me at my parents' house, and we enjoyed an active sex life. Eric slept over one night, and the three of us shared a bed for a while. He was going to pretend to be asleep while Evelyn and I made love, but Evelyn declined with him there and went to sleep elsewhere.

Meanwhile, my mother was developing severe heart failure. She had had heart surgery several years earlier and never had fully recovered. Now the end was imminent. Her last words to Evelyn were to take good care of me. I dearly loved my mother and felt her loss deeply. However, I had done most of my grieving after her surgery and had had time to prepare myself. And what I felt when she died did not compare to the total vitiation I felt six months later when my friendship with Eric was forced by his parents to end. In hindsight, it is easy to see what I might have done differently to possibly avoid our breakup. For example, once while I was watching television with Eric and his mother, the subject of man/boy love came up. I foolishly pursued a discussion with her on how I would treat the situation if a young son of mine were involved. I said that my reaction would depend on how he saw the relationship and that it would be in his best interest if I did not respond hysterically. It is clear now that I was subconsciously communicating what I thought her reaction should be to my friendship with her son. How I wish I had not started her thinking about the subject!

Eric's family had been planning to move and did so. I do not know that their moving was related to any suspicions about us, and I continued to visit them in their new home, about a 30-minute drive away. We exchanged Christmas gifts, but in January, the fatal blow was struck. I foolishly made him feel guilty one day when I got up to leave in a fabricated bit of mild anger because he did not want to rub my back. My behavior upset him very much. He followed me downstairs, yelling, and slammed the door after me. I believe this kind of reaction had been impending, because I had begun to perceive a change in attitude on the part of his parents. After this episode, he must have said something to his mother, because the next time I came over, she told me he did not want to see me anymore. Nevertheless, I often drove to his neighborhood, hoping to catch a glimpse of him near his home or school. He saw me once, and I told him to meet me at a nearby park to go sleigh-riding; he did so, and we had a good time. A friend who was with us remarked that it was obvious that he wanted to be with me. That was the last time I saw Eric. He attempted to find me at least once while visiting his old neighborhood, but I was not home at the time. Not long afterwards, he moved out of the country with his family. Through a mutual friend, I got Eric's phone number and finally spoke with him by phone when he was 15. He said what we had done was not right, but he was happy to hear from me. He took my number and promised to call, but soon after that conversation, I was arrested.

I had been crushed when Eric's mother told me I could no longer see Eric. I cried every day for weeks and whenever I thought about him afterwards. Then, when he left the country, it was like a piece inside of me died. It still hurts me to think about him, and I do not think I will ever fully recover.

It is difficult to express in words the love I felt for Eric. By comparison, I initially may have felt similar feelings for Allen, who was 12, but we were not together long enough for the same intensity to develop, and our ethnic differences set us apart as well. Dennis, at 14, was chronologically older than Eric and quite mature for his age, and therefore, we had been able to relate more as peers. Furthermore, we never experienced the closeness that physical intimacy can bring, although the lack of that closeness was more than compensated for by the gratification I felt in supporting his education, discipline, dedication to higher ideals of peace, love, and justice, and musical tastes and ability. I have no doubt that someday he will succeed in the tough world of professional music.

My relationship with Eric occurred during his 9th and 10th years of age. Although we enjoyed many of the same activities, we were not peers. Consequently, I could play a much larger role in developing Eric's personality. My emotion for him ran sky-high. I would have done anything for him. I loved that boy before we ever had sex, and if I had been able to foresee the future, I would gladly have foregone the sex so that our friendship could be maintained. I feel like I had, and then lost, a lifelong friend. I will see him again someday. He had a heart of gold. Sure, he could be a bit of a troublemaking brat at times, but he was not malicious, nor did he ever pass the bounds of normal childhood behavior. Usually, he was very respectful and helpful. I was especially pleased by the love he expressed for his family, which I encouraged. He even spoke of how he loved his sister, although he complained about her telling him what to do and although they fought occasionally. I also liked to hear him talk about the type of father he would be someday. His company was a tremendous pleasure, and he was a great help when I needed an errand done. What these three of my most significant relationships did have in common was that they were all good, loving children or adolescents to begin with. I just wanted to help them reach their full potential by providing them with unconditional love, whether or not sex was involved.

Between the time of my mother's death and my breakup with Eric six months later, Evelyn had left to return to her home. There, she received a letter from Eric's mother complaining of my involvement with Eric. Evelyn was skeptical about that accusation. Depressed over the recent loss of my mother and Eric and over Evelyn's absence, I took a trip to see Evelyn, as well as Peter—who was my closest adult confidant and from whom I kept no secrets. I greatly enjoyed the trip because I was able to express my true feelings, especially to Peter, who understood. I even divulged the truth to Evelyn, who said she thought she understood. Her continued acceptance of me deepened my love for her and was a definite factor in my later decision to marry her.

That short trip helped my spirits somewhat, but upon my return home, I felt that something was missing in my life. I met Richard, age 9, when each of us was alone late one night at a video game arcade. We became friends after meeting a couple of times, and soon he was accompanying me to other arcades or to my house, where he let me examine him. He obtained permission to sleep at my house one night. In our underwear, preparing for bed, we were horsing around. He rejected my attempt to fondle him, and I did not insist. My father was home, too, and he called me aside to ask just what I, "a 26-year-old man [was] doing with this kid." I explained that he was my friend and was going to spend the night, but my father disapproved and told me to take him home. I obeyed but was very angry and did not speak to my father for 10 days afterward. Nothing like this had ever happened between my father and me. Although it may be too much to ask the average person to understand and accept pedophilia, I always longed for that impossible dream of having an open, honest relationship with my parents. I was fortunate enough to have an otherwise good relationship with both my parents, however, and even to this day, my father continues to be very supportive.

## Hospital Clinical Work

During my last year as a medical student, I had begun a year of clinical clerkships. In my pediatrics rotations, there usually were one or two older children with whom I became friendly, to whom I devoted the little extra time I might have. My sexual attraction excludes younger children, but that orientation did not prevent me from being friends with them. I can remember two patients, one 4 months old and one 3 years old, of whom I was very fond. In general, my attempts at friendship usually were frustrated by the heavy work load and by a rapid turnover of most patients, both of which took some getting used to. On rare occasions, my efforts were rewarded by a note of thanks after the child left the hospital.

There was a 12-year-old male patient of whom I was very fond. He had been admitted for a testicular problem, which I examined daily. He was always friendly to me, even though, unbeknownst to me at the time, I had made him uncomfortable during an examination. I had a great desire to continue our friendship and even followed him out of the hospital at his discharge to say goodbye. It was an unlikely coincidence when he was a patient of mine again, more than a year later, at a different hospital. We were friendly once more, but his father informed me of the discomfort I had caused his son the last time. I apologized and said that I meant no harm and that I would not let such a situation recur. I could see that the patient resembled his father in his calm, warm, understanding manner.

There was a neighborhood boy, 10, whom I had met a few years earlier while showing some children a souvenir from a vacation. He reminded me of a cherub. He immediately endeared himself to me when he said that he would accompany me on my next vacation. Though I did not take him seriously, I liked his attitude. I often saw him leading his pack of friends around the neighborhood. Sometimes I drove around just trying to catch a glimpse of him. He was beautiful to behold: curly blond hair, aqua-blue eyes, and a well-proportioned muscular body. A good athlete, he usually wore shorts but no shirt in the summer. He came to swim in my family's pool once or twice in a group, but I never spent any significant amount of time with him; so my attraction to him was almost purely physical. I happened to see him, now 12, on my last day of freedom, and I had a great desire to tell him how I felt. The circumstances were not appropriate, however. Of children I have only seen, he was one of my stronger attractions, and my experience regarding him was unusual in that what ordinarily attracts me are attributes such as personality, a need for nurturance, and/or receptivity to a positive role model.

## Girls

Another unusual experience occurred during a visit Evelyn made to my home some time after I had told her about my attraction to children. Two of my nieces, ages 8 and 10, who lived nearby brought over friends, a brother and sister, 8 and 10, respectively. It was only the second time Alice, the sister, had met me, but she planted a big, wet kiss on my lips. We were very friendly that day. Once, while I was holding her in the pool, she brought her body close to mine, pressing her vagina to my erect penis through our bathing suits. It only lasted a second but felt glorious. Evelyn was nearby, and she was suspicious. She even separated us once when Alice and I were just sitting side by side holding hands. Had the opportunity presented itself, Alice and I certainly would have become more intimate. I heard only a few years later that she already was sexually active.

A few years before that second meeting with Alice, sisters Judy, 8, and Julie, 10, had moved onto our street with their divorced mother. Judy took me as a friend, and we visited each other's house. Julie was physically precocious, and she could easily pass for 14 or even 16 because she had well-developed breasts. Sometimes we wrestled around or I kissed her on the lips, achieving orgasm in my pants, but we had no overt sex. I had erections when Judy sat on my lap but never an orgasm.

## Residency (Medical-Specialty) Training

The only other significant experience I had with a girl occurred during my first year of specialty training in pediatrics. A 9-year-old girl was admitted for a urinary-tract infection. We usually were alone each day as I examined her. Once, her hand was rubbing against my penis as I took her blood pressure. I was wearing thin surgical scrub pants and was excited to orgasm, staining my pants. Immediately after, I went to change but met her mother in the hall. I fretted, but all the mother asked me about was her daughter's condition.

Perhaps my attraction to peripubertal females is equal to my attraction to males, but in practice, I have been much more involved with boys. There seem to be less opportunities with girls, and even more suspicion surrounds such interactions. Also, the commonality of maleness is a head start in my relating to boys.

During one of my clinical rotations, I began to date Debby, a nurse. She was divorced and had two sons, David, 6, living with her, and Charles, 12, living with her mother. The first time I met David, he wore only a T-shirt, which he flashed up and down as he paraded around the living room. Three months later, I met Charles during one of his rare visits to his mother. I could not understand why, living so close by, he came so rarely to see her nor why he was not living with her. I met with him several times to discuss these questions, and we became friends. Once, his mother suspected he and a friend were high on marijuana. A user herself, she merely wanted to know whether he, too, was, so as to make sure he did not get an adulterated product or use it irresponsibly. One evening, Charles and I shared some marijuana and were feeling good; I embraced him. We lay on the bed as I gently caressed him. As I gradually reached his genitals, he did not protest, and thus began our sexual relationship. We had sex about once a week. I took him for a couple of ski weekends. Again, the chance to sleep naked together for an entire night and make long, leisurely love was so intensely gratifying that I'm afraid that, as a famous Greek philosopher, on his second conviction and long sentence for pedophilia, said, "It was worth it." The emotional intensity did not approach that of my relationship with Eric, or even that with Allen or Dennis, but of all the children and/or adolescents I was ever involved with, Charles was by far the best lovemaker. He bragged that he knew how to French kiss, and boy, did he! That relationship lasted several months.

Evelyn came to visit again. I explained that I would be on call one or two nights each week, but I actually was staying at Debby's house. Romantically, this was the wildest period of my life, as there frequently were days when I made love to Evelyn in the evening or morning before going to work, to Charles that afternoon, and then to Debby, his mother, that night. But clearly, I enjoyed myself most with Charles. David (who was 6-years-old) and I also were involved, in a minor way, in that he liked to rub his genitals against me when we wrestled or tickled. He did not stimulate me, and I let him do what he wanted to do for his own gratification. There had been times, preceding my introduction into their lives, that the brothers had been involved with each other.

My problems with Charles began after he showed up at his mother's home one day with his friend George. Attracted to George, I tried to tickle him, but getting no positive response, I stopped. Later, George must have made some unfavorable remark to Charles, whose attitude changed without any other obvious cause. Charles told his father something about our relationship, and his father made him report it to the police. However, all he told the police was that once during our ski trip I touched his buttocks. He was well known to them as a "problem child" and was simultaneously making other outlandish allegations against an aunt and so was not taken very seriously. A detective did investigate, to whom I spoke by phone. He wanted a meeting of all involved parties, but an attorney advised me against going. Debby was distraught that I suddenly stopped seeing her without warning. She did not believe Charles, and she still cared for me. For me, it was a good pretext to devote all my attention to Evelyn. I thought that the matter was finished, but the incident came back to haunt me years later. It had been enough to scare me off kids—but only for a while.

## Marriage

The scare also contributed to my decision to marry Evelyn the following year. She had come for an extended visit, and we did love each other, and I saw no reason to wait any longer. A friend of hers came from out of town to attend the wedding, bringing her 11-year-old son. They visited us at our hotel the morning following the wedding, because we were not leaving on our honeymoon until late afternoon. Evelyn and her friend went out for a while, leaving me with the boy. We wrestled and jumped on the bed, doing all those hotel-room type things, during which I was stimulated to another, covert orgasm—this on the morning after my wedding! I behaved myself during our honeymoon, but I noticed many cute boys.

I returned to work, continuing my medical-specialty training. When I was on call, I was responsible for the children's and adolescents' units, where I spent my occasional free time. I became friends with a fatherless, withdrawn, 10-year-old boy, Ben. Because his schizophrenic mother had been engaging him in intercourse, her visits with the boy had to be supervised. I was invited to provide the supervision, along with the social worker, for one of those visits. It was actually painful to observe their very dysfunctional interaction. Mother arrived 20 minutes late for the ½-hour visit and then was more concerned with having me set the correct time on her new digital watch than she was with interacting with Ben. Between them, there was little contact, physical or emotional. When he spoke to her, her responses were totally unrelated to what he had said. While I never was convinced that his withdrawal would resolve completely, I was sure that he would do much better if he lived in even a semblance of a sane, nonchaotic environment. Sometimes he crawled into my lap just to be held, and I grew very fond of him. I found him masturbating once when I walked into his room. I never developed a sexual attraction to him, perhaps because he seemed to already be so oversexed. Yet, I had a great parental instinct that

I felt as an intense need to nurture this boy. A foster home was being sought for him, and I went so far as to obtain and fill out an application. I was talked out of filing the form, however. My wife Evelyn, unable to bear children, changed her mind about taking Ben after she met him for the second time. That meeting took place at a government hospital, where he was not expecting our visit. His first words to me when we arrived to see him there were, "When are you coming again?" I felt guilty that I could not guarantee a continued and predictable presence in his life, and so I stopped seeing him. I still believe I could have been quite a beneficial influence on him.

I became so well known on the pediatrics units in the hospital where I was training that when my turn came for subsequent rotations to the units, three patients requested me as their doctor even before my arrival! One was Robert, 13. We were friendly over the course of his four-month hospitalization. One of our more significant activities was visiting a nearby nursing home, initiated at his request. There we befriended an 85-year-old female whom we visited often. They had in common that they both were orphaned as children. I was impressed by the special fondness Robert showed for old folks as he approached each one, took his or her hand, and said hello. I had no overtly sexual relationship with any patient but could be discreetly aroused to orgasm when one sat on my lap or during horseplay. That rotation was easily my favorite.

My wife Evelyn and I decided to adopt a baby. During a short visit to her hometown, we informed some friends, who were adoptive parents, of our intention. We were back home less than a month when we got the call. As I listened to the social worker describe the baby, I watched my brother-in-law set up a crib in our bedroom for my infant nephew, with whom my wife was to babysit. The simultaneous aspect of the phone call and the setting up of the crib seemed like a sign. Another sign was the fact that I had accumulated vacation time and had another vacation scheduled to begin just about the time the social worker called. I am convinced the hand of God was manifest in the adoption of my son, and what an angel he turned out to be! I admit that the first time I saw him I thought he was ugly and questioned whether I wanted to spend the next 20 years raising him. Those feelings quickly dissolved, however, as I got to know his calm, meek, loving nature. During his five short months of life, he had been parented by a teenage single mother, but now he bonded to me very quickly and strongly and I to him. The separation from him, now age 3, is the most difficult part of my incarceration.

I have been asked whether I thought I might become sexual with my own son when he is older. I do not foresee such a thing. I have no such attraction to him now, and if I were to develop one later, I would refrain from acting on it so as to avoid possible legal consequences to myself and the confusing, traumatic effects such consequences might have on him.

On my next vacation, I traveled alone. It was a most incredible trip through North Africa, but the highlight was five days spent in a quaint town. On my first evening there, I met Ibrahim, 11, who was selling cigarettes. He became my constant companion and assistant. We slept together and had sex. He was very respectful and came in handy, because he helped carry my gear as we visited ruins and other towns. He lived with his mother but rarely saw his father, from whom his mother was separated. I was profoundly gratified when I was able to buy him the only new pair of pants that he ever had owned. When the time came to leave, it was very difficult to do so. He insisted on accompanying me to the train station, where I could not help but break down. He took my address and some money and promised to write, but one cannot realistically expect another who is struggling to survive to use money for stamps.

Back at work, the combination of improbable circumstances and bad luck resulted in my being reassigned to the hospital where, years earlier, I had been involved with Debby and her son Charles. Surprisingly, Debby greeted me calmly as we met by chance in the hallway. A friend of hers told me she had been devastated after our breakup. Updated personnel information had preceded my arrival, and she knew that I had gotten married. Nevertheless, she agreed to have dinner with me, which I asked her to do in part because I felt guilty about having left her suddenly. That was a difficult meal as I listened to how I had come into and upset her life, then suddenly left her alone to pick up the pieces, not to mention David, who was involved also, who had kept trying to call me until that Christmas.

At the hospital, a 10-year-old dark-skinned boy was referred for evaluation as a potential suicide. He was not very verbal. He denied having any suicidal inclinations as well as having any other problems whatsoever. So I engaged him in play therapy, which sometimes included a bit of roughhousing that I found mildly stimulating.

## Incarceration

My downfall was a cute 8-year-old boy who wandered into the hospital receptionist's office, where I happened to be having tea. He was waiting for his mother, who was seeing a therapist. He sat and had tea and cookies and a pleasant chat with me until his mother came. By pure coincidence, almost the same scene was repeated a week later, by which time I had grown fond of Tommy.

About a month earlier, while Tommy was alone in his home, a drunken man had entered. Tommy had run to a neighbor, who had called the police. They ultimately charged his mother with child neglect, and she had been ordered to serve 30 days in jail and to then enter an alcoholism treatment program. A foster home was being sought for Tommy for 90 days so his mother could enter the program. The only alternative was for him to stay with his father, who had never seen him. I began to think, "Wouldn't it be nice to be this kid's foster father for 90 days?" I invited him to visit me at work for one weekend during which, I knew, I would not be very busy. When he and his mother arrived, he did not want her to leave. So the three of us visited together and had lunch. We all agreed that he would return alone later that evening, and he did so.

We played in my room in the hospital. In good, clean fun, I threw him in the air several times. He became frightened, although I did not realize it, and went into the hallway, and when he did not return soon, I went looking for him. I found him in the hospital security office. When I opened the door, he pointed and said, "There's the man who tried to hurt me!" Of course, I had done no such thing, and nothing sexual had occurred between us. Nevertheless, Tommy's mother was phoned, and a policeman was called to investigate. He spoke with Tommy and then told the boy's mother that her son did not appear to have been interfered with. Mother denied wanting to press any charges, but my name was taken.

A few days later, a detective who read the report recognized my name from the report Charles had made years earlier, and he went to interview Tommy. This time, false allegations were suggested to the boy, and then they were made against me. Still, there were no allegations that clothes had been removed. But on the basis of these two flimsy reports separated by years, a warrant for my arrest was issued. A full-scale witch-hunt was launched, and I was arrested, again and again.

Relevant here is my behavior even after my arrest. I was facing multiple, horribly inflated charges, but I was unwilling to stay away from kids completely, especially when it might be years before I would ever get to be with them again—and especially after I met Bobbie. I thought it safer to restrict myself to my own large city.

I was out of jail on a bail bond and had been suspended from work at the hospital. I had sent my wife and son to her family in an attempt to spare them from what was going on. Overwhelmed by what was happening, having no one to confide in, and foolishly trusting that my lawyer was vigorously preparing my defense, I wasted much time, using video games as an escape. At the arcade, I became friendly with a 14-year-old who seemed younger than his age and then, later, independently met his 8-year-old brother Bobbie. Bobbie was outside alone late one night and, during our conversation, mentioned that he had not eaten. So I invited him to have a hamburger. When we returned to the arcade after half an hour, the security guard asked me to step into the office. As it happened, a third brother had seen Bobbie enter my car and had called their parents, who had called the police. The police had called the security guard. Bobbie and I did not know about these calls, and we were puzzled to see the police and his parents arrive. When he told everyone that everything was fine, the police just warned me and left.

I continued to run into Bobbie and his brothers in the area of the arcade. Our friendship grew after that shaky start, and I got to know Bobbie's whole family. They were poor and had no car. I took Bobbie many places, now with his parents' permission, and sometimes took his brothers, too, like the time I took them all to an anti-apartheid demonstration in an effort to instill in them a sense of social responsibility. I also took them to parks and movies. I frequently took Bobbie to my house, where we enjoyed lying together watching television. He even spent the night several times, sleeping in my arms while I had orgasms from the mere physical contact. He was a fairly bright boy to whom I supplied books to read, and I could never understand why he was in special education. He was taking well to the attention I showed him, I had grown very fond of him, and it was very sad that our friendship had to end so I could come to prison.

## Closing Thoughts

I have always considered myself a humanitarian. To ameliorate the sufferings and problems of fellow human beings has been my goal. Though perhaps a bit idealistic, in my heart that is how I have felt. Pursuing a career as a physician was a big step in that direction. With my acceptance into medical-specialty training, I sought to further my accessibility to the difficulties of others. I have been, in my heart and mind, true to the ideals of the medical profession. Add to this my great love for mankind and my overall attitude of selfless self-love

In order to maximize the health of others, I have felt it necessary to first safeguard my own health. I do not smoke, drink to excess, or abuse drugs. My vegetarian diet is "overdetermined," one might say, by my awareness of its health benefits, my opposition to the pointless slaughter of animals, and my concern about world hunger. As an individual whose academic as well as personal life experience has embraced both the sciences and philosophy, I hold strongly to these practices; the benefits in them are not only physical but psychological and spiritual as well.

The health of the planet also is my concern. I take very seriously the work in which many social and environmental groups are engaged. In an attempt to ensure Mother Earth's continued habitability for my child(ren) and all others of the world, I have been involved in several causes. Consider this example: during my second year of medical-specialty training, I almost single-handedly organized a series of lectures titled "Medicine and the Nuclear Threat." In this effort, I obtained the cosponsorship of my department, the medical ethics committee, the residents' union, of which I was an officer, and my local chapter of International Physicians for the Prevention of Nuclear War (IPPNW), of which I was a member. Such a series of presentations was unprecedented at my hospital. Though my efforts on behalf of IPPNW represent only a very small contribution to the totality of all their activities that year, I do feel I earned, for those efforts, a tiny portion of the Nobel Peace Prize they subsequently were awarded.

I have never interfered with, injured, or thwarted the growth and development of another human being. I have never hurt a child. On the contrary, I have loved children in a way that covered every aspect of the human-love spectrum. Yet, now I reflect that perhaps there is such a thing as loving too much. This is not necessarily my viewpoint; clearly, however, it is that of the society that has stolen my future and placed me in bondage—a most cruel and offensive bondage. It is remarkable in my opinion that an individual can be imprisoned for such a long period—for a first offense, no less—and looted of life simply for trying to add to its fullness.

# 19
# The Abused/Abuser Hypothesis of Child Sexual Abuse: A Critical Review of Theory and Research

Randall J. Garland
Michael J. Dougher
*Department of Psychology*
*University of New Mexico*
*Albuquerque, New Mexico 87131*

## Introduction

A widespread belief among the general public and professionals alike is that "sexual abuse causes sexual abuse" (Finkelhor et al., 1986; Kempe and Kempe, 1984; Lanyon, 1986). That is, sexually abused children and adolescents who have engaged in sexual behavior with an adult (or a significantly older adolescent) are commonly thought to be at risk in later years of themselves becoming sexually involved with children and adolescents. This belief is referred to here as the "abused/abuser hypothesis of child and adolescent sexual abuse."

Given the popularity of the abused/abuser hypothesis, it is perhaps surprising to find that there is a dearth of evidence supporting it. This is not to say that there is a substantial body of contradictory evidence. Rather, only a handful of studies have actually investigated the presumed association, and the designs and methods of these studies have been less than ideal. Most of the relevant data come from retrospective studies of adults that do not allow for direct causal analysis.

Inasmuch as sexual behavior between adults and children and adults and adolescents intuitively appears to be a complex phenomenon determined by multiple factors, the uncritical acceptance of the abused/abuser hypothesis may lead to premature and faulty conclusions regarding the determinants of such behavior, as well as to social policy based on inadequate and inaccurate information. Clearly, the status of this hypothesis warrants scrutiny. Accordingly, this chapter critically reviews the theoretical formulations and major research findings (i.e., data and interpretations) pertaining to the abused/abuser hypothesis.

# Theoretical Formulations

Several theoretical formulations have been suggested relating childhood and adolescent sexual behavior with adults to subsequent sexually non-normative behavior in these children and adolescents when they become adults. Unfortunately, most of these theoretical formulations were developed to explain nonnormative sexual behavior in general rather than adult sexual behavior with children and adolescents in particular. These theoretical formulations can be loosely categorized as either cognitive-behavioral or psychodynamic.

## Cognitive-Behavioral Formulations

Conditioning and/or modeling processes have been proposed as the means by which childhood and adolescent sexual behavior with adults may be related to subsequent sexual behavior with children and adolescents when these former children and adolescents themselves become adults (Howells, 1981).

McGuire, Carlisle, and Young (1965) hypothesized that nonnormative sexual arousal may become conditioned through masturbatory fantasies paired with orgasm. These researchers suggested that early sexual experiences, such as sexual behavior with an adult, supply the material for these masturbatory fantasies and that through classical conditioning (i.e., conditioned stimulus = fantasy, unconditioned stimulus = orgasm), the fantasy stimuli become increasingly sexually arousing. McGuire and colleagues suggested that these masturbatory fantasies might become progressively more nonnormative as a result of memory distortion and selection over time. They also allowed that other factors, such as feelings of physical or social inadequacy, might be important determinants of a preference for nonnormative sexual fantasies over more conventional ones.

There are two mechanisms by which conditioning can increase the probability of an adult's becoming sexually involved with a child or an adolescent. First, adult sexual behavior with a child or an adolescent often clinically manifests itself in the affected child or adolescent as sexual precociousness and increased sexual behavior (Alter-Reid et al., 1986; Finkelhor et al., 1986; Yates, 1982). Theoretically, a child's or an adolescent's increased sexual behavior with peers could directly condition sexual arousal to children and could serve as the basis for subsequent conditioning through masturbatory fantasies. Second, through processes like memory distortion over time, the child or adolescent who had been sexually involved with an adult could develop a masturbatory fantasy that somehow results in the conditioning of sexual arousal to children (e.g., fantasizing the self in the role of the adult).

Modeling (observational learning) has also been suggested as a process by which childhood and adolescent sexual behavior with adults may be related to subsequent sexual behavior with children and adolescents (Freeman-Longo, 1986; Howells, 1981). The child or adolescent may learn through observation that adults can and do sexually interact with children, that they experience rewarding consequences as a result of such interaction, and that they are unlikely to be punished. No doubt, many such children and adolescents also are misinformed by the adult involved in the abuse about the propriety of such behavior (Burgess et al., 1978).

There is plausibility to these cognitive-behavioral formulations. In support of the conditioning hypothesis are the observations that sexual responses can be classically conditioned (Dougher et al., 1987; Rachman, 1966) and that some adjudicated adult sex offenders become sexually aroused (as assessed by penile plethysmography) by descriptions of their own childhood sexual experiences with adults (Freeman-Longo, 1986). However, in two important respects, these formulations are limited. First, at an empirical level, for obvious ethical reasons there is no systematic evidence that either conditioning or modeling processes are operative in the development of adult sexual behavior with children or adolescents. Second, at a theoretical level, it is obvious that neither conditioning nor modeling processes alone can be necessary and sufficient causes. Other variables, such as social inadequacy, appear necessary for explaining why the child or adolescent who has been sexually involved with an adult remains sexually interested in children or adolescents when this child or adolescent becomes an adult (Howells, 1981). Consideration of other variables is especially important for the conditioning hypothesis. Many prepubescent and pubescent children experience sexual arousal and even orgasm with peers but do not later in adulthood engage in sexual behavior with children or adolescents (Howells, 1981; Langfeldt, 1981). Thus, while conditioning and modeling mechanisms may be determinants of adult human sexual behavior with children and adolescents, by themselves they are not adequate explanations.

## Psychodynamic Formulations

Identification and/or mastery processes also have been suggested as mechanisms by which childhood and adolescent sexual behavior with adults may lead to later adult sexual involvement with children or adolescents.

It is often suggested that adult androphilic pedophilia may be the long-term outcome of a previous emotionally gratifying experience of sexual contact with an adult during childhood or adolescence (Halleck, 1965; Rush, 1980; Seghorn, Prentky, and Boucher, 1987; Storr, 1964; Summit, 1983). Theoretically, for the emotionally deprived and neglected male child, sexual interaction with an older male could prove comforting and enjoyable. Through the mechanism of identification with the older partner, the male child or adolescent could be predisposed to become sexually involved with other male children or adolescents when he is an adult. Such an individual may identify with young males as the recipients of his affection and can therefore easily rationalize his behavior.

This formulation is supported indirectly by certain findings. Emotional deprivation, especially involving an inadequate or absent relationship with the father, has been suggested and found to be a correlate of male child and adolescent sexual behavior with adult males (Bender, 1965; DeJong, Emmett, and Hervada, 1982a; Finkelhor, 1984; Halleck, 1965; Ingram, 1979; Oliven, 1965; Pierce and Pierce, 1985; Rush, 1980; Virkkunen, 1981). Also, it has been found that adult males' retrospective self-reports of sexual contact during childhood and adolescence are not uniformly negative (Finkelhor, 1979; Fritz, Stoll, and Wagner, 1981; Landis, 1956) and that some young males may contemporaneously evaluate such an interaction as positive (Sandfort, 1982). Furthermore, it has been clinically observed that children sometimes interpret a disrupted sexual relationship with an adult as a loss (Burgess et al., 1978; Burgess et al., 1984). Finally, researchers have noted that androphilic pedophiles often retrospectively self-report disrupted or poor relationships with their fathers (Gebhard et al., 1965; Mohr, Turner, and Jerry, 1964; Paitich and Langevin, 1976). However, despite these suggestive findings, there is at present little or no direct empirical support for this psychodynamic formulation.

A second psychodynamic formulation emphasizes both identification and mastery processes. In this formulation, "identification with the aggressor" and the conversion of passive experience into activity done to others are the means by which sexual trauma is said to be related to "perversion" (Rosen, 1979; Stoller, 1975, 1979, 1985). Stoller, particularly, has articulated the process by which sexual trauma may lead to perversion. It does have to be noted that this formulation pertains to perversion in general. However, the formulation can be easily applied to adult sexual behavior with children and adolescents.

Stoller theorizes that perverse fantasies or acts represent the recapitulation of actual trauma directed at an individual's sex or gender identity. Perverse fantasies and acts are the means by which an individual symbolically attempts to gain revenge for and mastery over a childhood sexual trauma. As a result of identification with the aggressor, the individual, through such activities, is capable of temporarily turning a passively endured childhood trauma into an actively controlled adult triumph. Such activities preserve erotic gratification and a sense of potency.

Stoller's formulation is more comprehensive than are others in that he describes how additional factors mediate the effects of early sexual experiences. He proposes that the child involved must be susceptible to trauma and that this susceptibility is attributable to early life experiences. Specifically, he suggests that excessive symbiosis with the mother and deficient identification with the father can render a male child especially vulnerable to sexual trauma. He presumes this potential cause-and-effect situation to be the case because such a male child's sense of gender identity ought to be less firmly established. Additionally, such a parent/child configuration may potentiate oedipal conflicts, which in turn contribute to future difficulties in the development of adult heterosexual behavior.

Studies of male children and adolescents involved in sexual behavior with adults and clinical observations of adjudicated adult sex offenders of children provide some indirect partial support for Stoller's formulation and suggest its relevance for a hypothesized abused/abuser relationship.

Aggressive, antisocial behavior in male children and male adolescents is a common correlate of the disclosure of sexual involvement with an adult (Burgess et al., 1984; Burgess, Hartman, and McCormack, 1987; Carmen, Rieker, and Mills, 1984; Friedrich and Luecke, 1988; Rogers and Terry, 1984; Summit, 1983). This behavior commonly involves a sexual element (Rogers and Terry, 1984). Male children and adolescents who have been sexually involved with an adult often recapitulate their sexual experiences, with the exception that they enact the role of the older individual (Burgess et al., 1984; Burgess, Hartman, and McCormack, 1987; Rogers and Terry, 1984). The functions of this behavior are theorized to be the concealment of feelings of helplessness, the mastery of anxiety, and the reestablishment of masculinity (Burgess et al., 1984; Burgess, Hartman, and McCormack, 1987; Rogers and Terry, 1984).

Stoller's psychodynamic formulation, too, is supported by the similarities between offense characteristics and retrospective self-report data in incarcerated adult sex offenders of children or adolescents. Freeman-Longo (1986) and Groth (1979) have reported that incarcerated adult sex offenders who as children or adolescents themselves were sexually involved with adults often replicate their sexual experiences with children or adolescents when they, the incarcerated offenders, are adults. The ages of the children or adolescents with whom they become involved and the types of sexual acts performed have been noted to correspond to their own previous childhood and adolescent sexual experiences with adults.

## Summary and Commentary

Several theoretical formulations for the abused/abuser hypothesis have been proposed. These formulations have invoked conditioning, modeling, identification, and mastery processes. While each formulation has some explanatory power and some indirect empirical support, none have been shown to offer superior explanatory and predictive potency over competing formulations. Additionally, each formulation awaits more systematic research.

Clearly, variables in addition to previous sexual behavior with an adult have to be considered in evaluating the merits of the abused/abuser hypothesis. By itself, childhood or adolescent sexual contact with an adult is inadequate to explain subsequent adult sexual behavior with children or adolescents. These additional variables probably should include characteristics of the involved child (e.g., social competence and the stability of gender identity) and of the sexual interaction itself (e.g., the quality of the child's relationship with the involved adult) and the sequelae of the sexual experience (e.g., masturbatory conditioning to sexual fantasies based on the sexual experience). Numerous researchers have suggested that sexual contact between adults and children and adults and adolescents has no inevitable consequences but that the consequences depend on a complex network of interrelated variables (Bender, 1965; Bender and Grugett, 1952; Constantine, 1980; Finch, 1973; Halleck, 1965; Rieker and Carmen, 1986; Seghorn, Prentky, and Boucher, 1987). What is indicated, therefore, is that research should attempt to identify those conditions under which the abused/abuser hypothesis has merit, inasmuch as previous sexual behavior with an adult does not in itself adequately explain adult sexual behavior with children and adolescents. Unfortunately, most of the research conducted to date has focused primarily on the prevalence of childhood or adolescent histories of sexual contact with adults among adult sex offenders of children and adolescents.

# Childhood and Adolescent Histories of Sexual Contact with Adults Among Identified Sex Offenders of Children and Adolescents

A number of studies have investigated the prevalence of childhood and adolescent histories of sexual behavior with adults among sex offenders of children and adolescents. Many of these studies have been relatively unsophisticated in that few attempts have been made to integrate these childhood and adolescent sexual experiences with other factors. Additionally, the sophistication of many of these studies has been compromised by methodological issues relating mainly to the composition of sex offender groups and to the utilization of comparison groups. The authors of this chapter will progress from the least to the most sophisticated of the prevalence studies in the following review.

## Research Findings

The least sophisticated of studies give the prevalence of self-reported childhood or adolescent sexual behavior with adults among more or less well-defined samples of sex offenders. These studies include no comparison groups, making it impossible to directly evaluate whether the prevalence of childhood or adolescent sexual contact with adults is greater for sex offenders than it is for individuals with similar demographic characteristics who are not sex offenders.

Regrettably, all of the reviewed studies of adolescent sex offenders fall into this category. Additionally, the adolescent studies utilized heterogeneous sex offender samples, including, for example, exhibitionists, voyeurs, rapists, and pedophiles.

Longo (1982) found that 47% of his sample of adolescent sex offenders reported that they had engaged in sexual behavior with an adult during childhood. Of Longo's sample, 40% were identified sex offenders of children. Fehrenbach et al. (1986) found a childhood history of sexual behavior with adults in 18% of their sample of adolescent sex offenders, 63% of whom were sex offenders of children. Finally, Becker et al. (1986), studying a sample consisting of 77% intrafamilial adolescent sex offenders of children, noted that 23% of them had previously engaged in sexual behavior with an adult when they were children.

Those studies of adult sex offenders of children that did not include comparison groups are Frisbie (1969) and Abel (unpublished manuscript, cited in Knopp, 1984). Frisbie (1969) found that 24% of a group of sex offenders of children reported childhood histories of sexual contact with an adult. Frisbie's data suggested that childhood sexual behavior with an adult was more prevalent among sex offenders of male or of both male and female children as compared to sex offenders exclusively of female children. Abel (unpublished manuscript, cited in Knopp, 1984), too, found a self-reported history of childhood sexual behavior with adults to be more prevalent among sex offenders of male children (40% prevalence rate) versus sex offenders of female children (20% prevalence rate).

Two studies of adult sex offenders of children and adolescents attempted to deal with the issue of comparison groups by comparing the prevalence rates of childhood and adolescent sexual contact with adults among sex offenders of children with such contact among rapists (Seghorn, Prentky, and Boucher, 1987; Tingle et al., 1986). Unfortunately, both studies placed sex offenders of male and of female children and adolescents into a common group, thus obscuring the detection of any potential differences in prevalence rates between these two subtypes of sex offenders of children and adolescents.

Seghorn, Prentky, and Boucher (1987) found that 23% of a sample of rapists and 57% of a sample of sex offenders of children and adolescents reported childhood and adolescent sexual contact with adults. Tingle et al. (1986) investigated both homosexual and heterosexual childhood and adolescent sexual behavior with adults among rapists and among sex offenders of children and adolescents. These investigators observed that 38% of the rapists and 56% of the sex offenders of children reported childhood or adolescent histories of sexual behavior with adults. Among the rapists, 62% had been sexually involved with males, 0% had been sexually involved with females, and 38% had been sexually involved with both males and females. For the sex offenders of children, 70% had been sexually involved with males, 13% had been sexually involved with females, and 17% had been sexually involved with both males and females.

Two studies investigated childhood and adolescent histories of sexual contact with adults among sex offenders of children and among multiple comparison groups (Condy et al., 1987; Groth, 1979). These studies were more sophisticated in that prevalence rates for sex offenders of children were compared with the rates for other sex offenders, nonsexual offenders, and/or normal nonoffenders. However, sex offenders of male and of female children again were placed into a common group.

Groth (1979) examined self-reported histories of childhood and adolescent sexual experiences in the backgrounds of sex offenders of children, of rapists, and of police officers. He found that less than 3% of the police officers reported either forcible sexual assault or coerced sexual contact with an adult during childhood or adolescence. In contrast, 13% of the rapists and 25% of the sex offenders of children reported such experiences. Condy et al. (1987) found that 37% of sex offenders of children, 57% of rapists, 47% of nonsexual offenders, and 16% of non-offenders reported sexual behavior with females at least five years older than themselves during their own childhood and early adolescence.

Finally, there are the most sophisticated of the studies, those that utilized differentiated groups of sex offenders of children and adolescents as well as multiple comparison groups.

Gebhard et al. (1965) investigated the prevalence of self-reported childhood sexual contact with adults among a number of groups, including nonoffenders, nonsexual offenders, and a variety of sex offenders. Among their findings concerning the prevalence of prepubertal sexual contact with adults (including sexual approaches, exhibitionism, and actual physical contact) were the following: (a) nonoffenders—3% heterosexual contact, 8% homosexual contact; (b) nonsexual offenders—10% heterosexual contact, 31% homosexual contact; (c) rapists—10% heterosexual contact, 22% homosexual contact; (d) nonincestuous offenders of female children—10% heterosexual contact, 24% homosexual contact; (e) incestuous offenders of female children—8% heterosexual contact, 19% homosexual contact; (f) sex offenders of male children—8% heterosexual contact, 32% homosexual contact; (g) nonincestuous offenders of female adolescents—16% hetero-sexual contact, 14% homosexual contact; (h) nonincestuous offenders of male adolescents—6% heterosexual contact, 35% homosexual contact; and (i) incestuous offenders of female adolescents—6% heterosexual contact, 13% homosexual contact.

Langevin et al. (1985) examined the prevalence of self-reported childhood sexual behavior with adults for nonoffenders, for incestuous offenders of female children and adolescents, and for nonincestuous offenders of female children and adolescents. These researchers found that 4% of the nonoffenders, 21% of the incestuous offenders, and 10% of the nonincestuous offenders reported adult/child sexual contact with adult males during childhood. Additionally, 15% of the nonoffenders, 24% of the incestuous offenders, and 41% of the nonincestuous offenders reported adult/child sexual contact with females four or five years older than themselves during childhood.

Finally, Langevin and Lang (1985) studied self-reported childhood sexual experiences in the backgrounds of nonoffenders, of sex offenders of male children, of sex offenders of female children, and of other sexually anomalous males (e.g., exhibitionists and voyeurs). These researchers found that 15% of the nonoffenders, 5% of the sex offenders of male children, 21% of the sex offenders of female children, and 8% of the other sexually anomalous males reported prepubertal sexual contact with females at least four years older than themselves. Also, 4% of the nonoffenders, 14% of the sex offenders of male children, 3% of the sex offenders of female children, and 21% of the other sexually anomalous males reported prepubertal sexual contact with males four or five years older than themselves. Finally, 4% of the nonoffenders, 14% of the sex offenders of male children, 0% of the sex offenders of female children, and 15% of the other sexually anomalous males reported prepubertal sexual contact with adult males.

## Summary and Commentary

There is significant variability in the prevalence of self-reported childhood and adolescent sexual behavior with adults among nonoffenders, nonsexual offenders, sex offenders of children and adolescents, and other types of sex offenders. The findings of the studies of adult sex offenders of children and adolescents are summarized in Table 19.I. If one ignores whether the reported intergenerational sexual behavior was heterosexual or homosexual in nature, childhood and adolescent sexual contact with adults was reported by 3-16% of the nonoffenders, 10-47% of the nonsexual offenders, 0-57% of the sex offenders of children, and 8-57% of the other sex offenders or the sexually anomalous males.

No doubt, sampling and methodological differences among the studies account for much of the variability in findings. A variety of methods were used to assess the prevalence of childhood and adolescent sexual behavior

TABLE 19.I. Percent of various groups reporting childhood or adolescent sexual contact with an adult

| Study | Undifferentiated Adult Sex Offenders of Children and Adolescents | Adult Sex Offenders of Female Children and Adolescents | Adult Sex Offenders of Male Children and Adolescents | Other Sex Offenders or Sexually Anomalous Males (e.g., rapists and voyeurs) | Nonsexual Offenders | Non-offenders |
|---|---|---|---|---|---|---|
| Gebhard et al. (1965) | — | 6-24 | 6-35 | 10-22 | 10-31 | 3-8 |
| Frisbie (1969) | 24 | — | — | — | — | — |
| Groth (1979) | 25 | — | — | 13 | — | <3 |
| Abel (unpub. ms., cited in Knopp) (1984) | — | 20 | 40 | — | — | — |
| Langevin et al. (1985) | — | 10-41 | — | — | — | 4-15 |
| Langevin and Lang (1985) | — | 0-21 | 5-14 | 8-21 | — | 4-15 |
| Tingle et al. (1986) | 56 | — | — | 38 | — | — |
| Condy et al. (1987) | 37 | — | — | 57 | 47 | 16 |
| Seghorn et al. (1987) | 57 | — | — | 23 | — | — |

Note: The percents listed include heterosexual and/or homosexual contact with an adult during childhood or adolescence. Ranges are given when the column headings reflect more than one group in the original study. Studies of adolescent sex offenders are not depicted in the table.

with adults, including reviews of clinical records, self-report questionnaires, and personal interviews. There were differences in how childhood and adolescent sexual behavior with adults was defined. Finally, the data were collected at different times and in different contexts.

Despite this variability, self-reported childhood and adolescent sexual behavior with adults is more prevalent among adjudicated sex offenders of children and adolescents than among comparison groups of nonoffender males. However, it also appears that the self-reported prevalence of childhood and adolescent sexual behavior with adults is roughly comparable among adjudicated sex offenders of children, adjudicated nonsexual offenders, and other types of adjudicated sex offenders. (Refer to Table 19.I.) The prevalence of homosexual child and adolescent sexual contact with adults appears greater for sex offenders of both sexes of children as compared to rapists (see, for example, Gebhard et al., 1965, and Tingle et al., 1986). Also, the prevalence of childhood and adolescent sexual contact with adults appears greater among sex offenders of male children and adolescents than it does among sex offenders of female children and adolescents (Abel, unpublished manuscript, cited in Knopp, 1984; Frisbie, 1969; Gebhard et al., 1965; Langevin and Lang, 1985). However, the significance of the latter two findings is obscured by the data that show that childhood and adolescent sexual behavior with adults, both homosexual and heterosexual, is comparably prevalent among adjudicated nonsexual offenders (Condy et al., 1987; Gebhard et al., 1965) and among other sexually anomalous males (e.g., exhibitionists and voyeurs) (Langevin and Lang, 1985). Thus, while the prevalence of childhood and adolescent sexual behavior with adults may differentiate nonoffender males from adjudicated sex offenders of children, it does not clearly differentiate the latter group either from other adjudicated sex offenders or from nonsexual offenders.

However, even this conclusion is tentative because of the methodological limitations of the studies reviewed. First, the majority of the studies reviewed used only adjudicated and incarcerated sex offenders. Finkelhor et al. (1986) have questioned whether this group can be considered representative of sex offenders of children and adolescents. This group most likely represents a very biased sample of all adults who have engaged in sexual behavior with children and adolescents. Such incarcerated sex offenders are likely to be the ones who are the most "pathological" and who come from the most disadvantaged segments of society. Second, none of the reviewed studies included formal matching procedures or any statistical means for controlling for differences among the research groups (e.g., ethnicity and presence and type of psychopathology). Thus, other, uncontrolled factors could have contributed to the variability of the self-reported prevalence of childhood and adolescent sexual contact with adults among the groups and, perhaps, even to future adjudication as an adult sex offender.

The conclusion that seems warranted from the review is that childhood and adolescent sexual contact with adults is neither a necessary nor a sufficient cause for becoming an adjudicated sex offender of children or adolescents.

A reasonable overall estimate of the percentage of adjudicated sex offenders of children and adolescents who report having experienced sexual contact with an adult during childhood or adolescence is approximately 30%. Childhood or adolescent sexual contact with an adult thus characterizes only a fraction of such adjudicated sex offenders. One might argue that more adjudicated offenders of children and adolescents actually had such experiences but have "repressed" them. If this argument is used, however, the reason or reasons why sex offenders of children and adolescents would be more prone to repress such sexual experiences than would other groups of individuals must be explained. Thus, sexual contact with an adult during childhood or adolescence is not a necessary cause for becoming an adjudicated adult sex offender of children and adolescents.

Sexual contact with an adult during childhood or adolescence also does not appear to be a sufficient cause for becoming an adjudicated sex offender of children and adolescents. If such contact were a sufficient cause, the implication would be that all adults who were sexually involved with an adult when they themselves were children or adolescents would become sex offenders of children or adolescents. Three points belie this notion. First, there is the prevalence of self-reported sexual contact with adults during childhood and adolescence among adjudicated nonsexual offenders and sex offenders not involved with children or adolescents. Second, although approximately 25% of adult females report that they were sexually involved with an adult when they were children or adolescents, less than 10% of adjudicated sex offenders of children or adolescents are female (Finkelhor et al., 1986). Third, although the base rate in the general adult male population of males who have been sexually involved with children or adolescents is unknown, it is unlikely that this rate would approach 10%, a typical estimate of the prevalence of sexual contact with an adult during childhood or adolescence among adult males (Finkelhor et al., 1986).

In summary, the abused/abuser hypothesis—the belief that sexual behavior between adults and children or adolescents causes those children and adolescents, as adults, to become sexually involved with other children and adolescents—is inadequate and incorrect. If sexual behavior between adults and children or adolescents is at all a significant factor in the intergenerational transmission of such behavior, it is a factor that acts in combination with other factors to produce such an outcome (cf. Finkelhor, 1984; Finkelhor et al., 1986; Langevin and Lang, 1985).

## Additional Factors To Be Considered

One means by which to understand how adult sexual behavior with a child or an adolescent could contribute to the intergenerational transmission of such behavior is to consider additional pertinent variables. Some of these variables can be grouped within the following specific categories: the affected child's or adolescent's characteristics (including the family), the nature and the context of the sexual interaction itself, and the sequelae of the sexual interaction. The question is, how does sexual contact with an adult during childhood or adolescence interact with the variables within these categories so as to lead to the intergenerational transmission of sexual behavior with children or adolescents? With the question framed in this way, attempts can be made to assess these variables in future retrospective studies of adjudicated sex offenders and in future prospective (longitudinal) studies of children and adolescents who are identified as having been sexually involved with an adult. This type of assessment will require the use of multivariate designs and, perhaps, more sophisticated developmental models (e.g., see Zivin, this volume).

What follow are examples of some of the potentially relevant variables. They are discussed under the four categories—the characteristics of the child or adolescent, the nature and the context of the sexual interaction, and the sequelae of the sexual interaction.

## Characteristics of the Child or Adolescent

There are a number of characteristics of the child or adolescent and the child's or adolescent's family that may interact with sexual contact with an adult to contribute to the intergenerational perpetuation of this behavior.

The child's or adolescent's sex is obviously important, although it may not only be biological sex per se but also something associated with it, such as socialization experiences (Finkelhor et al., 1986).

The child's or adolescent's age may be significant, although the literature is conflictual as to whether younger or older children or adolescents are more "traumatized" by sexual behavior with an adult (Abel, Becker, Cunningham-Rathner, 1984; Constantine, 1980; DeJong, Emmett, and Hervada, 1982b; Finkelhor, 1979).

Preexisting emotional disturbance or psychiatric disorder in the child or adolescent may contribute to the development of intergenerational sexual behavior in either of two ways. Emotional disturbance or psychiatric disorder may exacerbate the effects of any traumatic aspects of sexual interaction with an adult (Halleck, 1965). Conversely, emotional disturbance or psychiatric disorder may make sexual interaction with an adult an exceptionally positive experience, inasmuch as the child or adolescent may experience needed affection in such a relationship. Identification with the older partner may then occur and predispose the child or adolescent to act similarly in the future (Halleck, 1965; Rush, 1980; Seghorn, Prentky, and Boucher, 1987; Storr, 1964; Summit, 1983).

The interpersonal skills of the child or adolescent seem especially important for determining whether sexual behavior with an adult during childhood or adolescence leads to the intergenerational perpetuation of this behavior. Deficits in interpersonal relationships and skills may make it difficult for the child or adolescent to progress to age-appropriate forms of affection and sexuality. Also, interpersonal deficits may result in variant environmental channeling of sexual behavior, which could be especially significant in a child or an adolescent with previous sexual experience with an adult (Gagnon, 1965; McGuire, Carlisle, and Young, 1965; Schwartz and Masters, 1983).

The stability of the child's or adolescent's sense of gender identity (i.e., the degree to which he or she feels masculine or feminine) also is likely to be an important variable. Stoller (1975, 1979, 1985) speculated that this variable critically determines the degree of "trauma" rendered by early sexual experiences and that it plays an important role in the etiology of what he terms "perversion." Additionally, this variable may account for the predominantly male child's or adolescent's propensity for sexually aggressive behavior subsequent to sexual interaction with an adult (Burgess et al., 1984; Burgess, Hartman, and McCormack, 1987; Carmen, Rieker, and Mills, 1984; Rogers and Terry, 1984; Rush, 1980; Summit, 1983).

The child's or adolescent's knowledge and attitudes about sex, too, may be important (Constantine, 1980). Deficient sex knowledge may increase the child's or adolescent's anxiety over the sexual behavior with an adult (Constantine, 1980) and may allow for the intrusion of unusual elements into the child's or adolescent's understanding of and fantasies about sex (Gagnon, 1965). Negative attitudes about sex may make appropriate sexual adjustment in later years more difficult (Abel, Becker, and Cunningham-Rathner, 1984; Constantine, 1980).

In addition to the child's or adolescent's characteristics, the characteristics of the child's or adolescent's parents and family may significantly interact with the experience of sexual behavior with an adult. Psychological disturbance in the parents, parental histories of sexual abuse, and negative parental attitudes about sex are all likely to engender adverse long-term consequences for the child or adolescent (Abel, Becker, and Cunningham-Rathner, 1984; Seghorn, Prentky, and Boucher, 1987). Such variables may operate by rendering the child or adolescent more susceptible to trauma or by exacerbating the trauma.

Family dysfunction, too, is likely to contribute to the traumatic aspects of a child's or an adolescent's sexual interaction with an adult (Abel, Becker, and Cunningham-Rathner, 1984; Constantine, 1980; Halleck, 1965). In this regard, there is evidence that family pathology increases the chances that the child or adolescent who has been sexually involved with an adult will intergenerationally perpetuate this behavior (Burgess, Hartman, and

McCormack, 1987; Seghorn, Prentky, and Boucher, 1987). Burgess, Hartman, and McCormack (1987) and Friedrich and Luecke (1988) found that sexually aggressive behavior among young males having previous sexual experience with adults was more common among those having a family background of nonsupport, disorganization, and violence.

Thus, a number of characteristics of the child or adolescent and of the child's or adolescent's family may interact with sexual contact with an adult and may contribute to the intergenerational transmission of this behavior.

## Nature and Context of Adult/Child or Adult/Adolescent Sexual Interaction

The nature of the sexual interaction and the context in which the interaction occurs are important categories comprising variables that may influence the intergenerational perpetuation of sexual behavior among adults and children or adolescents. Included in the nature of the interaction are the characteristics of the relationship between the two partners. These characteristics constitute a variable that may mediate the extent to which the child or adolescent identifies with the adult and consequently the extent to which the child or adolescent is predisposed toward future sexual involvement with children or adolescents (Halleck, 1965; Rush, 1980; Seghorn, Prentky, and Boucher, 1987; Storr, 1964; Summit, 1983).

The child's or adolescent's perception of control over the sexual interaction and the use of force during the interaction, two more variables, appear to be related to the degree of trauma experienced by the child or adolescent. There is a consensus that threats or force greatly enhance the traumatic aspects of a child's or an adolescent's sexual interaction with an adult (Abel, Becker, and Cunningham-Rathner, 1984; Burgess et al., 1978; Condy et al., 1987; Constantine, 1980; Finch, 1973; Finkelhor, 1979, 1984; Finkelhor et al., 1986; Friedrich and Luecke, 1988; Rogers and Terry, 1984). While it is unclear how such variables relate to the future development of sexual interest in children or adolescents, these variables may be associated with identification with the aggressor and active recapitulation of trauma as discussed by Stoller (1975).

The sex of the adult may be a relevant variable for the long-term effects of sexual behavior between adults and children or adolescents. One difference here is that adult females are less likely to use force than adult males (Condy et al., 1987; Johnson and Shrier, 1987). Additionally, heterosexual interaction between an adult female and a male child or adolescent may not provoke the young male to doubt his masculinity or sexual orientation (Johnson and Shrier, 1987). Finally, there is in fact some empirical evidence (i.e., retrospective self-report data) to suggest that heterosexual interaction with adult females is not as traumatic for male children and adolescents as is homosexual interaction with adult males (Condy et al., 1987; Finkelhor, 1979).

The duration and frequency of interaction with an adult would intuitively seem to be associated with the long-term effects on the child or adolescent. Specifically, one might think that the duration of the relationship with the adult would be related to the extent to which the child or adolescent comes to identify with the adult. There is, in fact, some evidence for this association in male children and adolescents: The longer young males have been involved with the adult male sexual partner, the more likely they are to maintain emotional, social, and economic ties with the adult male and to engage in sexually aggressive behavior against other children and adolescents (Burgess et al., 1984; Burgess, Hartman, and McCormack, 1987).

Likewise, one might argue that the number of adults who have been sexually involved with a particular child or adolescent and the types of sexual activities involved (e.g., fondling; oral, anal, or vaginal penetration) would be important determinants of outcome. These authors could find no data pertaining to the number of adult sexual partners. There are some data regarding type of sexual interaction, however. Friedrich and Luecke (1988) found that sexually aggressive children were more likely to report oral, anal, and/or vaginal penetration with adults than were nonaggressive children who also had sexual contact with adults. On the other hand, Finkelhor (1979) found no significant relationship between type of sexual activity and retrospectively self-reported trauma.

There is ample evidence, however, that as the age disparity between the child or adolescent and the adult increases, so does the degree of trauma for the child or adolescent and the likelihood of negative consequences as assessed by retrospective self-report and clinical judgment (Abel, Becker, and Cunningham-Rathner, 1984; Constantine, 1980; Finkelhor, 1979, 1984; Finkelhor et al., 1986; Landis, 1956; Rogers and Terry, 1984; Simari and Baskin, 1982).

Another variable that may affect long-term adjustment is the social visibility of the adult/child or adult/adolescent sexual interaction or relationship. This variable is one of two included in the category of the context in which the sexual interaction occurs. Burgess et al. (1984) noted that in male children and adolescents, involvement in pornography was one of the factors associated with what they described as identification with the aggressor and concomitant sexually aggressive behavior. It may be that this factor of social visibility enhances the young male's need to reestablish his sense of masculinity through aggressive, antisocial behavior. On the other hand, it may be that aggressive, antisocial males can be more easily persuaded to participate in the production of pornography.

The circumstances under which adult/child or adult/adolescent sexual interaction was terminated is the final variable in the category of context. This variable is a potentially important, yet uninvestigated factor in the long-term adjustment of the child or adolescent (Finkelhor and Browne, 1985). A frequently endorsed position is that some children and adolescents participate willingly in sexual behavior relationships with older individuals (Constantine, 1980; Finch, 1967, 1973; Ingram, 1979; Oliven, 1965; Virkkunen, 1981). This willingness may be especially characteristic of emotionally deprived children as well as of homosexual adolescent males (Halleck, 1965; Ingram, 1979; Rush, 1980; Storr, 1964; Summit, 1983). The termination of the relationship, therefore, could constitute a significant loss for the child or adolescent (Burgess et al., 1978). In turn, such an experience could facilitate the child's or adolescent's identification with the lost, older individual, thereby possibly predisposing the child or adolescent to behave like that individual in the future (Storr, 1964).

## Sequelae of the Abusive Interaction

In the category of the sequelae of the sexual interaction or relationship, there are three sequelae that may substantially contribute to the child's or adolescent's long-term adjustment. These sequelae, i.e., variables, are the child's or adolescent's behavior following the termination of the interaction or relationship, the consequences for the involved adult, and the reactions of other individuals to the disclosure of the sexual interaction or relationship.

One relatively common reaction of children and adolescents to sexual behavior with an adult is excessive sexualization (Alter-Reid et al., 1986; Finkelhor et al., 1986; Yates, 1982). Obviously, excessive sexualization, in the form of increased masturbation, could contribute to the development of atypical sexual interests through masturbatory conditioning processes like the processes suggested by McGuire, Carlisle, and Young (1965).

Rogers and Terry (1984) noted that the consequences for the involved adult may be important, as young males appear to engage in sexually aggressive behavior more frequently when the legal system fails to punish the adult with whom they have had sexual contact.

Finally, the reactions of others have to be considered as an important sequela of sexual behavior between adults and children or adolescents (Constantine, 1980; Finkelhor and Browne, 1985; Rogers and Terry, 1984). Denying or minimizing the behavior, blaming the child or adolescent, and expressing unrealistic fears about the impact of the behavior are three reactions of parents, family, and others that may heighten the child's or adolescent's trauma (Abel, Becker, and Cunningham-Rathner, 1984; Rogers and Terry, 1984). Inasmuch as these reactions may call the male child's or adolescent's sense of masculinity into question, they may potentiate adverse consequences for the child or adolescent. No doubt the child's or adolescent's adjustment also will be affected by the nature of legal proceedings in which the child or adolescent may become involved (Burgess et al., 1978; Finkelhor, 1984).

## Summary and Commentary

Inasmuch as the long-term impact of adult human sexual behavior with children and adolescents is the result of numerous interacting variables, researchers have to take these variables into account. To do so is especially important if researchers are to understand how sexual behavior with an adult during childhood or adolescence may be etiologically related to the intergenerational perpetuation of similar behavior. Examples of potentially significant variables having to do with the characteristics of the child and of the sexual interaction and examples of the sequelae of the sexual interaction have been presented, though, undoubtedly, other variables have been overlooked.

# Conclusions

The belief that sexual abuse causes sexual abuse, the so-called "abused/abuser hypothesis," is simplistic and misleading. The available evidence indicates that sexual behavior between an adult and a child or an adolescent is neither a necessary nor a sufficient cause of similar behavior in the child or adolescent when he or she becomes an adult. If sexual behavior with an adult is at all related to a child's or an adolescent's repeating the behavior during adulthood, it is related only in the context of other, interacting variables. Unfortunately, at this point, researchers do not know what all these other variables are or how they interact with childhood or adolescent sexual behavior with adults to lead to the intergenerational perpetuation of the behavior.

Nevertheless, the fact that some relation, albeit a complex one, appears to exist between sexual contact with an adult during childhood and adolescence and sexual involvement with children or adolescents during adulthood argues strongly for continued research on the issue. However, attention has to be given to those variables that may mediate the long-term effects of sexual contact with an adult during childhood or adolescence. Sophisticated multivariate research endeavors and more sophisticated developmental models may eventually allow us to specify the conditions under which adult sexual behavior with children and adolescents contributes to the intergenerational perpetuation of this type of behavior.

# Summary

This chapter represents a comprehensive and critical review of the major theoretical formulations and empirical findings pertinent to the so-called "abused/abuser hypothesis of child sexual abuse." The conclusion reached is that sexual contact with an adult during childhood or adolescence is neither a necessary nor a sufficient cause of adult sexual interest in children or adolescents.

## References

Abel, G.G., Becker, J.V., and Cunningham-Rathner, J. Complications, consent, and cognitions in sex between children and adults. *International Journal of Law and Psychiatry*, 1984, *7*, 89-103.

Alter-Reid, K., Gibbs, M.S., Lachenmeyer, J.R., Sigal, J., and Massoth, N.A. Sexual abuse of children: A review of the empirical findings. *Clinical Psychology Review*, 1986, *6*, 249-266.

Becker, J.V., Kaplan, M.S., Cunningham-Rathner, J., and Kavoussi, R. Characteristics of adolescent incest perpetrators: Preliminary findings. *Journal of Family Violence*, 1986, *1*, 85-97.

Bender, L. Offended and offender children. *In* R. Slovenko (Ed.), *Sexual behavior and the law*. Springfield, Ill.: Charles C. Thomas, 1965, pp. 687-703.

Bender, L., and Grugett, A.E. A follow-up on children who had atypical sexual experience. *American Journal of Orthopsychiatry*, 1952, *22*, 825-837.

Burgess, A.W., Groth, A.N., Holmstrom, L.L., and Sgroi, S.M. *Sexual assault of children and adolescents*. New York: Lexington, 1978.

Burgess, A.W., Hartman, C.R., McCausland, M.P., and Powers, P. Response patterns in children and adolescents exploited through sex rings and pornography. *American Journal of Psychiatry*, 1984, *141*, 656-662.

Burgess, A.W., Hartman, C.R., and McCormack, A. Abused to abuser: Antecedents of socially deviant behavior. *American Journal of Psychiatry*, 1987, *144*, 1431-1436.

Carmen, E., Rieker, P.P., and Mills, T. Victims of violence and psychiatric illness. *American Journal of Psychiatry*, 1984, *141*, 378-383.

Condy, S.R., Templer, D.I., Brown, R., and Veaco, L. Parameters of sexual contact of boys with women. *Archives of Sexual Behavior*, 1987, *16*, 379-394.

Constantine, L.L. The impact of early sexual experiences: A review and synthesis of outcome research. *In* J. Samson (Ed.), *Childhood and sexuality: Proceedings of the International Symposium*. Montreal: Editions Etudes Vivantes, 1980, pp. 150-172.

DeJong, A.R., Emmett, G.A., and Hervada, A.A. Epidemiologic factors in sexual abuse of boys. *American Journal of Diseases of Children*, 1982a, *136*, 990-993.

DeJong, A.R., Emmett, G.A., and Hervada, A.A. Sexual abuse of children: Sex-, race-, and age-dependent variations. *American Journal of Diseases of Children*, 1982b, *136*, 129-134.

Dougher, M.J., Crossen, J.R., Ferraro, D.P., and Garland, R. The effects of covert sensitization on preference for sexual stimuli: A preliminary analogue experiment. *Journal of Behavioral Therapy and Experimental Psychiatry,* 1987, *18*(4), 638-649.

Fehrenbach, P.A., Smith, W., Monastersky, C., and Deisher, R.W. Adolescent sex offenders: Offender and offense characteristics. *American Journal of Orthopsychiatry,* 1986, *56,* 225-233.

Finch, S.M. Sexual activity of children with other children and adults. *Clinical Pediatrics,* 1967, *6,* 1-2.

Finch, S.M. Adult seduction of the child: Effects on the child. *Medical Aspects of Human Sexuality,* 1973, *7,* 170-187.

Finkelhor, D. *Sexually victimized children.* New York: Free Press, 1979.

Finkelhor, D. *Child sexual abuse: New theory and research.* New York: Free Press, 1984.

Finkelhor, D., and Browne, A. The traumatic impact of child sexual abuse: A conceptualization. *American Journal of Orthopsychiatry,* 1985, *55,* 530-541.

Finkelhor, D., Araji, S., Baron, L., Browne, A., Peters, S.D., and Wyatt, G. E. *A sourcebook on child sexual abuse.* Beverly Hills, Calif.: Sage, 1986.

Freeman-Longo, R.E. The impact of sexual victimization on males. *Child Abuse and Neglect,* 1986, *10,* 411-414.

Friedrich, W.N., and Luecke, W.J. Young school-age sexually aggressive children. *Professional Psychology: Research and Practice,* 1988, *19,* 155-164.

Frisbie, L. *Another look at sex offenders in California.* California Department of Mental Hygiene, Research Monograph No. 12, Sacramento, Calif., 1969.

Fritz, G.S., Stoll, K., and Wagner, N.N. A comparison of males and females who were sexually molested as children. *Journal of Sex and Marital Therapy,* 1981, *7,* 54-59.

Gagnon, J.H. Sexuality and sexual learning in the child. *Psychiatry,* 1965, *28,* 212-228.

Gebhard, P.H., Gagnon, J.H., Pomeroy, W.B., and Christianson, C.V. *Sex offenders: An analysis of types.* New York: Harper & Row, 1965.

Groth, A.N. Sexual trauma in the life histories of rapists and child molesters. *Victimology,* 1979, *4,* 10-16.

Halleck, S.L. Emotional effects of victimization. *In* R. Slovenko (Ed.), *Sexual behavior and the law.* Springfield, Ill.: Charles C. Thomas, 1965, pp. 673-686.

Howells, K. Adult sexual interest in children: Considerations relevant to theories of aetiology. *In* M. Cook and K. Howells (Eds.), *Adult sexual interest in children.* New York: Academic Press, 1981, pp. 55-94.

Ingram, M. The participating victim: A study of sexual offences against prepubertal boys. *In* M. Cook and G. Wilson (Eds.), *Love and attraction: An international conference.* Oxford: Pergamon Press, 1979, pp. 511-517.

Johnson, R.L., and Shrier, D. Past sexual victimization by females of male patients in an adolescent medicine clinic population. *American Journal of Psychiatry*, 1987, *144*, 650-652.

Kempe, R.S., and Kempe, C.H. *The common secret: Sexual abuse of children and adolescents.* New York: W.H. Freeman, 1984.

Knopp, F.H. *Retraining adult sex offenders: Methods and models.* Syracuse, N.Y.: Safer Society Press, 1984.

Landis, J.T. Experience of 500 children with adult sexual deviants. *Psychiatric Quarterly Supplement*, 1956, *30*, 91-109.

Langevin, R., and Lang, R.A. Psychological treatment of pedophiles. *Behavioral Sciences and the Law*, 1985, *3*, 403-419.

Langevin, R., Day, D., Handy, L., and Russon, A.E. Are incestuous fathers pedophilic, aggressive, and alcoholic? *In* R. Langevin (Ed.), *Erotic preference, gender identity, and aggression.* New York: Lawrence Erlbaum Associates, 1985, pp. 161-179.

Langfeldt, T. Sexual development in children. *In* M. Cook and K. Howells (Eds.), *Adult sexual interest in children.* New York: Academic Press, 1981.

Lanyon, R.I. Theory and treatment in child molestation. *Journal of Consulting and Clinical Psychology*, 1986, *54*, 176-182.

Longo, R.E. Sexual learning and experience among adolescent sexual offenders. *International Journal of Offender Therapy and Comparative Criminology*, 1982, *26*, 235-241.

McGuire, R.J., Carlisle, J.M., and Young, B.G. Sexual deviations as conditioned behavior: A hypothesis. *Behaviour Research and Therapy*, 1965, *2*, 185-190.

Mohr, J.W., Turner, R.E., and Jerry, M.B. *Pedophilia and exhibitionism.* Toronto: University of Toronto Press, 1964.

Oliven, J.F. *Sexual hygiene and pathology: A manual for the physician and the professions.* Philadelphia, Penna.: J.B. Lippincott, 1965.

Paitich, D., and Langevin, R. The Clarke Parent-Child Relations Questionnaire: A clinically useful test for adults. *Journal of Consulting and Clinical Psychology*, 1976, *44*, 428-536.

Pierce, R., and Pierce, L.H. The sexually abused child: A comparison of male and female victims. *Child Abuse and Neglect*, 1985, *9*, 191-199.

Rachman, S. Sexual fetishism: An experimental analogue. *Psychological Record*, 1966, *16*, 293-296.

Rieker, P.P., and Carmen, E. The victim-to-patient process: The disconfirmation and transformation of abuse. *American Journal of Orthopsychiatry*, 1986, *56*, 360-370.

Rogers, C.M., and Terry, T. Clinical intervention with boy victims of sexual abuse. *In* I.R. Stuart and J.G. Greer (Eds.), *Victims of sexual aggression: Treatment of children, women, and men.* New York: Van Nostrand Reinhold, 1984, pp. 91-104.

Rosen, I. The general psychoanalytical theory of perversion: A critical and clinical review. *In* I. Rosen (Ed.), *Sexual deviation* (2nd ed.). New York: Oxford University Press, 1979, pp. 29-64.

Rush, F. *The best kept secret*. New York: McGraw-Hill, 1980.

Sandfort, T. *The sexual aspect of paedophile relations: The experiences of twenty-five boys*. Amsterdam: Pan/Spartacus, 1982.

Schwartz, M.F., and Masters, W.H. Conceptual factors in the treatment of paraphilias: A preliminary report. *Journal of Sex and Marital Therapy*, 1983, *9*, 3-18.

Seghorn, T., Prentky, R.A., and Boucher, R.J. Childhood sexual abuse in the lives of sexually aggressive offenders. *Journal of the American Academy of Child and Adolescent Psychiatry*, 1987, *26*, 262-267.

Simari, C.G., and Baskin, D. Incestuous experiences within homosexual populations: A preliminary study. *Archives of Sexual Behavior*, 1982, *11*, 329-344.

Stoller, R.J. *Perversion: The erotic form of hatred*. New York: Pantheon, 1975.

Stoller, R.J. *Sexual excitement: Dynamics of erotic life*. New York: Pantheon, 1979.

Stoller, R.J. *Observing the erotic imagination*. New Haven: Yale University Press, 1985.

Storr, A. *Sexual deviation*. Baltimore, Md.: Penguin Books, 1964.

Summit, R.C. The child sexual abuse accommodation syndrome. *Child Abuse and Neglect*, 1983, *7*, 177-193.

Tingle, D., Barnard, G.W., Robbins, L., Newman, G., and Hutchinson, D. Childhood and adolescent characteristics of pedophiles and rapists. *International Journal of Law and Psychiatry*, 1986, *9*, 103-116.

Virkkunen, M. The child as participating victim. *In* M. Cook and K. Howells (Eds.), *Adult sexual interest in children*. New York: Academic Press, 1981, pp. 121-134.

Yates, A. Children eroticized by incest. *American Journal of Psychiatry*, 1982, *139*, 482-485.

# 20
# Sexual Development at the Neurohormonal Level: The Role of Androgens

J.B. Hutchison
R.E. Hutchison
*MRC Neuroendocrine Development and Behaviour Group*
*Institute of Animal Physiology*
*BABRAHAM*
*Cambridge CB2 4AT*
*United Kingdom*

## Introduction

Despite significant advances in methods of behavioral description and analysis, the developmental origins of sexuality in humans are virtually unknown. It is clear from the literature that atypical patterns of sexual behavior, such as bisexuality, homosexuality, transsexualism, and transvestism, and their development are difficult to define (Pillard and Weinrich, 1987). Similarly, classification of adult human sexual behavior with children and adolescents as a behavioral abnormality that is called "pedophilia" (see Money, this volume) has not been particularly successful. Given the clinical importance of abnormality that relates to the sexual abuse of children and adolescents, an understanding of causation is crucially important. If the behavior cannot be categorized satisfactorily, is it possible to identify factors that cause these abnormalities, particularly those relating to physiological mechanisms? Medical research is obviously a long way from finding any answers to this question. However, prenatal sex hormones appear to have a role in human behavioral development (Money and Ehrhardt, 1972). Recent advances in cellular neuroendocrinology using animal models are providing indications about the way in which these hormones influence both the developing brain and behavior. It should be possible at least to formulate some hypotheses, based on nonhuman species, that may cast some light on human sexual development.

In trying to relate hormones to behavior on the one hand and to brain functioning on the other, one finds a major difficulty to be the level of analysis. Behavioral theories of sexual preference take into account the complexity of development in the formulation of mathematical models (Immelmann, 1969; see Bateson, 1978, for a review) and of speculative hypotheses of "black boxes" controlling behavior. However, the evidence may be small for the size of the hypothesis. The endocrinologist, in dealing with experimental data and new technology, is happy to establish something new based on sound physiological evidence in a year, but this reductionist approach may not be relevant in the context of complex behavioral interaction. The problem is to bring the two approaches together. This chapter is not an exhaustive review of hormonal research on behavioral development but, rather, a selective attempt at reviewing the theoretical background and describing some new ideas relating to hormone action at the cellular level that may be applicable to male behavioral development. The chapter aims (a) to present evidence suggesting that while the enzymatic formation of hormones, particularly estrogens, in the brain is a crucial factor in the development of behavioral sex differences, other types of metabolism have to be considered; (b) to explore how metabolic pathways involved in the formation of hormones within the brain are influenced by environmental events; and (c) to discuss whether this cellular work, based mainly on animal models such as birds and rodents, is leading to general principles that can be applied to human development.

## Behavioral Background

The development of behavior relating to the sexual abuse of children has received little attention from psychoendocrinologists so far. One of the difficulties in thinking about the relationship between hormones and aberrant behavior is that so little is known about how sex hormones might normally influence the choice of a particular type of mate, not only in humans but also in animals. Steroid sex hormones, the androgens, are well known to be required for male sexual behavior, although the relationships are obscure in humans (Bancroft, 1978). Whether sex hormones have any specific role in the establishment and expression of mating preferences that can be distinguished from their more general actions on reproductive behavior does not appear to be known. The few studies addressing this problem have been concerned mainly with mate choice in the female. In a number of mammalian species, estrous females show a preference for intact as opposed to castrated males in choice tests (reviewed by Johnston, 1979). Anestrous female rodents, such as rats, show no preference. While this experimental approach indicates perception on the part of the female of male characteristics, which evidently depend on testicular hormones, it does not answer the more complex question of whether there are subtle individual differences in preferences for potential mates. These preferences might depend both on the effect of hormones on learning the characteristics of conspecifics and family members in early development and the subsequent recognition of features in adulthood that are themselves hormone-dependent secondary sexual characteristics (see J.B. Hutchison and R.E. Hutchison, 1983, for a review). Beach (1969) has pointed out from his study of beagle bitches that there appears to be a system of preferences for a particular bitch and rejection of others that depends on the social context of the behavioral interaction and the estrous condition of the female.

Learning is involved in the acquisition of social preferences (see Hinde, 1987, for a review). The classic example is "sexual imprinting," which is a process whereby birds learn not only about their immediate kin but also about their own species. This learning allows the choice of an "optimal mate" when the animal is reproductively active in adulthood. (For a review, see Bateson, 1983). For example, male zebra finches reared initially with Bengalese finches and subsequently kept with their own species show a preference for female Bengalese finches during courtship (Immelmann, 1969). Therefore, social context in early development exerts a profound effect on the choice of a mate. Do androgens have any direct influence on the acquisition or learning of characters that are later involved in the choice of a mate? This possibility has been tested experimentally through the use of male Japanese quail by separating the act of choosing a mate, or the expression of the choice, from the performance of copulatory behavior (R.E. Hutchison and Bateson, 1982). There is a positive correlation between plasma androgen concentration and preference for the type (color morph) of female that the male had been reared with (J.B. Hutchison and R.E. Hutchison, 1983). Testicular hormones appear to be involved, since castration eliminates the expression of this preference. However, testicular hormones do not appear to be required for the acquisition of the preference, since castration of males soon after hatching has no effect on the expression of mate choice when testosterone treatment is given in adulthood (R.E. Hutchison and Bateson, 1982). Therefore, although androgens are associated with the choice of a mate, at least in Japanese quail, the learning processes do not require hormonal action during early development.

Human sexual preferences could be said to involve some sort of sexual-imprinting process, and in popular accounts of human sexual development, this type of mechanism has been used to explain homosexuality, fetishism, and possibly, normal sexual behavior (see Bateson,

1978, 1983, for reviews). However, as Bateson points out, the evidence for an imprinting-like process is largely anecdotal. Humans appear to be homogamous (Lewis, 1975) and form pairbonds with people who have the same body type. Although sexual imprinting is unlikely to be involved in human sexual development, early social experience must play a part in the formation of future sexual bonds, which are themselves probably influenced by hormonal conditions in adulthood.

Sexual orientation, which refers to the degree of preference for members of the same (homosexual) or the other (heterosexual) sex (see Pillard and Weinrich, 1987, for definitions), has been of particular interest in developmental studies on humans. In a recent paper on psychoendocrine research relating to human sexual behavior, Meyer-Bahlburg (1984) has examined critically whether the hormonal approach to psychosexual development and sexual orientation should be abandoned in favor of social-learning theories. There is a long-standing psychological explanation of sex differences in terms of learning through imitation and rehearsal of a particular sexual identity that is assigned to the individual by family or culture. However, there are strong arguments in favor of the psycho-endocrine approach, the most pertinent of which are the prenatal endocrine abnormalities that affect sexual development. These abnormalities influence not only behavior but also the development of a sexually dimorphic neuro-endocrine system controlling the pituitary gonadotrophins. The disruptive effect of these hormonal abnormalities in early behavioral development cannot be explained entirely by learning (Meyer-Bahlburg, 1984). Two clinical aspects of human psychosexual development relating to androgen action have assumed importance in recent years. The first involves patients with speech disturbances (dyslexia and stuttering) who tend to be left-handed and suffer from immune disorders (myasthenia gravis and rheumatoid arthritis). These apparently dissimilar conditions may be associated with androgen action during early fetal development. High levels of circulating testosterone are thought to suppress development of the left cerebral hemisphere and thereby induce a reversal of hemispheric dominance, which in turn affects the early learning of language and expression of handedness (Geschwind and Behan, 1982). This idea is highly speculative and based on correlational evidence that obviously cannot be tested experimentally. The second and equally controversial theory of androgen action proposes a model of hormone-dependent development of homosexuality in humans (Dörner, 1988). This theory was based initially on experimental work with rats and, more recently, on endocrine studies in humans. According to this "dual mating control" theory, the medial preoptic area (POA) of the brain acts as a "center" for hormonal action on male sexual behavior. The ventromedial hypothalamus is involved in female sexual control. Human homosexuality can be regarded, in terms of this theory, as "central nervous pseudohermaphroditism" (Dörner, 1976), and the differentiation of the mating centers is governed by early androgen action.

Disturbances that lower fetal androgen levels would, according to the model, bias the genetic male brain in the female direction and lead to a predisposition towards homosexuality in adulthood. Despite its attractive simplicity, this theory presents many difficulties (see Meyer-Bahlburg, 1984). Beach (1979) has strongly criticized comparisons between human and rat "homosexuality" and points out that "commonality of descriptive terms as applied to different species does not guarantee identity of the concepts to which the terms apply." He further believes that it is imperative to "evaluate interspecific similarities and differences and the causes, mediating mechanisms and functional outcomes of behavior." Although there is no behavioral justification for comparing rat mating behavior with human sexual orientation, this latter endocrine hypothesis has focused medical attention on the importance of prenatal steroid action and particularly on the androgens. In recent years, it has been recognized that homosexuality and other aspects of human sexual orientation cannot be explained by inter-sexuality of the sex chromosomes, gonads, or somatic morphology (Meyer-Bahlburg, 1984). Biological factors involved in human sexual differentiation appear to affect behavioral development without influencing peripheral hormonal levels or the utilization of these hormones at the time of the differentiation of the genitals and other secondary sexual characteristics.

With increasing interest in the role of prenatal hormones in human behavioral differentiation, a new approach has emerged. Instead of attention being focused exclusively on fluctuations in blood levels of steroid hormones, research is being directed more towards target tissues in the brain on which androgens are known to act. The crucial questions now are: (a) Does the sensitivity of brain cells to steroid sex hormones change at certain stages of development? (b) What causes these changes? This emphasis and the new experimental data from studies of subprimate mammals and birds are leading to attempts to unravel the cellular, molecular, and genetic factors, including gene coding of the expression of events within the brain cells that modulate androgen action. One cellular aspect of research based mainly on animal work has assumed significance. This aspect involves analysis of enzyme systems, located in target areas of the brain, that produce active metabolites of androgens, particularly those that form estrogens from androgenic substrates. The study of the enzymes involved and of the nuclear receptors of the active steroid products has important implications for psychoneuroendocrine research, because abnormalities in metabolic pathways and the resultant deficiencies in active steroid products can influence behavioral development irreversibly. In view of the methodological difficulties in studying these enzyme systems in the brain, evidence for the participation of metabolic pathways in early brain maturation is often difficult to interpret. This research has not reached the stage where even remote links can be drawn between steroid-metabolizing enzymes and human behavioral development. However, there is a growing body of evidence from subhuman species that cellular events accompanying androgen action in the brain are crucial in understanding hormonal sex differentiation.

## Interpreting Developmental Effects of Hormones

The role of hormones in the sexual differentiation of behavior is still controversial. Three initial questions must be answered before progress can be made in understanding the hormonal bases of human development:

1. Is there sound physiological evidence that sex hormones influence the behavioral development of animals?
2. If so, where and how do they act, bearing in mind what is known about hormone action in adult animals?
3. Can concepts derived from animal research be applied to human psychosexual differentiation?

The answer to the first question, based on more than 20 years of research mainly on mating behavior in rats and bird species, is undoubtedly affirmative. Sufficient work has been done to show that part of the answer to the second question lies in the understanding of how developing brain cells are influenced by steroid sex hormones. At present, the third question is open to speculation. However, neuroendocrine research has advanced sufficiently to allow consideration of a few hypotheses and the difficulties that have arisen with these ideas.

It is worthwhile evaluating some of the constraints on hormonal action in the adult in order to obtain an indication as to how androgens may act in the developing brain. The first and most important principle is that while androgens undoubtedly influence behavior mainly by direct action on the brain, the effectiveness of these hormones depends on factors governing the sensitivity of target tissues. This principle means that there is not necessarily a direct relationship between the amount of hormone in the blood and the degree of behavioral response to the hormone. Androgen action on brain cells is influenced in two ways, which are not mutually exclusive: the hormone itself can change in amount and availability, or the sensitivity to the hormone of the brain mechanisms mediating behavior can change. Hormonal sensitivity depends not only on the genetic constitution of the individual but also on environmental stimuli involved in social interactions. The second principle is that while the major action of androgen is undoubtedly on the brain itself and on hypothalamic target sites in particular, androgens influence peripheral sensory systems that in turn mediate input to the brain. Therefore, although most developmental research is directed towards understanding cell/steroid interactions in the brain, these hormones have peripheral effects that can influence brain activity by an indirect route. For example, estradiol-17-beta, by enlarging the sensory field of afferent neurones supplying the genital and perineal skin areas in female rats, increases the receptive area and sensory input to the brain (Komisaruk, Adler, and J.B. Hutchison, 1972).

Current ideas on the developmental actions of hormones on behavior are derived in part from embryological work (Jost, 1972; Jost and Magre, 1984). There are thought to be three stages in sexual development from an undifferentiated primordium common to genetic males and females. First, gonadal sex is determined by the presence or absence of the male testis-determining gene on the Y chromosome; second, the reproductive tract and genital morphology are differentiated; third, sexual differentiation of the brain and behavior occurs as the final stage. A similar scheme has been proposed by Dörner (1988) for human sexual differentiation, in which gonadal-sex differentiation occurs in the 2- to 3-month-old fetus, genital and internal reproductive duct differentiation occurs soon afterwards, and differentiation of the external genitalia occurs in months 3-4 of fetal development. Neuronal and psychosexual differentiation occur later, starting in month 4 of prenatal life. The general principle derived from embryological studies is that, in mammals, the male phenotype develops only when a specific hormonal signal (androgen) is present. In the absence of this signal, reproductive tissues differentiate to the female type. The best example is the differentiation of the Müllerian (female) and Wolffian (male) ducts from undifferentiated primordia by the action of fetal testicular hormone. The Wolffian-duct development requires the presence of testosterone, whereas Müllerian-duct development has no apparent hormonal requirement in the genetic female. Jost's work (1972) also illustrated another important principle, in that the development of the Müllerian ducts is actively suppressed in the male by a second factor, the glycoprotein Müllerian Inhibitory Substance (MIS) secreted by testicular Sertoli cells. Differentiation requires two processes, masculinization and defeminization, or suppression of female characteristics. In this case, a steroid hormone maintains the male duct system, and the protein MIS suppresses female-duct development.

Behavioral development in rodents appeared initially to differ from the somatic processes of differentiation. Thus, the earlier studies of mating behavior in the rat (Harris and Levine, 1965; see also Goy and McEwen, 1980) and the guinea pig (Phoenix et al., 1959) suggested that the postnatal action of testosterone could account for behavioral masculinization without the accompanying action of a defeminizing agent. Initially, behavioral differentiation was seen to occur along a masculine/feminine continuum that depended on testosterone action. This finding led to the proposition of the classical "organizational" hypothesis that androgens, acting during the perinatal period, either before or immediately after birth, organize the pattern of sexual behavior to the male type irrespective of genetic sex. This differentiating effect, or "organization," is thought to be irreversible and to occur at a "critical," or time-limited, "window" in development. Both the suppression of feminine behavior and the enhancement of masculine behavior were assumed to occur as a consequence of the effects of testosterone, suggesting a one-hormone process. The feminine behavioral type was assumed to require no hormonal effect. The second assumption of this classical hypothesis was that in adulthood, hormones appropriate to the sex of the individual "activated" the behavior (Phoenix et al., 1959). Organization and activation not only occurred at different stages of life but also were assumed to be different processes (see Goy and McEwen, 1980, for a review). The organizational hypothesis has been extended to other vertebrates. In birds (specifically Japanese quail), the effects of steroids on behavior appear to be the reverse of the effects in mammals. Ovarian estrogens, acting in early embryonic development, are thought to irreversibly feminize the brain. Therefore, the male can be demasculinized by estrogen during critical periods of embryonic brain differentiation. The female is the sex that is actively differentiated, and the male requires no differentiating process that depends on hormones. This finding can be linked to the fact that in birds, unlike mammals, the female is the heterogametic sex. The organizational effects of hormones on sexual differentiation appear generally to be exerted on the heterogametic sex (Adkins, 1975). There also is an indication that the same hormones that are involved in the organization of sex-typical behavior later activate the behavior (Goy and McEwen, 1980).

The early-organization hypothesis can be summarized as follows:

1. In the heterogametic sex, the appropriate hormone of that sex irreversibly organizes brain mechanisms of behavior during a "critical period" early in development.

2. The organizational hypothesis implies that there is a continuum in behavioral development from female to male that may depend, in mammals, on how much androgen is present during the critical period of development. This notion has important implications, because the amount of androgen in the developing mammalian brain could determine the degree of behavioral masculinization.

3. There is no requirement for a defeminization process.

4. Organizational and activational effects of hormones differ and can be distinguished by three criteria, i.e.,
   a. The duration of the hormonal effect,
   b. Whether there is a limited period of sensitivity to the hormone,
   c. At what stage in life the hormonal effect occurs (see also Phoenix et al., 1959).

5. In terms of the original theory, organizational effects are irreversible; they occur in perinatal development during a brief, limited, "critical" period before the brain and other target tissues for the hormone have finally matured.

## Difficulties with the "Organizational" Hypothesis

One of the major difficulties with the hypothesis relates to the site of androgen action. Does the hormone act exclusively on the brain during development? Hormones, including the sex steroids, affect sensory receptors and thereby modify afferent input to the brain (Beach, 1971; J.B. Hutchison, 1978). The argument has been raised very forcefully by Beach (1971) that androgen deprivation or treatment must affect development of the sexual effectors such as the penis. For example, neonatal castration of a rat on day 1 of life impairs penile development and differentiation of sensory receptors (penile spines) and causes deficiencies in the organization of spinal reflex control nuclei (Breedlove and Arnold, 1981). Therefore, the neonatally castrated male is deficient in both sensory and effector systems for sexual behavior later in adult life. The lack of the early effects of androgen on sexual differentiation can be explained by this peripheral effect. Penile development can be maintained using synthetic androgens (Baum, 1979) that have only peripheral effects. Such neonatally castrated males have apparently normal penile development yet show no sexual behavior, suggesting that the effects of early androgen are largely central. Nevertheless, Beach's point is one that has to be taken seriously, since it is impossible to know whether the sensory receptor system and afferent input are functionally intact. Afferent input from the genitalia can be determined neurophysiologically, but as little is known about the sensory morphology of penile mechanoreceptors and the electrophysiology of the afferent neurones, validation is still a long way off.

A second difficulty lies with the supposition that sexual differentiation is a unitary event involving a one-hormone androgenic effect. The "ortho-gonal model" of sexual differentiation (Whalen, 1974; reviewed by Yahr, 1985) establishes that in contrast to the classical theory, in which sexual differentiation occurs along a continuum, masculine and feminine aspects of sexual behavior are differentiated at separate stages in development and probably independently. Hormonal action that suppresses feminine behavior does not necessarily enhance masculine behavior (see Yahr, 1988). The best evidence for this model has been obtained using testicular feminized males (TFMs), which are mutant male rats carrying the X-linked allele for testicular feminization. Such mutant rats, which do not have androgen receptors in target tissues, show abnormally low levels of masculine mating behavior (mounting) despite treatment with testosterone in adulthood. However, if castrated as neonates, these TFMs do show feminine behavior (lordosis) as adults following estrogen and progesterone administration, suggesting that defeminization of coital behavior occurs in these androgen-insensitive males (see the review by Olsen, 1985) as it does in normal males. The TFM mutants appear to be defeminized by hormonal secretions from the testes without being fully masculinized. The terms "masculinization" and "defeminization" were introduced by Whalen (1974) to emphasize the independence of the hormonal processes involved in the development of masculine and feminine behavior. These processes may occur at different stages of development (heterochrony, see Yahr, 1988). Thus, the current idea of the sexual differentiation of behavior as applied to mammals, including primates, is quite similar to the original embryological hypothesis applied to the differentiation of the reproductive tracts. However, as will be discussed further, both the classical theory and later modifications have been derived almost exclusively from studies of copulatory behavior in a single species, the rat. More recently, developmental work has been extended to other types of behavior and to other species (see Yahr, 1988, for a review; Baum, Stockman, and Lundell, 1985; Goy and McEwen, 1980).

A third difficulty with the organizational hypothesis is whether hormonal "activation" of sexual behavior in adulthood and "organization" during perinatal development are separable processes. The real difference between these processes is thought to lie in the transient nature of hormonal effects in the adult on mature neuroendocrine mechanisms compared with the permanent effects of hormones early in life. There are a number of possibilities that could, in theory, account for the physiological differences. The sites of steroid action in the brain may differ between the infant and adult; the cellular mechanisms, including steroid metabolism and receptor binding may differ; steroids may exert different actions depending on the maturational state of the target areas in the brain at the time of steroid exposure. However, Arnold and Breedlove (1985) have argued convincingly that the rigid distinction between organizational and activational processes is no longer tenable. This change in outlook has occurred because recent research on the avian brain has provided evidence that does not fit the idea that permanent organizing effects occur only during a critical period of early development. For example, estrogens demasculinize mechanisms underlying copulatory behavior in female Japanese quail embryos (Adkins, 1975). Thus, females treated with estrogen as embryos do not show male copulatory behavior. However, if female Japanese quail are ovariectomized at hatching, a demasculinizing effect of estradiol can be demonstrated in adulthood (R.E. Hutchison, 1978). In the absence of estrogens during the posthatching period, the behavioral mechanisms remain receptive to the organizing effects of estrogenic steroids until maturity. Two facets of the organizational hypothesis have to be reconsidered, therefore. First, there is no strict temporal limit to the "critical period" for the differentiating effects of estrogen. Second, given the right conditions, mechanisms underlying behavior can be organized by steroids in the adult animal. Estrogens may have separate effects in which an early embryonic action sensitizes behavioral mechanisms in the brain so that they respond to a second organizing effect of estrogen later in development (R.E. Hutchison, 1978; J.B. Hutchison and R.E. Hutchison, 1985; see also Schumacher and Balthazart, 1985).

The conclusion that steroid hormones can organize the adult brain is not based only on behavioral studies. There has been ample demonstration that steroids have effects involving the structural organization of the adult brain that previously have been thought to occur only in juveniles. The best example was discovered by Nottebohm (1980), who showed that androgens increased the volume and cell number of two brain nuclei controlling song, the nucleus hyperstriatum ventrale pars caudale (HVc) and the nucleus robustus archistriatalis (RA), in adult female canaries. Remarkably, in the male canary, these nuclei also show cyclical changes in size that seem to be related to seasonal variations in the plasma testosterone level. The adult avian brain has an androgen-sensitive plasticity that does not appear to be a feature of the mammalian brain.

The fourth difficulty with the "organizational" hypothesis, a difficulty that is more relevant to this chapter, is whether steroids other than androgens are involved in the sexual differentiation of brain mechanisms of behavior. Since TFM rats are relatively insensitive to androgens and show no female behavior as adults, it has been suggested that their potential for female sexual behavior is suppressed in perinatal development by testicular secretions of hormones other than androgen (Olsen, 1985). This discovery is of great interest, because the hormonal mechanisms operating in development during masculinization and defeminization must differ. Estrogens appear to have different developmental effects from androgens. However, the view that estrogens have sexually differentiating effects on behavioral mechanisms in the brain cannot be tested directly in rats because of the presence of an alpha-fetoprotein in the circulating blood that preferentially sequesters estradiol-17-beta. Plasma protein binding is thought to eliminate the circulating free estradiol that binds to receptors (see Yahr, 1985, for a review). Similarly, the effects of systemically injected androgens on behavioral development are difficult to interpret, because the hormones are converted to both active and inactive androgenic and estrogenic metabolites in the brain (reviewed by J.B. Hutchison and Steimer, 1984). The observation that estrogens are formed in the brain and bind to estrogen receptors can only suggest a possible mechanism. More conclusive evidence has come from studies of the effects of nonaromatizable androgens such as 5 alpha-dihydrotestosterone (5 alpha-DHT). This androgen is effective in masculinizing but not defeminizing copulatory behavior of the rat (see Olsen, 1985). A second strategy has been to use a receptor-binding antagonist such as Tamoxifen, which appears to prevent behavioral defeminization by blocking estrogen action in brain cells. An aromatase blocker, the synthetic steroid 1, 4, 5 - androstatriene-3, 17-dione (ATD), can also be used effectively to prevent defeminization of coital behavior. There is now a great deal of evidence to suggest that aromatization and the production of estrogen in the neonatal brain is involved in the suppression of female sexual traits in male rats. Taken together, the existing evidence suggests that enzyme activity that forms estrogens in the brain is involved in behavioral defeminization during male development. However, the evidence itself is not entirely conclusive. For example, events that accompany the use of a nonaromatizable androgen such as 5 alpha-DHT can be difficult to interpret. A failure to masculinize behavior can be caused by a failure of the hormone to reach the brain, in view of extensive peripheral metabolism of 5 alpha-DHT in the circulating blood or liver to catabolic metabolites (J.B. Hutchison and Steimer, 1984). Enzyme blockers such as ATD are not specific in their action on the aromatase system. They also interfere with the activity of enzymes that produce active metabolites of testosterone such as 5 alpha-DHT in the brain and may bind to steroid receptors. An additional problem is that generalizations made on the rat do not necessarily apply to other species. For example, in some primates, including humans, behavioral defeminization may not occur (Goy and Goldfoot, 1975).

## Enzyme Systems that Form Steroid Hormones in the Brain

Androgens are converted to various metabolites by enzymatic activity within brain cells (see reviews by Naftolin, Ryan, and Petro, 1972; J.B. Hutchison and Steimer, 1984). Estrogens are known to be formed from androgens found in the hypothalamus of all vertebrates examined so far (Callard, 1984). Therefore, the possibility exists that estrogens formed by aromatization within the brain in early development are responsible for the sexually differentiating effects of androgens on sexual behavior. Androgens appear to act as intracellular prehormones, or substrates, for enzyme action. A better understanding of how androgen-metabolizing pathways in the brain contribute to behavioral development depends not only on a knowledge of how the enzymes work in brain cells but also on the restrictions imposed by the techniques available. It is worthwhile to consider briefly some of these methods and their drawbacks. Work performed on the adult brain, mainly in an avian species, the ring dove, has contributed some new ideas on the behavioral role of steroid-metabolizing enzymes. The first concept is that these enzyme systems both "activate" (form active metabolites that influence behavior) and "inactivate" (form biologically inactive catabolic metabolites) androgens. Both processes influence effective levels of testosterone in the brain. The second concept is that the balance between activation and inactivation of androgen in brain cells is influenced by environmental stimuli.

### Adult Brain

Studies of androgen metabolism in the brain and the measurement of enzymatic activities are now possible using radio-labeled tracers of high specific activity, which usually are tritiated ($^3$H) steroids. Brain slices or tissue homogenates can be incubated *in vitro* with $^3$H-androgen under controlled conditions and the steroid products identified in terms of type, quantity, and rate of production. Metabolic activity can also be examined in discrete areas, such as in identified brain nuclei (e.g., preoptic nuclei) associated with androgenic effects on behavior, by means of microdissection procedures. A direct correlation can then be made between molecular mechanisms in the cell, such as enzymatic conversions or receptor binding of steroids, and the behavioral effects of these hormones. The effects of the peripheral metabolism of androgens, including catabolism in liver cells, is eliminated by using these *in vitro* methods. However, complementary studies on the intact brain *in vivo* are required for the assessment of the physiological significance of such findings, because the normal relationships among cell compartments and among brain cells are destroyed by the *in vitro* homogenization procedures. Afferent input may influence cells containing aromatase in the intact brain, and this also complicates interpretation of *in vitro* methods. The systemic administration of tritiated hormones to castrated animals is commonly used for the estimation of steroid uptake in the brain and the localization of hormone-sensitive areas. The application of this method to the study of brain metabolism has limitations, because brain cells are exposed to a wide range of steroids arising from peripheral metabolism (e.g., from liver or adipose tissue). The interpretation of the observed metabolic pattern of the intact brain is only possible if data from *in vitro* experiments also are available. This problem can be solved to some extent by injecting labeled androgen directly into the brain of the intact animal. Diffusion of the tracer is limited, metabolism can be studied in specific brain areas under more physiological *in vivo* conditions, and interference from peripheral metabolism is negligible. Microperfusion of the dove POA with $^3$H-testosterone has shown that metabolism to both active and inactive products occurs in the brain of the intact male (J.B. Hutchison, Steimer, and R.E. Hutchison, 1986). However, this method has not been used to any extent yet, and the knowledge of steroid metabolism in the brain is based largely on *in vitro* techniques.

Enzyme-catalyzing reactions that result in the formation of biologically active metabolites, such as 5 alpha-DHT and estradiol, are part of **activation pathways**. The initial enzyme reaction in both 5 alpha-reduction and aromatization is irreversible. In the case of aromatization, this reaction also is a limiting step. Because the circulating levels of estrogens in the male are low, the activity of the brain aromatase will effectively control the availability of active estrogenic metabolites for further cellular actions, including binding to nuclear receptors. A major component of androgen metabolism is catabolic with the formation of inactive metabolites. For example, the 5 beta-reduction of androgens, which forms a major component of enzyme activity in the avian brain, is irreversible and represents a major **inactivation pathway**. This pathway is also catabolic in the human fetal brain and hepatic tissues (Stylianou et al., 1961). The 5 beta-reduction of androgens is likely to occur at an early stage of the cellular action. Because of the high capacity for conversion of testosterone to inactive metabolites in the avian brain, 5 beta-reductase is also likely to interfere with both further metabolism and the binding of active steroids to intracellular receptors. Therefore, 5 beta-reduction can be considered to be a mechanism of primary inactivation. This process can be distinguished from secondary inactivation, which occurs after the receptor-steroid complex has influenced genomic transcription (see Figure 20.1a, 1b, 1c).

The ring dove is a unique model for the study of estrogen-forming enzymes in the brain, because estrogens have specific effects in the POA mechanisms of sexual behavior, effects that are separable from androgenic effects (J.B. Hutchison, 1978). There is no equivalent mammalian model as yet. The enzymatic complex catalyzing the transformation of androgens to estrogens is known as the "aromatase" and is thought to consist of two components. One is a form of cytochrome P450. The other is a flavoprotein NADPH-cytochrome P450 reductase. The principal sites of estrogen synthesis are the gonads and the placenta in mammals, and other tissues, such as fat, liver, bone marrow, and male genital skin, also form estrogens.

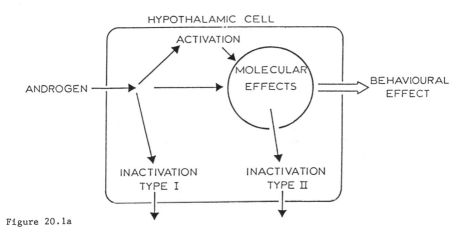

Figure 20.1a

Figure 20.1a. Androgens are converted to active metabolites (activation pathways: aromatase, 5 alpha-reductase) by intracellular enzymatic activity. Androgens also are converted to inactive catabolic metabolites (inactivation type I, 5 beta-reductase). Active steroids that influence gene expression also are degraded after binding to nuclear receptors (inactivation type II).

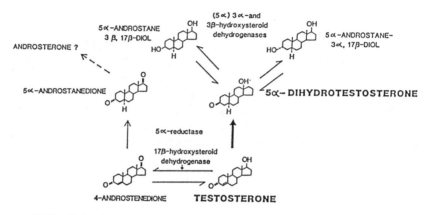

Figure 20.1b. Behaviorally active steroid metabolites (heavy print) formed from testosterone by enzymatic activity in the preoptic area and hypothalamus. These metabolites consist mainly of 5 alpha-reduced androgens and estrogens.

Brain aromatization was initially studied in the rat (Naftolin, Ryan, and Petro, 1972). Observations made subsequently indicate that hypothalamic aromatase activity in the ring dove brain is much higher than it is in the adult rodent (rat, hamster, gerbil) hypothalamus (J.B. Hutchison and Steimer, 1984, and unpublished observations). The anatomical distribution of the various enzymatic activities in the brain of the ring dove has been studied using a topographical microdissection procedure. The results of these studies show that aromatase activity is localized in the preoptic and hypothalamic areas. The 5 beta-reductase activity occurs in most parts of the adult brain, but it is markedly lower in known androgen-target areas that contain aromatase activity, including the POA and the basal hypothalamus. The distribution of 5 beta-reductase activity appears to be consistent with its presumed role as an inactivating enzyme. Thus, androgens are eliminated rapidly in nontarget areas, such as the cerebral cortex, but must be available for a minimum period of time in target areas, where their action is required. *In vitro* experiments carried out at physiological substrate concentrations show that the half-life of testosterone in nontarget areas of the dove brain, because of rapid inactivation by 5 beta-reduction, is approximately seven to

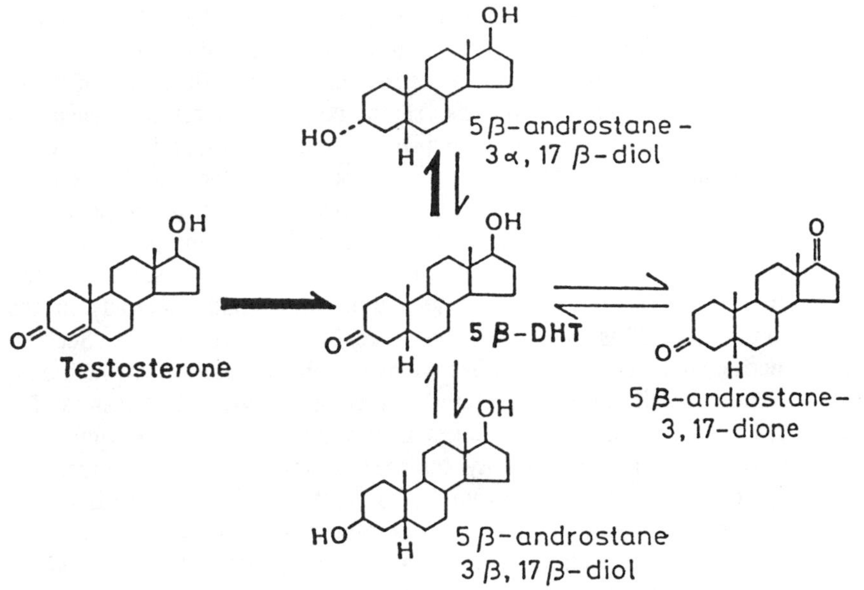

Figure 20.1c. Inactive steroid metabolites formed by intracellular 5 beta-reduction of testosterone in the hypothalamus. The 5 beta-reductase is particularly active in the avian brain and is not restricted to androgen-target areas such as the hypothalamus. This metabolic pathway has also been detected in mammals.

eight minutes. In specific target areas such as the POA, it is prolonged by a factor of five to ten (J.B. Hutchison and Steimer, 1984).

A knowledge of the kinetic characteristics of key enzymes will be required if a model is to be established of androgen metabolism in the brain and its regulation. Kinetic data, which are obtained by measuring enzyme activity at different substrate concentrations, can be useful in the understanding of the control of enzymes and their role in the cell. There is some kinetic information concerning the major pathways of androgen metabolism in the dove brain. The aromatase complex found in the POA of the male dove has a high affinity for its natural substrate (testosterone) and is most efficient at low substrate concentrations. However, the aromatase complex is rapidly saturated when the substrate concentration is increased, so that other pathways then will predominate. The same appears to apply to 5 alpha-reductase. In contrast, 5 beta-reductase appears to have a much higher capacity for the conversion of testosterone (J.B. Hutchison and Steimer, 1984), but its affinity for the substrate is also lower. Clearly, this latter pathway will be favored at higher substrate concentrations. Thus, kinetic data derived from studies on the dove brain suggest that metabolism may differ markedly according to the concentration of circulating androgen. At higher concentrations, the 5 beta-reduction pathway will predominate, whereas at lower testosterone concentrations, estrogenic and 5 alpha-reduced metabolites will be formed preferentially. Therefore, circulating androgens measured in the blood plasma give no real idea of how much active steroid is available for receptor binding in target brain cells.

A complicating feature in interpreting the effects of metabolism in brain cells is that many enzymes share common substrates such as testosterone. Consequently, alternative pathways are in competition, and the overall orientation of metabolism will depend on the modulation of particular enzyme activities. Probably two modes of control are involved. First, enzyme synthesis can be regulated by hormonal factors, an action that is likely to involve the classical receptor system and specific gene transcription. The control of aromatase activity by gonadal steroids in the hypothalamus may illustrate this type of regulation (see below). Second, enzyme activity can be directly affected by regulatory molecules, including steroids. These small molecules either can compete with the substrate for active sites or act by inducing changes in the conformation of the enzyme, which irreversibly alters its affinity for the substrate. These molecules are true enzyme regulators. For example, 5 alpha-DHT is a well-known inhibitor of aromatization. In addition, 5 beta-DHT affects aromatase activity in the brain. These regulatory steroids can either be products of competing pathways or derived from circulating steroids reaching the brain. Obviously, the complexity of these enzyme systems, particularly when account is taken of other competing factors such as receptor-binding proteins, is very great. To what degree enzyme activity is related to the receptor population for the steroid products is still unknown.

There is evidence from studies of the avian brain that the activity of steroid-metabolizing enzymes in some androgen-sensitive target areas of the brain (e.g., the POA) is not stable. The activity can change depending upon circulating androgen levels and environmental signals such as social stimuli and day length. In the dove, the activities of testosterone-metabolizing enzymes in both the preoptic and hypothalamic areas, and therefore the sensitivity of the brain to androgens, are influenced by the social environment, the endocrine status of the animal, and the animal's genetic sex. Testosterone is known, from recent work using the dove brain, to raise the activity of the preoptic aromatase. On average, the activity is increased three- to fivefold by systemic or intrahypothalamic testosterone treatment (Steimer and J.B. Hutchison, 1981; J.B. Hutchison and Steimer, 1984). Enzyme activity is not affected in nontarget brain areas that apparently are insensitive to testosterone, such as the cerebral cortex. Kinetic studies indicate that the observed increase in the activity of the POA aromatase probably results from induction of the enzyme (Steimer and J.B. Hutchison, 1989), since the maximum velocity ($V_{max}$) of conversion is increased without any change of affinity (measured by the $K_m$ of the enzyme) for the substrate (testosterone). This effect is likely to involve both the binding of the active steroid to specific receptors and genomic activation resulting in *de novo* synthesis of the aromatase complex. Testosterone could also activate the enzyme from an inactive form. The finding that the androgen level can change intracellular aromatase activity adds a new dimension to the understanding of the role of androgen-metabolizing enzymes in the brain, since the preoptic aromatase appears to serve as a regulator of androgen action in the male. In the event that more testosterone becomes available from the peripheral circulation, its action may either be amplified further or modified in androgen-target cells by the increased production of behaviorally effective estradiol. This idea appears to have wide application, because preoptic aromatase activity in other birds (quail, Schumacher and Balthazart, 1986) and rodents (the rat, Roselli, Horton, and Resko, 1985) has also been found recently to be increased by injected testosterone. Sociosexual stimuli also influence preoptic aromatase activity by means of changes in the circulating testosterone level and probably by acting directly on the preoptic enzyme system itself (J.B. Hutchison and Steimer, 1986) (see Figure 20.2).

## Developing Brain

If enzymes that form metabolites from androgen in the brain are active during development, does steroid metabolism in the developing brain have roles similar to its known roles in the adult brain? Are the same enzymes involved with a similar anatomical location in the developing brain as in the adult brain? These questions are important, because the classical theory of development implies that organizational and activational effects of androgens differ. Perhaps fetal steroid metabolism and its regulatory mechanisms also differ from the adult's. The ontogeny of androgen-metabolizing enzymes in

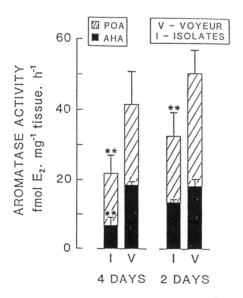

Figure 20.2a. Brain aromatase activity is influenced by behavioral stimuli in the male. The formation of estradiol-17-beta from testosterone is increased in the preoptic brain areas of male ring doves that were exposed to visual stimuli from interacting pairs for 2 or 4 days. "Voyeurs" were able to see and hear sexual behavior of courting pairs. "Isolates" were unable to see courtship activity but were exposed to the same auditory environment as the Voyeurs. (POA = preoptic area; AHA = anterior hypothalamus. $p < 0.01$, 2-tailed t-test. Bars represent standard error of the mean. Data from J.B. Hutchison and Steimer, 1986).

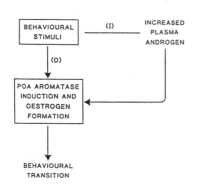

Figure 20.2b. Alternative interpretations of the effect of sociosexual stimuli on brain aromatase activity. Visual stimuli could influence preoptic aromatase directly (D) by changing the amount or activity of enzyme in the brain, possibly through intermediary neurotransmitter changes. Preoptic aromatase could also be influenced indirectly (I) by increased circulating testosterone levels resulting from exposure to behavioral stimuli. Since testosterone increases preoptic aromatase activity, the latter mechanism is more likely. The relative importance of the two routes is still unknown.

the brain is largely unknown. Only the brain aromatase has been studied in any detail. Several studies on the rat suggest that in the mammalian brain, aromatase activity is higher during perinatal development than it is in the adult (see Weisz, Brown, and Ward, 1982). Differences between the sexes in POA aromatase activity appear in neonatal development. During fetal and neonatal growth, there also are changes in blood androgen levels. For example, in the male rat, there is a postnatal increase in circulating testosterone, which does not occur to the same extent in females. Estradiol-17-beta concentrations increased dramatically after birth in the male rats but not in the females (Rhoda, Corbier, and Roffi, 1984). Whether fluctuations in circulating androgen levels are related to changes in the activity of androgen-metabolizing enzymes is not known. There are no data as yet from any mammalian species to suggest that the hypothalamic aromatase is influenced by hormonal conditions during development (Tobet et al., 1985). One reason for this lack of data is that it is almost impossible to alter testosterone levels in the fetal brain directly because of the intervention of the feto-placental endocrine unit. The effects of the injection of androgen into maternal tissues are difficult to interpret because of the peripheral and hepatic metabolism of testosterone in both the mother and the fetus. Studies in ferrets and rats during perinatal development indicate that the hypothalamic aromatase is not influenced by testosterone. However, hypothalamic estradiol levels have been shown to be consistently higher in neonatal male rats than in females. This postnatal rise in hypothalamic estradiol is correlated with a rise in circulating testosterone and is prevented by neonatal castration.

An avian model, the quail embryo, provides an opportunity for the study of developing brain enzymes in the absence of maternal steroids. It has been possible to examine the ontogeny of steroid-metabolizing enzymes in detail and, also, to intervene directly in the steroid environment of the developing embryo. The three major pathways of androgen metabolism, which are characteristic of the adult avian brain—aromatization, 5 alpha-reduction, and 5 beta-reduction—are all active in the embryo. During embryonic and posthatching life, hypothalamic and preoptic localization of the aromatase appears to be similar to that seen in the adult brain (J.B. Hutchison and Schumacher, 1986; see also Schumacher and Balthazart, 1987, in regard to adult quail). However, technical difficulties that result from the small size of the brain make it difficult to identify enzyme-rich cell areas. In postnatal quail chicks, testosterone enhances the activity of hypothalamic aromatase to adult levels (Schumacher, R.E. Hutchison, and J.B. Hutchison, 1988). The induction effect does not depend on the presence of gonadal hormones, because enzyme induction occurs in the POA of gonadectomized animals, nor are there sex differences in activity. This finding is of particular interest, because the aromatase induction effect is clearly sexually differentiated in adult quail (Schumacher and Balthazart, 1986). Therefore, there is a fundamental difference in enzyme activity between the developing brain and the adult brain. The sexual differentiation of the aromatase system occurs at some as yet unspecified stage late in development. Using the quail embryo, the current authors have also obtained an idea of when the capacity for the induction of the enzyme first appears in the embryonic brain. Induction by testosterone occurs as early as day 14 (hatching occurs on day 21). There is a linear relationship between the dose of testosterone and aromatase activity, but the effect obtained at posthatching (day 1) is fourteen times greater than the effect obtained at embryonic day 14. However, no increase at all was found in the aromatase activity of preoptic cells taken from day 10 embryos (Schumacher, R.E. Hutchison, and J.B. Hutchison, 1988). At present, it is difficult to understand why embryonic preoptic cells suddenly become sensitive to the inductive effects of testosterone. Does this change involve the development of receptors for testosterone, the removal of inhibitory factors affecting the enzyme, or, perhaps, the development of cells containing neurotransmitters that enhance aromatase activity? Alternatively, testosterone may activate genes that code for de novo synthesis of the enzyme.

## Environmental Effects on Development

In the adult avian brain, sociosexual stimuli that are involved in the coordination of male reproductive behavior increase preoptic aromatase activity and, consequently, the formation of behaviorally active estradiol-17-beta (J.B. Hutchison and Steimer, 1986). The formation of estrogen in the brain is also enhanced by increased circulating androgen not only in the adult but also in the developing brain. Is aromatase activity influenced by environmental stimuli in the developing mammalian brain? The only mammalian model for this work so far, the rat, has yielded some intriguing results. During the last week of gestation (days 18-19), there is a surge of circulating testosterone in the male with the result that testosterone levels are higher in male than in female fetuses (Weisz, Brown, and Ward, 1982). However, this surge in testosterone does not occur in male fetuses of mothers exposed to stressful stimuli (e.g., high-intensity light). One important consequence of the absence of the fetal testosterone surge is that there is a failure in normal behavioral masculinization and defeminization. The question addressed by Weisz and colleagues (1982) is whether the failure of differentiation in the progeny of stressed mothers results from a lack of estradiol formed from testosterone in the brain, the suggestion being that testosterone normally increases aromatase activity and enhances estrogen formation. For their study, they measured the conversion of androstenedione to estrone using the stereospecific incorporation of tritium from the 1-beta-$^3$H androgen into water. Therefore, total aromatase activity was measured rather than specific estrogenic metabolites such as estradiol. It should also be emphasized that the experiment did not measure the conversion of the natural substrate, testosterone, which has been found to be effective in sexual differentiation of the rat brain. The results, therefore, have to be interpreted with some caution. Nevertheless, they are of great interest, because stress decreases aromatase activity and, presumably, the production of estrogen within the brain of male fetuses. Hypothalamic aromatase activity is also decreased in female fetuses that do not show the surge in circulating testosterone on days 18 and 19. Apparently, the effects of environmental stress are exerted independently of circulating testosterone, possibly through the more general effects of stress, which, by changing the behavior of the mother, affect the fetus.

Recently, a positive correlation has been shown between plasma corticosterone levels of pregnant rats exposed to stress, and androstenedione levels in their female fetuses. Salivary cortisol levels in pregnant women who have experienced various stressful situations also appear to be related to testosterone measured in amniotic fluids of their female fetuses (Dörner et al., 1988). These endocrine correlations seem to suggest that stress influences the availability of fetal androgen. Dörner (1988) believes that a link can be drawn between these endocrine disturbances, stress, and the disruption of psychosexual orientation in later life. Environmental factors may have a profound influence on the active steroids formed in the brain by androgen-metabolizing enzymes. However, apart from difficulties in interpreting the behavioral effects of environmental stimuli, particularly "stress," the problem lies in trying to pin down the active cell areas in the developing brain that contain enzymes and in establishing the routes by which environmental stimuli have their effects. A further difficulty lies in trying to disentangle environmental effects that increase brain aromatase activity through raised circulating androgen levels from the more direct influence of environment exerted directly on the brain (see Figure 20.2b).

## A Role for the Inactivation of Androgen

In humans and other mammals, one aspect of sexual differentiation that has received considerable attention in recent years is whether "protective" mechanisms exist that prevent masculinization and defeminization of the brain by steroids circulating in genetic females. Steroids, particularly estrogens from the feto-placental unit, are available to influence the brain. Circulating estrogen concentrations are known to be higher during mammalian fetal development than in later life. The adrenals also secrete dehydroepiandrosterone sulphate, which is aromatized to estrogens. Two basic types of protective mechanisms have been suggested. The first involves changes in the sensitivity of female brain cells to steroids; the second is concerned with the availability of effective steroids. Of these mechanisms, the latter has received the most serious consideration. The alpha-fetoprotein in neonatal rats, which specifically sequesters estrogen in plasma, may provide a protective mechanism. This protein would prevent free estrogen from becoming available to influence target cells in the brain (reviewed in Toran-Allerand, 1984). However, it appears that the alpha-fetoprotein could equally well provide a transport mechanism that carries estrogens to brain cells (Döhler et al., 1984). Human alpha-fetoprotein does not bind estrogens. Therefore, other protective mechanisms must be present.

By determining the active-steroid environment of the developing brain, steroid-metabolizing enzymes, too, can be part of a protective mechanism. There is evidence that the inactivating 5 beta-reduction pathway in the avian brain could in theory provide such a protective mechanism. Both *in vivo* and *in vitro* metabolic studies of the adult male dove brain suggest that 5 beta-reductase interacts preferentially with testosterone entering brain cells and competes effectively with alternative pathways of androgen metabolism (J.B. Hutchison and Steimer, 1984). A number of lines of evidence indicate that the 5 beta-reduction of testosterone represents a major steroid inactivation pathway in brain cells. In view of the markedly higher levels of 5 beta-reductase activity in nontarget striatal, septal, and parolfactory areas of the adult brain than are in the hypothalamus, brain areas not directly implicated in androgen action could be "protected" from androgenic effects by a selective 5 beta-reductase activity. The inactivation of testosterone by 5 beta-reduction could be involved in the maintaining of brain areas in a differentiated functional state in adulthood. The question arising from this conjecture is whether metabolic inactivation of testosterone in brain cells plays any part in early brain organization. The distinct anatomical separation between brain areas in 5 beta-reductase activity, which is a feature of the adult brain in avian species (ring dove, quail), does not occur in the developing brain (J.B. Hutchison and Schumacher, 1986). The activity of 5 beta-reductase in male and female dove chicks is higher by an order of magnitude than is adult enzyme activity, and therefore, the half-life of testosterone in the POA of the embryo and newly hatched chick is considerably shorter than it is in the adult.

Does this high level of 5 beta-reductase activity provide a protective mechanism in the embryonic brain? There is one remarkable avian model of sexual differentiation that may throw some light on the role of an enzyme-inactivation mechanism. The song-control system in the brain telencephalic nuclei (RA and HVc) of the zebra finch is sexually dimorphic (Nottebohm and Arnold, 1976). Song occurs only in the male and is androgen dependent. The differentiation of adult song patterns depends on estrogen action during a brief posthatching period. The structural differentiation of the HVc and RA song-control nuclei that forms the male type also depends on the action of estrogen during the posthatching period. This discovery by Gurney and Konishi (1980) represents the only example known of an early differ-entiating effect of a steroid on behavior that can be related directly to structural changes in the brain. The source of the estrogen required for brain differentiation in the zebra finch is not known. However, it appears likely that the estrogen is derived from peripheral sources (e.g., the adrenals) in the male, since there is a massive surge of estrogen within the first four days of life (J.B. Hutchison and R.E. Hutchison, 1985). However, both the male and female have high testosterone levels in the peripheral plasma during this period, and the question arises as to what prevents masculinization of the female brain by estrogens formed from testosterone in the brain. As in other avian species, 5 beta-reduction is a major pathway of testosterone metabolism in the developing zebra finch brain. This enzymatic pathway could have a role in the sexual differentiation of the vocal-control system, since there is no sex difference in plasma testosterone levels during posthatching development. Both sexes have relatively high androgen concentrations in the blood that are likely to be inactivated rapidly by brain 5 beta-reduction. The surge in plasma estradiol, unaffected by 5 beta-reductase activity during days 3 and 4 after hatching, would differentiate the male vocal-control system. Testosterone would be inactivated selectively in both male and female brains by 5 beta-reduction. This idea is speculative, but the 5 beta-reduction pathway is proving to be a useful model system for studying enzyme inactivation of androgen in the developing brain, and 5 beta-reductase activity has been identified in the human fetal brain. Quite different enzymatic mechanisms are likely to be involved in the sexual differentiation of behavior depending on whether the active steroid is produced in the brain or peripherally (Figure 20.3).

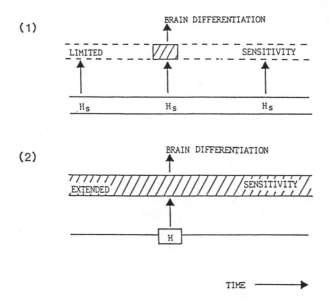

Figure 20.3. Different mechanisms for timing the action of sex hormones on the sexual differentiation of brain mechanisms of behavior. (1) The brain is sensitive to steroid action for a limited period; circulating steroids are present for prolonged periods in development. (2) The hormone is available for a limited period, but the brain is sensitive to the differentiating effects of steroids for an extended period. In (1), intracellular mechanisms such as enzymatic activation/inactivation of androgen limit the sensitivity of brain cells. In (2), the supply of sex steroids from the endocrine glands is the limiting factor. The latter mechanism appears to be applicable to the estrogen-sensitive development of the zebra finch vocal-control system. The former mechanism may apply to the hormonal differentiation of sexual behavior in other species of birds (e.g., Japanese quail) and in mammals such as rodents. ($H_s$ = hormone acting as a substrate for enzymatic conversion in the brain. H = hormone secreted peripherally for a limited period and acting in an unmetabolized form.)

## Androgen Metabolism in Primate Development

Research on subprimate mammals and birds indicates that the brain is irreversibly organized by steroids during development. Androgen-metabolizing enzymes, influenced by hormones and external environmental factors, are potentially important in determining the cellular action of androgen in brain areas. Are these findings applicable to the psychosexual development of humans and other primates? A question that can be answered readily is whether the potential for the formation of estrogen exists in the developing brain of subhuman primates. High aromatase activity has been identified in the brain of fetal rhesus monkeys at stages in development (e.g., day 100) comparable to the period in gestation when the organizing effects of androgens on behavior are thought to occur (Roselli and Resko, 1986). Despite high levels of estradiol in the maternal plasma, the fetus has low levels of circulating estrogen. Therefore, the fetal rhesus monkey appears to develop in a low-estrogen environment. Aromatase activity in preoptic, hypothalamic, and amygdala regions is an order of magnitude higher in the fetal than in the adult brain and can be detected as early as day 50 of gestation. There are small sex differences (higher in the male) in the amygdala but not in the preoptic and hypothalamic areas. Since fetal castration does not affect preoptic aromatase activity, it seems unlikely that the formation of high levels of estrogen in the brain depends on testicular androgens. In view of the inaccessibility of the fetal brain, there are technical difficulties in studying direct effects of steroids on hypothalamic aromatase activity. However, it has proved possible to establish whether preoptic aromatase activity is sensitive to changes in circulating androgen by treating rhesus monkey fetuses with the nonaromatizable androgen 5 alpha-DHT on day 100 of gestation. This treatment has no effect on preoptic aromatase activity (Roselli and Resko, 1986). However, this negative result is not entirely conclusive, because 5 alpha-DHT is rapidly metabolized peripherally and may not reach the fetal brain from systemic implants in sufficient concentrations to affect aromatase activity. When the steroid reaches the brain, further metabolism to catabolic 5 alpha-reduced metabolites probably occurs. Since there is a positive correlation between gonadotrophin-releasing hormone (GnRH) concentrations in hypothalamic areas and aromatase activity, there is a possibility that estrogens formed in the brain participate in the control of the fetal gonadotrophins (Roselli and Resko, 1986).

Surprisingly, in view of the evidence of estrogen action on the sexual differentiation of subprimate mammals and in light of the demonstration (Pomerantz et al., 1985) that high aromatase activity and estradiol receptors are present in the fetal rhesus brain, there is little direct evidence yet that estrogen plays a part in the development of primate behavior. In rhesus monkeys, 5 alpha-DHT masculinizes coital behavior as effectively as do the aromatizable androgens such as testosterone. This effect seems to exclude the necessity for participation of the aromatase system and estrogens in early behavioral development. The juvenile play of rhesus monkeys is masculinized by 5 alpha-DHT during gestation (Goy, 1981), but these findings do not exclude the possibility that the 5 alpha-DHT is acting through cell processes in the brain that normally are estrogen dependent. For example, exogenous 5 alpha-DHT is likely to induce brain aromatase activity and thereby increase estrogen formation. In addition, as Tobet and Baum (1987) have pointed out, the role of estrogen may be more subtle in primates than in other groups in that estrogen may "sensitize" target brain cells to subsequent effects of 5 alpha-DHT or testosterone. The evidence acquired by these researchers is based on some interesting experimental work in the ferret, a mammal that at least superficially appears to resemble rhesus monkeys in steroid requirements for brain differentiation. Testosterone given neonatally masculinizes coital behavior, whereas estrogen or 5 alpha-DHT does not, suggesting a specific role for testosterone. However, coital masculinization appears to be diminished by administering the aromatase blocker ATD to the mother before birth. Reduced aromatase activity in the fetal POA influences the development of male sexual behavior in adulthood. Therefore, there may be a biphasic process in which estrogen formed from androgen "sensitizes" target areas in the brain, perhaps by influencing the production of androgen receptors or the generation of particular enzyme systems such as the aromatase.

Despite the lack of convincing evidence suggestive of a role for estrogen in the sexual differentiation of rhesus monkeys, there is some support for a developmental action of estrogen from studies conducted on humans. Diethylstilbestrol (DES) given with progesterone to maintain pregnancy increases bi- and homosexuality as compared to control groups. Therefore, there may be an effect of an estrogen on human behavioral development. However, there are few data from hormonal studies of humans, and these studies are difficult to interpret (Ehrhardt et al., 1985; Meyer-Bahlburg, 1984). They do not take into account the view that estrogen may have a preorganizational, sensitizing role in the brain. Meyer-Bahlburg (1984) has made the interesting point that there is a consistent hormonal difference between homo- and heterosexual men. Homosexual men show a decrease in urinary androsterone towards levels seen in women. This observation is important, because neonatal androgen is known to influence the activity of sex-dependent hepatic enzymes that inactivate androgens in rats (Gustafsson et al., 1983). Therefore, prenatal testosterone may have widespread effects in determining the pattern of androgen metabolism in various tissues. Although attention has been focused exclusively on the aromatase and the central production of estrogen, changes in other metabolic pathways could alter the balance of steroid metabolites including inactive catabolic products. This possibility emphasizes the importance of studying the whole metabolic profile rather than specific enzyme systems in isolation. The best known and only clear-cut human example of an enzyme deficiency that influences androgen action is the 5 alpha-reductase deficiency syndrome (Guevedoches) studied by Imperato-McGinley et al. (1974) in the Dominican Republic. In this syndrome, male pseudohermaphrodites with incomplete virilization of the genitalia at birth have normal testosterone levels but have decreased formation of 5 alpha-DHT by intracellular 5 alpha-reductase activity in androgen-target tissues. The pseudohermaphrodites have female-like genitalia and are regarded as female during early development. Despite the social effects of being reared as girls, most of these cases adopted a masculine gender identity at puberty, probably under the influence of rising testosterone levels. Relatively few of these pseudohermaphrodites have been studied, and there is no indication yet whether generalizations can be made on the role of 5 alpha-reductase in human behavioral development. Dörner (1988) has emphasized that the 5 alpha-reductase deficiency syndrome demonstrates the importance of prenatal testosterone exposure in the development of male sexual orientation and male gender identity. However, in a separate study of 5 alpha-reductase deficiency (conducted in Papua New Guinea), Herdt and Davidson (1988) found that their subjects switched from a female to a male gender role "only under the greatest external public pressure" (p. 53). They found little support for the view that exposure of the brain to androgen *in utero* led to a change in gender role. While the defects in intracellular androgen metabolism can be identified biochemically, the sociosexual effects of any abnormality are more obscure. This point illustrates the difficulty of trying to assess the developmental role of androgen-metabolizing enzymes.

## Conclusions

Steroid sex hormones have an organizational role in brain development with respect to the sexual differentiation of mechanisms underlying behavior. Animal studies have shown that peaks in gonadal hormone levels occur at developmental stages that coincide with sensitive periods for the differentiation of both structural sex differences in the brain and sexual behavior. The physiological factors that control the timing and action of hormones on the brain during development are poorly understood. However, with increasing interest in the role of prenatal hormones, a new approach has come to light. Instead of research being focused exclusively on changes in peripheral levels of steroid hormones, attention is being directed more towards target tissues in the brain on which steroids, especially the androgens, are known to act. This emphasis and the new data from studies of subprimate mammals and of birds are leading to attempts to unravel the cellular, molecular, and genetic factors that modulate androgen action. One cellular aspect of research based on animal work has assumed significance. This aspect involves the analysis of steroid-metabolizing enzyme systems in areas of the brain through the use of radioisotope methods in which metabolites, formed from labeled precursor steroids, are studied *in vitro*. The intracellular conversion of androgens to biologically active metabolites is well known to be a prerequisite for hormonal action in peripheral target organs. In the human male, the production of a single 5 alpha-reduced metabolite (5 alpha-DHT) is required for the differentiation of the external genitalia. However, studies, particularly of the avian brain (ring dove, Japanese quail), have demonstrated that steroid metabolism relating to the behavioral action of androgen is more complex. An array of metabolites both biologically active and inactive are formed in brain areas associated with the behavioral effects of androgen. These enzyme systems cannot be studied realistically in isolation, because many different pathways of metabolism occur in the same brain areas. In view of the heterogeneity of brain tissue, it is not known yet whether these pathways occur in different cells or may co-exist in the same cell.

Studies, notably of the avian brain, have revealed three principles concerning the role of steroid-metabolizing enzymes in determining the behavior-related action of androgen. The **first principle** is that brain enzymes activate androgens to biologically effective forms. The production of estrogens from androgen by aromatase activity within brain cells is the best studied example. There is increasing evidence that estrogens are crucial not only for the differentiation of the "architecture" and cellular structure of the brain but also for sex differences in behavior. The **second principle** is that androgens are inactivated to biologically catabolic forms. Inactivating enzymes influence levels of testosterone available in target cells during sensitive periods of early development when hormones have their effects. In the avian brain, 5 beta-reductase activity is involved in converting androgens to inactive forms. The **third principle** is that environmental factors such as social stimuli and stress, known to affect behavioral development, also influence the activity of metabolic pathways that form both active and inactive metabolites from androgen. In birds, aromatase activity that converts testosterone to estradiol-17-beta in the POA is induced by elevated circulating androgen levels. Therefore, the enzyme systems are not stable. This point is important because it means that aromatase activity in the brain is sensitive to hormonal condition. Social stimuli also are likely to enhance hypothalamic aromatase activity, whereas stress, as demonstrated in the fetal rat brain, appears to decrease enzyme activity and the formation of estrogens at stages of development when these hormones are essential for sexual differentiation of the brain.

The study of the enzymes involved in the metabolism of androgen within the brain and the investigation of the nuclear receptors of the active steroid products have fundamental implications for research into psychosexual development, because (a) abnormalities in metabolic pathways during sensitive periods for steroid action and the resultant deficiency in active steroid products can influence behavioral development irreversibly and (b) the activity of steroid-metabolizing enzymes is sensitive to circulating androgen levels, suggesting that these enzymes provide a degree of plasticity in the developmental action of androgens on the brain.

Since many different pathways of metabolism and a variety of types of receptor systems are likely to occur in the same brain area, a better understanding of their cellular localization and of interactions between enzymes and metabolic products during developmental stages will be required before the role of metabolism in modulating androgen action can be fully interpreted. To resolve this relative lack of understanding, new approaches in the study of enzyme activation and inactivation will be required using selective enzyme inhibitors and antihormones. For the most part, these are not yet available with an adequate specificity of action.

## Summary

1. Androgens influence the differentiation of sex-typical behavior. Postnatal social experience appears to be more influential in human development than it is in the development of nonhuman species.

2. Learning is involved in the acquisition of male social preferences in developing postnatal animals. However, there is no evidence that hormones are involved in the development of mechanisms that later are required for the choice of a mate. Androgens influence expression of the choice in adulthood.

3. Work on animal models, notably rodents, indicates that androgen-specific differentiating effects can be distinguished from estrogen-specific events in pre- and postnatal development.

4. A steroid-metabolizing enzyme system, aromatase, forming estrogen from androgen in the brain, is involved in early behavioral development. This conclusion appears to be applicable to rodents and birds but has not been established yet for primates. The activity of the brain aromatase is influenced by environmental changes, notably stress and social stimuli.

5. Androgens also are inactivated in brain cells to catabolic products that may influence the level of effective hormone available for the sexual differentiation of behavior during early development.

6. The ontogeny of steroid-metabolizing enzymes in the brain is virtually unknown. However, from the little work that has been done, it appears that enzyme systems in the developing brain resemble the systems of the adult in being sensitive both to hormonal condition and environmental change. However, the mechanisms regulating these enzymes during development may differ from the mechanisms of the adult.

7. Further progress depends on the mapping of enzyme systems in brain cells and on establishing whether periods of sensitivity to steroids can be related to a particular pattern of metabolism in target areas of the brain. The use of highly specific enzyme blockers will be required for these studies. Since nearly all the work so far has been carried out using *in vitro* "test-tube" systems, there still is little knowledge of how the androgen-metabolizing enzymes function in the intact brain during development.

# References

Adkins, E.K. Hormonal basis of sexual differentiation in the Japanese quail. *Journal of Comparative and Physiological Psychology*, 1975, *89*, 61-71.

Arnold, A.P., and Breedlove, S.M. Organizational and activational effects of sex steroids on brain and behavior: A reanalysis. *Hormones and Behaviour*, 1985, *19*, 469-498.

Bancroft, J. The relationship between hormones and sexual behaviour in humans. *In* J.B. Hutchison (Ed.), *Biological determinants of sexual behaviour*. Chichester: John Wiley & Sons, 1978, pp. 493-521.

Bateson, P. Early experience and sexual preferences. *In* J.B. Hutchison (Ed.), *Biological determinants of sexual behaviour*. Chichester: John Wiley & Sons, 1978, pp. 29-55.

Bateson, P. The interpretation of sensitive periods. *In* A. Oliverio and M. Zappella (Eds.), *The behaviour of human infants*. New York: Plenum Press, 1983, pp. 57-70.

Baum, M.J. Differentiation of coital behaviour in mammals: A comparative analysis. *Neuroscience and Biobehavioral Reviews*, 1979, *3*, 265-284.

Baum, M.J., Stockman, E.R., and Lundell, L.A. Evidence of proceptive without receptive defeminization in male ferrets. *Behavioral Neuroscience*, 1985, *99*, 742-750.

Beach, F.A. Locks and beagles. *American Psychologist*, 1969, *24*, 971-989.

Beach, F.A. Hormonal factors controlling the differentiation, development and the display of copulatory behavior in the Ramstergig and related species. *In* L. Aronson and E. Tobach (Eds.), *Biopsychology of development*. New York: Academic Press, 1971, pp. 249-296.

Beach, F.A. Animal models for human sexuality. *In* Excerpta Medica series *Sex hormones and behavior. Ciba Foundation Symposium 62* (new series). Amsterdam, 1979, pp. 113-143.

Breedlove, M., and Arnold, A. Sexually dimorphic motor nucleus in rat spinal cord: Response to adult hormone manipulation, absence in androgen insensitive rats. *Brain Research*, 1981, *225*, 297-307.

Callard, G.V. Aromatization in brain and pituitary: An evolutionary perspective. *In* F. Celotti (Ed.), *Metabolism of hormonal steroids in the neuroendocrine structures*. New York: Raven Press, 1984, pp. 79-101.

Döhler, K.D., Hancke, J.L., Srivastava, S.S., Hofmann, C., Shryne, J.E., and Gorski, P.A. Participation of estrogens in female sexual differentiation of the brain; neuroanatomical, neuroendocrine and behavioural evidence. *Progress in Brain Research*, 1984, *61*, 99-117.

Dörner, G. *Hormones and brain differentiation*. Amsterdam: Elsevier, 1976.

Dörner, G. Neuroendocrine response to estrogen and brain differentiation in heterosexuals, homosexuals and transsexuals. *Archives of Sexual Behavior*, 1988, *17*, 57-75.

Dörner, G., Döcke, F., Gotz, F., Rohde, W., Stahl, F., and Tönjes, R. Sexual differentiation of gonadotrophin secretion, sexual orientation and gender role behavior. *Journal of Steroid Biochemistry*, 1987, *27*, 1081-1087.

Ehrhardt, A.A., Meyer-Bahlburg, H.F.L., Rosen, L.R., Feldman, J.F., Veridiano, N.P., Zimmerman, I., and McEwen, B.S. Sexual orientation after exposure to exogenous estrogen. *Archives of Sexual Behavior*, 1985, *14*, 57-78.

Geschwind, N., and Behan, P. Left-handedness: Association with immune diseases, migraine and developmental learning disorders. *Proceedings of the National Academy of Sciences*, 1982, *79*, 5097-5100.

Goy, R.W. Differentiation of male social traits in female rhesus macaques by prenatal treatment with androgens: Variation in type of androgen, duration and timing of treatment. *In* M.J. Novy and J.A. Resko (Eds.), *Fetal endocrinology*. New York: Academic Press, 1981, pp. 319-339.

Goy, R.W., and Goldfoot, D.A. Neuroendocrinology: Animal models and problems of human sexuality. *Archives of Sexual Behavior*, 1975, *4*, 405-420.

Goy, R.W., and McEwen, B.S. *Sexual differentiation of the brain*. Cambridge, Mass.: MIT Press, 1980.

Gurney, M.E, and Konishi, M. Hormone-induced sexual differentiation of brain and behavior in zebra finches. *Science*, 1980, *208*, 1380-1382.

Gustafsson, J-A., Mode, A., Norstedt, G., and Skett, P. Sex steroid induced changes in hepatic enzymes. *Annual Review of Physiology*, 1983, *45*, 51-60.

Harris, G.W., and Levine, S. Sexual differentiation of the brain and its experimental control. *Journal of Physiology*, 1965, *181*, 379-400.

Herdt, G.H., and Davidson, J. The Sambia "Turnim-Man": Sociocultural and clinical aspects of gender formation in male pseudohermaphrodites with 5-alpha-reductase deficiency in Papua New Guinea. *Archives of Sexual Behavior*, 1988, *17*, 33-56.

Hinde, R.A. *Individual relationships and culture*. Cambridge, England: Cambridge University Press, 1987.

Hutchison, J.B. Hypothalamic regulation of male sexual responsiveness to androgen. *In* J.B. Hutchison (Ed.), *Biological determinants of sexual behaviour*. Chichester: John Wiley & Sons, 1978, pp. 277-319.

Hutchison, J.B., and Hutchison, R.E. Hormonal mechanisms of mate choice in birds. *In* P. Bateson (Ed.), *Mate choice*. Cambridge, England: Cambridge University Press, 1983, pp. 389-405.

Hutchison, J.B., and Hutchison, R.E. Phasic effects of hormones in the avian brain during behavioural development. *In* R. Gilles and J. Balthazart (Eds.), *Neurobiology*. Berlin: Springer-Verlag, 1985, pp. 105-120.

Hutchison, J.B., and Schumacher, M. Development of testosterone-metabolizing pathways in the avian brain: Enzyme localization and characteristics. *Developmental Brain Research*, 1986, *25*, 23-42.

Hutchison, J.B., and Steimer, Th. Androgen metabolism in the brain: Behavioural correlates. *Progress in Brain Research*, 1984, *61*, 32-51.

Hutchison, J.B., and Steimer, Th. Preoptic formation of 17 beta-oestradiol is influenced by behavioural stimuli in the dove. *Brain Research*, 1986, *360*, 366-369.

Hutchison, J.B., Steimer, Th., and Hutchison, R.E. Formation of behaviorally active estrogen in the dove brain: Induction of preoptic aromatase by intracranial testosterone. *Neuroendocrinology*, 1986, *43*, 416-427.

Hutchison, R.E. Hormonal differentiation of sexual behaviour in Japanese quail. *Hormones and Behavior*, 1978, *11*, 363-387.

Hutchison, R.E., and Bateson, P. Sexual imprinting in male Japanese quail. The effects of castration at hatching. *Developmental Psychobiology*, 1982, *15*, 471-477.

Immelmann, K. Über den Einfluss Fruhkindlicher Erfahrungen auf die geschlechtliche Objekt fixierung bei Estrildiden. *Zeitschrift für Tierpsychologie*, 1969, *26*, 677-691.

Imperato-McGinley, J., Peterson, R.E., Gautier, T., and Sturla, E. Steroid 5 alpha-reductase deficiency in Man: An inherited form of male pseudohermaphroditism. *Science*, 1974, *186*, 1213-1243.

Johnston, R.E. Olfactory preferences, scent marking and "preceptivity" in female hamsters. *Hormones and Behavior*, 1979, *13*, 21-39.

Jost, A.A. A new look at the mechanisms controlling sex differentiation in mammals. *Johns Hopkins Medical Journal*, 1972, *130*, 38-53.

Jost, A.A., and Magre, S. Testicular development phases and dual hormonal control of sexual organogenesis. *In* M. Serio, M. Motta, M. Aznisi, and L. Martini (Eds.), *Sexual differentiation: Basic and clinical aspects*. New York: Raven Press, 1984.

Komisaruk, B.R., Adler, N.T., and Hutchison, J.B. Genital sensory field: Enlargement by estrogen treatment in female rats. *Science*, 1972, *178*, 1295-1298.

Lewis, R.A. Social influences on marital choice. *In* S.E. Dragstin and G.H. Elder (Eds.), *Adolescence in the life cycle*. New York: Wiley, 1975, pp. 211-225.

Meyer-Bahlburg, H.F.L. Psychoendocrine research on sexual orientation. Current status and future options. *Progress in Brain Research*, 1984, *61*, 375-398.

Money, J., and Ehrhardt, A.A. *Man and woman, boy and girl*. Baltimore: Johns Hopkins University Press, 1972.

Naftolin, F., Ryan, K.J., and Petro, Z. Aromatization of androstenedione by the anterior hypothalamus of adult male and female rats. *Endocrinology*, 1972, *90*, 295-298.

Nottebohm, F. Testosterone triggers growth of brain vocal control nuclei in adult female canaries. *Brain Research,* 1980, *189,* 429-436.

Nottebohm, F., and Arnold, A.P. Sexual dimorphism in vocal control areas of the song bird brain. *Science,* 1976, *194,* 211-213.

Olsen, K.L. Aromatization: Is it critical for the differentiation of sexually dimorphic behaviors? *In* R. Gilles and J. Balthazart (Eds.), *Neurobiology.* Berlin: Springer-Verlag, 1985, pp. 149-164.

Phoenix, Ch.H., Goy, R.W., Gerall, A.A., and Young, W.C. Organizing action of prenatally administered testosterone propionate on the tissues mediating mating behavior in the female guinea pig. *Endocrinology,* 1959, *55,* 369-382.

Pillard, R.C., and Weinrich, J.D. The Periodic Table model of the gender transpositions: Part 1. A theory based on masculinization and defeminization of the brain. *The Journal of Sex Research,* 1987, *23,* 425-454.

Pomerantz, S.M., Fox, T.O., Sholl, S.A., Vito, C.C., and Goy, R.W. Androgen and estrogen receptors in fetal rhesus monkey brain and anterior pituitary. *Endocrinology,* 1985, *116,* 83-89.

Rhoda, J., Corbier, P., and Roffi, J. Gonadal steroid concentrations in serum and hypothalamus of the rat at birth: Aromatization of testosterone to 17 beta-estradiol. *Endocrinology,* 1984, *114,* 1754-1760.

Roselli, C.E., and Resko, J.A. Effects of gonadectomy and androgen treatment on aromatase activity in the fetal monkey brain. *Biology of Reproduction,* 1986, *35,* 106-112.

Roselli, C.E., Horton, L.E., and Resko, J.A. Distribution and regulation of aromatase activity in the rat hypothalamus and limbic system. *Endocrinology,* 1985, *117,* 2471-2477.

Schumacher, M., and Balthazart, J. Sexual differentiation is a biphasic process in mammals and birds. *In* R. Gilles and J. Balthazart (Eds.), *Neurobiology.* Berlin: Springer-Verlag, 1985, pp. 203-219.

Schumacher, M., and Balthazart, J. Testosterone-induced aromatase is sexually dimorphic. *Brain Research,* 1986, *370,* 285-293.

Schumacher, M., and Balthazart, J. Neuroanatomical distribution of testosterone-metabolizing enzymes in the Japanese quail. *Brain Research,* 1987, *422,* 137-148.

Schumacher, M., Hutchison, R.E, and Hutchison, J.B. Ontogeny of testosterone-inducible brain aromatase activity. *Brain Research,* 1988, *441,* 98-110.

Steimer, Th., and Hutchison, J.B. Androgen increases formation of behaviourally effective oestrogen in the dove brain. *Nature* (London), 1981, *292,* 345-347.

Steimer, Th., and Hutchison, J.B. Is the androgen-dependent increase in preoptic estradiol-17-beta formation due to aromatase induction? *Brain Research,* 1989, *480,* 335-339.

Stylianou, M., Forchielli, E., Tummillo, M., and Dorfman, R.I. Metabolism *in vitro* of (4-$^{14}$C)-testosterone by a human liver homogenate. *Journal of Biological Chemistry,* 1961, *236,* 692-694.

Thompson, N.L., and McCandless, B.R. The homosexual orientation and its antecedents. *In* A. Davids (Ed.), *Child personality and psychopathology: Current topics 3.* New York: Wiley, 1976, pp. 157-197.

Tobet, S.A., and Baum, M.J. Role for prenatal estrogen in the development of masculine sexual behavior in the male ferret. *Hormones and Behavior,* 1987, *21,* 419-429.

Tobet, S.A., Shim, J.H., Osiecki, S.T., Baum, M.J., and Canick, J.A. Androgen aromatization and 5-alpha-reduction in ferret brain during perinatal development: Effects of sex and testosterone manipulation. *Endocrinology,* 1985, *116,* 1869-1877.

Toran-Allerand, C.D. On the genesis of sexual differentiation of the central nervous system: Morphogenetic consequences of steroidal exposure and possible role of a-fetoprotein. *Progress in Brain Research,* 1984, *61,* 63-98.

Weisz, J., Brown, B.L., and Ward, I.C. Maternal stress decreases steroid aromatase activity in brains of male and female rat fetuses. *Neuroendocrinology,* 1982, *35,* 374-379.

Whalen, R.E. Sexual differentiation: Models, methods and mechanisms. *In* R.C. Friedman, R.M. Richart, and R.L. Van de Wiele (Eds.), *Sex differences in behavior.* New York: Wiley, 1974, p. 467.

Yahr, P. Searching for the neural correlates of sexual differentiation in a heterogeneous tissue. *In* R. Gilles and J. Balthazart (Eds.), *Neurobiology.* Berlin: Springer-Verlag, 1985, pp. 180-203.

Yahr, P. Sexual differentiation of behavior in the context of developmental psychobiology. *In* E.M. Blass (Ed.), *Handbook of behavioral neurobiology 9.* New York: Plenum Press, 1988, pp. 197-243.

# 21
# The Complexity of the Concept of Behavioral Development: A Summary

Gail Zivin
*Department of Psychiatry and Human Behavior*
*Jefferson Medical College*
*Philadelphia, Pennsylvania 19107*

## Introduction

The behavior and feeling patterns that this volume examines appear to be inordinately complex, difficult-to-predict results of developmental processes. While many sets of contributing variables are suggested in the chapters of this volume, none of the authors would claim to present an overall picture of how sexual/affectional development typically proceeds or goes awry. But even if one had indisputable evidence for the contribution of one or all of these suggested factors, the choice would still be open on the general model of development into which these factors fit.

The typical developmental model would have multiple simultaneous linear (and, possibly, curvilinear) interactions between genetically given and environmental variables. The factors would appear in this model as variables. However, increasing numbers of developmental researchers are finding such a model unsatisfying in at least three ways:

　　1. It assigns to its variables characteristics that are rather too simple, homogeneous, and linear to account for the continuity of some factors in the face of the change in others.

2. It assigns simple, linear (or curvilinear) types of interaction between variables; at its most complex, this type of interaction allows only enhancement or suppression among variables. It does not allow more interesting, and often more plausible, types of interaction in which variables mutually transform each other or allow the emergence of new variables.
3. It does not assist in the discerning of the shape, direction, or priority of variables' actions amid the mass of multiple simultaneous interactions.

Some recent innovations in developmental theory present a systems model that meets these objections. These newer concepts share a general assumption that the individual is located in and composed of dynamic systems the variables (or "components") of which are in continuous interactions (or "transactions") that have the potential for transforming the components or allowing new components to emerge. Systems are composed of multiple levels, and interactions can occur between variables on different levels.

Can both linear and systemic concepts be used together? There are three possible answers to this question. A theorist who emphasizes opportunistic modularity in the evolution of the structure of organisms might suggest that a blend of both types of concept accurately represents the heterogeneous outcome of evolution. Another theorist might be so struck by the apparent irreconcilability of systemic and linear explanations and by the validity of one type that he or she might urge the adoption of only one type (Fogel and Thelen, 1987; Oyama, 1985). A third theorist might emphasize the transitory utility of concepts and the difficulty of establishing the validity of their metaphysical premises. From this position, the two types of conception might supplement each other, one providing useful still snapshots and the other providing high-speed integration. The current author trusts that the following presentations, of concepts of both types, will suggest to the reader how best to fashion a general developmental model that accommodates the explanatory factors presented in the other chapters of this volume. While this author sees the simultaneous utility of both types of conception, the systemic conceptions seem better suited to taking into account multiple simultaneous factors while reconciling apparently contradictory findings on their contributions to a final behavioral outcome.

# Developmental Concepts

The traditional concepts will be reviewed briefly before the newer ones are presented. It is informative to contrast the old and new concepts concerning their implications regarding **nonlinearity** vs. **linearity** of action, **steady state** vs. **dynamic change** of variables, and emphasis on **input and outcome** vs. **process.**

## The Traditional Concepts

Following are the six concepts that traditionally are applied in formulating a general model of the development of behavior:

1. **Stage** refers to a period in development in which there is a notably special organization of the individual. Stages are most powerful as explanatory concepts when they compose a necessary **linear** sequence, the **input** to one stage being the **output** of the prior stage. While development toward the next stage is always in process, the language of stage theories tends to emphasize the **steadiness** or homogeneity of the structure of a stage to aid in contrasting it with other stages.

2. **Sequence** also refers to a linear order of developmental organizations. Here, the order is not necessary, but it is typical and therefore normative. This concept, therefore, has the same nonsystemic characteristics noted above for "stage."

3. **Maturation** refers to the **linear** unfolding of genetically preprogrammed sequences of internally **steady** or homogeneous organizations. Its use typically emphasizes the behavioral **outputs** of these organizations.

4. **Critical period** refers to the necessity of an occurrence of an **input** during one specified time period for the producing of a highly specific **output** that cannot be reached at any other time. The individual usually is conceived of as having genetic preprogramming that generates the brief **steady** condition requiring the input and that orchestrates the change, by means of the input, to a new steady condition. The change is classically **linear**, going from a condition of preacquisition to an irreversible one of postacquisition.

5. **Sensitive period** broadens the necessary time period of the "critical period" concept and perhaps softens the degree to which the form of the outcome is assumed to be preprogrammed. Nevertheless, this concept remains linear in the notion of acquisition and in assuming the effective conditions to be largely static.

6. **Environment or experience.** While in general there is little that is as potentially varied as environment or experience, many developmental explanations use these concepts to suggest homogeneous, essentially **steady-state** factors. Such analyses contrast with them other factors that are also used to imply a homogeneous and static condition, such as "temperament," "social class," or "proband."

# The Newer Concepts

## Principles and Processes

Several of the newer concepts are captured in principles articulated by Cairns (1979). Five principles are condensed here from seven to convey the basic implications for studying developmental phenomena that are found in the newer concepts.

1. Behavior, social or nonsocial, requires a systemic, wholistic analysis having many levels, from neurobiological through sociocultural.
2. Bidirectional feedback can occur across levels, making behavior development probabilistic, not fixed by particular factors.
3. Development is a dynamic process that promotes the reorganization and adaptation of behavior over time.
4. Comparison requires polythetic analysis, which is "attention to the dissimilarities as well as the similarities of the function of a pattern."
5. Development does not stop having bidirectional feedback across levels at a certain age. Developmental behavior is probabilistic throughout the life span.

Fogel and Thelen (1987) have recently written an important article that presents to developmental psychologists a striking suggestion of some of the processes underlying change that occurs in dynamic systems. The authors start with the assumption that "behavior outcome is never 'hard wired,' but is characterized by an inherent indeterminacy . . ." (p. 749). They explain the stability of behavior in the face of inherent indeterminacy by positing crucial components of dynamic systems: **coordinative structures**. These components are functional groupings of factors that happen to fit together in only a limited number of ways. These fits result in particular behavioral outcomes. The many simultaneous biophysical and environmental schedules that co-occur within and around the individual restrict the presence of all the necessary factors. These limitations contribute to the self-organizing nature of dynamic systems and yield the typical sequences of change observed over the life cycle. (Genetic "programs" contribute merely scheduled factors that contribute to the fit of the whole.) A factor the presence of which is crucial for promoting a change is termed a "**control parameter**." The control parameter for one change in a subsystem is likely to be different from the control parameter for its next change. Just as the other component factors of a coordinative structure may be either within or outside the individual's skin, so also may a control parameter be inside or outside the individual.

An example may help clarify these abstractions. Fogel and Thelen present an example of behavior change that is compelling because it had previously so obviously seemed to be the simple product of linear, genetically programmed, neurological development. The behavior change is the disappearance of the newborn infant's step reflex. During the first month of life, human infants will perform stepping movements if held upright while alert and aroused to move. The movements disappear in the second month. It traditionally had been assumed that this change is the result of central nervous system inhibition of lower reflexes. However, Thelen showed (in Thelen, Fisher, and Ridley-Johnson, 1984) an increased biomechanical demand on the infant's leg muscles created by increased fat; the biomechanical demand prevents the reflex from being expressed in action although it still is present for potential expression. Thelen's group demonstrated that the stepping reflex reappeared in older babies when this demand was reduced by their being submerged waist-high in water. Thus, the **control parameter** of the stepping **coordinative structure** had been arousal to movement, but this parameter passed, at two months, to biomechanical demand on the leg muscles.

In sum, Fogel and Thelen propose a view of developing individuals as dynamic, self-organizing systems, whose apparent unfolding of usual developmental change is the result of usual but adventitious interactions between factors. These interactions yield coordinative structures the developmental changes of which are led by various control parameters. Control parameters can occur at component levels rather than at executive levels of behavioral organization. Note how this component-level control yields "self-organizing" systems. This perspective contrasts with the traditional view that genetic programming is at some executive level. Fogel and Thelen's position on the degree of self-organization and component-level control of systems development is not shared by all systems-oriented developmental theorists. However, the balance of their model does represent the new consensus that the individual is composed of and participates in multiple, nonlinear, mutually transforming subsystems. These subsystems are composed of factors within and outside the individual, mutually coordinating and presenting an orderly appearance of behavioral development.

## Concepts

Particular concepts convey the flavor of the systems conception of behavioral development. Two such concepts have such far-reaching implications for traditional thinking concerning development that they were the topic of a symposium held at a recent meeting of the Society for Research in Child Development (Feiring and Crnic, 1987). These concepts are those of **multipotentiality** and **equifinality**.

### Multipotentiality

This concept refers to the property that one set of variables can lead to varied outcomes. The concept does not suggest that the factors that create the variability are unknown or unknowable. It refers, simply, to normal variations in the trajectories of any set of starting factors, variations that result from cumulations of slight variations in their interactions. Most theorists accept some slight degree of multipotentiality in most phenomena. If the observer is not of a systems orientation, this potential for multiple outcomes tends to be seen as measurement or experimental "error." What is new about the concept of multipotentiality is that its use emphasizes that multiple outcomes occur, not simply as a background phenomenon, but as a central feature of systems. Its use thus asserts that explanations must include explanations of multiple outcomes.

An example of multipotentiality that is central to this volume is the preference for age and gender of sexual partners. From the findings reported in other chapters, it seems clear that one's preference is the systemic result of multiple factors—such as history of hormone release, stimuli associated with early sexual arousal, emotional valences of the environment occurring in early sexual experiences, and the presence of stress and relief associated with early sexual arousal. In the language of Fogel and Thelen, these and other factors contribute to the coordinative structure of sexual preference, even though it is unknown which of these factors may be control parameters at particular points in development.

*Equifinality*

This concept is the inverse of multipotentiality: varied inputs may interact with other factors to become similar outcomes. Both concepts emphasize the adaptive nature with which factors in systems change while being constrained by their general roles in the system. An example of equifinality in adult behavior with children and adolescents is the potential for different factors to motivate (different) adults to approach a child sexually. Various chapters in this volume have suggested that life histories promoting unusual expressions of various motives can account for such an approach to a child—for example, dominance motives, caretaking motives, and affiliative motives. The notion of equifinality allows all of these motive systems to be considered as being potentially equivalent factors. An important typical occurrence in a life that leads to an unusual expression of any of these motive systems would then become the control parameter effecting a shift in the sexual preference coordinative structure toward sexual approach to a child.

*Reciprocal Mediation*

Flavell has introduced into developmental psychology **reciprocal mediation**, a concept that specifically points out the nonlinear and transformative nature of variables that interact in a system. This term refers to the phenomenon of changes in more than one factor in a system changing one another. An example of reciprocal mediation might be taken from Finkelhor (1984). He indicates that each of four preconditions for adult/child sexual involvement (i.e., motivation to sexually abuse, absence of external inhibitors, absence of internal inhibitors, and lack of resistance by the child) becomes more compelling when any occur together.

*Differentiation of "Environment"*

Finally, in the field of developmental behavior genetics, certain concepts that have produced explanations of a linear nature currently are being applied from a new, systems viewpoint. The field employs methodology that apportions percentages of observed variation in a feature between twins to genetics or environment. Some of the statistical methodology requires the assumption that environments are homogeneous across children in one household and heterogeneous between households. Scarr (1987) and Plomin (1987) are in the forefront of the introduction of a more differentiated view of environment and its effects for behavior-genetics methodology. The view emphasizes that households provide different environments to their different children along many dimensions and often do so in complex interaction with early, biologically influenced characteristics of the children, such as temperament and birth order. While the multivariate statistical model underlying traditional behavior genetics analyses is linear and composed of static time slices, this new conceptual complexity in the heterogeneity of environmental effects is a move toward systems conceptualizations that require new and less linear analytic models. Thus, perhaps, some behavior genetics study of the future might attempt to explain how largely identical genetic coding for timing of hormone release could contribute to different sexual preference systems because of differing environmentally present control parameters.

# Conclusion

The newer, systems perspective concerning the development of behavior provides a theoretically based approach to synthesizing apparently contradictory research in this area. This approach is much more substantive than the old assertion that different researchers are simply studying different parts of the elephant. By assuming nonlinear, mutually transformative processes of change, researchers are freed from having to see contributing factors as merely enhancing or suppressing one or more variables. By accepting the functional interchangeability of biophysical and environmental factors in a system, researchers may really move beyond the nature/nurture dichotomy. By seeing subsystems of behavior as being composed of factors and control parameters that may be interchangeable if they fit the timing of the subsystem's coordinative structure, researchers may more sharply understand, retest, and synthesize seemingly contradictory research results concerning the "most important factors" in the development of sexual preferences for atypical gender and age choices.

# References

Cairns, R.B. *Social development: The origins and plasticity of interchanges*. San Francisco: Freeman, 1979.

Feiring, C., and Crnic, K.A. (Chairs). Equifinality: Approaches and problems in studying diversity in development. Symposium presented at the Biennial Meeting of the Society for Research in Child Development, Baltimore, Md., April 1987.

Finkelhor, D. *Child sexual abuse: New theory and research*. New York: The Free Press, 1984, Ch. 5.

Flavell, J.H. Structures, stages, and sequences in cognitive development. *In* W.A. Collins (Ed.), *The concept of development*, Minnesota Symposium on Child Psychology, Vol. 15. Hillsdale, N.J.: Lawrence Erlbaum Associates, 1982, pp. 1-27.

Fogel, A., and Thelen, E. Development of early expressive and communicative action: Reinterpreting the evidence from a dynamic systems perspective. *Developmental Psychology*, 1987, *23*, 747-761.

Oyama, S. *The ontogeny of information: Developmental systems and evolution*. Cambridge, England: Cambridge University Press, 1985.

Plomin, R. Adoption studies: Nurture as well as nature. Paper presented at the Biennial Meeting of the Society for Research in Child Development, Baltimore, Md., April 1987.

Scarr, S. (Chair). What adoption studies tell us about environmental effects on development. Symposium presented at the Biennial Meeting of the Society for Research in Child Development, Baltimore, Md., April 1987.

Thelen, E., Fisher, D.W., and Ridley-Johnson, R. The relationship between physical growth and a newborn reflex. *Infant Behavior and Development*, 1984, *7*, 479-493.

# 22
# Human Erotic Age Orientation: A Conclusion

Jay R. Feierman
*Department of Psychiatry*
*University of New Mexico*
  *and*
*Department of Behavioral Medicine*
*Presbyterian Healthcare Services*
*Albuquerque, New Mexico 87112*

## Introduction

### All Categories Are Arbitrary?

"Pedophile" and "ephebophile" are categorical labels for individuals who have in common a preferential sexual attraction to the attributes of children and adolescents, respectively. Given the multiplicity of human attributes, why are some individuals, who are attracted to certain human attributes, encumbered by labels such as "homosexual" or "pedophile" while other individuals, who are attracted to other human attributes, such as stature, skin complexion, or body shape, go unlabeled and therefore uncategorized? If all categories are arbitrary, why are some individuals, like "homosexuals" and "pedophiles," labeled and others not?

Within a biosocial framework, it is reasonable to assume that those perceivable attributes whose variance in expression preferentially affected variance in individual fitness in human phylogeny will be perceived, categorized, and labeled by individual humans. Certainly, the biological sex (perceived as gender) and the age of a sexual partner are attributes whose perturbations markedly would affect variance in individual fitness. In fact, if one were to pick only two attributes in a potentially procreative sexual partner, biological sex and age certainly would be the two most obvious candidates. It is therefore not surprising that apparent deviations of sexual attraction from the "procreative norm" will be perceived, categorized, and labeled so that knowledge about such labels and their underlying referents can be culturally transmitted across generations.

In the specific case of the categories "pedophilia" and "ephebophilia" in contemporary Western industrialized societies, such labeling, with its resultant social ostracism, humiliation, and banishment of the labeled individual, has three potential benefits to the individual fitness of the labeling individual: (1) the relative increase in the social status of the labeling individual by the diminishing of the social status of the labeled individual (see Okami, this volume); (2) the social avoidance of the labeled individual, especially in the context of a potential procreative mate (see Silva, this volume); and (3) the avoidance by the labeling (male) individual of showing any phenotypic expressions in himself indicative of the label if such predispositions are present. It is the last of the three so-called "benefits" that is a self-inflicted paradox, inasmuch as the "cost" of such self-knowledge is an indeterminable sentence of never to be discussed inner turmoil and pain.

There is, of course, the culturally transmitted belief that the categories pedophilia and ephebophilia, like homosexuality, are the result of some yet to be fully specified social-learning experience, such as in the "abused/abuser hypothesis," that potentially might be avoided if the outcome, as in homosexuality, were somehow labeled and then spoken about as a category (see Garland and Dougher, this volume). This belief may explain, to some degree, the sharp increase in verbalized homophobia in social groups of "at risk" male adolescents, often in the form of derogatory humor, and the near hysteria surrounding even the mention of the word "pedophilia" in some rightfully protective, parental-age adult social groups.

## All Mutually Exclusive Categories Are False

There was a time when something or someone was believed to be either dead or alive, male or female, pregnant or not pregnant, sinful or not sinful. Time has since taught us that there are small segments of nucleic acids that fall between living and nonliving, that one can be partly alive, partly male, partly pregnant, and partly sinful. Such is also the case with pedo- and ephebophilia. An individual is not exclusively a pedo- or an ephebophile or not a pedo- or an ephebophile, even though the dichotomous grammar of our perceptual and conceptual processes persuades us this way. The more meaningful questions to be asked of any adult male are (1) **To what degree** are youthful attributes sexually attractive? and (2) **To what**

**degree** can those behaviors that are proscribed by society or that actually are illegal be inhibited?

Especially in regard to gynephilic ephebophilia is the boundary of social appropriateness quite blurred for many self-respecting and other-respected adult male members of contemporary industrialized societies. The age of marriage, the "age of consent," and the resultant chronological definition of "nubile" female are steadily moving upward, while many upstanding adult male citizens' gnawing phylogenetic memories come dangerously close to never to be crossed boundaries.

Also, for many adult males, in contrast to adult females and for reasons that have been developed within this volume (see Eibl-Eibesfeldt, this volume), the boundaries between parental and romantic love continue to be blurred. This condition should not be surprising, given the phylogenetic origins of romantic love. Because aspects of male sexual behavior have functional proximity to aspects of male parental behavior, keeping their sexual and parental motor patterns separated will always be more difficult for males than for females.

## Neotenization and Nubility Perpetuation

All human males who are alive today are the offspring of ancestral males who, on average, found the attributes of females more sexually attractive than the attributes of males and who, on average, found the attributes of nubile females more sexually attractive than the attributes of truly juvenile or postmenopausal females. "Nubility," like nobility, is conferred from birth, but unlike nobility, nubility has a somewhat flexible, though nevertheless inevitable, period of expiration. Contributing to this flexibility are the two selective processes **neotenization** and **nubility perpetuation**. The former process carries over juvenile characteristics into the truly nubile period, and the latter process pushes the morphological markers of definite adulthood out of the entire reproductive period. These two selective processes are both genetically and culturally transmitted across generations and, also, are reflected somewhat in the morphological appearance of males. (This point relates to note 1, which is presented later in this chapter.)

### Neotenization

So that the newborn's head can fit through the pelvis of the adult human female, human infants are born with a relatively immaturely developed central nervous system, most of the maturation of which takes place during the early years of postpartum life. As a result of this **altricial** condition in which humans are born, with the added natural selection for the maintenance of plasticity for learning well into the adult period, human nubile females have retained numerous juvenile behavioral and morphological attributes. Behavioral examples of the reproductive neotenization of the human nubile female are the retention of both play behavior and nurturing-eliciting releasing stimuli during courtship. Morphological examples of the reproductive neotenization of the human nubile female are the suppression of facial and body hair in females as compared to males.

## Nubility Perpetuation

In many species of nonhuman primates, the juvenile individuals have different morphological features, e.g., "natal coats," when compared to the sexually mature, breeding adults. Humans, too, have easily recognized morphological signs of definite adulthood, with variation both among and within populations, such as the graying of the hair and the wrinkling of the skin. These easily recognized morphological signs of definite human adulthood are contrasted to the also easily recognized morphological signs of puberty that comprise the secondary sexual characteristics, such as the "feminine" hour-glass distribution of fat tissue in females.

These easily recognized morphological signs of definite human adulthood, such as gray hair, do not serve as unambiguous indicators of human-female breeding status, however. Rather, it is proposed, such signs have been "pushed back" into later adulthood in varying degrees by different societies (populations) by male sexual selection for nubile-female attributes throughout the entire female breeding period, a process termed the "nubility perpetuation" of reproductive-age females. Two global observations support this sexual-selection proposition: (1) There are marked differences in mean age of onset of gray hair among populations; (2) Skin wrinkling has a late mean age of onset in populations with late mean age of onset of gray hair.[1] In some societies more than in others, barely pubescent and definitely reproductively competent females are morphologically very similar to each other.

Adding to this similarity between barely pubescent and definitely reproductively competent females is the falling age of menarche that has been shown in numerous societies in which there are historical data. Numerous factors are believed to be responsible for the earlier age of menarche, including nutritional status, light, and natural and sexual selection. Associated with this earlier age of menarche, however, is a several-year period of adolescent-female subfecundity.

In addition to the genetically transmitted processes of female neotenization and nubility perpetuation are their culturally transmitted analogs (serve the same function). The shaving of leg hair by nubile females is an example of culturally transmitted reproductive neotenization. The wearing of undergarments that uplift the breasts and flatten the abdomen, the using of facial creams to retard the development of skin wrinkles, and the coloring of hair to hide its gray color are all examples of culturally transmitted nubility perpetuation.

All of these genetically and culturally transmitted processes blur the distinction between reproductively competent adults and children and adolescents. Therefore, all of these processes must be considered to be determinants, at some level, of pedo- and ephebophilia.

# Evolution

## Why in God's Name Would . . . ?

If ever there was a challenge for evolutionary biologists to make sense of a biology-related phenomenon, it would be to make sense of the mechanisms of evolution underlying human pedo- and ephebophilia. Whereas a similar challenge has been met somewhat reasonably in terms of the "nest helper" concept of adult homosexuality, hypothesizing that another type of nest helper would have to **erotically** love and sexually interact with the children for whom he was caring may be stretching the limits of the nest-helper concept too far.

Perhaps partly for philosophical as well as for sociopolitical reasons, it would be desirable for members of "erotic minorities," such as pedo- and ephebophiles, to have a meaningful, individual *raison d'être* per se from the perspective of evolutionary biology. However, this individual adaptationist, or selectionist, conceptualization of human pedo- and ephebophilia per se appears to have little direct scientific support at this time (see Dienske, this volume). The pertinent nonhuman-primate data, which have been reviewed and discussed in this volume, also do not lend support to such an interpretation, although they also do not refute such an interpretation, which still leaves open the possibility.

## Nonhuman and Human Primates

An important point regarding the nonhuman-primate data is that they are mainly species-typical, normative data rather than species-atypical, variant data, the latter being the types of data that would be required for describing the concepts human pedo- and ephebophilia. If a primatological description of human-primate sexual behavior were to be written by an outside observer, it is quite likely that pedo- and ephebophilia and pedo- and ephebosexual behavior, being species-atypical, would not be observed and, therefore, would not even be described. Even adult/adult homosexual behavior could be nearly invisible, as it is in many societies.

Also, our knowledge of adult/nonadult sexual behavior in nonhuman primates is very incomplete at this time. More species and more behavior have to be described before transspecies generalities, into which humans can be placed, can be suggested. In the meantime, only some preliminary statements can be made.

There is another common difficulty encountered in making comparisons between some nonhuman- and human-primate sexual behavior. The interindividual sexual behavior of savannah-living nonhuman primates under natural conditions can be observed. In contrast, human interindividual sexual behavior typically is not conducted in the presence of other members of the social group and, therefore, is difficult to observe or study directly. Aspects of it that are conducted in the presence of this group, such as public displays of small amounts of interpersonal affection, often involve classes of individuals between whom more amorous or overtly sexual interactions would, away from the social group, be societally proscribed. Therefore, the range of interindividual sexual behavior cannot be inferred on the basis of public displays. In addition, when studies are conducted of "all occurrences" of interindividual sexual behavior of certain nonhuman primates living under various conditions of captivity, the sexual behavior that is observed often resembles "barnyard behavior"; as a consequence, these data can only supplement naturalistic studies.

The witnessed adolescent/adult copulatory behavior under natural conditions in the species of nonhuman primates reviewed (see Anderson and Bielert, this volume) does not reveal very many clues as to the nonhuman-primate origins of human pedo- and ephebosexual behavior, with perhaps one very interesting exception typified by the unimale-type hamadryas baboon. In this species and in others, the adult male follows and cares for a sexually immature, juvenile female years before she is reproductively competent. This behavior differs somewhat from the human pattern of pedophilia in that the adult male baboon's behavior toward the juvenile is more parental than sexual during the juvenile period but then makes a transition into overt sexual copulatory behavior with the beginning of the juvenile's transition into sexual maturity. The significance of this pattern, however, is that adult-male parental-like behavior makes a transition into adult-male copulatory behavior in the same adult male individual over time. This making of a transition suggests that there is a degree of "functional proximity" between these two motivational states—parental and sexual—in another, albeit nonhuman, adult male primate. In addition, the female baboon is an early adolescent when the male's behavior becomes sexual toward her.

Most of the other adult/nonadult copulatory motor behavior observed in nonhuman primates under natural conditions appears to be play or practice motor patterns by nonadult males, which at best appears to be tolerated by the adult females. There have been no published reports to date of individual adult-male nonhuman primates who were observed to show preferential **sexual** interest in a young juvenile under natural conditions, in contrast to the situation in human pedo- and ephebophilia, even though in multimale breeding groups there is differential access among adult males to adult estrous females, who are preferred over younger females.

The mechanisms of inbreeding avoidance described in nonhuman primates are strong support for the nonhuman-primate origins of the same phenomenon in humans, but these mechanisms of familiarity/lack of interest and dispersal relate only obliquely to the mechanisms of adult erotic interest/lack of interest in juveniles per se (see Pusey, this volume).

The functions of nonhuman primate paternalism (see Taub, this volume) give a list of clues as to possible "biological motives" for human pedo- and ephebophilia. However, none of the nonhuman-primate motives appear to capture the **erotic** sexual attraction and the acting out of the sexual-motor-patterns component between human adult males and nonadults. There is significance, however, in the "particular friendships" that develop between adult males and particular nonrelated nonadults, "friendships" that to some degree resemble aspects of the nonsexual components of pedo- and ephebophile relationships (see Silva, this volume).

The use by the bonobos of sexual motor patterns for tension regulation and reconciliation among all age and sex combinations in the social group (see de Waal, this volume) has some functional counterparts among humans. One such counterpart is the use by humans of nonsexual affiliative motor patterns for reconciliation in the presence of the social group. In addition, it certainly is probable that outside of the observation of the social group, some adult humans reconcile by using sexual motor patterns in a fashion similar to bonobos. However, bonobos' display of intergenerational sexual motor patterns in the service of tension regulation and reconciliation within the social group appears to have a somewhat different "biological motive" than the sexual aspects of human pedo- and ephebophile relations that occur outside of the social group.

## On Chins, Spandrels, and Pedo- and Ephebophiles

It appears, therefore, that neither exact homologs (same behavior in the same context) nor exact analogs (same function) of human pedo- and ephebophilia are readily evident in what we now know from nonhuman-primate sexology. Given this lack of phylogenetic evidence for similarly executed and motivated behavior in the nearest living species to humans, there still is an alternative biosocial perspective the components of which have been discussed earlier in this volume:

> **Pedo- and ephebophilia are not functionally adaptive in the individual pedo- or ephebophile per se but, rather, are the by-products of natural and sexual selection for adult-male and adult-female heterosexuality in their male and female kin.**

Given the inevitable biological variability in the degree to which the **average** developing male and female brains are hormonalized, pedo- and ephebophilia can be conceptualized as a type of "**sacrificial altruism**" that is required, as an involuntary class of behavior, of a small percentage of males in the breeding population so that the average male can have an average amount of appropriately directed mating behavior.

The difference between "sacrificial altruism" and "kin selection" is that in the latter concept, there is implied an active, seemingly individually altruistic (but actually genetically selfish) fitness-benefitting act toward kin, such as is seen in the behavior of some of the social insects. In the former concept, the "help" may be as much by omission as by commission, inasmuch as such individuals are the "by-products" of the inevitable biological variation around a selected central tendency. So that most males will "love" children and adolescents just the right amount (see Mackey, this volume), some males will unfortunately love them too little and some too much. Such males, who love children and adolescents to a degree more than average or less than average, will be carried along in a population in the tails of frequency distributions as long as the fitness benefits of their existence that are available to their kin outweigh the costs.

Until a functional-adaptation hypothesis of human pedo- and ephebophilia can be supported with convincing data, either from the nonhuman or the human literature, the "by-product of selection" hypothesis seems a reasonable hypothesis to tentatively entertain. This hypothesis also fits with the two-dimensional model of brain masculinization and defeminization that was developed earlier in this volume by the structuring of a rank-order relationship of hormonalization between pedo- and ephebophilia and species-typical heterosexuality. It is simply inevitable that some adult males in a population will be sexually attracted to individuals who are younger and more feminine than self but whose attributes are more young and less feminine than can be found within the range of fertile females.

Thus, pedo- and ephebophiles, like chins and spandrels,[2] may have no primary adaptive function in themselves but, instead, may be rank-ordered by-products of selection for more adaptive attributes in their kin. In addition, given the degree to which human learning is governed by open genetic programs, such proclivities can be strengthened through both nonreinforced, critical-period, juvenile-imprinting-like phenomena (see D'Udine, this volume) and the more traditionally reinforced conditioning of adult life (see Domjan, this volume).

## Cause

Complex phenomena such as adult human male pedo- and ephebophilia do not have simple, reductionist, unitary causes. Rather, there are numerous factors at numerous levels that interact complexly (see Zivin, this volume) to bring about both the pedo- and ephebophilic predispositions and the overt pedo- and ephebosexual behaviors. Some of the main factors operating at the levels of the social group, the individual, the tissue, and the molecule will now be briefly reviewed.

## At the Level of the Social Group

At the level of the social group, the primary determinants of pedo- and ephebophilia, with their sometimes resultant pedo- and ephebosexual behaviors, are the parental-like interactions that adult males in certain **social roles** play with children and adolescents. The roles of **priest** ("father"), **teacher**, and **coach** are good examples.

Also very important at the level of the social group are the reconstituted families in which nonrelated adult males find themselves in surrogate parental roles with previously unknown children and adolescents. The role of **"stepfather"** is certainly the obvious example.

## At the Level of the Individual

It would seem that at the level of the individual, the most obvious example of a potential determinant of future pedo- and ephebophilia should be a highly pleasurable, eroticizing, sexual experience that occurred during a critical formative period in childhood or early adolescence with another child or adolescent (see D'Udine, this volume). Interestingly, however, self-reports of such experiences rarely are different from the usual self-reports of childhood sexual exploration in nonpedo- and nonephebophile males. In contrast, pedo- or ephebophilia could also result from a highly unpleasant or double-binded-entrapment type of sexual experience between a child or an adolescent and an adult (opponent-process learning), where only an individual without adult attributes (e.g., a child or an adolescent) could become eroticized and incorporated into the developing lovemap (see Money, this volume).

The effect of a seemingly emotionally neutral or self-reportedly positive sexual relationship between a child or an adolescent and an adult is nonspecific. Such a relationship is neither a necessary nor a sufficient cause of later pedo- and ephebophilia, however. These kinds of relationships appear to have variable effects on psychosexual development. Often, the negative effects are not realized at the time of the relationship, and often, they are brought out in the context of psychotherapy experienced later in life. The self-reports of positive effects rarely are self-disclosed, and when they are, they usually are not in the professional literature.

Another contributing determinant of pedo- and ephebophilia at the individual level would be the conditioning of a child or an adolescent (as the previously unconditioned stimulus) to sexually evocative status during the adulthood of an adult male (see Domjan, this volume). One can imagine a child or an adolescent inadvertently being paired with sexual arousal and that particular child or adolescent, or his or her categorized attributes, subsequently taking on sexually evocative properties.

Finally at the level of the individual would be those situations in which circumstances, such as the lack of sexual opportunity with age-appropriate sexual partners or the disinhibiting influence of alcohol or senility, result in adult human sexual behavior with a child or an adolescent. Such circumstances have been called in the literature "regressed pedophilia" in contrast to "fixed pedophilia," where the child or adolescent is a preferred sexual partner.

## At the Level of the Tissue

There are two sets of tissues that are involved in the understanding of the causal determinants of pedo- and ephebophilia: (1) the neural tissues in the brain, which underlie sexually dimorphic sexual behaviors (see Medicus and Hopf, this volume; Hutchison and Hutchison, this volume), and (2) the tissues that are responsible for the primary sexual characteristics of the external genitals, seen at birth, and the tissues that are responsible for the secondary sexual characteristics, which develop at puberty.

Paraphilias, such as pedo- and ephebophilia, are developed through the eroticization of attributes of childhood and adolescence that usually (normatively) are not associated with sexual arousal in adult human males. The exaggerated (diminutive) size as well as the highly discriminable visual characteristics of the budding signs of puberty of children and adolescents make them ideal (human) objects of paraphilic sexual attraction (see Feierman, this volume, Chapter 1).

## At the Level of the Molecule

Interestingly, more about human sexual behavior is directly known at the molecular level than at the tissue level, because most of the molecules of interest can be extracted from the peripheral blood of humans, while the main human tissues of interest lie within the inaccessible confines of the cranium. At the molecular level, there has been a lot of recent work on understanding the molecular (hormonal) basis of erotic sex (gender) preferences, although the molecules that are being measured are thought to be an indirect reflection of the differential reactivity of the underlying neural tissue (see Gladue, this volume).

The molecular neurobiology of testosterone and its estrogen-like metabolites in pedo- and ephebophilic males is a potential area of very promising research. However, even a cursory reading of Hutchison and Hutchison's chapter (this volume) should convince the reader who is uninitiated in biochemistry that simplistic, reductionist biochemical models are a great oversimplification and a misrepresentation of the facts. It is not surprising that older molecular (hormonal) studies that searched for hormonal blood-level differences in homosexual versus heterosexual males were destined not to succeed.

The technology to measure neurohormones directly and the reactivity of pertinent neural tissues indirectly now is ahead of the supply of interested and sufficiently trained investigators who might apply this technology to an understanding of both erotic sex (gender) and age orientations. To date, there are only a small number of investigators worldwide who are engaged in this potentially productive area of research. Nevertheless, it is certainly conceivable that in the future there will be neurohormonal blood tests, probably indirectly measuring the reactivity of particular neural tissues, that will allow the specifying of the degree to which one's brain predisposes one to be sexually attracted to atypical age and gender attributes in other individuals.

## Function

The difference between "adaptive function" and "function" from a biosocial perspective is the difference between using a coat hanger as an object upon which to suspend a coat and using it, for example, as an object with which to open locked doors; it is the difference between using a coin as a unit of exchange and using it as an object with which to turn a screw (see Dienske, this volume). That the coat hanger evolved (cultural evolution) to fulfill one adaptive function does not prevent a clever individual or an entire society from utilizing the existing structure in the service of another, added function (see Diamond, this volume; Schiefenhövel, this volume).

What does an adult human male do with an erotic age and possibly also a sexual (gender) orientation (i.e., lovemap) that misses the potentially procreative mark? What does an individual do with a coat hanger if one has no interest in coats; a coin and no desire for what it can legitimately buy? Unfortunately, adult male individuals with such variant age orientations, like species-atypical males the world over, proceptively search for individuals who fit the object of their sexual desire (i.e., their lovemap).

That some such adult males will discover that children and adolescents meet these needs is not at all surprising, given that children and adolescents, like age-appropriate potentially procreative females, are younger and more feminine than self (see Bullough, this volume). A given percentage of adult human males will inevitably be sexually attracted to individuals who are somewhat younger and somewhat less feminine than individuals found within the range of age-appropriate females. It is also quite understandable how a pedo- or an ephebophile's appetitive sexual behavior, like a coat hanger unbending, can facultatively adapt to the behavioral repertoire necessary to proceptively "court" a child or an adolescent.

It is most likely, therefore, that pedo- and ephebophilia are individual, facultative proclivities that are bent out of the tails of hormonal frequency distributions around the optimum brain masculinization and brain defeminization of the "average male." The "function" of pedo- and ephebophilia for the unfortunate adult male individual in whom their determinants reside is very similar to the function of the object of any other human male's erotic desires: fulfillment (see Dienske, this volume). The specific adaptive function of pedo- and ephebophilia per se to the individual pedo- and ephebophile, however, apart from the previously discussed sacrificial altruism, has yet to be convincingly demonstrated.

In the meantime, for contemporary Western industrialized societies, a social function for individual pedo- and ephebophiles who are caught acting out and then publicly adjudicated also is evident: the ostensible function is that the consequences of their behavior will deter other similarly motivated individuals. Pedo- and ephebophiles also are burdened with the functions of carrying, protecting, storing, and yes, even passing on the "by-products" of our genetic evolution that perhaps in moderation or in another body or in another generation will do someone else some good.

## Development

### When I Grow Up, I Want To Be . . . .

"When I grow up, I want to be . . ." are words that are heard frequently from children. There are a myriad of factors that eventually lead a particular child's or adolescent's life in one direction or another. Recently, much has been written about the development in childhood and adolescence of individuals who eventually grow up to be homosexual. Western industrialized societies have become somewhat more tolerant of "homosexual rights" in the process of granting other minorities such freedoms. There are now numerous well-written biographies and films on the lives of socially respectable and productive homosexual individuals. These materials, as well as interested and compassionate professionals and nonprofessionals, are available to an adolescent or a young-adult male who is personally dealing with his homosexuality.

These resources simply are not available in most Western industrialized societies for an adolescent or a young-adult male who is dealing with a preferential sexual attraction to children or younger adolescents. If in the process of learning about his sexuality such a male unfortunately acted his attraction out, in any way, and if in many jurisdictions he were to tell a human services professional (physician, psychologist, social worker, counselor, teacher, minister, and so forth) that he had done so, he very likely would be arrested. Almost all jurisdictions have "reporting laws" that make the reporting of such information to police or social service agencies mandatory. It is, therefore, not surprising that adolescent and adult males who are dealing with this issue rarely discuss it with anyone.

## Ostracism, Humiliation, and Banishment

When an adult human male with a sexual attraction to children or adolescents is found to be acting out this attraction in a Western industrialized society and if the adult male has any significant social status in his community, such is the material for headlines in newspapers. Then there follows a period of public ostracism, humiliation, and banishment. In many jurisdictions, this banishment occurs in penal institutions.

In various jurisdictions, penal institutions generally function to accomplish some combination of punishment, deterrence, protection, and rehabilitation, often with the emphasis on the first three rather than on the last. Pedo- and ephebosexual behavior are dealt with by many penal systems like other felonious criminal behaviors, such as burglary, robbery, rape, and murder, and many penal institutions offer pedo- and ephebophiles little or no effective psychological or medical therapy during their period of incarceration. Even after they are released, pedo- and ephebophiles often find very little help. In the United States, for example, self-help groups such as Sexaholics Anonymous, which are based on the principles of Alcoholics Anonymous, are distinguished by the relative absence of pedo- and ephebophiles. Also, most nongovernmental practitioners avoid the members of this population because of the tremendous liability associated with being responsible for their therapy.

There are specialized clinics in some jurisdictions to which such individuals can go for help, if not before, then at least after their encounter with the criminal justice system. With help—which often includes some combination of antiandrogen hormones (to lower sex drive), behavior modification, social skills training, and support groups—recidivism for acted-out, illegal pedo- and ephebosexual behavior is markedly reduced. Very rarely, however, will a pedo- or an ephebophile come for help before he has been apprehended by the criminal justice system. Part of the reason for this situation is the fear of being "turned in," as was noted previously, by the very therapist from whom he sought help. Another very significant reason for the lack of treatment before criminal apprehension is the fear of ostracism, humiliation, and banishment from noncriminal justice, social institutions. For example, can one imagine a male primary school teacher being continued in employment if it were discovered that he was being treated for never-acted-out pedophilia?

# Conclusions

## If Not But For the Grace of God and Natural Selection . . . .

In the course of professional work over the past 13 years, this author/
editor has had the opportunity to attend, in numerous jurisdictions within the
continental United States, sentencing hearings for pedo- and ephebophiles
who have been found guilty of pedo- or ephebosexual behavior. During
such hearings, because the individuals who were being sentenced were
public figures of high social status in their respective communities, media,
especially television, nearly always were present.

At the conclusion of such hearings, one could appreciate the meaning
of the term "judgemental," inasmuch as virtually all sentences were handed
down within the framework of castigating and derogatory comments. Such
comments, I believe, are what the larger social group wanted to hear, along
with the sight of television footage or newspaper photographs of the
publicly humiliated, submissively postured defendant waiting to be banished.

Often I have wondered during such times whether the sentencing judge
would be able to meet his own standards of continence if the object of his
own adult male sexual desires were similarly illegal.

## Acceptance

Pedo- and ephebophiles with strong religious convictions, which is the
population with which I am the most familiar, often take solace in their
belief that "this is the way God made me." Most pedo- and ephebophiles
with whom I have had contact over the years have begrudgingly accepted
the reality that the object of their sexual desires is socially proscribed as
illegal. Most, I believe, could have lawfully lived with this reality with a
little help before their downfall.

Most were not given the opportunity to receive this help, however,
because of the way that their behavioral proclivities were received by their
societies. Perhaps much of this reception was a result of the lack of
understanding of pedo- and ephebophilia. I hope so.

## Notes

[1] Another consideration is that gray hair once served as an indicator of
potential dominance and of adult-male breeding status. In this scenario,
when males preferentially sexually selected more nubile-looking, nongray,
reproductively competent females over gray, reproductively competent
females, they also inadvertently raised the age at which their own male sons
became gray, creating a potential balanced polymorphism for the age at
which an individual's hair turns gray.

[2]A spandrel is the inverted-triangle-shaped space between the right or the left exterior curve of an arch and an enclosing right angle, a space that is a by-product of the basic configuration of the arch.

# Author Index

# Subject Index

Italicized page numbers indicate material in figures and tables. Numerals in parentheses indicate endnotes.